GRAMMAR

FOR THE WELL-TRAINED MIND

PURPLE WORKBOOK

- REVISED EDITION -

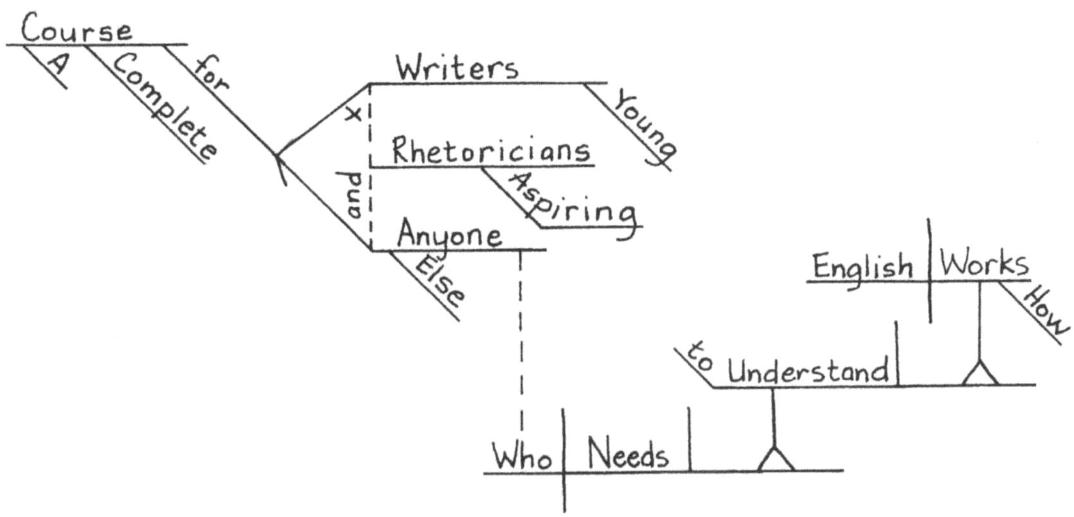

By Susan Wise Bauer
and Audrey Anderson,
Diagrams by Patty Rebne

Layout and Design by Shannon Zadrozny

WELL-TRAINED MIND PRESS

Names:	Bauer, Susan Wise, author. | Anderson, Audrey, 1986- author. | Rebne, Patty, illustrator. | Zadrozny, Shannon, designer.
Title:	Grammar for the well-trained mind. Purple workbook / by Susan Wise Bauer, with Audrey Anderson ; diagrams by Patty Rebne ; layout and design by Shannon Zadrozny.
Other titles:	Purple workbook
Description:	Revised edition. | [Charles City, Virginia] : Well-Trained Mind Press, [2024] | Interest grade level: 5-12. | Summary: Newly revised for ease of use, the Purple Workbook, along with the accompanying Key and the Core Instructor Text, make up a full year of Grammar for the Well-Trained Mind: a complete course that takes students from basic definitions ... through advanced sentence structure and analysis--all the grammar skills needed to write and speak with eloquence and confidence. This innovative program combines the three essential elements of language learning: understanding and memorizing rules (prescriptive teaching), repeated exposure to examples of how those rules are used (descriptive instruction), and practice using those rules in exercises and in writing (practical experience).--Publisher.
Identifiers:	ISBN: 978-1-944481-60-5 (paperback)
Subjects:	LCSH: English language--Grammar--Problems, exercises, etc.--Juvenile literature. | English language-- Rhetoric--Problems, exercises, etc.--Juvenile literature. | LCGFT: Problems and exercises. | BISAC: JUVENILE NONFICTION / Language Arts / Grammar. | EDUCATION / Teaching / Subjects / Language Arts. | JUVENILE NONFICTION / Language Arts / General.
Classification:	LCC: LB1631 .B3952 2024 | DDC: 428.00712--dc23

Table of Contents

FOREWORD

Welcome to *Grammar for the Well-Trained Mind*!

This innovative grammar program will take you from basic definitions ("A noun is the name of a person, place, thing, or idea") all the way through detailed analysis of complex sentence structure. Once you complete it, you'll have all the skills needed for the study of advanced rhetoric—persuasive speech and sophisticated writing.

WHAT MAKES UP THE FULL PROGRAM

Each year of study in *Grammar for the Well-Trained Mind* requires three books.

The nonconsumable *Core Instructor Text* is used for each year of study. It contains scripted dialogue for the instructor, all rules and examples, and teaching notes that thoroughly explain ambiguities and difficulties.

There are four *Student Workbooks* with accompanying *Keys*. Each consumable workbook provides a full course of exercises and assignments. Each corresponding key gives complete, thoroughly explained answers. Your goal is to complete all four *Workbooks* before the student finishes high school. (See *How the Program Works*, below.)

Two optional reference books are also available. All rules and definitions, with accompanying examples, have been assembled into a handy reference book, *The Grammar Guidebook*. This handbook will serve the student for all four years of study—and will continue to be useful as the student moves through advanced high school writing, into college composition, and beyond. In addition, all diagramming rules covered in the course are summarized in *The Diagramming Dictionary: A Complete Reference Tool for Young Writers, Aspiring Rhetoricians, and Anyone Else Who Needs to Understand How to Diagram English Sentences.*

HOW THE PROGRAM WORKS (FOR THE STUDENT)

Language learning has three elements.

First: You have to understand and memorize *rules*. We call this "prescriptive learning"—grasping the explicit principles that govern the English language and committing them to memory. *Grammar for the Well-Trained Mind* presents, explains, and drills all of the essential rules of the English language. Each year, the student reviews and repeats these rules.

Second: You need *examples* of every rule and principle ("descriptive learning"). Without examples, rules remain abstract. When you memorize the rule "Subjunctive verbs express situations that are unreal, wished for, or uncertain," you also need to memorize the example "I would not say such things if I were you!" Each year, the student reviews and repeats the same examples to illustrate each rule.

Third: You need *practice*. Although the four workbooks repeat the same rules and examples, each contains a completely new set of exercises and writing assignments, along with a *Key* providing complete answers.

The combination of *repetition* (the same rules and examples each year) and *innovation* (brand-new practice materials in every workbook) will lead you to complete mastery of the English language.

HOW TO USE GRAMMAR FOR THE WELL-TRAINED MIND

When you first use the program, begin with the *Core Instructor Text* and any one of the *Workbooks* with its accompanying *Key* (*Purple*, *Red*, *Blue*, or *Yellow*). Keep *The Grammar Guidebook* and *The Diagramming Dictionary* on hand for reference.

During this first year, you won't necessarily grasp every principle thoroughly. Simply go through the dialogue with your instructor, complete the exercises, check the answers, and discuss any mistakes.

You may need more than one year to complete your first *Workbook*; the exercises increase in complexity and difficulty from Week 20 on. That's absolutely fine. Feel free to take as much time as necessary to finish this workbook.

When your first *Workbook* is completed, you and your instructor will go back to the beginning of the *Core Instructor Text* and start over, this time using a *Workbook/Key* combination of a different color. You'll go over the same dialogue, the same rules, and the same examples—with an entirely fresh set of exercises. This combination of repeated information along with new and challenging exercises will truly begin to build your competence in the English language.

Follow this same procedure for the third and fourth years of study, using workbooks of the remaining two colors, along with their matching keys.

Regular reviews are built into the program. Every three weeks, take some extra time to do the exercises reviewing what was covered in the three weeks before. After Week 27, the reviews double in scope: twelve exercises review the material all the way back to the beginning of the course. These reviews, beginning with Review 9, become one week's work each. During review weeks, try to do three exercises per day, and then go back and review the rules and principles of any exercise in which you miss two or more sentences/examples.

WHICH WORKBOOK?

Because each workbook makes use of the same rules and examples, you may use any one of the four workbooks during your first year in the program. It is highly recommended, however, that you then go back and finish the earlier workbooks as well. The program is designed to take *at least* four years, no matter where you begin.

IMPORTANT PRINCIPLES OF LEARNING

As you study, keep the following in mind.

- Language is a rich, complicated tapestry. It is occasionally logical, and sometimes irrational. Mastering its complexities takes time and patience. Don't expect to master—or even completely understand—every principle the first time through. Repetition and practice will eventually bring clarity. Be diligent—don't abandon the curriculum because of frustration! But accept occasional confusion as a natural part of learning. If you don't understand subjunctives the first time through, for example, accept it, move on, and then repeat the following year. Eventually, the concepts will come into focus.
- Always ask for help if you need it. This isn't a test. It's a learning process.
- From Week 19 (halfway through the course) on, you are encouraged to read sentences out loud. Reading out loud is an important part of evaluating your own writing. Follow the directions—don't ignore them and read silently.
- Take as long as you need to finish each lesson. As noted above, it's perfectly acceptable to take more than one year to finish a workbook (particularly the first time through). The earlier lessons are shorter and simpler; they increase in both complexity and length as the book goes on. But especially in the later lessons, don't worry if you need to divide a lesson over two days, or take more than one week to complete a week's worth of lessons. In subsequent years, you'll go much more quickly through the earlier lessons, giving you time to stop and concentrate on areas of challenge later on.

ABOUT DIAGRAMMING

Grammar for the Well-Trained Mind uses diagramming exercises throughout.

Diagramming is a learning process. Think of the diagrams as experimental projects, not tests. Attempt the diagram, look at the answer, and then try to figure out why any differences exist. Expect these assignments—particularly in the second half of the book—to be challenging. Ask for help when you need it. Always diagram with a pencil (or on a whiteboard or blackboard), and expect to erase and redo constantly.

Also remember that diagramming is not an exact science! If you can explain clearly why you've made a particular choice, the diagram might be correct even if the key differs. To quote a 1914 grammar text: "Many constructions are peculiar, idiomatic, and do not lend themselves readily to any arrangement of lines" (Alma Blount and Clark S. Northup, *An English Grammar for Use in High and Normal Schools and in Colleges*).

WEEK 1

Introduction to Nouns and Adjectives

— LESSON 1 —

Introduction to Nouns
Concrete and Abstract Nouns

A noun names a person, place, thing, or idea.
Concrete nouns can be observed with our senses. Abstract nouns cannot.

Exercise 1A: Abstract and Concrete Nouns

Decide whether the underlined nouns are abstract or concrete. Above each noun, write *A* for abstract or *C* for concrete. If you have difficulty, ask yourself: Can this noun be touched, seen, or experienced with another one of the senses? If so, it is a concrete noun. If not, it is abstract.

All that glitters is not gold. (English and Spanish)

Forget injuries; never forget kindness. (Chinese)

Study the past if you would define the future. (Chinese)

We learn little from victory, much from defeat. (Japanese)

The shrimp that falls asleep gets carried away by the current. (Spanish)

He who conquers his anger has conquered an enemy. (German)

The oldest trees often bear the sweetest fruit. (German)

Pride is no substitute for a dinner. (Ethiopian)

A leaky house can fool the sun, but it can't fool the rain. (Haitian)

Exercise 1B: Abstract Nouns

Each row contains two abstract nouns and one concrete noun. Find the concrete noun and cross it out.

hunger	thirst	bread
delight	frosting	pleasure
confusion	victory	torch
shock	fear	monster
guard	sadness	tranquility
self-control	boredom	mob

— LESSON 2 —

Introduction to Adjectives
Descriptive Adjectives, Abstract Nouns
Formation of Abstract Nouns from Descriptive Adjectives

An adjective modifies a noun or pronoun.
Adjectives tell what kind, which one, how many, and whose.
Descriptive adjectives tell what kind.
A descriptive adjective becomes an abstract noun when you add -*ness* to it.

cheerful	cheerfulness
grumpy	grumpiness

Exercise 2A: Descriptive Adjectives, Concrete Nouns, and Abstract Nouns

Decide whether the underlined words are concrete nouns, abstract nouns, or descriptive adjectives. Above each, write *DA* for descriptive adjective, *CN* for concrete noun, or *AN* for abstract noun.

The cowardly lion wished for courage.

The shy tinman wished for love.

The silly scarecrow wished for intelligence.

The lost little girl wished for the power to go home.

The Yellow Brick Road led through a field of crimson poppies.

The travelers were overcome with sleepiness when they smelled the flowers.

Exercise 2B: Turning Descriptive Adjectives into Abstract Nouns

Change each descriptive adjective to an abstract noun by adding the suffix *-ness*. Write the abstract noun in the blank beside the descriptive adjective. Remember this rule: **When you add the suffix *-ness* to a word ending in *-y*, the *y* changes to *i*.** (For example, *grumpy* becomes *grumpiness*.)

sad ____________________

truthful ____________________

effective ____________________

ugly ____________________

silly ____________________

sluggish ____________________

eager ____________________

bulky ____________________

Exercise 2C: Color Names

Underline all the color words in the following paragraph. Then write *A* for adjective or *N* for noun above each underlined color word. If you are not sure, ask yourself, "[Color name] *what*?" If you can answer that question, you have found a noun that the color describes. That means the color is an adjective.

Rachel held her sister Dana's hand as they walked up the turquoise path into the yellow candy store. Candy of every imaginable flavor covered the walls. Dana immediately headed to the magenta jellybeans. Rachel laughed; Dana's favorite color was magenta, and she always wanted magenta clothes and notebooks for school. Rachel raced over to the bright red strawberries covered in white chocolate. Right next to the strawberries were green bonbons. She usually liked green, but this trip was not about color. It was about taste!

— LESSON 3 —

Common and Proper Nouns
Capitalization and Punctuation of Proper Nouns

A common noun is a name common to many persons, places, things, or ideas.
A proper noun is the special, particular name for a person, place, thing, or idea.
Proper nouns always begin with capital letters.

Capitalization Rules

1. Capitalize the proper names of persons, places, things, and animals.

boy	Peter
store	Baskin-Robbins
book	*Little Women*
horse	Black Beauty
sea	Sea of Galilee
port	Port of Los Angeles
island	Isle of Skye

2. Capitalize the names of holidays.

Memorial Day
Christmas
Independence Day
Day of the Dead

3. Capitalize the names of deities.

Minerva (ancient Rome)
Hwanin (ancient Korea)
God (Christianity and Judaism)
Allah (Islam)
Gitche Manitou or Great Spirit (Native American—Algonquin)

4. Capitalize the days of the week and the months of the year, but not the seasons.

Monday	January	winter
Tuesday	April	spring
Friday	August	summer
Sunday	October	fall

5. Capitalize the first, last, and other important words in titles of books, magazines, newspapers, movies, television series, stories, poems, and songs.

book	*Alice's Adventures in Wonderland*
magazine	*National Geographic*
newspaper	The *Chicago Tribune*
movie	*A River Runs Through It*
television series	*The Waltons*
television show	"The Chicken Thief"
story	"The Visit of the Magi"
poem	"The Night Before Christmas"
song	"Joy to the World"
chapter in a book	"The End of the Story"

6. Capitalize and italicize the names of ships, trains, and planes.

ship	*Titanic*
train	The *Orient Express*
plane	The *Spirit of St. Louis*

Exercise 3A: Capitalizing Proper Nouns

Write a proper noun for each of the following common nouns. Don't forget to capitalize all of the important words of the proper noun. Underline the names of the book and movie you choose, to show that those names should be in italics if they were typed.

Common Noun	**Proper Noun**
friend	____________________
book	____________________
movie	____________________
store	____________________
city	____________________
holiday	____________________

Exercise 3B: Proper Names and Titles

On your own paper, rewrite the following sentences properly. Capitalize and punctuate all names and titles correctly. If you are using a word processing program, italicize where needed; if you are writing by hand, underline in order to show italics.

I just finished reading the secret garden.

My uncle subscribes to the magazine time.

My favorite campfire song is bingo.

The sinking of the titanic was a terrible disaster.

Lewis Carroll's poem jabberwocky has many made-up words.

Exercise 3C: Proofreading for Proper Nouns

In the following sentences from *The Story of the World, Volume 3,* by Susan Wise Bauer, indicate which proper nouns should be capitalized by underlining the first letter of the noun three times. This is the proper proofreader mark for *capitalize*. The first word in the first sentence is done for you.

But not very many europeans traveled to russia, and those who settled in russia lived apart from the russians, in special colonies for foreigners.

peter's only port city, archangel, was so far north that it was frozen solid for half the year.

The sea of azov led right into the black sea, which led to the mediterranean. azov belonged to the ottoman turks.

The turks waved their turbans in surrender. azov had fallen!

— LESSON 4 —

Proper Adjectives
Compound Adjectives (Adjective-Noun Combinations)

1. Capitalize the proper names of persons, places, things, and animals.

2. Capitalize the names of holidays.

3. Capitalize the names of deities.

4. Capitalize the days of the week and the months of the year, but not the seasons.

5. Capitalize the first, last, and other important words in titles of books, magazines, newspapers, movies, television series, stories, poems, and songs.

6. Capitalize and italicize the names of ships, trains, and planes.

A proper adjective is formed from a proper name. Proper adjectives are capitalized.

	Proper Noun	Proper Adjective
Person	Aristotle	the Aristotelian philosophy
Place	Spain	a Spanish city
Holiday	Valentine's Day	some Valentine candy
Month	March	March Madness

Shakespeare wrote a number of sonnets.
I was reading some Shakespearean sonnets yesterday.

Mars is the fourth planet from the sun.
The Martian atmosphere is mostly carbon dioxide.

On Monday, I felt a little down.
I had the Monday blues.

The English enjoy a good cup of tea and a muffin.
Gerald enjoys a good English muffin.

The German-speaking tourists were lost in Central Park.
The archaeologist unearthed some pre-Columbian remains.

Words that are not usually capitalized remain lowercase even when they are attached to a proper adjective.

A compound adjective combines two words into a single adjective with a single meaning.

When the mine collapsed, it sent a plume of dust sky high.
I just had a thirty-minute study session.

N ADJ
sky high

ADJ N
thirty minute

N ADJ
user friendly

ADJ N
high speed

The sky-high plume of dust could be seen for miles.
My study session was thirty minutes.

Those directions are not user friendly!
I prefer user-friendly directions.

The connection was high speed.
He needed a high-speed connection.

Exercise 4A: Forming Proper Adjectives from Proper Nouns

Form adjectives from the following proper nouns. (Some will change form and others will not.) Write each adjective into the correct blank below. If you are not familiar with the proper nouns, you may look them up online on Encyclopaedia Britannica, Wikipedia, or some other source (this will help you complete the sentences as well). This exercise might challenge your general knowledge! (But you can always ask your instructor for help.)

Great Wall	Ireland	January	Victoria
Italy	Los Angeles	Shinkansen	Canada
Goth	Friday	Double Ninth Festival	Christmas

Traditionally, ________________________ cakes are made by layering lard, rice flour paste, and a bean paste diluted with white sugar, but each area of China has its own variation on the recipe.

The _________________ festival known as Plough Monday marked the return to work after Twelfth Night.

_________________ cathedrals were built by medieval journeymen—guilds of craftsmen who were expert woodcarvers, blacksmiths, stonemasons, plasterers, ironworkers, and glaziers.

During the _________________ period in England, many farmers left their land to live in cities and work in factories.

By _________________ standards, Hollywood Hills and Culver City are just a stone's throw from each other.

The diagonal section of the Huangyaguan section of the Ming Wall is called Heartbreak Hill by many runners in the _________________ Marathon.

My favorite _________________ cookies are gingerbread men and spritz.

The _________________ train carries over 143 million passengers from Tokyo to Shin-Osaka every year, sometimes at speeds as high as 200 miles per hour.

I found the recipe for *gelato di fragola* in my ________________ cookbook.

On Bloody Sunday (21 November 1920), fourteen British military operatives and fourteen ________________ civilians were killed in Dublin.

Er Shun, a giant panda on loan to the ________________ zoo in Toronto, gave birth to twin cubs in October of 2015; each one was the size of a stick of butter.

It was such a difficult week that we were all more than ready for the ________________ holiday and the long weekend.

Exercise 4B: Capitalization of Proper Adjectives

In the following sentences, correct each lowercase letter that should be capitalized by using the proofreader's mark (three underlines beneath each). Circle each proper adjective. Finally, write an *S* (for "same") above the proper adjectives that have not changed form from the proper noun.

the portuguese explorers were the first european travelers to reach the australian region, but spanish navigators were not far behind.

thomas abercrombie was a legendary national geographic photographer who worked in the arabian desert, the antarctic continent, the entire middle eastern region, and the south pole. he photographed jacques cousteau, the first indian white tiger brought to the north american continent, and the islamic pilgrimage to mecca.

the october farmers' market was a panorama of colorful leaves, halloween costumes, pumpkins, and heirloom squash. the blue hubbard and golden hubbard varieties were my favorite.

the laws of the elizabethan age allowed french and dutch protestants to have their own london churches, although english citizens were not supposed to enter them. diplomats from catholic countries were allowed to celebrate mass, but only in their own homes, and english subjects were banned from those services as well.

Exercise 4C: Hyphenating Attributive Compound Adjectives

Hyphens prevent misunderstanding! Explain to your instructor the differences between each pair of phrases. The first is done for you. If you're confused, ask your instructor for help.

a small-town boy
a small town boy

a small-town boy is a boy from a small town
a small town boy is a town boy of diminished size: a small boy who is also a town boy

a violent-crime conference
a violent crime conference

a high-chair cover
a high chair cover

a cross-country runner
a cross country runner

an ill-fated actress
an ill fated actress

WEEK 2

Introduction to Personal Pronouns and Verbs

— LESSON 5 —

Noun Gender
Introduction to Personal Pronouns

Exercise 5A: Introduction to Noun Gender

How well do you know your animals? Fill in the blanks with the correct name (and don't worry too much if you don't know the answers . . . this is mostly for fun).

Animal	Male	Female	Baby	Group of Animals
cattle	bull	____________	____________	drove of cattle
chicken	rooster	____________	chick	________________
deer	____________	____________	fawn	herd of deer
owl	____________	owl	____________	________________
horse	____________	____________	foal	________________
rabbit	____________	____________	bunny	________________
mouse	____________	doe	____________ OR__________	mischief of mice
swan	____________	pen	____________	__________OR________

Nouns have gender.
Nouns can be masculine, feminine, or neuter.
We use *neuter* for nouns that have no gender, and for nouns whose gender is unknown.

Subha Datta set off for the forest, intending to come back the same evening. He began to cut down a tree, but he suddenly had a feeling that he was no longer alone. As it crashed to the ground, he looked up and saw a beautiful girl dancing around and around in a little clearing nearby. Subha Datta was astonished, and let the axe fall. The noise startled the dancer, and she stood still.

Subha Datta thought he was dreaming.

Although she did not yet know it, the fairy had not convinced Subha Datta.

A pronoun takes the place of a noun.
The antecedent is the noun that is replaced by the pronoun.
Personal pronouns replace specific nouns.

I	we
you	you (plural)
he, she, it	they

Exercise 5B: Nouns and Pronouns

Write the correct pronoun above the underlined word(s). The first one is done for you.

They
Astronomers predicted that the comet would crash into Jupiter on or about July 25, 1994.
(Theo Koupelis, *In Quest of the Universe*)

This particular slab of black basalt was different from anything that had ever been discovered. The slab carried three inscriptions.
(Hendrik van Loon, *The Story of Mankind*)

Jenny and I read a book about inventors.

Benjamin Franklin not only invented objects such as the lightning rod, but Benjamin Franklin also invented the expression "pay it forward" to teach people to repay kindness by being kind to others.

Wilbur and Orville Wright had always loved construction. Wilbur and Orville Wright began as bicycle mechanics and eventually constructed the first successful airplane!

The wheel is one of the most important inventions of all time. The wheel was probably invented for chariots in ancient Mesopotamia, which is now part of Iraq.

"Why," said Effie, "I know what it is. It is a dragon like the one St. George killed." And Effie was right.

(E. Nesbit, *The Book of Dragons*)

Exercise 5C: Substituting Pronouns

Does the passage below sound awkward? It should, because it's not what the Brothers Grimm actually wrote. Choose the nouns that can be replaced by pronouns, cross them (and any accompanying words, such as *the*) out, and write the appropriate pronouns above them.

Then Dullhead fell to at once to hew down the tree, and when the tree fell Dullhead found amongst the roots a goose, whose feathers were all of pure gold. Dullhead lifted the goose out, carried the goose off, and took the goose to an inn where Dullhead meant to spend the night.

Now the landlord of the inn had a beautiful daughter, and when the daughter saw the goose, the daughter was filled with curiosity as to what this wonderful bird could be and the daughter longed for one of the golden feathers.

Exercise 5D: Pronouns and Antecedents

Circle the personal pronouns in the following sentences, and draw an arrow from each pronoun to its antecedent. If the noun and pronoun are masculine, write *M* in the margin. If they are feminine, write *F*; if neuter, write *N*. Some sentences have two personal pronouns. The first is done for you.

Although Helen Keller was blind and deaf, she became a famous author and speaker. F

The man selected a cake covered with violet icing and bit into it. It appeared to be filled with jam.

Sylvia was not much comforted. She moved along to the middle of the seat and huddled there.

—Joan Aiken, *The Wolves of Willoughby Chase*

Andreas Vesalius showed immense curiosity about the functioning of living things. He often caught and dissected small animals and insects.

—Kendall Haven, *100 Greatest Science Discoveries of All Time*

The Wart copied Archimedes in zooming up toward the branch which they had chosen.

—T. H. White, *The Once and Future King*

Mother Teresa was born in Albania; she worked for 45 years caring for the poor people of India.

Mahatma Gandhi led peaceful protests against the persecution of poor people and women in India. He disobeyed unfair laws but quietly suffered the punishment.

Even though he spent 27 years in prison, Nelson Mandela, a follower of Gandhi, helped to bring democracy for all races to South Africa.

Being the scientist that he was, Carver decided that he would take the peanut apart.
—Robert C. Haven, *Seven African-American Scientists*

"Why," said Effie, "I know what it is. It is a dragon like the one St. George killed." And she was right.
—E. Nesbit, *The Book of Dragons*

— LESSON 6 —

Review Definitions

Introduction to Verbs

Action Verbs, State-of-Being Verbs

Parts of Speech

A noun names a person, place, thing, or idea.
A common noun is a name common to many persons, places, things, or ideas.
Concrete nouns can be observed with our senses. Abstract nouns cannot.
An adjective modifies a noun or pronoun.
Adjectives tell what kind, which one, how many, and whose.
Descriptive adjectives tell what kind.
A descriptive adjective becomes an abstract noun when you add *-ness* to it.

A verb shows an action, shows a state of being, links two words together, or helps another verb.

Part of speech is a term that explains what a word does.

State-of-Being Verbs

am	were
is	be
are	being
was	been

Exercise 6A: Identifying Verbs

Mark each underlined verb *A* for action verb or *B* for state-of-being verb. Condensed slightly from W.S.B. Mathews, *A Popular History of the Art of Music.*

We here <u>enter</u> upon one of the most interesting and important chapters in the history of music.

The art of polyphony originated at the same period as the pointed arch and the great cathedrals of Europe. In music, polyphony represents the same bounding movement of mind, filled with high ideals. In the same country arose the Gothic arch, the beauties of Notre Dame in Paris, and the involved and massive polyphony of music.

Polyphonic is a term which relates itself to two others. They are Monodic and Homophonic. The musical art of the ancients was an art in which a single melodic formula doubled in a lower or higher octave, but where no harmony was; variety came through rhythm alone. Monodic art was an art of melody only. Our modern art of homophony is like that, in having but a single melody at each moment of the piece; but it differs from the ancient in the addition of a harmonic support for the melody tones. This harmonic accompaniment rules everything in modern music. It is within the power of the composer to support the melody tone with the chord which would most readily suggest itself, within the limitations of the key. Instances of this use of harmonic accompaniment are numerous in Wagner's works, and form the most obvious peculiarity of his style.

Halfway between these two types of musical art stands polyphony, which means etymologically "many sounds," but which in musical technique is "multiplicity of melodies." In a true polyphony, every tone of the leading voice possesses melodic character, but all the tones are themselves elements of other, independently moving melodies. The essence of polyphony is canonic imitation. The simplest form of this is the "round," in which one voice leads off with a phrase, and immediately a second voice begins with the same melody at the same pitch, and follows after. At the proper interval a third voice enters. Thus, when there is only one voice, we have monody; when the second voice enters we have combined sounds of two elements; and when the third enters we have chords of three tones.

A round goes on in an endless sequence until the performers stop arbitrarily. There is no innate reason why it might not continue indefinitely!

Exercise 6B: Action Verbs and State-of-Being Verbs

Provide an appropriate action and state-of-being verb for each of the following nouns. The first is done for you.

	State-of-Being	Action
The rabbit	was (or is)	hopped
Dinosaurs		
The sun		
Trains		
I		
The student		
Molecules		
The wind		
Wolves		
You		

Exercise 6C: Strong Action Verbs

Good writers use descriptive and vivid verbs. First underline the action verbs in the following sentences. Then rewrite a different, vivid verb in the space provided. The first is done for you. You may use a thesaurus if necessary.

Ellen spoke to her friend after their fight.	apologized
Edgar moved away from the angry tiger.	
The starving man ate his dinner.	
The delicate lamp broke on the floor.	
The frightened little girl asked for her mother.	
After the snowstorm, Carrie came down the hill in her sled.	

Alexander the Great beat his enemies. ____________________

The Blackfoot moved across the land. ____________________

— LESSON 7 —

Helping Verbs

Part of speech is a term that explains what a word does.

Exercise 7A: Action and Helping Verbs

Underline the action verbs in both columns of sentences once. The sentences in the second column each contain at least one helping verb. Underline these helping verbs twice. The first is done for you.

These sentences are adapted from *A Complete Geography*, by Ralph Tarr and Frank McMurry.

COLUMN 1	COLUMN 2
Waves form in the ocean.	Waves are formed by winds which blow over the water.
Waves endanger small ships.	Waves are constantly endangering small ships.
Waves damage the coast.	The constant beating of the waves is slowly eating the coast away.
Tides rise and fall.	Tides are caused by the moon and the sun.
The sun pulls on the earth.	The ocean is drawn slightly out of shape when the sun's pull affects it.
Spring tides rise high.	The high tides at full and new moon are called spring tides.

Helping Verbs

am, is, are, was, were
be, being, been
have, has, had
do, does, did
shall, will, should, would, may, might, must
can, could

Exercise 7B: Helping Verbs

Fill in each blank in the story with a helping verb. Sometimes, more than one helping verb might be appropriate. This excerpt is adapted from *King Arthur: Tales of the Round Table*, by Andrew Lang.

Long, long ago, after Uther Pendragon died, there was no king in Britain, and every knight hoped for the crown himself. Laws ________________ broken on every side, and the corn grown by the poor ________________ trodden underfoot, and there was no king to bring evildoers to justice.

When things were at their worst, Merlin the magician appeared and rode fast to the place where the Archbishop of Canterbury lived. They took counsel together, and agreed that all the lords and gentlemen of Britain ________________ ride to London and meet on Christmas Day in the Great Church. So this ________________ done.

On Christmas morning, as they left the church, they saw in the churchyard a large stone, and on it a bar of steel, and in the steel a naked sword ________________ held, and about it ________________ written in letters of gold, "Whoever pulls out this sword is by right of birth King of England."

The knights ________________ anxious to be King, and they tugged at the sword with all their might; but it never stirred. The Archbishop watched them in silence. When they ________________ exhausted themselves from pulling, he spoke: "The man is not here who ________________ lift out that sword, nor ________________ I know where to find him. But this is my counsel—that two knights ________________ chosen, good and true men, to keep guard over the sword."

This was done. But the gentlemen-at-arms cried out that every man had a right to try to win the sword, and they decided that, on New Year's Day, a tournament ________ be held and any knight who wished ________________ enter the lists.

Among them was a brave knight called Sir Ector, who brought with him Sir Kay, his son, and Arthur, Kay's foster-brother. Now Kay ________________ unbuckled his sword the evening before, and in his haste to be at the tournament ________________ forgotten to put it on again, and he begged Arthur to ride back and fetch it for him. But when Arthur reached the house the door ________________ locked, for the women ___________ gone out to see the tournament, and though Arthur tried his best to get in, he could not. Then he rode away in great anger, and said to himself, "Kay ________________ not be without a sword this day. I ________________ take that sword in the churchyard and give it to him." He galloped fast till he reached the gate of the churchyard. Here he jumped down and tied his horse tightly to a tree; then, running up to the stone, he seized the handle of the sword, and drew it easily out.

— LESSON 8 —

Personal Pronouns

First, Second, and Third Person

Capitalizing the Pronoun *I*

	Personal Pronouns	
	Singular	**Plural**
First person	I	we
Second person	you	you
Third person	he, she, it	they

Although they are not very hungry, I certainly am.

ich i I

As the German-built plane rose into the air, I experienced a strange loneliness.

Exercise 8A: Capitalization and Punctuation Practice

Correct the following sentences. Mark through any incorrect small letters and write the correct capitals above them. Insert quotation marks if needed. Use underlining to indicate any italics.

on the night of may 6, 1915, as his ship approached the coast of ireland, Captain william thomas turner left the bridge and made his way to the first-class lounge, where passengers were taking part in a concert and talent show, a customary feature of cunard crossings.

on the morning of the ship's departure from new york, a notice had appeared on the shipping pages of new york's newspapers. placed by the german embassy in washington, it reminded readers of the existence of the war zone and cautioned that "vessels flying the flag of great britain, or of any of her allies, are liable to destruction" and that travelers sailing on such ships "do so at their own risk." though the warning did not name a particular vessel, it was widely interpreted as being aimed at turner's ship, the lusitania, and indeed in at least one prominent newspaper, the new york world, it was positioned adjacent to cunard's own advertisement for the ship.

rev. henry wood simpson, of rossland, british columbia, put himself in god's hands, and from time to time repeated one of his favorite phrases, "holy ghost, our souls inspire." he said later he knew he would survive.

his life jacket held him in a position of comfort, "and i was lying on my back smiling up at the blue sky and the white clouds, and i had not swallowed much sea water either."

but, strangely, there was also singing. first tipperary, then rule, brittania! next came abide with me.

wilson believed that if he went then to congress to ask for a declaration of war, he would likely get it.

—Erik Larson, *Dead Wake*

the supposedly snobbish french leave all personal pronouns in the unassuming lowercase, and germans respectfully capitalize the formal form of "you" and even, occasionally, the informal form of "you," but would never capitalize "i."

the growing "i" became prevalent in the 13th and 14th centuries, with a geoffrey chaucer manuscript of the canterbury tales among the first evidence of this grammatical shift.

—Caroline Winter, "Me, Myself and I," in *The Times Magazine* 8/3/2008

Exercise 8B: Person, Number, and Gender

Label each personal pronoun in the following selection with its person (*1*, *2*, or *3*) and number (*S* or *PL*). For third-person singular pronouns only, indicate gender (*M*, *F*, or *N*). The first two are done for you.

1S
I was standing with Mr. and Mrs. Elbert Hubbard when the torpedo struck the ship.
3SN
It was a heavy, rather muffled sound; a second explosion quickly followed, but I do not think it was a second torpedo, for the sound was quite different. I turned to the Hubbards and suggested, "You should go down to get life jackets." They had ample time to go there and get back to the deck, but both seemed unable to act.

I went straight down to find a life belt, took a small leather case containing business papers, and went back up on deck to the spot where I had left the Hubbards. They had gone; I never saw the Hubbards again.

A woman passenger nearby called out to Captain Turner, "Captain, what should we do?" He answered, "Ma'am, stay right where you are. The ship is strong and she will be all right." So she and I turned and walked quietly aft and tried to reassure the passengers we met. There was no panic, but there was infinite confusion.

—Slightly condensed from Charles E. Lauriat, *The Lusitania's Last Voyage* (1931)

WEEK 3

Introduction to the Sentence

— LESSON 9 —

The Sentence
Parts of Speech and Parts of Sentences
Subjects and Predicates

A sentence is a group of words that contains a subject and predicate.

part of speech noun verb

The cat sits on the mat.

part of the sentence subject predicate

The subject of the sentence is the main word or term that the sentence is about.
Part of speech is a term that explains what a word does.
Part of the sentence is a term that explains how a word functions in a sentence.
The predicate of the sentence tells something about the subject.

part of speech ____________ ____________

The *Tyrannosaurus rex* crashes through the trees.

part of the sentence ____________ ____________

Exercise 9A: Parts of Speech vs. Parts of the Sentence

Label each underlined word with the correct part of speech AND the correct part of the sentence.

part of speech __________ ________

The cat licks its paws.

part of the sentence __________ ________

part of speech ________ ________

I actually prefer dogs.

part of the sentence ________ ________

part of speech ________ ________

The dog runs down the road.

part of the sentence ________ ________

part of speech ________ ________

He runs down the road.

part of the sentence ________ ________

Exercise 9B: Parts of Speech: Nouns, Adjectives, Pronouns, and Verbs

Label each underlined word with the correct part of speech. Use *N* for noun, *A* for adjective, *P* for pronoun, and *V* for verb.

One day, while I was playing with my new doll, Miss Sullivan put my big rag doll into my lap also, spelled "d-o-l-l" and tried to make me understand that "d-o-l-l" applied to both. Earlier in the day we had had a tussle over the words "m-u-g" and "w-a-t-e-r." Miss Sullivan had tried to impress it upon me that "m-u-g" is *mug* and that "w-a-t-e-r" is *water*, but I persisted in confounding the two. In despair she had dropped the subject for the time, only to renew it at the first opportunity. I became impatient at her repeated attempts and, seizing the new doll, I dashed it upon the floor.

—From Helen Keller, *The Story of My Life*

Exercise 9C: Parts of the Sentence: Subjects and Predicates

In each of the following sentences, underline the subject once and the predicate twice. Find the subject by asking, "Who or what is this sentence about?" Find the predicate by asking, "Subject what?" The first is done for you.

George ate the banana. *Who or what is this sentence about?* George.
George what? George ate.

Owls are birds of prey.

Owls see in both the day and night.

Vultures eat carrion.

Hawks hunt live prey.

Ospreys catch fish.

Kites prefer insects.

Falcons steal the nests of other birds.

— LESSON 10 —

Subjects and Predicates
Diagramming Subjects and Predicates
Sentence Capitalization and Punctuation
Sentence Fragments

A sentence is a group of words that contains a subject and predicate.
The subject of the sentence is the main word or term that the sentence is about.
The predicate of the sentence tells something about the subject.

He does.
They can.
It is.

Hurricanes form over warm tropical waters.

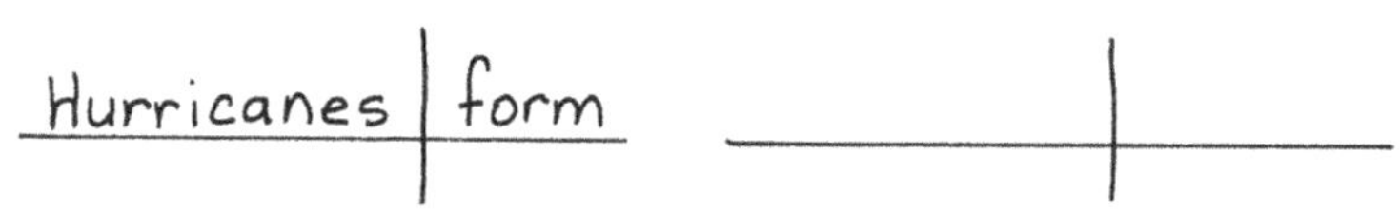

A sentence is a group of words that contains a subject and a predicate.
A sentence begins with a capital letter and ends with a punctuation mark.

No running in the kitchen.

> Can we measure intelligence without understanding it? Possibly so; physicists measured gravity and magnetism long before they understood them theoretically. Maybe psychologists can do the same with intelligence.
> **Or maybe not.**
> —James W. Kalat, *Introduction to Psychology* (Cengage Learning, 2007)

Because he couldn't go.
Since I thought so.

A sentence is a group of words that usually contains a subject and a predicate.
A sentence begins with a capital letter and ends with a punctuation mark.
A sentence contains a complete thought.

Exercise 10A: Sentences and Fragments

If the group of words expresses a complete thought, write *S* for sentence in the blank. If not, write *F* for fragment.

birds can land on the ground __________

small birds flapping their wings __________

or landing on the water __________

large birds can only hover for a short time __________

hummingbirds can beat their wings 52 times per second __________

because their feet act like skids __________

some birds are flightless __________

Exercise 10B: Proofreading for Capitalization and Punctuation

Add the correct capitalization and punctuation to the following sentences. In this exercise you will use proofreader's marks. Indicate letters which should be capitalized by underlining each letter three times. Indicate ending punctuation by using the proofreader's mark for inserting a period: ⊙. Indicate words which should be italicized by underlining them and writing *ITAL* after the sentence. If a word has to be both italicized AND capitalized, underline it once first, and then add triple underlining *beneath* the first underline. The first two are done for you.

once there was a very curious monkey named george ⊙

we booked a cruise on a ship called sea dreams ⊙ ITAL

the titanic had a sister ship called the olympic

the titanic had a gym, a swimming pool, and a hospital with an operating room

the millionaire john jacob astor and his wife were on board

the titanic hit an iceberg on april 14

when the ship began to sink, women and children were loaded into the lifeboats first the survivors in the lifeboats heard the band playing until the end

the carpathia brought the survivors to new york

Exercise 10C: Diagramming Subjects and Predicates

Find the subjects and predicates in the following sentences. Diagram each subject and predicate on your own paper. You should capitalize on the diagram any words which are capitalized in the sentence, but do not put punctuation marks on the diagram. If a proper name is the subject, all parts of the proper name go onto the subject line of the diagram. The first one is done for you.

Joseph Duckworth earned an Air Medal.

Many hurricanes form in the southwest North Pacific.

Few hurricanes arise on the equator.

Sometimes, hurricanes develop over land.

Satellites photograph hurricanes.

Radar tracks hurricanes.

Meteorologists issue hurricane warnings.

Red flags with black centers are warnings of approaching hurricanes.

— LESSON 11 —

Types of Sentences

A sentence is a group of words that usually contains a subject and a predicate.
A sentence begins with a capital letter and ends with a punctuation mark.
A sentence contains a complete thought.

A purple penguin is playing ping-pong.

A statement gives information. A statement always ends with a period.
Statements are declarative sentences.

An exclamation shows sudden or strong feeling.
An exclamation always ends with an exclamation point.
Exclamations are exclamatory sentences.

A command gives an order or makes a request.

A command ends with either a period or an exclamation point.
Commands are imperative sentences.

Sit!
Stand!
Learn!

The subject of a command is understood to be *you*.

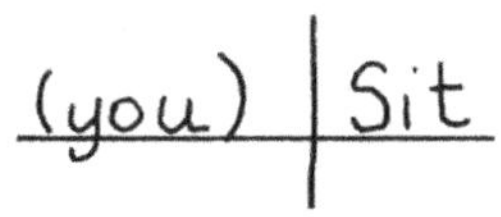

A question asks something.
A question always ends with a question mark.
Questions are known as interrogative sentences.

He is late.
Is he late?

Exercise 11A: Types of Sentences: Statements, Exclamations, Commands, and Questions

Identify the following sentences as *S* for statement, *E* for exclamation, *C* for command, or *Q* for question. Add the appropriate punctuation to the end of each sentence.

	Sentence Type
Aunt Karen is teaching me how to make strawberry pie	___________
Do we make the piecrust or the filling first	___________
Don't touch that stove	___________
Roll the dough until it is very thin	___________
I stirred the filling, and Aunt Karen poured it into the pan	___________
How long do we bake the pie	___________
This pie is delicious	___________
Eat this	___________
Do you mind if we sit down	___________
I am getting tired	___________

Exercise 11B: Proofreading for Capitalization and Punctuation

Proofread the following sentences. If a small letter should be capitalized, draw three lines underneath it. Add any missing punctuation.

what a beautiful morning

please come with me on a bike ride

my bicycle tires are flat

will you help me with the air pump

did you pack the water bottles and snacks

don't forget to put on sunscreen

let's go

Exercise 11C: Diagramming Subjects and Predicates

On your own paper, diagram the subjects and predicates of the following sentences. Remember that the understood subject of a command is *you*, and that the predicate may come before the subject in a question.

Learn quietly.
Are you hungry?
Sometimes, students work hard.
Other times, students stare out of windows.
The book is open.
Close the book.
Did you?
You did a good job today.

— LESSON 12 —

Subjects and Predicates
Helping Verbs
Simple and Complete Subjects and Predicates

The subject of the sentence is the main word or term that the sentence is about.

The simple subject of the sentence is *just* the main word or term that the sentence is about.

Mary	had a little lamb.
Its fleece	was white as snow.
...the lamb	was sure to go.

The complete subject of the sentence is the simple subject and all the words that belong to it.

The predicate of the sentence tells something about the subject.
The simple predicate of the sentence is the main verb along with any helping verbs.
The complete predicate of the sentence is the simple predicate and all the words that belong to it.

Complete Subject	**Complete Predicate**
Lambs born in the spring	must remain with their mothers until July.
Plentiful turnips	should be provided for them.

Exercise 12A: Complete Subjects and Complete Predicates

Match the complete subjects and complete predicates by drawing lines between them.

The hard storm	huddled close together under a low-branching tree.
The chickens	became cool and clear.
The horses	appeared, first one, then six, then twenty.
Out in the meadow, the sheep	ran for the open door of the hen-house.
The wind	were already in their comfortable stalls with hay.
The loud thunder	flew across the sky.
The clouds, too,	swayed the branches.
At last the air	came in the night when the farmers were asleep.
Next, the stars	made the lambs jump.

Exercise 12B: Simple and Complete Subjects and Predicates

In the following sentences (adapted from Connie Willis's wonderful novel *Bellwether*), underline the simple subject once and the simple predicate twice. Then, draw a vertical line between the complete subject and the complete predicate. The first is done for you.

The little ewe | kicked out with four hooves in four different directions, flailing madly.

A deceptively scrawny ewe had mashed me against the fence.

The flock meekly followed the bellwether.

The sheep were suddenly on the move again.

Out in the hall, they wandered aimlessly around.

In the stats lab, a sheep was munching thoughtfully on a disk.

A fat ewe was already through the door.

Exercise 12C: Diagramming Simple Subjects and Simple Predicates

On your own paper, diagram the simple subjects and simple predicates from Exercise 12B.

— REVIEW 1 —

Weeks 1-3

Topics
Concrete/Abstract Nouns
Descriptive Adjectives
Common/Proper Nouns
Capitalization of Proper Nouns and First Words in Sentences
Noun Gender
Pronouns and Antecedents
Action Verbs/State-of-Being Verbs
Helping Verbs
Subjects and Predicates
Complete Sentences
Types of Sentences

Review 1A: Types of Nouns

Fill in the blanks with the correct description of each noun. The first is done for you.

	Concrete / Abstract	Common / Proper	Gender (M, F, N)
teacher	C	C	N
Alki Beach	______	______	______
Miss Luzia	______	______	______
jellyfish	______	______	______
terror	______	______	______
Camp Greenside	______	______	______
determination	______	______	______
daughter-in-law	______	______	______
gentleman	______	______	______
vastness	______	______	______
President Jefferson	______	______	______

Review 1B: Types of Verbs

Underline the complete verbs in the following sentences. Identify helping verbs as *HV*. Identify the main verb as *AV* for action verb or *BV* for state-of-being verb. The first is done for you.

Erosion, rain, and winds have (HV) created (AV) the Grand Canyon over many years.

A massive flood could have contributed to the formation of the Grand Canyon.

Even experienced geologists are puzzled by this phenomenon.

Many rock layers compose the cavernous walls.

The Grand Canyon is considered one of the seven natural wonders of the world.

The Great Barrier Reef and Mount Everest are other natural wonders.

My grandparents and I might be at the Grand Canyon next September.

The Grand Canyon will be my first wonder of the world.

Maybe next I will travel to Australia for the Great Barrier Reef.

By the time I am 50 I will have seen all seven wonders of the world!

Review 1C: Subjects and Predicates

Draw one line under the simple subject and two lines under the simple predicate in the following sentences. Remember that the predicate may be a verb phrase with more than one verb in it.

Hot air balloons were constructed long before the invention of airplanes.

French scientists invented hot air balloons in the late 1700s.

They originally were very dangerous.

These first contraptions utilized a cloth balloon and a live fire.

Later modifications improved the safety of hot air balloons.

Soon, even tourists could ride in hot air balloons.

However balloonists also attempted more impressive feats.

Many have died in their attempts to break new ballooning records.

Three bold adventurers in the 1970s flew in a balloon across the Atlantic Ocean.

Review 1D: Parts of Speech

Identify the underlined words by writing the following abbreviations above them: *N* for noun, *P* for pronoun, *A* for adjective, *AV* for action verb, *HV* for helping verb, or *BV* for state-of-being verb.

The following excerpt is from the novel *Out of My Mind*, by Sharon Draper (Atheneum, 2010), pp. 3-4.

When people look at me, I guess they see a girl with short, dark, curly hair strapped into a pink wheelchair. By the way, there is nothing cute about a pink wheelchair. Pink doesn't change a thing.

They'd see a girl with dark brown eyes that are full of curiosity. But one of them is slightly out of whack.

Her head wobbles a little.

Sometimes she drools.

She's really tiny for a girl who is age ten and three quarters.

... After folks... finished making a list of my problems, they might take time to notice that I have a fairly nice smile and deep dimples—I think my dimples are cool.

I wear tiny gold earrings.

Sometimes people never even ask my name, like it's not important or something. It is.

My name is Melody.

Review 1E: Capitalization and Punctuation

Use proofreading marks to indicate correct capitalization and punctuation in the following sentences. Be careful: Some of these may have more than one sentence, so ending punctuation will need to be inserted to split sentences correctly!

Small letter that should be capitalized: ≡ beneath the letter.

Italics: single underline	insert period: ⊙	insert exclamation point: ^!
insert question mark: ^?	insert quotation marks: ^"	insert comma: ^,

the first day of winter was tuesday, december 21⊙

mr. collins, my history teacher, taught us about osiris, an ancient egyptian god

francisca sat outside café gutenberg and read gulliver's travels

does thanksgiving always fall on a thursday

in canada, thanksgiving is celebrated on the second monday in october

the trans-siberian railway, the longest railway in the world, runs from moscow to vladivostok

the opera california youth choir, a korean american choir, performed mozart's requiem in los angeles

did geraldine bring a copy of today's washington post

do we need to finish the call of the wild by friday for ms. hannigan's class

Review 1F: Types of Sentences

Identify the following sentences as *S* for statement, *C* for command, *E* for exclamation, or *Q* for question. If the sentence is incomplete, write *F* for fragment instead.

The following sentences were adapted from Pam Muñoz Ryan's *The Dreamer* (Scholastic, 2010), a fictional story about the poet Pablo Neruda (pp. 16-19).

	Sentence Type
The next day, Mamadre was far more watchful, and Neftalí could not escape from his bed.	________
"Tell me all that you can see."	________

"I see rain." __________

"Tell me about the stray dog." __________

"What color is it?" __________

"I cannot say." __________

"Maybe brown." __________

"Tell me about the boot that is missing." __________

"It has no shoestrings." __________

"I will rescue it and add it to my collections." __________

"You do not know where it has been." __________

"Or who has worn it." __________

To what mystical land does an unfinished staircase lead? __________

WEEK 4

Verb Tenses

— LESSON 13 —

Nouns, Pronouns, and Verbs
Sentences
Simple Present, Simple Past, and Simple Future Tenses

A noun names a person, place, thing, or idea.
A pronoun takes the place of a noun.
A verb shows an action, shows a state of being, links two words together, or helps another verb.

State-of-Being Verbs

am	were
is	be
are	being
was	been

Helping Verbs
am, is, are, was, were
be, being, been
have, has, had
do, does, did
shall, will, should, would, may, might, must
can, could

A sentence is a group of words that usually contains a subject and a predicate. A sentence begins with a capital letter and ends with a punctuation mark. A sentence contains a complete thought.

A verb in the present tense tells about something that happens in the present.
A verb in the past tense tells about something that happened in the past.
A verb in the future tense tells about something that will happen in the future.

Exercise 13A: Simple Tenses

	Simple Past	Simple Present	Simple Future
I			will grab
You	behaved		
She		jogs	
We	enjoyed		
They		guess	

Form the simple future by adding the helping verb *will* in front of the simple present.
A suffix is one or more letters added to the end of a word to change its meaning.

Forming the Simple Past
To form the past tense, add *-ed* to the basic verb.

sharpen–sharpened
utter–uttered

If the basic verb ends in *-e* already, only add *-d*.

rumble–rumbled
shade–shaded

If the verb ends in a short vowel sound and a consonant, double the consonant and add *-ed*.

scam–scammed
thud–thudded

If the verb ends in *-y* following a consonant, change the *y* to *i* and add *-ed*.

cry–cried
try–tried

Exercise 13B: Using Consistent Tense

When you write, you should use consistent tense—if you begin a sentence in one tense, you should continue to use that same tense for any other verbs in the same sentence. The following sentences use two verb tenses. Cross out the second verb and rewrite it so that the tense of the second verb matches the tense of the first one.

The first sentence is done for you.

hugged
Annie leaped up and ~~hugs~~ her mother.

Alison walked to the ticket booth and picks up tickets for her first football game.

Her brother accompanied her to the game and will explain the rules.

The game will continue for a long time, and the players work hard.

The running back steals the ball and scored a touchdown!

Alison and her brother jump in the air and will cheer for the team.

It will be a fun trip home because her brother stops for ice cream to celebrate.

Exercise 13C: Forming the Simple Past Tense

Using the rules for forming the simple past, put each one of the following verbs in parentheses into the simple past. Write the simple past form in the blank. Be sure to spell the past forms of regular verbs correctly, and to use the correct forms of irregular verbs.

These sentences are taken from *The Emerald City of Oz*, by L. Frank Baum.

The Nome King was in an angry mood, and at such times he was very disagreeable. Every one kept away from him, even his Chief Steward Kaliko.

Therefore the King _______________ (storm) and _______________ (rave) all by himself, walking up and down in his jewel-studded cavern and getting angrier all the time. Then he _______________ (remember) that it was no fun being angry unless he had some one to frighten and make miserable, and he _______________ (rush) to his big gong and __________ (make) it clatter as loud as he could.

In came the Chief Steward, trying not to show the Nome King how frightened he was.

"Send the Chief Counselor here!" _______________ (shout) the angry monarch.

Kaliko ran out as fast as his spindle legs could carry his fat, round body, and soon the Chief Counselor _______________ (enter) the cavern. The King _______________ (scowl) and _______________ (say) to him:

"I'm in great trouble over the loss of my Magic Belt. Every little while I want to do something magical, and find I can't because the Belt is gone. That makes me angry, and when I'm angry I can't have a good time. Now, what do you advise?"

"Some people," said the Chief Counselor, "enjoy getting angry."

"But not all the time," ________________ (declare) the King. "To be angry once in a while is really good fun, because it makes others so miserable. But to be angry morning, noon and night, as I am, grows monotonous and prevents my gaining any other pleasure in life. Now what do you advise?"

"Why, if you are angry because you want to do magical things and can't, and if you don't want to get angry at all, my advice is not to want to do magical things."

Hearing this, the King _____________ (glare) at his Counselor with a furious expression and _____________ (tug) at his own long white whiskers until he ___________ (pull) them so hard that he _____________ (yell) with pain.

"You are a fool!" he _____________ (exclaim).

"I share that honor with your Majesty," said the Chief Counselor.

The King _____________ (roar) with rage and _____________ (stamp) his foot.

"Ho, there, my guards!" he _____________ (cry). "Ho" is a royal way of saying, "Come here." So, when the guards had hoed, the King said to them, "Take this Chief Counselor and throw him away."

Then the guards took the Chief Counselor, and bound him with chains to prevent his struggling, and _____________ (lock) him away. And the King _____________ (pace) up and down his cavern more angry than before.

— LESSON 14 —

Simple Present, Simple Past, and Simple Future Tenses
Progressive Present, Progressive Past, and Progressive Future Tenses

A verb in the present tense tells about something that happens in the present.
A verb in the future tense tells about something that will happen in the future.
A verb in the past tense tells about something that happened in the past.

study will study studied

Forming the Simple Past:
To form the past tense, add *-ed* to the basic verb.
If the basic verb ends in *e* already, only add *-d.*
If the verb ends in a short vowel sound and a consonant, double the consonant and add *-ed.*
If the verb ends in *-y* following a consonant, change the *y* to *i* and add *-ed.*

Exercise 14A: Forming the Simple Past and Simple Future Tenses

Form the simple past and simple future of the following regular verbs.

Past	Present	Future
	add	
	share	
	pat	
	cry	
	obey	
	dance	
	groan	
	jog	
	kiss	

Yesterday, I cried. I was crying for a long time.
Today, I learn. I am learning my grammar.
Tomorrow, I will celebrate. I will be celebrating all afternoon.

A progressive verb describes an ongoing or continuous action.

Exercise 14B: Progressive Tenses

Circle the ending of each verb. Underline the helping verbs.

was chewing

will be dancing

am decorating

will be exercising

am floating

was gathering

will be copying

The progressive past tense uses the helping verbs *was* and *were*.
The progressive present tense uses the helping verbs *am*, *is*, and *are*.
The progressive future tense uses the helping verbs *will be*.

Spelling Rules for Adding *-ing*
If the verb ends in a short vowel sound and a consonant, double the consonant and add *-ing*.
skip–skipping
drum–drumming

If the verb ends in a long vowel sound plus a consonant and an *-e*, drop the *-e* and add *-ing*.
smile–smiling
trade–trading

Exercise 14C: Forming the Past, Present, and Progressive Future Tenses

Complete the following chart. Be sure to use the spelling rules above.

	Progressive Past	Progressive Present	Progressive Future
I run	I was running	I am running	I will be running
I chew			
I grab			
I charge			
You call	You were calling	You are calling	You will be calling
You fix			
You destroy			
You command			
We dare	We were daring	We are daring	We will be daring
We educate			
We jog			
We laugh			

Exercise 14D: Simple and Progressive Tenses

Fill in the blanks with the correct form of the verb in parentheses.

The scientist Antoni van Leeuwenhoek _______________ (progressive past of *experiment*) when he _______________ (simple past of *test*) the water of the inland lake Berkelse Mere.

When he _______________ (simple past of *look*) through his lens, he _______________ (simple past of *discover*) that microscopic creatures _______________ (progressive past of *swim*) in the water.

The French surgeon Ambroise Pare _______________ (progressive past of *cauterize*) wounds when he ran out of boiling oil.

He _______________ (simple past of *use*) salve instead, but he _______________ (simple past of *remark*) to another doctor, "In the morning, the wounds _______________ (progressive future of *fester*)."

In the morning, the wounds he _______________ (simple past of *treat*) with salve _______________ (progressive past of *heal*) better than the wounds that were treated with cauterization.

Johannes Kepler _______________ (progressive past of *study*) the orbit of Mars.

Finally, Kepler _______________ (simple past of *decide*) that the orbit must be elliptical.

— LESSON 15 —

Simple Present, Simple Past, and Simple Future Tenses
Progressive Present, Progressive Past, and Progressive Future Tenses
Perfect Present, Perfect Past, and Perfect Future Tenses

A progressive verb describes an ongoing or continuous action.

Yesterday, I was studying tenses.
Today, I am studying tenses.
Tomorrow, I will be studying something else!

NEWS BULLETIN!
A diamond theft occurred at the National Museum yesterday. The thief had already fled the scene when a security guard discovered that the diamond was missing.

A perfect verb describes an action which has been completed before another action takes place.

I practiced my piano.
I was practicing my piano all day yesterday.
I had practiced my piano before I went to bed.

Perfect Past	Perfect Present	Perfect Future
I had practiced yesterday.	I have practiced.	I will have practiced tomorrow.
I had eaten before bed.	I have eaten already.	I will have eaten by bedtime tomorrow.
I had seen the movie a week ago.	I have seen the movie once.	I will have seen the movie before it leaves the theater.

Perfect past verbs describe an action that was finished in the past before another action began.

Helping verb: *had*

Perfect present verbs describe an action that was completed before the present moment.

Helping verbs: *have, has*

Perfect future verbs describe an action that will be finished in the future before another action begins.

Helping verb: *will have*

Exercise 15A: Perfect Tenses

Fill in the blanks with the missing forms.

Simple Past	Perfect Past	Perfect Present	Perfect Future
I jogged	I had jogged	I have jogged	I will have jogged
I planted			
I refused			
I shrugged			
We cheered	We had cheered	We have cheered	We will have cheered
We sighed			
We managed			
We listened			
He missed	He had missed	He has missed	He will have missed
He knitted			
He juggled			
He hammered			

Exercise 15B: Identifying Perfect Tenses

Identify the underlined verbs as perfect past, perfect present, or perfect future. The first one is done for you.

perfect present
I have decided to set up a salt water fish tank in my room today.

I had read a book about marine biology before deciding to set up my tank.

I have put coral and damselfish in my tank, and I am buying a clown fish tomorrow morning.

I have tried to regulate the salt and light levels in the tank, so that the corals and fish can live in an environment similar to the ocean.

Last night I was looking for my clown fish because I had failed to see him all day.

I had become afraid for my clown fish, but he was hiding in the coral!

In fifteen years I will have finished studying marine science, and I will be working at a dolphin center.

Exercise 15C: Perfect, Progressive, and Simple Tenses

Each underlined verb phrase has been labeled as past, present, or future. Add the label *perfect*, *progressive*, or *simple* to each one. The first has been done for you.

progressive PRESENT / perfect PRESENT

Roopa is living with her parents and two little sisters in Chennai, India. She has lived there all her life.

PAST / PAST

Roopa was eating her lunch of curry and bread while she looked out the window.

PAST / PAST

Women were hurrying through the streets. They wore colorful saris with jasmine flowers in their hair.

PAST / PAST / FUTURE

Monsoon season had started already. Soon, thought Roopa, the rains will be flooding the streets.

PRESENT / FUTURE

When the monsoon rages, the palm trees will bend close to the ground under the pressure of the wind and rain.

PAST PAST
Roopa had finished her food by now. She picked up her cup of chai tea, happy that she

PAST
was sitting inside, safe and dry.

— LESSON 16 —

Simple Present, Simple Past, and Simple Future Tenses
Progressive Present, Progressive Past, and Progressive Future Tenses
Perfect Present, Perfect Past, and Perfect Future Tenses
Irregular Verbs

go	run	are	know	make
go-ed	run-ned	ar-ed	know-ed	mak-ed
went	ran	were	knew	made

Exercise 16A: Irregular Verb Forms: Simple Present, Simple Past, and Simple Future

Fill in the chart with the missing verb forms.

	Simple Past	Simple Present	Simple Future
I			will eat
You			will feel
She	wrote		
We		are	
They		get	
I			will have
You		go	
He	kept		

	Simple Past	Simple Present	Simple Future
We		make	
They		think	
I	ran		
You			will sing
It		speaks	
We			will know
They	swam		
I		write	
You		throw	
We			will become
They	taught		

	Simple Past	Simple Present	Simple Future	Progressive Past	Progressive Present	Progressive Future	Perfect Past	Perfect Present	Perfect Future
go	went	go	will go	was going	am going	will be going	had gone	have gone	will have gone
eat	ate	eat	will eat	was eating	am eating	will be eating	had eaten	have eaten	will have eaten

Exercise 16B: Irregular Verbs, Progressive and Perfect Tenses

Fill in the remaining blanks. The first is done for you.

Simple Present	Progressive Past	Progressive Present	Progressive Future	Perfect Past	Perfect Present	Perfect Future
give	was giving	am giving	will be giving	had given	have given	will have given
feel						
write						
grow						
keep						
make						
think						
run						
sing						
speak						
know						

Simple Present	Progressive Past	Progressive Present	Progressive Future	Perfect Past	Perfect Present	Perfect Future
swim						
write						
throw						
become						
teach						
is						

WEEK 5

More About Verbs

— LESSON 17 —

Simple, Progressive, and Perfect Tenses
Subjects and Predicates
Parts of Speech and Parts of Sentences
Verb Phrases

I yawn today. Yesterday, I yawned. Tomorrow, I will yawn.
I am yawning today. Yesterday, I was yawning. Tomorrow, I will be yawning.

A progressive verb describes an ongoing or continuous action.

I have yawned today already.
Yesterday, I had yawned before I had my dinner.
Tomorrow, I will have yawned by the time the sun goes down.

A perfect verb describes an action which has been completed before another action takes place.

Exercise 17A: Simple, Progressive, and Perfect Tenses
All of the bolded verbs are in the past tense. Label each bolded verb as *S* for simple or *PERF* for perfect.

Now in these subterranean caverns **lived** a strange race of beings, called by some gnomes, by some kobolds, by some goblins. There **was** a legend current in the country that at one time they **lived** above ground, and were very like other people. But for some reason or other, concerning which there were different legendary theories, the king **had laid** what they thought too severe taxes upon them, or **had required** observances of them they did not like, or **had begun** to treat them with more severity, in some way or other, and impose stricter laws; and the consequence was that they **had** all **disappeared** from the face of the country. According to the legend, however, instead of going to some other country, they **had** all **taken** refuge in the subterranean caverns, whence they never **came** out but at night, and then seldom **showed** themselves in any numbers, and never to many people at once. It was only in the least frequented and most difficult parts of the mountains that they were said to gather even at night in the open air. Those who **had caught** sight of any of them **said** that they **had** greatly **altered** in the course of generations; and no wonder, seeing they **lived** away from the sun, in cold and wet and dark places.

—From *The Princess and the Goblin*, by George MacDonald

had rejoiced
will have rejoiced

A phrase is a group of words serving a single grammatical function.

have greatly rejoiced
They will have all rejoiced

The subject of the sentence is the main word or term that the sentence is about.

The simple subject of the sentence is *just* the main word or term that the sentence is about.

The predicate of the sentence tells something about the subject.

The simple predicate of the sentence is the main verb along with any helping verbs.

Part of speech is a term that explains what a word does.

A noun names a person, place, thing, or idea.

A pronoun takes the place of a noun.

Part of the sentence is a term that explains how a word functions in a sentence.

A verb shows an action, shows a state of being, links two words together, or helps another verb.

Exercise 17B: Identifying and Diagramming Subjects and Predicates, Identifying Verb Tenses

Underline the subject once and the predicate twice in each sentence. Be sure to include both the main verb and any helping verbs when you underline the predicate. Identify the tense of each verb or verb phrase (*simple past*, *present*, or *future*; *progressive past*, *present*, or *future*; *perfect past*, *present*, or *future*) on the line. Then, diagram each subject and predicate on your own paper.

These sentences are taken from *The Light Princess and Other Fairy Stories*, by George MacDonald.

Her atrocious aunt had deprived the child of all her gravity. ______________________

One day an awkward accident happened. ______________________

The princess had come out upon the lawn. ______________________

She had almost reached her father. ______________________

He was holding out his arms. ______________________

A puff of wind blew her aside. ______________________

We have fallen in! ______________________

He was swimming with the princess. ______________________

I have quite forgotten the date. ______________________

By that time, they will have learned their lesson. ______________________

She found her gravity! ______________________

Down the narrow path they went. ______________________

They reached the bottom in safety. ______________________

— LESSON 18 —

Verb Phrases
Person of the Verb
Conjugations

	Progressive Past	Progressive Present	Progressive Future
I run	I was running	I am running	I will be running
you call	you were calling	you are calling	you will be calling
he jogs	he was jogging	he is jogging	he will be jogging
we fix	we were fixing	we are fixing	we will be fixing
they call	they were calling	they are calling	they will be calling

PERSONS OF THE VERB

	Singular	Plural
First person	I	we
Second person	you	you
Third person	he, she, it	they

Simple Tenses

REGULAR VERB, SIMPLE PRESENT

	Singular	Plural
First person	I pretend	we pretend
Second person	you pretend	you pretend
Third person	he, she, it pretends	they pretend
First person	I wander	we wander
Second person	you wander	you wander
Third person	he, she, it wanders	they wander

REGULAR VERB, SIMPLE PAST

	Singular	Plural
First person	I wandered	we wandered
Second person	you wandered	you wandered
Third person	he, she, it wandered	they wandered

REGULAR VERB, SIMPLE FUTURE

	Singular	Plural
First person	I will wander	we will wander
Second person	you will wander	you will wander
Third person	he, she, it will wander	they will wander

Perfect Tenses

REGULAR VERB, PERFECT PRESENT

	Singular	Plural
First person	I have wandered	we have wandered
Second person	you have wandered	you have wandered
Third person	he, she, it has wandered	they have wandered

REGULAR VERB, PERFECT PAST

	Singular	Plural
First person	I had wandered	we had wandered
Second person	you had wandered	you had wandered
Third person	he, she, it had wandered	they had wandered

REGULAR VERB, PERFECT FUTURE

	Singular	Plural
First person	I will have wandered	we will have wandered
Second person	you will have wandered	you will have wandered
Third person	he, she, it will have wandered	they will have wandered

Exercise 18A: Third-Person Singular Verbs

In the simple present conjugation, the third-person singular verb changes by adding an *-s*. Read the following rules and examples for adding *-s* to verbs in order to form the third-person singular. Then, fill in the blanks with the third-person singular forms of each verb.

The first of each is done for you.

Usually, add *-s* to form the third person singular verb.

First-Person Verb	Third-Person Singular Verb
I shatter	it shatters
I skip	she ________
I hike	he ________

Add *-es* to verbs ending in *-s*, *-sh*, *-ch*, *-x*, or *-z*.

First-Person Verb	Third-Person Singular Verb	
we brush	he	brushes
we hiss	it	______
we catch	she	______

If a verb ends in *-y* after a consonant, change the *y* to *i* and add *-es*.

First-Person Verb	Third-Person Singular Verb	
I carry	it	carries
I study	she	______
I tally	he	______

If a verb ends in *-y* after a vowel, just add *-s*.

First-Person Verb	Third-Person Singular Verb	
we stray	she	strays
we buy	he	______
we play	it	______

If a verb ends in *-o* after a consonant, form the plural by adding *-es*.

First-Person Verb	Third-Person Singular Verb	
I go	she	goes
I do	it	______
I echo	he	______

Exercise 18B: Simple Present Tenses

Choose the correct form of the simple present verb in parentheses, based on the person. Cross out the incorrect form.

Hana Suzuki is fourteen. Every morning, she (eat/eats) rice and soup.

She is Japanese, and she (live/lives) in Canada with her family.

She has twin brothers. They (gobble/gobbles) their food and always (finish/finishes) before she does.

"You (chew/chews) too fast," her mother (say/says).

"But the food (taste/tastes) better if you (eat/eats) it quickly," they always (argue/argues).

"I (think/thinks) that you (enjoy/enjoys) the food more if you (slow/slows) down."

But they never (hear / hears).

They always (run / runs) out of the house too soon!

Exercise 18C: Perfect Present Tenses

Write the correct form of the perfect present verb in the blank. These sentences are drawn from Charles Dickens's novel *Oliver Twist.*

"I am very hungry and tired," replied Oliver, the tears standing in his eyes as he spoke. "I ________________ [*walk*] a long way—I have been walking these seven days."

"Speak the truth; and if I find you ________________ [*commit*] no crime, you will never be friendless while I live."

"He ________________ [*go*], sir," replied Mrs. Bedwin.

"I consider, sir, that you ____________________ [*obtain*] possession of that book under very suspicious and disreputable circumstances."

"There, my dear," said Fagin, "that's a pleasant life, isn't it? They ________________ [*go*] out for the day."

"We ____________________ [*consider*] your proposition, and we don't approve of it."

— LESSON 19 —

Person of the Verb

Conjugations

State-of-Being Verbs

English	**Latin**		
conjugate	*conjugare*	*con*	+ *jugare*
to join a verb to each person in turn	to join together	with	+ to yoke

REGULAR VERB, SIMPLE PRESENT

	Singular	**Plural**
First person	I conjugate	we conjugate
Second person	you conjugate	you conjugate
Third person	he, she, it conjugates	they conjugate

REGULAR VERB, SIMPLE PAST

conjugated

REGULAR VERB, SIMPLE FUTURE

will conjugate

REGULAR VERB, PERFECT PRESENT

	Singular	Plural
First person	I have conjugated	we have conjugated
Second person	you have conjugated	you have conjugated
Third person	he, she, it has conjugated	they have conjugated

REGULAR VERB, PERFECT PAST

had conjugated

REGULAR VERB, PERFECT FUTURE

will have conjugated

REGULAR VERB, PROGRESSIVE PRESENT

am conjugating

STATE-OF-BEING VERB, SIMPLE PRESENT

	Singular	Plural
First person	I am	we are
Second person	you are	you are
Third person	he, she, it is	they are

Exercise 19A: Forming Progressive Present Tenses

Fill in the blanks with the correct helping verbs.

Regular Verb, Progressive Present

	Singular	Plural
First person	I ______________ conjugating	we ______________ conjugating
Second person	you ______________ conjugating	you ______________ conjugating
Third person	he, she, it ______________ conjugating	they ______________ conjugating

STATE-OF-BEING VERB, SIMPLE PRESENT

	Singular	Plural
First person	I am	we are
Second person	you are	you are
Third person	he, she, it is	they are

STATE-OF-BEING VERB, SIMPLE PAST

	Singular	Plural
First person	I was	we were
Second person	you were	you were
Third person	he, she, it was	they were

STATE-OF-BEING VERB, SIMPLE FUTURE

	Singular	Plural
First person	I will be	we will be
Second person	you will be	you will be
Third person	he, she, it will be	they will be

STATE-OF-BEING VERB, PERFECT PRESENT

	Singular	Plural
First person	I have been	we have been
Second person	you have been	you have been
Third person	he, she, it has been	they have been

STATE-OF-BEING VERB, PERFECT PAST

	Singular	Plural
First person	I had been	we had been
Second person	you had been	you had been
Third person	he, she, it had been	they had been

STATE-OF-BEING VERB, PERFECT FUTURE

	Singular	Plural
First person	I will have been	we will have been
Second person	you will have been	you will have been
Third person	he, she, it will have been	they will have been

STATE-OF-BEING VERB, PROGRESSIVE PRESENT

	Singular	Plural
First person	I am being	we are being
Second person	you are being	you are being
Third person	he, she, it is being	they are being

STATE-OF-BEING VERB, PROGRESSIVE PAST

	Singular	Plural
First person	I was being	we were being
Second person	you were being	you were being
Third person	he, she, it was being	they were being

STATE-OF-BEING VERB, PROGRESSIVE FUTURE

	Singular	Plural
First person	I will be being	we will be being
Second person	you will be being	you will be being
Third person	he, she, it will be being	they will be being

Exercise 19B: Forming Progressive Past and Future Tenses

Fill in the blanks with the correct helping verbs.

Regular Verb, Progressive Present

	Singular	Plural
First person	I _____________ conjugating	we _____________ conjugating
Second person	you _____________ conjugating	you _____________ conjugating
Third person	he, she, it __________ conjugating	they _____________ conjugating

Regular Verb, Progressive Past

	Singular	Plural
First person	I _____________ conjugating	we _____________ conjugating
Second person	you _____________ conjugating	you _____________ conjugating
Third person	he, she, it __________ conjugating	they _____________ conjugating

Regular Verb, Progressive Future

	Singular	Plural
First person	I ____________ conjugating	we ____________ conjugating
Second person	you ____________ conjugating	you ____________ conjugating
Third person	he, she, it ____________ conjugating	they ____________ conjugating

— LESSON 20 —

Irregular State-of-Being Verbs

Helping Verbs

Forms of the State-of-Being Verb *Am*

SIMPLE PRESENT

	Singular	Plural
First person	I am	we are
Second person	you are	you are
Third person	he, she, it is	they are

SIMPLE PAST

	Singular	Plural
First person	I was	we were
Second person	you were	you were
Third person	he, she, it was	they were

SIMPLE FUTURE

	Singular	Plural
First person	I will be	we will be
Second person	you will be	you will be
Third person	he, she, it will be	they will be

PERFECT PRESENT

	Singular	Plural
First person	I have been	we have been
Second person	you have been	you have been
Third person	he, she, it has been	they have been

PERFECT PAST

	Singular	Plural
First person	I had been	we had been
Second person	you had been	you had been
Third person	he, she, it had been	they had been

PERFECT FUTURE

	Singular	Plural
First person	I will have been	we will have been
Second person	you will have been	you will have been
Third person	he, she, it will have been	they will have been

PROGRESSIVE PRESENT

	Singular	Plural
First person	I am being	we are being
Second person	you are being	you are being
Third person	he, she, it is being	they are being

PROGRESSIVE PAST

	Singular	Plural
First person	I was being	we were being
Second person	you were being	you were being
Third person	he, she, it was being	they were being

PROGRESSIVE FUTURE

	Singular	Plural
First person	I will be being	we will be being
Second person	you will be being	you will be being
Third person	he, she, it will be being	they will be being

Exercise 20A: Simple Tenses of the Verb *Have*

Try to fill in the missing blanks in the chart below, using your own sense of what sounds correct as well as the hints you may have picked up from the conjugations already covered. Be sure to use pencil so that any incorrect answers can be erased and corrected!

Simple Present

	Singular	Plural
First person	I ___have___	we ________
Second person	you ________	you ________
Third person	he, she, it ________	they ________

Simple Past

	Singular	Plural
First person	I ______	we ______
Second person	you ______	you ______
Third person	he, she, it ______	they ______

Simple Future

	Singular	Plural
First person	I will ______	we ______
Second person	you ______	you ______
Third person	he, she, it ______	they ______

Exercise 20B: Simple Tenses of the Verb *Do*

Try to fill in the missing blanks in the chart below, using your own sense of what sounds correct as well as the hints you may have picked up from the conjugations already covered. Be sure to use pencil so that any incorrect answers can be erased and corrected!

Simple Present

	Singular	Plural
First person	I do	we ______
Second person	you ______	you ______
Third person	he, she, it ______	they ______

Simple Past

	Singular	Plural
First person	I ______	we ______
Second person	you ______	you ______
Third person	he, she, it ______	they ______

Simple Future

	Singular	Plural
First person	I will ______	we ______
Second person	you ______	you ______
Third person	he, she, it ______	they ______

I will be	I shall be	I shall be!
You will run	You will run	You shall run!
He, she, it will sing	He, she, it will sing	He, she, it shall sing!
We will eat	We shall eat	We shall eat!
You will shout	You will shout	You shall shout!
They will cavort	They will cavort	They shall cavort!

I **will** go to bed early.
When I was young, I **would** always go to bed early.

I **would** like to go to bed early.
I **should** probably go to bed now.

I **would** eat the chocolate caramel truffle.
I **should** eat the chocolate caramel truffle.
I **may** eat the chocolate caramel truffle.
I **might** eat the chocolate caramel truffle.
I **must** eat the chocolate caramel truffle.
I **can** eat the chocolate caramel truffle.
I **could** eat the chocolate caramel truffle.

Am, is, are, was, were, be, being, and *been* are forms of the verb *am.*
Have, has, and *had* are forms of the verb *has.*
Do, does, and *did* are forms of the verb *do.*
Shall and *will* are different forms of the same verb.
Should, would, may, might, must, can, and *could* express hypothetical situations.

WEEK 6

Nouns and Verbs in Sentences

— LESSON 21 —

Person of the Verb
Conjugations
Noun-Verb/Subject-Predicate Agreement

SIMPLE PRESENT

	Singular	Plural
First person	I enjoy	we enjoy
Second person	you enjoy	you enjoy
Third person	he, she, it enjoys	they enjoy

PERFECT PAST

	Singular	Plural
First person	I had been	we had been
Second person	you had been	you had been
Third person	he, she, it had been	they had been

PROGRESSIVE FUTURE

	Singular	Plural
First person	I will be running	we will be running
Second person	you will be running	you will be running
Third person	he, she, it will be running	they will be running

Complete Conjugation of a Regular Verb

SIMPLE PRESENT

	Singular	Plural
First person	I grab	we grab
Second person	you grab	you grab
Third person	he, she, it grabs	they grab

SIMPLE PAST

I grabbed, etc.

SIMPLE FUTURE

I will grab, etc.

PERFECT PRESENT

	Singular	Plural
First person	I have grabbed	we have grabbed
Second person	you have grabbed	you have grabbed
Third person	he, she, it has grabbed	they have grabbed

PERFECT PAST

I had grabbed, etc.

PERFECT FUTURE

I will have grabbed, etc.

PROGRESSIVE PRESENT

	Singular	Plural
First person	I am grabbing	we are grabbing
Second person	you are grabbing	you are grabbing
Third person	he, she, it is grabbing	they are grabbing

PROGRESSIVE PAST

	Singular	Plural
First person	I was grabbing	we were grabbing
Second person	you were grabbing	you were grabbing
Third person	he, she, it was grabbing	they were grabbing

PROGRESSIVE FUTURE

I will be grabbing, etc.

Exercise 21A: Person and Number of Pronouns

Identify the person and number of the underlined pronouns. Cross out the incorrect verb in parentheses. The first one is done for you.

These sentences are taken from *The Once and Future King*, by T.H. White.

	Person	Singular/Plural
They (do / ~~does~~) love to fly.	third	plural
He (was / were) seeing one ray beyond the spectrum.		
We (has / had) better fly.		
You (is / are) beginning to drop out of the air.		
It (is / are) confusing to keep up with you.		
I (was / were) a fish.		
You (has / have) to glide in at stalling speed all the way.		
They (prefer / prefers) to do their hunting then.		

SIMPLE PRESENT

	Singular	Plural
Third person	he, she, it grabs	they grab
	the man grabs	the men grab
	the woman grabs	the women grab
	the eagle grabs	the eagles grab

PERFECT PRESENT

	Singular	Plural
Third person	he, she, it has grabbed	they have grabbed
	the boy has grabbed	the boys have grabbed
	the girl has grabbed	the girls have grabbed
	the bear has grabbed	the bears have grabbed

PROGRESSIVE PRESENT

	Singular	Plural
Third person	he, she, it is grabbing	they are grabbing
	the father is grabbing	the fathers are grabbing
	the mother is grabbing	the mothers are grabbing
	the baby is grabbing	the babies are grabbing

PROGRESSIVE PAST

	Singular	Plural
Third person	he, she, it was grabbing	they were grabbing
	the king was grabbing	the kings were grabbing
	the queen was grabbing	the queens were grabbing
	the dragon was grabbing	the dragons were grabbing

Exercise 21B: Identifying Subjects and Predicates

Draw two lines underneath each simple predicate and one line underneath each simple subject in the following sentences. If a phrase comes between the subject and the predicate, put parentheses around it to show that it does not affect the subject-predicate agreement.

Leafcutter ants live in the southern United States and South America.

These creatures, strong and resourceful, create gardens and complex societies.

The tiny leafcutter ant carries almost ten times its own body weight.

The ants within the kingdom consist of a queen ant, soldier ants, and worker ants.

The queen of the colony lays eggs.

The soldiers, bigger than the workers, protect the colony.

The workers cut leaves for their gardens.

Exercise 21C: Subject-Verb Agreement

Cross out the incorrect verb in parentheses so that subject and predicate agree in number and person. Be careful of any confusing phrases between the subject and predicate.

Caitlin (go/goes) to the beach to surf every weekend.

The waves, glittering under the sun, (crash/crashes) against the shore.

She (use/uses) her small surfboard because the waves are huge.

The other surfers in the ocean (smile/smiles) at her.

Boards of all shapes and colors (float/floats) on the water.

"I (has/have) all day to surf!" she (think/thinks) happily.

— LESSON 22 —

Formation of Plural Nouns
Collective Nouns

A collective noun names a group of people, animals, or things.

Exercise 22A: Collective Nouns

Write the collective noun for each description. Then fill in an appropriate singular verb for each sentence. (Use the simple present tense!) The first is done for you.

Description		Collective Noun	Verb	
mother, father, sister, brother	The	family	eats	together.
nine baseball players	The	________	________	the game.
many students learning together	The	________	________	the test.
people playing different musical instruments	The	________	________	the piece.
52 playing cards	The	________	________	incomplete.
many mountains	The	________	________	high and icy.
a group of stars that forms a picture	This	________	________	brightly.

Exercise 22B: Plural Noun Forms

Read each rule and the example out loud. Then rewrite the singular nouns as plural nouns in the spaces provided.

Usually, add *-s* to a noun to form the plural.

Singular Noun	Plural Noun
desk	desks
willow	________
spot	________
tree	________

Add *-es* to nouns ending in *-s*, *-sh*, *-ch*, *-x*, or *-z*.

Singular Noun	Plural Noun
mess	messes
splash	
ditch	
fox	
buzz	

If a noun ends in *-y* after a consonant, change the *y* to *i* and add *-es*.

Singular Noun	Plural Noun
family	families
salary	
baby	
hobby	

If a noun ends in *-y* after a vowel, just add *-s*.

Singular Noun	Plural Noun
toy	toys
donkey	
valley	
guy	

Some words that end in *-f or -fe* form their plurals differently. You must change the *f* or *fe* to *v* and add *-es*.

Singular Noun	Plural Noun
leaf	leaves
shelf	
wife	
thief	

Words that end in *-ff* form their plurals by simply adding *-s*.

Singular Noun	Plural Noun
sheriff	sheriffs
cliff	
tariff	

Some words that end in a single *-f* can form their plurals either way.

Singular Noun	Plural Noun
scarf	scarfs/scarves
hoof	

If a noun ends in *-o* after a vowel, just add *-s*.

Singular Noun	**Plural Noun**
patio	patios
radio	________________
rodeo	________________
zoo	________________

If a noun ends in *-o* after a consonant, form the plural by adding *-es*.

Singular Noun	**Plural Noun**
potato	potatoes
hero	________________
volcano	________________
echo	________________

To form the plural of foreign words ending in *-o*, just add *-s*.

Singular Noun	**Plural Noun**
piano	pianos
burrito	________________
kimono	________________
solo	________________
soprano	________________

Irregular plurals don't follow any of these rules!

Singular Noun	**Irregular Plural Noun**
child	children
foot	feet
tooth	teeth
man	men
woman	________________
mouse	mice
goose	geese
deer	________________
fish	fish

Exercise 22C: Plural Nouns

Complete the following excerpt by filling in the plural form of each noun in parentheses. There is *one* collective noun (singular in form) in the passage. Find and circle it.

The following is slightly condensed from the introduction to *The Pirate's Who's Who*, by Philip Gosse (1924).

Surely (pirate) _____________ are as much entitled to a biographical dictionary of their own as are (clergyman) _____________, (race-horse) _____________, or (artist) _____________. Have not the medical (man) _____________ their Directory, the (lawyer) _____________ their List, the (peer) _____________ their Peerage? There are (book) _____________ which record the (particular) _____________ of (musician) _____________, (dog) _____________, and even white (mouse) _____________. Above all, there is that astounding and entertaining volume, *Who's Who*, found in every club smoking-room, and which grows more bulky year by year, stuffed with information about the (life) _____________, the (hobby) _____________, and the (marriage) _________ of all the most distinguished (person) _____________ in every profession. But there has been until now no work that gives immediate and trustworthy information about the lives, and—so sadly important—the (death) _____________ of our pirates.

Delving in the *Dictionary of National Biography*, it has been a sad disappointment to the writer to find so little space devoted to the careers of these picturesque if, I must admit, often unseemly persons. There are, of course, to be found a few pirates with household (name) _____________ such as Kidd, Teach, and Avery. But I compare with indignation the meagre show of pirates in that monumental work with the rich profusion of (divine) _____________! Even during the years when piracy was at its height, the pirates are utterly swamped by the (theologian) _____________. Can it be that these two (profession) ______________ flourished most vigorously side by side, and that when one began to languish, the other also began to fade?

My original intention was that only pirates should be included. To admit (privateer) ______________, (corsair) ______________, and other (sea-rover) ______________ would have meant the addition of a vast number of names, and would have made the work unwieldy. But the difficulty has been to define the exact meaning of a pirate. A pirate was not a pirate from the cradle to the gallows. He usually began his life at sea as an honest mariner. He perhaps mutinied with other of the ship's crew, killed or otherwise disposed of the captain, seized the ship, and sailed off.

Often it happened that, after a long naval war, (ship) ______________ were laid up and (navy) ______________ reduced, thus flooding the countryside with begging and starving (seaman) ______________. These were driven to go to sea if they could find a berth, often half-starved and brutally treated, and always underpaid, and so easily yielded to the temptation of joining some vessel bound vaguely for the "South Sea," where no (question) ______________ were asked and no (wage) ______________ paid, but every hand on board had a share in the adventure.

— LESSON 23 —

Plural Nouns
Descriptive Adjectives
Possessive Adjectives
Contractions

An apostrophe is a punctuation mark that shows possession. It turns a noun into an adjective that tells whose.

Possessive adjectives tell whose.

An adjective modifies a noun or pronoun.
Adjectives tell what kind, which one, how many, and whose.
Descriptive adjectives tell what kind.
A descriptive adjective becomes an abstract noun when you add -*ness* to it.

Form the possessive of a singular noun by adding an apostrophe and the letter *s*.

Exercise 23A: Introduction to Possessive Adjectives

Read the following nouns. Choose a person that you know to possess each of the items. Write that person's name, an apostrophe, and an *s* to form a possessive adjective.

Example: Aunt Catherine	Aunt Catherine's	coffee mug
	______________	pickup truck
	______________	anteater
	______________	knitting needles
	______________	bus ticket to Seattle, Washington
	______________	cat food

Form the possessive of a plural noun ending in -*s* by adding an apostrophe only.

Form the possessive of a plural noun that does not end in -*s* as if it were a singular noun.

Exercise 23B: Singular and Plural Possessive Adjective Forms

Fill in the chart with the correct forms. The first is done for you. Both regular and irregular nouns are included.

Noun	Singular Possessive	Plural	Plural Possessive
plant	plant's	plants	plants'
child			
family			
pirate			
match			
class			
sheep			
tortilla			
galley			
video			
ox			

	SINGULAR		PLURAL	
	Pronoun(s)	**Possessive Adjective**	**Pronoun(s)**	**Possessive Adjective**
First person	I	my	we	our
Second person	you	your	you	your
Third person	he, she, it	his, her, its	they	their

INCORRECT	CORRECT
I's book	my book
you's candy	your candy
he's hat	his hat
she's necklace	her necklace
it's nest	its nest
we's lesson	our lesson
they's problem	their problem

Contraction	**Meaning**
he's	he is
she's	she is
it's	it is
you're	you are
they're	they are

A contraction is a combination of two words with some of the letters dropped out.

Exercise 23C: Common Contractions

Drop the letters in grey print and write the contraction on the blank. The first is done for you.

Full Form	**Common Contraction**	**Full Form**	**Common Contraction**
I am	I'm	let us	______
he is	______	is not	______
we are	______	were not	______
you have	______	do not	______
she has	______	can not	______
they had	______	you are	______
he will	______	it is	______
you would	______	they are	______

— LESSON 24 —

Possessive Adjectives
Contractions
Compound Nouns

A contraction is a combination of two words with some of the letters dropped out.

Contraction	**Meaning**	**Not the Same as**
he's	he is	his
she's	she is	her
it's	it is	its
you're	you are	your
they're	they are	their

It's hard for a hippopotamus to see its feet.
It is *hard for a hippopotamus to see its feet.*
It's hard for a hippopotamus to see ***it is*** *feet.*

You're fond of your giraffe.
You are *fond of your giraffe.*
You're fond of ***you are*** *giraffe.*

They're searching for their zebra.
They are *searching for their zebra.*
They're searching for ***they are*** *zebra.*

Exercise 24A: Using Possessive Adjectives Correctly

Cross out the incorrect word in parentheses.

My sunglasses are lost. Could I borrow (yours / your's)?

When (your / you're) finished reading, could you lend me (your / you're) magazine?

(Its / It's) swelteringly hot today!

The car won't start. (Its / It's) battery must be dead.

(His / He's) rollerblades are too tight.

Did you remember (your / you're) backpack? I think (its / it's) still on the chair.

(They're / Their) so absentminded. (They're / Their) always losing (they're / their) belongings.

Whose pencil is that? (Its / It's) not a red pencil; (its / it's) blue, and (its / it's) eraser is chewed.

(Their / They're) restaurant is known for (its / it's) fabulous desserts.

(It's / Its) not fair that (she's / hers) always using (your / you're) pencils instead of (she's / hers).

A compound noun is a single noun composed of two or more words.

One word	shipwreck, haircut, chalkboard
Hyphenated word	self-confidence, check-in, pinch-hitter
Two or more words	air conditioning, North Dakota, *The Prince and the Pauper*

Exercise 24B: Compound Nouns

Underline each simple subject once and each simple predicate (verb) twice. Circle each compound noun.

The post office will close early today.

Sunrise comes very late in the wintertime.

My mother-in-law forgot her checkbook.

I was running for the bus stop with all my dry cleaning in my arms.

The commander-in-chief arrived with great pomp and circumstance.

I really need a truckful of manure for my garden.

I had a horrendous headache last night.

"You Brush Your Teeth" is a song about toothbrushes.

If a compound noun is made up of one noun along with another word or words, pluralize the noun.

passerby passersby passerbys

If a compound noun ends in *-ful*, pluralize by putting an *-s* at the end of the entire word.

truckful trucksful truckfuls

If neither element of the compound noun is a noun, pluralize the entire word.

grown-up growns-up grown-ups

If the compound noun includes more than one noun, choose the most important to pluralize.

attorney at law attorneys at law attorney at laws

Exercise 24C: Plurals of Compound Nouns

Write the plural of each singular compound noun in parentheses in the blanks to complete the sentences.

Both of our (brother-in-law) ____________________ are (chef de cuisine) ____________________ at Ethiopian restaurants in Washington, D.C.

All three (sergeant major) ____________________ have testified at multiple (court-martial) ____________________.

The four (secretary of state) ____________________ had a top-secret meeting.

I like to put three (teaspoonful) ____________________ of curry spice into my chicken curry.

Those annoying (good-for-nothing) ____________________ have stolen all of the (bagful) ____________________ of canned goods I was collecting for the food bank.

My mother keeps two (tape measure) ____________________ in each of her (toolbox) ____________________.

The (Knight Templar) ____________________ were almost wiped out in France in 1307.

Matija Bećković and Charles Simić are both past (poet laureate) ____________________ of Serbia.

— REVIEW 2 —

Weeks 4-6

Topics
Simple, Progressive, and Perfect Tenses
Conjugations
Irregular Verbs
Subject/Verb Agreement
Possessives
Compound Nouns
Contractions

Review 2A: Verb Tenses

Write the tense of each underlined verb phrase above it: *simple past, present,* or *future*; *progressive past, present,* or *future*; or *perfect past, present,* or *future*. The first is done for you. Watch out for words that interrupt verb phrases but are not helping verbs (such as *not*).

progressive present
I am reading *The Word Snoop*.

By the time I have finished this book, I will have learned everything there is to know about the English language!

The next section that I will be reading is about silent letters.

After I have completed the section on silent letters, I will study the history of punctuation.

The following sentences are taken from *The Word Snoop*, by Ursula Dubosarsky (New York: Dial Books, 2009).

It is time to talk about silent letters.

They are the ones that creep sneakily into words at the beginning, middle, or end when you are not expecting them.

What are you doing there, silent letters!

You frightened me!

English is not the only language with silent letters, but it has more than most.

This can be really hard when you are learning to spell, as you have probably realized already.

Then other people thought it would be good if English looked more like Latin, so a *b*, for example, was dumped back into the word *doubt*, even though it had been taken out because no one pronounced it that way anymore.

And have you ever wondered about words like *psalm* and *rhubarb*?

They came from ancient Greek words.

Quite a few of today's silent letters have not always been so quiet.

Imagine yourself back when you were learning the alphabet for the very first time.

You will have to crack the special code if you want to know what I am saying.

Review 2B: Verb Formations

Fill in the charts with the correct conjugations of the missing verbs. Identify the person of each group of verbs.

PERSON: ___________

	Past	Present	Future
SIMPLE	she	she	she will wiggle
PROGRESSIVE	she	she	she
PERFECT	she had wiggled	she	she

PERSON: ___________

	Past	Present	Future
SIMPLE	I shuffled	I	I
PROGRESSIVE	I	I	I will be shuffling
PERFECT	I	I	I

PERSON: ___________

	Past	Present	Future
SIMPLE	you itched	you	you
PROGRESSIVE	you	you	you
PERFECT	you	you	you will have itched

PERSON: ___________

	Past	Present	Future
SIMPLE	they	they sneeze	they
PROGRESSIVE	they	they	they
PERFECT	they had sneezed	they	they

Review 2C: Person and Subject/Verb Agreement

Circle the correct verb in parentheses.

The following sentences are taken from *The 2,548 Best Things Anybody Ever Said*, by Robert Byrne (New York: Simon & Schuster, 1990).

It (is/are) a good thing for an uneducated man to read books of quotations.
—Winston Churchill

I (hates/hate) quotations.
—Ralph Waldo Emerson

We (doesn't/don't) know a millionth of one percent about anything.
—Thomas Alva Edison

He (writes/write) so well he (makes/make) me feel like putting my quill back in my goose.
—Fred Allen

I (considers/consider) exercise vulgar. It (makes/make) people smell.
—Alec Yuill Thornton

If you (isn't/aren't) fired with enthusiasm, you'll be fired with enthusiasm.
—Vince Lombardi

Children (is/are) guilty of unpardonable rudeness when they (spits/spit) in the face of a companion; neither are they excusable who spit from windows or on walls or furniture.
—St. John Baptist de La Salle

Seriousness (is / are) the only refuge of the shallow.
—Oscar Wilde

Of all the animals, the boy (is / are) the most unmanageable.
—Plato

Plato (is / are) a bore.
—Friedrich Nietzsche

In expressing love we (belongs / belong) among the most undeveloped countries.
—Saul Bellow

Only young people (worries / worry) about getting old.
—George Burns

The two biggest sellers in any bookstore (is / are) the cookbooks and the diet books. The cookbooks (tells / tell) you how to prepare the food and the diet books (tells / tell) you how not to eat any of it.
—Andy Rooney

Review 2D: Possessives and Compound Nouns

Circle the TEN possessive words in the following excerpt. Include possessive words formed from both nouns and pronouns.

Find and underline the SIX compound nouns. Write the plurals of those compound nouns on the blanks at the end of the excerpt.

The following excerpt is taken from *Mary Poppins*, by P.L. Travers (New York: Harcourt Books, 1997).

Jane, with her head tied up in Mary Poppins's bandanna handkerchief, was in bed with earache . . .

So Michael sat all the afternoon on the window-seat telling her the things that occurred in the Lane. And sometimes his accounts were very dull and sometimes very exciting.

"There's Admiral Boom!" he said once. "He has come out of his gate and is hurrying down the Lane. Here he comes. His nose is redder than ever and he's wearing a top-hat. Now he is passing Next Door—"

"Is he saying, 'Blast my gizzard!'?" enquired Jane.

"I can't hear. I expect so. There's Miss Lark's second housemaid in Miss Lark's garden. And Robertson Ay is in our garden, sweeping up the leaves and looking at her over the fence. He is sitting down now, having a rest."

. . . "Mary Poppins," said Jane, "there's a cow in the Lane, Michael says."

"Yes, and it's walking very slowly, putting its head over every gate and looking round as though it had lost something."

__________ __________ __________

__________ __________ __________

Review 2E: Plurals and Possessives

Write the correct possessive, plural, and plural possessive forms for the following nouns.

Noun	Possessive	Plural	Plural Possessive
ghost	__________	__________	__________
ox	__________	__________	__________
trolley	__________	__________	__________
thrush	__________	__________	__________
Johnson	__________	__________	__________
rodeo	__________	__________	__________
city	__________	__________	__________
person	__________	__________	__________

Review 2F: Contractions

Finish the following excerpt about Helen Keller by forming contractions from the words in parentheses.

The excerpt is from *Miss Spitfire: Reaching Helen Keller*, by Sarah Miller (Boston, Mass.: Atheneum Press, 2007).

How do I dare hope to teach this child—Helen—when __________ (I have) never taught a child who can see and hear? __________ (I have) only just graduated from the

Perkins Institution for the Blind myself. Worse, ___________ (it is) not simply that Helen ___________ (cannot) hear words or see signs . . . The very notion that words exist, that objects have names, has never even occurred to her . . . At least I know that task ___________ (is not) impossible; Perkins's famous Dr. Howe taught my own cottage mate Laura Bridgeman to communicate half a century ago, and ___________ (she is) both deaf and blind. Even so, ___________ (I am) afraid . . .

More than that, ___________ (I am) afraid Helen's family expects too much from me. If ___________ (they have) read the newspaper articles about Laura, _________ (they are) prepared for a miracle. They ___________ (do not) know Laura's "miraculous" education was hardly perfect . . .

If the Kellers are hoping for another Laura Bridgeman, I ___________ (do not) know how I—an untrained Irish orphan—can please them. I ___________ (cannot) tell them there may never be another Laura Bridgeman . . .

___________ (There is) not a relative alive ___________ (who would) have me, and I ___________ (would not) know where to find them now anyhow. ___________ (I would) die of shame if I had to go back to Perkins a failure.

WEEK 7

Compounds and Conjunctions

— LESSON 25 —

Contractions
Compound Nouns
Diagramming Compound Nouns
Compound Adjectives
Diagramming Adjectives
Articles

A contraction is a combination of two words with some of the letters dropped out.

Exercise 25A: Contractions Review

Write the two words that form each contraction on the blanks to the right. Some contractions have more than one correct answer. The first is done for you.

Contraction	Helping Verb	Other Word
we're	are	we
I've	________	________
mightn't	________	________
doesn't	________	________
mustn't	________	________
that's	________	________
you'd	________	________
it's	________	________
you're	________	________

Our air conditioning is working!

Exercise 25B: Diagramming Adjectives and Compound Nouns

On your own paper, diagram every word of the following sentences.

Unfortunate mix-ups happen.
Your desk lamp illuminates.
Early trout fishing succeeds.
Star Wars entertains.

The large-headed monster had twenty-seven teeth.

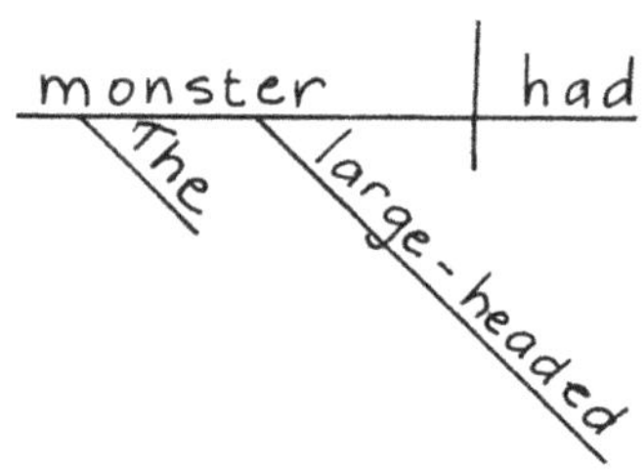

The articles are *a, an*, and *the*.

Exercise 25C: Compound Nouns

Draw a line to match each word in Column A with the correct word in Column B to form a single-word compound noun. Then rewrite the new compound noun on the space provided.

Column A	Column B	New Compound Noun
farm	fly	____________
pot	sill	____________
butter	post	____________
court	house	____________
lamp	pie	____________
window	martial	____________

Exercise 25D: Compound Adjectives

Correctly place hyphens in the following phrases.

sixty one students

a thirty minute presentation

bluish green water

a first class ticket

twenty four black and white copies

two thirds majority

man eating grizzly bear

Exercise 25E: Diagramming Adjectives, Compound Nouns, and Compound Adjectives

On your own paper, diagram every word in the following sentences. These are adapted from Jules Verne's *Twenty Thousand Leagues Under the Sea.*

An iron-plated monster had risen.
The hideous, powerful sea-monster thrashed.
The magnificent chestnut-brown sea otter hissed.
A colossal, billowing storm-cloud threatened.
The monster's formidable death-rattle shook.

— LESSON 26 —

Compound Subjects
The Conjunction *And*
Compound Predicates
Compound Subject-Predicate Agreement

The fireman hurries.
The policeman hurries.
The fireman and the policeman hurry.

Simple Present	
I hurry	we hurry
you hurry	you hurry
he, she, it hurries	they hurry

Compound subjects joined by *and* are plural in number and take plural verbs.

A conjunction joins words or groups of words together.

The farmer plants.
The farmer harvests.
The farmer plants and harvests.

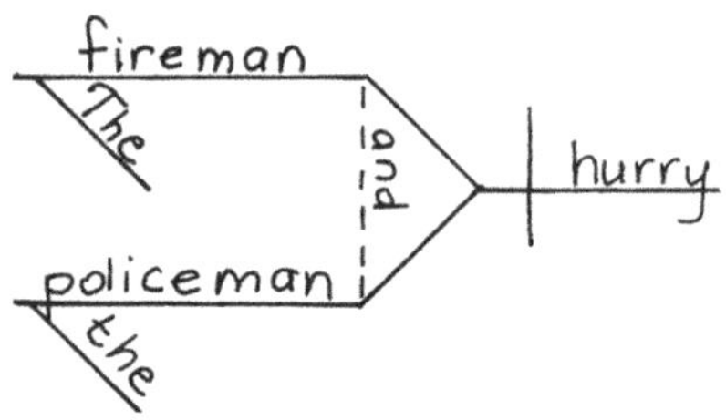

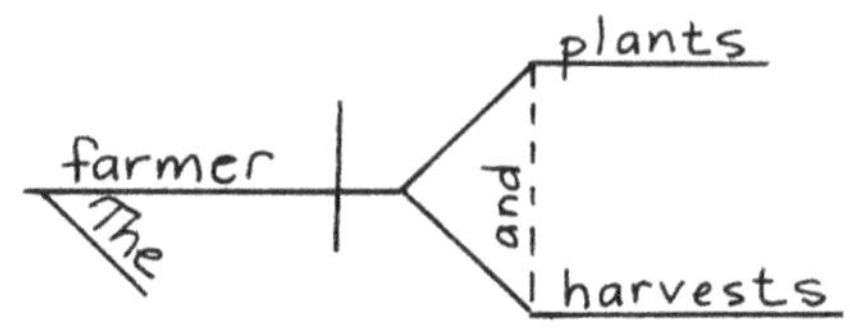

Exercise 26A: Identifying Subjects, Predicates, and Conjunctions

Underline the subject(s) once and the predicate(s) twice in each sentence. Circle the conjunctions that join them. The first one is done for you.

These sentences are adapted from *Discoverer of the Unseen World: A Biography of Antoni van Leeuwenhoek*, by Alma Payne Ralston.

Here he scooped up a generous sample of the marshy water and put it into a container.

The following night he assembled his simple equipment and prepared to observe the Berkelse Mere water by the light of a single candle.

He put the container in the office-laboratory where he did all of his work and study and waited until the following night.

Particles, green streaks, and little animalcules filled the slide.

The motion of most of these animalcules in the water was so swift and so various.

The streaks were arranged after the manner of copper or tin worms and moved rapidly as he watched.

Exercise 26B: Diagramming Compound Subjects and Predicates

Underline the subject(s) once and the predicate(s) twice in the following sentences. Circle any conjunctions.

When you are finished, diagram the subjects (and any articles modifying the subjects), predicates, and conjunctions (ONLY) of each sentence on your own paper.

The last three sentences in the exercise are taken from L. Frank Baum's *Tik-Tok of Oz*.

Marcos and Carolina are making cookies with their mother.

Marcos and Carolina cut and design the cookies.

Marcos adds and stirs the ingredients.

The Rainbow's Daughter and the Rose Princess approached them.

The Shaggy Man grasped the bundle of copper and dumped it upon the ground.

They had raised him and had balanced him upon his feet.

Exercise 26C: Forming Compound Subjects and Verbs

Combine each of these sets of simple sentences into one sentence with a compound subject and/or a compound predicate joined by *and*. Rewrite the new sentences on your own paper.

The architect plans buildings.
The architect designs buildings.

The audiologist helps children who cannot hear well.
The speech pathologist helps children who cannot hear well.

The electrician installs wires.
The electrician repairs wires.

The software designer conceptualizes new websites.
The graphic designer conceptualizes new websites.
The software designer creates new websites.
The graphic designer creates new websites.

Exercise 26D: Subject-Verb Agreement with Compound Subjects

Choose the correct verb in parentheses to agree with the subject by crossing out the incorrect verb.

The pilot, copilot, and flight attendants (manage/manages) the aircraft.

The pilot and the copilot (fly/flies) the plane.

The flight attendants (assist/assists) the passengers.

The airplane mechanic and the security guard (ensure/ensures) the safety of the passengers.

The air traffic controller (communicate/communicates) with and (guide/guides) the airplanes.

— LESSON 27 —

Coordinating Conjunctions
Complications in Subject-Predicate Agreement

A conjunction joins words or groups of words together.
A coordinating conjunction joins similar or equal words or groups of words together.

and, or, nor, for, so, but, yet

Indonesia and Greater Antilles are groups of islands.
I will nap or go running.
They will not help me, nor you.
I ran after them, for I needed help.
I stubbed my toe, so now my foot hurts.
I was exhausted, but my sister was still full of energy.
He was laughing, yet he seemed sad.

Exercise 27A: Using Conjunctions

Fill the blanks in the sentences below with the appropriate conjunctions. You must use each conjunction at least once. (There is more than one possible answer for many of the blanks.)

The copper man lost his balance ____________ tumbled to the ground in a heap.
— L. Frank Baum, *Tik-Tok of Oz*

There was always the danger of English ____________ Spanish ships appearing on the green waters of the Gulf.
— Thomas B. Costain, *The Mississippi Bubble*

Pare ____________ his fellow surgeons treated gunshot wounds by cauterizing them with boiling oil of elder.
— John Simmons, *Doctors and Discoveries*

The sun was setting outside, __________ the light that came through the windows was red ____________ gold, __________ it did not reach all the way into the corners of the room.

The princess was a sweet little creature, ___________ at the time my story begins was about eight years old, I think, ___________ she got older very fast.
— George MacDonald, *The Princess and the Goblin*

The goblins were now, not ordinarily ugly, __________ either absolutely hideous, or ludicrously grotesque in face __________ form.

— George MacDonald, *The Princess and the Goblin*

There are two __________ three old towers in the field, forlorn, with wall __________ towers suggesting a splendor that has now departed.

Riches cannot save us from pain, __________ can they be taken with us into another world.

During the summer, the lake lost this clearness __________ became whitish in color.

I could not sleep, __________ I was troubled in mind.

The copper man was silent, __________ Betsy wound him up with the key beneath his left arm.

— L. Frank Baum, *Tik-Tok of Oz*

The song of the icy sea is not loud, __________ it can be heard to a great distance.

No bather would have a chance if he once got within the grasp of such a monster, __________ could a canoe resist the strength of its pull.

— John Timbs, *Eccentricities of the Animal Creation*

Compound subjects joined by *and* are plural in number and take plural verbs.

I am friendly.
George and I are friends.

The policeman or the fireman hurries.

The dog and the cat are sleeping on the sofa.
The dog or the cat is sleeping on the sofa.
The dogs or the cat is sleeping on the sofa.

When compound subjects are joined by *or,* the verb agrees with the number of the nearest subject.

The pies were scrumptious.
The pies on the table were scrumptious.
The box of pencils is on the top shelf.

A can of red beans sits on the table.

The young man at all of the meetings was bored.

Fractions are singular if used to indicate a single thing.
Fractions are plural if used to indicate more than one thing.

Three-fourths of the pie was missing.
Three-fourths of the socks were missing.

Expressions of money, time, and quantity (weight, units, and distance) are singular when used as a whole, but plural when used as numerous single units.

Thirty dollars is too much to pay for that shirt.
Thirty dollars are spread across the table.

Seven years is a long time to wait.
The minutes tick by.

A thousand pounds is far too heavy for that truck.
Fifty gallons of water are divided among the refugees.
Four miles is too far to walk.

Collective nouns are usually singular. Collective nouns can be plural if the members of the group are acting as independent individuals.

The herd of cattle was grazing quietly.
The herd of cattle were scattered throughout the plains.

Exercise 27B: Subject-Predicate Agreement: Troublesome Subjects

Choose the correct verb in parentheses to agree with the subject noun or pronoun in number. Cross out the incorrect verb.

After breakfast, half of the bananas (are/is) left, but two-thirds of the bread (have/has) already been eaten.

The patients (was/were) still alive.

I (am/is) moved by an exceedingly powerful desire for knowledge of the heavens.

The choir and the orchestra (listen/listens) carefully to the conductor.

The trombone players or the saxophonist (is/are) behind the beat.

My family always (eat/eats) a lot in the morning.

The cars on the bridge (zoom/zooms) quickly by.

The celebrity couple (was/were) filing for divorce.

The raccoon or the squirrels (has / have) been eating from the birdfeeder.

Nearly three-fourths of the sky (was / were) covered in fog.

An animal in the bushes (growl / growls) menacingly.

Fifteen hundred dollars (was / were) handed out to eleven hundred lottery winners.

Three weeks (is / are) not enough time to finish my paper!

Two-thirds of his shirt (was / were) eaten by the tiger.

The band (begin / begins) to play.

Fifty miles (lie / lies) between the ultramarathoner and the finish line.

The hockey team (was / were) arguing amongst themselves.

He and the rest of his shirt (has / have) escaped.

Exercise 27C: Fill in the Verb

Provide the correct third-person number (singular or plural) of a verb (any verb!) that makes sense.

The truthfulness of these men and women __________ indeed exemplary.

A profusion of sweet treats __________ to extra pounds around the holidays.

Socrates and Plato __________ the best-known philosophers of ancient Greece.

The discomfort and unhappiness __________ very great in that place.

The ship, with all the sailors aboard, __________.

Sides A, B, and C __________ a triangle.

My father, my brother, or my sister __________ with me to the movies.

The nation __________ very powerful.

The council __________ divided in their opinions.

— LESSON 28 —

Further Complications in Subject-Predicate Agreement

Many nouns can be plural in form but singular in use: measles, mumps, rickets, politics, mathematics, economics, news.

Mathematics is my favorite subject.

Singular literary works, works of art, newspapers, countries, and organizations can be plural in form but are still singular in use.

Little Women was written by Louisa May Alcott.
The United States is south of Canada.

Many nouns are plural in form and use but singular in meaning: pants, scissors, pliers, glasses.

Pants are too hot in the summertime.

In sentences beginning with *There is* or *There are*, the subject is found after the verb.

There is a skunk in the brush.
There are three skunks in the brush.

***Each* and *every* always indicate a singular subject.**

In Masai villages, each woman cares for her own cattle.
In Masai villages, each of the women cares for her own cattle.
In Masai villages, each cares for her own cattle.

In Masai villages, women care for their own cattle.

Every man needs friends.
Men need friends.

Compound nouns that are plural in form but singular in meaning take a singular verb.

Fish and chips is my favorite British dish.

Compound subjects joined by *and* take a singular verb when they name the same thing.

The owner and manager of the ice cream shop is also working behind the counter.

Nouns with Latin and Greek origins take the singular verb when singular in form and the plural verb when plural in form.

The data suggest otherwise.

Singular	**Plural**
medium	media
datum	data
criterion	criteria
phenomenon	phenomena
focus	foci
appendix	appendices

Exercise 28A: Subject-Verb Agreement: More Troublesome Subjects

Choose the correct verb in parentheses and cross out the incorrect verb.

The *New York Times* (arrive / arrives) every day at 5:00 a.m.

My mother's eyeglasses (are / is) missing, but she reads the paper anyway.

Our friend and neighbor (is / are) going away for a long vacation.

"Politics (are / is) an interesting subject," she mumbles.

The reviewers as well as the editor (believe / believes) that the book is worth reading.

The suspect's whereabouts (is / are) unknown at this time.

Luckily, there (are / is) muffins baking in the oven.

Each of the cherries (is / are) perfectly ripe.

Forty percent of the staff (is / are) discontent with the working conditions.

Haunted house phenomena (is / are) more common than you might think.

There before him (was / were) a veritable swimming pool.

Here (was / were) a chance for him.

Kinetics (is / are) my favorite class in school.

Every one of the soldiers (is / are) afraid of the coming invasion.

Almost no data (was / were) gathered from the last set of experiments.

Mumps (was / were) a common childhood disease before immunizations became common.

Genetics (determine / determines) the color of your eyes.

You or he (are / is) the right person for the job.

Forty percent of my time (is / are) spent on homework.

The appendices (was / were) found at the end of the paper.

The chef and owner (has / have) come out to say hello to the diners.

Exercise 28B: Correct Verb Tense and Number

Complete each of these sentences from the *Norwegian Fairy Book* by writing the correct number and tense of the verb indicated.

There __________ in Kvam a marksman by the name of Per Gynt. [simple present of *live*]

There __________ more forests on the Fjäll, and all sorts of beasts dwell in them. [simple present of *am*]

With the exception of three dairy-maids, all the herd-folk __________ [progressive present of *leave*]

The three beautiful princesses in the castle __________ for rescue. [progressive past of *long*]

Forty-two trolls __________ towards the peasants. [progressive present of *march*]

Dogs or a crying child __________ the service. [progressive present of *disturb*]

Fifty shillings __________ the cost of a fine sword. [simple present of *am*]

A pair of gold shears __________ by the fireplace. [progressive past of *hang*]

A pattern of black and blue spots __________ his whole body. [simple present of *cover*]

The master and commander __________ the ship to set sail. [simple present of *order*]

A chest of bright silver coins __________ beneath the roots. [simple present of *lie*]

Once upon a time there __________ seven sons of a king. [simple past of *am*]

Once upon a time there __________ a king with seven sons. [simple past of *am*]

WEEK 8

Introduction to Objects

— LESSON 29 —

Action Verbs
Direct Objects

A direct object receives the action of the verb.

Cara built a bonfire.
We roasted marshmallows over the bonfire.
Tom ate the delicious cookie.
Julia, hot and thirsty, drank the fresh-squeezed lemonade.
She visited her grandfather.
He had forgotten her name.
She found peace.

We roasted marshmallows.

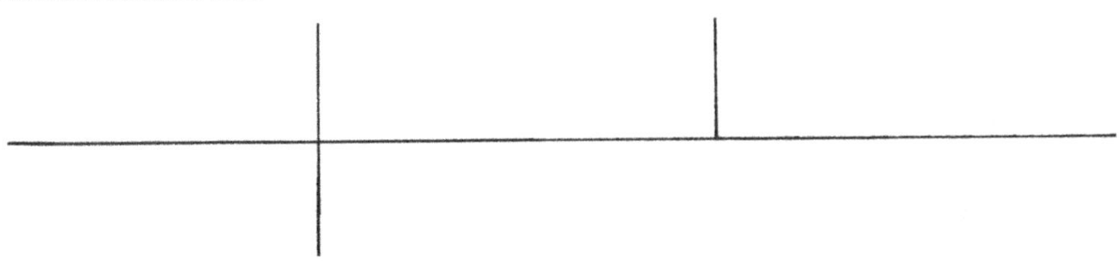

We roasted soft marshmallows and beefy hot dogs.

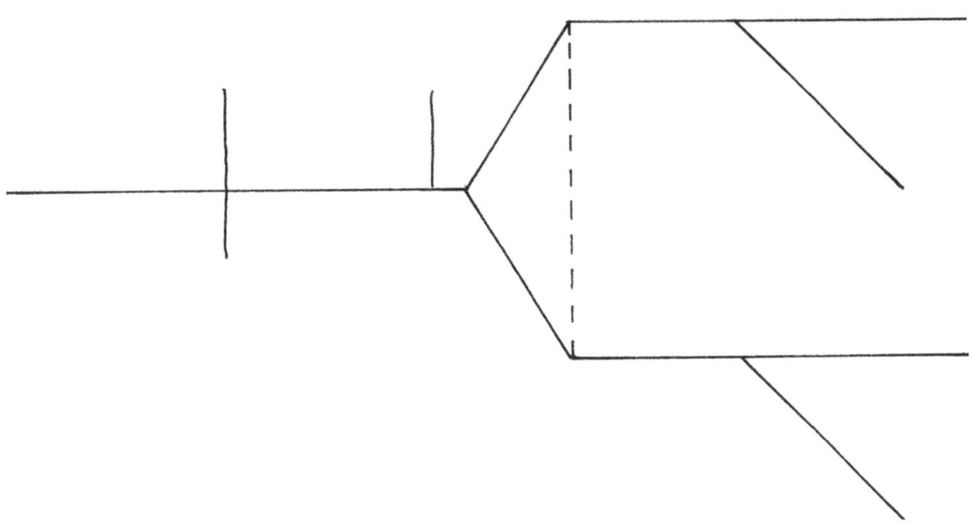

My friend and I rode roller coasters and ate popcorn and cotton candy.

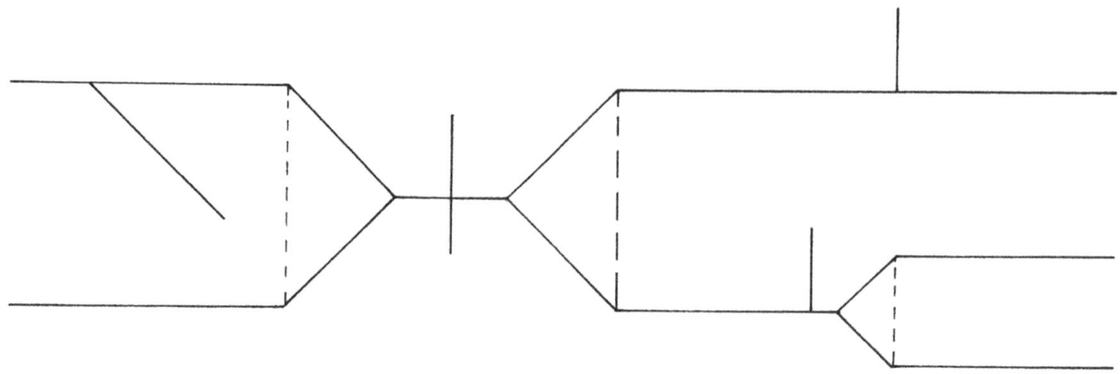

Exercise 29A: Direct Objects

In the following sentences, underline the subjects once and the predicates twice. Circle each direct object.

Simon visited his great-aunt in Quebec.

He spends time with her every summer.

His aunt cooked crepes for him for lunch.

At home, he made crepes for his friends and added chocolate, bananas, and cream.

The little princess could see the sky only during the day.

They had got a king and a government.

They heartily cherished the ancestral grudge.

Nature recycles dead leaves.

The dead leaf material protects the soil.

Juliana recycles too.

She built a bin for compost.

She added dried leaves, food scraps, and grass clippings.

Many bugs and worms lived in her compost bin.

The compost nourished her garden.

The herbs and flowers grew and produced leaves and blooms.

Exercise 29B: Diagramming Direct Objects

On your own paper, diagram the subjects, verbs, direct objects, and any necessary conjunctions in the sentences from Exercise 29A.

— LESSON 30 —

Direct Objects
Prepositions

I broke my breakfast plate!
The pottery plate broke into pieces.

A preposition shows the relationship of a noun or pronoun to another word in the sentence.

Prepositions
aboard, about, above, across
after, against, along, among, around, at

before, behind, below, beneath
beside, between, beyond, by

down, during, except, for, from
in, inside, into, like

near, of, off, on, over
past, since, through, throughout

to, toward, under, underneath
until, up, upon
with, within, without

Exercise 30A: Identifying Prepositions

In the following sentences from George MacDonald's *The Princess and the Goblin*, find and circle each preposition.

These mountains were full of hollow places; huge caverns, and winding ways, some with water running through them, and some shining with all colours of the rainbow when a light was taken into them. There would not have been much known about them, had there not been mines there, great deep pits, with long galleries and passages running from them, which had been dug to get at the ore of which the mountains were full. In the course of digging, the miners came upon many of these natural caverns. A few of them had openings onto the side of a mountain, or into a ravine.

Exercise 30B: Word Relationships

The following sentences all contain action verbs. Underline each subject once and each action verb twice. If the sentence has an action verb followed by a direct object, write *DO* above the direct object.

If the sentence contains a preposition, circle the preposition and draw a line to connect the two words that the preposition shows a relationship between. The first is done for you.

The train (in) the depot puffed loudly.

He opened the door suddenly.

My father is hanging pictures today.

The brook under the bridge flows sluggishly.

I opened the door of the car immediately.

The car in the distance slowed.

She suddenly slowed the car.

The twelve white cabins beside the blackened lot sit deserted.

Dark draperies hung upon the walls.

The tunnel through the mountain flooded.

The dog was hiding under the porch.

The clockmaker wound the clock every morning.

Exercise 30C: Diagramming Direct Objects

On your own paper, diagram the subjects, predicates, and direct objects only from the sentences above. If a sentence does not have a direct object, do not diagram it.

— LESSON 31 —

Definitions Review
Prepositional Phrases
Object of the Preposition

A noun names a person, place, thing, or idea.
An adjective modifies a noun or pronoun.
A pronoun takes the place of a noun.
A verb shows an action, shows a state of being, links two words together, or helps another verb.
A conjunction joins words or groups of words together.
A coordinating conjunction joins similar or equal words or groups of words together.
A phrase is a group of words serving a single grammatical function.
A preposition shows the relationship of a noun or pronoun to another word in the sentence.

Prepositions
aboard, about, above, across
after, against, along, among, around, at
before, behind, below, beneath
beside, between, beyond, by
down, during, except, for, from
in, inside, into, like
near, of, off, on, over
past, since, through, throughout
to, toward, under, underneath
until, up, upon
with, within, without

A brook sluggishly flows (through) low ground.

Dark draperies hung (upon) the walls.

The tunnel wound (into) the green hill.

A prepositional phrase begins with a preposition and ends with a noun or pronoun. That noun or pronoun is the object of the preposition.

Put your hand beneath your workbook.

Calvin ran across the floor.

I baked a pie for my mother.

Exercise 31A: Objects of Prepositional Phrases

Fill in the blanks with a noun as the object of the preposition to complete the prepositional phrases.

Georgie hid his string beans underneath his ________________.

Everett always wanted to travel across ________________.

Above the ________________ soared the eagle.

Samantha has the best hide-and-seek spot, between the ____________ and ____________.

Wally cried when he fell down the ________________.

Ronald does not venture into the woods after ________________.

Exercise 31B: Identifying Prepositional Phrases

Can you find all ten of the prepositional phrases in the following excerpt from Arthur Conan Doyle's *The Hound of the Baskervilles*? Underline the complete prepositional phrases. Circle the prepositions. Label each object of the preposition with OP. (A *gig* is a small horse-drawn carriage.)

I can well remember driving to his house in the evening some three weeks before the fatal event. He chanced to be at his hall door. I had descended from my gig and was standing before him, when I saw his eyes fix themselves over my shoulder and stare past me with an expression of the most dreadful horror.

Exercise 31C: Remembering Prepositions

Can you remember all 46 prepositions without looking back at your list? On your own paper, write them down in alphabetical order. The first letter of each preposition and the number of prepositions that begin with that letter are found below, as a memory aid.

A	B	D	E	F	I	L
aboard	______	______	______	______	______	______
______	______	______		______	______	
______	______				______	
______	______					
______	______					
______	______					
______	______					
______	______					
______						
______						

N	O	P	S	T	U	W
______	______	______	______	______	______	______
	______			______	______	______
	______			______	______	______
	______			______	______	
					______	

— LESSON 32 —

Subjects, Predicates, and Direct Objects
Prepositions
Object of the Preposition
Prepositional Phrases

The subject of the sentence is the main word or term that the sentence is about.
The simple subject of the sentence is *just* the main word or term that the sentence is about.
The complete subject of the sentence is the simple subject and all the words that belong to it.

The warrior saw on the opposite mountain two great globes of glowing fire.

The predicate of the sentence tells something about the subject.
The simple predicate of the sentence is the main verb along with any helping verbs.
The complete predicate of the sentence is the simple predicate and all the words that belong to it.
A direct object receives the action of the verb.
A preposition shows the relationship of a noun or pronoun to another word in the sentence.

Prepositions
aboard, about, above, across
after, against, along, among, around, at
before, behind, below, beneath
beside, between, beyond, by
down, during, except, for, from
in, inside, into, like
near, of, off, on, over
past, since, through, throughout
to, toward, under, underneath
until, up, upon
with, within, without

A prepositional phrase begins with a preposition and ends with a noun or pronoun. That noun or pronoun is the object of the preposition.

DO
The warrior | saw on the opposite mountain two great globes of glowing fire.

The warrior saw two great globes.

The Dragon King with his retainers accompanied the warrior to the end of the bridge, and took leave of him with many bows and good wishes.

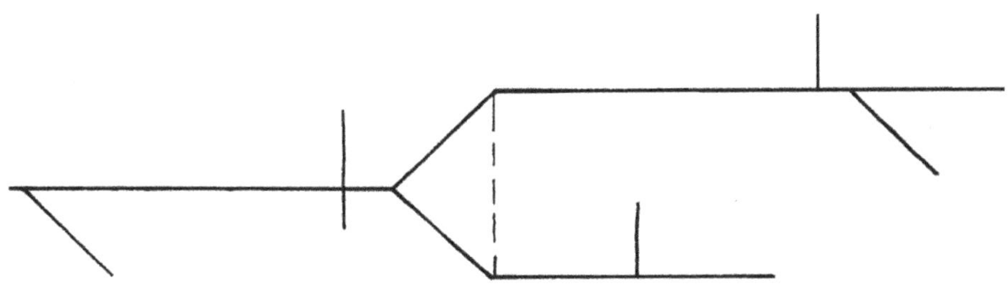

Exercise 32A: Identifying Prepositional Phrases and Parts of Sentences

In the following sentences, adapted from *Japanese Fairy Tales*, by Yei Theodora Ozaki, circle each prepositional phrase. Once you have identified the prepositional phrases, underline subjects once and predicates twice, and label direct objects with *DO*.

The kind-hearted, hard-working old man and the cross-patch wife lived in Japan with the old man's tame sparrow.

The old woman spoiled the happiness of her home by her scolding tongue.

After a hard day's work, the old man opened the cage of the sparrow, talked to her, gave treats, and played with her.

The old woman hated the sparrow and quarrelled with her husband about the little bird.

She drove the sparrow into exile with spite and spread the laundry in the sun.

In the evening, the old man came into the house with anticipation and was disappointed.

The old man shed painful tears after dark.

He rose before dawn and searched for the sparrow over the hills, through the woods, in bamboo forests.

Lady Sparrow was with her family.

She thanked him with many polite bows for all the kindnesses of the past years.

Exercise 32B: Diagramming

On your own paper, diagram all of the uncircled parts of the sentences from Exercise 32A.

WEEK 9

Adverbs

— LESSON 33 —

Adverbs That Tell How

A sneaky squirrel stole my sock slowly.
A sneaky squirrel stole my sock sleepily.
A sneaky squirrel stole my sock cheerfully.
A sneaky squirrel stole my sock rapidly.

An adverb describes a verb, an adjective, or another adverb.

An **exceptionally** sneaky squirrel stole my sock slowly.
A sneaky squirrel stole my sock **very** rapidly.

Adverbs tell how, when, where, how often, and to what extent.

Adjective	**Adverb**
serious	seriously
fierce	__________
thorough	__________
crazy	crazily
scary	__________
cheery	__________

He left hurriedly.
Hurriedly, he left.
He hurriedly left.

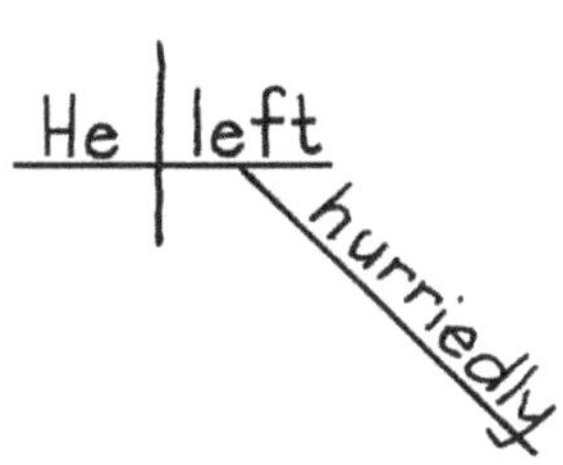

Exercise 33A: Identifying Adverbs That Tell How

Underline the adverbs telling *how* in the following sentences, and draw arrows to the verbs that they modify. Some sentences contain more than one adverb.

Elizabeth I angrily charged Essex, on his allegiance, not to leave Ireland without her permission.

The Taj Mahal stands magnificently in the city of Agra, India.

The grand structure extravagantly honors Queen Mumtaz Mahal, wife of Emperor Shah Jahan.

After the death of the queen, Emperor Shah Jahan mourned despondently and inconsolably for two years.

The Emperor painstakingly constructed the Taj Mahal over a period of 22 years.

Within the marble walls of the Taj Mahal, the Emperor could properly honor his beloved wife.

Fittingly, this architectural masterpiece has been called one of the Seven Wonders of the World.

As he said once laughingly, it is the best opportunity to tell him all of the things he should hear.

Immediately he pulls his feet from his sandals.

She sang sweetly and played handsomely on the lute.

Exercise 33B: Forming Adverbs from Adjectives

Turn the following adjectives into adverbs.

Adjective	Adverb	Adjective	Adverb
odd	____________	handy	____________
angry	____________	beautiful	____________
fond	____________	clever	____________
hesitant	____________	shrewd	____________
gaudy	____________		

Exercise 33C: Diagramming Adverbs

On your own paper, diagram the following sentences.

They rested peacefully.
Suddenly he stopped.
Rosa played hockey aggressively.
James kindly fixed sweet lemonade.
Did they work diligently?
The new tadpoles were wiggling furiously.

— LESSON 34 —

Adverbs That Tell When, Where, and How Often

Exercise 34A: Telling When

Angeline dropped her recipe cards for French toast. Help her to get organized by numbering the following sentences from 1 to 5, so that she can make breakfast.

_______ Later, fry the soaked bread on both sides in a hot skillet.

_______ Second, beat three eggs with a bit of milk, sugar, and cinnamon.

_______ Finally, enjoy with fresh maple syrup and cream.

_______ First, slice a loaf of French bread into thick slices.

_______ Next, place the bread in the egg mixture and soak for ten minutes.

An adverb describes a verb, an adjective, or another adverb.
Adverbs tell how, when, where, how often, and to what extent.

Yesterday I washed my dog outside.

The dog ran away.

Then the dog lay down.

Now my dog is sleeping there.

My glasses are lying there.
My red book is sitting here.

There are my glasses.
Here is my red book.

Now my dog is sleeping there.

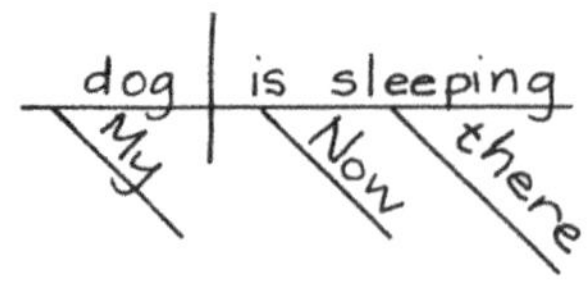

There are my glasses.

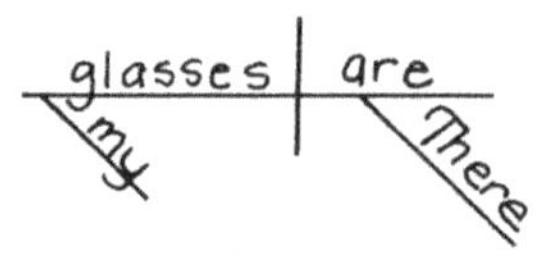

Here is my red book.

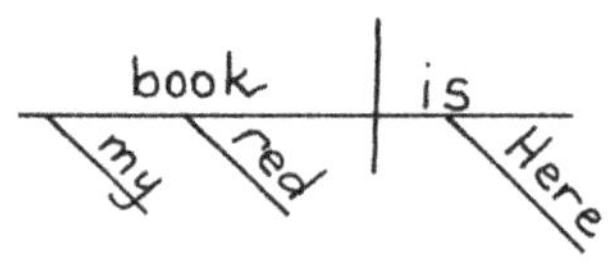

***Here* and *there* are adverbs that tell where.**

I wash my dog weekly.
Richie is always looking for adventure.
I will often be eating.

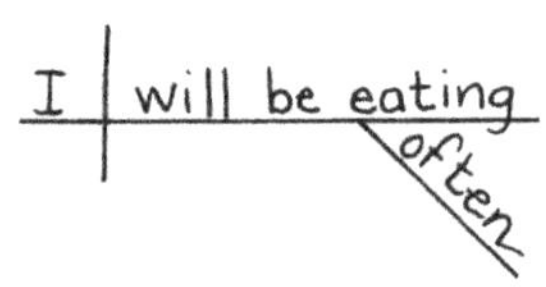

When will you arrive?
Where is my hat?
How are you doing?

you will arrive When.

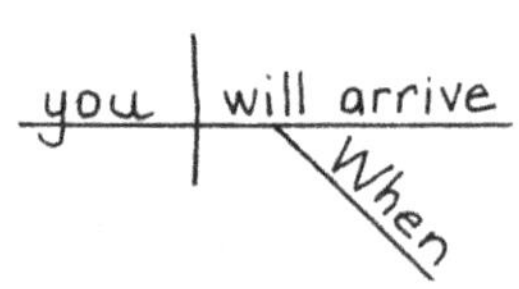

my hat is Where.

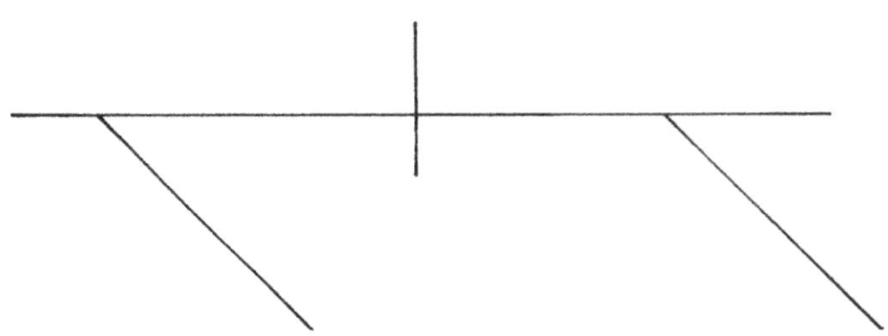

Exercise 34B: Distinguishing Among Different Types of Adverbs

Put each of the following adverbs in the correct category according to the question that it answers.

tomorrow	occasionally	there	now
carefully	inside	above	first
comfortably	always	rarely	fast

When	Where	How	How Often
____________	____________	____________	____________
____________	____________	____________	____________
____________	____________	____________	____________

Exercise 34C: Identifying Adverbs of Different Types

Underline the 13 adverbs in the following sentences that tell *when*, *where*, or *how often*.

Estefan has never missed a soccer practice.

The team practices daily outside.

First, the team runs laps.

There they go!

Later they practice drills.

Soccer is usually called *futebol* or *football* in Brazil.

Brazil's national team has repeatedly won the World Cup.

Those who saw him for the first time were often charmed by the eager cordiality of his address.

She had worn some of the dresses once or twice.

It was always strong and confident and it was never dull.

Exercise 34D: Diagramming Different Types of Adverbs

On your own paper, diagram the following sentences.

Tomorrow I am camping there.
Where are you sleeping?
When did you eat dinner?
I will never forget you.
Leo rang his bell twice and tapped his foot impatiently.

— LESSON 35 —

Adverbs That Tell To What Extent

An adverb describes a verb, an adjective, or another adverb.
Adverbs tell how, when, where, how often, and to what extent.

The extremely humid day was unpleasant.
Sharon runs quite quickly.
Larry shrieked especially loudly.

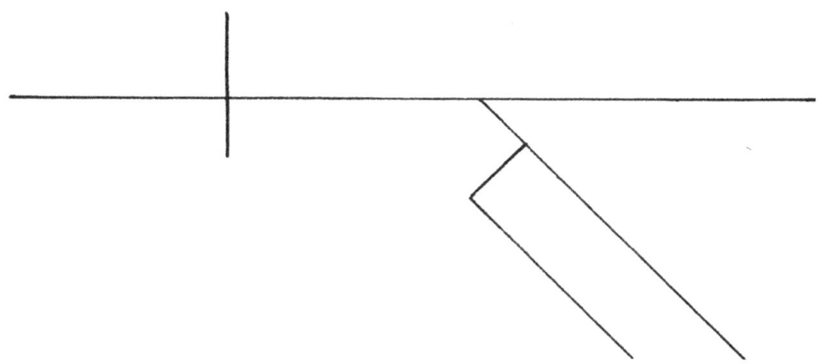

Extremely skittish Larry ran away.

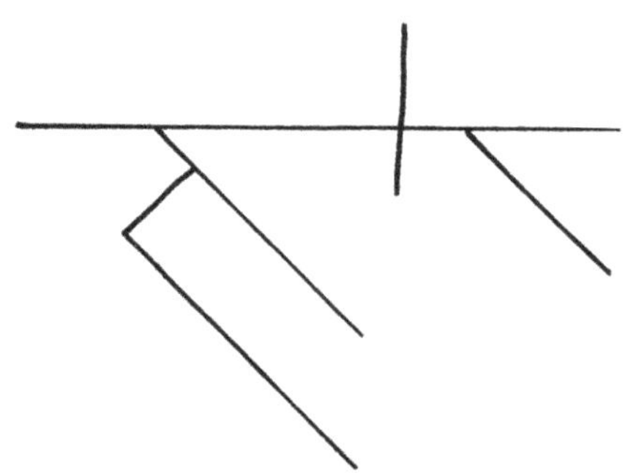

Exercise 35A: Identifying the Words Modified by Adverbs

Draw an arrow from each underlined adverb to the word it modifies.

Mom told us <u>rather</u> <u>unexpectedly</u> about the plans to move to a new house.

Jordan and I were not <u>especially</u> excited about the idea.

We had worked <u>very</u> <u>hard</u> to make friends in this neighborhood.

The new town would be <u>much</u> larger and <u>less</u> familiar.

We rode with Dad to see our brand new house.

Dozens of enormously grand trees very gently shaded the porch.

A beautifully designed tree house had already been built in the back yard.

Mom and Dad had tried particularly hard to find a place that we would like.

Maybe the kids across the street could come right now to see our tree house!

His face may have been ugly, but all admit that it was remarkably expressive.

His attitude at the piano was perfectly quiet and amazingly dignified.

"Unnaturally patient," says one pupil, "he would have a passage repeated a dozen times till it was to his mind"; "infinitely strict in the smallest detail," says another, "until the right rendering was obtained."

(The following sentences are from Stacy Schiff's *Cleopatra: A Life*.)

She was incomparably richer than anyone else in the Mediterranean.

Cleopatra descended from a long line of murderers and faithfully upheld the family tradition but was, for her time and place, remarkably well-behaved.

Exercise 35B: Diagramming Different Types of Adverbs

On your own paper, diagram every word of the following sentences.

Very talented Lily can jump extremely high.

Traffic stopped quite suddenly.

Drive much more carefully!

Luke gave very strict orders extraordinarily sharply.

Aunt Lou fixes especially fine meals.

Your excessively rude cousin pinched me particularly hard.

— LESSON 36 —

Adjectives and Adverbs
The Adverb *Not*
Diagramming Contractions
Diagramming Compound Adjectives and Compound Adverbs

An adjective modifies a noun or pronoun.
Adjectives tell what kind, which one, how many, and whose.

An adverb describes a verb, an adjective, or another adverb.
Adverbs tell how, when, where, how often, and to what extent.

It matters naught.

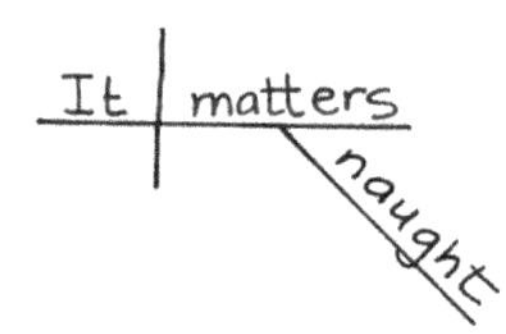

It does not matter.

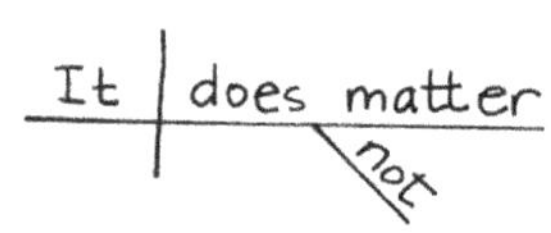

A contraction is a combination of two words with some of the letters dropped out.

It doesn't matter.

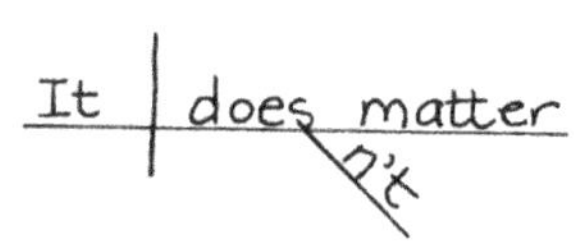

It's not there.

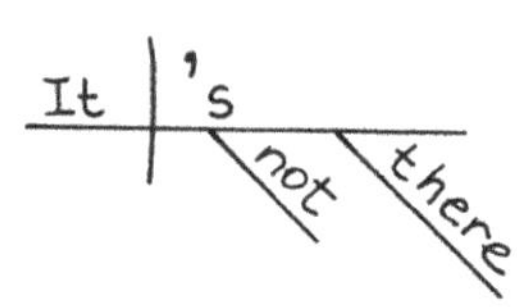

Tall and wide arches weren't often built.

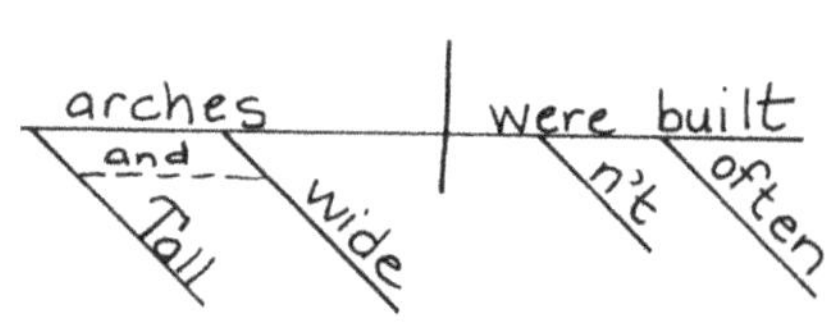

The idea was deeply and widely held.

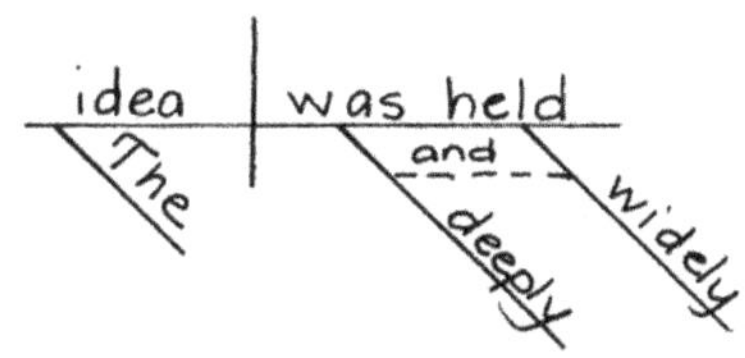

Exercise 36A: Practice in Diagramming

On your own paper, diagram every word of the following sentences. These are adapted from Jack London's *The Call of the Wild.*

Buck didn't read the newspapers or journals.

Men had found a yellow metal and were rushing out.

The prospectors wanted strong and heavy dogs.

They didn't always buy dogs.

They crassly and dishonestly stole Buck.

Buck now faced a great and difficult problem.

A great fear seized him and contracted his muscles spasmodically and instinctively.

Twelve alert and active dogs drew the sled.

He was struggling and delayed the start.

He was not always running forward.

— REVIEW 3 —

Weeks 7-9

Topics
Parts of Speech
Compound Parts of Sentences
Prepositions
Prepositional Phrases
Objects of Prepositions
Subjects and Predicates
Subject-Verb Agreement
Verbs and Direct Objects

Review 3A: Parts of Speech

Identify the underlined words as *N* for noun, *ADJ* for adjective, *ADV* for adverb, *PREP* for preposition, or *CONJ* for conjunction. The first sentence is done for you.

The following excerpt is taken from *A Wrinkle in Time*, by Madeleine L'Engle (New York: Yearling, 1973), pp. 3-8.

It was a dark (ADJ) and (CONJ) stormy (ADJ) night.

In her attic bedroom Margaret Murry, wrapped in an old patchwork quilt, sat on the foot of her bed and watched the trees tossing in the frenzied lashing of the wind. Behind the trees clouds scudded frantically across the sky. Every few moments the moon ripped through them, creating wraith-like shadows that raced along the ground.

The house shook.

Wrapped in her quilt, Meg shook.

She wasn't usually afraid of weather. –It's not just the weather, she thought. –It's the weather on top of everything else. On top of me. On top of Meg Murry doing everything wrong. . . .

"Why didn't you come up to the attic?" Meg asked her brother, speaking as though he were at least her own age. "I've been scared stiff."

"Too windy up in that attic of yours," the little boy said. "I knew you'd be down. I put some milk on the stove for you." . . .

How did Charles Wallace always know about her? How could he always tell? He never knew—or seemed to care—what Dennys or Sandy were thinking. It was his mother's mind, and Meg's, that he probed with frightening accuracy.

Review 3B: Recognizing Prepositions

Circle the 46 prepositions in the following bank of words. Try to complete the exercise without looking back at your list of prepositions.

beside or under to nowhere except was with

like near and since that for fly

also around bring us upon aboard sail of

anyone beyond into through though throughout across

below inside what among here past about

from being during thing above off mine

beneath after but at against until should

between by wrong along this toward before

fry underneath up down right left over within without

out front behind side in so on board

Review 3C: Subjects and Predicates

In these sentences from poems by Edward Lear, draw one line under the subject and two lines under the predicate. Watch out for compound subjects and predicates!

The owl and the pussycat went to sea in a beautiful pea-green boat.

They took some honey, and plenty of money, wrapped up in a five-pound note.

The owl looked up to the stars above and sang to a small guitar.

Hand in hand, on the edge of the sand, they danced by the light of the moon.

Two Owls and a Hen, four larks and a Wren, have all built their nests in my beard!

The Cups and the Saucers danced madly about.

The Plates and the Dishes looked out of the casement.

The Soup-ladle peeped through a heap of Veal Patties and squeaked with a ladle-like scream of surprise.

The Tea-kettle hissed and grew black in the face.

They galloped away to a beautiful shore.

In silence they rode and made no observation.

Review 3D: Complicated Subject-Verb Agreement

Cross out the incorrect verb form in parentheses.

Yann or Marilou (is / are) the best candidate for class president.

The class (votes / vote) at 10:00 on Thursday.

The class (was / were) whispering amongst themselves about the upcoming election.

"Five dollars (is / are) too much to pay for school lunch," Yann claims.

Yann and his running mates (plans / plan) to lower the price of the daily lunch.

But Marilou (has / have) decided to get a new basketball hoop for the playground.

The principal or the teachers (is / are) counting the votes.

Aesop's Fables (does / do) not seem terribly interesting as the class waits to hear the election results.

The envelope with the results (rests / rest) temptingly on the table.

The teacher's glasses (slides / slide) down her nose when she announces the winner.

Two-thirds of the students (has / have) voted for Marilou.

The news (spreads / spread) quickly throughout the class.

After school there (is / are) a grand party.

Yann and Marilou graciously (shakes / shake) hands.

Review 3E: Objects and Prepositions

In the following paragraph from Charles Dickens's novel *A Tale of Two Cities,* identify the underlined words as *DO* for direct object or *OP* for object of a preposition. For each direct object, find and underline twice the action verb that affects it. For each object of the preposition, find and circle the preposition to which it belongs.

There is one compound object of a preposition, and one compound adjective. When you find them, write *compound OP* and *compound adj* in the margin next to them. Draw arrows from each compound form to the appropriate label in the margin.

The coach lumbered on again, with heavier wreaths of mist closing round it as it began the descent. The guard soon replaced his blunderbuss in his arm-chest, and, having looked to the rest of its contents, and having looked to the supplementary pistols that he wore in his belt, looked to a smaller chest beneath his seat, in which there were a few smith's tools, a couple of torches, and a tinder-box. For he was furnished with that completeness that if the coach-lamps had been blown and stormed out, which did occasionally happen, he had only to shut himself up inside, keep the flint and steel sparks well off the straw, and get a light with tolerable safety and ease (if he were lucky) in five minutes.

WEEK 10

Completing the Sentence

— LESSON 37 —

Direct Objects
Indirect Objects

She gave **Odysseus** bread and sweet wine and sent him forth.

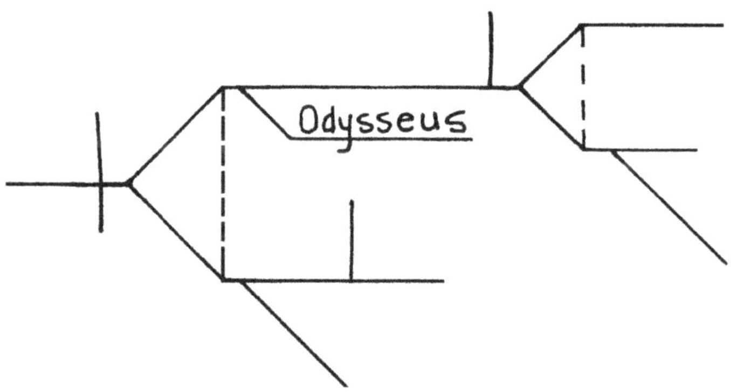

A direct object receives the action of the verb.
An indirect object is the noun or pronoun for whom or to whom an action is done.
An indirect object comes between the action verb and the direct object.

Odysseus asked the stranger a question.
Brandon sent his cousin and uncle an email.

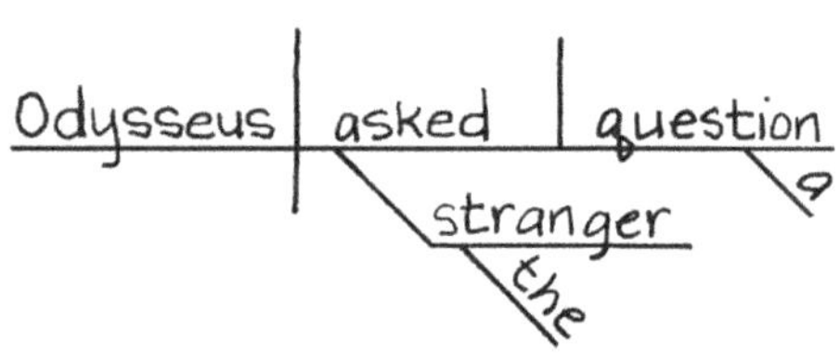

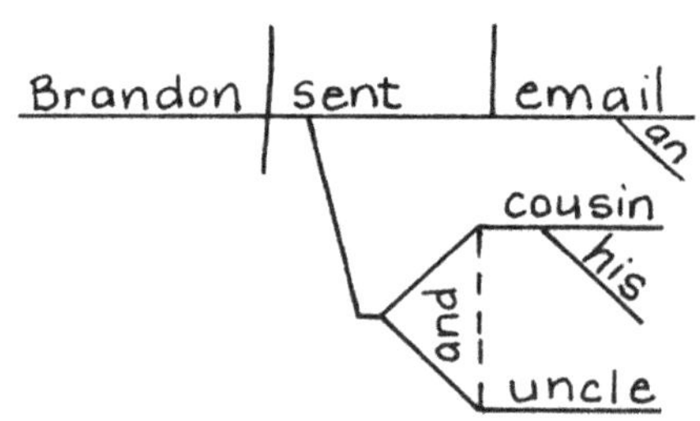

Exercise 37A: Identifying Direct Objects

Underline the action verbs and circle the direct objects in these sentences, adapted from *The Mississippi Bubble*, by Thomas B. Costain. Remember that you can always eliminate prepositional phrases first if that makes the task easier.

French guns could sweep the horizon.

The lookout could keep a sharp eye on the beach.

Any settlement would need a strong fort.

The outer wall had bastions.

This made a snug little harbor.

The defenders could meet the attacks.

Exercise 37B: Identifying Direct Objects, Indirect Objects, and Objects of Prepositions

Underline every object in the following sentences. Label each one: *DO* for direct object, *IO* for indirect object, or *OP* for object of the preposition.

At Christmas, Benjamin makes his aunt an ornament.

Sarah's mother cooks the family a huge dinner in October for Canadian Thanksgiving.

For each of the eight days of Hanukkah, Maddie's parents give her and her brother a present.

On Australia Day, Ramon bakes his sister meat pie.

Mr. Takahashi always brings his nieces and nephews souvenirs from different Japanese cities.

Hong's grandfather gives him money for Chinese New Year.

Exercise 37C: Diagramming Direct Objects and Indirect Objects

On your own paper, diagram the following sentences.

Isabella made us cocoa.
Aunt Debbie taught me Polish.
Sean bought us brunch.
Uncle Walter mailed Joey the cookies.
I knitted Grandma the mittens.
She gave me and my brother hugs and kisses.
Can you give me help?

— LESSON 38 —

State-of-Being Verbs
Linking Verbs
Predicate Adjectives

The tiny, jewel-colored hummingbird is strong and frantically energetic.

A verb shows an action, shows a state of being, links two words together, or helps another verb.

A linking verb connects the subject to a noun, pronoun, or adjective in the complete predicate.

A predicate adjective describes the subject and is found in the complete predicate.

The subject of the sentence is the main word or term that the sentence is about.
The simple subject of the sentence is *just* the main word or term that the sentence is about.
The complete subject of the sentence is the simple subject and all the words that belong to it.

The predicate of the sentence tells something about the subject.
The simple predicate of the sentence is the main verb along with any helping verbs.
The complete predicate of the sentence is the simple predicate and all the words that belong to it.

State-of-Being Verbs

am	were
is	be
are	being
was	been

I am.

I am hungry.

They are being.

They are being loud.

The sunset was.

The sunset was spectacular.

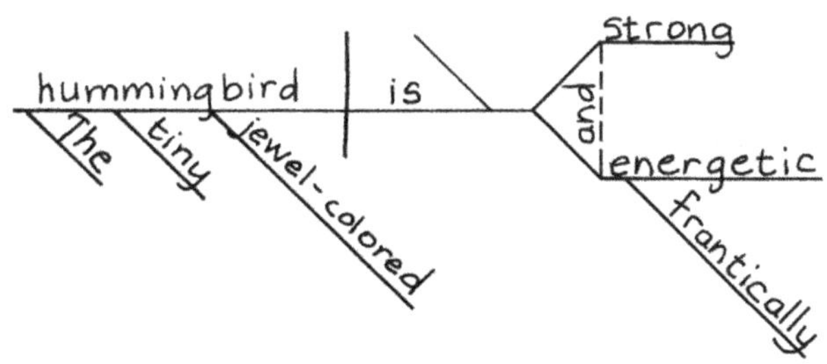

LV PA
Hummingbirds are tiny.

AV DO
Tiny hummingbirds sipped sweet nectar.

Exercise 38A: Action Verbs and Linking Verbs

In the following sentences, adapted from *A Christmas Carol*, by Charles Dickens, underline the subjects once and the predicates twice. If the verb is a linking verb, write *LV* over it, circle the predicate adjective, and label it *PA*. If the verb is an action verb, write *AV* over it, circle the direct object, and label it *DO*. The first is done for you.

> Hint #1: Predicate adjectives and direct objects will never be found in prepositional phrases. Remember—eliminating prepositional phrases can help you find the other parts of the sentence more easily.
>
> Hint #2: Don't forget that *not* is an adverb—never part of the verb.

LV PA
The knocker on the door was very large.

Scrooge had seen the knocker, night and morning, during his whole residence.

Scrooge saw Marley's face.

It was not angry and ferocious.

The eyes were wide open and perfectly motionless.

He turned the key and shut the door.

Scrooge was not fearful of echoes.

Darkness is cheap.

Scrooge liked it.

Quite satisfied, he closed his door and locked it.

The fire was low and dim.

Someone was dragging a heavy chain.

He heard the noise much louder on the floors below.

Exercise 38B: Diagramming Direct Objects and Predicate Adjectives

On your own paper, diagram *only* the subjects, predicates, and direct objects or predicate adjectives from the sentences in Exercise 38A.

— LESSON 39 —

Linking Verbs
Predicate Adjectives
Predicate Nominatives

I am unpopular.
I am a flower.
I am a berry.

A predicate adjective describes the subject and is found in the complete predicate.
A predicate nominative renames the subject and is found in the complete predicate.

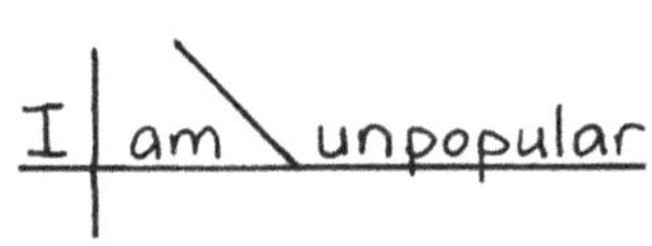

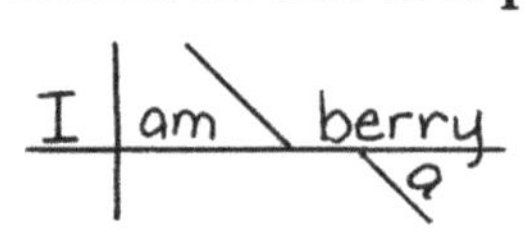

Iguanas are reptiles.
Iguanas = reptiles (predicate nominative)

Iguanas are scaly.
scaly iguanas (predicate adjective)

reptiles iguanas not a predicate adjective
iguanas $\neq$ scaly not a predicate nominative

Exercise 39A: Finding Predicate Nominatives and Adjectives

Underline the linking verbs in the following sentences, and circle the predicate nominatives or adjectives. Draw a line from each predicate nominative or adjective to the subject that it describes. There may be more than one of each.

Ethiopia is a country in eastern Africa.

Amharic is the national language of Ethiopia.

Ethiopian foods can be extremely spicy.

Common Ethiopian dishes are veggies, meat, and sourdough flatbread.

Everyone is happy there.

His face was round.

His name is Mr. Mo.

A growing lad is always hungry.

Exercise 39B: Distinguishing Between Predicate Nominatives and Adjectives

Underline the predicate nominatives and predicate adjectives in the following sentences. Identify them by writing *PN* above the predicate nominatives and *PA* above the predicate adjectives.

The Western landscape is mountainous.

That large shadow was a mountain.

A good education is a great advantage.

Matthew's education was advantageous in his career search.

The selling point of the car was its color.

In the setting sun, the sky was bright and colorful.

The saxophone music was soulful and beautiful.

The appeal of the music was its soul and beauty.

European fortifications were crude.

One is saline, bitter, and stinking.

The walls were dirty.

It was entirely separate.

It was cold, bleak, biting weather.

Exercise 39C: Diagramming

On your own paper, diagram every word of the following sentences.

Rainforests are magnificent.
Bats are flying mammals.
Most bats are insectivores.
Bat caves can be dark and creepy.
Be careful!
Dark clouds gathered.
Loud thunder frightened little Timmy.
Are you afraid?
Heavy rains nourished thirsty plants.

— LESSON 40 —

Predicate Adjectives and Predicate Nominatives
Pronouns as Predicate Nominatives
Object Complements

A linking verb connects the subject to a noun, pronoun, or adjective in the complete predicate.

A pronoun takes the place of a noun.
The antecedent is the noun that is replaced by the pronoun.

I	we
you	you (plural)
he, she, it	they

It is I.
The winner is you.
My best friend is she.

It = I
winner = you
friend = she

(plural noun) ______________________________ are we.

(singular noun) ______________________________ has been you.

(plural noun) ______________________________ were they.

We elected Marissa leader.
The explorers found the camp abandoned.
He painted the fence white.

An object complement follows the direct object and renames or describes it.

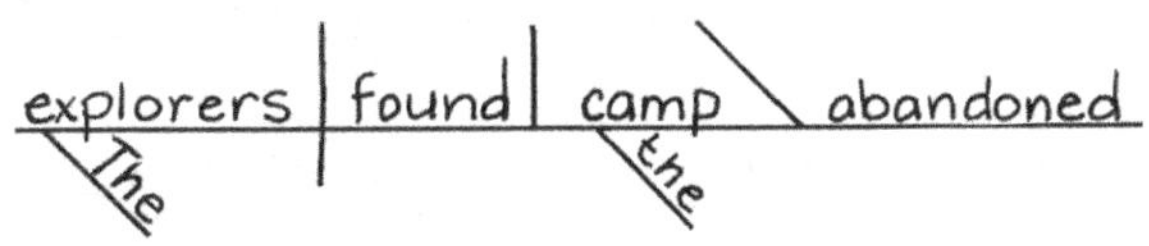

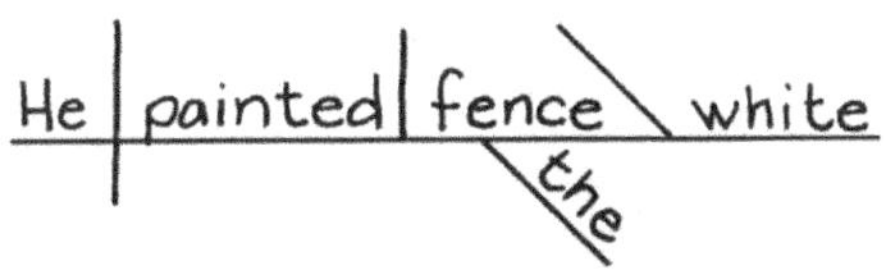

An adjective that comes right before the noun it modifies is in the *attributive position.*

They are user-friendly directions.

An adjective that follows the noun is in the *predicative position.*

Those directions are user friendly.

My friend dyed his hair purple.
My friend dyed his purple hair.
My friend dyed his purple hair orange.

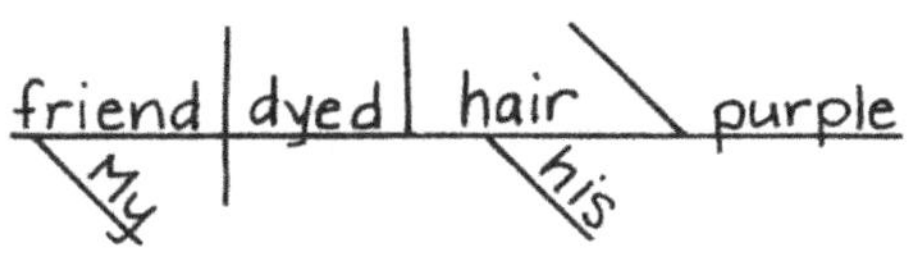

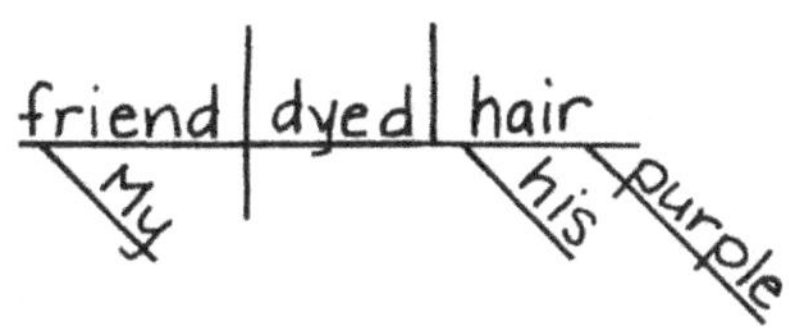

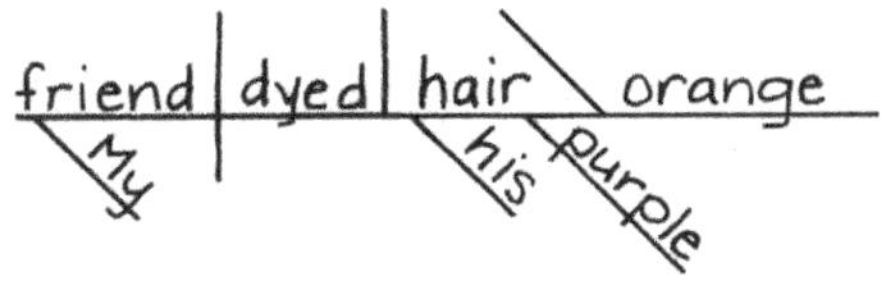

Exercise 40A: Reviewing Objects and Predicate Adjectives and Nominatives

Identify the underlined words as *DO* for direct object, *IO* for indirect object, *OP* for object of a preposition, *PN* for predicate nominative, or *PA* for predicate adjective.

- For each direct object (or direct object/indirect object combination), find and underline twice the action verb that affects it.
- For each object of the preposition, find and circle the preposition to which it belongs.
- For each predicate nominative and predicate adjective, find and draw a box around the linking verb that it follows.
- When you are finished, answer the questions at the end of the selection.

The following excerpts are slightly adapted from *A Thousand Never Evers*, by Shana Burg (New York: Delacorte Press, 2008), pp. 1-5.

Now get this: a boy in Jackson is so rich that when he finished high school, his daddy bought him a brand-new car. At least that's what I heard. In my family, we don't have that kind of money, but my uncle gives a whole dollar to any Pickett who graduates Acorn Elementary School. It's tradition.

So here I am, soaring through the sky on my swing that hangs from the oak tree, when Uncle Bump calls out the door of his shed, "Go on. Get your brother. He'll take you." He stretches a dollar bill between both hands and I jump right off. . . .

I nod so my brother will think I know what he's talking about. But I wonder why he can't answer my questions plain and simple. If he's so smart, why doesn't he tell me this: Why do they call it the movement? How can he swipe under his nose and stop crying? And why did Medgar Evers's mama give him such a silly name?

1. Find the compound adjective in this passage. Write it in the blank below and cross out the incorrect choice.

__________________________ is in the attributive/predicative position.

2. Find the object complement in this passage. Write it in the blank below and cross out the incorrect choices.

__________________________ is an adjective/noun that describes/renames the direct object.

Exercise 40B: Parts of the Sentence

Label the following in each sentence: *S* (subject), *LV* (linking verb), *AV* (action verb), *DO* (direct object), *OC-A* (object complement-adjective), *OC-N* (object complement-noun), *IO* (indirect object), or *PN* (predicate nominative).

The king considered Anne beautiful.

The king considered Anne politely.

The king offered Anne Boleyn a crown.

The king crowned Anne Boleyn queen.

She found the situation perplexing.

The old woman kept the cottage neat.

The old woman kept the cottage carefully.

The sound struck the merrymakers dumb.

The teacher appointed you monitor.

The monitor was you.

The dim light rendered large objects barely visible.

Exercise 40C: Diagramming

Diagram the sentences from Exercise 40B on your own paper.

WEEK 11

More About Prepositions

— LESSON 41 —

Prepositions and Prepositional Phrases
Adjective Phrases

Prepositions
aboard, about, above, across
after, against, along, among, around, at
before, behind, below, beneath
beside, between, beyond, by
down, during, except, for, from
in, inside, into, like
near, of, off, on, over
past, since, through, throughout
to, toward, under, underneath
until, up, upon
with, within, without

A preposition shows the relationship of a noun or pronoun to another word in the sentence.
A prepositional phrase begins with a preposition and ends with a noun or pronoun. That noun or pronoun is the object of the preposition.
A phrase is a group of words serving a single grammatical function.

I could have been running away.

Speed of Sound

Ring of Fire

Bridge Over Troubled Water

Time of Your Life

The Sound of Silence

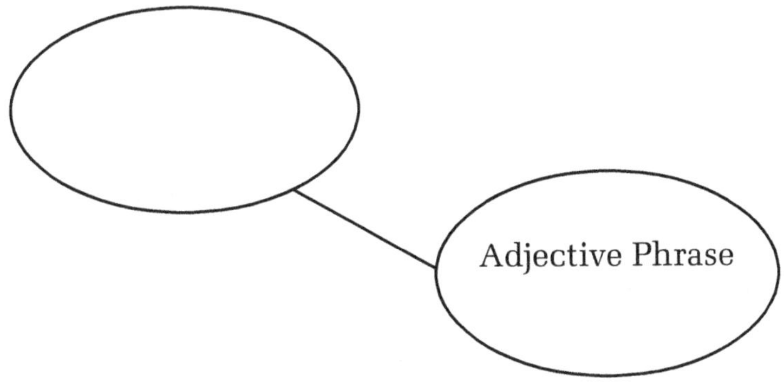

Prepositional phrases that act as adjectives are also called adjective phrases.

The boy with the freckles was whistling.
The old man on the bench hummed a tune.
Arthur borrowed a book of mine.

Adjective phrases usually come directly after the words they modify.

Caleb climbed a tree with thick branches.

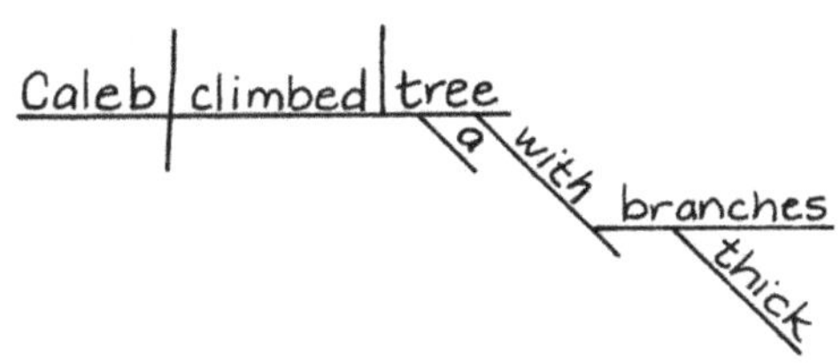

The children in the house were sleeping.

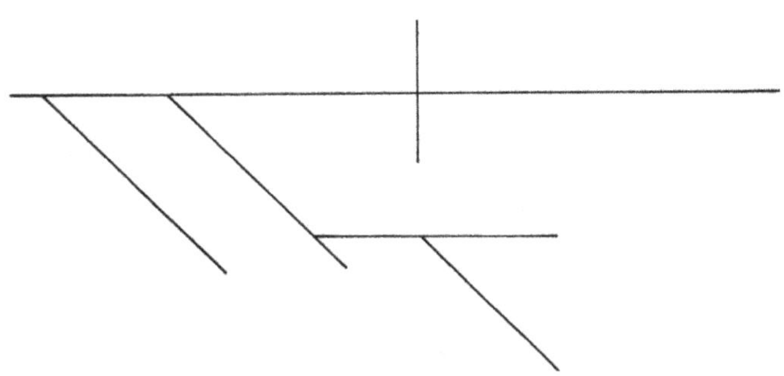

Exercise 41A: Identifying Adjective Phrases

Underline the adjective phrases in the following sentences. Draw an arrow from each phrase to the word it modifies. The first is done for you.

Queen Victoria was a great ruler <u>of England</u>.

She started some of our most popular fashions.

Many brides before Queen Victoria wore black wedding dresses.

White was a color for funerals.

But Queen Victoria wanted to wear a wedding dress with beautiful white lace.

Queen Victoria in her spotless white gown stunned the nation.

Women today still follow this trend of hers.

> The following sentences are from Ian Ridpath's *The Illustrated Encyclopedia of Astronomy and Space.*

The total number of comets is enormous.

The study of their physical structure and behavior . . . is now an increasingly important field of research.

The Sun's heat melts the nucleus, releasing huge volumes of gas.

Exercise 41B: Diagramming Adjective Phrases/Review

Diagram the following sentences on your own paper. Follow this procedure, and ask yourself the suggested questions if necessary.

1) Find the subject and predicate and diagram them first.
   What is the verb?
   Who or what [verb]?

2) Ask yourself: Is the verb an action verb? If so, look for a direct object.
   Who or what receives the action of the verb?
   If there is a direct object, check for an indirect object.
   To whom or for whom is the action done?

Remember that there may be no direct object or no indirect object—but you can't have an indirect object without a direct object. If there is an indirect object, it will always come between the verb and the direct object.

3) Ask yourself: Is the verb a state-of-being verb? If so, look for a predicate nominative or predicate adjective.
   Is there a word after the verb that renames or describes the subject?

4) Find all prepositional phrases. Ask yourself: Whom or what do they describe?

5) Place all other adjectives and adverbs on the diagram. If you have trouble, ask for help.

Brides in India wear red.

Many of our traditions have unusual origins.

History can tell us stories about ourselves.

Queen Victoria was a great ruler of England.

Many brides before Queen Victoria wore black wedding dresses.

White was a color for funerals.

Queen Victoria, in her spotless white gown, stunned the nation.

— LESSON 42 —

Adjective Phrases
Adverb Phrases

Prepositional phrases that act as adverbs are also called adverb phrases.
An adverb describes a verb, an adjective, or another adverb.
Adverbs tell how, when, where, how often, and to what extent.

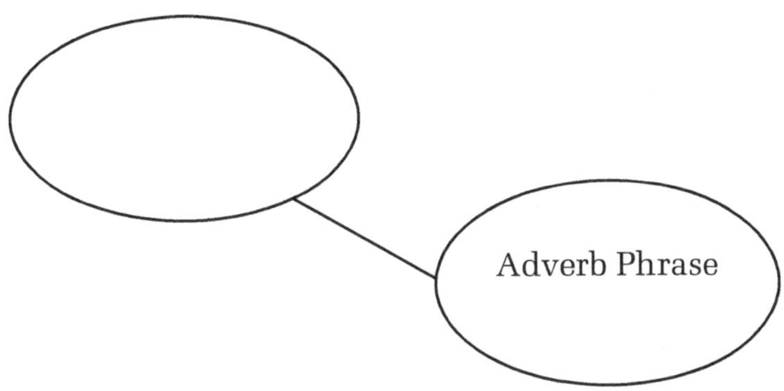

Fly Me to the Moon

I Fall to Pieces

Wake Me at Sunset

Sitting on the Dock of the Bay

Cameron scuba-dives in Hawaii.
At 6:00 a.m., Cameron wakes.

Adverb phrases can be anywhere in a sentence.

With great confidence, Hank Aaron swung the bat through the air.

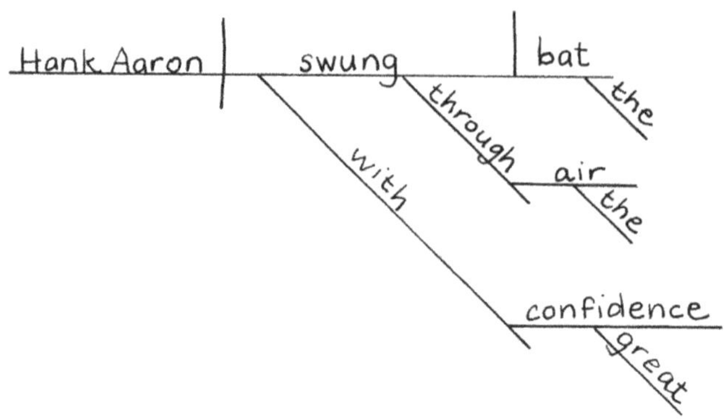

In summer, the car was hot beyond belief.

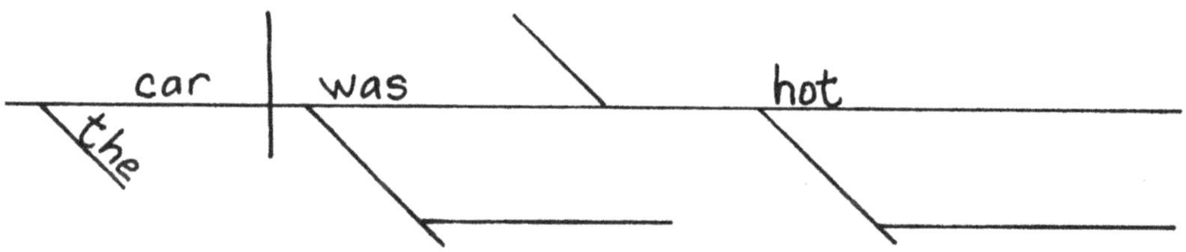

Exercise 42A: Identifying Adverb Phrases

Underline the adverb phrases in the following sentences and circle the preposition that begins each phrase. Draw an arrow from the phrase to the word it modifies. The first is done for you.

Ozzie's family traveled to California for a volcano tour.

In northern California they toured Mount Shasta.

Through some volcanic craters, you can see bubbling lava.

Active volcanoes have erupted during recent history.

Extinct volcanoes have not erupted in millennia.

Gas builds up in the volcano with increasing pressure.

Volcanic eruptions are caused by this buildup.

With incredible force, the volcano can shoot dangerous gas and ash into the air.

At this stage, the storm goes into decline.

Some species are born larger and immediately drop to the bottom.

The octopus lays her eggs in capsules and attaches them to a rock with a string-like substance.

She defends the nest against intruders.

Exercise 42B: Diagramming Adverb Phrases

On your own paper. diagram the following five sentences from *The Adventures of Tom Sawyer*, by Mark Twain.

Tom eagerly drew his sore toe from the sheet and held it up for inspection.
Tom was panting with his exertion by this time.
Sid yawned, stretched, and then brought himself up on his elbow with a snort and stared at Tom.
Tom was suffering in reality now.
The pain vanished from the toe.

— LESSON 43 —

Definitions Review
Adjective and Adverb Phrases
Misplaced Modifiers

An adjective modifies ______________________________.

Adjectives tell ______________________________.

A preposition shows ______________________________
word in the sentence.

A prepositional phrase ______________________________
______________________ **or pronoun.**

____ object of the preposition.

A phrase is ____ function.

Prepositional phrases that ____ adjective phrases.

Adjective phrases usually ____.

An adverb describes ____.

Adverbs tell ____ extent.

____ are also called adverb phrases.

Prepositions

a _______________, a _______________, a _______________, a _______________

a __________, a __________, a __________, a __________, a __________, a __________

b _______________, b _______________, b _______________, b _______________

b _______________, b _______________, b _______________, b _______________

d ____________, d ____________, e ____________, f ____________, f ____________

i _______________, i _______________, i _______________, l _______________

n ____________, o ____________, o ____________, o ____________, o ____________

p _______________, s _______________, t _______________, t _______________

t _______________, t _______________, u _______________, u _______________

u _______________, u _______________, u _______________

w _______________, w _______________, w _______________

The cat scratched Brock's sister with the striped tail.

A misplaced modifier is an adjective phrase in the wrong place.

The beautiful girl was dancing with the handsome man in the red dress.

On the pizza, Molly ate the mushrooms.

I cut my finger while I was cooking badly.

I saw that the toast was burned with a glance.

I spotted the dog chewing on the sofa leg from the stairs.

Exercise 43A: Distinguishing Between Adjective and Adverb Phrases

Underline all of the prepositional phrases in the following sentences. Write *ADJ* above the adjective phrases and *ADV* above the adverb phrases.

On her birthday, Etta received a powerful telescope with a tripod.

With her new telescope, she could see four of the moons of Jupiter.

She tracked their movement over several weeks.

At the beginning of the month, they were spaced almost equally distant.

By the middle of the month, one of the moons was hidden behind Jupiter.

After her telescope experiment, Etta viewed the stars of the night sky with renewed awe.

A thunderstorm goes through a number of stages.

Rain drops may remain in a liquid form for some time.

The octopus climbed out of the tank, slithered to the corner of the table, felt with its tentacles for a table leg that it could not see, slid down the table leg, dragged itself across the deck and dropped to the safety of the sea below.

From Derek K. Hitchins, *Systems Engineering: A 21st Century Systems Methodology*

Even the largest octopus can squeeze through a narrow opening in the top of an aquarium. Once it escapes, an octopus can live a long time on land.

From Katie Kubesh, Kimm Bellotto, and Niki Mcneil, *Predators of the Deep*

Exercise 43B: Correcting Misplaced Modifiers

Circle the misplaced adjective and adverb phrases in the following sentences. Draw an arrow to the place where the phrase should be. The first is done for you.

The lady bought two peaches with large, dangly earrings.

Inside the doughnut, Derek licked the cream filling.

I fondly remembered the chicken my grandmother fried in my mind.

The doctor inside the patient's joint felt the hard lump.

Alistair gave a rosemary plant to his mother in a hand-painted pot.

With three legs, Welles built a kitchen stool.

Erin of chocolate and peanut butter baked cookies.

The man squirted honey into his tea with long hair and ripped shoes.

Under the bed, Gertrude found the missing earring.

The boy picked up the lizard with checkered pants.

My uncle told us how he used to scrub dirty dogs at the table.

— LESSON 44 —

Adjective and Adverb Phrases

Prepositional Phrases Acting as Other Parts of Speech

The ship went down into the Gulf of Guinea and, with many stops on the way, approached the mouth of the Congo.

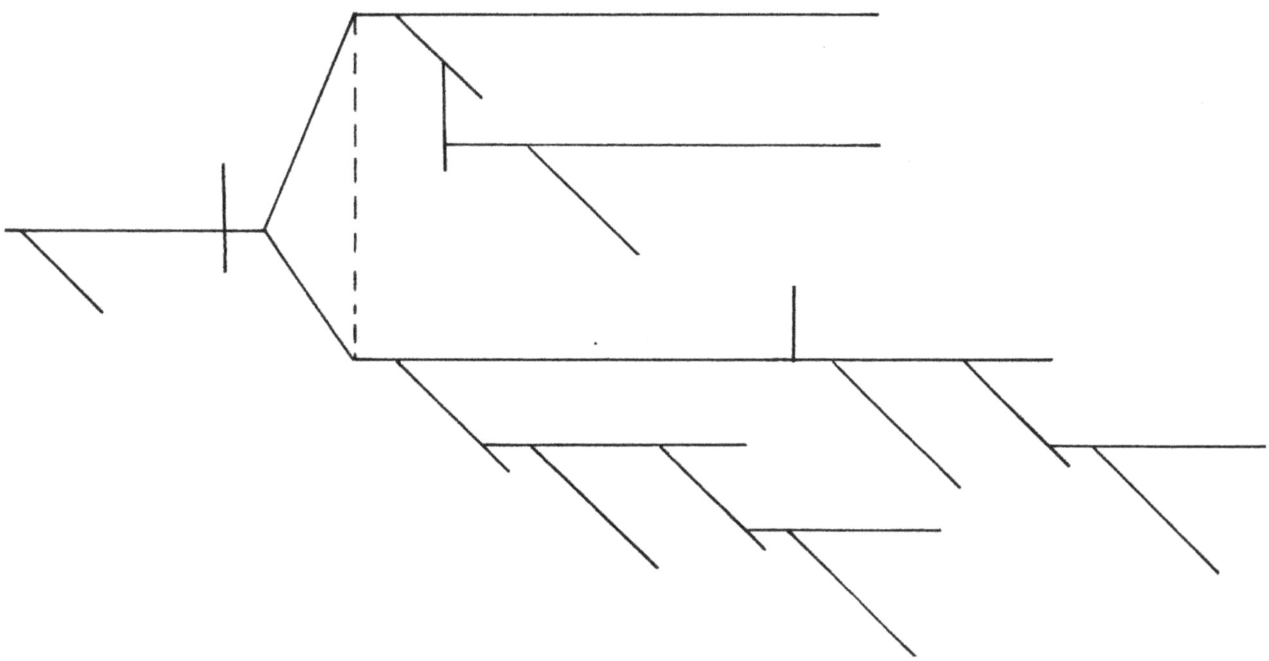

A swamp is not a safe place.

Under the bridge is not a safe place.

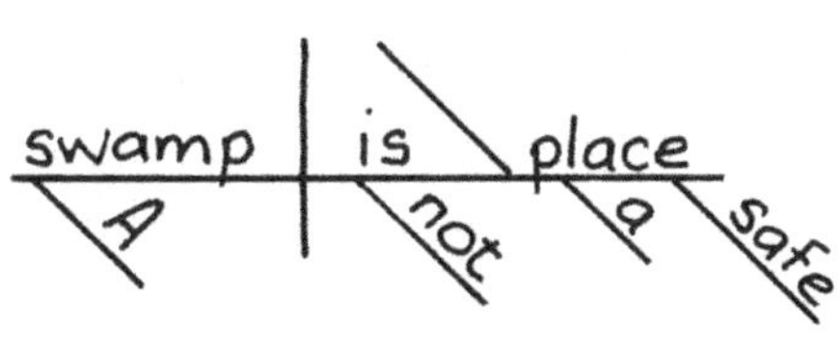

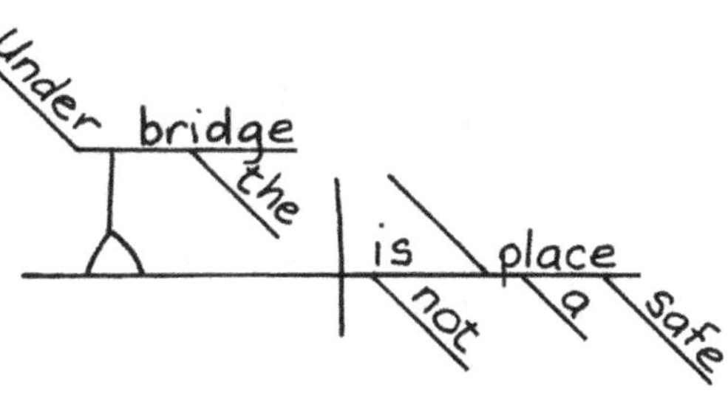

The best place for the treasure is my closet.

The best place for the treasure is under the bed.

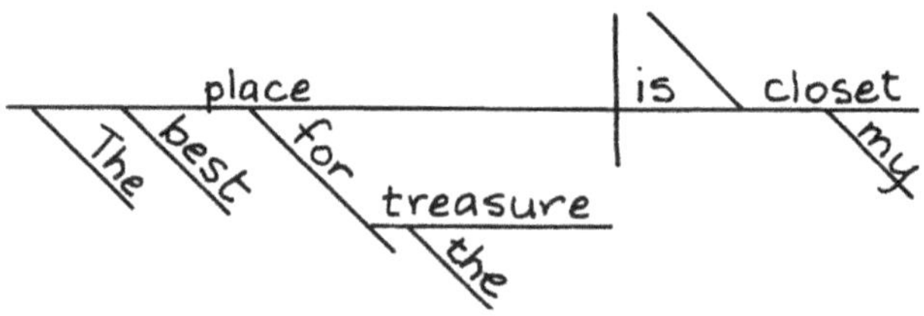

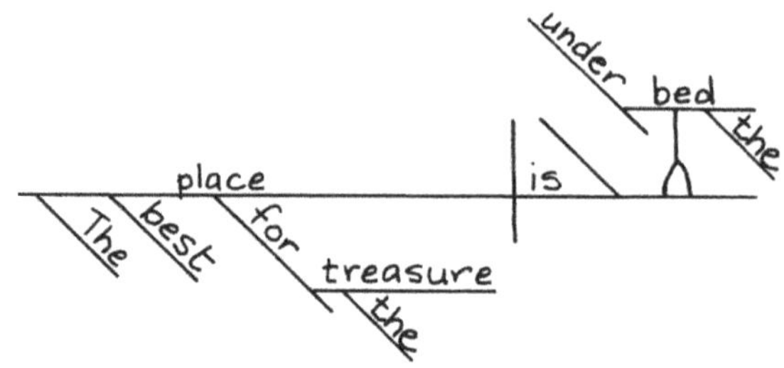

He stepped from the dark.

He stepped from behind the tree.

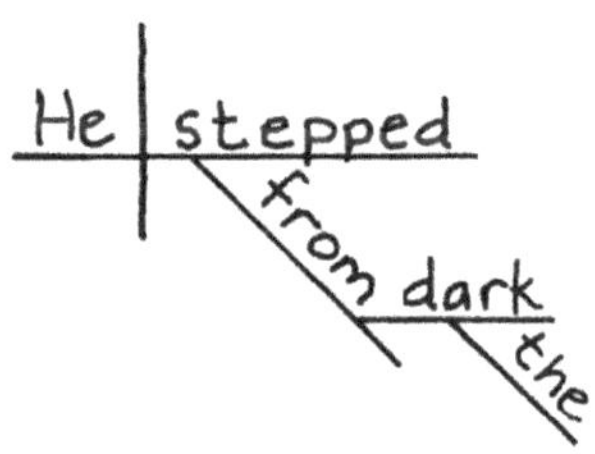

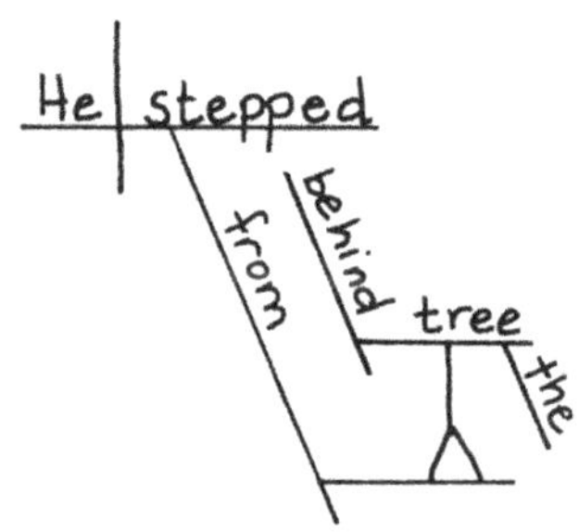

The man is happy.

The man is in love.

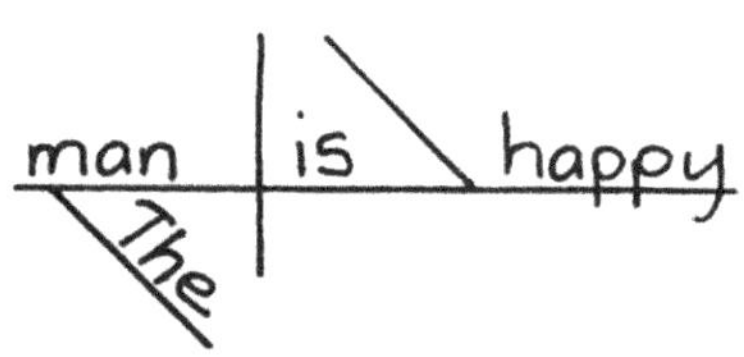

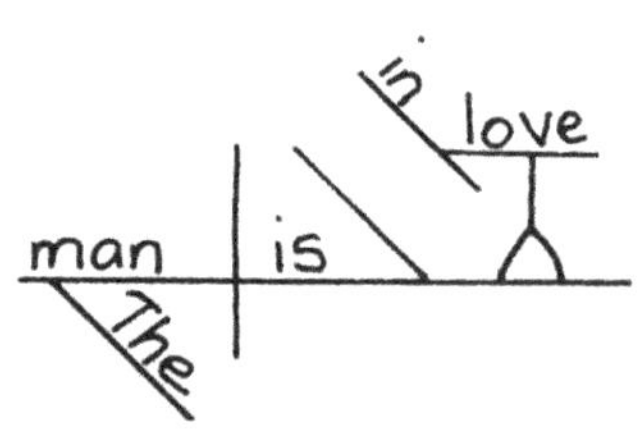

Exercise 44A: Prepositional Phrases Acting as Other Parts of Speech

In each sentence below, circle any prepositional phrases. Underline the subject of the sentence once and the predicate twice. Then, label the prepositional phrase as *ADJ* (adjective phrase), *ADV* (adverb phrase), *S* (subject), *PA* (predicate adjective), *PN* (predicate nominative), or *OP* (object of the preposition).

The waiters are in elaborate green uniforms.

The house on the secluded lane is on fire.

In the south was her lost home.

Molting makes a snake moody and depressed.

The best time for us is after dinner.

We drove through the large gateway, up a slight hill, to the door of the great white house.

Before breakfast is too early!

Beyond the fence is the park.

My favorite ride is in a private jet.

A growl rumbled from beneath the roof.

Exercise 44B: Diagramming

On your own paper, diagram the sentences from 44A.

WEEK 12

Advanced Verbs

— LESSON 45 —

Linking Verbs
Linking/Action Verbs

State-of-Being/Linking Verbs
am, is, are, was, were
be, being, been

Additional Linking Verbs
taste, feel, smell, sound, look
prove, grow,
remain, appear, stay
become, seem

I tasted the candy.

The candy tasted delicious.

The fried chicken tasted crispy.

The chicken tasted the birdseed.

Thomas felt the baby chick.
Thomas felt sad.

ACTION	LINKING
He proved the theory.	He proved unreliable.
The farmer grew wheat.	The farmer grew tired.
The dog remained on the porch.	The dog remained wary.
The cloud appeared in the sky.	The cloud appeared threatening.
We stayed home.	We stayed happy with our home.

The student became confused.
The grammar seemed difficult.

Exercise 45A: Distinguishing Between Action Verbs and Linking Verbs

Underline the verbs in the following sentences. Identify them as *AV* for action verb or *LV* for linking verb. If the verb is followed by a direct object (*DO*), predicate adjective (*PA*), or predicate nominative (*PN*), label it.

Remember that a verb with *no* direct object, predicate adjective, or predicate nominative will most likely be an action verb. Also remember that direct objects, predicate adjectives, and predicate nominatives are never found in prepositional phrases.

Maggie smelled the week-old milk.

The milk smelled strange.

She threw the milk away.

Casey remained in the cellar during the tornado.

He stayed calm in the stressful situation.

The storm seemed endless.

Casey was nervous.

His little sister was holding his hand.

Soon the sky became clear and still.

The sapling became an oak.

Trees grow on either side of the road.

It looks untidy.

Castles of various sorts were common.

Peking reflected the dominance of the imperial household.

Exercise 45B: Distinguishing Among Different Kinds of Nouns

Underline all of the nouns in the following sentences. Identify them as *S* for subject, *IO* for indirect object, *DO* for direct object or *PN* for predicate nominative.

Susana planted a garden.

Susana grew tomatoes, basil, and peppers.

Susana gave her little plants water and care.

Soon the seeds were tiny little green shoots.

The veggies became ready to harvest.

Susana picked the vegetables and made her sister a delicious salad.

Now Susana is a chef!

Exercise 45C: Diagramming Action Verbs and Linking Verbs

On your own paper, diagram the following sentences.

They seem anxious.
Daniel fixed Mom dinner.
Toads are amphibians.
Toads are hopping.
He tasted couscous.
This tastes delectable.

— LESSON 46 —

Conjugations
Irregular Verbs
Principal Parts of Verbs

Verbs in the simple past, simple present, and simple future describe actions that simply happen.
Verbs in the progressive past, progressive present, and progressive future describe actions that go on for a while.
Verbs in the perfect past, perfect present, and perfect future describe actions which have been completed before another action takes place.

Exercise 46A: Forming Simple, Perfect, and Progressive Tenses

Fill in the missing blanks in the chart below.

Simple Present

	Singular	Plural
First person	I breathe	we __________
Second person	you __________	you breathe
Third person	he, she, it __________	they breathe

Simple Past

	Singular	Plural
First person	I ____________	we ____________
Second person	you ____________	you ____________
Third person	he, she, it ____________	they breathed

Simple Future

	Singular	Plural
First person	I ____________	we ____________
Second person	you will breathe	you ____________
Third person	he, she, it ____________	they ____________

Perfect Present

	Singular	Plural
First person	I ____________	we ____________
Second person	you ____________	you ____________
Third person	he, she, it has breathed	they ____________

Perfect Past

	Singular	Plural
First person	I ____________	we ____________
Second person	you ____________	you had breathed
Third person	he, she, it ____________	they ____________

Perfect Future

	Singular	Plural
First person	I will have breathed	we ____________
Second person	you ____________	you ____________
Third person	he, she, it ____________	they ____________

Progressive Present

	Singular	Plural
First person	I ____________	we are breathing
Second person	you ____________	you ____________
Third person	he, she, it ____________	they ____________

Progressive Past

	Singular	Plural
First person	I ____________	we ____________
Second person	you were breathing	you ____________
Third person	he, she, it ____________	they ____________ breathing

Progressive Future

	Singular	Plural
First person	I will be breathing	we ____________
Second person	you ____________	you ____________
Third person	he, she, it ____________	they ____________

Simple Present	Simple Past	Simple Future
build	built	will build
buy	bought	will buy
choose	chose	will choose
sell	sold	will sell

Exercise 46B: Latin Roots

The following English words were created from Latin words. Draw lines matching the English word with the Latin root word. You do not need to know Latin to do well on this exercise!

English word	Latin root	Meaning
ambulance	A. *frango*	("to break")
audible	B. *claudo*	("to close")
exclude	C. *audio*	("to hear")
dictate	D. *habito*	("to live")
edible	E. *fugio*	("to flee")
fragile	F. *ambulo*	("to walk")
refugee	G. *edo*	("to eat")
habitat	H. *dico*	("to speak")

English verbs have three principal parts.

First principal part: the simple present (present)

(I) conjugate *(I)* ______________

Second principal part: the simple past (past)

(I) conjugated *(I)* ______________

Third principal part: the perfect past, minus helping verbs (past participle)

(I have) conjugated *(I have)* ______________

Exercise 46C: Principal Parts of Verbs

Fill in the chart with the missing forms.

	First Principal Part Present	Second Principal Part Past	Third Principal Part Past Participle
I	climb	climbed	climbed
I	flop		flopped
I			sniffled
I	juggle		
I		announced	
I			winked
I	plan		
I		waved	
I	roast		
I			lifted

Exercise 46D: Distinguishing Between First and Second Principal Parts

Identify the underlined verb as 1 for first principal part or 2 for second principal part.

These sentences are taken from *The Greely Arctic Expedition: As Fully Narrated by Lieut. Greely, U.S.A., And Other Survivors.*

The crystal mountains dash against each other backward and forward.

We passed from a heated cabin at 30° above zero to 47° below zero in the open air without inconvenience.

The sea-gulls fly away screaming.

Her great masts and massive ribs of solid timber cracked.

Nothing remained of the great ship.

— LESSON 47 —

Linking Verbs
Principal Parts
Irregular Verbs

Linking Verbs
am, is, are, was, were
be, being, been
taste, feel, smell, sound, look
prove, grow
remain, appear, stay
become, seem

Present	Past	Past Participle
(I) taste	(I) tasted	(I have) tasted
(I) become	(I) became	(I have) become
(I) feel	(I) felt	(I have) felt

COMMON IRREGULAR VERBS

Present	Past	Past Participle				
SAME PRESENT, PAST, and PAST PARTICIPLE:						
beat	beat	beat	(OR	beat	beat	beaten)
burst	burst	burst				
cost	cost	cost				
cut	cut	cut				
fit	fit	fit				
let	let	let				
put	put	put				
quit	quit	quit				
hit	hit	hit				
hurt	hurt	hurt				
set	set	set				
shut	shut	shut				
SAME PAST and PAST PARTICIPLE:						
bend	bent	bent				
send	sent	sent				
lend	lent	lent				
bleed	bled	bled				
feed	fed	fed				
feel	felt	felt				
keep	kept	kept				
lead	led	led				
leave	left	left				
meet	met	met				
read	read	read				
sleep	slept	slept				
bring	brought	brought				
buy	bought	bought				
catch	caught	caught				
fight	fought	fought				
seek	sought	sought				
teach	taught	taught				
think	thought	thought				
lay	laid	laid				
pay	paid	paid				
say	said	said				
sell	sold	sold				
tell	told	told				

lose	lost	lost
shoot	shot	shot
find	found	found
wind	wound	wound
dig	dug	dug
sit	sat	sat
win	won	won
stand	stood	stood
understand	understood	understood
hear	heard	heard
make	made	made
build	built	built

DIFFERENT PAST AND PAST PARTICIPLE:

awake	awoke	awoken
bite	bit	bitten
break	broke	broken
choose	chose	chosen
forget	forgot	forgotten
freeze	froze	frozen
get	got	gotten
give	gave	given
drive	drove	driven
eat	ate	eaten
fall	fell	fallen
hide	hid	hidden
rise	rose	risen
shake	shook	shaken
speak	spoke	spoken
steal	stole	stolen
take	took	taken
write	wrote	written
ride	rode	ridden
become	became	become
begin	began	begun
come	came	come
run	ran	run
drink	drank	drunk

shrink	shrank	shrunk
ring	rang	rung
sing	sang	sung
swim	swam	swum
draw	drew	drawn
fly	flew	flown
grow	grew	grown
know	knew	known
tear	tore	torn
wear	wore	worn
do	did	done
go	went	gone
lie	lay	lain
see	saw	seen

— LESSON 48 —

Linking Verbs
Principal Parts
Irregular Verbs

Linking Verbs
am, is, are, was, were
be, being, been
taste, feel, smell, sound, look
prove, grow
remain, appear, stay
become, seem

Verbs in the simple past, simple present, and simple future describe actions that simply happen.
Verbs in the progressive past, progressive present, and progressive future describe actions that go on for a while.
Verbs in the perfect past, perfect present, and perfect future describe actions which have been completed before another action takes place.

PRINCIPAL PARTS
present, past, past participle

Exercise 48A: Principal Parts

Fill in the blanks in the following chart of verbs.

Present	Past	Past Participle
meet	______	______
wind	______	______
______	was	______
______	______	read
______	fit	______
begin	______	______
______	______	come
run	______	______
______	______	drunk
______	shrank	______
______	______	rung
sing	______	______
swim	______	______
______	______	learned
______	______	known
______	wore	______
______	______	done
go	______	______
______	lay	______
______	saw	______
______	______	caught
hide	______	______
speak	______	______
______	______	stolen
______	took	______
write	______	______
______	______	walked
______	______	ridden
hear	______	______
make	______	______

Present	Past	Past Participle
________	________	sent
________	________	hurt
lead	________	________
________	listened	________
________	________	shut
________	________	lent
________	laid	________
________	________	told
lose	________	________
dig	________	________
________	chose	________
________	________	become

Exercise 48B: Forming Correct Past Participles

Write the correct third principal part (past participle) in each blank. The first principal part is provided for you in parentheses. The first is done for you.

I have ___made___ (make) a chocolate cake for my grandmother.

My grandmother has ____________ (come) from Oregon to visit!

She has ____________ (bring) hot cocoa with her to share.

I had already ____________ (read) the book about the history of chocolate that she had ____________ (give) me during our last visit.

The book was ____________ (write) by a historian and culinary anthropologist.

By the time we finished talking about the book, my grandmother and I had ____________ (drink) three cups of cocoa.

We decided that we had ____________ (be) very studious historians.

Exercise 48C: Forming Correct Past Tenses

Write the correct second principal part (past) in each blank. The first principal part is provided for you in parentheses. The first is done for you.

I ___told___ (tell) my grandmother what I had learned about the history of chocolate.

Chocolate ____________ (come) from a bean called *cacao*.

An unknown person in Latin America _______________ (am) the first to make chocolate.

They _______________ (drink) chocolate as a spicy beverage.

Spanish conquistadors _______________ (bring) the *cacao* beans back to Spain.

They _________________ (put) sugar in the chocolate and _______________ (make) desserts from it.

As she ___________ (eat) a big bite of chocolate cake, my grandmother ___________ (say) that she _______________ (am) grateful to the first person who ever made chocolate.

Exercise 48D: Proofreading for Irregular Verb Usage

Find and correct the SIX errors in irregular verb usage in the following excerpts from the Norwegian folktale "Why the Sea is Salt." Cross out the incorrect forms and write the correct ones above.

But Christmas is a time when even selfish people give gifts. So he gived his brother a fine ham, but telled him never to let him see his face again.

The merchant knowed how to start the mill, but he did not know how to stop it; no matter which way he turned it, it goed on grinding and grinding. The heap of salt growed higher and higher, until at last the ship went down, making a great whirlpool where it sinked.

Exercise 48E: Diagramming

On your own paper, diagram the following four sentences.

Who made you the judge of your brother?

The gratin of potato and cheese smelled absolutely delightful.

In the morning is the best time for exercise.

Queen Abigail smelled the bouquet of roses and lilies without enthusiasm.

— REVIEW 4 —

Weeks 10-12

Topics
Direct and Indirect Objects
Linking Verbs
Predicate Adjectives
Predicate Nominatives
Articles
Adjective Phrases
Adverb Phrases
Action vs. Linking Verbs
Irregular Verbs
Principal Parts (Present, Past, Past Participle)

Review 4A: Action vs. Linking Verbs

Identify the underlined verbs as *A* for action or *L* for linking.

Over half of earth's living creatures dwell in the depths of the sea.

The identities of many of these creatures remain unknown.

Deep-sea creatures are perhaps the most bizarre animals on earth.

Many deep-sea animals may seem nightmarish but in reality are harmless.

The fish have developed over time in the dark, cold depths of the sea and have grown quite ugly.

Because of the shortage of light and food, the fish have grown unusual adaptations.

Because their eyes are large, and their skin is devoid of pigment, these creatures appear alien-like.

The grisly fangtooth fish may look fearsome, but it only grows to a length of six inches.

We can only imagine what strange, undiscovered animals must live even farther under the waters!

Review 4B: Predicate Adjectives and Predicate Nominatives

Underline the linking verb in each of the following sentences. If the sentence concludes with a predicate nominative or predicate adjective, circle each and write *PA* for predicate adjective or *PN* for predicate nominative above it.

Grandpa Harold is my mother's father.

He is my only grandparent.

Grandpa Harold's hair has grown gray and thin.

His back has become somewhat bent.

But his laugh is still clear and joyous.

Sometimes he seems younger than my serious cousin Leslie.

She is a teenager, but she seems much more mature.

Her perfume smells spicy and floral.

Review 4C: Adjective and Adverb Phrases

In the following excerpt from Russell Freedman's *Give Me Liberty! The Story of the Declaration of Independence,* identify each underlined prepositional phrase as *ADJ* for adjective phrase or *ADV* for adverb phrase.

William Gray, a master rope maker, knew there was going to be trouble in Boston that night. He wanted no part of it. As dusk fell, he closed the shutters of his house and shop. After supper, he sent his apprentice, fourteen-year-old Peter Slater, upstairs and locked the boy in his room.

Peter waited until the house was quiet. Then he knotted his bedding together, hung it out the window, and slid to freedom. He wasn't a rope maker's apprentice for nothing.

He hurried along dark cobbled streets to a secret meeting place, a blacksmith's shop where a crowd of men and boys seemed to be getting ready for a costume party. They were smearing their faces with coal dust and red paint and wrapping old blankets around their shoulders, disguising themselves as Mohawk Indians. . . .

Review 4D: Forming Principal Parts

Complete the following excerpt (from *Animals on the Edge: Science Races to Save Species Threatened with Extinction*, by Sandra Pobst) by writing the correct principal part (PP) of the verb (first, second, or third) in parentheses.

Some people ____________ (*wonder*, 1st PP) why we should ____________ (*make*, 1st PP) the effort to save animals that are in danger of becoming extinct. After all, species have __________ (*be*, 3rd PP) going extinct throughout history as natural conditions ___________ (*change*, 2nd PP).

The changes occurring today, however, ______________ (*be*, 1st PP) primarily the result of human activity. As the world's population has _____________ (*grow*, 3rd PP), forests have been ____________ (*cut*, 3rd PP) down, prairies ____________ (*plow*, 3rd PP) under for farms, cities have _______________ (*expand*, 3rd PP), and factories and cars have ________________ (*spew*, 3rd PP) pollution into the air and water. Illegal killing of animals has also _________ (*increase*, 3rd PP) as some cultures highly ____________ (*value*, 1st PP) products made from protected animals.

Review 4E: Irregular Verbs

Find and correct the SIX errors in irregular verb usage in the following excerpt from *Island of the Blue Dolphins*, by Scott O'Dell. Cross out each incorrect form and write the correct form above it.

I finded nothing in the canoes under the cliff. Then, remembering the chest the Aleuts had brung to shore, I setted out for Coral Cove. I had saw that chest on the beach during the battle but did not remember that the hunters had took it with them when they fleed.

Review 4F: Misplaced Modifiers

Circle the misplaced adjective and adverb phrases in the following sentences. Draw an arrow to the place where each phrase should be.

The girl caught a lake trout with two blond braids.

The canoe rocked precariously in the waves with two seats.

From the plate, the dog gobbled the cake that had fallen.

The snake wriggled through the grass with the red stripes.

Marta accidentally bumped a man carrying books with her elbow.

Uncle Bruce told us stories about his trip to the Caribbean in the dining room.

I heard that the mayor is coming to our school from Hillary's brother.

In the campfire, the boy with the ripped jeans toasted his marshmallow.

Review 4G: Diagramming

On your own paper, diagram the following sentences.

Before the invention of money, people bartered for goods.
Luke trades Matt a chicken for a basket of apples.
Barter can be complex and problematic.
Cowry shells became money in ancient Chinese society.
Money was invented for simplification.
Over the years, silver and gold became standards of currency.
Today we give stores paper money.
Will all money be electronic in the future?

WEEK 13

Advanced Pronouns

— LESSON 49 —

Personal Pronouns
Antecedents
Possessive Pronouns

Lindsay woke up when Lindsay heard Lindsay's mother call Lindsay. Lindsay ate Lindsay's breakfast and brushed Lindsay's teeth and got ready for Lindsay's day.

A pronoun takes the place of a noun.
The antecedent is the noun that is replaced by the pronoun.

Personal Pronouns

	Singular	**Plural**
First person	I	we
Second person	you	you (plural)
Third person	he, she, it	they

Exercise 49A: Personal Pronouns and Antecedents

Circle the personal pronouns in the following sentences, adapted from *A Christmas Carol*, by Charles Dickens. Draw an arrow from each pronoun to the antecedent. In the margin, write the gender (*F*, *M*, or *N*) and number (*S* or *PL*) of each pronoun.

Scrooge gazed at the ghostly face. He could see it clearly.

Though the eyes were wide open, they were perfectly motionless.

Darkness is cheap, and Scrooge liked it.

Scrooge was not a man to be frightened by echoes. He fastened the door.

Personal Pronouns (Full List)

I, me, my, mine

you, your, yours

he, she, him, her, it

his, hers, its

we, us, our, ours

they, them, their, theirs

Possessive Adjectives (same as Possessive Pronouns)

my	our
your	your
his, her, its	their

Peter's sword	__________ sword
The Pevensie children's wardrobe	__________ wardrobe
The tree's silver leaves	__________ leaves
Lucy's cordial	__________ cordial

The tree's silver leaves glistened.
Its silver leaves glistened.

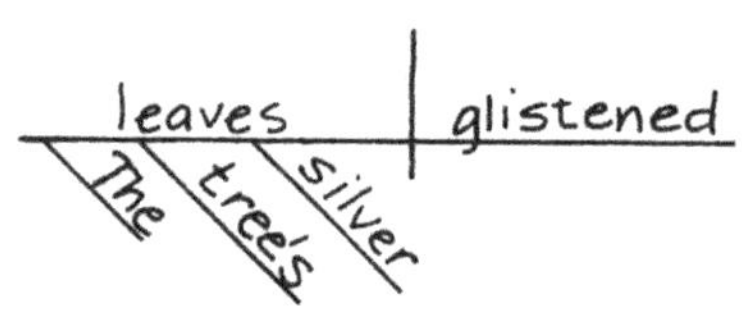

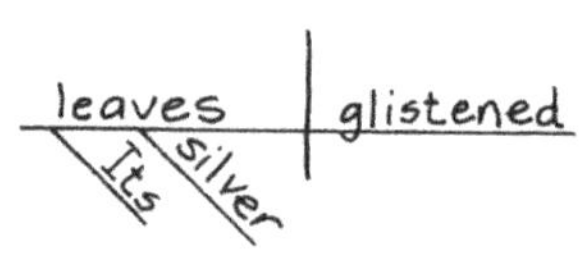

Lucy's cordial healed Edmund.

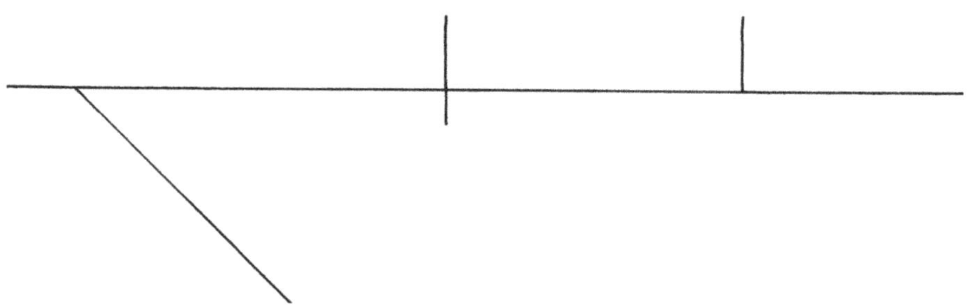

Her cordial healed Edmund.

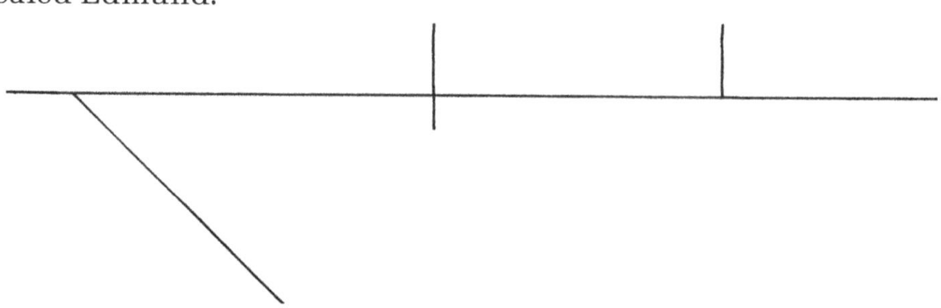

The chocolate is my candy.
The chocolate is mine candy.
The chocolate is mine!

He is your baby brother.
He is yours baby brother.
The baby brother is yours!

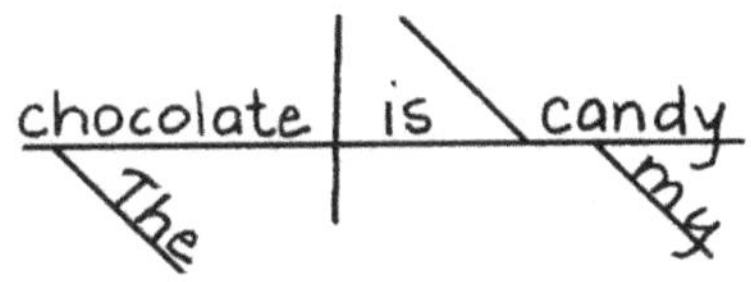

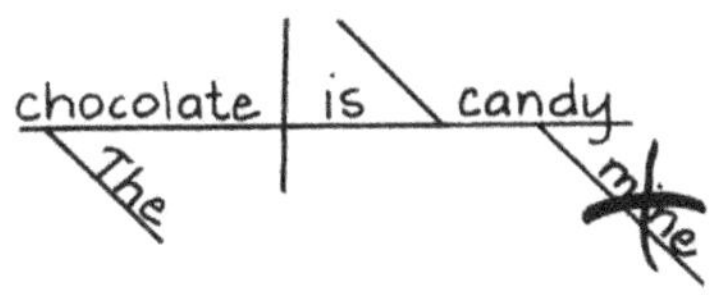

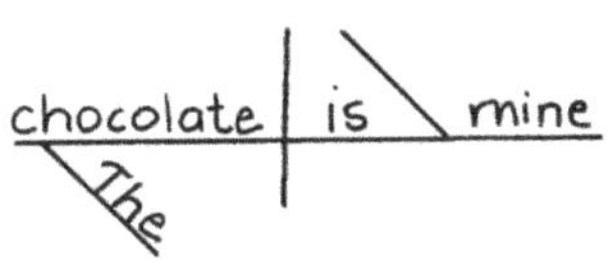

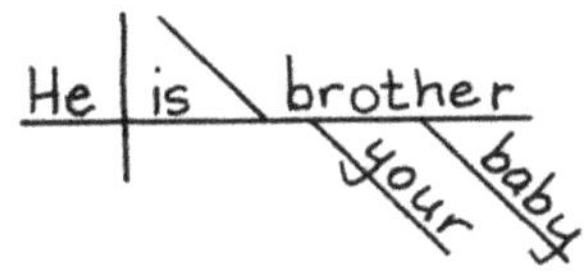

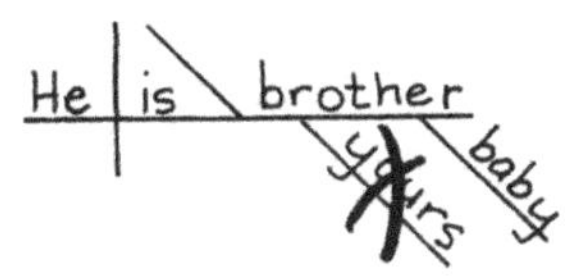

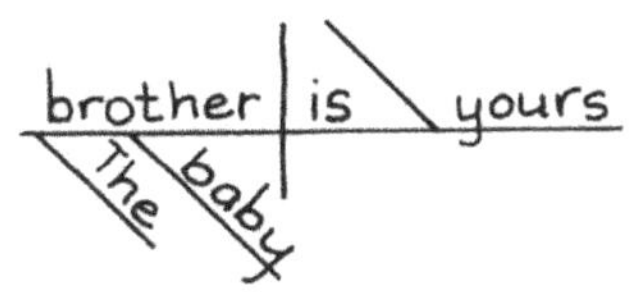

Exercise 49B: Identifying Possessive Pronouns

Underline the possessive pronouns in the following sentences from *The Travels of Marco Polo*. Each possessive pronoun is acting as an adjective. Draw an arrow from the pronoun to the noun it modifies. There may be more than one pronoun in each sentence.

On its summit is erected an ornamental pavilion, which is likewise entirely green.

Here, on the southern side of the new city, is the site of his vast palace.

In the rear of the body of the palace are large buildings containing several apartments, where is deposited the private property of the monarch, or his treasure in gold and silver bullion, precious stones, and pearls, and also his vessels of gold and silver plate.

Exercise 49C: Using Possessive Pronouns

Write the correct possessive pronoun above the underlined noun(s).

Theodore Roosevelt loved bull terrier dogs. After biting many people, Theodore Roosevelt's pet dog was sent away from the White House.

Theodore Roosevelt's daughter Alice received a present from the Empress of China.

The Empress's gift was a small Pekingese dog.

The first animal launched into orbit in space was a Russian female dog, Laika.

Laika, a stray from the streets of Russia, had already proven Laika's ability to withstand harsh conditions.

My family and I named my family's and my first pet dog Laika after the famous astronaut dog.

Animals depend on animals' owners.

The Wesley sisters take turns looking after the Wesley sisters' pet dog.

It's Stephanie's turn today.

This puppy is Penny's, but that one is my puppy.

There is a problem with this dog collar. The collar's buckle is broken.

Exercise 49D: Diagramming Pronouns

On your own paper, diagram every word in the following sentences.

The *North Star* made her way into a small inlet in the ice.
She was caught by the ice, and was completely destroyed.
Her great masts and her massive ribs of solid timber cracked and broke.

— LESSON 50 —

Pronoun Case

Personal Pronouns (Full List)
I, me, my, mine
you, your, yours
he, she, him, her, it
his, hers, its
we, us, our, ours
they, them, their, theirs

My crown, I am; but still my griefs are mine.
—William Shakespeare, *Richard II*

Object pronouns are used as objects in sentences.
me, you, him, her, it, us, them

Mark each bolded pronoun as *DO, IO*, or *OP.*

> For **me**, my lords, I love **him** not, nor fear **him.**
> —William Shakespeare, *Henry VIII*

> Give **us** notice of his inclination.
> —William Shakespeare, *Richard III*

> A virtuous and a Christian-like conclusion,/To pray for **them** that have done scathe to **us**.
> —William Shakespeare, *Richard III*

Subject pronouns are used as subjects and predicate nominatives in sentences.
I, you, he, she, it, we, they

Mark each bolded pronoun as *S* or *PN.*

> **I** am **he**.
> —William Shakespeare, *Richard III*

> Stand **we** in good array; for **they** no doubt,/Will issue out again and bid us battle.
> —William Shakespeare, *Henry VI*

> **I** blame her not, **she** could say little less;/**She** had the wrong. But what said Henry's queen?
> —William Shakespeare, *Henry VI, Part III*

You need to learn grammar. I will teach you.

I met her at the park. She was wearing her jacket.

It is not very hard. I will learn it.

CORRECT	***INCORRECT***
I am he.	I am him.
The students are we.	The students are us.
The teachers are they.	The teachers are them.

The kitten licked Jim. The kitten licked __________.

The winners were Judy and Diane. The winners were __________.

Give the prize to Madison (OP) and him (OP). NOT: Give the prize to *he.*

S S
Dad and I made brownies. NOT: *Me* made brownies.

Exercise 50A: Subject and Object Pronouns

Underline all the personal pronouns in the following paragraph. Identify them as *S* for subject, *O* for object, or *P* for possessive.

This description of a pyroclastic flow was written by the Roman lawyer Pliny the Younger after he lived through the eruption of Mount Vesuvius in the year 79. This translation by Betty Radice comes from *The Letters of the Younger Pliny* (Penguin Books, 1963), Book VI.

Ashes were already falling, not as yet very thickly. I looked round: a dense black cloud was coming up behind us, spreading over the earth like a flood . . . We had scarcely sat down to rest when darkness fell, not the dark of a moonless or cloudy night, but as if the lamp had been put out in a closed room. You could hear the shrieks of women, the wailing of infants, and the shouting of men; some were calling their parents, others their children or their wives, trying to recognize them by their voices . . . A gleam of light returned, but we took this to be a warning of the approaching flames rather than daylight. However, the flames remained some distance off; then darkness came on once more and ashes began to fall again, this time in heavy showers. We rose from time to time and shook them off, otherwise we should have been buried and crushed beneath their weight.

Exercise 50B: Using Personal Pronouns Correctly

Choose the correct word(s) in parentheses and cross out the incorrect choice(s). Be sure to choose the grammatically correct choice for writing and not the choice that sounds the best.

My brother and sister and (me/I) decided to clean the yard for our father's birthday.

My mother helped (us/we) to find the tools.

Daniela and (him/he) raked, and I trimmed the bushes.

Mom lent (Diego and me/Diego and I) a hand when we bagged the leaves.

At the end of the day, (us/we) were very tired but very pleased.

Dad gave Daniela, Diego, and (me/I) a huge compliment.

He said that the best gifts of all were (us/we).

Exercise 50C: Diagramming Personal Pronouns

On your own paper, diagram the following sentences. Personal pronouns are diagrammed exactly like the nouns or adjectives they replace.

They offered us advice.

We beat them!

It is I.

He fixed me lunch.

I understand you.

Their companions were we.

— LESSON 51 —

Indefinite Pronouns

Gollum wanted the ring. He longed for it.
Everyone hoped that Frodo would succeed.

Indefinite pronouns are pronouns without antecedents.

Indefinite Pronouns
Singular

anybody	anyone	anything
everybody	everyone	everything
nobody	no one	nothing
somebody	someone	something
another	other	one
either	neither	each

Plural
both, few, many, several

Singular or Plural
all, any, most, none, some

All of the cake was eaten.

All of the pieces were eaten.

Most of the people . . .

None of the water . . .

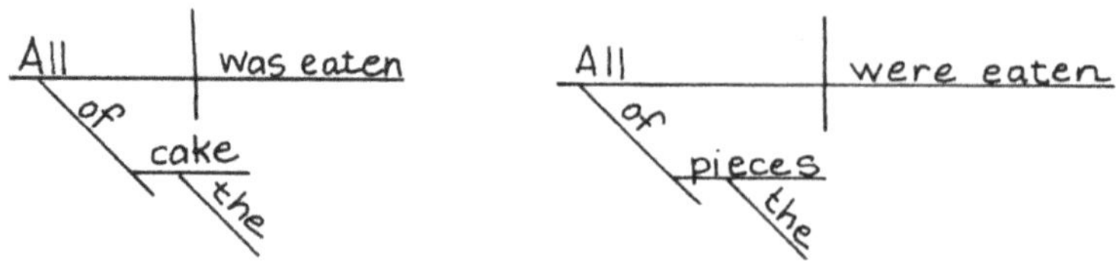

Many of the guests arrived early.

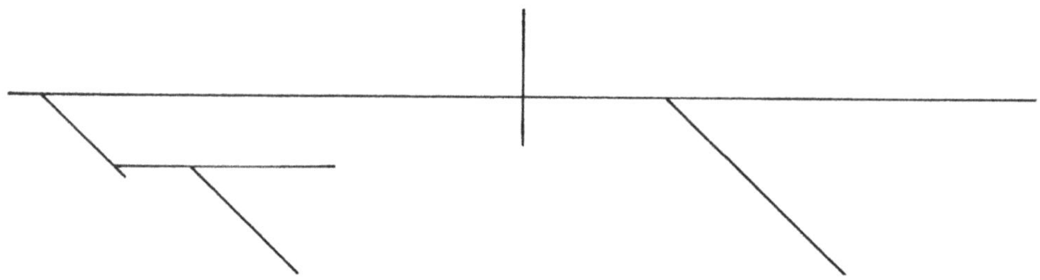

Many guests arrived early.

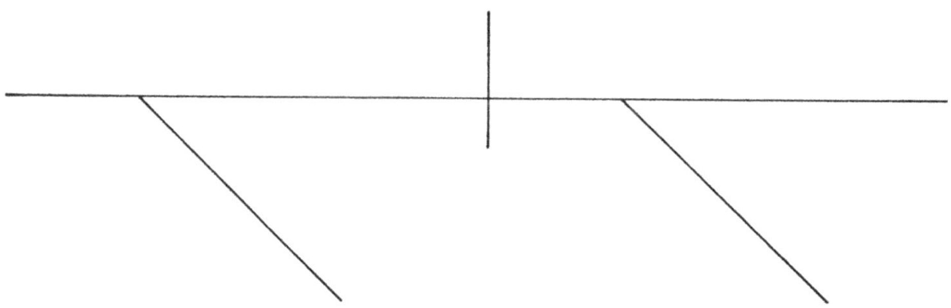

Exercise 51A: Identifying Indefinite Pronouns

Underline all of the indefinite pronouns in the following sentences. Each sentence may contain more than one pronoun.

Sitting-room, bedroom, lumber-room. All as they should be. Nobody under the table, nobody under the sofa; a small fire in the grate; spoon and basin ready; and the little saucepan of gruel (Scrooge had a cold in his head) upon the hob. Nobody under the bed; nobody in the closet; nobody in his dressing-gown, which was hanging up in a suspicious attitude against the wall.

—From Charles Dickens, *A Christmas Carol*

The summer heat has withered everything except the mesquite, the *palo verde*, the grease wood, and the various cacti.

—From John Charles Van Dyke, *The Desert: Further Studies in Natural Appearances*

Nothing besides gilding and painting presents itself to the eye.

—From Marco Polo and Johns Masefield, *The Travels of Marco Polo the Venetian*

Exercise 51B: Subject-Verb Agreement: Indefinite Pronouns

Choose the correct verb in parentheses. Cross out the incorrect verb.

Both of the Travis twins (is / are) throwing a birthday party.

Everyone (has / have) been invited!

All of the decorations (was / were) purchased and hung.

A few of the guests (has / have) arrived already, but some (is / are) going to be late.

Most of the cupcakes (has / have) been made.

But some of the icing (is / are) missing!

(Does / Do) anyone know where the icing is?

One of the Travis twins (was / were) holding up Tiger, the cat.

All of his furry face (was / were) covered in icing.

Exercise 51C: Diagramming Indefinite Pronouns

On your own paper, diagram the following sentences, drawn from *Oliver Twist*, by Charles Dickens.

Nobody knows him.
Neither of them are employed.
Few people were stirring.
They were both daughters.
Both of them were wrapped in shabby outer garments.

— LESSON 52 —

Personal Pronouns
Indefinite Pronouns

Personal Pronouns
I, me, my, mine
you, your, yours
he, she, him, her, it
his, hers, its
we, us, our, ours
they, them, their, theirs

Subject pronouns: ____

____

_________________________ am delighted to be doing grammar.

_________________________ are delighted to be doing grammar.

_________________________ is delighted to be doing grammar.

Object pronouns: ____

____

The walrus splattered water all over _________________________.

The rain drenched Kim and _________________________________.

Possessive pronouns/possessive adjectives in attributive position: _____________________

____

I grabbed ____________________________________ umbrella.

The cloud began dropping _____________________ moisture.

The soaked tourists ran for _____________________ cars.

Possessive pronouns/possessive adjectives in predicate position: ______________________

____

That raincoat is _____________________________________.

Those waterproof ponchos are _________________________.

Indefinite pronouns are pronouns without antecedents.

Singular Indefinite Pronouns

anybody	anyone	anything
everybody	everyone	everything
nobody	no one	nothing
somebody	someone	something
another	other	one
either	neither	each

Everyone _________ in the kitchen.

Nobody ___________ in the dining room.

Neither of them ___________ in the garden.

Plural Indefinite Pronouns
both, few, many, several

Both __________ cooking eggplants.

A few of the crowd __________ objecting to eggplant.

Several __________ quite happy with the prospect of eggplant.

Singular or Plural Indefinite Pronouns
all, any, most, none, some

All of the fire engines __________ there.

All of the mansion __________ destroyed in the fire.

Is everyone coming to get __________ Christmas present?

____

Are they all coming to get their Christmas presents?

Exercise 52A: Subject and Object Pronouns

In the following sentences from E. Nesbit's *The Railway Children*, cross out the incorrect pronoun.

And (he / him) did not like the feeling which thinking this gave (he / him).

That night at tea (he / him) asked Mother if (she / her) had a green leather note-book with silver corners.

(She / Her) had not; but when (she / her) heard what (he / him) wanted it for (she / her) gave (he / him) a little black one.

"It has a few pages torn out," said (she / her), "but it will hold quite a lot of numbers."

After all, it was (she / her) who had thought of packing up the odds and ends of things to eat.

"Is (he / him) all killed?" asked Phyllis.

"All (we / us) can do, you and (I / me) and Daddy, is to be brave, and patient."

"Phil and (I / me) are going away."

"(I / Me) don't know how to thank you for making it possible for (I / me)."

"Father and (I / me) used to go on the river at Marlow before (we / us) were married."

"Besides parting from Father, (he/him) and (I/me) have had a great sorrow—oh, terrible—worse than anything you can think of."

"If you take his feet and Phil and (I/me) take his head, (we/us) could carry him."

"(I/Me) know that you love mother and Peter and Phil and (I/me)."

"Phil and (I/me) can wash (they/them)," said Bobbie, "if you'll iron (they/them), Mother."

(She/Her) and her mother and that awful sheet of newspaper were alone in the room together.

Exercise 52B: Possessive and Indefinite Pronouns

In these sentences from E. Nesbit's *The Enchanted Castle,* cross out the incorrect word in each set of parentheses.

"I ought to," she said, "if anybody (does/do)."

The sun was blazing in at the window; the eight-sided room was very hot, and everyone (was/were) getting cross.

Everyone (was/were) very hungry, and more bread and butter had to be fetched.

Something enormously long and darkly grey came crawling towards him, slowly, heavily. The moon came out just in time to show (its/their) shape.

No one (was/were) to be seen.

And the nearer they came to the Temple of Flora, in the golden hush of the afternoon, the more certain each (was/were) that they could not possibly have done otherwise.

Both the others (was/were) used to Gerald's way of telling a story while he acted it.

Everyone grew calmer and more contented with (his/their) lot.

Part of the shelf near it held, not bright jewels, but rings and brooches and chains, as well as queer things that she did not know the names of, and all (was/were) of dull metal and odd shapes.

Then everyone sat or lay down on (his/their) couch and the feast began.

All (was/were) still as the sweet morning itself.

There (was/were) a few bunches of flowers among the vegetables, and the children hesitated, balanced in choice.

But none of the houses (turns /turn) into enchanted castles.

A few words (was/were) exchanged.

None of the children (was / were) at all sure what the utmost rigour of the law might be.

Some (was / were) dipping (his / their) white feet among the gold and silver fish, and sending ripples across the faces of the seven moons.

Some (was / were) pelting each other with roses so sweet that the girls could smell them even across the pool.

Others (was / were) holding hands and dancing in a ring, and two (was / were) sitting on the steps playing cat's-cradle which is a very ancient game indeed with a thread of white marble.

Some of us (is / are) very hungry.

Exercise 52C: Writing Sentences from Diagrams

Use the diagrams below to reconstruct these sentences from E. Nesbit's *Five Children and It.* Write the original sentence on the blank below each diagram. Pay careful attention to each part of speech! Punctuate each sentence properly.

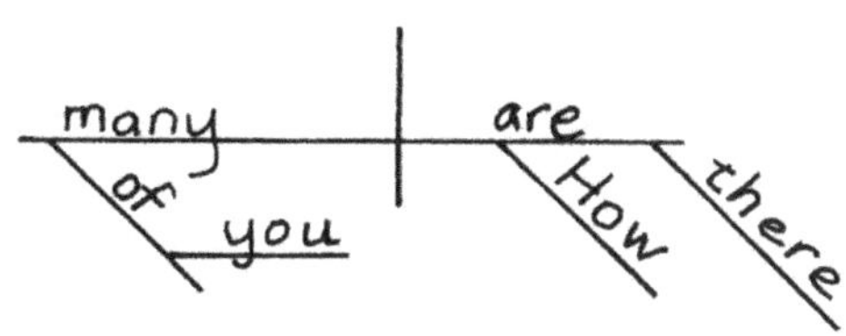

___

___

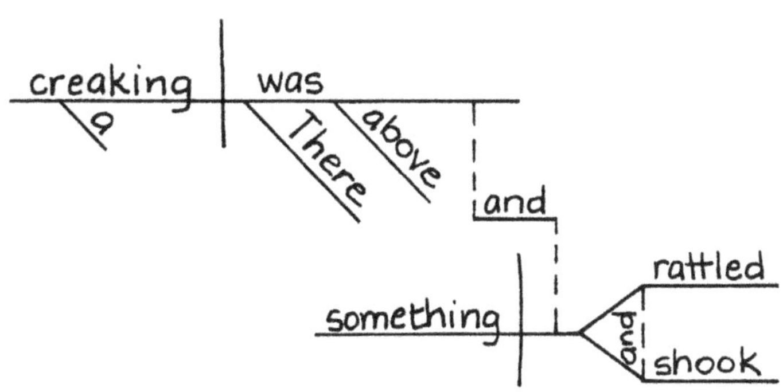

___

___

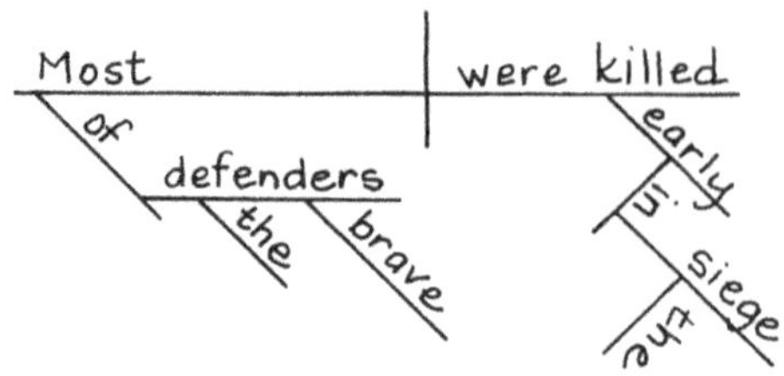
Most
were killed
of
defenders
the
brave
early
in
siege
the

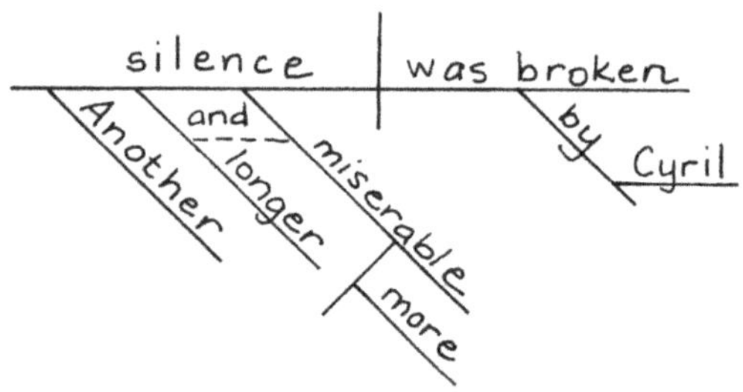
silence
was broken
Another
and
longer
miserable
more
by
Cyril

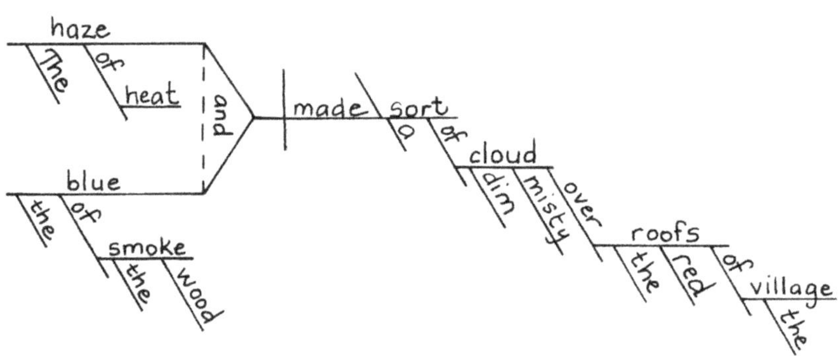
haze
The
of
heat
and
blue
the
of
smoke
the
wood
made
sort
a
of
cloud
dim
misty
over
roofs
the
red
of
village
the

WEEK 14

Active and Passive Voice

— LESSON 53 —

Principal Parts
Troublesome Verbs

She set the set of sorted stuff
Beside the seat where she had sat.

English verbs have three principal parts.
The first principal part is the simple present.
The second principal part is the simple past.
The third principal part of a verb is found by dropping the helping verb from the perfect past.

Exercise 53A: Principal Parts of Verbs

Fill in the chart with the missing forms.

	First Principal Part Present	Second Principal Part Past	Third Principal Part Past Participle
I	clap		
I		quit	
I		hid	
I			avoided
I	keep		
I			said
I	see		
I		broke	

Troublesome Irregular Verbs

Verb	Principal Parts	Definition
sit	(sit, sat, sat)	to rest or be seated
set	(set, set, set)	to put or place something
lie	(lie, lay, lain)	to rest or recline
lay	(lay, laid, laid)	to put or place something
rise	(rise, rose, risen)	to get up or go up
raise	(raise, raised, raised)	to cause something to go up or grow up
let	(let, let, let)	to allow
leave	(leave, left, left)	to go away from or allow to remain

Exercise 53B: Using Correct Verbs

Choose the correct verb in parentheses. Cross out the incorrect verb.

Katrin loves to (lay/lie) in her bed on cold mornings in Iceland.

But today Katrin (rose/raised) early from bed, because her *amma,* or grandmother, is turning 80 years old today.

Amma (rose/raised) six children, including Katrin's father.

Katrin's father (lay/laid) the marinated salmon on the grill.

Katrin's parents had (let/left) her alone for the afternoon and (let/left) her go horseback riding.

After she returned, she and her mother (set/sat) the table.

Her mother had (laid/lain) the embroidered cloth napkins next to the plates.

After eating dinner, they all (set/sat) at the table for hours and talked and laughed.

Very late that night, Katrin (lay/laid) down to sleep.

Exercise 53C: Correct Forms of Troublesome Verbs

Fill in the blanks with the correct form of the indicated verb.

I ____________ some time in a situation which no language can describe. (*lie*)
—Karl Friedrich Hieronymous, *The Adventures of Baron Munchausen*

She then gathers more pollen, ____________ another egg, and builds another partition. (*lay*)
—Anna Botsford Comstock, *Handbook of Nature Study*

She always ____________ a space for a vestibule near the door. (*leave*)
—Anna Botsford Comstock, *Handbook of Nature Study*

After listening for some time, I ___________ my head and looked around. (*raise*)
—Karl Friedrich Hieronymous, *The Adventures of Baron Munchausen*

This means that if you ___________ in one in Hawaii you might be boiled like a lobster. (*sit*)
—Bill Bryson, *A Short History of Nearly Everything*

Exercise 53D: Proofreading for Correct Verb Usage

Find and correct *six* errors in verb usage by crossing out the incorrect verbs and writing the correct forms above them.

Last year, my brother and I rose a crop of peanuts. Our parents let a quarter of the garden free for us to plant the peanuts. As soon as the sun had rose, we ran to the garden to plant our peanuts. We planted unroasted peanuts that we had bought from the grocery store. Soon they sprouted, producing little green shoots that raised out of the ground. We were patient and waited a long time, but we never saw any peanuts. The leaves began to turn yellow, so we decided to pull up the plants. My brother pulled up the first plant and lay it on the ground. The dirt fell off the roots, and we saw the peanuts laying there on the grass. They had been growing underground the whole time.

— LESSON 54 —

Verb Tense

Active and Passive Voice

past	simple
present	progressive
future	perfect

A simple verb simply tells whether an action takes place in the past, present, or future.
A progressive verb describes an ongoing or continuous action.
A perfect verb describes an action which has been completed before another action takes place.

Exercise 54A: Reviewing Tenses

Write the tense of each underlined verb above it. These two excerpts are from the Sherlock Holmes story "The Adventure of the Speckled Band," written by Arthur Conan Doyle. The first is done for you.

perfect present

"It seems that a young lady has arrived in a considerable state of excitement, who insists upon seeing me. She is waiting now in the sitting-room. Now, when young ladies wander about the metropolis at this hour of the morning and knock sleepy people up out of their beds, I presume that it is something very pressing which they have to communicate."

He had ceased to strike, and was gazing up at the ventilator, when suddenly there broke from the silence of the night the most horrible cry to which I have ever listened.

The door had been fastened upon the inner side, and the windows were blocked by old-fashioned shutters with broad iron bars.

He fastened the door upon the inner side.

In a sentence with an active verb, the subject performs the action.
In a sentence with a passive verb, the subject receives the action.

I punched you.
You were punched by me.

The Egyptians constructed pyramids.
Pyramids were constructed.
Pyramids were constructed by the Egyptians.

Active Verb	Passive Verb
Present Freddy tricks the alligator.	**is/are + past participle** The alligator is tricked by Freddy.
Past Freddy tricked the alligator.	**was/were + past participle** The alligator was tricked by Freddy.
Future Freddy will trick the alligator.	**will be + past participle** The alligator will be tricked by Freddy.
Progressive Present Freddy is tricking the alligator.	**is/are being + past participle** The alligator is being tricked by Freddy.

Progressive Past
Freddy was tricking the alligator.

was/were being + past participle
The alligator was being tricked by Freddy.

***Progressive Future**
Freddy will be tricking the alligator.

***will be being + past participle**
The alligator will be being tricked by Freddy.

Perfect Present
Freddy has tricked the alligator.

has/have been + past participle
The alligator has been tricked by Freddy.

Perfect Past
Freddy had tricked the alligator.

had been + past participle
The alligator had been tricked by Freddy.

Perfect Future
Freddy will have tricked the alligator.

will have been + past participle
The alligator will have been tricked by Freddy.

*The passive form of progressive future verbs is awkward and not often used.

State-of-being verbs do not have voice.

Exercise 54B: Distinguishing Between Active and Passive Voice

Identify the following sentences as *A* for Active or *P* for Passive. If you're not sure, ask yourself: Is the subject *doing* the verb, or is the verb *happening to* the subject?

The Battle of Marathon was fought thousands of years ago between Athens and Persia. ________

Many interesting legends have been told about the battle. ________

The Athens army was outnumbered. ________

The Athens army asked Sparta for help. ________

A messenger boy named Pheidippides was sent to Sparta to request aid. ________

The Persians were defeated! ________

Pheidippides had been delivering messages for days! ________

Nonetheless, the messenger boy carried news of victory 26 miles back to Athens. ________

Today, the famous 26.2-mile race is called a marathon. ________

The following sentences are taken from *The Adventures of Baron Munchausen*, by Karl Friedrich Hieronymous.

We sailed from Amsterdam with dispatches from their High Mightinesses the States of Holland. ________

The natives of the island were half-starved by his oppressive and infamous impositions. ________

In about six weeks we arrived at Ceylon. ________

We were received with great marks of friendship and true politeness. ________

The skin of the crocodile was stuffed in the usual manner. ________

The lion's skin was properly preserved. ________

We measured the crocodile. ________

Exercise 54C: Forming the Active and Passive Voice

Fill in the chart below, rewriting each sentence so that it appears in both the active and the passive voice. Be sure to keep the tense the same. The first is done for you.

ACTIVE	PASSIVE
The Greeks created the Olympic Games.	The Olympic Games were created by the Greeks.
	The first Olympic race was won by a cook named Coroebus.
France was hosting the first modern Olympics.	
The Olympics bring together many countries.	
A famous athlete will light the Olympic torch.	
	Many people have been inspired by Olympic champions.

— LESSON 55 —

Parts of the Sentence
Active and Passive Voice

My arms and legs were strongly fastened to the ground.

I felt something alive on my left leg.

I saw a tiny human creature with a bow and arrow.

They ran back in a fright.

Some of them were hurt by the fall.

— LESSON 56 —

Active and Passive Voice
Transitive and Intransitive Verbs

Active Voice
Present
The farmer grows wheat.
Past
I made a cake.
Future
The princess will keep the key.

Progressive Present
The farmer is growing wheat.
Progressive Past
I was making a cake.
Progressive Future
The princess will be keeping the key.

Perfect Present
The farmer has grown wheat.
Perfect Past
I had made a cake.
Perfect Future
The princess will have kept the key.

I laugh out loud.
The baby slept soundly.

Passive Voice
am/is/are + past participle
Wheat is grown by the farmer.
was/were + past participle
The cake was made by me.
will be + past participle
The key will be kept by the princess.

is/are being + past participle
Wheat is being grown by the farmer.
was/were being + past participle
The cake was being made by me.
will be being + past participle
The key will be being kept by the princess.

has/have been + past participle
Wheat has been grown by the farmer.
had been + past participle
The cake had been made by me.
will have been + past participle
The key will have been kept by the princess.

The queen will sit in the front row.
He died.

transire (Latin for "to pass over")

Transitive verbs express action that is received by some person or thing.
Intransitive verbs express action that is not received by any person or thing.

Common Intransitive Verbs

cough	go	arrive
sit	lie	rise
shine	sneeze	am, is, are, was, were

Common Transitive Verbs

love	eat	help
set	lay	raise
cut	hug	save

I am sitting on the front porch.
I lay down on the grass.
I will have risen early in the morning.

I am setting the heavy box down.
I laid my weary head on my arms.
I will have raised my hand at least once by the end of class.

Verbs That Can Be Used as Transitive or Intransitive

turn	break	speak
fly	run	spread
taste	eat	sing

The cook turns the meat on the spit.

I will spread gochujang mayonnaise on the burger bun.

He is singing a difficult aria.

The captain turned towards the sunset.

The mist spread across the river's surface.

He's singing in the shower.

The cook turns the meat on the spit.

____

I will spread gochujang mayonnaise on the burger bun.

____

He is singing a difficult aria.

____

Exercise 56A: Transitive and Intransitive Verbs

Underline each verb in the following sentences. Write *T* above each transitive verb and *IT* above each intransitive verb. Circle the direct object of each transitive verb.

Most of these sentences are adapted from *Mexico: An Encyclopedia of Contemporary Culture and History* (ABC-CLIO, 2004).

He was sleeping in the Iberia hotel.

The advent of modernism laid the groundwork for a distinctly Mexican poetry.

Diego Rivera complained about the stifling training at the National Academy of San Carlos.

Samuel Ruiz sent priests and other volunteers to support peasant activism.

The solution to Mexico's problems lay in political reform at the national level.

Comedy-fantasies like Carlos Vela's *Cinco de chocolate y uno de fresa* entertained audiences.

Mexico broke diplomatic relations with the Axis but did not declare war until May 1942.

The city was sitting atop dry lake beds in a valley.

Francisco Villa broke publicly with the First Chief of the Constitutionalist Army.

The government looked to the oil industry as a major source of revenue.

The road to power ran through the federal bureaucracy.

Many years of bloody fighting lay ahead.

Especially popular with students and the middle class, he ran a strong campaign.

Rebel groups even ate in company cafeterias.

Changes in immigration laws in 1990 raised Mexico's annual quota.

The Maya laid siege to Merida in 1848.

The best Golden Age films entertained and instructed.

Exercise 56B: Active and Passive Verbs

In the blanks below, rewrite each sentence with an active verb so that the verb is passive. Rewrite each sentence with a passive verb so that the verb is active.

These sentences are adapted from *Mexico: A Primary Source Cultural Guide*, by Alan Cobb (Rosen Publishing Group, 2004).

Quetzalcoatl brought a small tree to the Toltecs.

___

The tree grew flowers and then brown pods.

___

Quetzalcoatl picked the pods and dried them.

___

The women were taught to roast and grind the pods by Quetzalcoatl.

___

He instructed the Toltecs to mix the pods with hot water and hot peppers.

___

First honey, and then milk and sugar, was added by the Toltecs to this bitter drink.

___

The gods gave them their sacred chocolate drink.

___

Exercise 56C: Diagramming

On your own paper, diagram every word in the following sentences.

She took her coat down and locked the door of the cottage behind her and walked down the dim road towards the curve.

Napoleon was alarmed by the news of the loss of the battle and the retreat of the army beyond the Seine.

You can buy a "Goat for Peace" for your aunt's birthday.

A goat is a milk and fertilizer factory and can provide self-sufficiency.

WEEK 15

Specialized Pronouns

— LESSON 57 —

Parts of Speech
Parts of the Sentence
Intensive and Reflexive Pronouns

Anita made herself a huge brownie sundae!

Reflexive pronouns refer back to the subject.
Usually, reflexive pronouns act like objects.

Part of speech is a term that explains what a word does.
Part of the sentence is a term that explains how a word functions in a sentence.

He adapted himself to their knowledge.
He gave himself a task.
He praises in himself what he blames in others.

myself, himself, herself, itself, yourself, yourselves, ourselves, themselves

Intensive pronouns emphasize a noun or another pronoun.

The Queen of England herself gave the speech.
The Queen of England gave the speech herself.

DO
The Queen of England gave herself.

IO
The Queen of England gave herself the speech.

OP
The Queen of England gave the speech to herself.

Aristotle himself observed these variations.

He jumped into the sea and drowned himself.

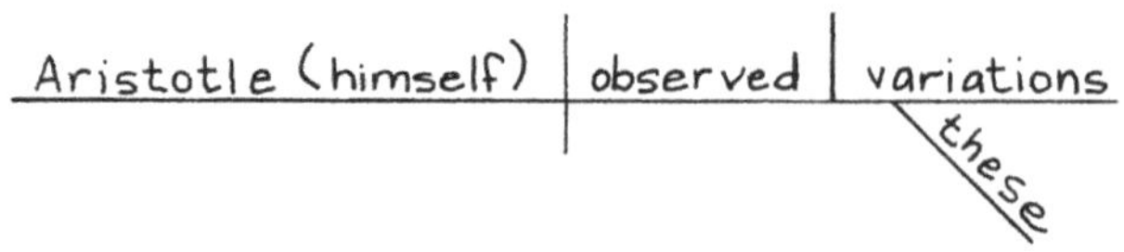

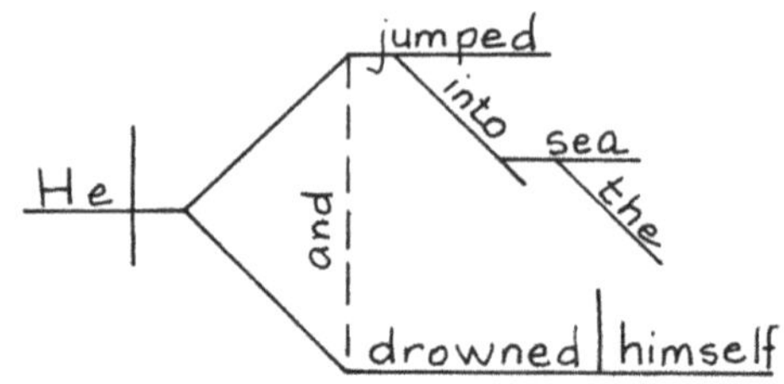

Do NOT use theirselves, hisself, or ourself.

Diana and myself cooked a casserole.
Diana and I cooked a casserole.
I myself cooked a casserole.
Take care of yourself.

Exercise 57A: Identifying Intensive and Reflexive Pronouns

Underline the intensive and reflexive pronouns in the following sentences. Above each pronoun, write *I* for intensive or *R* for reflexive. If the pronoun is reflexive, also mark it as *DO* (direct object), *IO* (indirect object), or *OP* (object of the preposition). The first is done for you.

R DO
Esther treated herself to a giant brownie sundae.

Control yourselves!

The mayor himself presented the award.

We ourselves cleaned the entire house.

I bought myself a new board game.

I myself bought the new board game.

> The following sentences are adapted from *Galileo: Astronomer and Physicist*, by Paul Hightower.

Some professors came to see Galileo make a fool of himself.

The book itself was a brilliant and important work.

He constructed himself a working model of the new telescope.

Galileo wrote to Kepler, "I count myself happy in the search for truth."

The stars themselves did not move.

Exercise 57B: Using Intensive and Reflexive Pronouns Correctly

Each of the following sentences contains errors in the usage of intensive and reflexive pronouns. Cross out the incorrect word and write the correction above it.

Felix cut hisself when he tripped over the root.

We asked ourself what we should do.

Stuart gave him and myself excellent advice.

The Guzman brothers theirselves made the rhubarb pie.

Chelsea and himself ate the entire dessert!

We ourselves picked up Emory and herself from the train station.

Exercise 57C: Diagramming Intensive and Reflexive Pronouns

On your own paper, diagram every word in the following sentences.

He occupied himself with a collection of old books.
The three inner satellites are themselves eclipsed by the shadow of Jupiter.
A new problem now presented itself to the scientist.
The power of the earth draws the moon to itself.

— LESSON 58 —

Demonstrative Pronouns
Demonstrative Adjectives

Questions	Punch Lines
What did the teacher say to make the student eat his quiz?	That opens up a whole new can of worms.
What did the customer in the butcher shop hear that scared him?	This will be a piece of cake!
What did the fisherman say when he dropped his bucket of bait?	These cost an arm and a leg.

Demonstrative pronouns demonstrate or point out something. They can take the place of a single word or a group of words.

this, that, these, those

"Your cousin wrote this," said Aunt Alexandra. "He was a beautiful character."

"Didn't know it was this dark. Didn't look like it'd be this dark earlier in the evening."

Demonstrative adjectives modify nouns and answer the question *which one*.

That was the only time I ever heard Atticus say it was a sin to do something . . .

"I destroyed his last shred of credibility at that trial, if he had any to begin with."

It was times like these when I thought my father, who hated guns and had never been to any wars, was the bravest man who ever lived.

I was beginning to notice a subtle change in my father these days, that came out when he talked with Aunt Alexandra.

"Dill, those were his own witnesses."

Mrs. Merriweather was one of those childless adults who find it necessary to assume a different tone of voice when speaking to children.

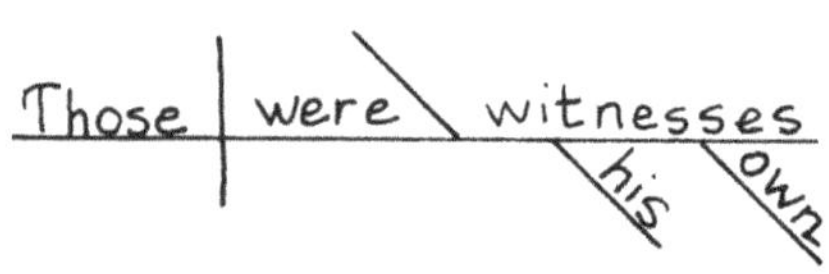

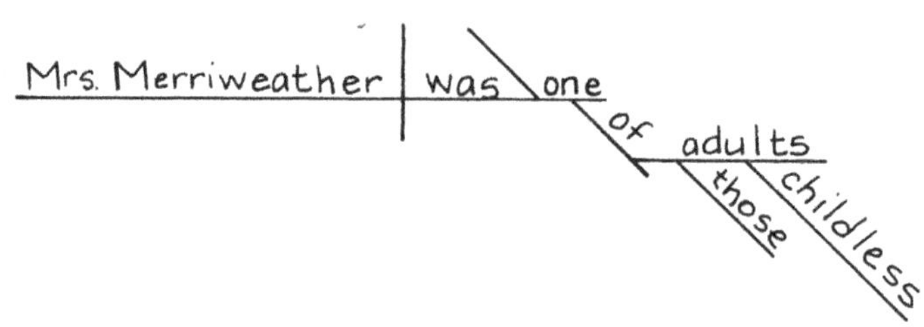

(The above sentences are from *To Kill a Mockingbird*, by Harper Lee.)

Did you see the coaster? That is one scary ride.

Raindrops on roses and whiskers on kittens, bright copper kettles and warm woolen mittens, brown paper packages tied up with strings—these are a few of my favorite things.

Exercise 58A: Demonstrative Pronouns and Demonstrative Adjectives

In the sentences below, label every occurrence of *this*, *that*, *these*, and *those* as either *DP* (for demonstrative pronoun) or *DA* (for demonstrative adjective). Draw an arrow from each demonstrative adjective to the noun it modifies. Label each demonstrative pronoun as *S* (subject), *DO* (direct object), *IO* (indirect object), or *OP* (object of the preposition).

These sentences are slightly adapted from *The Civil Rights Movement*, by Elizabeth Sirimarco (Marshall Cavendish, 2005).

The driver asked us to stand up and let him have those seats.

Medgar Evers was effective, and that made him a target of hate.

This leaking old wreck of a shanty must be nearly half a century old.

"This time, on this issue," said Johnson, "there must be no hesitation and no compromise with our purpose."

That finally brought a reaction from a police officer.

"I quit being white, and free, and an American citizen when I climbed aboard that Jim Crow coach," wrote Sprigle.

All of this is on account of us wanting to register.

These strong feelings gave rise to the Black Power movement.

She was apparently calm, but those of us who knew her were aware of the great perturbation beneath her serene exterior.

The leaders passed these on to the followers.

Yes, this is the United States, I thought to myself.

We will achieve these goals because most Americans are law-abiding citizens.

It was during those days that the sonnet "If We Must Die" exploded out of me.

And he said, "Well, if you don't stand up, I'm going to call the police and have you arrested." I said, "You may do that."

Segregation was legal as long as blacks were provided with facilities "equal" to those of whites.

Exercise 58B: Demonstrative Pronouns

In the blank beneath each section, write a possible description of the thing or person that the underlined demonstrative pronoun stands for. Make sure to choose the correct number. (And use your imagination.)

That is completely disgusting.

___

Those are my very favorites.

___

This really hurts.

___

These smell horrible.

___

Exercise 58C: Diagramming

On your own paper, diagram every word in the following three sentences.

There must be no hesitation and no compromise with our purpose.
During those days, the sonnet itself exploded out of me.
All of this is on account of us.

— LESSON 59 —

Demonstrative Pronouns
Demonstrative Adjectives
Interrogative Pronouns
Interrogative Adjectives

Interrogative pronouns take the place of nouns in questions.
who, whom, whose, which, what

"Who started this?" said Uncle Jack.
"Talk like what in front of whom?" he asked.
Whose is that blanket?

Which is correct?

Whose blanket is missing?
What madness is this?
Which shoes are yours?

Interrogative adjectives modify nouns.

REMEMBER #1: Don't confuse *whose* and *who's.*
Whose orange flip-flops are those? *Interrogative pronoun*
Who's cooking dinner? *Contraction of* who is

I don't know whose/who's coming to dinner.

Whose/who's plate is still empty?

REMEMBER #2: Use *whom* as an object and *who* as a subject or predicate nominative.

CORRECT
Who started this? *She started this. They started this. I started this. Jack started this.*
Talk like what in front of whom? *In front of him? In front of her? In front of them? In front of Jack?*

Whom/Who is calling?

To whom/who did you speak?

REMEMBER #3: Diagram interrogative adjectives like any other adjective, and diagram interrogative pronouns like any other pronoun.

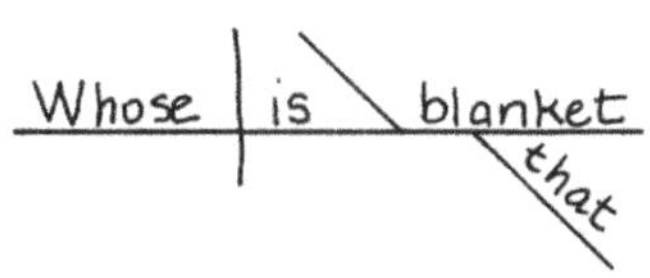

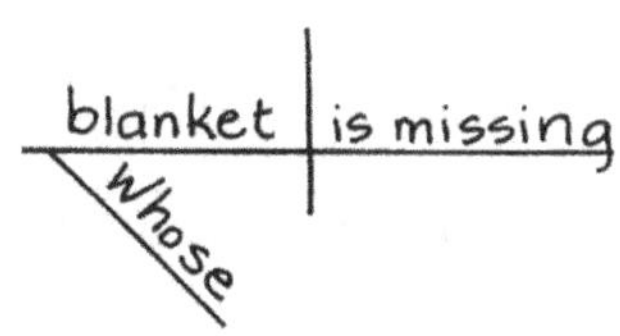

Exercise 59A: Identifying Demonstrative and Interrogative Pronouns

Underline all of the demonstrative and interrogative pronouns in the sentences. There may be more than one in each sentence.

This was lucky; he was about to begin to groan, as a "starter," as he called it, when it occurred to him . . . his aunt would pull it out, and that would hurt.

"Look here, Joe Harper, whose is that tick?"

This restored her and she said: "Tom, what a turn you did give me. Now you shut up . . . and climb out of this."

Who comes here into Sherwood Forest without my pass?

"Which of us does he mean?" gasped Huckleberry.

"What's the row there? Who's banging? What do you want?"

—Mark Twain, *The Adventures of Tom Sawyer*

This meant . . . some ships fought in the battle for a much longer time than others.

—Roy Adkins, *Nelson's Trafalgar: The Battle That Changed the World*

On entering the huts they found two large parrots (*guacamayos*) entirely different from those seen until then by the Spaniards.

—R.A. Van Middledyk, *The History of Puerto Rico: From the Spanish Discovery to the American Occupation*

Exercise 59B: Using Interrogative and Demonstrative Pronouns Correctly

Choose the correct word in parentheses. Cross out the incorrect word.

(Whose / Who's) going to the concert in the park tonight?

(Who / What) is the lead singer for the band tonight?

(Who / Whom) is that lovely girl in the yellow dress?

(This / These) is Marcela's favorite music.

(Whose / Who's) are these purple dancing shoes?

(These / Those) are my dance shoes right here, so (these / those) must be Keith's shoes over there.

(Who / Whom) did she ask to dance?

(Who's / Whose) dancing with Marcela now?

(Who / Whom) did you invite to dinner?

(This / These) has been a lovely evening.

(Who / Whom) is organizing the event next week?

With (who / whom) will you get a ride home?

Exercise 59C: Diagramming Interrogative and Demonstrative Pronouns

On your own paper, diagram the following sentences.

Whose are these lovely mittens?
He did what?
They talked lazily of this and that.
Who brought this?
For whom was the letter intended?
Which is the best road to San Diego?
You must try this cheesecake and those truffles!

— LESSON 60 —

Pronoun Review

Sentences Beginning with Adverbs

A pronoun takes the place of a noun.
An antecedent is the noun that is replaced by the pronoun.

Personal Pronouns
I, me, my, mine
you, your, yours
he, she, him, her, it
his, hers, its
we, us, our, ours
they, them, their, theirs

Indefinite pronouns are pronouns without antecedents.

Singular

anybody	anyone	anything
everybody	everyone	everything
nobody	no one	nothing
somebody	someone	something
another	other	one
either	neither	each

Plural

both	few	many	several

Singular or Plural

all	any	most	none	some

Reflexive pronouns refer back to the subject.
myself, himself, herself, itself, yourself, yourselves, ourselves, themselves

She tripped and hurt herself.
She herself tripped.

Intensive pronouns emphasize a noun or another pronoun.

Demonstrative pronouns demonstrate or point out something. They can take the place of a single word or a group of words.
this, that, these, those

Interrogative pronouns take the place of nouns in questions.
who, whom, whose, which, what

Interrogative adjectives modify nouns.

What are you doing? Don't you know what direction to go?

That is she.
What is that?
Which is yours?
Where are you?
There you are.
So it is.

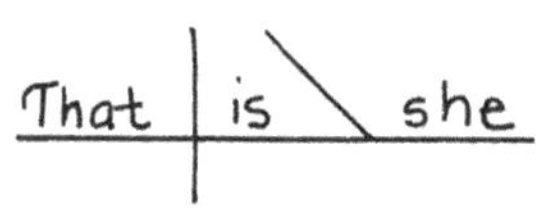

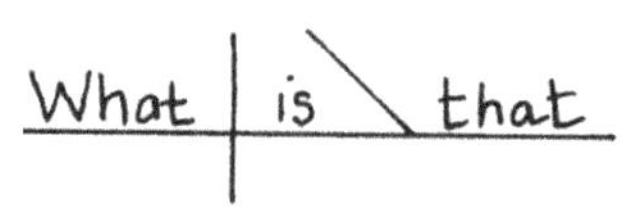

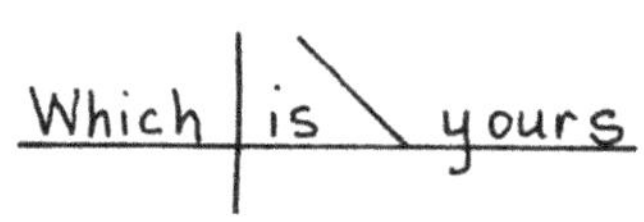

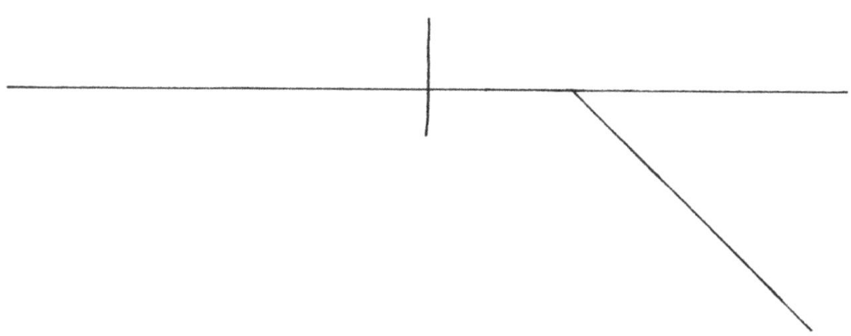

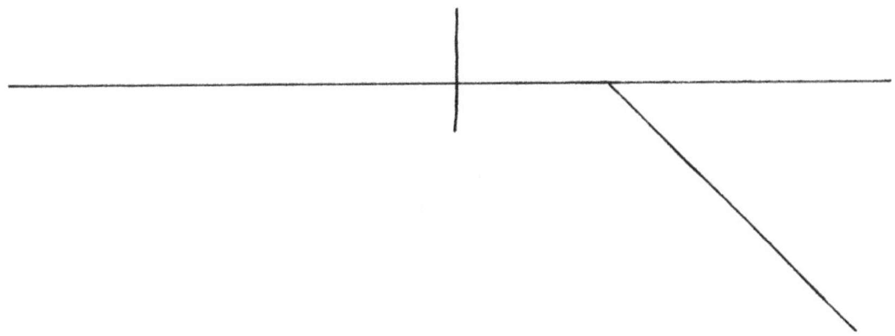

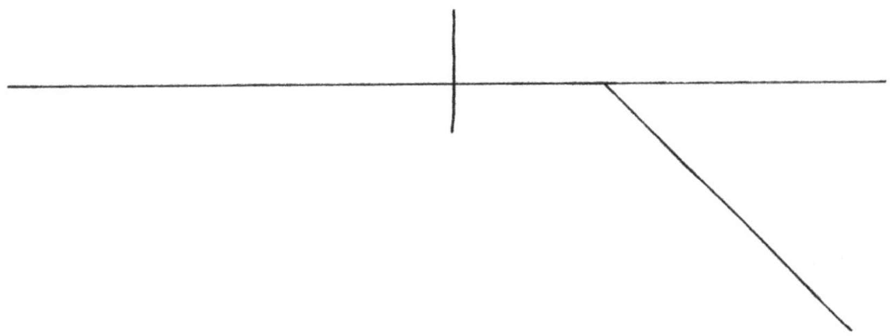

Exercise 60A: Singular/Plural Indefinite Pronouns

Cross out the incorrect verb in each sentence.

All of the family (were/was) at the ball.

None of us (are/is) able to help our nature.

Some of the gentlemen (were/was) gone to the stables.

(Are/Is) any of the pie left?

Most of the books (were/was) locked up behind glass doors.

Exercise 60B: Interrogatives and Demonstratives

In each of the following sentences, underline the interrogatives and demonstratives. If they are acting as adjectives, draw a line from each to the noun it modifies. If they are acting as other parts of the sentence, label them (*S* for subject, *DO* for direct object, *IO* for indirect object, or *OP* for object of the preposition).

These sentences are taken from a 19th-century fairy tale called "The Peasant and His Son."

Oho, my friend, what is the meaning of this?

These are most elaborate preparations.

I was in one of those three eggs.

Who took away your father's cow?

You will find that out in the evening, perhaps.

And you will expose yourself to this danger?

This is a very strange proceeding!

Whose daughter is she?

His feelings were wounded by these words.

Exercise 60C: Diagramming Practice

On your own paper, diagram every word of the following sentences, adapted from Charlotte Bronte's *Jane Eyre.*

The cold winter wind had brought with it somber clouds and a chilly rain.
Where are my powers for this dread undertaking?
Dreadful to me was the return from the walk with nipped fingers and toes.
There were the two wings of the building, the garden, and the hilly horizon.

— REVIEW 5 —

Weeks 13-15

Topics
Pronouns and Antecedents
Possessive Pronouns
Subject and Object Pronouns
Indefinite Pronouns (and Subject-Verb Agreement)
Troublesome Verbs
Active and Passive Voice
Conjugating Passive Voice
Intensive and Reflexive Pronouns
Demonstrative and Interrogative Pronouns

Review 5A: Types of Pronouns

Put each pronoun in the word bank in the correct category of pronoun.

this mine some whom
themselves me which
those itself they anyone
few our us
its whose I him
ourselves she that

Personal Subject _______________ _______________ _______________

Personal Object _______________ _______________ _______________

Personal Possessive _______________ _______________ _______________

Indefinite _______________ _______________ _______________

Demonstrative _______________ _______________ _______________

Interrogative _______________ _______________ _______________

Intensive/Reflexive _______________ _______________ _______________

Review 5B: Using Correct Pronouns

Cross out the incorrect pronoun in parentheses.

(Whose / Who's) coming with Nettie and (I / me) to the market?

(Whose / Who's) car will we use to get (there / their)?

The first person to arrive was (he / him).

Gena, Kayleigh, and (she / her) are arguing about (whose / who's) the best at grammar.

(There / their) was a fire near (there / their) house, and (their / they're) worried for (their / they're) neighbors.

(Who / Whom) is the boy that hurt (himself / hisself) this morning?

Christie and (I / myself) would prefer to build the fort by (ourself / ourselves).

(Who / Whom) are (they / them) speaking with?

The last two people on the train were Buford and (she / her).

Candace and (he / him) are sitting next to (who / whom)?

Review 5C: Pronouns and Antecedents

Circle the NINE personal pronouns (subject, object, and possessive) in the following excerpt from *Tuck Everlasting*, by Natalie Babbitt. Draw arrows to each pronoun's antecedent.

One pronoun does not have a written antecedent. Can you guess why?

One day at that time, not so very long ago, three things happened and at first there appeared to be no connection between them.

At dawn, Mae Tuck set out on her horse for the wood at the edge of the village of Treegap. She was going there, as she did once every ten years, to meet her two sons, Miles and Jesse.

At noontime, Winne Foster, whose family owned the Treegap wood, lost her patience at last and decided to think about running away.

And at sunset a stranger appeared at the Fosters' gate. He was looking for someone, but he didn't say who.

No connection, you would agree. But things can come together in strange ways.

Pronoun without a written antecedent: __________

Review 5D: Agreement with Indefinite Pronouns

Choose the correct word in parentheses to agree with the indefinite pronouns. Cross out the incorrect word.

(Is / Are) all of these books required reading for the summertime?

Some of these shirts (is / are) still wrinkled.

Has anyone left (her / their) necklace here on the chair?

No one here (knows / know) how to soft-boil an egg.

Both (was / were) late to the meeting because of the power outage.

(Has / Have) all of the milk been drunk?

(Is / Are) someone picking up some more milk on (his / their) way home?

Most of the audience (was / were) clapping enthusiastically.

Many (is / are) called, but few (is / are) chosen. —Matthew 22:14

Review 5E: Distinguishing Between Active and Passive Voice

Identify each sentence as *A* for active voice or *P* for passive voice. The verbs are underlined for you.

These sentences were adapted from *Walking the Appalachian Trail*, by Larry Luxenberg (Stackpole Books, 1994), an account of hiking the Appalachian Trail ("A.T."), a 2,147-mile-long trail along the eastern coast of the United States.

Each year as many as two thousand people start out to hike the whole A.T. ________

Hikers are well advised to camp at or near the first four shelters along the trail. ________

Ranger training includes frequent night patrols. ________

Hikers can also be assured that what these Rangers go through in their seventeen-day stint in these mountains is infinitely more difficult than the thru-hikers' transit. ________

Jeff is renowned on the A.T. for examining hikers' packs. ________

Tourists can still pan for gold in the area. ________

The name Dahlonega is said to be the Cherokee name for "precious yellow or gold." ________

Springer Mountain is revered among hikers for its prominent role on the A.T. ________

Because of the high winds, Robie jumped two miles upwind of Springer. _______

His canopy was caught in two trees. _______

Review 5F: Troublesome Verbs

Choose the correct verb form in parentheses. Cross out the incorrect form.

These sentences were taken from *The Dollmaker,* by Harriette Arnow (Simon & Schuster, 1983), the story of a mother raising her family in rural Appalachia.

She waited, calling to him with her eyes, but he never (raised / rose) his head.

She had (laid / lain) there in her bed and heard it and felt alone in the hearing.

Black coal smoke (raised / rose) from the post-office chimney.

Last night's thin snow still (lay / laid) in the cup-like hollows of the leaves.

Enoch, the nine-year-old, (sat / set) stiff and straight on the chair like a boy.

Gertie hesitated. She seldom (let / left) Cassie go visiting alone.

She pressed Cassie's face close against her coat, (lay / laid) her hands on her scarf-wrapped ears, all the while conscious of the watching, listening children.

Mrs. Hull took the lamp from the mail shelf and (sat / set) it on the meat counter.

He went into the main room to put on the clean overalls she had (lay / laid) out on the rocking chair.

Gertie watched a little saucer fall from a corner of the flimsy crumpling box and (lay / lie), a bright spot of red in the snow.

WEEK 16

Imposters

— LESSON 61 —

Progressive Tenses
Principal Parts
Past Participles as Adjectives
Present Participles as Adjectives

One Sunday afternoon in 1917, cousins named Frances Griffiths and Elsie Wright, aged nine and fifteen, saw some fairies and took clear snapshots of them with their box camera . . . In 1983, sixty-six years later, Elsie Wright and Frances Griffiths decided that it was time to confess what people had suspected all along. The fairies were paper dolls . . . propped up on the grass with pins.

—Kathryn Ann Lindskoog, *Fakes, Frauds, & Other Malarkey*

	First Principal Part Present	Second Principal Part Past	Third Principal Part Past Participle
	plan	planned	planned
	burst	burst	burst
	catch	caught	caught
	fall	fell	fallen

The planned vacation did not go well.

The burst balloon fit inside the honey jar.

The caught fish wriggled on the hook.

I climbed over the fallen tree.

The past participle of a verb can act as a descriptive adjective.

The freshly picked peaches were full of flavor.

As the clock struck twelve, he heard a rustling noise in the air.

By the side of the road, he saw a fox sitting.

Her mother stirred the pot of boiling water.

The snoring guards lay at the doorstep, fast asleep.

A simple verb simply tells whether an action takes place in the past, present, or future.

I thought, I think, I will think.

A perfect verb describes an action which has been completed before another action takes place.

I had thought, I have thought, I will have thought.

A progressive verb describes an ongoing or continuous action.

I was thinking, I am thinking, I will be thinking.

First Principal Part Present	Second Principal Part Past	Third Principal Part Past Participle	Present Participle
rustle	rustled	rustled	rustling
sit	sat	sat	sitting
snore	snored	snored	snoring
am	was	been	being

The present participle of a verb can act as a descriptive adjective.

The burst balloon fit inside the honey jar.

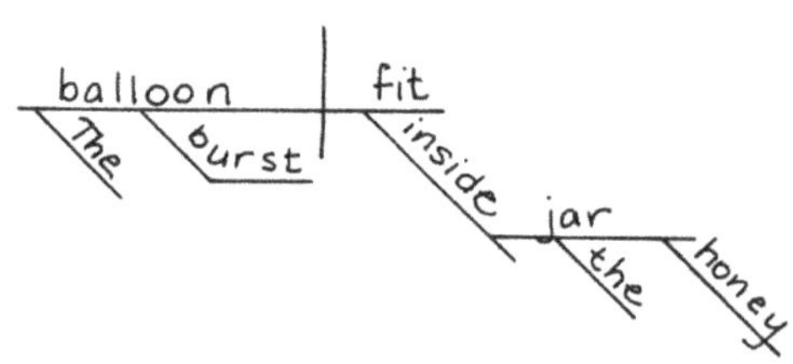

The snoring guards lay at the doorstep, fast asleep.

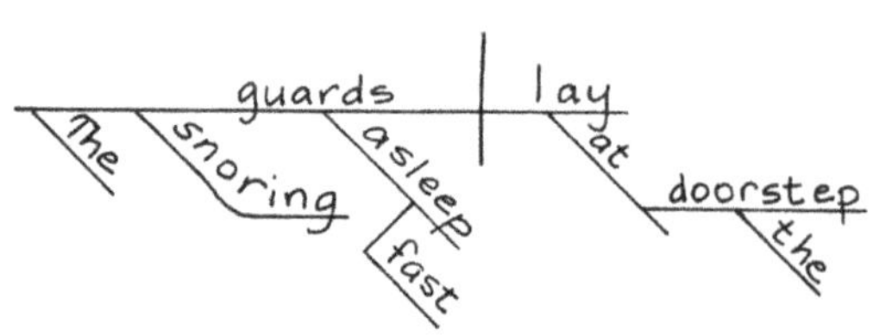

Sparkling stars shone.

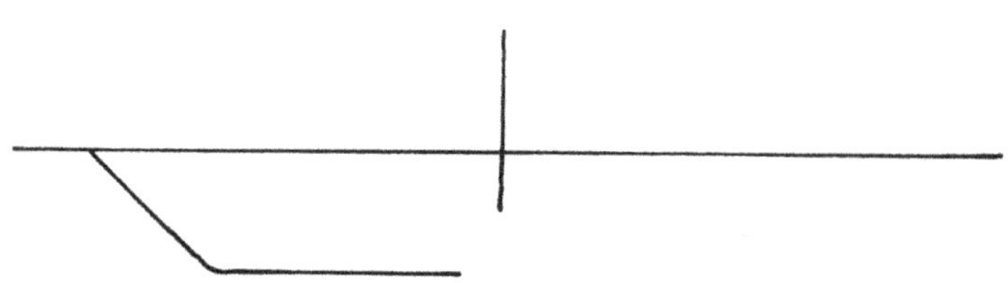

The forgotten cheese molded.

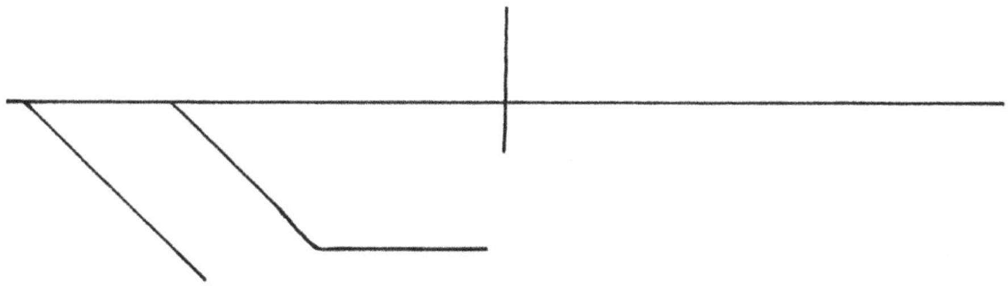

OPTIONAL:
The rustling leaves told us that the wind was rising.
The leaves, being rustled, signified the coming of fall.
Having rustled the leaves, the wind died down.
The leaves having been rustled, the wind died down.
The rustled leaves finally stilled.

Present (Active) Participle	Present (Passive) Participle	Perfect Present (Active) Participle	Perfect Present (Passive) Participle	Past Participle
add *-ing*	**being + past participle**	**having + past participle**	**having + been + past participle**	**add *-ed* (second principal part)**
rustling	being rustled	having rustled	having been rustled	rustled
eating				eaten
reading				read

Exercise 61A: Identifying Past Participles Used as Adjectives

Underline the past participles used as adjectives in the following sentences, taken from Jim Kjelgaard's classic novel *Big Red.* Draw a line from each past participle to the word modified.

Not long, just long enough to get a ripped foot or a slashed side before Danny could send home the shot that would kill the bear.

But all he saw was the plainly imprinted tale of how the red dog had come upon the bear.

He found the bear's trail in the scuffed leaves there.

But his tongue was a dry, twisted thing that clung to the roof of his mouth.

By a broken bramble, a bit of loosened shale, or an occasional paw print between the boulders, he worked out the direction that Old Majesty had taken.

Exercise 61B: Identifying Present Participles Used as Adjectives

Underline the present participles used as adjectives in the following sentences. Draw a line to each word modified.

The first four sentences are from *Big Red*; the last three are from Alma Payne Ralston's *Discoverer of the Unseen World.*

He had turned for the first time to face the pursuing dog.

Old Majesty had left his retreat by the beech tree, and with whipping front paws had tried to pin the red dog to the earth.

Old Majesty had climbed straight up the long, sloping nose of a hump-backed ridge and had run along its top.

He would come . . . with snapping jaws and slashing paws.

In reality the instrument was "a simple magnifying glass."

In the coming months, Galileo worked to create telescopes that were more and more powerful.

The telescope that Galileo created is known today as a refracting telescope.

Exercise 61C: Diagramming Participles Used as Adjectives

On your own paper, diagram the following sentences.

Whistling teakettles sound homey.

Boiling water steeps aromatic tea.

Chipped teacups leak.

Steaming mugs warm frozen fingers.

— LESSON 62 —

Parts of Speech and Parts of Sentences
Present Participles as Nouns (Gerunds)

The cuckoo is one of the great con artists of the animal world. It can trick other birds into raising its children by laying their eggs in the stranger's nest. When the cuckoo chicks hatch, the youngsters continue their parents' strategy by killing any other birds in the nest before they reveal their identity. Scientists have found the imposter cuckoo even fools the foster parent into thinking its chicks are still alive by flapping yellow patches on its wings. This also creates the illusion there more mouths to feed and tricks the foster parents into delivering more food.

—Augustus Brown, *Why Pandas Do Handstands: And Other Curious Truths About Animals*

The running rabbit was darting towards the briar patch.

Part of speech is a term that explains what a word does.

A noun names a person, place, thing, or idea.

Part of sentence is a term that explains how a word functions in a sentence.

subject   direct object   indirect object   object of a preposition

A gerund is a present participle acting as a noun.

Careful sailing was the duty of the captain's mate.

This day was lost from pure whim, for the pleasure of going ashore.

Providence gives the deserving their due.

With the other hand, he repressed the beatings of his heart.

Running is my favorite exercise.

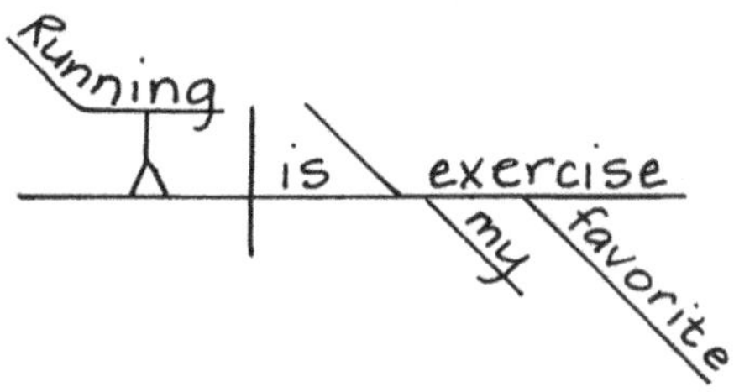

He feared falling.

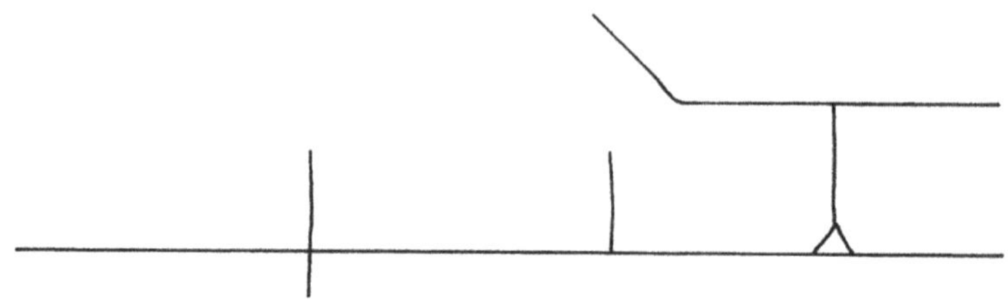

Exercise 62A: Identifying Gerunds

In the following sentences, adapted from H. A. Guerber's *Myths of the Norsemen from the Eddas and Sagas*, underline each subject once and each predicate twice. Write *DO* above any direct objects, *IO* above any indirect objects, and *OP* above any objects of prepositions. Circle each gerund.

The waving of Hrim's mane sent dew and frost to the earth.

The Northmen feared the winter chilling of the earth.

Dwarves spent their time in mining.

Heimdall's trumpet announced the coming of the frost-giants.

Odin offered the starving his own oxen.

Exercise 62B: Diagramming Gerunds

On your own paper, diagram every word in the following sentences.

Galloping exhausted the little mare.

The Giant was tired of working.

The great eagle's wings were flapping.

Loki heard flapping.

The cunning Ice Dwellers were planning an invasion.

— LESSON 63 —

Gerunds
Present and Past Participles as Adjectives
Infinitives
Infinitives as Nouns

The comings and goings of her acquaintances provided Mrs. Jennings great entertainment.

This circumstance was a growing attachment between her eldest girl and the brother of Mrs. John Dashwood.

The presence of the two Miss Steeles, lately arrived, gave Elinor pain.

An infinitive is formed by combining *to* and the first-person singular present form of a verb.

	Present Tense		**Infinitive**
	Singular	**Plural**	
First person	I give	we give	
Second person	you give	you give	______________
Third person	he, she, it gives	they give	
First person	I think	we think	
Second person	you think	you think	______________
Third person	he, she, it thinks	they think	
First person	I have	we have	
Second person	you have	you have	______________
Third person	he, she, it has	they have	

To err is human.
To forgive is divine.
—Alexander Pope

To wish was to hope.

To hope was to expect.
—Jane Austen

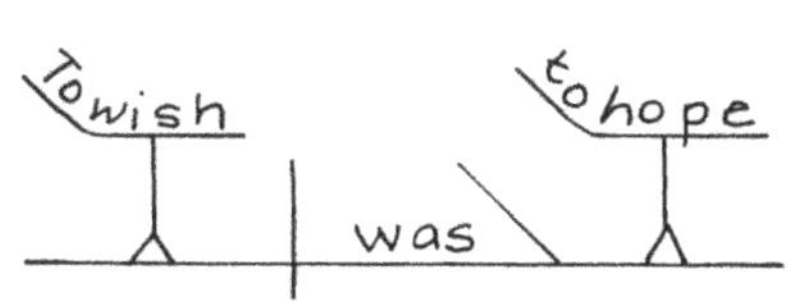

Exercise 63A: Identifying Gerunds and Infinitives

Underline the gerunds and infinitives in the following quotes. Identify the imposters as *G* for gerund or *I* for infinitive. Then, identify each gerund or infinitive as a subject (*S*), predicate nominative (*PN*), direct object (*DO*), or object of a preposition (*OP*).

To give your best is to receive the best. —Raymond Holliwell

Loving is never a waste of time. —Astrid Alauda

The old soldier did not fear to die; he hoped to conquer. —Alexandre Dumas

To imagine is everything; to know is nothing at all. —Anatole France

It is not how much we do, but how much love we put in the doing. It is not how much we give, but how much love we put in the giving. —Mother Teresa

To judge another is to lose an opportunity. —Unknown

I have never developed indigestion from eating my words. —Winston Churchill

To be or not to be… is the question. —Shakespeare, *Hamlet*

I love eating, I love drinking, I love painting. —Wang Meng

How many legs does a dog have if you call a tail a leg? Four. Calling a tail a leg doesn't make it a leg. —Abraham Lincoln

On all sides were heard rejoicing and congratulation. —Julius Caesar

Tracking over the boulders was painfully slow work. —Jim Kjelgaard, *Big Red*

There was one chance in fifty of killing that huge bear with a single shot. —Jim Kjelgaard, *Big Red*

Exercise 63B: Diagramming Gerunds and Infinitives

On your own paper, diagram the following sentences.

To give is to receive.
Loving is never a waste of time.
The old soldier did not fear to die.
I love eating.
On all sides were heard rejoicing and congratulations.
Tracking was painfully slow work.

— LESSON 64 —

Gerunds
Present and Past Participles
Infinitives
Gerund, Participle, and Infinitive Phrases

I love eating.

I love eating ____

____

A phrase is a group of words serving a single grammatical function.
I love eating pancakes with maple syrup, yellow cake with chocolate frosting, and grilled ribeye steaks.

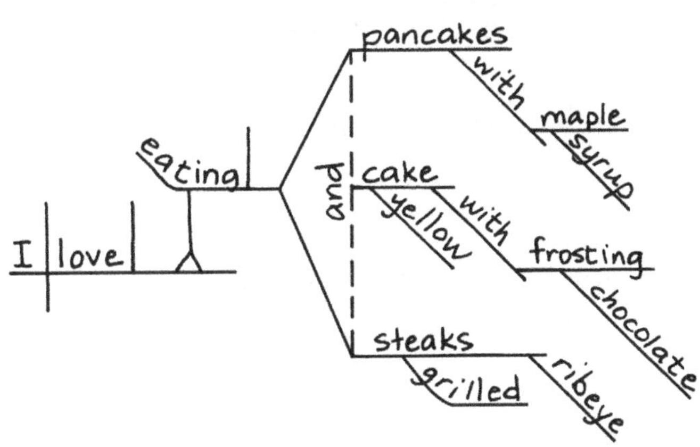

To give without expecting a reward is to receive an even greater gift.

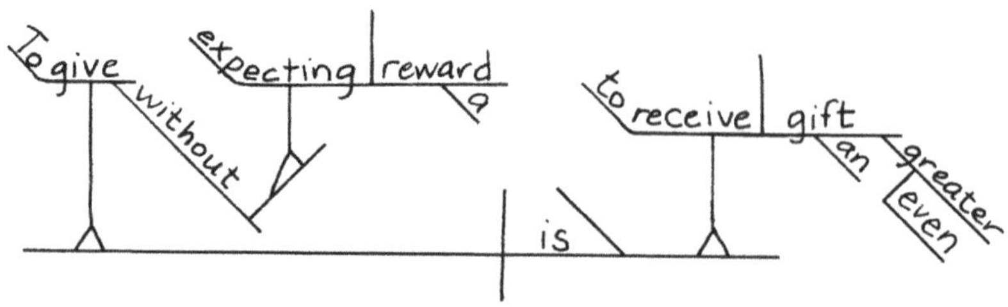

He saw the priceless antique vase shattered across the floor and scattered on the rug.

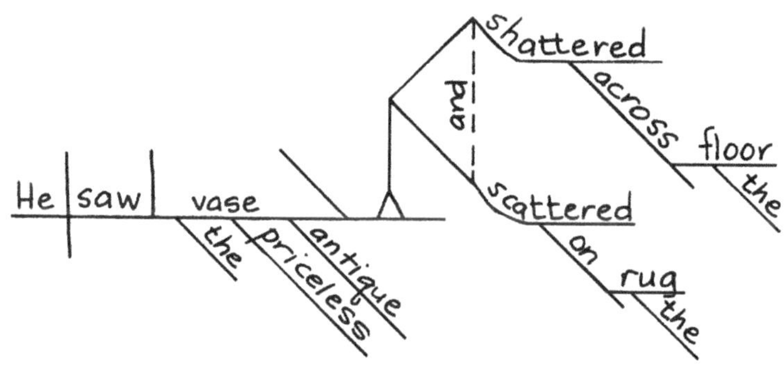

Exercise 64A: Identifying Phrases That Serve as Parts of the Sentence

In the following sentences, begin by underlining each prepositional phrase.

Then, circle each group of words that contains a gerund, infinitive, present participle, or past participle. Each one serves as a part of the sentence. (Those circled phrases might include some of your prepositional phrases!) Label each circled phrase. Your options are: *ADJ* (adjective), *ADV* (adverb), *S* (subject), *IO* (indirect object), *DO* (direct object), *OC* (object complement), *OP* (object of the preposition), *PN* (predicate nominative), or *PA* (predicate adjective).

These sentences are taken from *The Story of the Champions of the Round Table*, by Howard Pyle.

With terror growing greater in his heart, he saw the flame of fire consuming the town and the castle.

Meanwhile, Queen Helen and Folio sat together waiting for him to return.

Presently, they heard the sound of his horse's hooves coming down that rocky path.

I was to wait for arms and armor to aid me.

Thus Queen Helen found him, and finding him made no outcry of any kind.

Were they not broken of heart?

The fallen knight embraced Sir Lancelot about the knees.

Sir Percival and Sir Lamorak had obtained permission to ride forth together in companionship.

Exercise 64B: Diagramming

On your own paper, diagram all of the sentences from Exercise 64A.

WEEK 17

Comparatives and Superlatives, Subordinating Conjunctions

— LESSON 65 —

Adjectives

Comparative and Superlative Adjectives

An adjective modifies a noun or pronoun.
Adjectives tell what kind, which one, how many, and whose.

The positive degree of an adjective describes only one thing.
The comparative degree of an adjective compares two things.
The superlative degree of an adjective compares three or more things.

Most regular adjectives form the comparative by adding *-r* or *-er*.
Most regular adjectives form the superlative by adding *-st* or *-est*.

Positive	Comparative	Superlative
large	larger	largest
big	bigger	biggest
silly	sillier	silliest

Spelling Rules

If the adjective ends in *-e* already, add only *-r* or *-st*.

noble	nobler	noblest
pure	purer	purest
cute	_________	_________

If the adjective ends in a short vowel sound and a consonant, double the consonant and add *-er* or *-est*.

red	redder	reddest
thin	thinner	thinnest
flat	_________	_________

If the adjective ends in *-y*, change the *y* to *i* and add *-er* or *-est*.

hazy	hazier	haziest
lovely	lovelier	loveliest
lucky	________	________

Many adjectives form their comparative and superlative forms by adding the word *more* or *most* before the adjective instead of using *-er* or *-est*.

unusual	more unusual	most unusual
fascinating	more fascinating	most fascinating
fun	more fun	most fun

She is more lovely than the dawn.
She is lovelier than the dawn.

She is the most lovely of all women.
She is the loveliest of all women.

The taller boy glanced around uneasily.

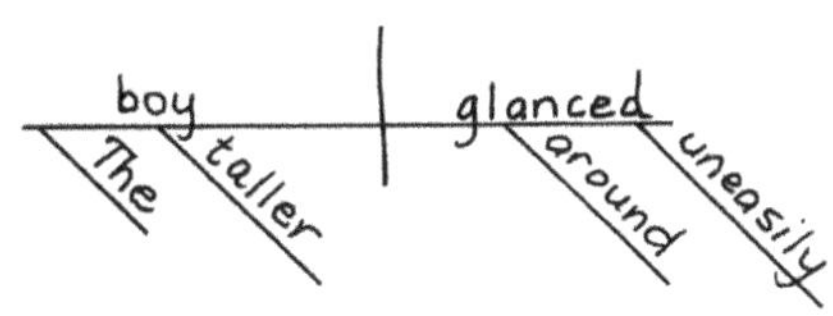

His more confident friend rang the doorbell.

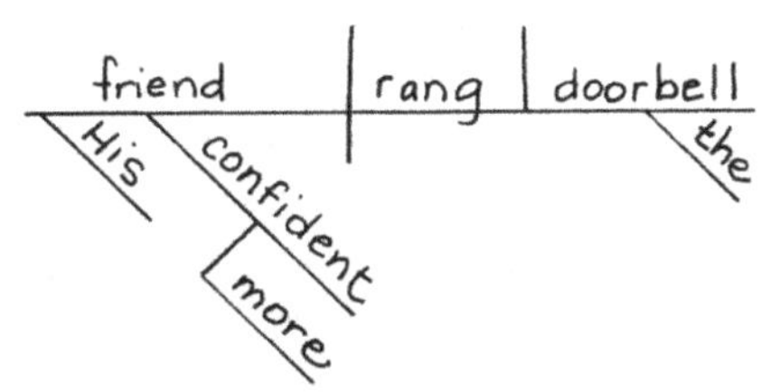

In comparative and superlative adjective forms, the words *more* and *most* are used as adverbs.

Exercise 65A: Identifying Positive, Comparative, and Superlative Adjectives

Identify the underlined adjective forms as *P* for positive, *C* for comparative, or *S* for superlative.

The first two sentences are from Matthew Pilkington's *A General Dictionary of Painters*; the third sentence is from Alison Weir's *The Six Wives of Henry VIII;* the last two sentences are from Albert Frederick Pollard's *Henry VIII.*

Jan Brueghel the Younger would also become a painter.

One of their finest joint performances was the picture of Adam and Eve in Paradise.

He was nearly forty-five now, growing <u>bald</u>, and running to fat . . . <u>more egotistical</u>, <u>more sanctimonious,</u> and <u>more sure</u> of his own divinity, while still seeing himself as a paragon of courtly and <u>athletic</u> knighthood.

His suspicion was aroused on the <u>slightest</u> pretext.

He was beginning to look grey and <u>old</u>, and was growing daily <u>more corpulent</u> and unwieldy.

Exercise 65B: Forming Comparative and Superlative Adjectives

Fill in the blank with the correct form of the adjective in parentheses. All of these comparisons will end in *-er* or *-est.*

This summer has been much ______________________ than last summer. (*hot*)

Grandpa says that this winter will be the __________ winter that he has ever seen. (*snowy*)

Redwood trees are the __________ trees in the world. (*tall*)

The Redwood National Forest was even __________ than I had imagined! (*grand*)

The Great Barrier Reef is the __________ coral reef system in the world. (*large*)

The stout infantfish lives in the Great Barrier Reef and is the ______________________ fish in the sea. (*tiny*)

Golden retriever dogs are much ____________ and ______________________ than Chihuahuas. (*big, gentle*)

Golden retrievers may be the ______________________ dogs in the world. (*friendly*)

Exercise 65C: Diagramming Comparative and Superlative Adjectives

On your own paper, diagram the following sentences. The first three sentences are from J. J. Scarisbrick's *Henry VIII.*

Cromwell had been the most faithful servant.
He seemed most assured and trustful.
The smallest gesture could have opened the doors to forgiveness and reconciliation.
On this lovely autumn day, studying seemed most inappropriate.
A more shocking discovery was around the corner.

— LESSON 66 —

Adverbs
Comparative and Superlative Adverbs
Coordinating Conjunctions
Subordinating Conjunctions

An adverb describes a verb, an adjective, or another adverb.
Adverbs tell how, when, where, how often, and to what extent.

The positive degree of an adverb describes only one verb, adjective, or adverb.
The comparative degree of an adverb compares two verbs, adjectives, or adverbs.
The superlative degree of an adverb compares three or more verbs, adjectives, or adverbs.

Most adverbs that end in *-ly* form their comparative and superlative forms by adding the word *more* or *most* before the adverb instead of using *-er* or *-est*.

thoughtfully	more thoughtfully	most thoughtfully
sadly	more sadly	most sadly
angrily	more angrily	most angrily

A few adverbs ending in *-y* change the *-y* to *i* and add *-er* or *-est*.

early	earlier	earliest

He worked more efficiently.

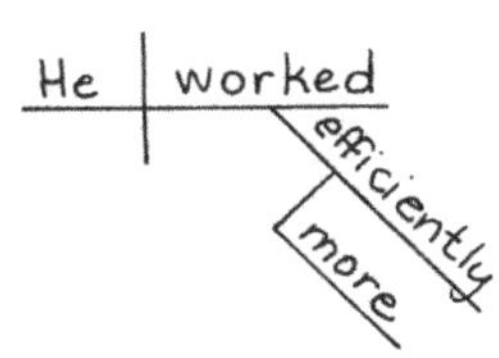

He worked more efficiently than his brother.

A conjunction joins two words or groups of words together.
and, or, nor, for, so, but, yet

A coordinating conjunction joins equal words or groups of words together.

The sun and the moon give us light.
The moon shines fitfully yet brightly.

A subordinating conjunction joins unequal words or groups of words together.

to subordinate: to place in a lower order or rank; to make secondary
sub: from *Latin preposition sub,* beneath, under
ordinate: from *Latin verb ordo,* to rank

He worked more efficiently than his brother.

He worked more efficiently than his brother [worked].

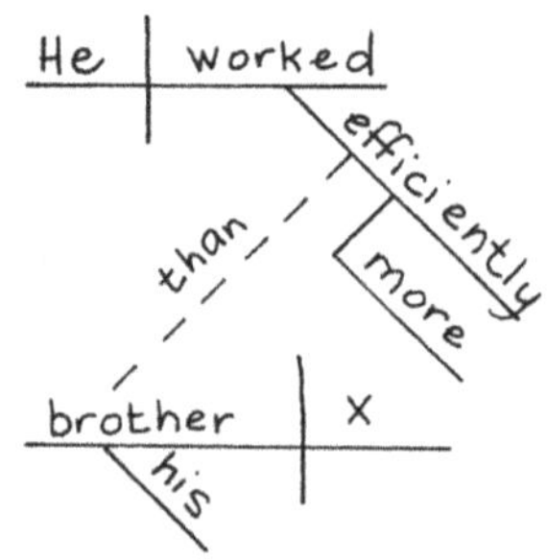

He is older than his brother.
He is older than his brother [is].

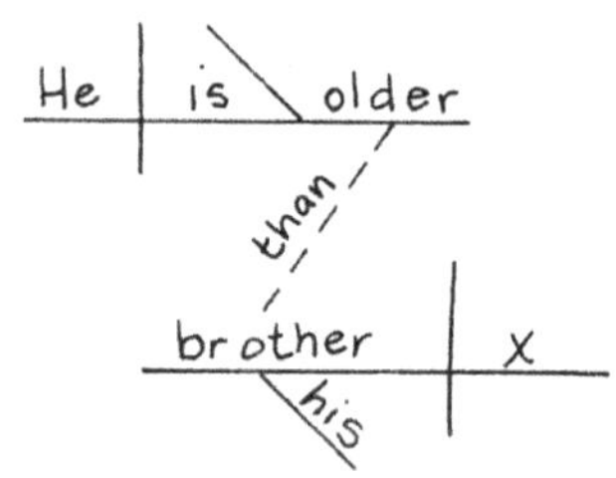

Exercise 66A: Diagramming Comparatives

Diagram the first two sentences on the frames provided. Diagram the remaining sentences on your own paper.

The hare runs faster than the dog.

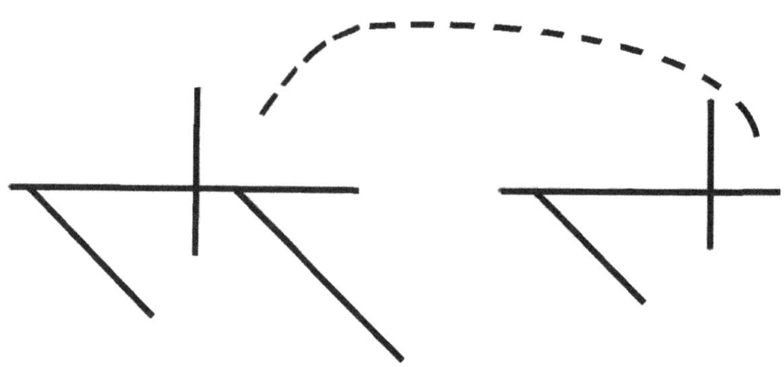

My right hand is working better than my left hand.

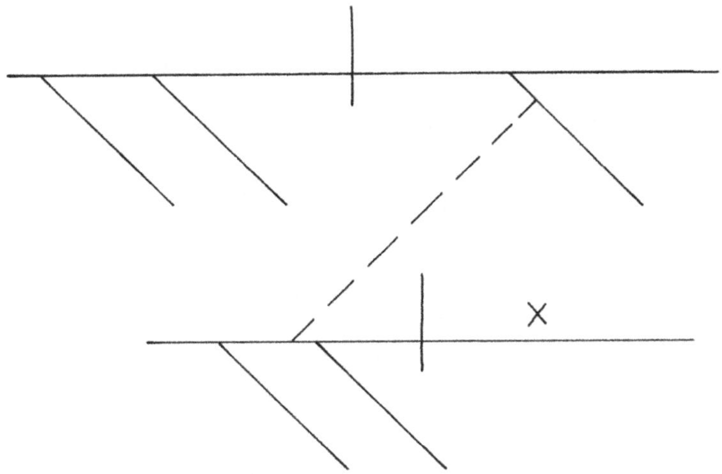

Today's movie is even sillier than yesterday's movie.
My brain thinks more slowly than yours does.
This cupcake is yummier than that one.

Exercise 66B: Identifying Positive, Comparative, and Superlative Adverbs

Identify the underlined adverb forms as *P* for positive, *C* for comparative, or *S* for superlative.

The first sentence is from Alan Schom's *Napoleon Bonaparte;* the last two sentences are from Alison Weir's *The Six Wives of Henry VIII.*

He <u>rarely</u> moved, apart from his long bony hands.

If he walked any <u>more slowly</u>, he would have been standing still.

The child scooted <u>closer</u> and clutched her hand <u>more tightly</u>.

His was the <u>most grotesquely</u> twisted nose she had ever seen.

She played the <u>most awkwardly</u> and yet the <u>most skillfully</u> of any of the members of the tennis team.

Worse still, it oozed pus <u>continually</u>, and had to be dressed daily, not a pleasant task for the person assigned to do it as the wound stank <u>dreadfully</u>.

He would become <u>increasingly</u> subject to savage and unreasonable rages.

Exercise 66C: Forming Comparative and Superlative Adverbs

Fill in the blank with the correct form of the adverb in parentheses.

Of all of the mountains in Africa, Mt. Kilimanjaro stands the ____________. (*tall*)

The cheetah runs the ____________ of all the earth's land animals. (*fast*)

Courtney moved into the house across the street and now lives much ____________ to me than before. (*close*)

Freddy came to the party ____________ than I did and left ____________. (*late, early*)

Tess can ride the roller coaster first; she has been waiting the ____________ of everyone. (*long*)

The birthday package arrived ____________ than I had expected. (*soon*)

— LESSON 67 —

Irregular Comparative and Superlative Adjectives and Adverbs

Exercise 67A: Best and Worst Jobs

Put the following jobs in the columns according to your opinion. (There are no *correct* answers—it all depends on you.)

ice cream taster	garbage collector	fashion designer
children's book illustrator	grass cutter	professional sky diver

good: ____________________________ **bad:** ____________________________

better: ____________________________ **worse:** ____________________________

best: ____________________________ **worst:** ____________________________

Irregular Comparative and Superlative Adjectives

Adjective	**Comparative Form**	**Superlative Form**
good	better	best
bad	worse	worst
little	less	least
much	more	most
many	more	most

I have more legs than a snake.
The octopus has the most legs of the three.

Irregular Comparative and Superlative Adverbs

Adverb	**Comparative Form**	**Superlative Form**
well	better	best
badly	worse	worst
little	less	least
much	more	most
far	farther	farthest

Do not use *more* with an adjective or adverb that is already in the comparative form. Do not use *most* with an adjective or adverb that is already in the superlative form.

Use an adjective form when an adjective is needed and an adverb form when an adverb is needed.

INCORRECT	CORRECT	S LV ADV PA
The team played good.	The team played well.	I am (not) well.
The tomato smells badly.	The tomato smells bad.	

Common Linking Verbs
am, is, are, was, were, be, being, been
taste, feel, smell, sound, look, prove, grow, remain, appear, stay, become, seem

The music sounds beautiful/beautifully.

Exercise 67B: Using Comparatives and Superlatives Correctly

Choose the correct form in parentheses. Cross out the incorrect form.

Maury eats (more wisely / wiser) than Frida.

Frida works (more hard / harder) than Maury does, so she fixes her meals (more quickly / quicker).

Buttons, their pet rabbit, probably eats the (most healthily / healthiest) of all.

When Frida eats lots of vegetables, she feels much (more cheerily / cheerier) and (more calmly / calmer).

Frida sings "Happy Birthday" (more cheerily / cheerier) than Maury does.

Frida goes jogging (more often / oftener) than Maury does.

Sometimes Maury goes jogging with Frida, but he jogs (more slowly / slower) than she does.

Frida doesn't mind. She is (more happy / happier) when she has company on her jogs.

Exercise 67C: Using Correct Comparative Forms of Modifiers

Choose the correct form in parentheses. Cross out the incorrect form. The last two sentences are from Albert Frederick Pollard's *Henry VIII.*

In a basketball game, the team that plays (best / better) wins.

Coach says that even if we play the (best / better) team in the league, we still have a chance.

If we play (harder / more harder) than they do and want to win (more / the most), then maybe we will beat them.

Sometimes even a very good team will play (worse / worst) than our team.

Today we will play against the Eagles. Compared to us, the Eagles have the (best / better) record.

They have (the most / more) wins in the entire league.

However, our record is not too much (more worse / worse) than theirs.

Let's play our (best / most best) game ever!

Vocal and instrumental pieces of his own composition, preserved among the manuscripts at the British Museum, rank among the (better / best) productions of the time.

His temper was getting (worse / worst).

Exercise 67D: Using Correct Adverbs and Adjectives

Choose the correct word in parentheses. Cross out the incorrect word.

The last sentence is from Isaac Newton Arnold's *The History of Abraham Lincoln, and the Overthrow of Slavery.*

I don't feel (good / well) today. I have a headache and a sore throat.

Ursula played so (good / well)! We would not have won the tournament without her.

The opponents did not play (bad / badly), but Ursula is extremely (good / well) at tennis.

Harriet smells (bad / badly). She should have showered!

Harriet smells (bad / badly). She can't tell if milk is sour by sniffing it.

Rattlesnakes taste (good / well). They have an organ called a Jacobson's organ that increases their sense of taste and smell.

Rattlesnakes taste (good / well). If you fry them, they taste just like chicken.

He analyzed (good / well); he saw and presented what lawyers call the very *gist* of every question.

— LESSON 68 —

Coordinating and Subordinating Conjunctions
Correlative Conjunctions

When my mother makes *tacos al pastor*, she uses ancho chilies and pasilla chilies and cumin seed and garlic and pork roast and fresh cilantro.

A coordinating conjunction joins equal words or groups of words together.
and, but, for, nor, or, so, yet

For dessert, I will have *tres leches* cake with fresh raspberries or caramel sandwich cookies with ice cream.
In my opinion, pork without pineapple is much better than pork with pineapple.

A subordinating conjunction joins unequal words or groups of words together.

We are cooking either pork roasts or goat chops tonight.
The patient was neither worse nor better.

Correlative conjunctions work in pairs to join words or groups of words.
Coordinating correlative conjunctions join equal words or groups of words.
both . . . and
not only . . . but/but also
either . . . or
neither . . . nor
although/though . . . yet/still
if . . . then

In the beginning, both the Sun and the Moon were dark.

Not only the town itself, but also the ranches in the neighborhood are built on hilltops.

Although he did not remember the way, still he pressed on.

If we run faster, then we will escape.

Though weary, still he presses on.

If unseated, then he will be unable to continue jousting.

Subordinating correlative conjunctions join unequal words or groups of words.
although/though . . . yet/still
if . . . then

In the beginning, the Sun and the Moon were dark.
In the beginning, both the Sun and the Moon were dark.

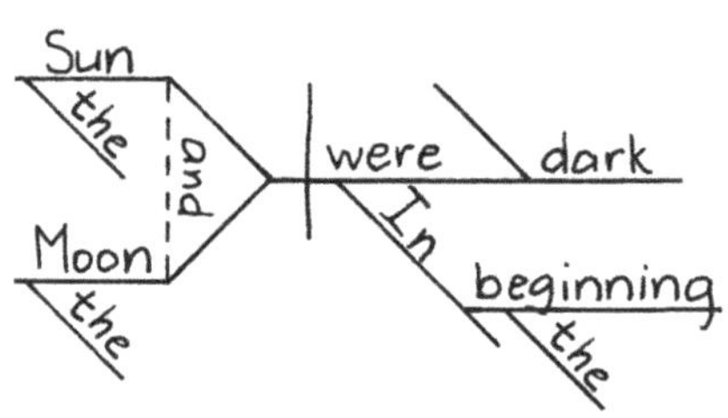

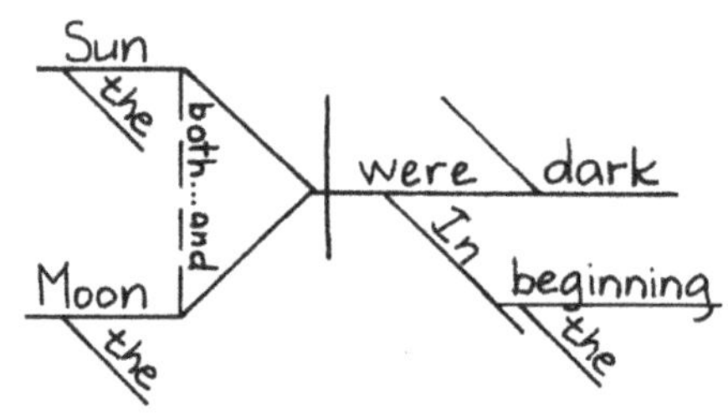

Although he did not remember, still he pressed on.

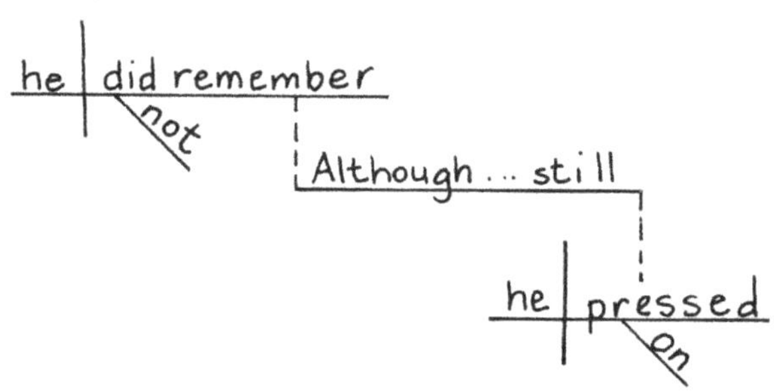

Both the grey foxes and the lion are watching for rabbits.

Not only the grey foxes but also the lion is watching for rabbits.
Either the mountain lion or the bears are growling.
Neither the butterflies nor the hummingbird was in the garden.

When compound subjects are connected by *not only . . . but/but also*, *either . . . or*, or *neither . . . nor*, the verb agrees with the subject that is closest to the verb.

Exercise 68A: Coordinating and Subordinating Correlative Conjunctions

In each of the following sentences, circle the correlative conjunctions. Underline the words or groups of words that the conjunctions connect. In the blank, write *C* for coordinating or *S* for subordinating.

These sentences are adapted from Stanley A. Wolpert's *India.*

Devout Hindus not only wash themselves in the bubbling green of Varanasi water but also drink it. ________

If we succumb, then we are done for. _______

The immediate aftermath of that horrible war brought neither prosperity nor contentment. _______

Though anathema to Muslims, yet pork is eaten by some Hindus (but not by others). _______

Not only time, but both river floods and monsoon rains have obscured ancient India's early millennia. _______

Most of the world had either begun to destroy nuclear-armed missiles or agreed to sign the test ban treaties. _______

Although kept as traditional as possible, still British regiments were forced to adapt to some Bengali customs. _______

All animals, both quadrupeds and birds, are larger than in other countries. _______

Diwali generally falls either in our solar October or November. _______

If the rains came late, then crows and other scavengers reaped the only harvest. _______

Ingenious ancient Indian philosophers also reasoned that it was possible to feel both cold and hot upon entering the same room. _______

Exercise 68B: Subject-Verb Agreement

Cross out the incorrect verb in each set of parentheses.

Not only the cat but also all of the dogs (is/are) waiting by the rat's den.

Either the prince or his servants (is/are) bringing the eighty pounds of mustard seed.

Both the tigers and the jackal (was/were) lurking in the bushes.

Not only the little fishes but also the crab (was/were) hiding beneath the lotus leaves.

Either the Raja's seven daughters or the Raja's wife (is/are) preparing rice with care.

Neither the Fakir nor the dogs (was/were) ever found.

Both the snake-king and the tiger-king (was/were) sympathetic to the Brahman.

Neither the oats nor the ear of corn (was/were) satisfying to the hungry horse.

Exercise 68C: Diagramming

On your own paper, diagram every word of the following sentences.

The King of Persia planned to destroy both him and his tribe.

Neither wealth nor power does your slave desire!

Either the new bride or the hospitable master of the house will welcome not only the expected guests but also the uninvited intruders.

Both his wife and his brothers were delighted to see the coming of the dawn.

WEEK 18

Clauses

— LESSON 69 —

Phrases
Sentences
Introduction to Clauses

A phrase is a group of words serving a single grammatical function.

A verb phrase is the main verb plus any helping verbs.

Four musketeers were waiting their turn.

A prepositional phrase begins with a preposition and ends with a noun or pronoun.

The center of the most animated group was a musketeer of great height.

A prepositional phrase that describes a noun or pronoun is called an adjective phrase.

He wore a long cloak of crimson velvet.

A prepositional phrase that describes a verb, adjective, or adverb is called an adverb phrase.

The young man advanced into the tumult and disorder.

(Sentences adapted from *The Three Musketeers*, by Alexandre Dumas.)

A clause is a group of words that contains a subject and a predicate.

Behind the dusty wardrobe.
Lucy opened the door.
Leaping and bounding.
They did not believe her.
He tasted the delicious candy.
Because he wanted more.

An independent clause can stand by itself as a sentence.

A sentence is a group of words that usually contains a subject and a predicate. A sentence begins with a capital letter and ends with a punctuation mark. A sentence contains a complete thought.

Can we measure intelligence without understanding it? Possibly so. *Physicists measured gravity and magnetism long before they understood them theoretically. Maybe psychologists can do the same with intelligence.*

Or maybe not.

—James W. Kalat, *Introduction to Psychology*

A dependent clause is a fragment that cannot stand by itself as a sentence.

Although Jamie didn't mean to eat the entire cake. __________

Whether they won or lost. __________

He picked up the pieces. __________

That milk is from Uncle Louie's cow. __________

Since she was already covered in mud. __________

Because my grandmother came to visit.
I cleaned up my room.

Because my grandmother came to visit, I cleaned up my room.

Dependent clauses begin with subordinating words.
Dependent clauses are also known as subordinate clauses.

Exercise 69A: Distinguishing Between Phrases and Clauses

Identify the following groups of words as *phrases* or *clauses*. The clauses may be independent or dependent, but you only need to identify them as *clauses*. In each clause, underline the subject once and the verb twice.

Twisting and winding __________

The rooster fought the hen __________

Because of the earthquake __________

Because the earthquake toppled a major building __________

Macy was shocked __________

Dribbling the basketball _______________

Although eels and jellyfish are not _______________

It wasn't Brady's fault _______________

Through the bathrooms of the big bungalow _______________

He was a mongoose _______________

Tickling under my chin _______________

Exercise 69B: Distinguishing Between Independent and Dependent Clauses

Identify the following clauses as independent (*IND*) or dependent (*DEP*).

Unless he could clean his room in the next hour _______________

He laid the bricks one by one _______________

As she munched chips on the train _______________

Since the new baby was born _______________

The balloon sailed high into the clouds _______________

If he hadn't heard the kitten mewing _______________

It would have been awful _______________

Rikki-tikki-tavi tingled all over _______________

When morning came _______________

Though Rikki-tikki-tavi had never met a live cobra before _______________

Exercise 69C: Turning Dependent Clauses into Complete Sentences

Choose three of the dependent clauses in Exercise 69B and attach independent clauses to them to form complete, complex thoughts. Write your three new sentences on your own paper. (The dependent clause can go before or after the independent clause.)

— LESSON 70 —

Adjective Clauses
Relative Pronouns

Intro 70: Introduction to Adjective Clauses

Match the dependent clause on the right with the correct independent clause on the left. The first one has been done for you.

Beethoven, A , was deaf.	~~A.~~ who composed "Ode to Joy"
Many ships have sunk in the Bermuda Triangle, ____________.	B. that supposedly lives in the lakes of Scotland
Da Vinci, ____________, was a vegetarian.	C. whom many have called the greatest scientist of all time
Einstein, ________, had speech problems as a child.	D. whose most famous painting is the *Mona Lisa*
Many people have reportedly seen the Loch Ness monster ______.	E. which is a mysterious area in the Caribbean

Dependent clauses can act as adjectives, adverbs, or nouns.

An adjective clause is a dependent clause that acts as an adjective in a sentence, modifying a noun or pronoun in the independent clause.

They banded together in small groups that whispered and discussed and disputed.

A man who passed by spoke to them.

Relative pronouns introduce adjective clauses and refer back to an antecedent in the independent clause.
who, whom, whose, which, that

The men **who had been champions before Finn came** rallied the others against him.

Among the young princes was a boy **whom the High King preferred**.

The Chain of Silence was shaken by the servant **whose duty and honor it was.**

The thing **which was presented to us** is not true.

The people believed in gods **that the king did not accept**.

Use *who, whom,* and *whose* to refer to persons.

Use *which* to refer to animals, places, and things.
Use *that* and *whose* to refer to persons, animals, places, or things.

She saw him, and he saw her.

Use *P* for prepositions, *OP* for objects of prepositions, *ADJ* for adjectives, *ADV* for adverbs, *IO* for indirect objects, *DO* for direct objects, and *OC* for object complements.

I who speak to you have seen many evils.

At the door is a gentleman for whom no seat has been found.

He was the boy whom they called Little Fawn.

They are men whose happiness lies in ambition.

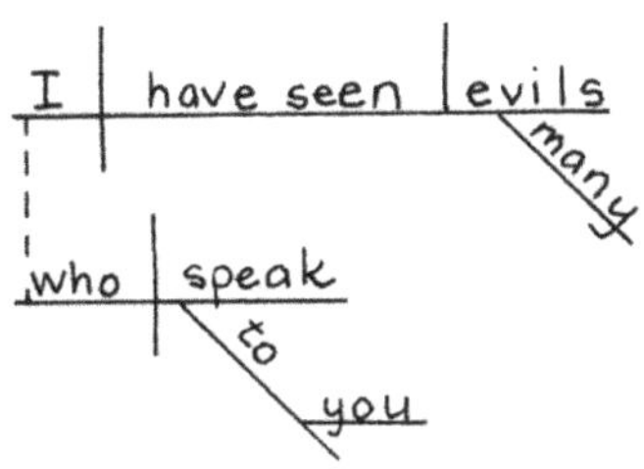

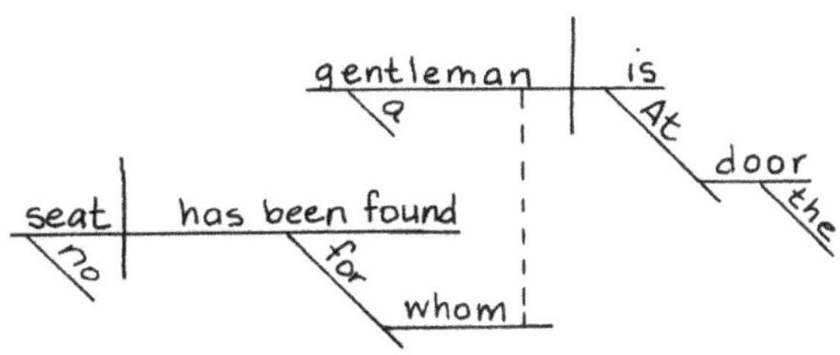

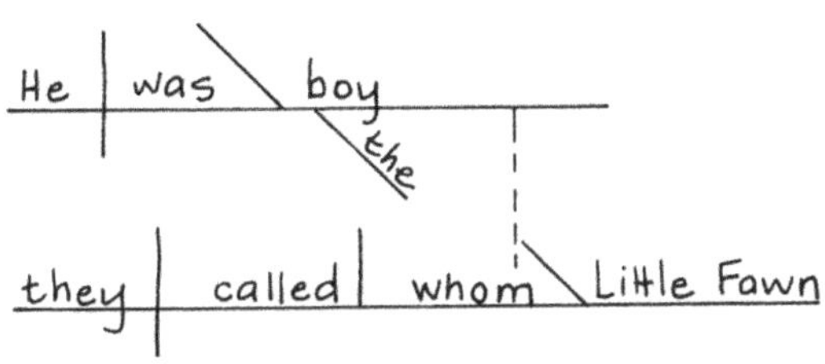

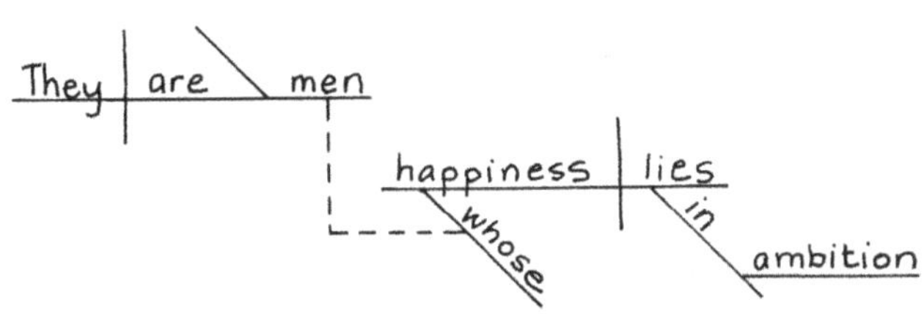

Exercise 70A: Identifying Adjective Clauses and Relative Pronouns

Underline the adjective clauses in the following sentences, and circle the relative pronouns. Draw an arrow from each relative pronoun to its antecedent.

Many ships that sail between Europe and North America pass through the Bermuda Triangle.

Stories that tell of mysterious disturbances in the Triangle have frightened captains for years.

One captain, whose ship eventually sank in the Triangle, reported strange green waters.

Pilots who were flying over the Bermuda Triangle have also experienced trouble.

One possible explanation is unusual magnetic activity, which may cause compasses to malfunction.

The Gulf Stream, which is a strong ocean current, could also affect waters in the Triangle.

Other explanations that people have offered are less scientific.

Many superstitious sailors blame Atlantis, which is a mythical underwater city.

Exercise 70B: Choosing the Correct Relative Pronoun

In each sentence, cross out the incorrect relative pronoun. Above the correct pronoun, write *S* for subject, *OP* for object of the preposition, or *DO* for direct object to show how the relative pronoun is used within the dependent clause.

These sentences are adapted from classic Welsh fairy tales.

One day the queen's daughter, (who/whom) was now fifteen, decided to go and see the world.

She often visited the house of an old miser (who/whom) lived nearby.

She dressed the children (who/whom) she did not like in rags.

One of them, (who/whom) seemed to be older than the rest, came up to him.

His favorite dog was a hound (who/whom) never missed his prey.

You have very bad neighbors, (who/whom) I do not trust.

They returned to the king, (who/whom) at once sent forth his army.

He searched for the infant, about (who/whom) he had had a vivid dream.

There was a lovely young woman (who/whom) the fairies often visited.

Exercise 70C: Diagramming Adjective Clauses

On your own paper, diagram every word of the following sentences.

I am meeting Shirin, whose textbook I borrowed.

Thomas Jefferson, who was the third President of the United States, built the University of Virginia.

The first person that arrives will receive a free baseball.

Horace ate the brownies that Mom had made for the picnic.

Ravi, whom I had given my number, called me this morning.

— LESSON 71 —

Adjective Clauses
Relative Adverbs
Adjective Clauses with Understood Relatives

A phrase is a group of words serving a single grammatical function.
A clause is a group of words that contains a subject and a predicate.

An independent clause can stand by itself as a sentence.
A dependent clause is a fragment that cannot stand by itself as a sentence.

Dependent clauses begin with subordinating words.
Dependent clauses are also known as subordinate clauses.

Adjective clauses are also known as relative clauses because they relate to another word in the independent clause.

Relative pronouns introduce adjective clauses and refer back to an antecedent in the independent clause.
who, whom, whose, which, that

This was the very spot **where** a proud tyrant raised an undying monument to his own vanity.

He was going back to serve his country at a time **when** death was the usual reward for such devotion.

The reasons **why** he vented his ill humor on the soldiers were many.
—Adapted from *The Scarlet Pimpernel*, by Baroness Emmuska Orczy

Relative adverbs introduce adjective clauses and refer back to a place, time, or reason in the independent clause.
where, when, why

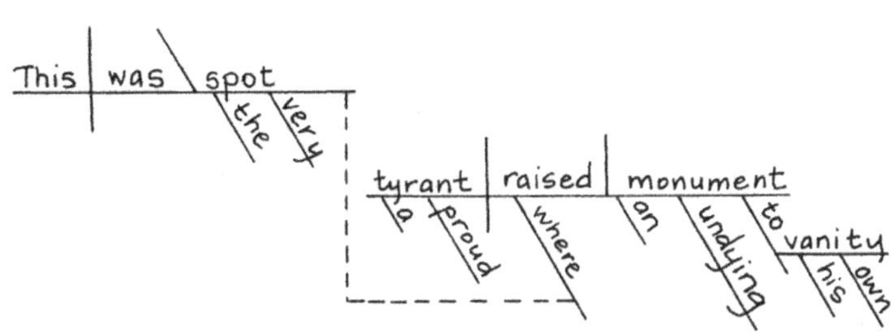

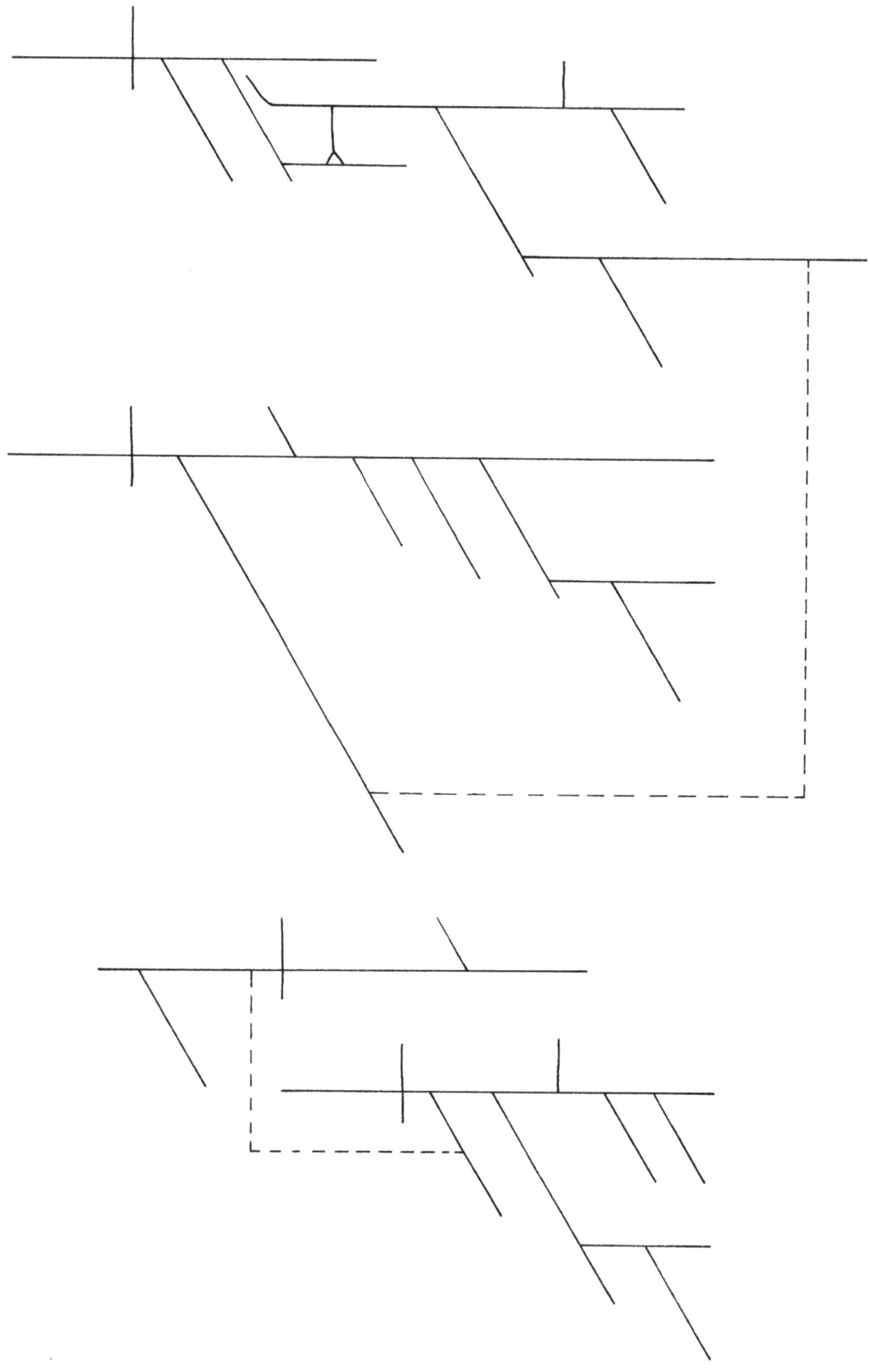

The evil men do lives after them.

I read the book you sent me.

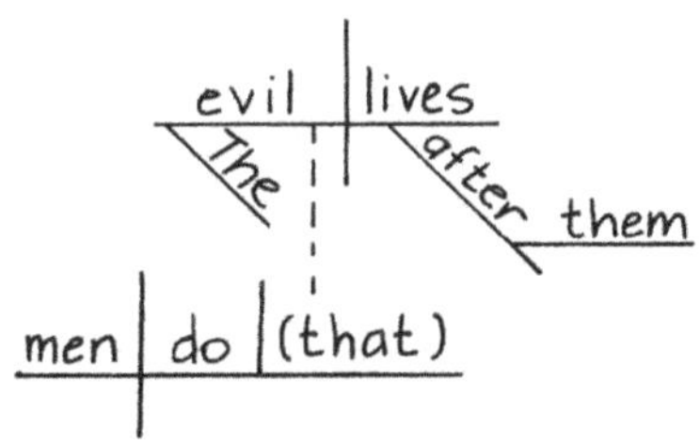

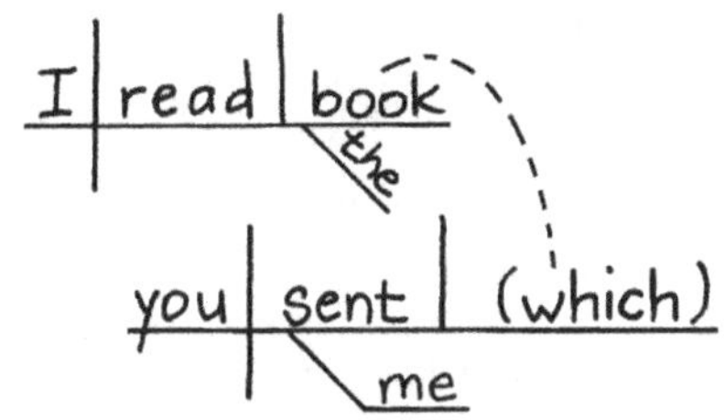

Exercise 71A: Relative Adverbs and Pronouns

In the following sentences, underline each adjective clause. Circle each relative word and label it as *RP* for relative pronoun or *RA* for relative adverb. Draw an arrow from each relative word back to its antecedent in the independent clause.

These sentences are taken from Herman Melville's classic novel *Moby Dick.* Some have been slightly adapted or condensed.

He's the bird what catches the worm.

The sea is a green pasture where our children's grand-children will go for bread.

In the distance lay a ship whose furled sails conveyed a warning.

Nantucket was her great original, the Tyre of this Carthage, the place where the first dead American whale was stranded.

You look out a glass window where the frost is all on the outside.

Some few hands are called ship-keepers, whose province it is to work the vessel.

Father Mapple was in the hardy winter of an old age which was merging into a second flowering youth.

The ostensible reason why Ahab did not go on board was the coming storm.

The Guernsey-man, who had just got into the chains, had slung his nose in a sort of bag.

We should be furnished with the reason why his sense of smell seems obliterated.

He scarce heeds the moment when he drops seething into the yawning jaws awaiting him.

This was written at a time when the whalebone was largely used in ladies' bodices.

I was he whom the Fates ordained to take the place of Ahab's bowsman.

Exercise 71B: Missing Relative Words

Draw a caret in front of each adjective clause and insert the missing relative pronoun. (For the purposes of this exercise, *which* and *that* may be used interchangeably.)

Reykjavik is one of the finest cities I have visited.

The elderly woman you met is not my grandmother.

The giraffe we saw was extremely tall and ravenously hungry.

The painting you admired was painted by me.

Of all the songs I have ever heard, this was the saddest.

The sloppy language the writer used is disgraceful.

The heritage seeds we planted have sprouted.

Exercise 71C: Diagramming

On your own paper, diagram the following sentences from your first two exercises.

The sea is a green pasture where our children's grand-children will go for bread.

Nantucket was her great original, the Tyre of this Carthage, the place where the first dead American whale was stranded.

He scarce heeds the moment when he drops seething into the yawning jaws awaiting him.

I was he whom the Fates ordained to take the place of Ahab's bowsman.

The giraffe we saw was extremely tall and ravenously hungry.

— LESSON 72 —

Adverb Clauses

A clause is a group of words that contains a subject and a predicate.

**A dependent clause is a fragment that cannot stand by itself as a sentence.
Dependent clauses begin with subordinating words.
Dependent clauses are also known as subordinate clauses.**

Dependent clauses can act as adjective clauses, adverb clauses, or noun clauses.

Adverb clauses modify verbs, adjectives, and other adverbs in the independent clause. They answer the questions where, when, how, how often, and to what extent.

When the supper was finished, the king expressed a wish.

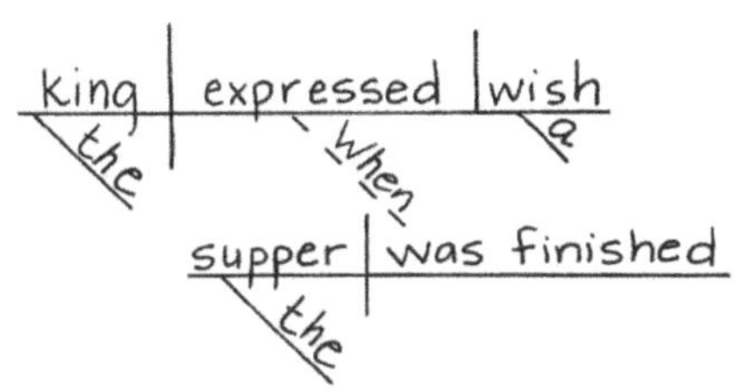

Adverb clauses can be introduced by adverbs.

Common Adverbs That Introduce Clauses
as (and its compounds: as if, as soon as, as though)
as if
how (and its compound: however)
when (and its compound: whenever)
whence
where (and its compounds: whereat, whereby, wherein, wherefore, whereon)
while
whither

A subordinating conjunction joins unequal words or groups of words together.

An honest enemy is better than an agreeable coward.

An honest enemy is better than an agreeable coward [is].

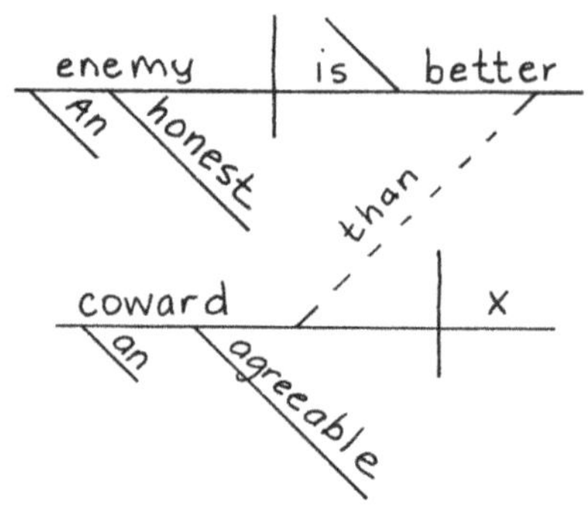

Subordinating conjunctions and subordinating correlative conjunctions often join an adverb clause to an independent clause.

Common Subordinating Conjunctions
after
although
as (as soon as)
because
before
if
in order that
lest
since
though
till
unless
until
although/though . . . yet/still
if . . . then

Because she loves Korean food, my aunt taught me to cook kimchi.

I will put six plates on the table unless our neighbors are also coming for dinner.

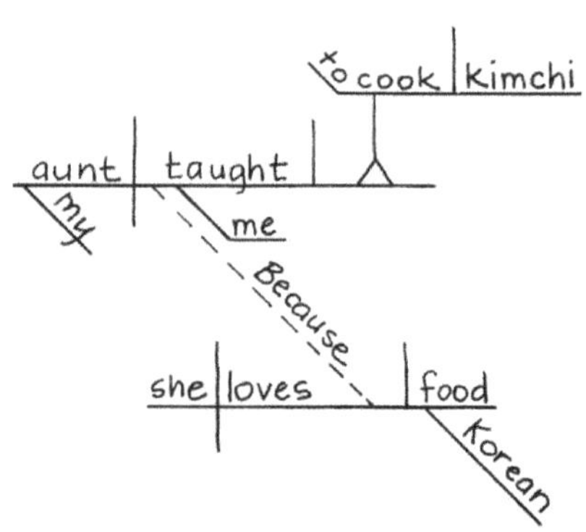

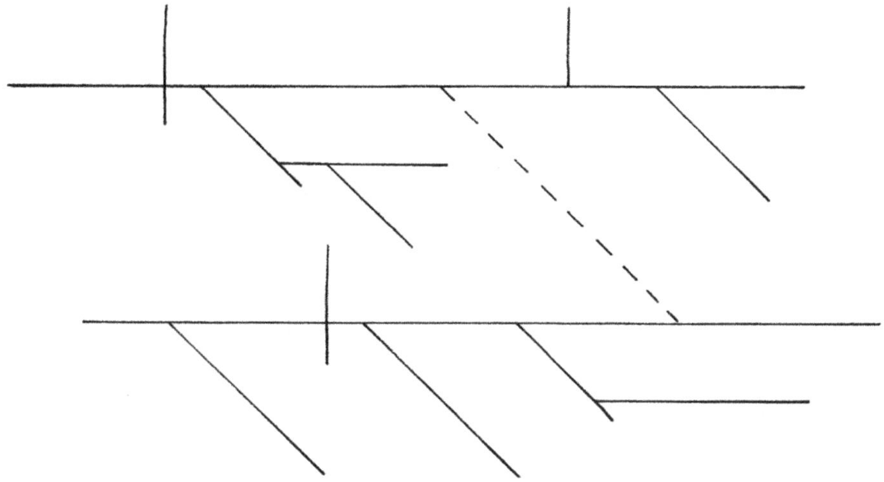

The task is difficult if you do not take care.

She was confident that she could reach the top of the mountain.

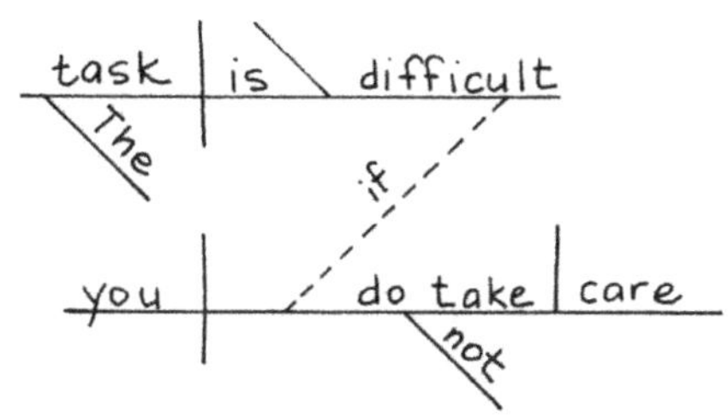

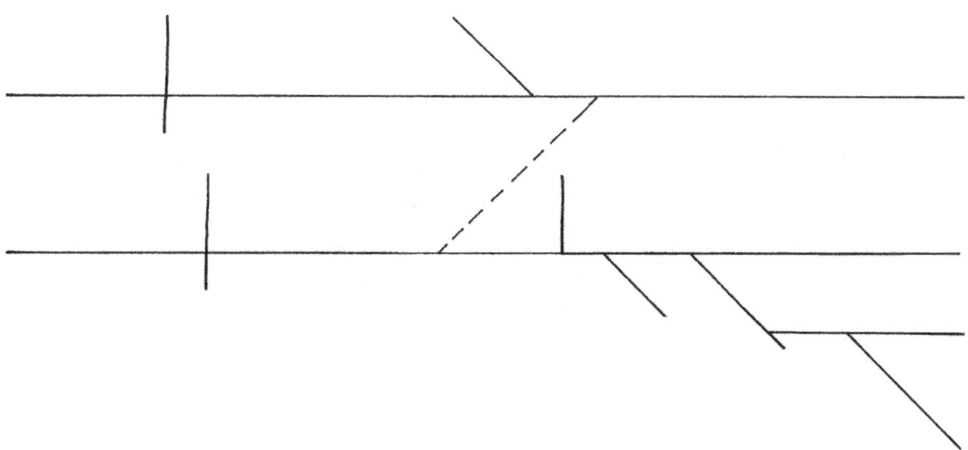

He sprinted quickly as though he were being chased by monsters.

The judge spoke severely because the attorney was not paying attention.

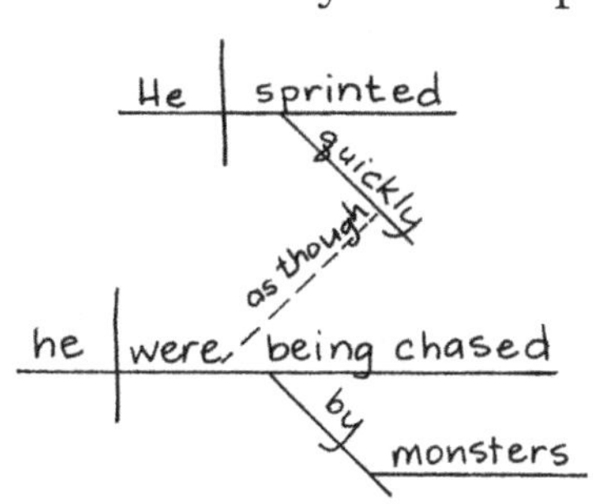

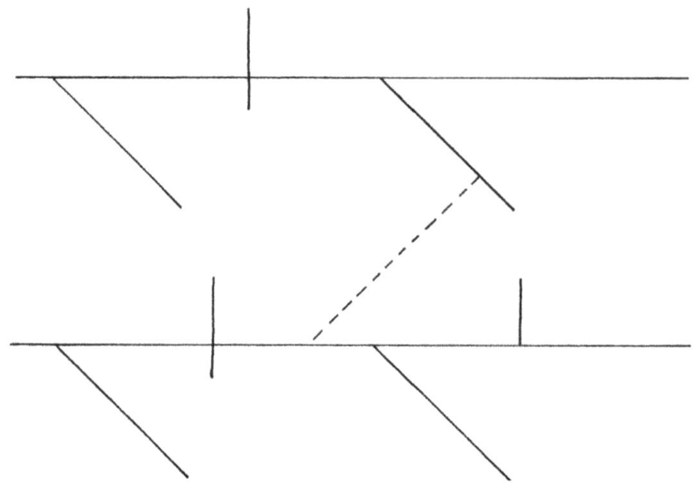

I will wait where I am.

I waited at the place where I had marked the ground.

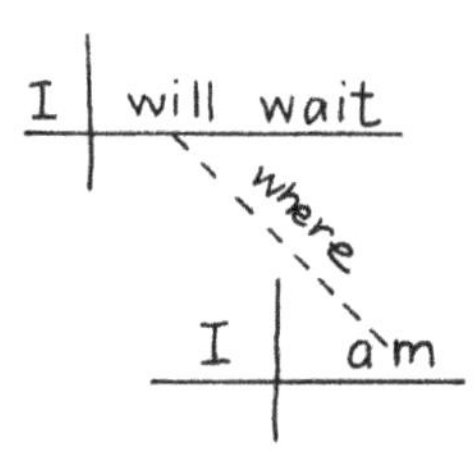

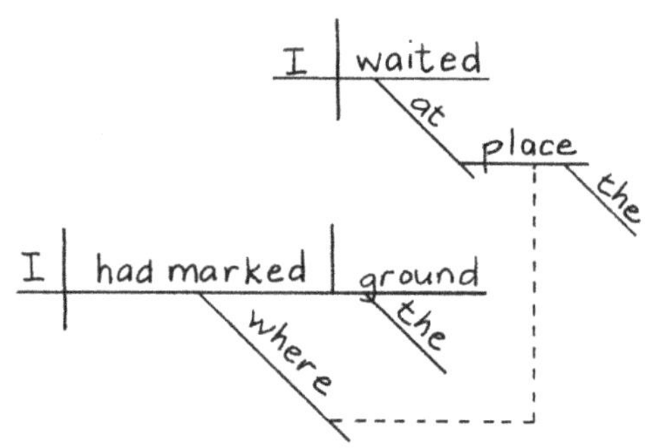

Exercise 72A: Adverb Clauses

In the following sentences, underline each adverb clause. Circle the subordinating word(s) at the beginning of each clause and label it *ADV* for adverb or *SC* for subordinating conjunction. Draw an arrow from the subordinating word back to the verb, adverb, or adjective that the clause modifies.

These sentences are adapted from Alexandre Dumas's *The Man in the Iron Mask.*

The countenance of Aramis darkened as the young man continued.

When you have related it, leave us.

It was dangerous because his attempts to escape were many.

He drew the message from his pocket swiftly since the king was already rising to leave.

Since the king has given secret orders, I no longer possess his confidence.

While these affairs were separating forever the four musketeers, Athos began to pay his tribute.

Louis XIV continued as if he had seen nothing.

The moon, too, as if she had placed herself at his orders, silvered the trees and lake with her own bright and quasi-phosphorescent light.

This luminous square decreases from one till three, slowly, as if it sorrowed to bid me farewell.

The king would burn the whole building and its contents, in order that it might not be made use of by anyone else.

Exercise 72B: Descriptive Clauses

In the following sentences, underline each dependent clause. Above each, write *ADVC* for adverb clause or *ADJC* for adjective clause. Circle each subordinating word(s) and label it as *ADV* for adverb, *RP* for relative pronoun, or *SC* for subordinating conjunction. Draw an arrow from the subordinating word back (or forward) to the word in the independent clause that the dependent clause modifies.

These sentences are adapted from Alexandre Dumas's *The Man in the Iron Mask.*

For as my conscience does not accuse me, I aver my innocence.

He fell back to the cavern where the three rowers awaited him.

As soon as he was assured by the sound of their descending footsteps, he put the lantern on the table.

Speak to me of the religious order whose chief you are.

It is not you who will have to thank me, but rather the nation whom you will render happy, the posterity whose name you will make glorious.

D'Artagnan recoiled, as though the syllables had knocked the breath out of his body.

You remember the story of the Roman general who always kept seven wild boars roasting.

You see before you, my dear monsieur, a man who considers himself disgraced.

Will you meet me at Paris, in order that I may know your determination?

But already Percerin, goaded by the idea that the king was to be told, had offered Lebrun a chair.

He drank in delicious draughts of that mysterious air which interpenetrates at night the loftiest forests.

Exercise 72C: Diagramming

On your own paper, diagram every word of the following sentences.

These sentences are adapted from Alexandre Dumas's *The Man in the Iron Mask.*

Although the courier made a great noise, Baisemeaux heard nothing.

The latter, whose hands trembled in a manner to excite pity, turned a dull and meaningless gaze upon the letter.

It was Aramis who brought me the invitation.

D'Artagnan, pushing on Porthos, who scattered the groups of people right and left, succeeded in gaining the counter.

Moliere fixed upon Porthos one of those looks which penetrate the minds and hearts of men.

— REVIEW 6 —

Weeks 16-18

Topics
Personal Pronouns: Subject, Object, Possessive, Reflexive
Verb Voice (Active and Passive)
Verb Tense
Adjectives
Gerunds and Participles
Phrases
Clauses (Independent and Dependent)

Review 6A: Pronouns

In the following sentences, taken from the classic 1913 novel *The Custom of the Country*, by Edith Wharton, circle each pronoun. Label each as *S* (subject form of the personal pronoun), *O* (object form of the personal pronoun), *P* (possessive form of the personal pronoun), *R* (reflexive), *INT* (intensive), *I* (indefinite), *D* (demonstrative), or *RP* (relative pronoun).

"Yes—I suppose so. He said he'd like to paint me. Mabel Lipscomb introduced him. I don't care if I never see him again," the girl said, bathed in angry pink.

She meant to watch and listen without letting herself go, and she sat very straight and pink, answering promptly but briefly, with the nervous laugh that punctuated all her phrases—saying "I don't care if I do" when her host asked her to try some grapes, and "I wouldn't wonder" when she thought anyone was trying to astonish her.

Mrs. Marvell met this gravely. "It would depend, I should say, on the kind of people she wished to see."

Some she knew without being able to name them—fixed figure-heads of the social prow—others she recognized from their portraits in the papers; but of the few from whom she could herself claim recognition not one was visible, and as she pursued her investigations the whole scene grew blank and featureless.

He paused before answering, and she sat watching his shadowy profile against the passing lamps. "My mother's ideas are old-fashioned; and I don't know that it's anybody's business but yours and mine."

She kept her eyes fixed on her book while he entered the room and moved about behind her, laying aside his hat and overcoat; then his steps came close and a small parcel dropped on the pages of her book.

The old Marquis and his wife, who were content, when they came up from Burgundy in the spring, with a modest set of rooms looking out on the court of their ancestral residence, expected their son and his wife to fit themselves into the still smaller apartment which had served as Raymond's bachelor lodging.

Whenever Undine saw him after an absence she had a curious sense of his coming back from unknown distances and not belonging to her or to any state of things she understood. Then habit reasserted itself, and she began to think of him again with a querulous familiarity.

Review 6B: Using Comparative and Superlative Adjectives Correctly

Choose the correct form in parentheses. Cross out the incorrect form.

Rainforests are the earth's (diversest/most diverse) natural places.

Rainforests are (sunnier/more sunny) and (damper/most damp) than other forests.

The floor of the rainforest is the (darkest/most dark) and (humidest/most humid) place in the rainforest.

The canopy, or leafy part of the forest, is (richer/richest) in wildlife than the forest floor.

Rainforests are the earth's (more valuable / most valuable) natural wonder, hosting over half of the world's plant and animal species.

Every year rainforests are destroyed, and today they are (scarcer / most scarce) than they have ever been.

We must be (carefuller / more careful) than our ancestors, in order to protect this precious resource.

Review 6C: Verbs

Underline the main verb in each sentence. In the space above it, write the tense (*SIMP PAST, PRES, FUT; PROG PAST, PRES, FUT; PERF PAST, PRES, FUT*) and voice (*ACT* for active or *PASS* for passive) of the verb. If the verb is active, also note whether it is transitive (*TR*) or intransitive (*INTR*). The first is done for you.

These sentences are taken from *A History of China*, by Wolfram Eberhard.

PERF PRES, ACT, INTR

Chinese scholars have succeeded in deciphering some of the documents discovered.

The still existing fragments of writing of this period are found almost exclusively on tortoiseshells or on other bony surfaces.

No preference was shown to the son of the oldest brother.

At the time of the Han Dynasty, all citizens (slaves excluded) had accepted family names.

Many of the old works have only come down to us in an imperfect state and with doubtful accuracy.

It will be remembered that Buddhism came to China overland and by sea in the Han epoch.

Nomads were still living in the middle of China.

The younger sons were given independent pieces of land.

Every feudal system harbours some seeds of a bureaucratic system of administration.

Review 6D: Identifying Dependent Clauses

Underline each dependent clause in the following sentences. Circle the subordinating word. Label each clause as either adjective (*ADJ*) or adverb clause (*ADV*), and draw a line from each subordinating word to the word it modifies.

These sentences are taken from "Rikki-Tikki-Tavi," by Rudyard Kipling.

This is the story of the great war that Rikki-tikki-tavi fought single-handed.

His war-cry, as he scuttled through the long grass, was: "Rikk-tikk-tikki-tikki-tchk!"

He looked at Rikki-tikki with the wicked snake's eyes that never change their expression.

He jumped up in the air as high as he could go, and just under him whizzed by the head of Nagaina, Nag's wicked wife.

She had crept up behind him as he was talking, to make an end of him; and he heard her savage hiss as the stroke missed.

The Coppersmith is a bird who makes a noise exactly like the beating of a little hammer on a copper pot.

From the thick grass at the foot of the bush there came a low hiss —a horrid cold sound that made Rikki-tikki jump back two clear feet.

Darzee was a feather-brained little fellow who could never hold more than one idea at a time in his head.

So he sang a very mournful song that he made up on the spur of the minute.

He was dizzy, aching, and felt shaken to pieces when something went off like a thunderclap just behind him.

Review 6E: Present and Past Participles

Underline each present participle and past participle in the following sentences. Indicate what part of the sentence each serves as with the labels *ADJ* for adjective, *ADV* for adverb, *S* for subject, *DO* and *IO* for direct and indirect object, and *OP* for object of the preposition. For adverbs and adjectives, draw an arrow back to the word modified.

Aloo tikki are made with mashed potatoes and cilantro, *garam* masala, and cumin.

Saute cumin seeds and onion in bubbling oil before adding other ingredients.

Divide the finished mixture into equal portions and shape into balls.

Flatten the balls on a greased tabletop.

Heat more oil in a frying pan and fry until the potato is golden.

You can make green pea *tikki* by mashing peas together with spinach and green chilis.

Aloo tikki is always hot and satisfying.

Eating *aloo tikki* is my favorite morning break activity.

The street vendor was very busy frying the morning's *aloo tikki*.

You can also buy *aloo tikki* at *chaat* shops found in New Delhi.

You will find *aloo tikki chaat* heaped with yogurt and pomegranate in Pitampura.

Review 6F: Diagramming

On your own paper, diagram every word of the following sentences (taken from H. E. Macomber's biography of Samuel Finley Morse in *Stories of Great Inventors*).

There are many, many things, common and useful to us now, which were unknown to the world in 1800.

Lighting by means of gas was yet unknown.

Even kerosene, which makes so poor a light, was then unused.

Though he did not snatch the thunder from the heavens, he gave the electric current thought, and bound the earth in light.

WEEK 19

More Clauses

— LESSON 73 —

Adjective and Adverb Clauses
Introduction to Noun Clauses

A clause is a group of words that contains a subject and a predicate.

I know that a noun is the name of a person, place, thing, or idea.

I know an old lady who swallowed a fly while she was sitting on the front porch.

Dependent clauses can act as adjective clauses, adverb clauses, or noun clauses.

An adjective clause is a dependent clause that acts as an adjective in a sentence, modifying a noun or pronoun in the independent clause.
Relative pronouns introduce adjective clauses and refer back to an antecedent in the independent clause.

Adverb clauses modify verbs, adjectives, and other adverbs in the independent clause.
They answer the questions where, when, how, how often, and to what extent.
Adverb clauses can be introduced by adverbs.
Subordinating conjunctions and subordinating correlative conjunctions often join an adverb clause to an independent clause.

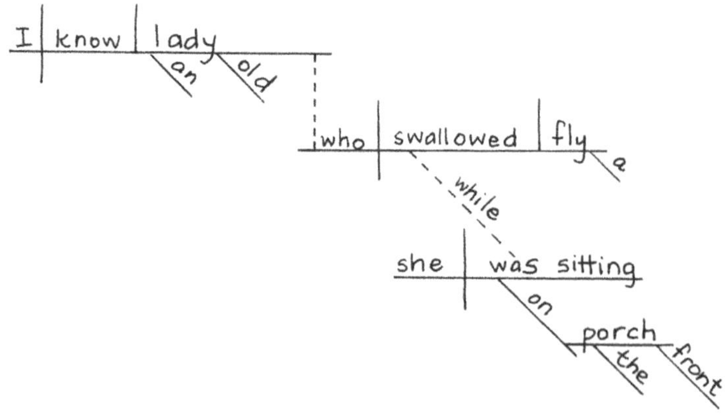

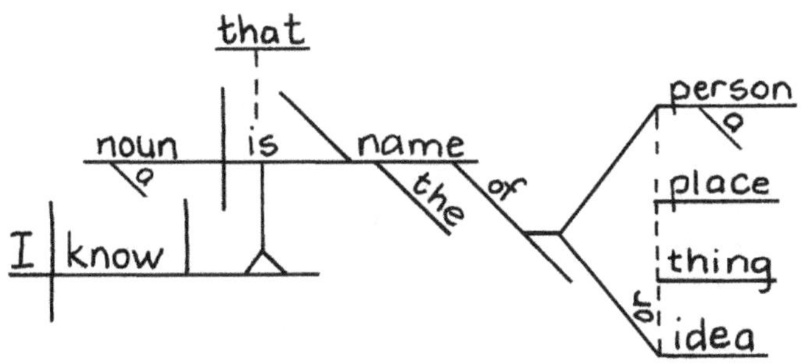

A noun clause takes the place of a noun.
Noun clauses can be introduced by relative pronouns, relative adverbs, subordinating conjunctions, or understood subordinating words.

I know where your lost keys are.

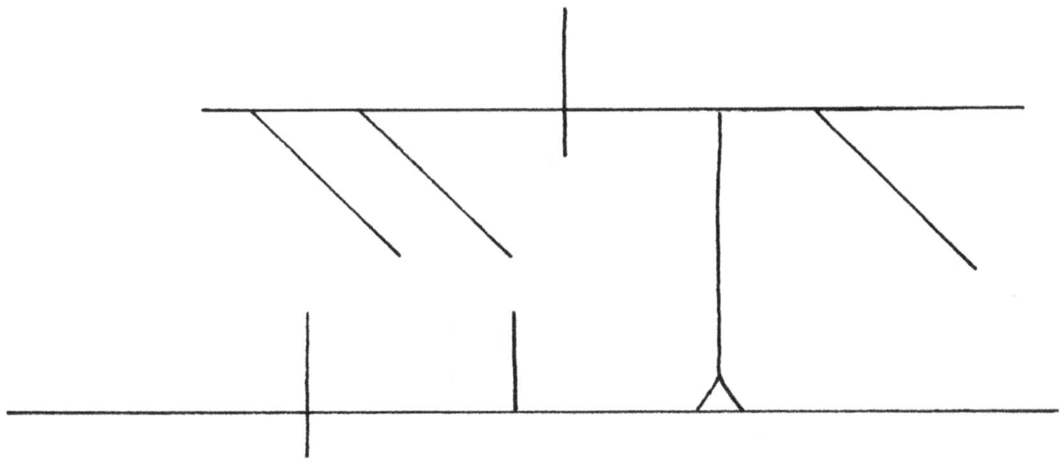

Whoever runs fastest will win the race.

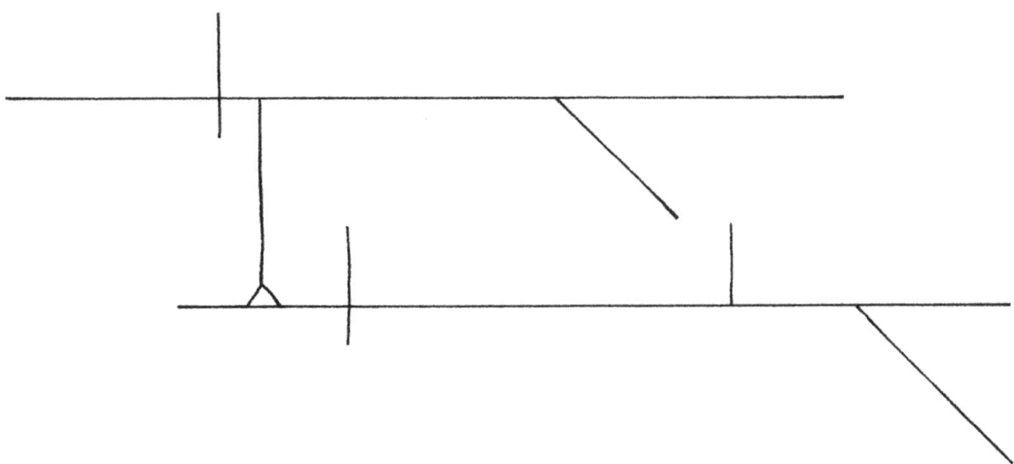

I really wish I had more chocolate.

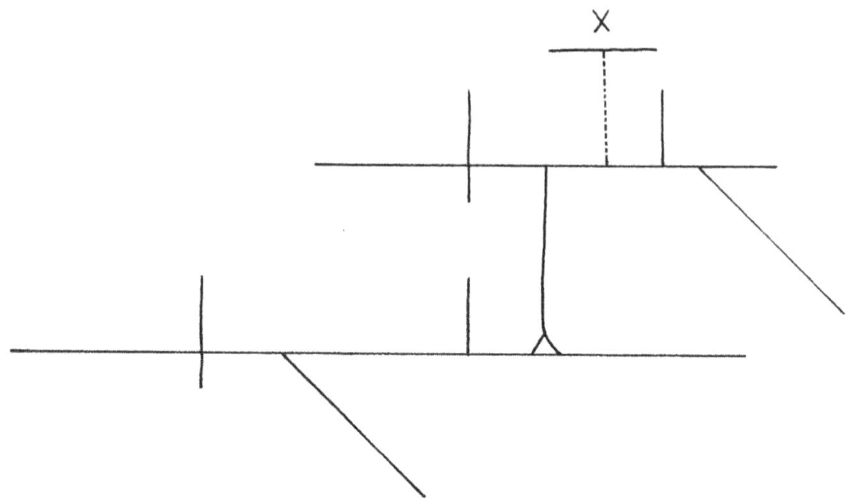

Nothing was as it should be.

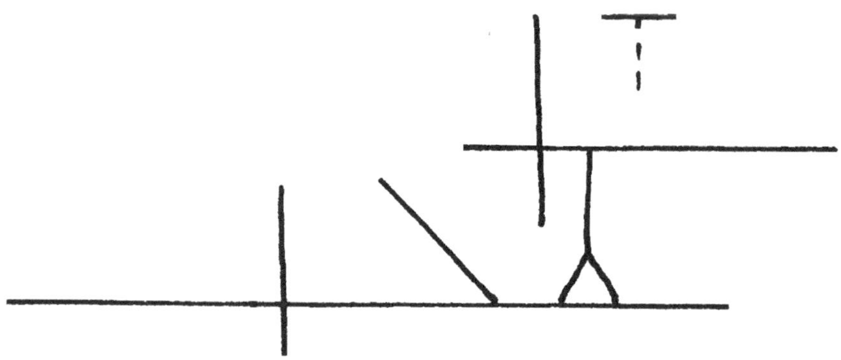

What matters most in this situation is how you feel about it.

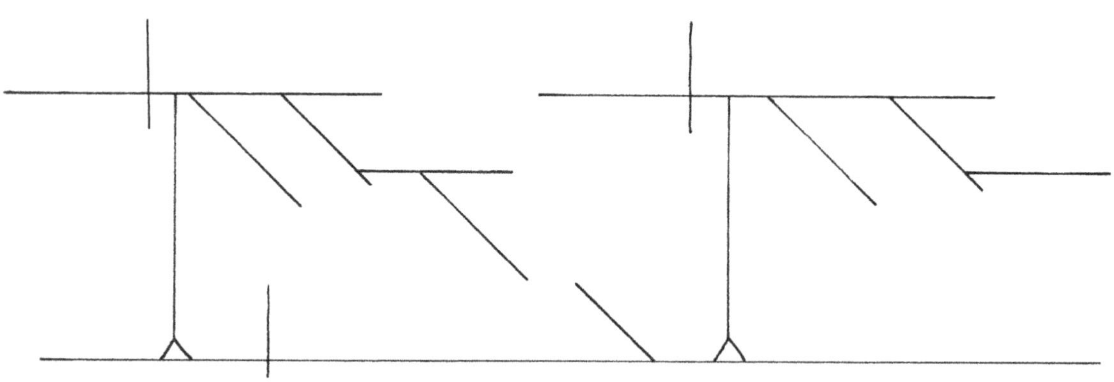

Exercise 73A: Identifying Clauses

In the following sentences, circle each dependent clause. Label each as *N* for noun, *ADJ* for adjective, or *ADV* for adverb. Indicate whether the noun clauses are subjects (*S*) or direct objects (*DO*). Draw a line from the subordinating word of each adjective and adverb clause back to the word it modifies.

Some of these clauses may have another clause within them! Do your best to find both, and ask your instructor for help if needed.

These sentences are taken from *Tarzan of the Apes*, by Edgar Rice Burroughs.

Though Lady Greystoke lived for a year after her baby was born, she was never again outside the cabin, nor did she ever fully realize that she was not in England.

That he had been able to turn his hands at all to such unaccustomed labor was a source of mild wonder to him.

But deep in the minds of the apes was rooted the conviction that Tarzan was a mighty fighter and a strange creature.

So peaceful was her end that it was hours before Clayton could awake to a realization that his wife was dead.

By the time Tarzan was ten years old he was an excellent climber, and on the ground could do many wonderful things which were beyond the powers of his little brothers and sisters.

Whatever his decision, the apes accept it as final, and return to their occupations satisfied.

Tarzan wondered why the men had gone into the jungle.

Occasionally they would enter a spot where the foliage above was less dense.

It was the surprise at the blinding flash and the deafening roar that had caused her hasty but temporary retreat.

Still more wonderful was how it contained the likeness of one who might be a brother.

Exercise 73B: Creating Noun Clauses

For each of the following sentences, write a noun clause that fits into the blank.

If you have trouble coming up with a dependent clause, try starting out with one of the following subordinating words: *that, how, why, what/whatever, who/whoever* (these are always subjects within the dependent clause), *whom/whomever* (these are always objects within the dependent clause), *where, whether.* (This is not an exhaustive list of the possibilities—just a jumping-off place for you.)

No one should know ____.

____ was not very clear.

Tell your father ____.

____ was extremely unfortunate.

The starving colonists ate ____.

Exercise 73C: Diagramming

On your own paper, diagram every word of the following sentences (taken from *Tarzan of the Apes*).

There was no simian in all the mighty forest through which he roved that dared to challenge his right to rule.

None of them could understand how a child could be so slow and backward in learning to care for itself.

His thoughts were interrupted by the station agent who entered asking if there was a gentleman by the name of Tarzan in the party.

— LESSON 74 —

Clauses Beginning with Prepositions

The sun itself, which makes time, is elder by a year now.

Any man's death diminishes me, because I am involved in mankind.

What we call fortune here has another name above.

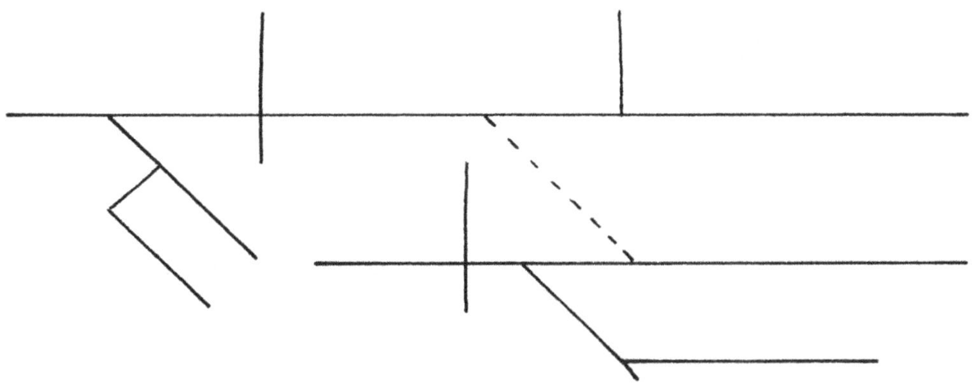

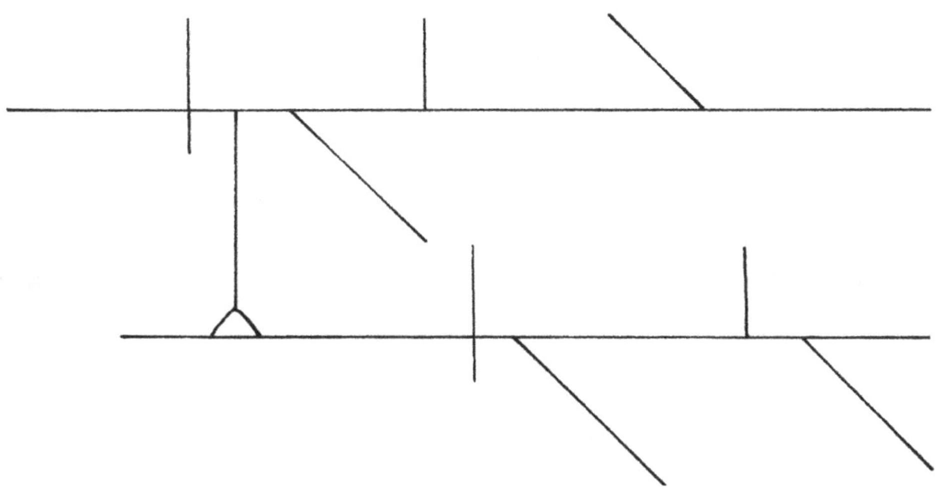

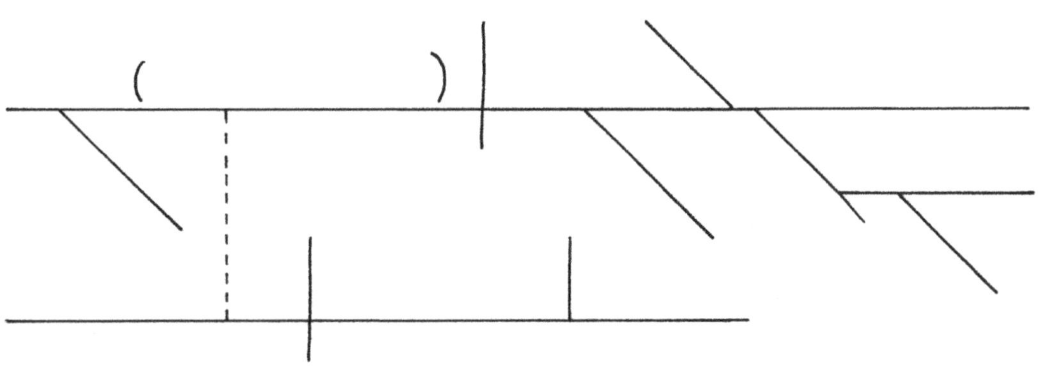

That carrack is the ship in which they are to sail.

He sent for his friends, of whom he took a solemn farewell.

Do not ask for whom the bell tolls.

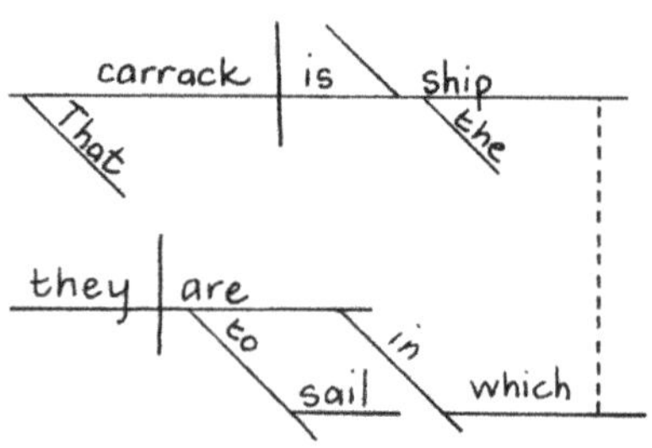

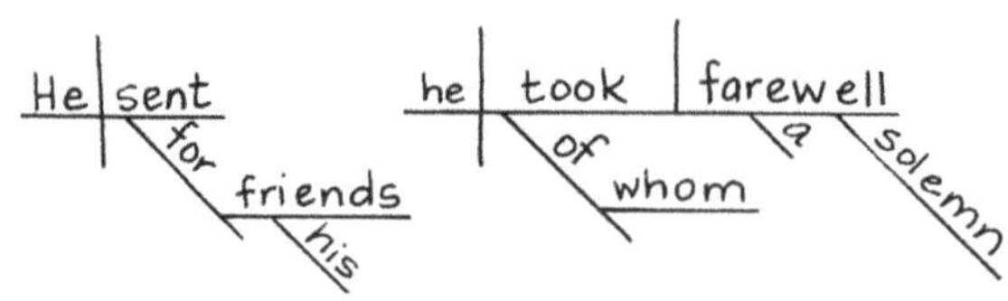

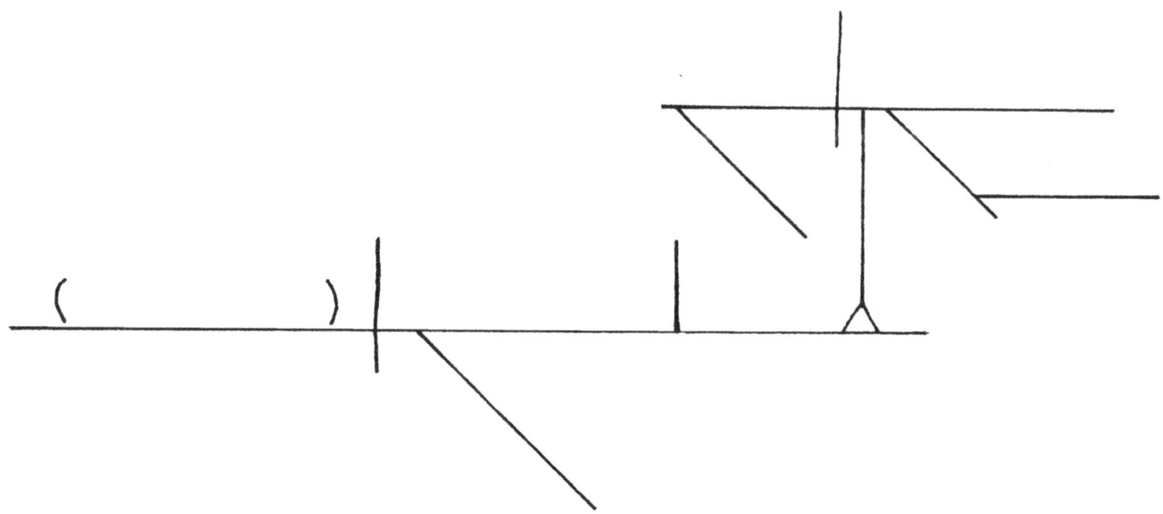

Who always acts as a subject or predicate nominative within a sentence. _Whom_ always acts as an object.

INCORRECT
He sent for his friends, of who he took a solemn farewell.
Do not ask for who the bell tolls.

ALSO INCORRECT (Informal)
He sent for his friends, who he took a solemn farewell of.
Do not ask who the bell tolls for.

CORRECT (Informal)
He sent for his friends, whom he took a solemn farewell of.
Do not ask whom the bell tolls for.

She is growing angry at the person who/whom she is arguing with.

____

Rude behavior is something I won't put up with!
Rude behavior is something up with which I will not put!

Exercise 74A: Adjective Clauses Beginning with Prepositions

In the following sentences, circle each adjective clause. Draw a line from the subordinating word back to the word the clause modifies. If the clause begins with a preposition, underline that preposition and label its object with *OP*.

These sentences are adapted from *Native America: A History*, by Michael L. Oberg.

Drought killed the crops upon which the Chumash relied for food.

French weapons flowed from the Caddos to the Comanches, with whom they allied.

The Caddos entered into a treaty in which they ceded their lands.

He was a Cherokee hunter who lived for a time with bears.

Anthropologists searched for Algonquian remnants with which they could understand the past.

She felt sympathy for the Dakotas, with whom she identified in many ways.

Uncas found himself walking a treacherous path between the English and the natives over whom he exerted his influence.

We wish to return to the state in which we lived before these strangers came.

Aupaumut hoped to employ strong relations with the United States as a barrier against the Iroquois among whom his people lived.

They were a power with whom their rivals had to reckon.

The people who came to be known as the Cherokees told a different story.

The scarcity of game prevented the Senecas from the same hunts to which their fathers were accustomed.

Exercise 74B: Correct Use of *Who* and *Whom*

Choose the correct pronoun within the parentheses; cross out the incorrect pronoun.

(Who / Whom) does this belong to?

I think you should buy flowers for the girl (who / whom) you are interested in.

She is an official against (who / whom) no charge can be brought.

The mansion was inhabited by an old woman (who / whom) spent her days knitting.

He is the only one of them all (who / whom) I could make my friend.

(Who / Whom) is coming along with us all?

(Who / Whom) should you talk to?

This is the lady to (who / whom) I am indebted.

I was looking for my aunt and the two friends (who / whom) she was travelling with.

For those of us (who / whom) arrived on time, the evening went well.

There are only a few to (who / whom) this privilege is granted.

That is the family (who / whom) we were talking about.

I'm glad someone is here of (who / whom) I can ask advice.

This request should go to my partner, (who / whom) is already aware of the problem.

Exercise 74C: Formal and Informal Diction

On your own paper, rewrite the following informal sentences in formal English, placing the preposition before its object. In four sentences, you will also need to insert a relative pronoun. The first has been done for you.

Read both versions of each sentence out loud, and place a star by any sentence that sounds better in informal English.

Whom should I turn to?

To whom should I turn?

The forest which the animals lived in was deep and dark.

Sarya finally learned whom the presents were intended for.

He is the one I owe my thanks to.

The men whom charges were brought against went on trial.

The girl he's talking to is the daughter of the president.

There are many other galaxies besides the ones we've given names to.

I'm very fond of the family I live with.

Exercise 74D: Diagramming

On your own paper, diagram every word of the following two sentences from Exercise 74A.

French weapons flowed from the Caddos to the Comanches, with whom they allied.

Uncas found himself walking a treacherous path between the English and the natives over whom he exerted his influence.

— LESSON 75 —

Clauses and Phrases
Misplaced Adjective Phrases
Misplaced Adjective Clauses

In many East Asian countries, the day a baby is born is considered its first birthday.

The first birthday after a baby is born is considered its second birthday.

A phrase is a group of words serving a single grammatical function.

A clause is a group of words that contains a subject and a predicate.

Western birthdays are often celebrated with a cake made especially for the occasion.

The first reference to a "birthday cake" dates from 1785, when the Oxford Dictionary listed the phrase for the first time.

The young woman went to the awards ceremony with her father in a gorgeous ball gown.

She gave the cookie to the little girl made of gingerbread.

Paige gave a birthday cake to her cousin which she had baked herself.

Adjective clauses and phrases should usually go immediately before or after the noun or pronoun they modify.

Exercise 75A: Correcting Misplaced Modifiers

Circle the misplaced adjective clauses and phrases in the following sentences. Draw an arrow to the place where each modifier should be.

The trees shaded the little girl with lush green branches.

The dog knocked over the vase that was running around the house.

The three girls walked down the street chewing gum.

I borrowed a sandwich for lunch with mayonnaise.

He gave a dog to his daughter named Rufus.

The lamp crashed onto the floor that Hillary had kicked.

With big fuzzy ears, I gave a stuffed elephant to my sister Angie.

Tourists crowd the streets of Venice carrying cameras.

Kevin made Aunt Jean a strawberry pie, who is his mother's older sister.

She tossed the fish in the bucket that was thrashing around.

We served pizza to the children on paper plates that were too floppy.

Exercise 75B: Diagramming

Each of the following sentences has at least one misplaced clause or phrase. On your own paper, diagram each sentence correctly, and then read the corrected sentence out loud to your instructor.

These sentences are adapted from Willa Cather's novel *O, Pioneers!*

The boys looked away from the shabby old barn with the flaming steeple towards the red church who were watching.

Huddled on the grey prairies, a mist of fine snow-flakes was curling and eddying about the cluster of low drab buildings.

Her cousins sat in the pews dressed in black and weeping profusely.

— LESSON 76 —

Noun, Adjective, and Adverb Clauses
Restrictive and Non-Restrictive Modifying Clauses

Type of clause	Function in the sentence	Introduced by . . .	Diagram by . . .	Also known as
Adjective clause	Modifies a noun or pronoun in the main clause. Answers the questions *Which one? What kind? How many? Whose?*	. . . a relative pronoun, relative adjective, or relative adverb that refers back to a noun or pronoun in the main clause. The most common are *who, whom, whose, that, which, where, when, why.*	. . . placing every word of the dependent clause on a separate diagram below the diagram of the main clause. Connect the relative pronoun, adjective, or adverb to the word it refers to in the main clause with a dotted line.	Relative clause, dependent clause, subordinate clause
Adverb clause	Modifies a verb, adjective, or adverb in the main clause. Answers the questions *Where? When? How? How often? To what extent?*	. . . subordinating conjunctions, such as *when, until, before, after, as, while, where, although, unless, because, since, though, so that, even though.* (**NOTE:** There are many other subordinating conjunctions.)	. . . placing every word of the dependent clause *except* for the subordinating word on a separate diagram below the diagram of the main clause. Draw a dotted line connecting the predicate of the dependent clause to the word modified in the independent clause, and write the subordinating word on the dotted line.	Subordinate clause, dependent clause

Type of clause	Function in the sentence	Introduced by . . .	Diagram by . . .	Also known as
Noun clause	Stands in as any part of the sentence that a noun can fill: subject, direct object, indirect object, predicate nominative, object of the preposition, appositive [see Lesson 94], object complement.	. . . most commonly, *that.* Can also be introduced by *who, whom, which, what, whether, why, when, where, how,* or other subordinating words.	. . . drawing a tree in the appropriate noun space on the diagram and placing each word in the noun clause on a diagram that sits on top of the tree. If the subordinating word only connects the dependent clause to the rest of the sentence and doesn't have a grammatical function *within* the dependent clause, diagram it on a line that floats above the predicate of the clause and is attached to the predicate by a dotted line.	Nominal clause, subordinate clause, dependent clause

Exercise 76A: Clause Review

For each of the three sentences below, complete these steps:

1) Find and circle the dependent clauses. Label each one as *adjective, adverb,* or *noun.*
2) Identify and underline the subordinating word.
3) For the adverb and adjective clauses, draw a line from the subordinating word back to the word modified. For the noun clauses, identify the part of the sentence that each clause is serving as.
4) Diagram each sentence on your own paper.

These sentences are taken from *The Magic of Oz,* by L. Frank Baum.

The Glass Cat, although it had some disagreeable ways and manners, nevertheless realized that Trot and Cap'n Bill were its friends.

There is the gold flower-pot containing the Magic Flower, which is very curious and beautiful.

The Wizard did not know whether it would be better for him to hide himself until they

moved on again.

A restrictive modifying clause defines the word that it modifies. Removing the clause changes the essential meaning of the sentence.

A non-restrictive modifying clause describes the word that it modifies. Removing the clause doesn't change the essential meaning of the sentence.

In much of Asia, the day that a baby is born is considered to be its first birthday.

Wei's second birthday, which would have been considered his first in North America, was

celebrated with a feast of long noodles and red-dyed eggs.

The movie, which lasted far too long, was quite boring.
I get very angry at people who talk during a movie.
My sister, who enjoys ballet and *muay thai* fighting, has gone to climb Denali.
She ran faster because there was a mountain lion behind her.

Only non-restrictive clauses should be set off by commas.

CORRECT
Hammurabi, who spent much of his life at war, created one of the first law codes.

INCORRECT
Hammurabi who spent much of his life at war created one of the first law codes.

CORRECT
The bricks that formed their city walls were made of mud.

INCORRECT
The bricks, that formed their city walls, were made of mud.

The king had no firm foundation on which to build. ____________________

The king had no firm foundation, on which to build. ____________________

Exercise 76B: Non-Restrictive Clauses and Missing Commas

In the following sentences, taken from James Stephens' classic collection *Irish Fairy Tales*, underline each dependent clause. Place commas around each non-restrictive clause. Use proofreader's marks: ^. Leave sentences with restrictive clauses as they are.

Although she was horrified by the battle her interests lay in another direction.

The idea that a stranger may expire on your doorstep from hunger cannot be tolerated.

There came a sickness that bloated the stomach and purpled the skin.

The feast of Tara was held at which all were gathered together.

Among the three hundred dogs which Fionn owned were two that he loved.

They stared dumbly at the stranger as though they were utterly dazed.

There is a dense wood where every thorn is as sharp as a spear.

He did not loosen his knees when he walked.

She was singing lullabies to a cat that was yelping on her shoulder.

I am kinder than you which no one can deny.

Exercise 76C: Restrictive Clauses and Unnecessary Commas

In the following sentences, taken from James Stephens' classic collection *Irish Fairy Tales,* underline each dependent clause. Delete the incorrect commas that have been placed around restrictive clauses. Use proofreader's marks: 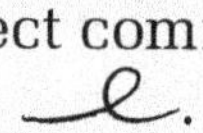. Leave sentences with non-restrictive clauses as they are.

I was so alone, that my own shadow frightened me.

They met him at the place, where games are played.

For although Fionn loved Goll, he did not like him.

When the men saw his condition, they were distressed at his illness.

Each breeze, that came from the right hand or the left, brought me a tale.

For a while it did not matter to Fionn, which way the hare jumped.

He remembered only an endless conversation, from which his mind slipped constantly away.

There is an eerie feeling abroad, which I do not like.

I was that, which I had dreamed.

WEEK 20

Constructing Sentences

— LESSON 77 —

Constructing Sentences

Exercise 77A: Making Sentences Out of Clauses and Phrases

The independent clauses below are listed in order and make up a story—but they're missing all their supporting pieces.

On your own paper, rewrite the story by attaching the dependent clauses and phrases in lists 2 and 3 to the independent clauses in List 1 to make complete sentences. You may insert dependent clauses that act as adjectives or adverbs into the beginning, middle, or end of independent clauses (usually by putting them right before or after the word they modify), and you may change any capitalization or punctuation necessary. But do not add or delete words.

The first sentence has been constructed for you.

Crossing out each clause or phrase as you use it will help you not to repeat yourself!

List 1. Independent Clauses

~~A terrible monster allowed no one to pass.~~
The Sphinx had the head of a woman.
The people were very much frightened.
They had lost their lives.
No one could harm the Sphinx.
The king had ridden off.
A messenger came.
He said.
Oedipus came.
The streets were filled.
The young prince soon learned the cause.
Oedipus immediately set out.
Oedipus walked.
What creature walks?
Oedipus answered.

Man creeps.
Man walks upright.
He supports his tottering steps.
The Sphinx, knowing, tried to get away.
Oedipus forced the Sphinx.

List 2. Dependent Clauses
that the creature of the riddle was man
if he wished to live
where it was dashed to pieces
since it ate up anyone
~~who could not answer a riddle~~
that the king and all of his servants had been killed
because he was sure
who could not guess its riddle
hoping to learn the answer to the riddle
listening to what they said
until he was stopped
that he could guess the riddle
which told him to answer a riddle
that its power was now at an end
although the bravest men had gone out to kill it
~~which it asked~~
unless he guessed the mysterious riddle

List 3. Phrases
and upon three at night
along the road
all talking at once
~~called the Sphinx~~
the body of a lion
drawing his sword
upon two at noon
with a staff
by the Sphinx
with excited people
after a few moments
over a cliff
in the morning of life
in the attempt
in the morning

and the wings of an eagle
onto the sharp stones below
of deep thought,
in old age
to find the monster
running into town
in manhood
in his chariot
to the city
upon four feet
soon afterwards
of their excitement
of Thebes
on hands and knees

FIRST SENTENCE

A terrible monster called the Sphinx allowed no one to pass who could not answer a riddle which it asked.

— LESSON 78 —

Simple Sentences
Complex Sentences

A sentence is a group of words that usually contains a subject and a predicate.
A sentence begins with a capital letter and ends with a punctuation mark.
A sentence contains a complete thought.

(The following sentences are from *The Cricket in Times Square*, by George Selden.)

A mouse was looking at Mario.

Gradually the dirt that had collected on the insect fell away.

A complex sentence contains at least one subordinate clause.
A simple sentence contains one independent clause and no subordinate clauses.

But in all his days, and on all his journeys through the greatest city in the world, Tucker had never heard a sound quite like this one.

No matter what else is in a simple sentence, it will only have *one* subject-predicate set in it.

Then he folded a sheet of Kleenex, tucked it in the box, and put the cricket in it.

The thrumming of the rubber tires of automobiles, and the hooting of their horns, and the howling of their brakes made a great din.

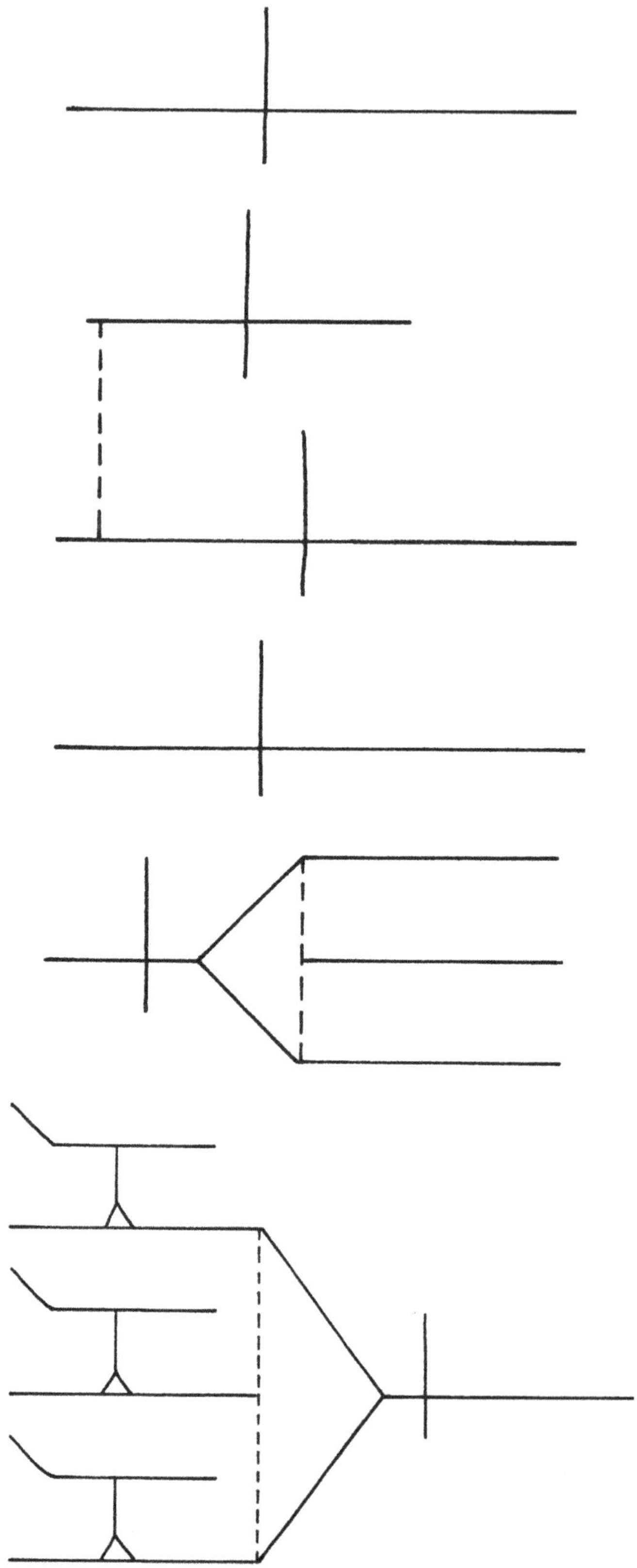

My closest friend and my greatest enemy met on the battlefield and fought bitterly.

Exercise 78A: Identifying Simple and Complex Sentences

In the sentences below, underline each subject once and each predicate twice. (Find the subjects and predicates in both independent and dependent clauses.) In the blank at the end of each sentence, write *S* for simple or *C* for complex.

These sentences are taken from *Knights of Art: Stories of the Italian Painters*, by Amy Steedman.

Many of the new artists shook off the old rules and ideas, and began to paint in quite a new way. _______________

There was one man especially, called Michelangelo, who arose like a giant, and with his new way and greater knowledge swept everything before him. _______________

As the boy grew up he clearly showed in what direction his interest lay. _______________

At school he was something of a dunce at his lessons. _______________

Every spare moment he spent making sketches on the walls of his father's house. _______________

Without needing a lesson he began to copy the statues in terra-cotta. _______________

Like all the other artists, he would often go to study Masaccio's frescoes in the little chapel of the Carmine. _______________

Michelangelo never forgot all that he owed to Lorenzo. _______________

Through the outer walls of stone he seemed to see the figure imprisoned in the marble. _______________

Michelangelo was obliged to lie flat upon a scaffolding and paint the ceiling above him. _______________

So, incomplete as they were, Michelangelo was obliged to uncover the frescoes that all Rome might see them. ______________

Exercise 78B: Forming Complex Sentences

On your own paper, rewrite each pair of simple sentences as a single complex sentence. The first is done for you. You will need to add a subordinating word to one of the sentences to turn it into a dependent clause.

There may be more than one way to rewrite each sentence, as you can see in the example.

Young Titian had great talent in painting. His uncle sent him to study with Giovanni Bellini.

Because young Titian had great talent in painting, his uncle sent him to study with Giovanni Bellini.

OR

Young Titian, whose uncle sent him to study with Giovanni Bellini, had great talent in painting.

Titian began to paint with a marvelous richness of color. His color made his name famous.

The Emperor Charles V was so delighted with Titian's work. He made Titian a knight.

Titian met Michelangelo. The great master looked at his paintings with much interest.

In his famous picture, the Virgin is all alone. She has left her companions behind.

The crowd stands watching her from below. The high priest waits for her above.

Exercise 78C: Diagramming

On your own paper, diagram the following four sentences. Beside each diagram, write the number of vertical lines dividing subjects from predicates, along with the label *S* for simple or *C* for complex.

This is the house Jack built.

The horse and the hound and the horn belonged to the farmer sowing his corn.

There was an old woman who lived in a shoe, who had so many children she didn't know what to do.

She gave them some broth without any bread and whipped them all soundly and put them to bed.

— LESSON 79 —

Compound Sentences
Run-on Sentences
Comma Splice

(The sentences in this lesson are taken from *Pride and Prejudice*, by Jane Austen.)

Bingley had never met with more pleasant people or prettier girls in his life; everybody had been most kind and attentive to him; there had been no formality, no stiffness; he had soon felt acquainted with all the room.

A compound sentence is a sentence with two or more independent clauses.

Everybody was surprised.
Darcy, after looking at her for a moment, turned silently away.

Everybody was surprised, and Darcy, after looking at her for a moment, turned silently away.

A coordinating conjunction joins similar or equal words or groups of words together.
and, or, nor, for, so, but, yet

Run-on sentence

INCORRECT (run-on sentences)
I ran quickly down the road, it was a very long way to the end.
The rabbit leaped out of the bushes, the children watched with eager interest.

CORRECT
I ran quickly down the road, **but** it was a very long way to the end.
The rabbit leaped out of the bushes, **and** the children watched with eager interest.

Comma Splice

Mr. Bennet, you are wanted immediately.

We are all in an uproar.

Mr. Bennet, you are wanted immediately; we are all in an uproar.

colon :
semicolon ;

The envelope contained a sheet of elegant, little, hot-pressed paper, well covered with a lady's fair, flowing hand.

Elizabeth saw her sister's countenance change as she read it.

The envelope contained a sheet of elegant, little, hot-pressed paper, well covered with a lady's fair, flowing hand; and Elizabeth saw her sister's countenance change as she read it.

The independent clauses of a compound sentence must be joined by a comma and a coordinating conjunction, a semicolon, or a semicolon and a coordinating conjunction. They cannot be joined by a comma alone.

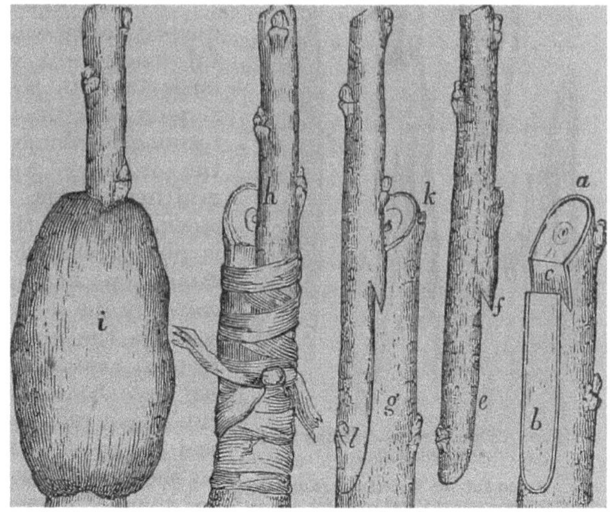

An illustration of splicing from A. J. Downing's 1889 manual *The Fruits and Fruit Trees of America*

Mr. Collins was not agreeable; his society was irksome, and his attachment to her must be imaginary.

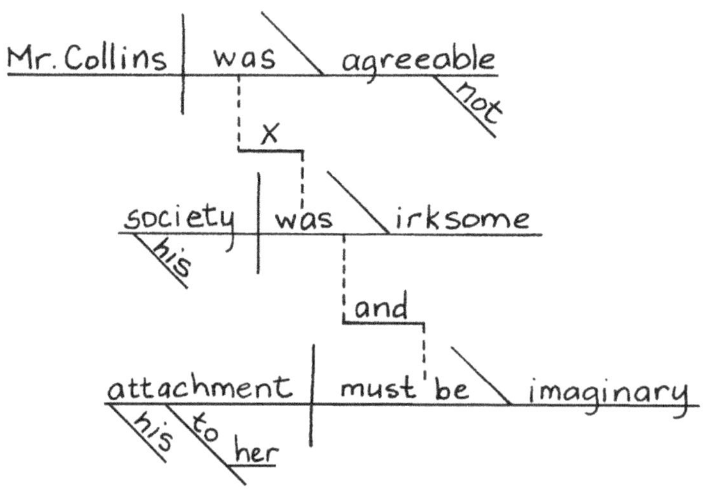

Mr. Collins is a conceited, pompous, narrow-minded, silly man; you know it, and you shall not defend Charlotte Lucas.

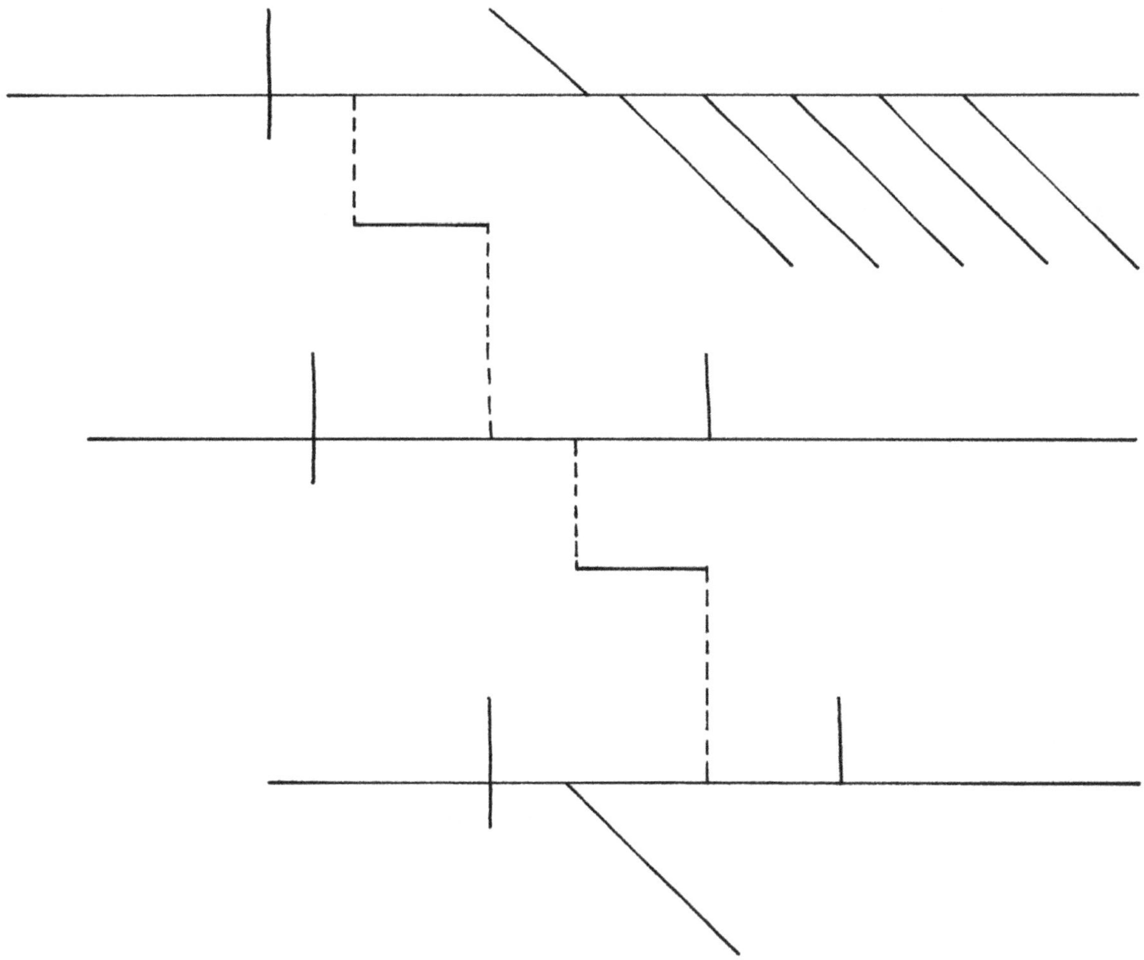

Coordinating Conjunction	Meaning/Function	Example
and	simply *in addition to*	I ran and he ran.
or	presents alternatives	He can teach or his assistant can teach.
nor	presents negative alternatives	He did not work, nor did he sleep.
for	*because*	I sang loudly, for I was happy.
so	showing results	He ate too much, so his stomach hurt.
but	*despite that*	I ran ten miles, but I wasn't tired.
yet	*nevertheless*	I had little money, yet I was content.

Exercise 79A: Forming Compound Sentences

Choose at least one independent clause from Column 1 and at least one independent clause from Column 2. Using correct punctuation and adding coordinating conjunctions as needed, combine the clauses into a compound sentence. (You may use more than two clauses, as long as your sentence makes sense!) Write your new compound sentences on your own paper. Use every clause at least once.

Column 1	Column 2
Master your temper.	The sun blazed down.
There was a strange look in his eyes.	The rains fell.
I might get up early.	It ought to be avoided
The fishermen could not launch their boats.	Treasures sink to the bottom.
It was August.	Your temper will master you.
The winds blew.	He was oddly cheerful.
The floods came.	I might sleep in.
Trash floats on the surface of the water.	The storm was raging fiercely.
The comma splice is a common mistake.	The corn grew green and thick.

Exercise 79B: Correcting Run-on Sentences (Comma Splices)

Using proofreader's marks (^ to insert a coordinating conjunction, ^, to insert a comma, ^; to insert a semicolon), correct each of the run-on sentences below.

The British Empire had to give up its colonies, the colony of Singapore needed to become an independent nation.

At the beginning of the 20th century, 72 percent of Singapore's population was Chinese the rest of its residents were primarily Indian, Arab, European, and British.

In 1909 Singapore belonged to the Straits Settlements colony, Penang and Malacca were in this colony as well.

During World War II, the Imperial Japanese occupied Singapore, after the Surrender of Japan the British claimed Singapore again.

In 1948, the Communist Party of Malaya tried to take over Singapore by force this caused a state of emergency lasting for twelve years.

In 1965 Singapore became independent as the Republic of Singapore it ruled itself from that point on.

British armed forces remained in Singapore until 1971, the Republic had to build up its own defenses after that.

Exercise 79C: Diagramming

On your own paper, diagram every word of the following sentences from *Mr. Popper's Penguins*, by Richard and Florence Atwater.

He was spattered here and there with paint and calcimine, and there were bits of wallpaper clinging to his hair and whiskers, for he was rather an untidy man.

I have painted all of the kitchens in Stillwater; I have papered all of the rooms in the new apartment building on Elm Street.

It will be nice to have you at home, but it is a little difficult to sweep with a man sitting around reading.

From the depths of the packing case, he suddenly heard a faint "Ork," and his heart stood still.

— LESSON 80 —

Compound Sentences

Compound-Complex Sentences
Clauses with Understood Elements

The rabbit jumped, and the lion roared, and the giraffe ambled.

The boy **who had the tickets** boarded the train, but his brother decided to hail a taxi instead; their mother knew **that they would both arrive home by bedtime.**

A compound-complex sentence is made up of two or more independent clauses, at least one of which is a complex sentence.

He was the proudest, most disagreeable man in the world, and everybody hoped that he would never come there again.

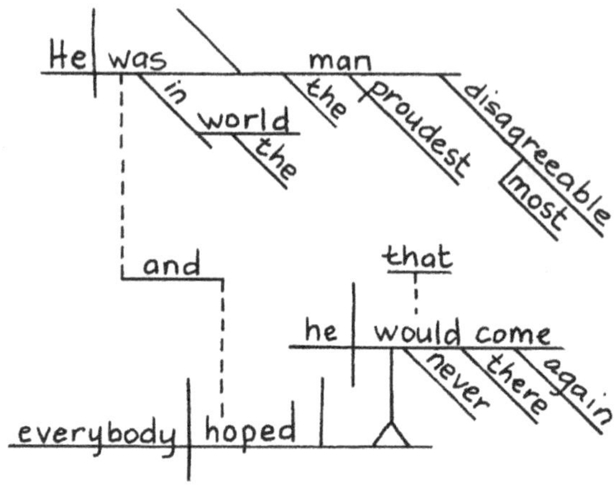

She could not recover from the surprise of what had happened; it was impossible to think of anything else; and, totally indisposed for employment, she resolved, soon after breakfast, to indulge herself in air and exercise.

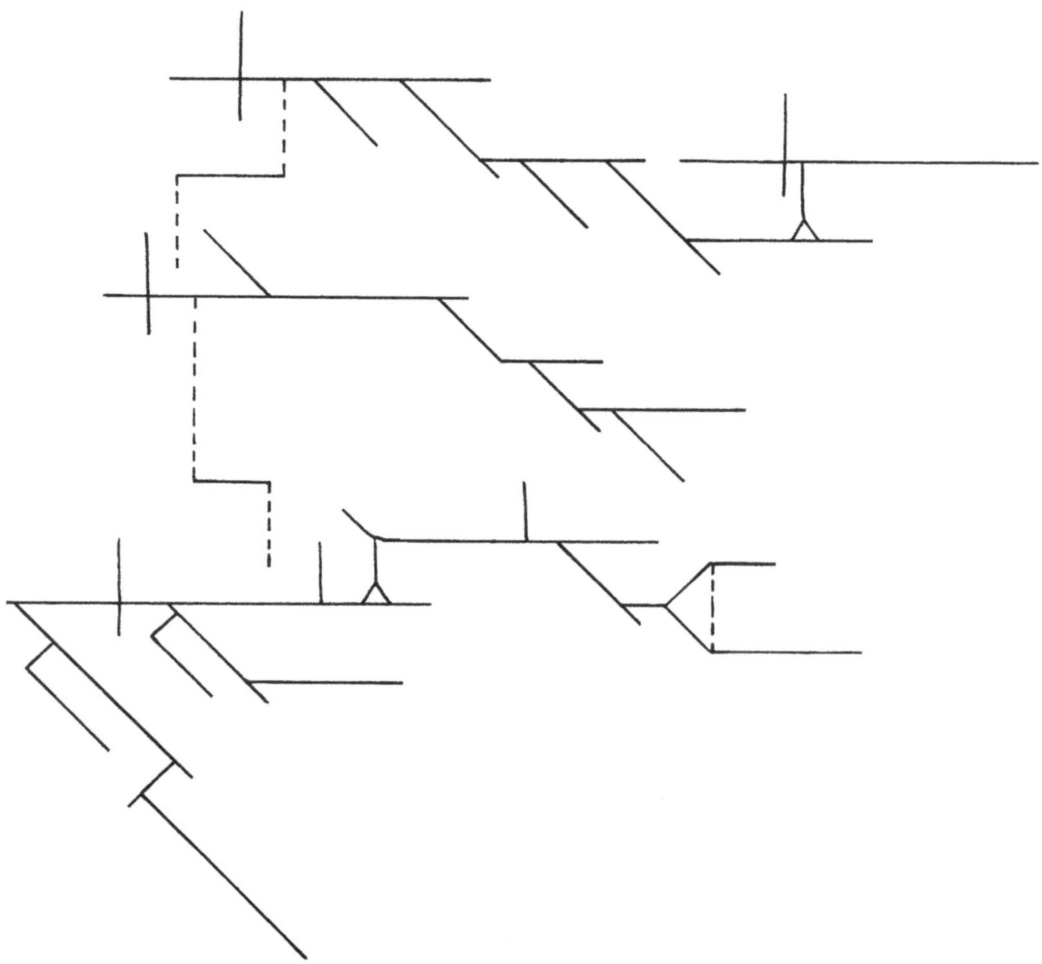

That was the weirdest thing I have ever seen.

The apples I bought yesterday had just been picked.

The speech he made was short and powerful.

He is vain, and you know he is not a sensible man.

He was at the same time haughty, reserved, and fastidious, and his manners, although well-bred, were not inviting.

The situation that troubled her remained the same, her peace equally disturbed by the circumstances.

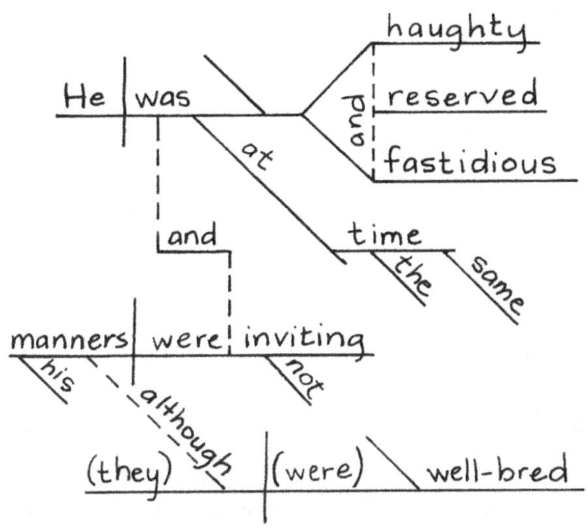

Exercise 80A: Analyzing Complex-Compound Sentences

The sentences below are all complex-compound sentences. For each sentence, carry out the following steps:

a) Cross out each prepositional phrase.

b) Circle any dependent clauses. Label them as *ADJ, ADV,* or *NOUN.* Draw a line from adjective and adverb clauses to the word modified. Label noun clauses with the part of the sentence that they function as.

c) Underline the subject of each independent clause once and the predicate twice.

d) Draw a vertical line between each simple and/or complex sentence.

e) Insert missing words (if any).

The first sentence has been done for you.

These sentences are taken from Isabel F. Hapgood's English translation of the complete five-volume novel *Les Miserables*, by Victor Hugo.

ADJ

Jean Valjean's mother had died ~~of a milk fever~~, (which had not been properly attended to;) | his father, a tree-pruner, ~~like himself~~, had been killed ~~by a fall from a tree~~.

Maubert Isabeau, the baker on the Church Square at Faverolles, was preparing to go to bed, when he heard a violent blow on the grated front of his shop; he arrived in time to see an arm passed through a hole made by a blow from a fist, through the grating and the glass.

While the bolt of his iron collar was being riveted behind his head with heavy blows from the hammer, he wept; his tears stifled him; they impeded his speech.

Then still sobbing, he raised his right hand and lowered it gradually seven times, as though he were touching in succession seven heads of unequal heights, and from this gesture they divined that the thing which he had done, whatever it was, was done for the sake of clothing and nourishing seven little children.

He admitted that he had committed an extreme and blameworthy act; the loaf of bread would probably not have been refused to him had he asked for it; in any case, it would have been better to wait until he could get it through compassion or through work.

From suffering to suffering, he had gradually arrived at the conviction that life is a war; and in this war, he was the conquered.

Exercise 80B: Constructing Complex-Compound Sentences

From each set of independent clauses, construct a single complex-compound sentence. You may turn any of the clauses into dependent clauses by adding subordinating words, insert any other words necessary, omit unnecessary words, and make any other needed changes, but try to keep the original meaning of each clause. You must use every clause in the set!

You may turn a clause into a prepositional phrase or another form, as long as your resulting sentence has at least two independent clauses and one dependent clause and contains all of the information in the listed clauses.

Write your new sentences on your own paper.

The first has been done for you.

We usually go to bed.
It is ten o'clock at night.
It is dark and cold outside.
We usually eat pie in the evening.
We usually go to bed when it is ten o'clock and dark and cold at night, but first we eat pie.
OR
When it is ten-o'clock at night and dark and cold outside, we eat pie and then go to bed.

The two boys sat on the beach.
The beach was at Sapzurro.
They could see through the clear green water to the white sand below.
The October afternoon was hot.
They sat in the shade of a clump of wax palms.

Benjamin Franklin discovered electricity.
He invented the lightning rod.
He wrote down thirteen virtues.
Order, silence, justice, and temperance were four of the virtues.

He wanted these virtues to become his habits.
He kept a little book to record his daily habits.

Frozen raindrops collide with each other and create an electrical charge.
The electrical charge travels to the ground.
We call this charge "lightning."
Lightning creates a sound wave behind it.
We call this sound wave "thunder."
Light waves travel faster than sound waves.
We see the lightning before we hear the thunder.

Tacos de papas are tacos filled with mashed potatoes.
The potatoes can be russet potatoes with butter and cumin.
They could be sweet potatoes with jalapeno peppers and red onions.
The tacos can be vegetarian.
They can also contain chorizo.
Spanish chorizo is sausage made from minced pork, smoked paprika, salt, and sometimes garlic.
Mexican chorizo is made from ground meat.
That ground meat can be pork, or beef, turkey, or venison.

Exercise 80C: Diagramming

On your own paper, diagram the following epigrams. (Epigram: a short clever saying)

I have found you an argument; I am not obliged to find you an understanding.
—Samuel Johnson

A tart temper never mellows with age; and a sharp tongue is the only edged tool that grows keener with constant use.
—Washington Irving

All actual heroes are essential men; and all men, possible heroes.
—Elizabeth Barrett Browning

Improve yourself by other men's writings, thus attaining easily what they acquired through great difficulty.
—Socrates (translated by Michael R. Burch)

WEEK 21

Conditions

— LESSON 81 —

Helping Verbs
Tense and Voice
Modal Verbs

Helping Verbs
am, is, are, was, were
be, being, been
have, has, had
do, does, did
shall, will, should, would, may, might, must
can, could

In a sentence with an active verb, the subject performs the action.
In a sentence with a passive verb, the subject receives the action.

The progressive past tense uses the helping verbs *was* and *were*.
The progressive past passive voice uses the helping verbs *was/were being.*
The progressive present tense uses the helping verbs *am, is,* and *are*.
The progressive present passive voice uses the helping verbs *is/are being.*
The progressive future tense uses the helping verbs *will* and *be*.
The progressive future passive voice uses the helping verbs *will be being.*

Perfect past verbs describe an action that was finished in the past before another action began.
The active voice uses the helping verb *had.*
The passive voice uses the helping verbs *had been.*
Perfect present verbs describe an action that was completed before the present moment.
The active voice uses the helping verb *have.*
The passive voice uses the helping verbs *has/have been.*
Perfect future verbs describe an action that will be finished in the future before another action begins.
The active voice uses the helping verb *will have.*
The passive voice uses the helping verbs *will have been.*

NOTE: *Shall and will are different forms of the same verb.*

I do not believe in aliens.

He does not believe in aliens.

We did not believe in aliens (until they landed).

Do you believe in aliens?
Does he believe in aliens?
Did we believe in aliens (after they landed)?

I do too believe in aliens!
He does believe in aliens!
We did believe in aliens (once they had landed)!

Use the helping verbs *do, does,* and *did* to form negatives, ask questions, and provide emphasis.

	SIMPLE PRESENT		SIMPLE PRESENT EMPHATIC	
First person	I believe	we believe	I do believe	we do believe
Second person	you believe	you believe	you do believe	you do believe
Third person	he, she, it believes	they believe	he, she, it does believe	they do believe

	SIMPLE PAST		SIMPLE PAST EMPHATIC	
First person	I believed	we believed	I did believe	we did believe
Second person	you believed	you believed	you did believe	you did believe
Third person	he, she, it believed	they believed	he, she, it did believe	they did believe

We should be prepared for the arrival of alien spacecraft.
On earth, a Martian would weigh three times more than on Mars.
Strange creatures may visit Earth in our lifetime.
Alien invaders might want to conquer us.
The arrival of aliens must change our world.
We can scarcely imagine what that change will be.
We could find out that the aliens are friendly.

Modal verbs express situations that have not actually happened.
would, can, could, may, might: **possibility**
must, should: **obligation**
may: **permission**
can: **ability**

I would love to go eat a huge cheeseburger.
I can either sleep or eat.

I could probably finish my work by supper.
I may go down to the hamburger stand on the boardwalk.
I might get a burger with onions and Swiss cheese.

I must stop eating this cheeseburger!
I really should eat more vegetables.

Yes, you may eat that burger!

I can exercise self-control!

SIMPLE PRESENT MODAL

First person	I could eat	we could eat
Second person	you could eat	you could eat
Third person	he could eat	they could eat

PERFECT PRESENT MODAL

First person	I should have eaten	we should have eaten
Second person	you should have eaten	you should have eaten
Third person	she should have eaten	they should have eaten

I should've finished my work early; I could've finished it, if I'd had peace and quiet; I would've finished it, if everyone hadn't kept interrupting me.

Exercise 81A: Using *Do, Does*, and *Did*

On your own paper, rewrite each sentence, putting it into the form described in brackets. Use the appropriate form of the helping verb along with any interrogatives or negatives necessary. Don't forget that you may have to change the form of the verb! The first one is done for you.

These sentences are taken from Jack Finney's *Invasion of the Body Snatchers.*

You heard of the Mattoon Maniac. [Change into a question.]

Did you hear of the Mattoon Maniac?

It happens. [Provide emphasis.]

I knew how to answer him. [Turn into a negative statement.]

A psychology instructor told me about an odd personality change. [Provide emphasis.]

I know how much noise I made. [Turn into a negative statement.]

We prefer the weird and thrilling to the dull and commonplace. [Provide emphasis.]

They drifted through space. [Provide emphasis.]

This street looks dead. [Change into a question.]

This incredible alien life form "thinks" this or "knows" it. [Change into a question.]

You know he isn't really Ira any more. [Change into a question.]

Exercise 81B: Modal Verbs

Fill in the blanks below with an appropriate helping verb (*should, would, may, might, must, can, could*) to form a modal verb. There may be more than one correct answer for each sentence. Use each helping verb at least once.

These sentences are taken from John Wyndham's wonderful novel *The Day of the Triffids.* After you finish the exercise, be sure to read the original sentences in the *Answer Key.*

Fires and weather ______________ have worked on it; it ______________ be visibly dead and abandoned. But now, at a distance, it ______________ still masquerade as a living city.

It was evident that most of the foraging parties ______________ have returned by this hour.

______________ we spend our time in prolonging misery when we believe that there is no chance of saving people in the end?

We ______________ do as he says. We ______________ show some, though only some, of these people where there is food. We ______________ do that for a few days, maybe for a few weeks, but after that—what?

I can't help feeling that there ______________ be something wrong about anything that starts with shooting.

Triffid stems do not snap—but they ______________ be mangled.

Some of us ______________ be feeling that it is the end of everything. It is not. But to all of you I will say at once that it ______________ be the end of everything—if we let it.

Any suspicion of illness ______________ be reported at once, since the effects of a contagious disease among us ______________ be serious.

Granted that they do have intelligence, then that ______________ leave us with only one important superiority—sight.

I couldn't get away from the feeling that they ______________ indeed be rattling out secret messages to one another.

Exercise 81C: Verb Tense and Voice

For each sentence below, underline each verb phrase (in both dependent and independent clauses), and identify the tense and voice of the verb. For state-of-being verbs, which are neither active nor passive in voice, identify the tense and write *state-of-being.* Mark modal verbs as *perfect past* or *simple present.* The first sentence is done for you.

These sentences are taken from H. G. Wells's classic science fiction novel *The War of the Worlds.* Some have been slightly condensed.

Simple Past Active (shouted); Progressive Present Active (is coming)

"Death!" I shouted. "Death is coming! Death!"

All night long the Martians were hammering and stirring, sleepless, indefatigable, at work upon the machines they were making ready, and ever and again a puff of greenish-white smoke whirled up to the starlit sky.

I wrenched the horse's head hard round to the right, and in another moment the dog-cart had heeled over upon the horse; the shafts smashed noisily and I was flung sideways and fell heavily into a shallow pool of water.

Lots will be worried by a sort of feeling that something is terribly wrong.

When his eyes were clear again, he saw the monster had passed and was rushing landward.

Beyond that, the tower of Shepperton Church—it has been replaced by a spire—rose above the trees.

If I had fully realized the meaning of all the things I had seen, I should have immediately worked my way back to rejoin my wife.

The thread of life that has begun here will have streamed out to our sister planet.

Across the immensity of space, the Martians have watched the fate of these pioneers of theirs, and perhaps on the planet Venus they have found a securer settlement.

I do not think that nearly enough attention is being given to the possibility of another attack from the Martians.

Presently the Martians will be coming this way again.

— LESSON 82 —

Conditional Sentences
The Condition Clause
The Consequence Clause

(The following sentences are from *The Phantom Tollbooth,* by Norton Juster.)

If you have any more questions, please ask the giant.

If one is right, then ten are ten times as right.

If you are not perfectly satisfied, your wasted time will be refunded.

A condition is a circumstance that restricts, limits, or modifies.

Snow only falls when three conditions are met: the temperature up high is freezing, the temperature at ground level is freezing, and there are water droplets in the air.

A condition clause describes a circumstance that has not yet happened.
A consequence clause describes the results that will take place if the condition clause happens.

Unless it gets warmer, I will stay inside.

I will not go for a walk if it remains this cold.

When the temperature reaches 70 degrees, I will go outside.

Should it rain, I will not come.

Had he been fired, he could have left immediately.

Refuse my conditions, and I will become your enemy!

A conditional sentence expresses the conditions under which an action may take place. It contains a condition clause and a consequence clause.

CONDITION CONSEQUENCE
If you have any more questions, please ask the giant. ____________________

CONDITION CONSEQUENCE
If one is right, then ten are ten times as right. ____________________

CONDITION CONSEQUENCE
If you are not perfectly satisfied, your wasted time will be refunded. ____________________

First conditional sentences express circumstances that might actually happen.

The predicate of the condition clause is in a ________________________ tense.

The predicate of the consequence clause is an ________________________ or is in a

________________________ or ________________________ tense.

If only Rhyme and Reason were here, things would improve.

If you walked as fast as possible and looked at nothing but your shoes, you would arrive at your destination more quickly.

Second conditional sentences express circumstances that are contrary to reality.

The predicate of the condition clause is in a ________________________ tense.

The predicate of the consequence clause is in the ________________________ tense.

Modal verbs express situations that have not actually happened.

Simple Present

I would improve	We would improve
You would improve	You would improve
He would improve	They would improve

Perfect Past

I could have arrived	We could have arrived
You could have arrived	You could have arrived
She could have arrived	They could have arrived

If we had told you then, you might not have gone.

If the kingdom had been divided equally, both sons would now rule as kings.

Third conditional sentences express past circumstances that never happened.

The predicate of the condition clause is in the ________________________ tense.

The predicate of the consequence clause is in the ________________________ or

________________________ tense.

Exercise 82A: Identifying Conditional Sentences

Some of the sentences in this exercise are conditional sentences—and others are not! Identify each conditional sentence by writing a *C* in the margin. For each conditional sentence, label the clauses as *condition* or *consequence.*

Although he was small and helpless, the mouse was a wise little creature.

If he did not find a place to hide, he would serve as dinner to the great owl.

And if he went within reach of the cat's claws, he would suffer for it.

As he thought and thought, his eyes grew brighter.

"As long as I am near the cat, the owl will not dare to come after me."

"While we have never been friends, dear cat, I have always considered you a noble enemy."

"If you will promise never to do me any harm, I will nibble through the string around your neck and set you free."

Although the mouse pretended to nibble the string, he took care not to bite it through.

He knew that she would eat him up unless he took great care.

Exercise 82B: Tense in Conditional Sentences

Fill in each blank below with the correct tense and form of the verb in brackets. Some sentences may have more than one possible correct answer.

First Conditional Sentences

If my sister __________ [*see*] me eating her candy, I __________ [state-of-being verb] in big trouble.

If he __________ [state-of-being verb] late, __________ [*go*] without him.

If that small child __________ [*eat*] too much, she __________ [state-of-being verb] sick.

If I __________ [*find*] the book, I __________ [*send*] it to you.

Unless the patient __________ [*stop*] smoking, he __________ [*become*] very ill.

If she ______________ [*follow*] my advice about those investments, she __________ [state-of-being verb] a very rich woman.

Second Conditional Sentences

If I __________ [*know*] what to do, I __________ [*do*] it.

If I __________ [*break*] my leg, I __________ not __________ [*run*] the marathon.

If I ______________ [*have*] the book, I ________________ [*send*] it to you.

If the patient __________ [*stop*] smoking, he __________ [*feel*] much better.

Third Conditional Sentences

If I __________ [*know*] what would happen, I __________ never __________ [*eat*] the apple.

If the policeman __________ [warn] her about the consequences, she ____________________ [*behave*] differently.

If I ________________ [*try*] to run a better campaign, I ________________ [state-of-being verb] President now.

If I __________ [*have*] the book, I ________________ [*send*] it to you.

If the patient __________ [*stop*] smoking, he __________ not __________ [*cough*] so much now.

__________ she __________ [*follow*] my advice about those investments, she __________ [state-of-being verb] a rich woman today.

Exercise 82C: Diagramming

On your own paper, diagram these sentences, taken from J. R. R. Tolkien's *The Hobbit.* A conditional clause should be diagrammed like any other dependent clause.

Goblins do not usually venture very far from their mountains, unless they are driven out and are looking for new homes, or are marching to war.

You would have dropped him, if a goblin had suddenly grabbed your legs from behind in the dark, tripped up your feet, and kicked you in the back!

That only makes eleven and not fourteen, unless wizards count differently than other people.

— LESSON 83 —

Conditional Sentences
The Subjunctive

First conditional sentences express circumstances that might actually happen.
The predicate of the condition clause is in a present tense.
The predicate of the consequence clause is in an imperative, present, or future tense.

If we surrender and I return with you, will you promise not to hurt this man?

So bow down to her if you want, bow to her.

If she is otherwise when I find her, I shall be very put out.

Unless I am wrong (and I am never wrong), they are headed dead into the fire swamp.

Second conditional sentences express circumstances that are contrary to reality.
The predicate of the condition clause is in a past tense.
The predicate of the consequence clause is in the simple present modal tense.

I would not say such things if I were you!

If I had a month to plan, maybe I could come up with something.

If we only had a wheelbarrow, that would be something.

Third conditional sentences express past circumstances that never happened.
The predicate of the condition clause is in the perfect past tense.
The predicate of the consequence clause is in the perfect present modal or simple present modal tense.

But they would have killed Westley, if I hadn't done it.

CONTRARY TO FACT	FACT
If we surrender	We surrender.
If you want	We want.
If she is	She is.
If I were	I was.
If we had	We had.

Subjunctive verbs express situations that are unreal, wished for, or uncertain.
Indicative verbs affirm or declare what actually is.

I eat gingerbread men.

If I eat too many gingerbread men, I will not want any dinner.

The three little pigs build houses.

If the three little pigs build straw houses, the wolf will blow them all down.

INDICATIVE SIMPLE PAST		
First person	I was	we were
Second person	you were	you were
Third person	he, she, it was	they were

SUBJUNCTIVE SIMPLE PAST		
First person	I were	we were
Second person	you were	you were
Third person	he, she, it were	they were

CORRECT	I would not say such things if I were you!
INCORRECT	I would not say such things if I was you!

CORRECT	I was cold.
CORRECT	If I were cold, I would put on a hat.
INCORRECT	If I was cold, I would put on a hat.

He was smart.

If he __________ smart, he would go immediately.

I insist that she leave the door open.

I recommend that he arrive early.

The professor asked that the student read out loud.

	INDICATIVE SIMPLE PRESENT		**SUBJUNCTIVE SIMPLE PRESENT**	
First person	I leave	we leave	I leave	we leave
Second person	you leave	you leave	you leave	you leave
Third person	he, she, it leaves	they leave	he, she, it leave	they leave

It is vital that a lifeguard _____________ the children swim. [subjunctive present of *watch*]

The lifeguard ______________________ the children swim. [indicative present of *watch*]

The woman demanded that the mechanic ___________ her car. [subjunctive present of *fix*]

The mechanic __________________ her car. [indicative present of *fix*]

My mother suggested that my sister _____________ to bed early. [subjunctive present of *go*]

My sister ________________ to bed early. [indicative present of *go*]

Exercise 83A: Subjunctive Forms in Song Lyrics

Fill in each blank with the correct state-of-being verb.

If I __________ a rich man, all day long I'd biddy biddy bum.

If I __________ a wealthy man, I wouldn't have to work hard.

If I __________ rich, I'd have the time that I lack to sit in the synagogue and pray.
—From the musical *Fiddler on the Roof*

If I __________ a swan, I'd be gone.

If I __________ a train, I'd be late again.

And if I __________ a good man, I'd talk with you more often than I do.
—From the Pink Floyd song "If"

If I __________ a carpenter, and you __________ a lady, would you marry me anyway?

If a miller __________ my trade, at a mill wheel grinding, would you miss your colour box?
—From the Tim Hardin song "If I Were a Carpenter"

If she __________ only mine, I would build a house so fine.

She __________ as pretty as a queen.
—From the bluegrass song "Lulu Walls"

Exercise 83B: Subjunctive Forms in Complex Sentences

In each pair of verb forms, cross out the incorrect form.

It (seem / seems) now as if my stomach (were / was) as empty as a rich man's brain.
The cook insisted that she (try / tries) the cuttlefish dish.
The doctor recommended that he (sits / sit) out the next game.
He made a proposal that the committee (buys / buy) more supplies.
The boy wished that he (were / was) there to join the meal.
If I (were / was) like you I could scale the wall.
The general (were / was) determined that the invasion (remain / remains) secret.
She demanded that he (leave / leaves) at once.
It was / were essential that he (saves / save) enough money for college.
It is vital that everyone (enter / enters) before the curtain rises.
The architect (was / were) anxious that his client (see / sees) the new building plans.
If he (was / were) president of Mars, he could (make / makes) laws for all the Martians.

— LESSON 84 —

Conditional Sentences
The Subjunctive
Moods of Verbs
Subjunctive Forms Using *Be*

Tense
A simple verb simply tells whether an action takes place in the past, present, or future.
A progressive verb describes an ongoing or continuous action.

A perfect verb describes an action which has been completed before another action takes place.

The air was bracing, yet with a cold edge which made the travelers grateful for the cloaks

Medwyn had given them.

Voice

In a sentence with an active verb, the subject performs the action.

In a sentence with a passive verb, the subject receives the action.

It is not given to men to know the ends of their journeys.

Mood

Indicative verbs express real actions.

Subjunctive verbs express unreal actions.

Imperative verbs express intended actions.

Modal verbs express possible actions.

"Drink," the stranger said again, while Taran took the flask dubiously. "You look as

though I were trying to poison you."

There can be no victory over the Cauldron-Born, but with luck, we can hold.

First conditional sentences express circumstances that might actually happen.
The predicate of the condition clause is in a present tense.
The predicate of the consequence clause is an imperative, present, or future tense.

Unless I am wrong (and I am never wrong), they are headed dead into the fire swamp.

Second conditional sentences express circumstances that are contrary to reality.
The predicate of the condition clause is in a past tense.
The predicate of the consequence clause is in the simple present modal tense.

If we only had a wheelbarrow, that would be something.

Third conditional sentences express past circumstances that never happened.
The predicate of the condition clause is in the perfect past tense.
The predicate of the consequence clause is in the perfect present modal or simple present modal tense.

But they would have killed Westley, if I hadn't done it.

SIMPLE PAST INDICATIVE
He left me behind.

SIMPLE PAST SUBJUNCTIVE SIMPLE PRESENT MODAL
If he left me behind, I would feel quite upset.

	INDICATIVE PRESENT (SIMPLE)		SUBJUNCTIVE PRESENT (SIMPLE)	
First person	I leave	we leave	I leave	we leave
Second person	you leave	you leave	you leave	you leave
Third person	he, she, it leaves	they leave	he, she, it leave	they leave

INDICATIVE He leaves at noon.
SUBJUNCTIVE It's important that he leave at noon.

	INDICATIVE PAST (SIMPLE)		SUBJUNCTIVE PAST (SIMPLE)	
First person	I was	we were	I were	we were
Second person	you were	you were	you were	you were
Third person	he, she, it was	they were	he, she, it were	they were

SIMPLE PRESENT MODAL PAST SUBJUNCTIVE
I would not say such things if I were you!

SIMPLE PRESENT INDICATIVE SIMPLE PAST SUBJUNCTIVE
CORRECT You look as though I were trying to poison you.

SIMPLE PRESENT INDICATIVE SIMPLE PAST INDICATIVE
INCORRECT You look as though I was trying to poison you.

I wish he were here.

A trace of a smile appeared on his face, as though he were savoring something pleasant.

	INDICATIVE PRESENT (SIMPLE)		SUBJUNCTIVE PRESENT (SIMPLE)	
First person	I am	we are	I be	we be
Second person	you are	you are	you be	you be
Third person	he, she, it is	they are	he, she, it be	they be

INDICATIVE — I am well-organized.
SUBJUNCTIVE — My job requires that I be well-organized.

INDICATIVE — You are on time.
SUBJUNCTIVE — I strongly suggest that you be on time.
SUBJUNCTIVE/MODAL — Tomorrow, you should be on time.

He suggested that she be given a new task.

The captain ordered that the anchor be lifted.

It is vital that we all be properly prepared.

The present passive subjunctive is formed by pairing *be* with the *past participle* of a verb.

enjoy ______________________
juggle ______________________
plan ______________________
roast ______________________

Exercise 84A: Parsing Verbs

Underline each predicate, in both main clauses and dependent clauses. Above each, write the tense, voice, and mood of the verb.

Tenses: Simple past, present, future; progressive past, present, future; perfect past, present, future
Voice: Active, passive (or state-of-being)
Mood: Indicative, subjunctive, imperative, modal, subjunctive/modal

These sentences are taken from Lloyd Alexander's novel *The High King,* the final book in the *Chronicles of Prydain* series.

The socket from which the dragon's crest had been torn was lined with flat stones, and in it, as in a narrow grave, lay Dyrnwyn, the black sword.

You have learned much, but learn this last and hardest of lessons.

Oh, if I were a giant again, you'd not find me lingering!

If any life be staked against Arawn Death-Lord, it must be mine.

They'll have no stomach for a fight now.

Huge blocks of ice thundered down the slope, bounding and rolling as if they had been no more than pebbles.

Mount up behind the King of Mona, if he can stand your company, and be quick about it.

This is the most terrible thing that has ever happened.

Taran had already dismounted and was racing down the slope, waving at the bard to follow him.

Exercise 84B: Forming Subjunctives

Fill in the blanks in the following sentences with the correct verb form indicated in brackets.

I ______________ [simple present indicative of *wish*] that my brother ______________ [simple past subjunctive of *am*] here.

The judge's decision ______________ [simple past indicative of *am*] that the driver ______________ [simple present passive subjunctive of *fine*] five hundred dollars.

If he ______________ [simple present passive subjunctive/modal of *convict*] of reckless driving, he ______________ [simple future indicative of *lose*] his license.

If the earth ______________ [simple past subjunctive of *am*] flat, adventurers ______________ [perfect present modal of *am*] unable to sail all the way around it.

Far ______________ [simple present subjunctive of *am*] it from me to question your motives!

If my boss ______________ [simple past subjunctive of *am*] unhappy with my performance, he ________________________ [perfect present modal of *say*] so.

If only he ___________________ [perfect past subjunctive of *determine*] to overcome his difficulties!

______________ [simple past subjunctive of *am*] he to ask me to marry him,

I _____________________ [simple present modal of *refuse*].

It _____________________ [perfect present subjunctive of *am*] better to avoid the conversation altogether.

Exercise 84C: Diagramming

On your own paper, diagram the following sentences.

These are the first three sentences from the chapter "Shadows" in Lloyd Alexander's *The Castle of Llyr.*

The feast that evening was surely the merriest the castle had ever seen. Kaw, perched on the back of Taran's chair, bobbed up and down and looked as if the banquet had been arranged entirely in his honour. King Rhuddlum beamed with good spirits; the talk and laughter of the guests rang through the Great Hall.

— REVIEW 7 —

Weeks 19-21

Topics
Phrases and Clauses
Adjective, Adverb, and Noun Clauses
Pronouns
Mood: Modal, Subjective, Imperative, Indicative
Conditional Sentences

Review 7A: Improving Sentences with Phrases

In the blanks below, supply phrases that meet the descriptions in brackets. You may supply more than one phrase in any blank, as long as at least one phrase fulfills the requirements (often, additional prepositional phrases may be needed). The first is done for you, with explanations provided.

The original sentences are taken from John Knowles's classic 1959 novel *A Separate Peace*. This is a challenging assignment—prepare to spend some time on it!

When you are finished, compare your sentences with the originals in the *Answer Key*.

[adverbial prepositional phrase answering the question *where*] [adjectival present participle phrase modifying *anyone*]

I had rarely seen anyone go __________, or anyone ____________ or even an open window.

[adverbial prepositional phrase answering the question *where*] [adjectival present participle phrase modifying *anyone*]

I had rarely seen anyone go into one of them*, or anyone* playing on a lawn *or even an open window.*

EXPLANATION: The phrase modifies the verb *go* and tells us where *anyone* is going. Although Knowles could have written "into the houses" (a single prepositional phrase), he chose to put two phrases together ("into one" + "of them").

EXPLANATION: The present participle *playing* describes what *anyone* is doing. Knowles has written a present participle phrase that includes a prepositional phrase ("on a lawn"). He could have written "playing happily" or another phrase containing *only* the participle and modifiers.

[adjectival prepositional phrase describing the houses; preposition should have a compound object]

Today ____ the houses looked both more elegant and more lifeless than ever.

[adverbial prepositional phrase answering the question *where*]

__________________________________ I reached a marble foyer and stopped

[adverbial prepositional phrase answering the question *where*]

____.

[adjectival prepositional phrase describing the wind] [adverbial prepositional phrase answering the question *when*]

__________________ the wind flung wet gusts at me; __________________

[adjectival present participle phrase describing *fool*] [adjectival infinitive phrase describing *fool*]

I would have felt like a fool __________, only __________________

[adverbial prepositional phrase answering the question *where*] [adverbial subordinate clause answering the question *when*]

A little fog hung __________ so that __________ I felt myself becoming isolated from everything __________.

[adjectival prepositional phrase describing *everything*]

[adjectival present participle phrase describing *trees*]

There were several trees __________.

[adjectival infinitive phrase describing *head*] [adjectival prepositional phrase describing *sounds*]

My head began __________, and the vague rustling sounds ______________ came to me ______________.

[adverbial prepositional phrase answering the question *how* (manner)]

[present participle phrase acting as a noun and serving as the direct object of *risk*]

I would have to spring far out or risk ______________.

[adjectival past participle phrase describing *radio*]

Our illegal radio, ______________, was broadcasting the news.

Review 7B: Improving Sentences with Clauses

Rewrite each sentence on your own paper, adding a dependent clause that meets the description in brackets. The first is done for you, with explanations provided.

The original sentences are taken from *A Christmas Carol*, by Charles Dickens. When you are finished, compare your sentences with the originals in the *Answer Key*.

[noun clause serving as the predicate nominative, renaming *doubt*]

There is no doubt that Marley was dead.

[The subject of the sentence is *doubt*; the linking verb *is* connects the subject to the clause explaining what the *doubt* is. *There* and *no* are adverbs modifying *is*.]

This must be distinctly understood, or nothing wonderful can come of the story

[adjective clause describing *story*]

____________________________________.

Scrooge had a very small fire, but the clerk's fire was so very much smaller

[adverb clause describing *how* much smaller]

____________________________________.

[adjective clause describing *shops*]

The brightness of the shops ____

[adverb clause telling *when*]

made pale faces ruddy ______________________.

[adjective clause describing *chambers*]

He lived in chambers ____.

[adjective phrase describing *noise*]

They were succeeded by a clanking noise, deep down below, ____________________.

[noun clause serving as the object of the infinitive *to have heard*]

Scrooge then remembered to have heard _____________________________________.

Review 7C: Conditional Clauses

Label the following sentences as first, second, or third conditional by writing *1*, *2*, or *3* in the blank next to each one. Underline each conditional clause. Circle each consequence clause.

These sentences are taken from *The Hobbit*, by J. R. R. Tolkien.

I'll cook beautifully for you, a perfectly beautiful breakfast for you, if only you won't have me for supper. ________

If we don't get blown off, or drowned, or struck by lightning, we shall be picked up by some giant and kicked sky-high for a football. ________

If their plan had been carried out, there would have been none left there next day; all would have been killed except the few the goblins kept from the wolves and carried back as prisoners to their caves. ________

Bilbo began to feel there really was something of a bold adventurer about himself after all, though he would have felt a lot bolder still if there had been anything to eat. ________

Now scuttle off, and come back quick, if all is well. ________

If precious asks, and it doesn't answer, we eats it, my precious. ________

They all thought their own shares in the treasure (which they quite regarded as theirs, in spite of their plight and the still unconquered dragon) would suffer seriously if the Wood-elves claimed part of it, and they all trusted Bilbo. ________

Yet if they had known more about it and considered the meaning of the hunt and the white deer that had appeared upon their path, they would have known that they were at last drawing towards the eastern edge, and would soon have come, if they could have kept up their courage and their hope, to thinner trees and places where the sunlight came again. ________

Review 7D: Pronoun Review

The following paragraphs are taken from Russian fairy tales. Circle every pronoun. Label each as personal (*PER*), possessive (*POSS*), reflexive (*REF*), demonstrative (*DEM*), or indefinite (*IND*). Beside this label, add the abbreviation for the part of the sentence (or clause) that the pronoun serves as: adjective (*ADJ*), subject (*SUBJ*), direct object (*DO*), indirect object (*IO*), or object of the preposition (*OP*).

The first has been done for you.

POSS/ADJ

On (her) deathbed the merchant's wife called her little daughter to her, took out from under the bed-clothes a doll, gave it to her, and said, "Listen, Vasilissa, dear; remember and obey these last words of mine. I am going to die. And now, together with my parental blessing, I bequeath to you this doll. Never show it to anybody; and whenever any misfortune comes upon you, give the doll food, and ask its advice. If you do this, it will tell you a cure for your troubles." Then the mother kissed her child and died.

This time there was no help for it; Prince Ivan had to confess everything, and then he took to entreating the Sun's Sister to let him go, that he might satisfy himself about his old home. So at last he persuaded her, and she let him go away to find out about his home. But first she provided him for the journey with a brush, a comb, and two youth-giving apples. However old anyone might be, if he should eat one of these apples, he would grow young again in an instant.

Review 7E: Parsing

In the sentences below, underline every verb or verb phrase that acts as the predicate of a clause (dependent or independent). Label each verb with the correct tense, voice, and mood.

> **Tenses:** Simple past, present, future; progressive past, present, future; perfect past, present, future
> **Voice:** Active, passive, or state-of-being
> **Mood:** Indicative, subjunctive, imperative, modal, subjunctive/modal

The first is done for you.

These sentences are taken from Tom Holland's history *Persian Fire*.

simple present, active, modal — simple past, state-of-being, indicative — simple past, active, indicative

While Darius would soon prove himself as bold as he was ruthless, he was never one to flaunt his crimes.

His calculations had been precise.

A rare opportunity was indeed now opening.

If the assassination squad could ambush him on open ground, somewhere on the road between Ecbatana and the heartland of royal power in Persia, then he might be dispatched with relative ease.

Horses, white horses, covered the plain—as many as 160,000 of them, it was said.

What happened next would be retold by all those who traced their lineage from the seven leaders of the assassination squad.

The wretch who weaves deceit will bring death into his country.

From that moment on, the King of Lydia had become the oracle's most generous patron.

If he were one of the greatest men of the kingdom—one of Darius's six co-conspirators, say—then he and his retinue might receive up to a hundred quarts of wine.

If rivals proved obdurate, they were best murdered on the quiet.

Review 7F: Diagramming

On your own paper, diagram every word of the following sentence from J. R. R. Tolkien's *The Fellowship of the Ring.*

And if he often uses the Ring to make himself invisible, he *fades*; he becomes in the end invisible permanently, and walks in the twilight under the eye of the Dark Power that rules the Rings.

WEEK 22

Parenthetical Elements

— LESSON 85 —

Verb Review

INDICATIVE TENSES

SIMPLE		Active	Passive
	Past	he followed he was	he was followed
	Present	he follows he is	he is followed
	Future	he will follow he will be	he will be followed
PROGRESSIVE			
	Past	he was following he was being	he was being followed
	Present	he is following he is being	he is being followed
	Future	he will be following he will be being	he will be being followed
PERFECT			
	Past	he had followed he had been	he had been followed
	Present	he has followed he has been	he has been followed
	Future	he will have followed he will have been	he will have been followed

MODAL TENSES
(would OR should, may, might, must, can, could)

SIMPLE		Active	Passive
	Present	he would follow he would be	
PERFECT			
	Past	he would have followed he would have been	

SUBJUNCTIVE TENSES

SIMPLE		Active	Passive
	Past	he followed he were	
	Present	he follow he be	

Complete the following chart with the third-person-singular form of the verb indicated in the left-hand column. If you need help, ask your instructor.

INDICATIVE TENSES

		Active	Passive
SIMPLE			
attack	Past	[he, she, it]	[he, she, it]
paint	Present	[he, she, it]	[he, she, it]
buy	Future	[he, she, it]	[he, she, it]
PROGRESSIVE			
drink	Past	[he, she, it]	[he, she, it]
forget	Present	[he, she, it]	[he, she, it]
guide	Future	[he, she, it]	[he, she, it]
PERFECT			
embarrass	Past	[he, she, it]	[he, she, it]
interrupt	Present	[he, she, it]	[he, she, it]
scold	Future	[he, she, it]	[he, she, it]

MODAL TENSES
(would OR should, may, might, must, can, could)

		Active	Passive
SIMPLE			
dance	Present	[he, she, it]	
PERFECT			
sleep	Past	[he, she, it]	

SUBJUNCTIVE TENSES

		Active	Passive
SIMPLE			
fall	Past	[he, she, it]	
fall	Present	[he, she, it]	

On your own paper, write sentences that use each of the forms above as the predicate of an independent or dependent clause. If you need help (or ideas), ask your instructor.

— LESSON 86 —

Restrictive and Non-Restrictive Modifying Clauses
Parenthetical Expressions

In after-years Piglet liked to think that he had been in Very Great Danger during the Terrible Flood, but the only danger he had really been in was in the last half-hour of his imprisonment, when Owl, who had just flown up, sat on a branch of his tree to comfort him, and told him a very long story about an aunt who had once laid a seagull's egg by mistake, and the story went on and on, rather like this sentence, until Piglet, who was listening out of his window without much hope, went to sleep quietly and naturally, slipping slowly out of the window towards the water until he was only hanging on by his toes, at which moment luckily a sudden loud squawk from Owl, which was really part of the story, woke Piglet up and just gave him time to jerk himself back into safety and say, "How interesting, and did she?" when—well, you can imagine his joy when at last he saw the good ship *The Brain of Pooh* (Captain, C. Robin; 1st Mate, P. Bear) coming over the sea to rescue him.

—From *Winnie-the-Pooh*, by A. A. Milne

A restrictive modifying clause defines the word that it modifies. Removing the clause changes the essential meaning of the sentence.

A non-restrictive modifying clause describes the word that it modifies. Removing the clause doesn't change the essential meaning of the sentence.

Only non-restrictive clauses should be set off by commas.

Parentheses ( ) can enclose words that are not essential to the sentence.
singular: parenthesis
plural: parentheses

when Owl who had just flown up sat on a branch of his tree to comfort him

until Piglet who was listening out of his window without much hope went to sleep quietly

a sudden loud squawk from Owl which was really part of the story woke Piglet up

Parenthetical expressions often interrupt or are irrelevant to the rest of the sentence.

Punctuation goes inside the parentheses if it applies to the parenthetical material; all other punctuation goes outside the parentheses.

Parenthetical material only begins with a capital letter if it is a complete sentence with ending punctuation.

As soon as he saw his companion fall, the other soldier, with a loud cry, jumped out of the boat on the far side, and he also floundered through the water (which was apparently just in his depth) and disappeared into the woods of the mainland.

If you can swim (as Jill could) a giant bath is a lovely thing.

He had only once been in a ship (and then only as far as the Isle of Wight) and had been horribly seasick.

The cabin was very tiny but bright with painted panels (all birds and beasts and crimson dragons and vines) and spotlessly clean.

From the waist upward he was like a man, but his legs were shaped like a goat's (the hair on them was glossy black) and instead of feet he had goat's hoofs.

Get me a score of men-at-arms, all well mounted, and a score of Talking Dogs, and ten Dwarfs (let them all be fell archers), and a Leopard or so, and Stonefoot the Giant.

Edmund had had no gift, because he was not with them at the time. (This was his own fault, and you can read about it in the other book.)

Because it was such an important occasion they took a candle each (Polly had a good store of these in her cave).

I read the *Chronicles of Narnia* (all seven of them!) in three days.
Did you know that C. S. Lewis wrote the *Chronicles of Narnia* (all seven of them)?
C. S. Lewis and J. R. R. Tolkien were good friends (amazing, isn't it?).

Exercise 86A: Restrictive and Non-Restrictive Modifying Clauses

In the following sentences, mark each bolded clause as either *ADV* for adverb or *ADJ* for adjective, and draw an arrow from the clause back to the word modified. Some sentences contain more than one modifying clause.

Then, identify each bolded modifying clause as either restrictive (*R*) or non-restrictive (*N*).

Finally, set off all of the non-restrictive clauses with commas. Use the proofreader's mark: ^, for comma insertion. When you are finished, compare your punctuation with the original.

These sentences are slightly condensed from Lewis Carroll's *Alice's Adventures in Wonderland.* The original commas around the non-restrictive clauses have been removed.

How funny it'll seem to come out among the people **that walk with their heads downward**!

She found herself in a long, low hall **which was lit up by a row of lamps hanging from the roof.**

Soon her eye fell on a little glass box **that was lying under the table**: she opened it, and found in it a very small cake **on which the words "EAT ME" were beautifully marked in currants**.

Now I'm opening out like the largest telescope **that ever was.**

However, she soon made out that she was in the pool of tears **which she had wept when she was nine feet high.**

They were indeed a queer-looking party **that assembled on the bank**—the birds with draggled feathers, the animals with their fur clinging close to them, and all dripping wet, cross, and uncomfortable.

At last the Mouse **who seemed to be a person of authority among them** called out, "Sit down, all of you, and listen to me! I'll soon make you dry enough!"

William the Conqueror **whose cause was favored by the pope** was soon submitted to by the English **who wanted leaders**.

"I have tasted eggs, certainly," said Alice **who was a very truthful child**.

While she was looking at the place where it had been it suddenly appeared again.

It was very provoking to find that the hedgehog had unrolled itself, and was in the act of crawling away: besides all this, there was generally a ridge or furrow in the way **wherever she wanted to send the hedgehog to.**

Those **whom she sentenced** were taken into custody by the soldiers **who of course had to leave off being arches to do this** so that by the end of half an hour or so there were no arches left, and all the players, except the King, the Queen, and Alice, were in custody and under sentence of execution.

So she stood still **where she was** and waited.

Exercise 86B: Identifying Parenthetical Expressions

Identify each parenthetical expression as a phrase, dependent clause, or sentence.

CHALLENGE EXERCISE

Provide a fuller description of each expression. What kind of phrase, clause, or sentence? What does it do or modify?

When you are finished, ask your instructor for the fuller explanations. Compare your descriptions to these explanations.

She generally gave herself very good advice (though she very seldom followed it), and sometimes she scolded herself so severely as to bring tears into her eyes.

By this time she had found her way into a tidy little room with a table in the window, and on it (as she had hoped) a fan and two or three pairs of tiny white kid gloves.

"Curiouser and curiouser!" cried Alice (she was so much surprised, that for the moment she quite forgot how to speak good English).

"It is a very good height indeed!" said the Caterpillar angrily, rearing itself upright as it spoke (it was exactly three inches high).

"When I'm a Duchess," she said to herself (not in a very hopeful tone though), "I won't have any pepper in my kitchen at all."

As soon as she had made out the proper way of nursing it (which was to twist it up into a sort of knot, and then keep tight hold of its right ear and left foot, so as to prevent its undoing itself), she carried it out into the open air.

They very soon came upon a Gryphon, lying fast asleep in the sun. (If you don't know what a Gryphon is, look at the picture.)

The judge, by the way, was the King; and as he wore his crown over the wig (look at the frontispiece if you want to see how he did it), he did not look at all comfortable, and it was certainly not becoming.

Exercise 86C: Punctuating Sentences with Parenthetical Expressions

Correct each of the following sentences, using the proofreader's marks listed below.

Insert quotation marks:
insert comma:
insert period:
insert question mark:
insert exclamation point:
delete:
move punctuation mark:

If the sentence is correct, write *C* in the margin next to it.

If young writers could learn grammar without a textbook, this workbook wouldn't be necessary (But, to be honest, a few intuitive types do figure it out on their own).

After seven weeks of instruction, the grammar class was frustrated with the teacher's knowledge. (or, to be frank, the lack thereof.)

I looked up the publication information for our grammar book (Harcourt Brace, 2002), but I still don't think that it reflects modern grammar usage.

We checked our grammar book's explanation of parenthetical elements (we all thought it was adequate, if not great) against the explanation in the nineteenth-century grammar book (so hard to read!)

I really do love grammar (and writing.)

Could you bring me a new grammar book quickly? (and cheaply)

That will help me to punctuate parentheses properly (and easily).

It's a simple enough job, if you know exactly what you're saying (and where to put the punctuation)

I've been researching grammar books (crazy hobby, isn't it)? for over a year now.

— LESSON 87 —

Parenthetical Expressions
Dashes

(The sentences in this lesson are from Lewis Carroll's novel *Through the Looking-Glass.)*

A little provoked, she drew back, and after looking everywhere for the queen (whom she spied out at last, a long way off), she thought she would try the plan, this time, of walking in the opposite direction.

There was a Beetle sitting next to the Goat (it was a very queer carriage-full of passengers altogether).

Or—let me see—suppose each punishment was to be going without a dinner; then, when the miserable day came, I should have to go without fifty dinners at once!

I can see all of it when I get upon a chair—all but the bit behind the fireplace.
I can see all of it when I get upon a chair, all but the bit behind the fireplace.

But the beard seemed to melt away as she touched it, and she found herself sitting quietly under a tree—while the Gnat (for that was the insect she had been talking to) was balancing itself on a twig just over her head, and fanning her with its wings.

Parentheses ( ) can enclose words that are not essential to the sentence.
Parenthetical expressions often interrupt or are irrelevant to the rest of the sentence.
Punctuation goes inside the parentheses if it applies to the parenthetical material; all other punctuation goes outside the parentheses.
Parenthetical material only begins with a capital letter if it is a complete sentence with ending punctuation.

Dashes — — can enclose words that are not essential to the sentence.
Dashes can also be used singly to separate parts of a sentence.

I read Lewis Carroll's poem "Jabberwocky" which, I thought, was very weird.
I read Lewis Carroll's poem "Jabberwocky" which—I thought—was very weird.
I read Lewis Carroll's poem "Jabberwocky" which (I thought) was very weird.

Commas make a parenthetical element a part of the sentence.
Dashes emphasize a parenthetical element.
Parentheses minimize a parenthetical element.

1. You can set off parenthetical elements in three different ways.
2. You can turn a dependent clause into a parenthetical element just by putting it inside dashes or parentheses.

3. You can use a dash in place of a comma to emphasize the part of the sentence that follows.

The independent clauses of a compound sentence must be joined by a comma and a coordinating conjunction, a semicolon, or a semicolon and a coordinating conjunction. They cannot be joined by a comma alone.

CORRECT
Alice ventured to taste it, and finding it very nice (it had, in fact, a sort of mixed flavour of cherry tart, custard, pineapple, roast turkey, toffee, and hot buttered toast) she very soon finished it off.

INCORRECT
Alice ventured to taste it, and finding it very nice, it had, in fact, a sort of mixed flavour of cherry tart, custard, pineapple, roast turkey, toffee, and hot buttered toast, she very soon finished it off.

Exercise 87A: Types of Parenthetical Expressions

Identify each parenthetical expression as a phrase, dependent clause, or sentence.

CHALLENGE EXERCISE

- Provide a fuller description of each expression. What kind of phrase, clause, or sentence? What does it do or modify?
- When you are finished, ask your instructor for the fuller explanations. Compare your descriptions to these explanations.

These sentences are taken from *Through the Looking-Glass*, by Lewis Carroll.

"Here are the Red King and the Red Queen," Alice said (in a whisper, for fear of frightening them), "and there are the White King and the White Queen sitting on the edge of the shovel."

"What manner of things?" said the Queen, looking over the book (in which Alice had put "The White Knight is sliding down the poker. He balances very badly"). "That's not a memorandum of your feelings!"

"I should see the garden far better," said Alice to herself, "if I could get to the top of that hill: and here's a path that leads straight to it—at least, no, it doesn't do that—" (after going a few yards along the path, and turning several sharp corners), "but I suppose it will at last."

For a few minutes all went on well, and she was just saying, "I really shall do it this time—" when the path gave a sudden twist and shook itself (as she described it afterwards), and the next moment she found herself actually walking in at the door.

"So young a child," said the gentleman sitting opposite to her (he was dressed in white paper), "ought to know which way she's going, even if she doesn't know her own name!"

"Indeed I shan't!" Alice said rather impatiently. "I don't belong to this railway journey at all—I was in a wood just now—and I wish I could get back there."

"Crawling at your feet," said the Gnat (Alice drew her feet back in some alarm), "you may observe a Bread-and-Butterfly. Its wings are thin slices of bread-and-butter, its body is a crust, and its head is a lump of sugar."

"I mean to get under the—under the—under this, you know!" putting her hand on the trunk of the tree.

"If I wasn't real," Alice said—half-laughing through her tears, it all seemed so ridiculous—"I shouldn't be able to cry."

Exercise 87B: Punctuating Parenthetical Expressions

On either side of each bolded parenthetical expression, place parentheses, dashes, or commas. There are not necessarily *correct* answers for these, but compare them to the originals when you have finished.

These sentences are taken from *The Strange Case of Dr. Jekyll and Mr. Hyde*, by Robert Louis Stevenson.

I met with one accident which as it brought on no consequence I shall no more than mention.

Poole admitted the visitor as he spoke into a large, low-roofed, comfortable hall, paved with flags, warmed after the fashion of a country house by a bright, open fire, and furnished with costly cabinets of oak.

He felt what was rare with him a nausea and distaste of life.

A good picture hung upon the walls, a gift as Utterson supposed from Henry Jekyll, who was much of a connoisseur.

I was struck besides with the shocking expression of his face, with his remarkable combination of great muscular activity and great apparent debility of constitution, and last but not least with the odd, subjective disturbance caused by his neighbourhood.

I believe his murderer for what purpose, God alone can tell is still lurking in his victim's room.

Evil I fear would come evil was sure to come of that connection.

He began to go wrong wrong in mind though of course I continue to take an interest in him for old sake's sake as they say.

The fellow had a key, and what's more he has it still.

The smile withered from his face happily for him yet more happily for myself, for in another instant I had certainly dragged him from his perch.

This then is the last time short of a miracle that Henry Jekyll can think his own thoughts or see his own face now how sadly altered! in the glass.

He was small and very plainly dressed, and the look of him even at that distance went somehow strongly against the watcher's inclination.

And then all of a sudden he broke out in a great flame of anger, stamping with his foot, brandishing the cane, and carrying on as the maid described it like a madman.

Exercise 87C: Using Dashes for Emphasis

On your own paper, rewrite the next four sentences, substituting dashes for the underlined punctuation marks and making any other capitalization or punctuation changes needed.

These sentences are taken from *White Fang*, by Jack London.

They did not go far (a couple of days' journey).

Running at the forefront of the pack was a large grey wolf, one of its several leaders.

He had bred true to the straight wolf-stock. In fact, he had bred true to old One Eye himself, with but a single exception, and that was he had two eyes to his father's one.

So to him the entrance of the cave was a wall, a wall of light.

— LESSON 88 —

Parenthetical Expressions
Dashes
Diagramming Parenthetical Expressions

We met the new neighbors today, who, we think, are very pleasant people.
It was a glorious morning—a cool, sunny, sweet-scented morning.
The chef decided to put liver, which was one of his favorites, on the dinner menu.
The liver (which most diners didn't order) was cooked with onions and red wine.

Recognizing Parenthetical Elements

Dashes and parentheses always turn a clause or phrase into a parenthetical element—even if there's actually a grammatical relationship between the clause or phrase and the rest of the sentence.

If a clause or phrase is set off by commas, but doesn't have a clear grammatical relationship to the rest of the sentence, it is parenthetical.

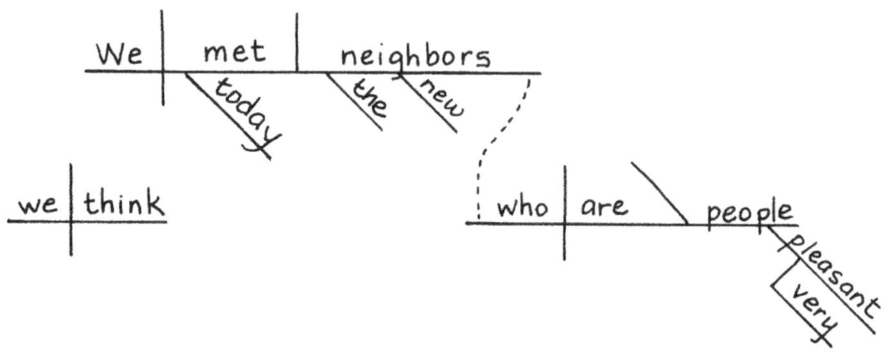

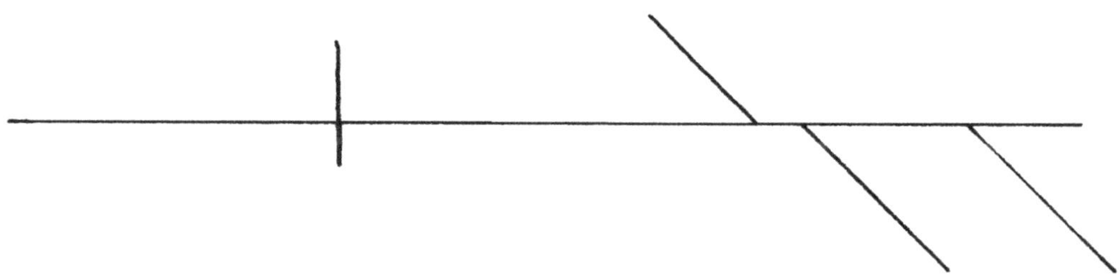

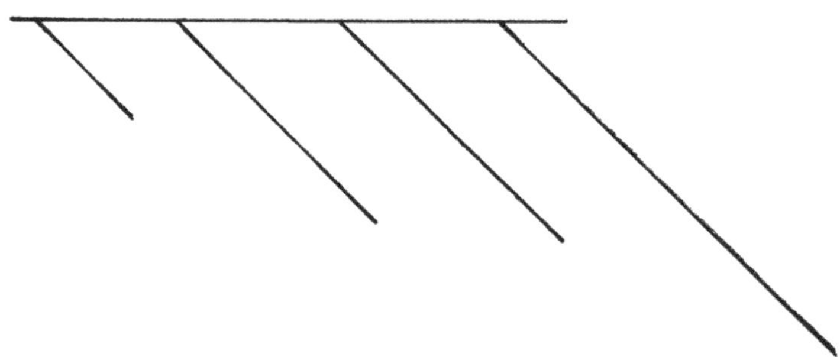

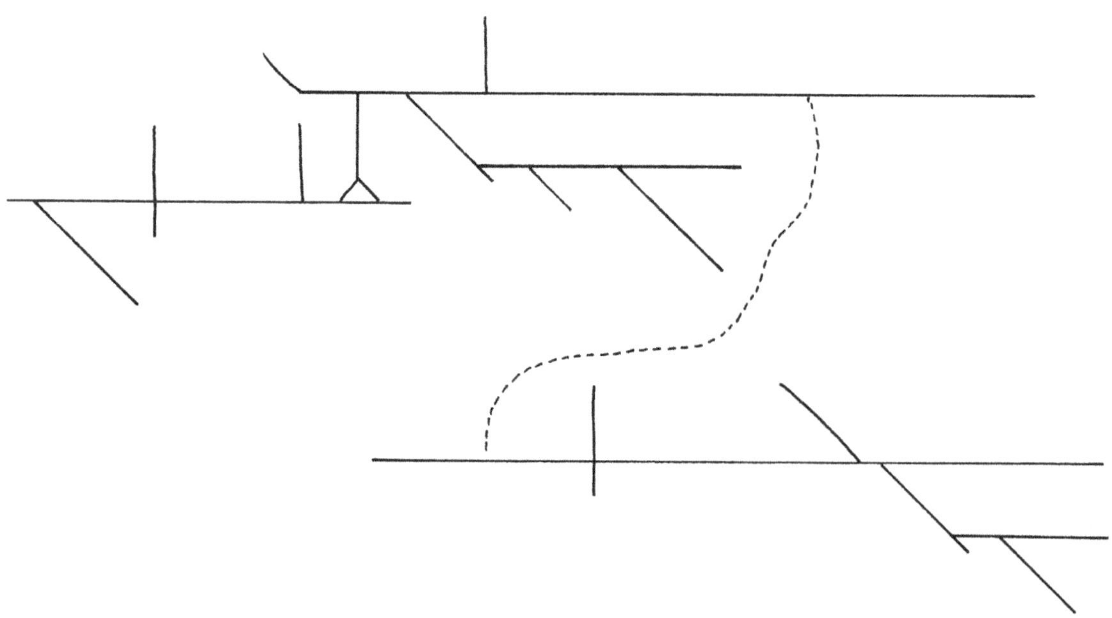

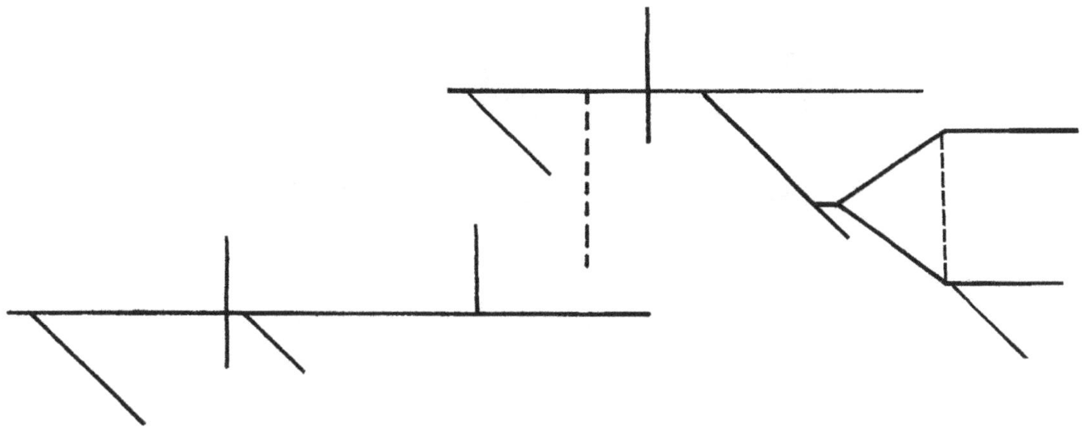

The train—can you believe it?—was on time (a rare and happy occurrence!).

Exercise 88A: Diagramming Parenthetical Expressions

On your own paper, diagram each of the following sentences.

The following sentences are slightly condensed from O. Henry's classic short story "The Gift of the Magi."

Quietness and value—Jim and the chain had quietness and value.

He was only twenty-two—with a family of his own!

There lay the Combs—the combs that Della had seen in a shop window and loved for a long time.

The magi, as you know, were wise men—wonderfully wise men—who brought gifts to the newborn Christ-child.

The following sentences are slightly condensed from *A Christmas Carol*, by Charles Dickens.

Marley's chain was made (for Scrooge observed it closely) of cash-boxes, keys, padlocks, ledgers, deeds, and heavy purses wrought in steel.

The clerk, with the long ends of his white comforter dangling below his waist (for he boasted no greatcoat), went down a slide on Cornhill.

Mrs. Cratchit made the gravy (ready beforehand in a little saucepan) hissing hot.

There was a little saucepan of gruel (Scrooge had a cold in his head) upon the hob.

WEEK 23

Dialogue and Quotations

— LESSON 89 —

Dialogue

"I'm sorry, Ender," Valentine whispered. She was looking at the band-aid on his neck.

Ender touched the wall and the door closed behind him. "I don't care. I'm glad it's gone."

"What's gone?" Peter walked into the parlor, chewing on a mouthful of bread and peanut butter.

Ender did not see Peter as the beautiful ten-year-old boy that grown-ups saw, with dark, thick, tousled hair and a face that could have belonged to Alexander the Great. Ender looked at Peter only to detect anger or boredom, the dangerous moods that almost always led to pain. Now as Peter's eyes discovered the band-aid on his neck, the telltale flicker of anger appeared.

Valentine saw it too. "Now he's like us," she said, trying to soothe him before he had time to strike.

—From *Ender's Game*, by Orson Scott Card

Dialogue: the actual words characters speak
Narrative: the rest of the story

Dialogue is set off by quotation marks.

A dialogue tag identifies the person making the speech.
When a dialogue tag comes after a speech, place a comma, exclamation point, or question mark inside the closing quotation marks.

"I ate the cookie," my brother said.
"I ate seventeen cookies!" my brother exclaimed.
"Do you think I'll be sick?" my brother asked.

INCORRECT:
"I ate the cookie." My brother said.

When a dialogue tag comes before a speech, place a comma after the tag. Put the dialogue's final punctuation mark inside the closing quotation marks.

My brother said, "I ate the cookie."

My brother exclaimed, "I ate seventeen cookies!"

My brother asked, "Do you think I'll be sick?"

Speeches do not need to be attached to a dialogue tag as long as the text clearly indicates the speaker.

"I've watched through his eyes, I've listened through his ears, and I tell you he's the one. Or at least as close as we're going to get."

"That's what you said about the brother."

"The brother tested out impossible. For other reasons. Nothing to do with his ability."

"Same with the sister. And there are doubts about him. He's too malleable. Too willing to submerge himself in someone else's will."

"Not if the other person is his enemy."

"So what do we do? Surround him with enemies all the time?"

"If we have to."

—From *Ender's Game*, by Orson Scott Card

Usually, a new paragraph begins with each new speaker.

CORRECT:
"I'm not afraid to say what I think," George retorted. "I wish you could be honest too."
"I'm not afraid to say what I think," George retorted, "whether or not you like it."

INCORRECT (Run-on sentence):
"I'm not afraid to say what I think," George retorted, "I wish you could be honest too."

INCORRECT (Ends with a sentence fragment):
"I'm not afraid to say what I think," George retorted. "Whether or not you like it."

When a dialogue tag comes in the middle of a speech, follow it with a comma if the following dialogue is an incomplete sentence. Follow it with a period if the following dialogue is a complete sentence.

Exercise 89A: Punctuating Dialogue

The excerpt below is from H. G. Wells's classic science fiction novel *The Time Machine.* All of the dialogue is missing quotation marks, and some of it is missing ending punctuation as well. Do your best to supply the missing punctuation marks.

When you are finished, compare your version with the original.

I took my eyes off the Time Traveller's face, and looked round at his audience. The Medical Man seemed absorbed in the contemplation of our host. The Editor was looking hard at the end of his cigar—the sixth. The Journalist fumbled for his watch. The others, as far as I remember, were motionless.

The Editor stood up with a sigh. What a pity it is you're not a writer of stories he said, putting his hand on the Time Traveller's shoulder.

You don't believe it?

Well—

I thought not. The Time Traveller turned to us. Where are the matches he said.

He lit one and spoke over his pipe, puffing. To tell you the truth . . . I hardly believe it myself . . . And yet—

His eye fell with a mute inquiry upon the withered white flowers upon the little table. Then he turned over the hand holding his pipe, and I saw he was looking at some half-healed scars on his knuckles.

The Medical Man rose, came to the lamp, and examined the flowers. The blooms are very odd he said. The Psychologist leant forward to see, holding out his hand for a specimen.

I'm hanged if it isn't a quarter to one said the Journalist.

How shall we get home

Plenty of cabs at the station said the Psychologist.

It's a curious thing said the Medical Man but I certainly don't know the natural order of these flowers. May I have them

The Time Traveller hesitated. Then suddenly he said Certainly not

Where did you really get them said the Medical Man.

The Time Traveller put his hand to his head. He spoke like one who was trying to keep hold of an idea that eluded him. They were put into my pocket when I travelled into Time. He stared round the room. I can feel that it is all going. This room and you and the atmosphere of every day is too much for my memory. Did I ever make a Time Machine, or a model of a Time Machine? Or is it all only a dream? They say life is a dream, a precious poor dream at times—but I can't stand another that won't fit. It's madness. And where did the dream come from? . . . I must look at that machine. If there is one!

He caught up the lamp swiftly, and carried it, flaring red, through the door into the corridor. We followed him. There in the flickering light of the lamp was the machine sure enough, squat, ugly, and askew; a thing of brass, ebony, ivory, and translucent glimmering quartz. Solid to the touch—for I put out my hand and felt the rail of it—and with brown spots and smears upon the ivory, and bits of grass and moss upon the lower parts, and one rail bent awry.

The Time Traveller put the lamp down on the bench, and ran his hand along the damaged rail. It's all right now he said. The story I told you was true. I'm sorry to have brought you out here in the cold.

He took up the lamp, and, in an absolute silence, we returned to the smoking-room.

Exercise 89B: Writing Dialogue Correctly

On your own paper, rewrite the following sentences as dialogue, using the past tense for the dialogue tags. Use the notations in parentheses to help you.

You may choose to place dialogue tags before, in the middle, or after dialogue, or to leave the tags out completely. But you must have at least one sentence with a dialogue tag that comes before, at least one sentence with a dialogue tag that comes after, at least one speech with the dialogue tag in the middle, and at least one speech with no dialogue tag at all.

When you are finished, compare your answers with the original. The first is done for you.

Sentences are taken from *Anne of Green Gables*, by Lucy Maud Montgomery.

(Anne asks) What am I to call you? Shall I always say Miss Cuthbert? Can I call you Aunt Marilla?

(Marilla answers) No; you'll call me just plain Marilla. I'm not used to being called Miss Cuthbert and it would make me nervous.

(Ann protests) It sounds awfully disrespectful to just say Marilla.

(Marilla says) I guess there'll be nothing disrespectful in it if you're careful to speak respectfully. Everybody, young and old, in Avonlea calls me Marilla except the minister.

(Anne says, wistfully) I'd love to call you Aunt Marilla. I've never had an aunt or any relation at all—not even a grandmother. It would make me feel as if I really belonged to you. Can't I call you Aunt Marilla?

(Marilla says) No. I'm not your aunt and I don't believe in calling people names that don't belong to them.

(Anne says) But we could imagine you were my aunt.

(Marilla says, grimly) I couldn't.

(Anne says, wide-eyed) Do you never imagine things different from what they really are?

(Marilla says) No.

(Anne says, drawing a long breath) Oh! Oh, Miss—Marilla, how much you miss!

(Marilla retorts) I don't believe in imagining things different from what they really are.

First answer:

"What am I to call you?" asked Anne. "Shall I always say Miss Cuthbert? Can I call you Aunt Marilla?"

Exercise 89C: Proofreading

Using the following proofreader's marks, correct these incorrect sentences. They are from the O. Henry short story "The Ransom of Red Chief."

insert quotation marks:	insert comma:
insert period:	insert question mark:
insert exclamation point:	delete:
move punctuation mark:	

"Hey, little boy!" says Bill, "Would you like to have a bag of candy and a nice ride"?

The boy catches Bill neatly in the eye with a piece of brick.

"That will cost the old man an extra five hundred dollars", says Bill, climbing over the wheel.

"What you getting up so soon for, Sam" asked Bill.

"Me?" says I, "Oh, I got a kind of a pain in my shoulder. I thought sitting up would rest it."

"You're a liar" says Bill! "You're afraid. You was to be burned at sunrise, and you was afraid he'd do it. And he would, too, if he could find a match. Ain't it awful, Sam? Do you think anybody will pay out money to get a little imp like that back home?"

"Sure." said I "A rowdy kid like that is just the kind that parents dote on. Now, you and the Chief get up and cook breakfast, while I go up on the top of this mountain and reconnoiter."

— LESSON 90 —

Dialogue

Direct Quotations

The stranger said, "I have come far seeking Mali and have found great wealth here. But I must tell your king that great wealth that the world has not seen is worth less to your children's children than a rumor of water to a people dying of thirst."

The elders wondered silently about this stranger who presumed to lecture the king of Mali, but they were much too polite to say anything that might make a guest feel less than welcome.

"You will have to go to Niani, the capital city, to speak with the *mansa*—that is, the king—of Mali," said Musa Weree, with a smile that seemed to mask a secret.

But the stranger showed no interest in Niani. "The king has heard me!" he said.

—From *Mansa Musa: The Lion of Mali*, by Khephra Burns

During the two months he remained in Mali, Ibn Battuta paid grudging respect to the safety and justice of the kingdom: "A traveler may proceed alone among them, without the least fear of a thief or robber," he noted.

In Sulayman's twenty-four years on the throne, Mali remained firmly under his authority. Sulayman surrounded himself with the trappings of an emperor: gold arms and armor; ranks of courtiers and Turkish mamluks, warrior slaves bought from Egypt, surrounding him. They were required to keep solemn and attentive in his presence: "Whoever sneezes while the king is holding court," al-'Umari explains, "is severely beaten."

—From *The History of the Renaissance World*, by Susan Wise Bauer

Dialogue: the exact words of a speaker
Direct quotation: the exact words of a writer

Dialogue tags attach dialogue to a speaker.
Attribution tags attach direct quotations to a writer.

When an attribution tag comes after a direct quote, place a comma, exclamation point, or question mark inside the closing quotation marks.

"Many ships sank that day," the chronicler wrote.
"Seventeen ships sank that day!" the chronicler lamented.
"Who can say how many lives were lost?" the chronicler mourned.

INCORRECT:
"Many ships sank that day." The chronicler wrote.

When an attribution tag comes before a direct quote, place a comma after the tag. Put the dialogue's final punctuation mark inside the closing quotation marks.

According to the chronicler, "Many ships sank that day."
The chronicler tells us, "Seventeen ships sank that day!"
One witness asked, "Who can say how many lives were lost?"

When an attribution tag comes in the middle of a direct quotation, follow it with a comma if the remaining quote is an incomplete sentence. Follow it with a period if the remaining quote is a complete sentence.

"Many ships," the chronicler tells us, "sank that day."
"Seventeen ships sank that day," the chronicler tells us. "Who can say how many lives were lost?"

Speeches do not need to be attached to a dialogue tag as long as the text clearly indicates the speaker.

Every direct quote must have an attribution tag.

CORRECT:

> The soldiers chased Yazdegerd north into the province of Kirman, but the Arab army was caught in a blizzard and froze. "The snow reached the height of a lance," al-Tabari says. Only the commander, one soldier, and a slave girl survived, the latter because her owner slit open the stomach of a camel and packed her inside it to keep her warm.
>
> —*The History of the Medieval World*, by Susan Wise Bauer

INCORRECT:

> The soldiers chased Yazdegerd north into the province of Kirman, but the Arab army was caught in a blizzard and froze. "The snow reached the height of a lance." Only the commander, one soldier, and a slave girl survived, the latter because her owner slit open the stomach of a camel and packed her inside it to keep her warm.

Exercise 90A: Punctuating Dialogue

The six sentences below, from E. B. White's *The Trumpet of the Swan,* are missing punctuation. Write in all of the missing punctuation marks (insert them directly rather than using proofreader's marks). When you are finished, compare your answers to the original.

One evening a few weeks later, when the cygnets were asleep, the swan said to the cob Have you noticed anything different about one of our children, the one we call Louis

Different replied the cob In what way is Louis different from his brothers and sisters? Louis looks all right to me. He is growing well; he swims and dives beautifully. He eats well. He will soon have his flight feathers

Oh, he looks all right said the swan. And heaven knows he eats enough. He's healthy and bright and a great swimmer. But have you ever heard Louis make any sound, as the others do? Have you ever heard him use his voice or say anything? Have you ever heard him utter a single beep or a single burble

Come to think of it, I never have replied the cob, who was beginning to look worried.

Have you ever heard Louis say good night to us, as the others do? Have you ever heard him say good morning, as the others do in their charming little way, burbling and beeping

Now that you mention it, I never have said the cob Goodness! What are you getting at?

Exercise 90B: Punctuating Direct Quotations

Write in all of the missing punctuation marks (insert them directly rather than using proofreader's marks). When you are finished, compare your answers to the original sentences.

Pinney concludes with the observation There is little reason to make the swan an unclean animal.

As a young woman, Goodall liked to go along her English river where she saw water birds, moor hens, kingfishers, and swans The swans were a bit scary she says especially when they had a nest or babies, because then they are sometimes aggressive. I knew one man who once had his leg broken when an angry swan, thinking he was after one of her babies, attacked him.

While on a hunting expedition on rivers of Missouri and Kentucky, Audubon writes of the Trumpeter To form a perfect conception of the beauty and elegance of these Swans, you must observe them when they are not aware of your proximity.

Waterfowl migration according to Simpson and Day is very apparent in the Northern Hemisphere where vast numbers leave northern breeding areas, moving south to warmer regions along fairly defined flyways.

—Alice L. Price, *Swans of the World: In Nature, History, Myth and Art*

A garden dung-heap recommends Mr. Baily overgrown with artichokes, mallows, and other weeds, is an excellent cover for chickens, especially in hot weather.

There is no sort of insect notes Mr. Dickson which fowls will not eat. They are exceedingly fond of flies, beetles, grasshoppers, and crickets, but more particularly of every sort of grub, caterpillar, and maggot.

Mr. Baily adds Do not give fowls meat, but always have the bones thrown out to them after dinner; they enjoy picking them, and perform the operation perfectly.

We never ourselves now attempt to assist a chick from the shell explains Mr. Wright.

—Hugh Piper, *Poultry: A Practical Guide*

Exercise 90C: Attribution Tags

In the following paragraphs, adapted from the classic nineteenth-century animal guide *Beeton's Book of Poultry and Domestic Animals*, find and underline the direct quotes that are missing their attribution tags. When you are finished, ask your instructor to check your work.

Then, compare the paragraphs with the originals found in the *Answer Key*. Circle each attribution tag in the *Answer Key*.

It is essential that the keepers of Dorkings must provide a good long run for the chickens. If this is carefully done, the Dorkings will thrive and grow well. There are two species: the white and the colored. White Dorkings are the favorite of many poultry raisers. "They lay well, and are excellent sitters and mothers." However, the colored Dorking is also a handsome bird.

The fantail pigeon is the most elegant of all the pigeons. It is pure white with a long, delicately curved neck, so long that at times the bird's head will nestle among the tail feathers. The fantail pigeon is also known by other names. One of the most successful pigeon breeders calls it a *broad-tailed shaker.* "They are called shakers," he writes, "because they constantly shake their heads up and down; broad-tailed, from the great number of feathers they have in their tails."

The limbs of the Manx cat are gaunt, its fur close-set, its eyes staring and restless, and it possesses no tail. As one cat-fancier says, "A black Manx cat, with its staring eyes and its stump of a tail, is an almost unearthly looking beast." The Angol cat, on the other hand, is one of the most beautiful of cats, with long and silky fur, and a remarkably full and brush-like tail.

George Henry Lewes has furnished us with some curious facts about the tail of the tadpole. If it is cut off, the tail will continue to live for several days, and not only live but grow. "I have kept tails alive for up to eleven days, and they not only grow, but twist about with a rapid swimming movement when irritated." However, when the tails reach the point when they require circulation of blood for their further development, they die.

The Dhole, or Kholsun, is a wild dog living in the depths of the Indian jungles. Like other wild dogs, it forms packs and hunts down game. The dhole is a brave dog, and has no fear even of the terrible tiger. "From the observations which have been made, hardly any animal, with the exception of the elephant and the rhinoceros, can cope with the dhole." Only the leopard is safe, because the dogs cannot follow their spotted quarry into the tree branches.

The Rocky Mountain squirrel lurks, bat-like, in the gloom of the pine forests during the day, and becomes active at night. The Australian physician and naturalist George Bennet says, "Their flying membrane is a folding of the skin along either side, clothed by a dense fur, enabling the squirrel to take leaps of almost incredible extent." Flying squirrels are also found in Sri Lanka and in India.

— LESSON 91 —

Direct Quotations
Ellipses
Partial Quotations

> A few clouds of dust moving to and fro signify that the army is encamping. Humble words and increased preparations are signs that the enemy is about to advance. Violent language and driving forward as if to the attack are signs that he will retreat. When the light chariots come out first and take up a position on the wings, it is a sign that the enemy is forming for battle. Peace proposals unaccompanied by a sworn covenant indicate a plot. When there is much running about and the soldiers fall into rank, it means that the critical moment has come. When some are seen advancing and some retreating, it is a lure.
>
> —Sun Tzu, *The Art of War*, trans. Lionel Giles

> The good general not only deceives the enemy himself, but assumes that his enemy is always deceiving him: "Humble words and increased preparations are signs that the enemy is about to advance," Sun Tzu explains. "Violent language and driving forward as if to the attack are signs that he will retreat . . . Peace proposals unaccompanied by a sworn covenant indicate a plot." Both Confucius and Sun-Tzu, roughly contemporary as they are, offer a philosophy of order, a way of dealing with a disunified country; stability through the proper performance of social duties, or stability through intimidation.
>
> —Susan Wise Bauer, *The History of the Ancient World*

Ellipses show where something has been cut out of a sentence.

élleipsis Greek for "omission"
ellipsis (singular), ellipses (plural)

The Roman historian Varro mentions an early division of Rome's people into three "tribes" of some kind.

The attackers were thoroughly thrashed, since the army of debtors that came

charging out to meet them was, as Livy puts it, "spoiling for a fight."

The present participle of a verb can act as a descriptive adjective.

The city needed laws "which every individual citizen could feel that he had . . .

consented to accept."

Every direct quote must have an attribution tag.
A second or third quote from the same source does not need another attribution tag, as long as context makes the source of the quote clear.

A clause is a group of words that contains a subject and a predicate.
A dependent clause is a fragment that cannot stand by itself as a sentence.
Dependent clauses begin with subordinating words.
Dependent clauses are also known as subordinate clauses.

Adjective clauses are also known as relative clauses because they relate to another word in the independent clause.
Relative pronouns introduce adjective clauses and refer back to an antecedent in the independent clause.
A noun clause takes the place of a noun.

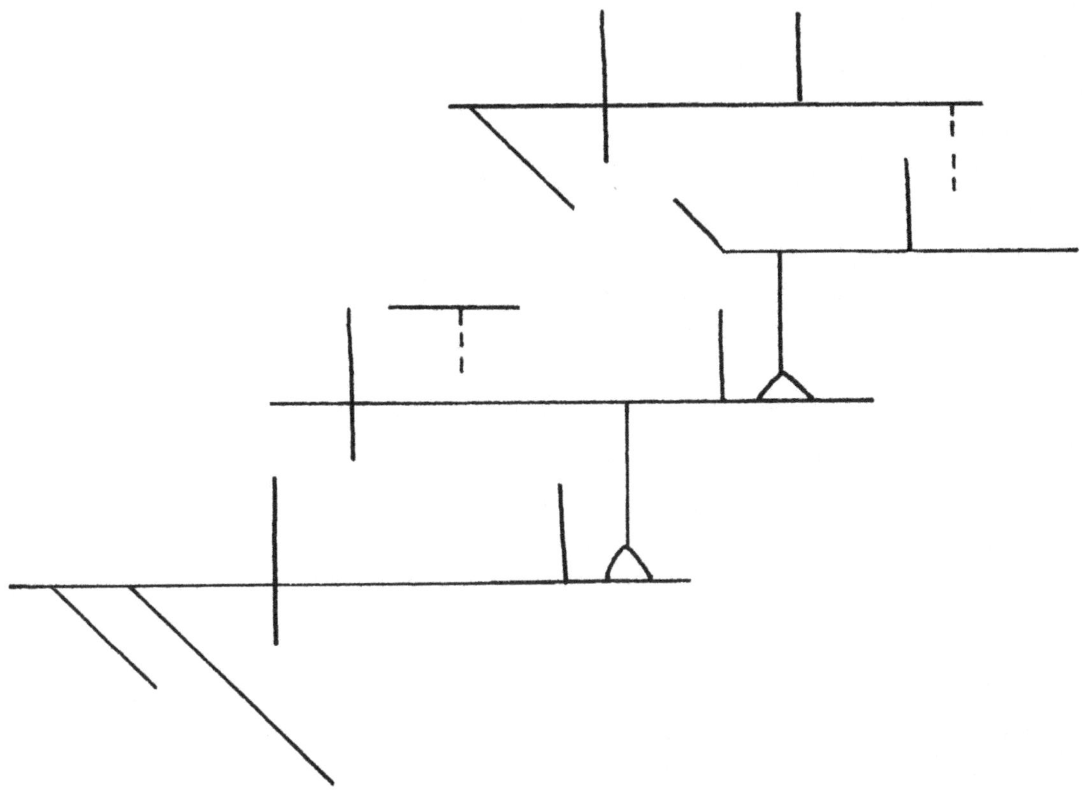

The city of Veii, Livy writes, had "inflicted worse losses than she suffered," which means that the siege had significantly weakened the Roman army.

> Such was the fall of Veii, the wealthiest city of Etruria. Even her final destruction witnessed to her greatness, for after a siege of ten summers and ten winters, during which she inflicted worse losses than she suffered, even when her destined hour had come she fell by a stratagem and not by direct assault.
>
> —Livy, *The Early History of Rome*

He had heard, "in the silence of the night," an inhuman voice saying, "Tell the magistrates that the Gauls are coming."

Direct quotes can be words, phrases, clauses, or sentences, as long as they are set off by quotation marks and form part of a grammatically correct original sentence.

Exercise 91A: Using Ellipses

The following three paragraphs are taken from Charles Morris's *The 1906 San Francisco Earthquake and Fire: As Told by Eyewitnesses.*

This excerpt is 368 words long. On your own paper, rewrite it so that it has no more than 200 words. Use ellipses wherever you omit words. Do not cut the opening or closing words of any paragraph. Make sure that you don't end up with run-on sentences or fragments!

When you are finished, compare your version with the condensed version found in the *Answer Key.*

> The work of fighting the fire was the first and greatest duty to be performed, but from the start it proved a very difficult, almost a hopeless, task. With fierce fires burning at once in a dozen or more separate places, the fire department of the city would have been inadequate to cope with the demon of flame even under the best of circumstances. As it was, they found themselves handicapped at the start by a nearly total lack of water. The earthquake had disarranged and broken the water mains and there was scarcely a drop of water to be had, so that the engines proved next to useless. Water might be drawn from the bay, but the center of the conflagration was a mile or more away, and this great body of water was rendered useless.
>
> The only hope that remained to the authorities was to endeavor to check the progress of the flames by the use of dynamite, blowing up buildings in the line of progress of the conflagration. This was put in practice without loss of time, and soon the thunder-like roar of the explosions began, blasts being heard every few minutes, each signifying that some building had been blown to atoms. But over the gaps thus made the flames leaped, and though the brave fellows worked with a desperation and energy of the most heroic type, it seemed as if all their labors were to be without avail, the terrible fire marching on as steadily as if a colony of ants had sought to stay its devastating progress.
>
> It was with grief and horror that the mass of the people gazed on this steady march of the army of ruin. They were seemingly half dazed by the magnitude of the disaster, strangely passive in the face of the ruin that surrounded them, as if stunned by despair and not yet awakened to a realization of the horrors of the situation. Among these was the possibility of famine. No city at any time carries more than a few days' supply of provisions, and with the wholesale districts and warehouse regions invaded by the flames the shortage of food made itself apparent from the start. Water was even more difficult to obtain, the supply being nearly all cut off.

Exercise 91B: Partial Quotations

On your own paper, rewrite the five statements below so that each one contains a partial quotation. Draw the partial quotation from the bolded sentences that follow each statement. The authors of the bolded sentences are provided for you—be sure to include an attribution tag for each direct quote!

You may change and adapt the statements freely.

One of your sentences should contain a very short one- to three-word quote; one should contain a prepositional phrase, gerund phrase, participle phrase, or infinitive phrase; and one should quote a dependent clause.

If you need help, ask your instructor to show you sample answers.

Jane Seymour was the third wife of Henry VIII.

"But the predominant impression given by her portrait . . . is of a woman of calm good sense. And contemporaries all commented on Jane Seymour's intelligence . . . She was also naturally sweet-natured (no angry words or tantrums here) and virtuous—her virtue was another topic on which there was general agreement."

—Antonia Fraser, historian

In the nineteenth century, candy-makers could add anything they wanted to candy.

"Unscrupulous manufacturers would resort to any number of devious and even dangerous practices to sell their goods. Some, for example, varnished their candies with shellac to make them shinier and more attractive. Brick dust was added to some candies to make them redder, while other candies contained lead, insect parts and other contaminants."

—Joël Glenn Brenner, financial journalist

Vampire bats drink the blood of other animals.

"Vampire bats are unique among mammals for their habit of subsisting on the blood of other warm-blooded vertebrates . . . The bats do preferentially bite the capillary-rich tips of fingers, toes and noses; and through a small circular aperture made in the victim's skin, they indeed can lap large quantities of blood for their size—thanks to an anticoagulant in their saliva that also can lead to excessive bleeding in their victims after they drink their fill and flap away."

—Bill Wasik and Monica Murphy, science writers

Brain development happens very quickly in babies.

"When babies are born, their brains have about the same number of connections as adults have. That doesn't last long. By the time children are 3 years old, the connections in specific regions of their brains have doubled or even tripled."

—John Medina, molecular biologist

Medieval town clocks could be very elaborate.

"The clock made about 1350 for the cathedral of Strasbourg . . . included a moving calendar and an astrolabe whose pointers indicated the movements of the sun, moon and planets. The upper compartment was adorned with a statue of the Virgin before whom

at noon the Three Magi bowed while a carillon played a tune. On top of the whole thing stood an enormous cock which, at the end of the procession of the Magi, opened its beak, thrust forth its tongue, crowed and flapped its wings."

—Carlo M. Cipolla, economic historian

Exercise 91C: Diagramming

On your own paper, diagram every word of the following sentences.

These are slightly adapted from *Rabid: A Cultural History of the World's Most Diabolical Virus*, by Bill Wasik and Monica Murphy.

These are difficult! Do your best, and then compare your answers with the *Answer Key*.

Skunks do not attack (or even approach) humans except when in the demented throes of rabies.

It was a yellow bat—a species that eats nothing but insects—but today it seemed determined to make a meal of the boy.

After hearing reports of a rabid wolf marauding through the region of Arbois, furiously biting man and beast, Pasteur and his friends witnessed one victim being brought to the blacksmith's shop for treatment.

He devised a simple experimental protocol; twenty-five sheep would be vaccinated against anthrax, fifty including these would be infected, and an additional ten would be untreated controls.

— LESSON 92 —

Partial Quotations

Ellipses

Block Quotes

Colons

Brackets

If a direct quotation is longer than three lines, indent the entire quote one inch from the margin in a separate block of text and omit quotation marks.

If you change or make additions to a direct quotation, use brackets.

> And I doubt not but posterity will find many things, that are now but Rumors, verified into practical Realities. It may be some ages hence, a voyage to the Southern unknown Tracts, yea possibly the Moon, will not be more strange than one to America. To them, that come after us, it may be as ordinary to buy a pair of wings to fly into remotest Regions; as now a pair of Boots to ride a Journey. And to confer at the distance of the Indies by Sympathetick

conveyances, may be as usual to future times, as to us in a litterary correspondence. The restauration of gray hairs to Juvenility, and renewing the exhausted marrow, may at length be effected without a miracle: And the turning of the now comparative desert world into a Paradise, may not improbably be expected from late Agriculture.

Now those, that judge by the narrowness of former Principles, will smile at these Paradoxical expectations: But questionless those great Inventions, that have in these later Ages altered the face of all things; in their naked proposals, and meer suppositions, were to former times as *ridiculous.* To have talk'd of a *new Earth* to have been discovered, had been a Romance to Antiquity. And to sayl without sight of Stars or shoars by the guidance of a Mineral, a story more absurd, than the flight of Daedalus.

—Joseph Glanvill, *Scepsis Scientifica: Or, Confest Ignorance, The Way to Science; In an Essay of the Vanity of Dogmatizing and Confident Opinion*

In 1661, the English philosopher Joseph Glanvill predicted the invention of "many things, that are now but Rumors." Among them were space travel, airplanes, and conversation over long distances. In his essay *Scepsis Scientifica,* Glanvill admits that these inventions seem farfetched, but he argues that the discovery of a new continent must have seemed just as unlikely:

> It may be some ages hence, a voyage to the Southern unknown Tracts, yea possibly the Moon, will not be more strange than one to America. To them, that come after us, it may be as ordinary to buy a pair of wings to fly into remotest Regions; as now a pair of Boots to ride a Journey. And to confer at the distance of the Indies by Sympathetick conveyances, may be as usual to future times, as to us in a litterary correspondence . . . [T]hose great Inventions, that have in these later Ages altered the face of all things . . . were to former times as *ridiculous.* To have talk'd of a *new Earth* [the North and South American continents] to have been discovered, had been a Romance [Glanvill means a "fairy tale"] to Antiquity.

Glanvill goes on to point out that navigating a ship by compass ("the guidance of a Mineral," as he puts it) instead of by the stars must have seemed just as impossible to ancient sailors as moon travel does to people of his own day.

When using a word processing program, leave an additional line space before and after a block quote.

Block quotes should be introduced by a colon (if preceded by a complete sentence) or a comma (if preceded by a partial sentence).

As the English philosopher Joseph Glanvill predicted in 1661,

> It may be some ages hence, a voyage to the Southern unknown Tracts, yea possibly the Moon, will not be more strange than one to America. To them, that come after us, it may be as ordinary to buy a pair of wings to fly into remotest Regions; as now a pair of Boots to ride a Journey.

If you change or make additions to a direct quotation, use brackets.

Exercise 92A: Writing Dialogue Correctly

The following speeches, from *Little Women*, by Louisa May Alcott, are listed in the correct order, but are missing the dialogue tags. On your own paper, rewrite the speeches as dialogue, making use of the dialogue tags below. You must place at least one dialogue tag before a speech, one in the middle of a speech, and one following a speech.

A list of the rules governing dialogue follows, for your reference.

When you are finished, compare your dialogue to the original passage in the *Answer Key*.

List 1. Dialogue (in Correct Order)

Meg, I wish you'd go and see the Hummels. You know Mother told us not to forget them.

I'm too tired to go this afternoon.

Can't you, Jo?

Too stormy for me with my cold.

I thought it was almost well.

It's well enough for me to go out with Laurie, but not well enough to go to the Hummels.

Why don't you go yourself?

I have been every day, but the baby is sick, and I don't know what to do for it. I think you or Hannah ought to go.

Ask Hannah for some nice little mess, and take it round, Beth, the air will do you good. I'd go but I want to finish my writing.

My head aches and I'm tired, so I thought maybe some of you would go.

Amy will be in presently, and she will run down for us.

List 2. Dialogue Tags (Not in Correct Order)

asked Beth

said Beth, ten days after Mrs. March's departure

Beth said earnestly

Beth said

Meg asked
suggested Meg
replied Meg, rocking comfortably as she sewed
said Jo, laughing, but looking a little ashamed of her inconsistency
said Jo, adding apologetically

List 3. For Reference: Rules for Writing Dialogue

A dialogue tag identifies the person making the speech.

When a dialogue tag comes after a speech, place a comma, exclamation point, or question mark inside the closing quotation marks.

When a dialogue tag comes before a speech, place a comma after the tag. Put the dialogue's final punctuation mark inside the closing quotation marks.

Speeches do not need to be attached to a dialogue tag as long as the text clearly indicates the speaker.

Usually, a new paragraph begins with each new speaker.

When a dialogue tag comes in the middle of a speech, follow it with a comma if the following dialogue is an incomplete sentence. Follow it with a period if the following dialogue is a complete sentence.

Exercise 92B: Using Direct Quotations Correctly

On your own paper, rewrite the following three paragraphs, inserting at least one quote from each of the following three sources into the paragraph. Use the following guidelines:

a) At least one quote must be a block quote.
b) At least one quote must be a complete sentence.
c) At least one quote must be a partial sentence incorporated into your own sentence.
d) Each quote must have an attribution tag.
e) At least one quote must be condensed, using ellipses.
f) You must make at least one change or addition that needs to be put in brackets.

A list of the rules governing direct quotations follows, for your reference.

You may make whatever changes are needed to the paragraphs. When you are finished, compare your paragraphs to the sample answer in the *Answer Key.*

These paragraphs are adapted from Chapter Ten of *The History of the Renaissance World*, by Susan Wise Bauer.

List 1. Paragraphs

After Babur the Tiger died in 1530, he left his oldest son Humayan in charge of his empire. But not long after Humayan came to the throne, he was driven out of India by invaders. He spent the next fifteen years trying to get the throne of India back! Finally, Humayan was able to return to his palace in Delhi. But he had lost much of his father's empire.

Just one year after Humayan returned to India, he slipped on the steps of his library, hit his head, and died. In 1556, his thirteen-year-old son Akbar was crowned emperor in his place. Akbar was young, but he was determined to restore the glory of his grandfather's empire. He launched a furious campaign to reconquer the lands that Humayan had lost. And after he got those lands back under his control, he added even more cities to his empire. By the time he died, after a reign of forty-nine years, Akbar ruled an empire that covered half of India.

Like his grandfather Babur, Akbar was a fair and just ruler. Although he himself was a Muslim, Akbar believed that he would need to be popular with his Hindu subjects if he wanted to stay on the throne. So he married a Hindu princess and allowed Hindu worship to continue in his country.

List 2. Sources

"Humayan walked out upon the terrace of the library, and sat down there for some time to enjoy the fresh air. When the Emperor began to descend the steps of the stair from the terrace, the crier, according to custom, proclaimed the time of prayer. The King stood still upon this occasion and repeated his creed, then sat down upon the second stair till the proclamation was ended. When he was going to rise, he supported himself on a staff, which unfortunately slipped upon the marble, and the King fell headlong from the top to the bottom of the stair; he was taken up insensible and laid upon his bed; he soon recovered his speech, and the physicians administered all their art but in vain; for upon the 11th of the month, about sunset, his soul took flight to Paradise."

—Alexander Dow, translator and historian

"Akbar further underscored toleration as a major concern of state by declaring his policy of sulh-i kul, universal toleration. That extended the canopy of justice to all, regardless of religious affiliation."

—Catherine Asher, historian

"During his reign of nearly half a century Akbar had his fill of fighting. Noted as an administrator and a broadminded statesman, he was forced to distinguish himself first as a soldier. At the outset of his reign he possessed only the Punjab and Delhi, and he had to struggle even to maintain himself on the throne of Delhi. Twenty years of severe fighting was needed to bring the country into subjection and numerous campaigns ensued during the twenty years to round off the boundaries of the kingdom."

—*The Cyclopedia of India: Biographical, Historical, Administrative, Commercial*

List 3. For Reference: Rules for Using Direct Quotations

When an attribution tag comes after a direct quote, place a comma, exclamation point, or question mark inside the closing quotation marks.

When an attribution tag comes before a direct quote, place a comma after the tag. Put the dialogue's final punctuation mark inside the closing quotation marks.

When an attribution tag comes in the middle of a direct quotation, follow it with a comma if the remaining quote is an incomplete sentence. Follow it with a period if the remaining quote is a complete sentence.

Direct quotes can be words, phrases, clauses, or sentences, as long as they are set off by quotation marks and form part of a grammatically correct original sentence.

An ellipsis shows where something has been cut out of a sentence.

Every direct quote must have an attribution tag.

If a direct quotation is longer than three lines, indent the entire quote one inch from the margin in a separate block of text and omit quotation marks.

If you change or make additions to a direct quotation, use brackets.

WEEK 24

Floating Elements

— LESSON 93 —

Interjections
Nouns of Direct Address
Parenthetical Expressions

Oh dear, I've dropped my keys.
Oops! The keys fell through the grate into the sewer.
Alas, I will not be able to unlock my door.
Whew! That was a close one.
Whoa, let's just slow down here for a minute.
Hush, I'm on the phone.

inter between
jacere to throw

Interjections express sudden feeling or emotion. They are set off with commas or stand alone with a closing punctuation mark.

Friends, Romans, countrymen, lend me your ears!
Stars, hide your fire!
I am afraid, my dear, that you are too late.
Run, baby, run.
Get down, dog!

Nouns of direct address name a person or thing who is being spoken to. They are set off with commas. They are capitalized only if they are proper names or titles.

Parentheses ( ) can enclose words that are not essential to the sentence.
Parenthetical expressions often interrupt or are irrelevant to the rest of the sentence.
Punctuation goes inside the parentheses if it applies to the parenthetical material; all other punctuation goes outside the parentheses.
Parenthetical material only begins with a capital letter if it is a complete sentence with ending punctuation.
Parenthetical expressions can also be set off by commas.

The doctor was so late, in fact, that the baby was born before he arrived.

To be sure, she will tell a very plausible story.

When Marco Polo travelled to China he crossed, as it were, the horizon of European knowledge.

Fear was, no doubt, the greatest enemy the army had.

In a word, he supported the other candidate.

These things are always difficult, you know.

Short parenthetical expressions such as the following are usually set off by commas: *in short, in fact, in reality, as it were, as it happens, no doubt, in a word, to be sure, to be brief, after all, you know, of course.*

Whew! That was a close one.

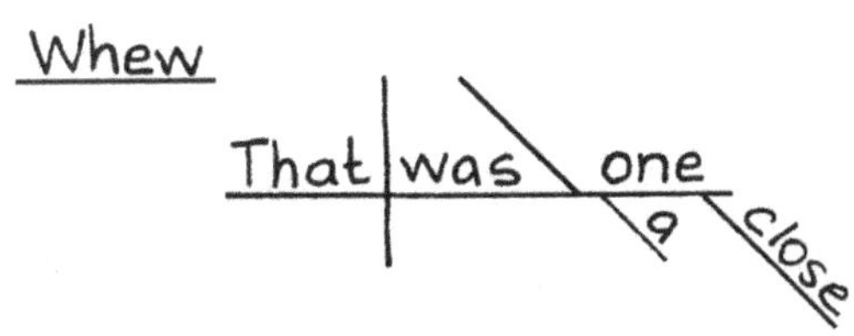

Friends, Romans, countrymen, lend me your ears!

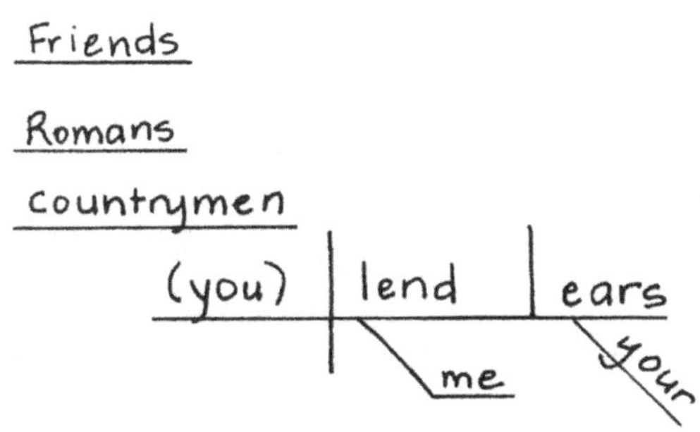

In a word, he supported the other candidate.

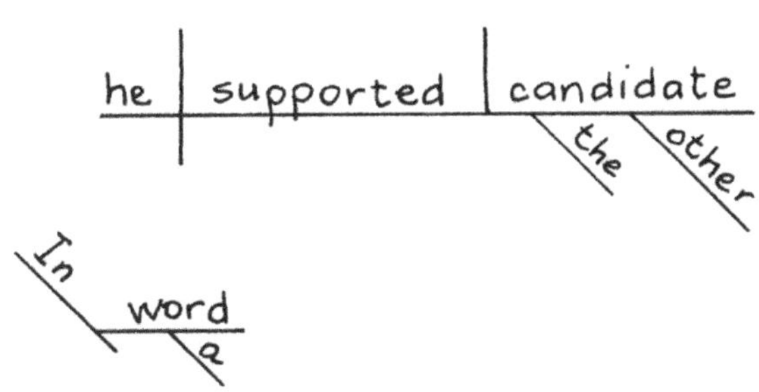

The following sentences are taken from *The Scarlet Pimpernel*, by Baroness Emmuska Orczy.

Your heroism, your devotion, which I, alas, so little deserved, have atoned for that unfortunate episode of the ball.

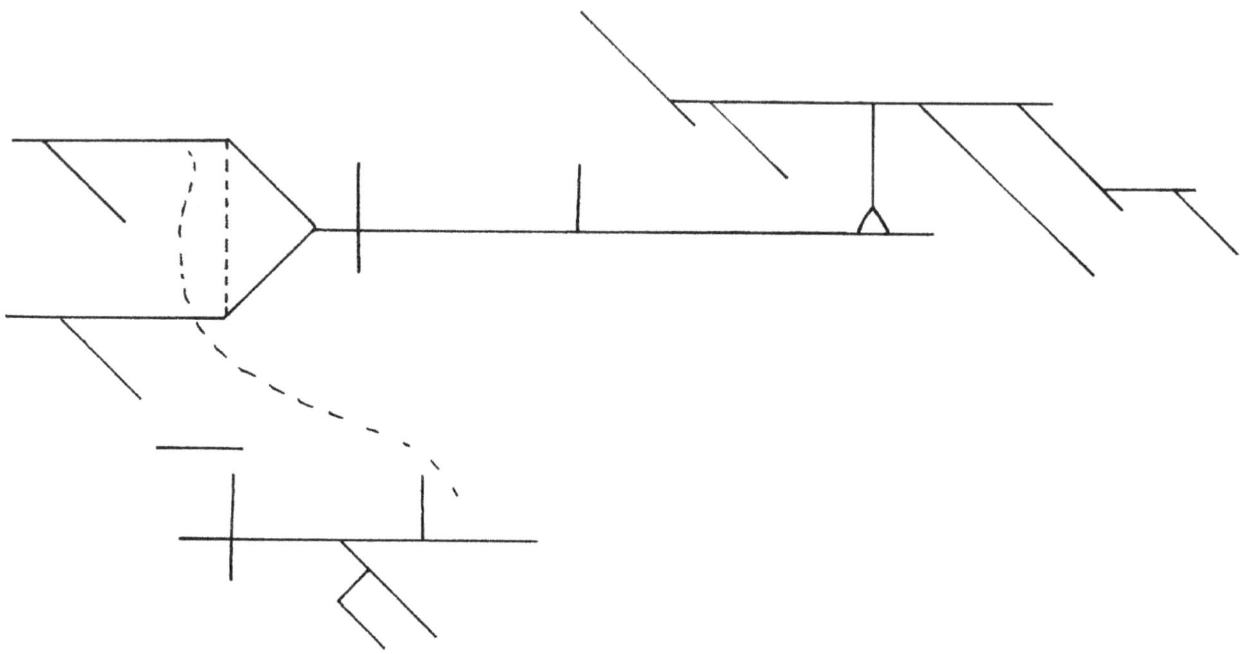

Do you impugn my bravery, Madame?

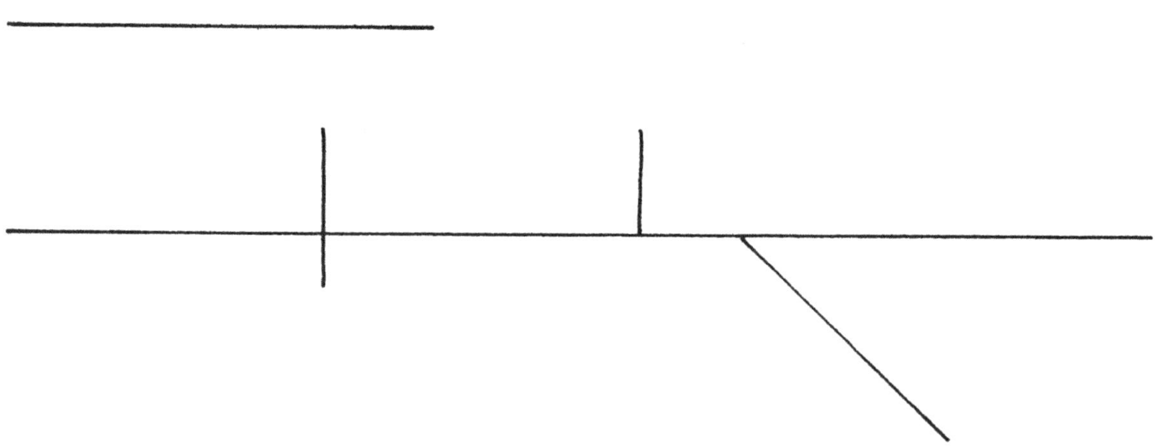

This restriction, of course, did not apply to her, and Frank would, of course, not dare to oppose her.

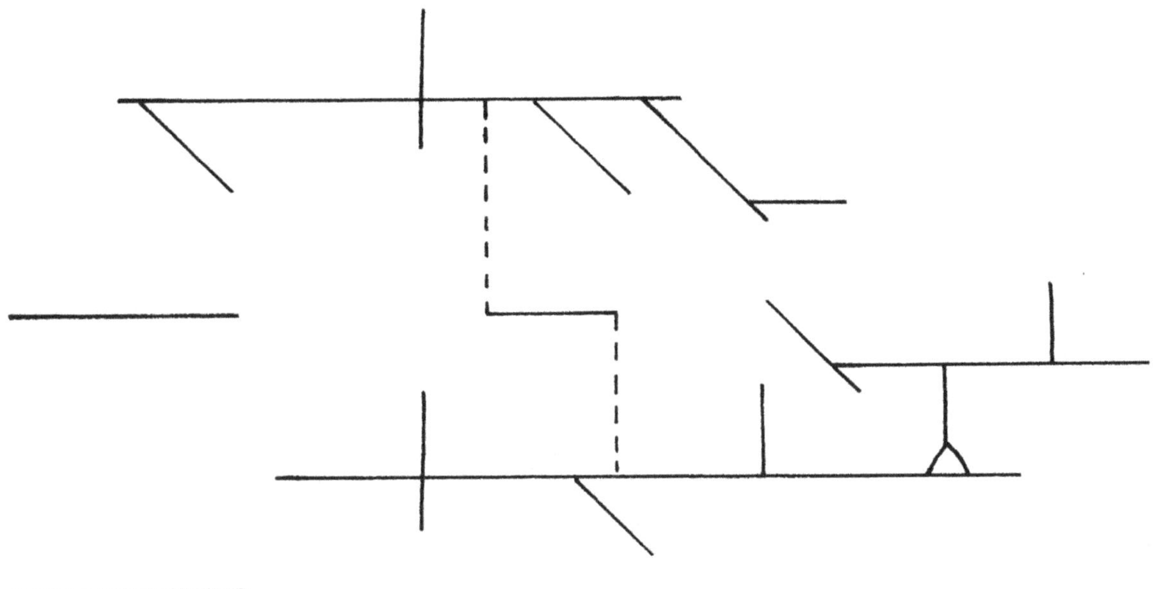

The storm will, no doubt, snarl the traffic.

There is no doubt that the storm is coming.

We aren't ready yet, you know.

You know that we aren't ready yet.

The snow caused school to be cancelled, of course.

In case of snow, school is cancelled as a matter of course.

Exercise 93A: Using Floating Elements Correctly

On your own paper, rewrite the following sentences in List 1, inserting interjections, nouns of direct address, and parenthetical expressions from List 2. You must use every item in List 2 at least once. Every sentence in List 1 must have at least one insertion. Interjections may either come before or after sentences on their own, or may be incorporated directly into the sentence.

List 1. Sentences

Pluto is no longer considered to be a planet.
This milk has spoiled.
I think I'd better kill that rattlesnake.
Go take a nap.
You finally understand quadratic equations!

Is that dog really a St. Bernard-Chihuahua mix?
That is the exact book I was looking for.

List 2. Interjections, Nouns of Direct Address, Parenthetical Expressions

come what may
children
congratulations
sweetheart
Mother
eureka
oh, well
Mr. President
no doubt
in fact
of course

Exercise 93B: Parenthetical Expressions

In the following pairs of sentences, underline each subject once and each predicate twice. In each pair, cross out the parenthetical expression that is not essential to the sentences. If the expression is used as an essential part of the sentence, circle it and label it with the correct part of the sentence (e.g., *prep phrase acting as adj*, etc.). If it acts as a modifier, draw an arrow back to the word it modifies.

The meeting was, after all, a failure.

After all that preparation, the meeting was a failure.

You must appeal, in a word, to the reader's imagination.

There is great power in a word that is carefully chosen.

As it happens, I will be too late to see the presentation.

Thanks to the live broadcast, we will be able to see the presentation as it happens.

To be sure of yourself is a good quality, but can also become a weakness.

The laws governing self-defense are, to be sure, complicated and confusing.

In fact, autobiographies are notoriously unreliable.

Autobiographies are often unreliable in fact.

Exercise 93C: Diagramming

On your own paper, diagram every word of the following sentences.

These are slightly adapted from Sir Walter Scott's historical novel *Waverley*.

Oh, Squire, we should have followed you through flood and fire, to be sure!

Alas, Mr. Waverley, I have no better advice.

Distance, in truth, produces the same effect.

The starlight was lost as the stars faded before approaching day, and the head of the marching column, continuing its descent, plunged as it were into the heavy ocean of fog, which rolled its white waves over the whole plain, and over the sea by which it was bounded.

— LESSON 94 —

Appositives

Rome, the Eternal City, is built on seven hills that lie on both sides of the Tiber River.

Dubrovnik, the Pearl of the Adriatic, is a walled seaside fortress in Croatia.

Helsinki, the White City of the North, gets no sunshine at all for about fifty days every winter.

In Mumbai, the City of Dreams, almost seven million people ride the trains every day.

Chinese tin miners founded the Malaysian city Kuala Lumpur, the Golden Triangle, in 1857.

The people of Sydney, the Harbour City, celebrate Harbour Day, a commemoration of the first convict ships landing in Sydney Cove, on January 26.

An appositive is a noun, pronoun, or noun phrase that usually follows another noun and renames or explains it.

Rome's first ruler, Romulus, killed his brother and seized power.
In the Middle Ages, many Spanish Jews, *Conversos*, migrated to Dubrovnik.
A 1981 movie about the USSR, *Reds*, was actually filmed in Helsinki.

Rome is built on seven hills that lie on both sides of the Tiber River.
Dubrovnik is a walled seaside fortress in Croatia.
Helsinki gets no sunshine at all for about fifty days every winter.

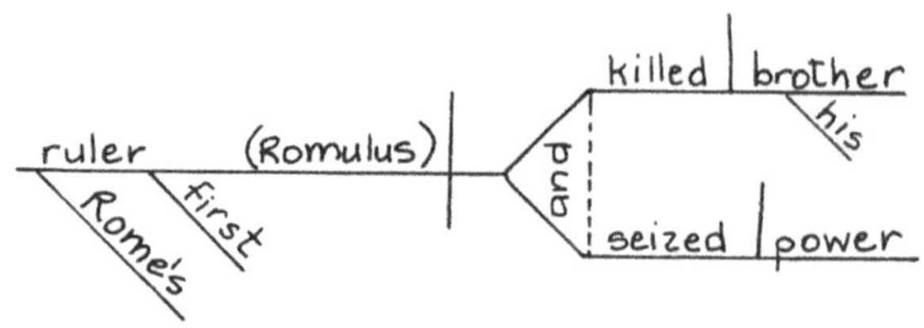

In Mumbai, the City of Dreams, almost seven million people ride the trains every day.

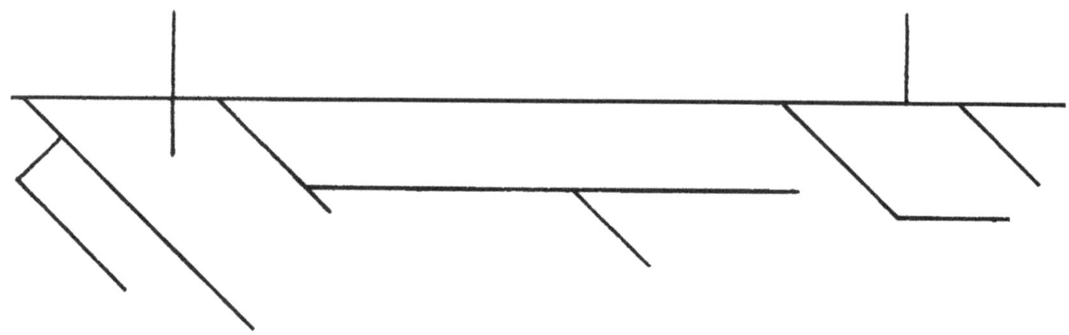

Chinese tin miners founded the Malaysian city Kuala Lumpur, the Golden Triangle, in 1857.

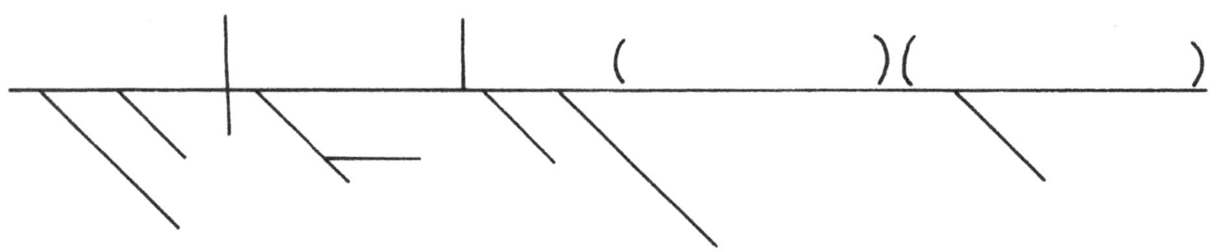

An appositive is a noun, pronoun, or noun phrase that usually follows another noun and renames or explains it.

The wisest philosopher of the ancients, Socrates wrote nothing.

A better-known destination, Marseilles is less picturesque than the surrounding villages.

An ancient breed, the Kuvasz protects helpless livestock.

Appositives are set off by commas.

The wisest philosopher of the ancients, Socrates, wrote nothing.

A better-known destination, Marseilles, is less picturesque than the surrounding villages.

An ancient breed, the Kuvasz, protects helpless livestock.

An appositive that occurs within a sentence has commas both before and after it. An appositive at the beginning of a sentence has one comma that follows it. An appositive at the end of a sentence has one comma that precedes it.

My grandfather, Aquilino Ramos, makes the best pork adobo I've ever eaten.

The best supper ever, pineapple chicken adobo waited for us on the table.

My grandfather prepared a fantastic meal, squid adobo with tomatoes.

An appositive is a noun, pronoun, or noun phrase that usually follows another noun and renames or explains it. Appositives are set off by commas.

Exercise 94A: Using Appositives

Rewrite the following sentences on your own paper, inserting at least one appositive or appositive phrase from List 1 into each of the sentences in List 2, and using correct punctuation. You may insert more than one appositive into each sentence, but you must use each appositive or phrase in List 1 at least once.

List 1. Appositives

Henry
the Duke of Normandy
the year of Indian independence
George III
Lahore
their ancestral home
the Virgin Queen
the founder of the Sikh Empire
the author of *Robinson Crusoe*
Haryana and Punjab
the blind poet

List 2. Sentences

John Milton wrote *Paradise Lost.*
Daniel Defoe wrote over 250 works.
Jane Austen's brother became her literary agent.
William the Conqueror became the first Norman king of England.
Virginia was named in honor of Elizabeth.
The king of England was paying little attention to the colonies.
Maharaja Ranjit Singh ruled his kingdom from Aurangzeb's old fortress.
After 1947, the Sikhs emigrated out of the Punjab and settled throughout India.
In 1966, the Punjab was again divided into two separate states.

Exercise 94B: Identifying Appositives

In each of the following sentences, underline the subject of each independent clause once, and the predicate twice. Circle each appositive or appositive phrase.

These sentences are taken from Constance Garnett's translation of *Crime and Punishment*, by Fyodor Dostoyevsky.

I am Raskolnikov, a student; I came here a month ago.

He was a man over fifty, bald and grizzled, of medium height, and stoutly built.

The persons still in the tavern were a man who appeared to be an artisan, drunk, but not extremely so, sitting before a pot of beer, and his companion, a huge, stout man with a grey beard.

This man, this most reputable and exemplary citizen, will on no consideration give you money.

Her stockings, her stockings I have sold for drink!

She married her first husband, an infantry officer, for love, and ran away with him from her father's house.

You can judge the extremity of her calamities, that she, a woman of education and culture and distinguished family, should have consented to be my wife.

Boots, cotton shirt-fronts—most magnificent, a uniform—they got up all in splendid style, for eleven roubles and a half.

The first morning I came back from the office I found Katerina Ivanovna had cooked two courses for dinner—soup and salt meat with horseradish—which we had never dreamed of till then.

And here I, her own father, took thirty copecks of that money for a drink.

There is the house of Kozel, the cabinet-maker, a German, well-to-do.

In the far distance, a copse lay, a dark blur on the very edge of the horizon.

A few paces beyond the last market garden stood a tavern, a big tavern.

Exercise 94C: Diagramming (Challenge!)

On your own paper, diagram every word of the following five sentences from Exercise 94B.

NOTE: The last three sentences each contain a diagramming challenge! Try to come up with solutions on your own—how can you make the sentence structure clear? If you get frustrated, ask your instructor for help. And when you're finished, compare your diagrams to those in the *Answer Key*.

Her stockings, her stockings I have sold for drink!

I am Raskolnikov, a student; I came here a month ago.

The persons still in the tavern were a man who appeared to be an artisan, drunk, but not extremely so, sitting before a pot of beer, and his companion, a huge, stout man with a grey beard.

Boots, cotton shirt-fronts—most magnificent, a uniform—they got up all in splendid style, for eleven roubles and a half.

The first morning I came back from the office I found Katerina Ivanovna had cooked two courses for dinner—soup and salt meat with horseradish—which we had never dreamed of till then.

— LESSON 95 —

Appositives
Intensive and Reflexive Pronouns
Noun Clauses in Apposition
Object Complements

myself, himself, herself, itself, yourself, yourselves, ourselves, themselves

Reflexive pronouns refer back to the subject.
Intensive pronouns emphasize a noun or another pronoun.

I may have expressed myself badly.

I myself was never top in anything!

An appositive is a noun, pronoun, or noun phrase that usually follows another noun and renames or explains it. Appositives are set off by commas.

I may have expressed myself badly.

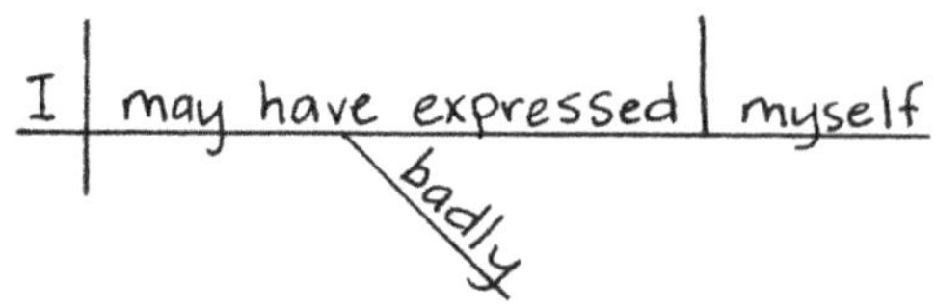

I myself was never top in anything!

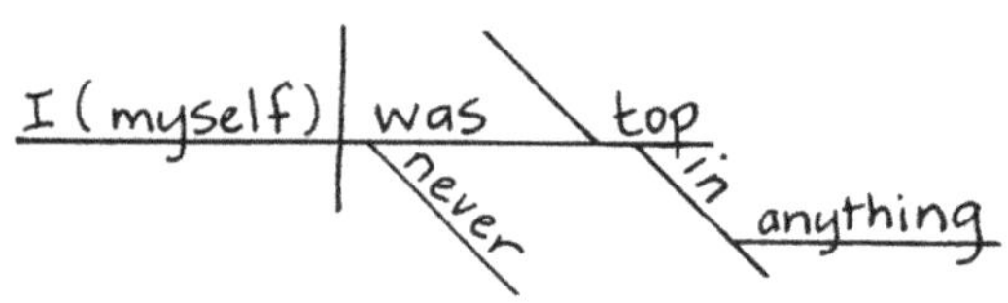

The author, Fyodor Dostoyevsky, was born in Moscow in 1821.

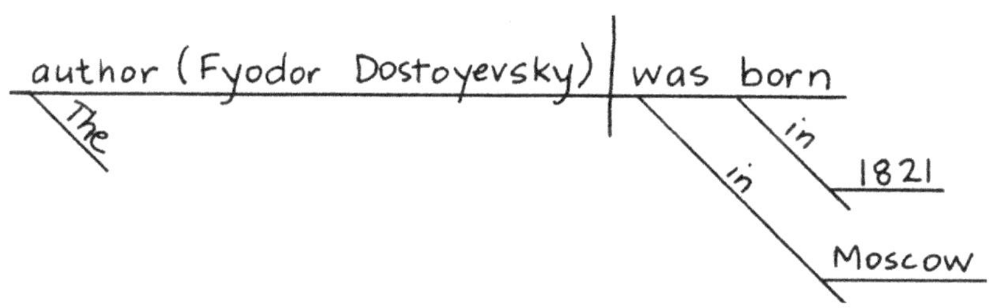

Exercise 95A: Reflexive and Intensive Pronoun Review

In the following sentences from Fyodor Dostoyevsky's novel *The Idiot*, underline each reflexive or intensive pronoun. Put parentheses around each intensive pronoun. Label each reflexive pronoun with the correct part of the sentence (*S, DO, IO, PA, PN, OP*, etc.).

"No, he didn't, for I saw it all myself," said Colia.

Might he suggest, for instance, such a thing as a marriage between himself and one of the general's daughters?

Everyone gasped; some even crossed themselves.

"Prince, be so kind as to come to me for a moment in the drawing-room," said Nina Alexandrovna herself, appearing at the door.

It hid itself under the cupboard and under the chest of drawers, and crawled into the corners.

Why, it was yourself who advised me to bring him over.

Judge for yourselves.

But I'll tell you why I have been awaiting you so impatiently, because I believe that Providence itself sent you to be a friend and a brother to me.

You see, prince, I'll tell you privately, Evgenie and ourselves have not said a word yet.

Not that Varia was afraid of standing up for herself.

Yet we feel that we ought to limit ourselves to the simple record of facts, without much attempt at explanation, for a very patent reason: because we ourselves have the greatest possible difficulty in accounting for the facts to be recorded.

They had themselves decided that it would be better if the prince did not talk all the evening.

A dependent clause can act as an appositive if it renames the noun that it follows.
The article's argument, that studying grammar is good for your brain, didn't convince me.

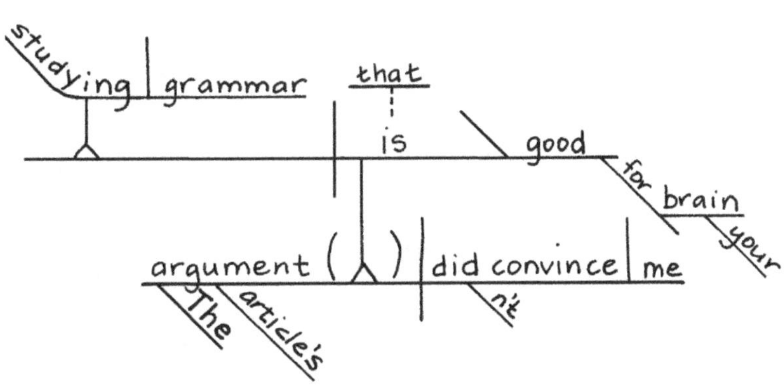

Don't forget our story, that we left early and didn't stop on the way.

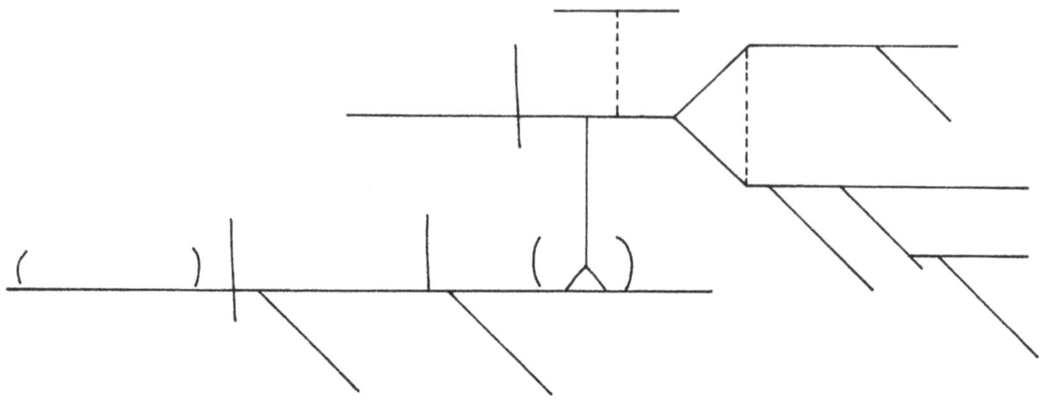

Dependent clauses can act as adjective clauses, adverb clauses, or noun clauses.

An adjective clause is a dependent clause that acts as an adjective in a sentence, modifying a noun or pronoun in the independent clause. Relative pronouns introduce adjective clauses and refer back to an antecedent in the independent clause.

A noun clause takes the place of a noun. Noun clauses can be introduced by relative pronouns, relative adverbs, or subordinating conjunctions.

Reread the story that made you happy.

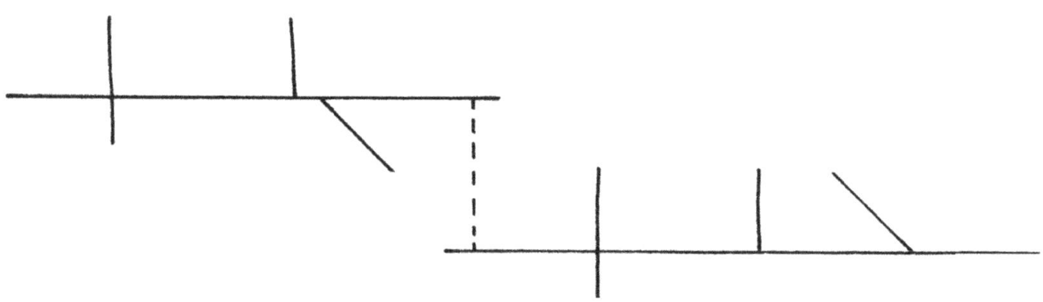

An object complement follows the direct object and renames or describes it.

The story, a long boring tale that seemed to go on forever, took up most of the evening.

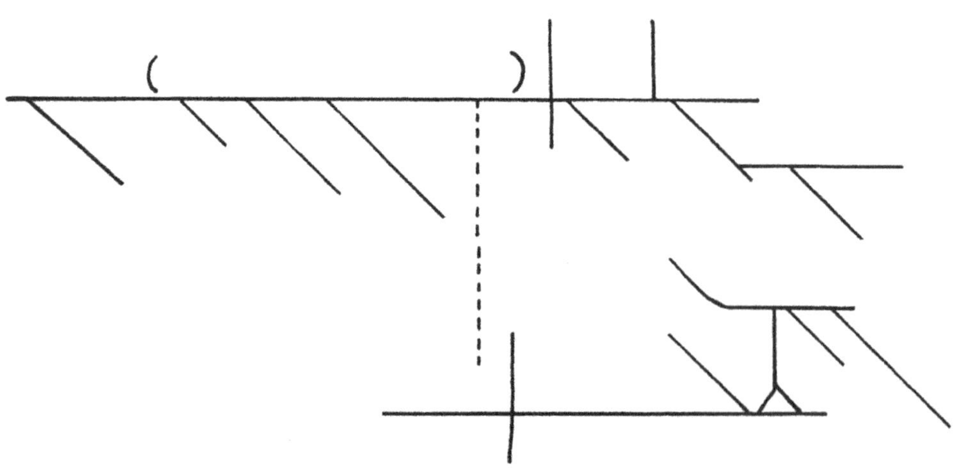

Exercise 95B: Distinguishing Noun Clauses in Apposition from Adjective Clauses

In the following sentences, identify each noun, noun phrase, or noun clause acting as an appositive by underlining it and writing the abbreviation *APP* above it. Draw an arrow from each appositive back to the noun it renames or explains.

Circle each adjective clause and draw an arrow from each circle back to the noun that the adjective clause modifies.

He sincerely believed the impossible, that aliens were living among us.

The court's conclusion, that the convicted man deserved a retrial, was immediately challenged in the press.

I smashed the spider that was dangling from the corner of my bed.

The mystery, how the treasure had disappeared without a trace, was still unsolved.

The truth, that I was bored and wanted to leave, would have hurt my host's feelings.

The sailors hoped to capture the ship which was was anchored close by.

The skater's conviction, that he would win an Olympic medal, sustained him through long hours of practice.

The shepherd, a gnarled mountain man who carried an ancient weathered crook, whistled to his dog, a whippet-thin border collie.

He hefted the weapon, a sword that had been forged by his grandfather, and turned towards the enemy.

My mother's advice, that I should leave early to avoid traffic, turned out to be very good advice indeed.

The musical instrument that I love the most is the violin.

Her hope, that he would return from the war unharmed, began to fade away.

His greatest fault, that he works so slowly, is a difficult one to overcome.

The book never really answers the question, which ambition is better to pursue.

Vegetables that are grown organically are much more expensive.

My car, the blue one that is parked by the fire hydrant, won't start.

Exercise 95C: Diagramming

On your own paper, diagram every word of these two sentences from Frederick Marryat's classic adventure novel *The Pirate.* Do your best to place each word on the diagram, but ask your instructor if you need help.

Our little party was now threatened with a new danger, that we might be run over by the frigate, which was now within a cable's length of us, driving the seas before her in one widely extended foam, as she pursued her rapid and impetuous course.

The indignation and rage which were expressed by the captain as he rapidly walked the deck in company with first mate—his violent gesticulation—proved to the crew that there was mischief brewing.

— LESSON 96 —

Appositives
Noun Clauses in Apposition
Absolute Constructions

I am absolutely serious, my friend.

The whole story is absolutely untrue.

There is absolutely no question as to the alibi!

He appeared to be in an absolute frenzy.

Her face and voice were absolutely cold and expressionless.

Having no near relations or friends, I was trying to make up my mind what to do, when I ran across John Cavendish. (Adjective)

Our efforts having been in vain, we had abandoned the matter. **(Absolute construction)**

Semantic: having to do with meaning

(Greek *sēmantikós*, "having meaning")

An absolute construction has a strong semantic relationship but no grammatical connection to the rest of the sentence.

To tell the truth, an idea, wild and extravagant in itself, had once or twice that morning flashed through my brain.

Dr. Bauerstein remained in the background, his grave bearded face unchanged.

He has lived by his wits, as the saying goes.

> To tell the truth, an idea, wild and extravagant in itself, had once or twice that morning flashed through my brain.

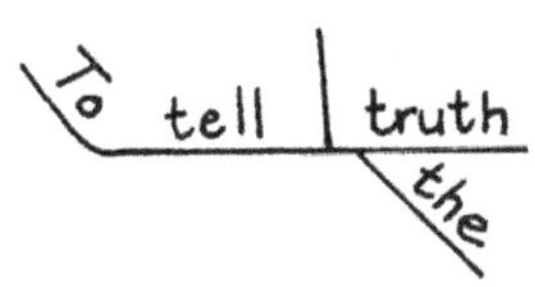

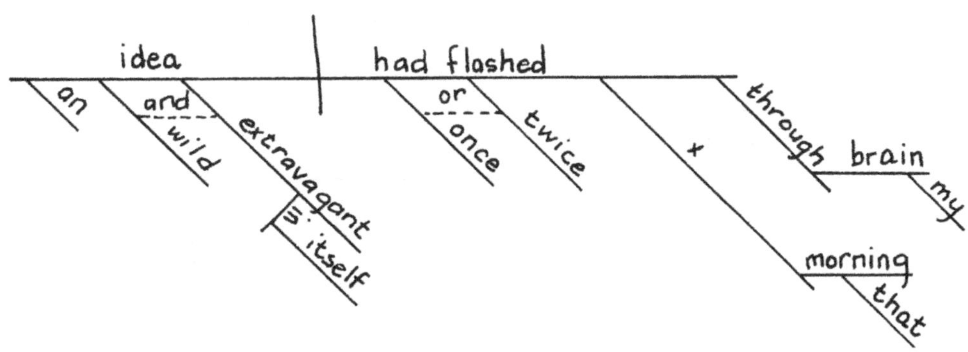

Dr. Bauerstein remained in the background, his grave bearded face unchanged.

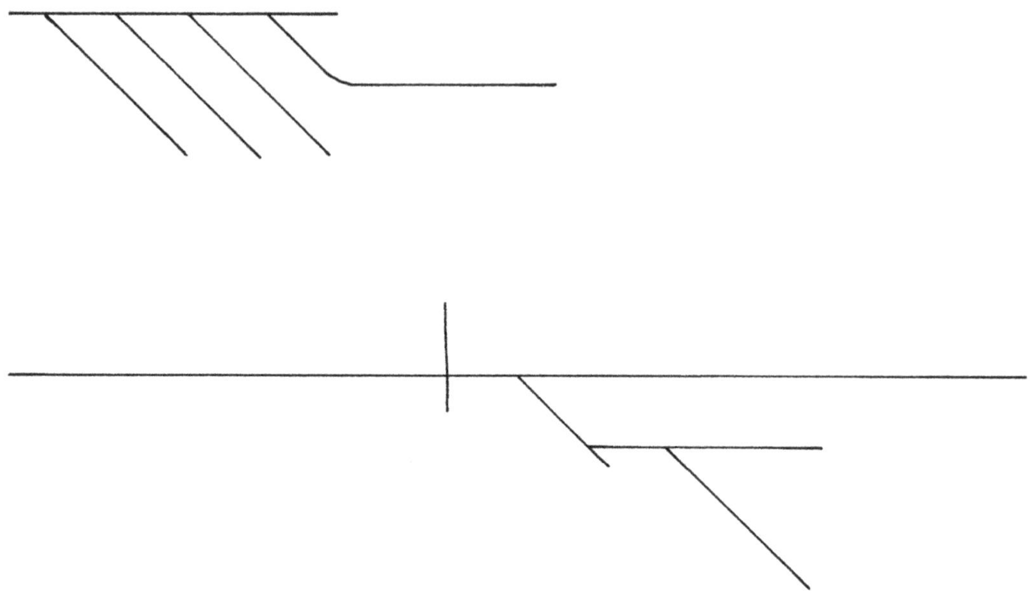

He has lived by his wits, as the saying goes.

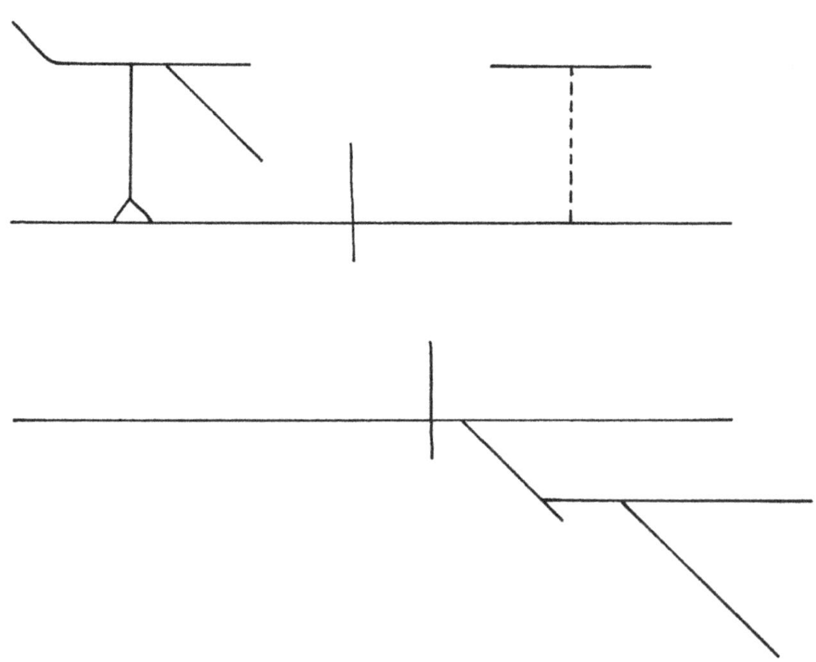

Exercise 96A: Identifying Absolute Constructions

The excerpts below are taken from classic works of poetry and prose. Circle the absolute construction in each one. Label each absolute construction as *CL* for clause or *PHR* for phrase. For clauses, underline the subject of each clause once and the predicate twice.

A fellow presently passing by, Adams asked him if he could direct him to an ale-house.
—Henry Fielding

As to the door being locked, it is a very ordinary lock.
—Agatha Christie

Thinkest thou this heart could feel a moment's joy,

Thou being absent?
—Henry Wadsworth Longfellow

We sitting, as I said, the cock crew loud.
—Alfred, Lord Tennyson

He went down, rider and steed, before his lance.
—Edward Bulwer-Lytton

He was buried in Westminster Abbey, the stone that bears his inscription resting at the

feet of Addison.
—Thomas Macaulay

He speaks three or four languages, word for word.
—William Shakespeare

As to my cargo, it was, a great part of it, lost.
—Daniel Defoe

Here lies, his head upon the lap of earth,

A youth to fortune and to fame unknown.

—Thomas Gray

Exercise 96B: Appositives, Modifiers, and Absolute Constructions

The sentences below, taken from *The Mysterious Affair at Styles*, by Agatha Christie, each contain phrases or clauses set off by dashes. Some are appositives, some are modifiers, and some are absolute constructions. Identify then by writing *APP*, *MOD*, or *AC* above each one. For appositives and modifiers, draw an arrow back to the word being renamed or modified.

Very well—but it's all extremely mysterious.

We will look at the chest—but no matter—we will examine it all the same.

It was the expression on his face that was extraordinary—a curious mingling of terror and agitation.

She had bolted the door leading into his room—a most unusual proceeding on her part.

She was not extravagantly loved—no.

Call for me in passing—the last house in the village.

A very dark shadow is resting on this house—the shadow of murder.

Miss Howard had been on afternoon duty on Tuesday, and—a convoy coming in unexpectedly—she had kindly offered to remain on night duty.

Mary Cavendish was there, shaking the girl—who must have been an unusually sound sleeper—and trying to wake her.

My idea was—a very ridiculous one—that she had intended to poison him.

But I decided that if I made any interesting and important discoveries—as no doubt I should—I would keep them to myself.

I think—I am sure—he cared for me at first.

They had already arranged their infamous plot—that he should marry this rich, but rather foolish old lady, induce her to make a will leaving her money to him, and then gain their ends by a very cleverly conceived crime.

Did you—while you happened to be alone for a few seconds—unlock the poison cupboard, and examine some of the bottles?

Exercise 96C: Diagramming

On your own paper, diagram every word of the following sentences, taken from Agatha Christie's mystery novel *Murder on the Orient Express.*

Round her neck was a collar of very large pearls which, improbable though it seemed, were real.

Poirot passed along the corridor, a somewhat slow progress, as most of the people travelling were standing outside their carriages.

There was a kind of cool efficiency in the way she was eating her breakfast and in the way she called to the attendant to bring her more coffee, which bespoke a knowledge of the world and of travelling.

To look up the antecedents of all these people, to discover their *bona fides*—that takes time and endless inconvenience.

— REVIEW 8 —

Weeks 22-24

Topics

Parenthetical Expressions
Dashes, Colons, and Brackets
Dialogue and Dialogue Tags
Direct Quotations and Attribution Tags
Ellipses and Partial Quotations
Block Quotes
Interjections
Nouns of Direct Address
Appositives
Noun Clauses in Apposition
Absolute Constructions

Review 8A: Definition Fill-in-the-Blank

You learned many definitions in the past three weeks! Fill in the blanks in the definitions below with one of the terms from the list. Many of the terms will be used more than once.

commas	comma	parentheses
line space	dashes	coordinating conjunction
semicolon	colon	paragraph
appositive	appositives	absolute construction
period	attribution tag	exclamation point
parenthetical expression	interjections	dialogue tag
question mark	brackets	ellipses
restrictive modifying clause	nouns of direct address	quotation marks
non-restrictive modifying clause	closing quotation marks	short parenthetical expressions

A ____________________________________ defines the word that it modifies. Removing the clause changes the essential meaning of the sentence.

A ____________________________________ describes the word that it modifies. Removing the clause doesn't change the essential meaning of the sentence.

Only a ____________________________________ should be set off by commas.

____________________ can enclose words that are not essential to the sentence.

A ____________________ often interrupts or is irrelevant to the rest of the sentence.

Punctuation goes inside the ____________________ if it applies to the ____________________; all other punctuation goes outside the ____________________.

A ____________________ only begins with a capital letter if it is a complete sentence with ending punctuation.

A ____________________ can also be set off by commas.

____________________ such as the following are usually set off by commas: *in short, in fact, in reality, as it were, as it happens, no doubt, in a word, to be sure, to be brief, after all, you know, of course.*

____________________ can enclose words that are not essential to the sentence.

____________________ can also be used singly to separate parts of a sentence.

____________________ make a parenthetical element a part of the sentence.

____________________ emphasize a parenthetical element.

____________________ minimize a parenthetical element.

The independent clauses of a compound sentence must be joined by a ____________ and a ____________________, a ____________, or a ________________ and a ____________________. They cannot be joined by a ____________ alone.

When a ____________________ comes before a speech, place a ____________________ after the tag. Put the dialogue's final punctuation mark inside the ____________________.

Speeches do not need to be attached to a ____________________ as long as the text clearly indicates the speaker.

Usually, a new ______________________________ begins with each new speaker.

When a ______________________________ comes in the middle of a speech, follow it with a ______________________________ if the following dialogue is an incomplete sentence. Follow it with a _______________ if the following dialogue is a complete sentence.

When an ______________________________ comes after a direct quote, place a __________________________, _________________________, or ______________________________ inside the closing quotation marks.

When an ______________________________ comes before a direct quote, place a ______________________________ after the tag. Put the dialogue's final punctuation mark inside the ______________________________.

When an ______________________________ comes in the middle of a direct quotation, follow it with a ______________________________ if the remaining quote is an incomplete sentence. Follow it with a _______________ if the remaining quote is a complete sentence.

Every direct quote must have an ______________________________.

______________________________ show where something has been cut out of a sentence.

A second or third quote from the same source does not need another _______________, as long as context makes the source of the quote clear.

Direct quotes can be words, phrases, clauses, or sentences, as long as they are set off by ______________________________ and form part of a grammatically correct original sentence.

If a direct quotation is longer than three lines, indent the entire quote one inch from the margin in a separate block of text and omit ______________________________.

If you change or make additions to a direct quotation, use ________________________.

When using word processing software, leave an additional ____________________ before and after a block quote.

Block quotes should be introduced by a ____________________ (if preceded by a complete sentence) or a ____________________ (if preceded by a partial sentence).

____________________ express sudden feeling or emotion. They are set off with ____________________ or stand alone with a closing punctuation mark.

____________________ name a person or thing who is being spoken to. They are set off with ____________________. They are capitalized only if they are proper names or titles.

An ____________________ is a noun, pronoun, or noun phrase that usually follows another noun and renames or explains it. ____________________ are set off by ____________________.

A dependent clause can act as an ____________________ if it renames the noun that it follows.

An ____________________ has a strong semantic relationship but no grammatical connection to the rest of the sentence.

Review 8B: Punctuating Restrictive and Non-Restrictive Clauses, Compound Sentences, Interjections, and Nouns of Direct Address

The sentences below contain restrictive clauses, non-restrictive clauses, interjections, and nouns of direct address. Some are compound sentences. But all of them have lost their punctuation! Insert all necessary punctuation directly into the sentences (use the actual punctuation marks rather than proofreader's marks).

These sentences are taken from Harriet Jacobs's 1861 memoir *Incidents in the Life of a Slave Girl, Written by Herself.*

Ah Ellen is that you he said in his most gracious manner

Five of them were my grandmothers children and had shared the same milk that nourished her mothers children

Alas the thought was familiar to me and had sent many a sharp pang through my heart

She may be an ignorant creature degraded by the system that has brutalized her from childhood but she has a mothers instincts and is capable of feeling a mothers agonies

Forgive me for what mother For not letting him treat me like a dog

We that loved him waited to bid him a long and last farewell

I asked her to prepare a poultice of warm ashes and vinegar and I applied it to my leg which was already much swollen

My uncle Phillip who was a carpenter had very skillfully made a concealed trap door which communicated with the storeroom

I had slunk down behind a barrel which entirely screened me but I imagined that Jenny was looking directly at the spot and my heart beat violently

My grandmother loved this old lady whom we all called Miss Fanny

This wounded my grandmother's feelings for she could not retain ill will against the woman whom she had nourished with her milk when a babe

There the prisoners rest together they hear not the voice of the oppressor the servant is free from his master

Well Martha I've brought you a letter from Linda

Review 8C: Dialogue

In the following passage of dialogue, taken from Harriet Beecher Stowe's classic anti-slavery novel *Uncle Tom's Cabin*, all of the punctuation around, before, and after the lines of dialogue is missing. Insert all necessary punctuation directly into the sentences (use the actual punctuation marks rather than proofreader's marks).

Marie was busy, turning over the contents of a drawer, as she answered Well, of course, by and by, Eva, you will have other things to think of besides reading the Bible round to servants. Not but that is very proper; I've done it myself, when I had health. But when you come to be dressing and going into company, you won't have time. See here! she added these jewels I'm going to give you when you come out. I wore them to my first ball. I can tell you, Eva, I made a sensation.

Eva took the jewel-case, and lifted from it a diamond necklace. Her large, thoughtful eyes rested on them, but it was plain her thoughts were elsewhere.

How sober you look, child! said Marie.

Are these worth a great deal of money, mamma?

To be sure, they are. Father sent to France for them. They are worth a small fortune.

I wish I had them said Eva to do what I pleased with!

What would you do with them?

I'd sell them, and buy a place in the free states, and take all our people there, and hire teachers, to teach them to read and write.

Eva was cut short by her mother's laughing.

Set up a boarding-school! Wouldn't you teach them to play on the piano, and paint on velvet?

I'd teach them to read their own Bible, and write their own letters, and read letters that are written to them said Eva, steadily. I know, mamma, it does come very hard on them that they can't do these things. Tom feels it—Mammy does,—a great many of them do. I think it's wrong.

Come, come, Eva; you are only a child! You don't know anything about these things said Marie Besides, your talking makes my head ache.

Marie always had a headache on hand for any conversation that did not exactly suit her.

Review 8D: Parenthetical Expressions, Appositives, Absolute Constructions

Each one of the sentences below (from Frederick Douglass's 1845 memoir *Narrative of the Life of Frederick Douglass, an American Slave, Written by Himself*) contains an element not closely connected to the rest of the sentence: parenthetical, appositive, or absolute.

In each sentence, find and circle the unconnected element (word, phrase, or clause).

Above it, write *PAR* for parenthetical, *APP* for appositive, or *AB* for absolute.

In the blank at the end of the sentence, note whether the element is set apart with commas (*C*), parentheses (*P*), or dashes (*D*).

She was nevertheless left a slave—a slave for life—a slave in the hands of strangers. ________

I started off to Covey's in the morning (Saturday morning) wearied in body and broken in spirit. ________

We went, as usual, to our several fields of labor. _______

As to my own treatment while I lived on Colonel Lloyd's plantation, it was very similar to that of the other slave children. _______

There being little else than field work to do, I had a great deal of leisure time. _______

In the afternoon of that day, we reached Annapolis, the capital of the state. _______

His reply was, as well as I can remember, that Demby had become unmanageable. _______

I shall never forget the ecstasy with which I received the intelligence that my old master (Anthony) had determined to let me go to Baltimore, to live with Mr. Hugh Auld, brother to my old master's son-in-law, Captain Thomas Auld. _______

The slave was made to say some very smart as well as impressive things in reply to his master—things which had the desired though unexpected effect; for the conversation resulted in the voluntary emancipation of the slave on the part of the master. _______

In hottest summer and coldest winter, I was kept almost naked—no shoes, no stockings, no jacket, no trousers, nothing on but a coarse tow linen shirt, reaching only to my knees. _______

Review 8E: Direct Quotations

The following paragraph about Abraham Lincoln, from *The Emancipation Proclamation: Ending Slavery in America*, by Adam Woog, contains two different direct quotations from Lincoln himself. Those quotations are bolded, but they are not properly punctuated. Rewrite the paragraph on your own paper, spacing and punctuating both quotations correctly.

When you are finished, circle any places where words have been left out of the direct quotations.

Underline any places where words have been added to the direct quotations.

Abraham Lincoln became a celebrity through his eloquent appearances in debates with his opponent, Stephen Douglas. In one of these now-famous debates, Lincoln stated that slavery was **the issue that will continue in this country when these poor tongues of Judge Douglas and myself shall be silent.** He went on **It is the eternal struggle between these two principles—right and wrong—throughout the world . . . The one is the common right of humanity, and the other the divine right of kings . . . No matter what shape it comes [in] . . . it is the same tyrannical principle.** As the public learned during these debates, Lincoln was not a polished politician.

Review 8F: Diagramming

On your own paper, diagram every word of the following sentences—twice! Each sentence can legitimately be diagrammed in two different ways. (Remember, the English language doesn't operate by strictly scientific laws. Sometimes grammar is a matter of interpretation.) Try to diagram both options for each. One option will contain a floating element (a parenthetical expression or an absolute), while the second will place all words on a single diagram.

These sentences are taken from *The Underground Railroad*, by Raymond Bial.

If you need help, or a hint, ask your instructor.

The Underground Railroad was, in fact, an informal yet intricate network of routes leading north, eventually to Canada.

Yet I believed I could accurately capture the spirit of drama in these otherwise quiet places—both the courage of flight and the nobility of the aid extended to fugitive slaves.

I was left with a feeling of reverence for those brave people—both runaways and workers on the Railroad—who had gone before us.

WEEK 25

Complex Verb Tenses

— LESSON 97 —

Verb Tense, Voice, and Mood
Tense Review (Indicative)
Progressive Perfect Tenses (Indicative)

Moods
- Indicative
- Subjunctive
- Imperative
- Modal

(The following sentences are from Beverly Cleary's novel *Fifteen*.)

He spoke rapidly, as if he were anxious to get the words out of the way.

Mood: ______________________

And be home by ten thirty.

Mood: ______________________

To hide her discomfort she took small bites of ice cream.

Mood: ______________________

Should they talk awhile, or should she suggest that they leave, or should she wait for him to suggest it?

Mood: ______________________

Indicative verbs express real actions.
Subjunctive verbs express unreal actions.
Imperative verbs express intended actions.
Modal verbs express possible actions.

Here everything looked brand-new, as if the furniture had been delivered only the day before.

Mood: ______________________

Voice: ______________________

Now the fat pug dog rose and shook himself, scattering his hair over the carpet.

Mood: ______________________

Voice: ______________________

Voice
In a sentence with an active verb, the subject performs the action.
In a sentence with a passive verb, the subject receives the action.

Tense
A simple verb simply tells whether an action takes place in the past, present, or future.
A progressive verb describes an ongoing or continuous action.
A perfect verb describes an action which has been completed before another action takes place.

Exercise 97A: Review of Indicative Tenses

The following partially completed chart shows the active and passive tenses of the regular verb *refuse* (in the third-person singular), the irregular verb *tell* (in the third-person plural), and the irregular verb *bring* (in the first-person singular). Review your indicative tenses by completing the chart now.

		Active	Passive
SIMPLE TENSES			
refuse *tell* *bring*	Past	he refused they I	he they were I
refuse *tell* *bring*	Present	he they I bring	he is they I
refuse *tell* *bring*	Future	he they will tell I	he will be they I

		Active	Passive
PROGRESSIVE TENSES			
refuse *tell* *bring*	Past	he they I was	he was being refused they I
refuse *tell* *bring*	Present	he they I am bringing	he is they I
refuse *tell* *bring*	Future	he they will be I	he they I will be being brought
PERFECT TENSES			
refuse *tell* *bring*	Past	he they had told I	he had been they I
refuse *tell* *bring*	Present	he has they I	he they I have been brought
refuse *tell* *bring*	Future	he they I will have brought	he they I

A progressive perfect verb describes an ongoing or continuous action that has a definite end.

progressive perfect past
I had been running for half an hour before I decided to stop.
progressive perfect present
I have been running all morning.
progressive perfect future
I will have been running for an hour by the time you arrive.

PAST

Simple	I rejoiced over my grammar!
Progressive	I was rejoicing over my grammar.
Perfect	I had rejoiced over my grammar.
Progressive Perfect	I had been rejoicing over my grammar, until I realized I had done the wrong exercises.

PRESENT

Simple	I enjoy this schoolwork!
Progressive	I am enjoying this schoolwork.
Perfect	I have enjoyed this schoolwork.
Progressive Perfect	I have been enjoying this schoolwork, but unfortunately I have to stop now and go play Minecraft.

FUTURE

Simple	I will expect to receive a prize!
Progressive	All afternoon, I will be expecting to receive a prize.
Perfect	By dinner time, I will have expected to receive my prize.
Progressive Perfect	By dinner time, I will have been expecting to receive a prize for at least four hours.

PROGRESSIVE PERFECT PAST

Active The house had been showing signs of wear.

Passive The house had been being shown to prospective buyers for months.

PROGRESSIVE PERFECT PRESENT

Active I have been sending letters out every day.

Passive I have been being sent to the post office by my mother every day.

PROGRESSIVE PERFECT FUTURE

Active Come June, the professors will have been teaching Latin for two years.

Passive Come June, the students will have been being taught Latin for two years.

PROGRESSIVE PERFECT TENSES

Past	**Active**	**Passive**
Active: helping verb had + *helping verb* been + *present participle* *Passive: helping verb* had + *helping verb phrase* been being + *past participle*	I had been amusing you had been amusing he, she, it had been amusing we had been amusing you had been amusing they had been amusing	I had been being amused you had been being amused he, she, it had been being amused we had been being amused you had been being amused they had been being amused
Present	**Active**	**Passive**
Active: helping verb have *or* has + *helping verb* been + *present participle* *Passive: helping verb* have *or* has + *helping verb phrase* been being + *past participle*	I have been amusing you have been amusing he, she, it has been amusing we have been amusing you have been amusing they have been amusing	I have been being amused you have been being amused he, she, it has been being amused we have been being amused you have been being amused they have been being amused

PROGRESSIVE PERFECT TENSES

Future	Active	Passive
Active: helping verb phrase will have been *+ present participle*	I will have been amusing you will have been amusing he, she, it will have been amusing	I will have been being amused you will have been being amused he, she, it will have been being amused
Passive: helping verb phrase will have been being *+ past participle*	we will have been amusing you will have been amusing they will have been amusing	we will have been being amused you will have been being amused they will have been being amused

Perfect Future Passive	The students will have been taught Latin very thoroughly.
Progressive Perfect Future Passive	Come June, the students will have been being taught Latin for two years.
Progressive Perfect Future Passive (Understood)	Come June, the students will have been taught Latin for two years.

Exercise 97B: Parsing Verbs

In the following sentences, underline the main verb of every clause (both independent and dependent). Above each verb, write the tense and voice. (All verbs are in the indicative mood.)

You may abbreviate: *PROG, PERF, SIMP, PAST, PRES, FUT,* and then either *ACT* or *PASS*, or *SB* for state-of-being.

When he reaches the summit of Everest, he will have been climbing for over eleven hours.

He had been wondering for the past few years what had happened to the seer who made the prophecy.

They removed the feeder because too many birds had been being killed by stray cats.

By this point, the new cook will have been being introduced to her duties for several days.

He had been tempted for years by the dreams of freedom; they were calling him to move West into the wide open spaces.

An hour that is spent walking is an hour well spent, because you will have been thinking for all that time.

The exhaustion that I had been experiencing, off and on, ever since my arrival swept over me again.

He has been implying that I am behind on my rent, even though I paid up on the first of the month as usual.

Ever since the Russians beat them into space, the Americans had been desperately striving to seize the initiative.

The director will have been wondering how a performance which began so well suddenly fell apart.

Exercise 97C: Completing Sentences

Complete the following sentences by providing an appropriate verb in the tense and voice indicated beneath each blank. For state-of-being verbs, simply provide an appropriate state-of-being verb in the tense indicated.

The historian ______________________ his readers for over twenty years.
(progressive perfect present, active)

By this time next week, I ______________________ at this company for eight years.
(progressive perfect future, active)

I ______________________ in that sauna all morning.
(progressive perfect present, active)

The nuts ______________________ in the brandy and cinnamon mixture all morning.
(progressive perfect present, active)

By dinner, he ______________________ his room for five solid hours.
(progressive perfect future, active)

He ______________________ (simple future, passive), because he ______________________ (progressive perfect future, active) a complete meal.

That stupid dog ______________________ in the slimy pond again.
progressive perfect present, active

The operatic soprano ______________________ ever since she ______________ able to talk.
progressive perfect present, active — simple past, state-of-being

My mother ______________, but not with grief; she ______________________ onions for the spaghetti sauce.
progressive present, active — progressive perfect present, active

The pilot ______________________ ever since he ______________________ his license in 2009.
progressive perfect present, active — simple past, active

— LESSON 98 —

Simple Present and Perfect Present Modal Verbs
Progressive Present and Progressive Perfect Present Modal Verbs

Modal verbs express situations that have not actually happened.
should, would, may, might, must, can, could

Would, may, might, can, could: **possibility**

He was afraid that, in a little while, death ______________ meet him.

I fear that we ______________ never see him in this life again.

Oh, that I ______________ strike a blow for him before I die!

Only a knight of true valor ______________ hope to win.

Madam, how then ______________ I help you?

Must, should: **obligation**

I ______________ find a man whom I can truly love.

You ______________ do homage to King Arthur for your kingdom.

May: **permission**

______________ I go to Camelot, to see the jousting?

Can: **ability**

Nothing ______________ heal his wound on this side of the water.

	Simple Present Modal (Active)	
First person	I could help	we could help
Second person	you could help	you could help
Third person	he, she, it could help	they could help

	Perfect Present Modal (Active)	
First person	I should have helped	we should have helped
Second person	you should have helped	you should have helped
Third person	he, she, it should have helped	they should have helped

MODAL TENSES

	Simple Present	**Simple Past**	**Simple Future**
Active	I should help	none	none
Passive	I should be helped	none	none
	Progressive Present	**Progressive Past**	**Progressive Future**
Active	I could be helping	none	none
Passive	I could be being helped	none	none
	Perfect Present	**Perfect Past**	**Perfect Future**
Active	I would have helped	none	none
Passive	I would have been helped	none	none
	Progressive Perfect Present	**Prog Perfect Past**	**Prog Perfect Future**
Active	I might have been helping	none	none
Passive	I might have been being helped	none	none

Use the simple present or progressive present when the situation isn't happening in the present.

Since I slept badly last night, I might go take a nap.

mood	indicative	modal
tense	________	________
voice	________	________

People are being left in the hospital when they could be being nursed at home.

mood	indicative	________
tense	________	________
voice	________	________

Use the perfect present or the progressive perfect present when the situation didn't happen in the past.

I was eating cheese and crackers when I could have been sitting down to a big juicy steak.

mood	indicative	______________
tense	progressive past	______________
voice	active	______________

While the floors were being scrubbed, I could have vacuumed the rugs.

mood	indicative	______________
tense	progressive past	______________
voice	passive	______________

Modal Present: Simple or Progressive
Modal Past: Perfect or Progressive Perfect

MODAL TENSE FORMATION

Simple Present

Active	I can help	modal helping verb + first-person singular
Passive	I should be helped	modal helping verb + *be* + past participle

Progressive Present

Active	I might be helping	modal helping verb + *be* + present participle
Passive	I could be being helped	modal helping verb + *be* + *being* + past participle

Perfect Present

Active	I would have helped	modal helping verb + *have* + past participle
Passive	I may have been helped	modal helping verb + *have* + *been* + past participle

Progressive Perfect Present

Active	I must have been helping	modal helping verb + *have* + *been* + present participle
Passive	I could have been being	modal helping verb + *have* + *been* + *being* + past participle

Exercise 98A: Parsing Verbs

Write the tense, mood, and voice of each verb above it. The first is done for you.

These sentences have been slightly adapted from *King Arthur's Knights*, by Henry Gilbert.

simple past, indicative, active

The king refused to give the signal to sit to meat until he should have experienced some strange adventure.

The cook and his scullions came to and fro with anxious faces, for they feared that the meat could be overdone.

Each great baron, strong in men, plotted to win the overlordship when the king should be gone.

If Lancelot had dared his enemies to prove his treason, they would have been instantly discountenanced.

Others believed that what rumour said might be coming true.

I fear war must come of it all.

Men were all amazed, and would have gone instantly to see this marvel, but the archbishop bade them stay.

No man or child could be seen anywhere.

The kings and lords for angry spite would have slain Arthur, but the archbishop threatened them with the most dreadful ban of Holy Church.

His wound could be bleeding afresh.

Many of the dead may have been slain by their own kindred.

The dead shall lie uncoffined, for no prayers may be said over them.

Exercise 98B: Forming Modal Verbs

Fill in the blanks with the missing modal verbs. Using the helping verbs indicated, put each action verb provided into the correct modal tense.

You ______________________________ back to the beginning of the book only after you have read the end.

helping verb: *can*
simple present active of *go*

The rice beds ______________________________ to just the right depth, and the first rice seeds sown, before the farmers can rest.

helping verb: *must*
perfect present passive of *flood*

After counting the rings of the giant live oak, the researcher believed that it ____________ during Tecumseh's lifetime.

helping verb: *could*
progressive perfect present active of *grow*

An article in *Palaeodiversity* suggests that dinosaurs ______________________________ hallucinogenic fungi.

helping verb: *might*
perfect present active of *eat*

Cosmologists ______________________________ their ideas about infinity.

helping verb: *may*
progressive present active of *change*

Instead of learning to use weapons, the young men ______________________________ to be compassionate.

helping verb: *should*
progressive perfect present passive of *teach*

Everybody has to die, but I always believed that an exception __________________________ in my case. (William Saroyan).

helping verb: *would*
simple present passive of *make*

The additional food bank is helpful, but there are so many other important needs that

______________________________ instead!

helping verb: *could*
progressive present passive of *meet*

— LESSON 99 —

Modal Verb Tenses
The Imperative Mood
The Subjunctive Mood
More Subjunctive Tenses

Indicative verbs express real actions.
Subjunctive verbs express unreal actions.
Imperative verbs express intended actions.
Modal verbs express possible actions.

Turn to the end of your book.
Eat more vegetables!
Go away.

Be checked by a doctor before you come back to work.

The present passive imperative is formed by adding the helping verb *be* to the past participle of the verb.

Subjunctive verbs express situations that are unreal, wished for, or uncertain.

If we kept our ponies up in the winter time, we gave them fodder to eat.

We kept our ponies up in the winter time, and we gave them fodder to eat.

	Simple Present Subjunctive State-of-Being Verb		Simple Past Subjunctive State-of-Being Verb	
First person	I be	we be	I were	we were
Second person	you be	you be	you were	you were
Third person	he, she, it be	they be	he, she, it were	they were

Should you be in town, come by and see me.

If I were a bird, I would fly across the water.

	Simple Present Subjunctive Action Verb: Active		Simple Present Subjunctive Action Verb: Passive	
First person	I leave	we leave	I be left	we be left
Second person	you leave	you leave	you be left	you be left
Third person	he, she, it leave	they leave	he, she, it be left	they be left

He leaves early to avoid traffic.
I suggest that he leave early to avoid traffic.

The present passive subjunctive is formed by pairing *be* with the past participle of a verb.

The tent was left behind.
The guide recommended that the tent be left behind.

	Simple Past Subjunctive Action Verb: Active		Simple Present Subjunctive Action Verb: Passive	
First person	I left	we left	I were left	we were left
Second person	you left	you left	you were left	you were left
Third person	he, she, it left	they left	he, she, it were left	they were left

If I left early, I might be able to pick up the milk.
I left early to pick up the milk.

If I were left behind, I would be upset.
I was left behind, which made me very upset.

Simple Future Subjunctive Action Verb: Active	Simple Future Subjunctive Action Verb: Passive
None	None

Use the simple past subjunctive state-of-being verb, plus an infinitive, to express a future unreal action.

If I were to die tomorrow, I would have no regrets.

PROGRESSIVE TENSES

	Progressive Present Subjunctive Action Verb: Active	
First person	I am leaving	we are leaving
Second person	you are leaving	you are leaving
Third person	he, she, it is leaving	they are leaving

	Progressive Present Subjunctive Action Verb: Passive	
First person	I am being left	we are being left
Second person	you are being left	you are being left
Third person	he, she, it is being left	they are being left

If I be running late, I must throw myself upon your kind mercies.

If I am running late, I will call you.

It is unlikely that I am being penalized.

	Progressive Past Subjunctive Action Verb: Active	
First person	I **were** leaving	we were leaving
Second person	you were leaving	you were leaving
Third person	he, she, it **were** leaving	they were leaving

	Progressive Past Subjunctive Action Verb: Passive	
First person	I **were** being left	we were being left
Second person	you were being left	you were being left
Third person	he, she, it **were** being left	they were being left

If I were running in the race, I would certainly win.

I was running in the race.

If I were being left behind, I would make a huge fuss.

I was being left behind.

Progressive Future Subjunctive
Action Verb: Active

None

Progressive Future Subjunctive
Action Verb: Passive

None

PERFECT TENSES

	Perfect Present Subjunctive Action Verb: Active	
First person	I have left	we have left
Second person	you have left	you have left
Third person	he, she, it has left	they have left

	Perfect Present Subjunctive Action Verb: Passive	
First person	I have been left	we have been left
Second person	you have been left	you have been left
Third person	he, she, it has been left	they have been left

	Perfect Past Subjunctive Action Verb: Active	
First person	I had left	we had left
Second person	you had left	you had left
Third person	he, she, it had left	they had left

	Perfect Past Subjunctive Action Verb: Passive	
First person	I had been left	we had been left
Second person	you had been left	you had been left
Third person	he, she, it had been left	they had been left

Perfect Future Subjunctive
Action Verb: Active

None

Perfect Future Subjunctive
Action Verb: Passive

None

PROGRESSIVE PERFECT TENSES

	Progressive Perfect Present Subjunctive Action Verb: Active	
First person	I have been leaving	we have been leaving
Second person	you have been leaving	you have been leaving
Third person	he, she, it has been leaving	they have been leaving

	Progressive Perfect Present Subjunctive Action Verb: Passive	
First person	I have been being left	we have been being left
Second person	you have been being left	you have been being left
Third person	he, she, it has been being left	they have been being left

	Progressive Perfect Past Subjunctive Action Verb: Active	
First person	I had been leaving	we had been leaving
Second person	you had been leaving	you had been leaving
Third person	he, she, it had been leaving	they had been leaving

	Progressive Perfect Past Subjunctive Action Verb: Passive	
First person	I had been being left	we had been being left
Second person	you had been being left	you had been being left
Third person	he, she, it had been being left	they had been being left

Progressive Perfect Future Subjunctive
Action Verb: Active

None

Progressive Perfect Future Subjunctive
Action Verb: Passive

None

Exercise 99A: Complete the Chart

Fill in the missing forms on the following chart. Use the verbs indicated above each chart, in order. The first form on each chart is done for you.

INDICATIVE

(confuse, trick, read, add, allow, paint, pass, save, school, lead, kiss, mark)

Indicative Tense	Active Formation	Examples	Passive Formation	Examples
Simple present	Add *-s* in third-person singular	I confuse he, she, it ______	*am/is/are* + past participle	I am confused you ______ he, she, it ______

Indicative Tense	Active Formation	Examples	Passive Formation	Examples
Simple past	Add *-d* or *-ed*, or change form	I ____________	was/*were* + past participle	I ____________ you ____________
Simple future	+ *will* OR *shall*	they ____________	*will be* + past participle	it ____________
Progressive present	*am*/*is*/*are* + present participle	I ____________ you ____________ he, she, it ____________	*am*/*is*/*are* *being* + past participle	I ____________ you ____________ he, she, it ____________
Progressive past	*was*/*were* + present participle	I ____________ you ____________ he, she, it ____________	*was*/*were* *being* + past participle	I ____________ you ____________ he, she, it ____________
Progressive future	*will be* + present participle	I____________	*will be being* + past participle	it ____________
Perfect present	*has*/*have* + past participle	I ____________ you ____________ he, she, it ____________	*has*/*have been* + past participle	I ____________ you ____________ he, she, it ____________
Perfect past	*had* + past participle	they ____________	*had been* + past participle	you ____________
Perfect future	*will have* + past participle	we ____________	*will have been* + past participle	they ____________

Indicative Tense	Active Formation	Examples	Passive Formation	Examples
Progressive perfect present	*have/has been* + present participle	I ______________ he, she, it ______________	*have/has been being* + past participle	I ______________ he, she, it ______________
Progressive perfect past	*had been* + present participle	you ______________	*had been being* + past participle	you ______________
Progressive perfect future	*will have been* + present participle	you ______________	*will have been being* + past participle	they ______________

MODAL
(match, quarry, nibble, obey)

Modal Tense	Active Formation	Examples	Passive Formation	Examples
Simple present	modal helping verb + simple present main verb	I could match you ______________ he, she, it ______________	modal helping verb + *be* + past participle	I ______________ they ______________
Progressive present	modal helping verb + *be* + present participle	I ______________	modal helping verb + *be* + *being* + past participle	it ______________
Perfect present	modal helping verb + *have* + past participle	you ______________	modal helping verb + *have* + *been* + past participle	it ______________

Modal Tense	Active Formation	Examples	Passive Formation	Examples
Progressive perfect present	modal helping verb + *have been* + present participle	I ________________	modal helping verb + *have been being* + past participle	we ________________

IMPERATIVE
(number, feed)

Imperative Tense	Active Formation	Examples	Passive Formation	Examples
Present	simple present form without subject	Number ! ________________!	*be* + past participle	________________! ________________!

SUBJUNCTIVE
(fear, feel, rattle, wave, wear, call, carry, dash)

Subjunctive Tense	Active Formation	Examples	Passive Formation	Examples
Simple present	no change in any person	I fear you ________________ he, she, it ________________ we ________________ you ________________ they ________________	*be* + past participle	I ________________ they ________________
Simple past	**same as indicative:** add *-d* or *-ed*, or change form	I ________________ you ________________ he, she, it ________________	*were* + past participle	he ________________ you ________________

Subjunctive Tense	Active Formation	Examples	Passive Formation	Examples
Progressive present	**same as indicative:** *am/is/are* + present participle	I ___ you ___ he, she, it ___	**same as indicative:** *am/is/are being* + past participle	I ___ you ___ he, she, it ___
Progressive past	*were* + present participle	I ___ you ___ he, she, it ___	*were being* + past participle	I ___ you ___ he, she, it ___
Perfect present	**same as indicative:** *has/have* + past participle	I ___ he, she, it ___ they ___	**same as indicative:** *has/have been* + past participle	I ___ he, she, it ___ they ___
Perfect past	**same as indicative:** *had* + past participle	we ___	**same as indicative:** *had been* + past participle	we ___
Progressive perfect present	**same as indicative:** *have/has been* + present participle	I ___ you ___ he, she, it ___	**same as indicative:** *have/has been being* + past participle	I ___ you ___ he, she, it ___
Progressive perfect past	**same as indicative:** *had been* + present participle	you ___	**same as indicative:** *had been being* + past participle	you ___

Exercise 99B: Parsing

Write the mood, tense, and voice of each underlined verb above it. The first is done for you.

These sentences are taken from Mary Shelley's classic novel *Frankenstein*. The first is done for you.

indicative simple present active

The sun is yet high in the heavens; before it descends to hide itself behind your snowy precipices and illuminate another world, you will have heard my story and can decide.

She is to be tried today, and I hope, I sincerely hope, that she will be acquitted.

The moon had reached her summit in the heavens and was beginning to descend.

Instead of being spent in study, as you promised yourself, the year has been consumed in my sick room.

Perhaps, if my first introduction to humanity had been made by a young soldier, burning for glory and slaughter, I should have been imbued with different sensations.

Shall I create another like yourself, whose joint wickedness might desolate the world. Begone! I have answered you; you may torture me, but I will never consent.

If he were vanquished, I should be a free man.

If for one instant I had thought what might be the hellish intention of my fiendish adversary, I would rather have banished myself forever from my native country and wandered a friendless outcast over the earth than have consented to this miserable marriage.

—LESSON 100—

Review of Moods and Tenses
Conditional Sentences

First conditional sentences express circumstances that might actually happen.
The predicate of the condition clause is in a present tense.
The predicate of the consequence clause is an imperative or is in a present or future tense.

If we surrender and I return with you, will you promise not to hurt this man?
So bow down to her if you want, bow to her.
If she is otherwise when I find her, I shall be very put out.
Unless I am wrong (and I am never wrong), they are headed dead into the fire swamp.

Second conditional sentences express circumstances that are contrary to reality.
The predicate of the condition clause is in a past tense.
The predicate of the consequence clause is in the simple present modal tense.

I would not say such things if I were you!
If I had a month to plan, maybe I could come up with something.
If we only had a wheelbarrow, that would be something.

Third conditional sentences express past circumstances that never happened.
The predicate of the condition clause is in the perfect past tense.
The predicate of the consequence clause is in the perfect present modal or simple present modal tense.

But they would have killed Westley, if I hadn't done it.

If I were you, I would go home.

If I were you, I would be dancing with joy.

If I had been wrong, I would say so now.

If I had been wrong, I would be apologizing with sincerity.

If I had been wrong, I would have said so.

If I had been wrong, I would have been running for my life.

(The examples that follow are adapted from Mary Shelley's *Frankenstein*.)

First conditional sentences express circumstances that might actually happen.
The predicate of the condition clause is in a present tense.
The predicate of the consequence clause is an imperative or is in a present or future tense.

If I fail, you will see me again soon, or never.

If you believe that she is innocent, rely on the justice of our laws.

If I could bestow animation upon lifeless matter, I might renew life.

Second conditional sentences express circumstances that are contrary to reality.
The predicate of the condition clause is in a past tense.
The predicate of the consequence clause is in the simple or progressive present modal tense.

Unless such symptoms had been shown early, a sister or brother could never suspect the other of fraud.

If you cherished a desire of revenge against me, you would be rejoicing in my destruction.

Third conditional sentences express past circumstances that never happened.
The predicate of the condition clause is in the perfect past tense.
The predicate of the consequence clause is in any modal tense.

If she had earnestly desired it, I should have willingly given it to her,

If you had known me as I once was, you would not recognize me in this state of degradation.

If the voice of conscience had been heeded, Frankenstein would yet have lived.

Exercise 100A: Conditional Sentences

Identify the following sentences (taken from *Japanese Fairy Tales*, by Yei Theodora Ozaki) as first, second, or third conditional by writing a *1*, *2*, or *3* in the margin next to each.

If it goes on much longer like this, not only shall I lose all my children, but I myself must fall a victim to the monster. ________

The warrior saw that he had now only one arrow left in his quiver, and if this one failed he could not kill the centipede. ________

If I had made a mistake, I would have begged you to forgive me! ________

I shall soon take my leave if you will give me the big box—that is all I want! ________

Very well, Ojisan, we will give you the tortoise if you give us the money! ________

It must be very far away, if it exists at all! ________

If you would like to see the Sea King's land, I will be your guide. ________

If you open it, something dreadful will happen to you! ________

If the Princess Hase were to write a poem and offer it in prayer, might it not stop the noise of the rushing river and remove the cause of the Imperial illness? ________

If only you had spoken in time I should have remembered it, and should have brought it along with me! ________

Exercise 100B: Parsing

Write the correct mood, tense, and voice above each underlined verb. These sentences are taken from *Japanese Fairy Tales*, by Yei Theodora Ozaki.

While he was speaking, a train of fishes appeared, all dressed in ceremonial, trailing garments.

Then the happy fisherman, following his bride, the Sea King's daughter, was shown all the wonders of that enchanted land where youth and joy go hand in hand and neither time nor age can touch them.

Surely someone has been telling you lies, and you are dazed, and you know not what you say—or some evil spirit has taken possession of your heart.

The old man tried to pacify her by showing her the box of presents he had brought back with him, and then he told her of all that had happened to him, and how wonderfully he had been entertained at the sparrow's house.

Seized with curiosity as to who could be studying so diligently in such a lonely spot, he dismounted, and leaving his horse to his groom, he walked up the hillside and approached the cottage.

Never neglect to keep the anniversaries of your ancestors, and make it your duty to provide for your children's future.

It seemed as if she were made of light, for the house was filled with a soft shining, so that even in the dark of night it was like daytime.

They said that they had worked for over a thousand days making the branch of gold, with its silver twigs and its jeweled fruit, that was now presented to her by the Knight, but as yet they had received nothing in payment.

You must sit where you are and not move, and whatever happens don't go near or look into the inner room.

The Happy Hunter said he blamed himself; if he had understood how to fish properly he would never have lost his hook, and therefore all this trouble had been caused in the first place by his trying to do something which he did not know how to do.

A great darkness now overspread the heavens, the thunder rolled and the lightning flashed, and the wind roared in fury, and it seemed as if the world were coming to an end.

I have made the badger soup and have been waiting for you for a long time.

When the branch was finished, he took his journey home and tried to make himself look as if he were wearied and worn out with travel.

Exercise 100C: Diagramming

On your own paper, diagram every word of the following sentences from *Japanese Fairy Tales*, by Yei Theodora Ozaki.

I cannot forgive you unless you bring me back my own hook.

The warrior saw that he had now only one arrow left in his quiver, and if this one failed he could not kill the centipede.

But the Sun and the Moon still hesitated, saying that they had heard that one of the pillars of heaven had been broken as well, and they feared that, even if the roads had been remade, it would still be dangerous for them to sally forth on their usual journeys.

WEEK 26

More Modifiers

—LESSON 101—

Adjective Review

Adjectives in the Appositive Position
Correct Comma Usage

It was a dark and stormy night; the rain fell in torrents, except at occasional intervals, when it was checked by a violent gust of wind which swept up the streets (for it is in London that our scene lies), rattling along the house-tops, and fiercely agitating the scanty flame of the lamps that struggled against the darkness.

—From *Paul Clifford*, by Edward Bulwer-Lytton

An adjective modifies a noun or pronoun.
Adjectives tell what kind, which one, how many, and whose.
Descriptive adjectives tell what kind.
A descriptive adjective becomes an abstract noun when you add *-ness* to it.
Possessive adjectives tell whose.

Hastings kissed the duke's hand in silence.

Nouns become adjectives when they are made possessive.
Form the possessive of a singular noun by adding an apostrophe and the letter *s*.

duchess ____________________

Form the possessive of a plural noun ending in *-s* by adding an apostrophe only.

emperors ____________________

Form the possessive of a plural noun that does not end in *-s* as if it were a singular noun.

noblemen ____________________

Since choice was mine, I chose the man love could not choose, and took this sad comfort to my heart.

—From *The Last of the Barons*, by Edward Bulwer-Lytton

An adjective that comes right before the noun it modifies is in the attributive position. An adjective that follows the noun it modifies is in the predicative position.

On the floor is the image of a dog in mosaic, with the well-known motto "Cave canem" upon it.

My name is well known, methinks, in Pompeii.
—From *The Last Days of Pompeii*, by Edward Bulwer-Lytton

Possessive Pronouns (Adjectives)

Attributive	**Predicative**
my	mine
your	yours
his, her, its	his, hers, its
our	ours
your	yours
their	theirs

The eyes were soft, dark, and brilliant, but dreamlike and vague; the features in youth must have been regular and beautiful, but their contour was now sharpened by the hollowness of the cheeks and temples.

His face was far less handsome than Marmaduke Nevile's, but infinitely more expressive, both of intelligence and command,—the features straight and sharp, the complexion clear and pale, and under the bright grey eyes a dark shade spoke either of dissipation or of thought.
— From *The Last of the Barons*, by Edward Bulwer-Lytton

Appositive adjectives directly follow the word they modify.

The sea, blue and tranquil, bounded the view.

To add to the attractions of his house, his wife, simple and good-tempered, could talk with anybody, take off the bores, and leave people to be comfortable in their own way.

It was a spot remote, sequestered, cloistered from the business and pleasures of the world.

The latter was a fine dark-eyed girl, tall, self-possessed, and dressed plainly indeed, but after the approved fashion.
—From *Alice: or, The Mysteries*, by Edward Bulwer-Lytton

When three or more nouns, adjectives, verbs, or adverbs appear in a series, they should be separated by commas.

"Wrinkles" in the comma rule:

1. **When three or more items are in a list, a coordinating conjunction before the last term is usual but not necessary.**

    The horse spun, bucked, kicked with abandon.
    The horse spun, bucked, and kicked with abandon.

    Chickens, roosters, ducks filled the yard.
    Chickens, roosters, and ducks filled the yard.

    I ran quickly, efficiently, easily.
    I ran quickly, efficiently, and easily.

    It was a spot remote, sequestered, cloistered.
    It was a spot remote, sequestered, and cloistered.

    It was a dark, stormy, frightening night.
    It was a dark, stormy, and frightening night.

2. **When three or more items are in a list and a coordinating conjunction is used, a comma should still follow the next-to-last item in the list.**

    The fourteen-year-old loved her sisters, Taylor Swift, and Jennifer Lawrence.
    The fourteen-year-old loved her sisters, Taylor Swift and Jennifer Lawrence.

    Oranges, apples, and plums filled the fruit bowl.
    Oranges, apples and plums filled the fruit bowl.

3. **When two or more adjectives are in the attributive position, they are only separated by commas if they are equally important in meaning.**

    Monday was a tiring, difficult day.
    Monday was a tiring and difficult day.
    Monday was a difficult, tiring day.

    The old man was wearing a grey wool overcoat.
    The old man was wearing a grey and wool overcoat.
    The old man was wearing a wool grey overcoat.

    INCORRECT: Monday was a tiring difficult day.
    INCORRECT: The old man was wearing a grey, wool overcoat.

Exercise 101A: Identifying Adjectives

Underline every adjective (including verb forms used as adjectives) in the following sentences. Above each adjective, write *DESC* for descriptive or *POSS* for possessive. Then, label each as in the attributive (*ATT*), appositive (*APP*), or predicative (*PRED*) position.

Finally, draw an arrow from each adjective to the word it modifies. Do not underline articles.

These sentences are taken from *A Strange Story*, by Edward Bulwer-Lytton.

And the tall guttering candle by the bedside, and the flicker from the fire, threw their reflection on the ceiling just over my head in a reek of quivering blackness.

An ascent, short, but steep and tortuous, conducted at once to the old Abbey Church, nobly situated in a vast quadrangle, round which were genteel and gloomy dwellings.

She seemed listless and dejected, and was very pale; but she denied that she felt unwell.

As to his antecedents, he had so frankly owned himself a natural son, a nobody, a traveller, an idler; his expenses were so unostentatious; he was so wholly the reverse of the character assigned to criminals, that it seemed as absurd to bring a charge of homicide against a butterfly or a goldfinch as against a seemingly innocent and delightful favourite of humanity and nature.

My bride was on the floor prostrate, insensible: my first dreadful thought was that life had gone.

The entrance of the arcade was covered with parasite creepers, in prodigal luxuriance, of variegated gorgeous tints,—scarlet, golden, purple; and the form, an idealized picture of man's youth fresh from the hand of Nature, stood literally in a frame of blooms.

I applied the flame of the candle to the circle, and immediately it became lambent with a low steady splendour that rose about an inch from the floor; and gradually from the light there emanated a soft, gray, transparent mist and a faint but exquisite odour.

Exercise 101B: Punctuation Practice

The sentences below are missing all of their punctuation marks! Using everything you have learned about punctuation, insert correct punctuation. You may simply write the punctuation marks in, rather than using proofreader's marks.

These sentences are slightly adapted from Horace Walpole's 1764 novel, *The Castle of Otranto*, generally thought to be the first gothic novel.

They heard a confused noise of shrieks horror and surprise

He examined the bleeding mangled remains of the young prince

The portrait of his grandfather which hung over the pitted oak bench where they had been sitting uttered a deep sigh

He printed a thousand kisses on her clay cold hands and uttered every expression that love sincere deep and despairing could dictate

The lower part of the castle was hollowed into several intricate cloisters it was not easy to find the door that opened into the dark awful cavern

His steady composed manner and the gallantry of his last reply which were the first words she heard distinctly interested her

His person was noble handsome and commanding but his countenance soon engrossed her whole attention

Surprise doubt tenderness respect succeeded each other in the youths face

Pride ambition and his reliance on ancient prophecies which had pointed out a possibility of preserving his family combated that thought

His hot headed impious passion subsided

Savage inhuman monster What have you done

Exercise 101C: Diagramming

On your own paper, diagram the following sentences from *The Mysteries of London*, an 1844 gothic novel by George W. M. Reynolds.

The sun had set behind huge piles of dingy purple clouds, which, after losing the golden hue with which they were for awhile tinged, became somber and menacing.

He was a man about fifty years of age, with a jolly red face, a somewhat bulbous nose, small laughing eyes, short grey hair standing upright in front, whiskers terminating above his white cravat.

When the two ruffians stooped down to take him up again, fear surmounted all other sentiments, all feelings, all inclinations; and his deep—his profound—his heartfelt agony was expressed in one long shriek, loud and piercing.

—LESSON 102—

Adjective Review
Pronoun Review
Limiting Adjectives

(All sentences in this lesson are taken from *The Two Towers*, by J. R. R. Tolkien.)

They had come to the desolation that lay before Mordor: the lasting monument to the dark labour of its slaves that should endure when all their purposes were made void; a land defiled, diseased beyond all healing—unless the Great Sea should enter in and wash it with oblivion.

brown curling hair	old tired horse
long black hair	white horse
snowy hair	running horse
his hair	king's horse

Descriptive adjectives *describe* by giving additional details.
Limiting adjectives *define* by setting limits.

Descriptive Adjectives	**Limiting Adjectives**
Regular	Possessives
Present participles	Articles
Past participles	Demonstratives
	Indefinites
	Interrogatives
	Numbers

The articles are *a*, *an*, and *the*.

Demonstrative pronouns demonstrate or point out something. They take the place of a single word or a group of words.

this, that, these, those

Demonstrative adjectives modify nouns and answer the question *which one*.

If those unhappy hobbits are astray in the woods, it might draw them hither.

The prisoners are NOT to be searched or plundered; those are my orders.

Indefinite pronouns are pronouns without antecedents.

Singular

anybody	anyone	anything
everybody	everyone	everything
nobody	no one	nothing
somebody	someone	something
another	other	one
either	neither	each

Plural

both few many several

Singular or Plural

all any most none some

I do not understand all that goes on myself, so I cannot explain it to you. Some of us are still true Ents, and lively enough in our fashion, but many are growing sleepy, going tree-ish, as you might say.

Indefinite adjectives modify nouns and answer the questions *which one* and *how many*.

We will ride for a few hours, gently, until we come to the end of the valley.

The cord hurts us, yes it does, it hurts us, and we've done nothing.

Some are quite wide awake, and a few are, well, ah, well, getting Entish.

Each Palantir replied to each, but all those in Gondor were ever open to the view of Osgiliath.

Interrogative pronouns take the place of nouns in questions.

who, whom, whose, what, which

Interrogative adjectives modify nouns.

Then if not yours, whose is the wizardry?

At whose command do you hunt Orcs in our land?

Which way do we go from here?

How far back his treachery goes, who can guess?

Cardinal numbers represent quantities (one, two, three, four . . .).
Ordinal numbers represent order (first, second, third, fourth . . .).

Treebeard was at their head, and some fifty followers were behind him.

Fifteen of my men I lost, and twelve horses, alas!

"Not Elves," said the fourth, the tallest, and as it appeared, the chief among them.

Gollum was the first to get up.

It was his turn to sleep first, and he was soon deep in a dream.

Exercise 102A: Identifying Adjectives

The following paragraph has been condensed slightly from the opening of "The Fall of the House of Usher," by Edgar Allan Poe. Underline every word that acts as an adjective.

Do not include phrases or clauses acting as adjectives. Also, do not include articles. (There are just too many!)

Label each one using the following abbreviations:

Descriptive Adjectives		**Limiting Adjectives**	
Regular	*DA-R*	Possessives	*LA-P*
Present participles	*DA-PresP*	~~Articles~~	~~*LA-A*~~
Past participles	*DA-PastP*	Demonstratives	*LA-D*
		Indefinites	*LA-IND*
		Interrogatives	*LA-INT*
		Numbers	*LA-N*

During the whole of a dull, dark, and soundless day in the autumn of the year, when the clouds hung oppressively low in the heavens, I had been passing alone, on horseback, through a singularly dreary tract of country, and at length found myself, as the shades of the evening drew on, within view of the melancholy House of Usher. I know not how it was—but, with the first glimpse of the building, a sense of insufferable gloom pervaded my spirit. I say insufferable; for the feeling was unrelieved by any of that half-pleasurable, because poetic, sentiment, with which the mind usually receives even the sternest natural images of the desolate or terrible. I looked upon the scene before me—upon the mere house, and the simple landscape features of the domain—upon the bleak walls—upon the vacant eye-like windows—upon a few rank sedges—and upon a few white trunks of decayed trees—with an utter depression of soul which I can compare to no earthly sensation more properly than to the after-dream of the reveller upon opium—the bitter lapse into every-day life—the hideous dropping off of the veil. There was an iciness, a sinking, a sickening of the heart—an unredeemed dreariness of thought. What was it—I paused to think—what was it that so unnerved me in the contemplation of the House of Usher? It was a mystery insoluble; nor could I grapple with the shadowy fancies that crowded upon me as I pondered. I was forced to fall back upon the unsatisfactory conclusion, that while, beyond doubt, there are combinations of very simple natural objects which have the power of thus affecting us, still the analysis of this power lies among considerations beyond our depth. It was possible, I reflected, that a different arrangement of the particulars of the scene, of the details of the picture, would be sufficient to modify, or perhaps to annihilate its capacity for sorrowful impression; and, acting upon this idea, I reined my horse to the precipitous brink of a black and lurid tarn that lay in unruffled lustre by the dwelling, and gazed down—but with a shudder even more thrilling than before—upon the remodelled and inverted images of the gray sedge, and the ghastly tree-stems, and the vacant and eye-like windows.

Exercise 102B: Analysis

The passage above shows you how a good writer uses adjectives: a mix of colorful descriptive adjectives and sparer, simpler limiting adjectives.

The total word count of the excerpt is 394 words. Now count each type of adjective and fill out the following chart:

Descriptive Adjectives		**Limiting Adjectives**	
Regular	__________	Possessives	__________
Present participles	__________	~~Articles~~	__________
Past participles	__________	Demonstratives	__________
		Indefinites	__________
		Interrogatives	__________
		Numbers	__________
Total Descriptive Adjectives	__________	Total Limiting Adjectives	__________

Total Adjectives Used __________

Good prose can't be reduced to *just* formulas—but formulas can give you some extra help in writing well. The total word count of the excerpt is 394 words. You can figure out what fraction of the total word count is taken up by adjectives by dividing the total word count by the total number of adjectives used. Work that sum now, and ask your instructor for help if necessary.

⟌ 394

The sum above tells you that 1 out of every ______________ [insert answer to division problem!] words in this passage is an adjective. In other words, adjectives do not make up more than about 1/______ of this descriptive writing.

Now let's look at the relationship between limiting and descriptive adjectives. Complete the following division problem:

[number of limiting adjectives] ______ | ___________ [number of descriptive adjectives] =

The sum above tells you that 1 out of every ________________ [insert answer to second division problem!] adjectives used is a limiting adjective. In other words, limiting adjectives do not make up more than about ________________ of this descriptive writing.

Ask your instructor to share the last part of this exercise with you.

Exercise 102C: Using Adjectives

On your own paper, rewrite the passage below. It is taken from Edgar Allen Poe's sea adventure *Narrative of A. Gordon Pym*—but all of the adjectives (except for articles) have been removed.

Where adjectives could be removed without making the sentence ungrammatical, they have simply been deleted without a trace. Where removing an adjective made the sentence unreasonable, a blank has been inserted instead. So you *know* that adjectives go in the blanks—but you'll have to find a lot of other places to put them as well!

You can also insert adverbs, additional articles, and conjunctions as necessary to make your insertions work.

Use the same proportions as the passage in Exercise 102B. This excerpt originally had 325 words, so use 45-48 total adjectives, not including articles.

Use no more than seven to nine limiting adjectives. Use at least three different kinds of limiting adjectives (your choice!).

The remainder should be descriptive adjectives. Use at least three participles (present or past) as adjectives.

When you are finished, compare your work with the original passage in the *Answer Key.*

The brig came on slowly, and now more steadily than before, and—I cannot speak calmly of ____________ event— ____________ hearts leaped up wildly within us, and we poured out ____________ souls in shouts and thanksgiving to God for the deliverance that was so palpably at hand. Of a sudden, and all at once, there came wafted over the ocean from the vessel (which was now close upon us) a smell, a stench, such as the world has no name for—no conception of. I gasped for breath, and turning to ____________ companions, perceived that they were ____________ than marble. But we had now no time left for question or surmise—the brig was within feet of us, and it seemed to be ____________ intention to run under ____________ counter, that we might board her without putting out a boat. We rushed aft, when, suddenly, a yaw threw her off full ____________ points from the course she had been running, and, as she passed under our stern at the distance of about ____________ feet, we had a view of ____________ decks. Shall I ever forget the horror of ____________ spectacle? Bodies, among whom were females, lay scattered about between the counter and the galley in the state of putrefaction. We plainly saw that not a soul lived in ____________ vessel! Yet we could not help shouting to the dead for help! Yes, long and loudly did we beg, in the agony of the moment, that those images would stay for us, would not abandon us to become like them, would receive us among their company! We were raving with horror and despair—thoroughly ____________ through the anguish of our disappointment.

—LESSON 103—

Misplaced Modifiers
Squinting Modifiers
Dangling Modifiers

The party organizer passed around stuffed mushrooms to the guests on tiny bamboo mats.

Churning inexorably towards the coast, we breathlessly watched the weather reports about the hurricane.

Miranda spotted a blue heron on the way home.

The movie star rode through the crowds of fans in a limousine.

The inconsiderate child was kicking the back of the airplane seat.
The child was kicking the inconsiderate back of the airplane seat.

Mari upset almost every colleague she worked with.
Mari almost upset every colleague she worked with.

I slept for barely an hour.
I barely slept for an hour.

A misplaced modifier is an adjective, adjective phrase, adverb, or adverb phrase in the wrong place.

The chocolate fudge cake that I baked recently fell off the table onto the dirty floor.

Doing fifty chin-ups quickly strengthens your biceps.

My friend said on Monday we would go camping.

A squinting modifier can belong either to the sentence element preceding or the element following.

After reading more on the subject, the article turned out to be incorrect.
The experiment failed, not having procured the correct ingredients.
Exhausted by long days at work, the secretary's joy was unbounded when the office closed because of snow.

A dangling modifier has no noun or verb to modify.

How to Fix a Dangling Modifier

1. Provide the missing word in the main clause.

   After reading more on the subject, I discovered that the article was incorrect.

2. Turn the dangling phrase into a clause by putting the missing word(s) into the phrase itself.

After I read more on the subject, the article turned out to be incorrect.

INCORRECT: Having been delayed by traffic, the bride's frustration was easily understood.

1. Provide the missing noun or verb in the main clause.

____

____

2. Turn the dangling phrase into a clause by putting the missing noun or verb into the phrase itself.

____

____

Exercise 103A: Correcting Misplaced Modifiers

Circle each misplaced modifier and draw an arrow to the place in the sentence that it should occupy.

I can't even consider leaving you without pain.

He was a man with one ear named William White.

My brother would like to play a piece on the piano of his own composing.

The housekeeper could see that the floor had been mopped with half an eye.

The fishermen were up before daybreak at 3 a.m.

Here are some ideas for protecting your property from the sheriff's department.

After robbing the bank, the getaway car took the robbers to the airport.

The dress that she wore to the wedding, splattered with cake frosting, has been cleaned.

Carefully baked by my mother, my brother brought cookies to the party.

Lost: A cow belonging to an old woman with brass knobs on her horns.

Exercise 103B: Clarifying Squinting Modifiers

Circle each squinting modifier. On your own paper, rewrite each sentence twice, eliminating the ambiguity by moving the squinting modifier to produce sentences with two different meanings. Insert commas and change capitalization/punctuation as needed.

The first is done for you. (Warning: the last one has a catch!)

Writing out the points on 3x5 cards (clearly) gave the second debater an edge.

Clearly, writing out the points on 3x5 cards gave the second debater an edge.

Writing out the points clearly on 3x5 cards gave the second debater an edge.

Aspiring pianists who practice often become proficient in a short time.

Children who watch TV rarely turn out to be readers.

The ancient Greeks understood human dignity at least as well as we do.

The vet explained eventually the dog would need to go back to the SPCA.

The pollen I breathed in intensely made me cough.

The king promised after his coronation to declare war on the kingdom's enemies.

Tell the caller if he is in the living room I will not see him.

Although the patient at first improved gradually he became sicker.

I only spoke to him.

Exercise 103C: Rewriting Dangling Modifiers

On your own paper, rewrite each of these sentences twice, using each of the strategies described in the lesson.

Hiking down the trail, the birds sang beautifully and the sweet scent of flowers drifted past.

The ferry departed, having eaten our lunch.

Looking at the mountain from the east, it has a plume of snow and ice blowing from its peak.

Tearing open the envelope, a thick wad of bills fell out.

After pointing out my errors, I was sent out of the room.

—LESSON 104—

Degrees of Adjectives

Comparisons Using *More*, *Fewer*, and *Less*

Good, better, best,
Never let it rest,
Till your good is better,
And your better, best.
—Julia Richman, *School Work 3*, No. 2 (June 1904)

And summer days were sad and long,
And sad the uncompanioned eyes,
And sadder sunset-tinted leaves.
Of all sad words of tongue or pen,
The saddest are these: "It might have been!"
—John Greenleaf Whittier

The positive degree of an adjective describes only one thing.
The comparative degree of an adjective compares two things.
The superlative degree of an adjective compares three or more things.

Most regular adjectives form the comparative by adding *-r* or *-er*.
Most regular adjectives form the superlative by adding *-st* or *-est*.

positive	comparative	superlative
______________	______________	______________

Irregular adjectives may change form completely.

positive	comparative	superlative
______________	______________	______________

For a moment the general did not reply; he was smiling his curious red-lipped smile. Then he said slowly, "No. You are wrong, sir. The Cape buffalo is not the most dangerous game." He sipped his wine. "Here in my preserve on this island," he said in the same slow tone, "I hunt more dangerous game."

—Richard Connell, "The Most Dangerous Game" (1924)

Many adjectives form their comparative and superlative forms by adding the word *more* or *most* before the adjective instead of using *-er* or *-est*. In comparative and superlative adjective forms, the words *more* and *most* are used as adverbs.

positive	comparative	superlative
______________	______________	______________

So long as people will drink, drink will be made; and so long as drink is made, there will be those to sell it. Well, the more the restrictions, the fewer to sell; the fewer to sell, the less sold; the less sold, the less made; the less made, the less drunk; the less drunk, the fewer the inebriates—and that's what the temperance people are after.

—*The Grip*, Vol. 20, 1882

The more thoroughly we searched, the fewer treasures we found.
The more love I offered, the less enthusiasm he showed.

Use *fewer* for concrete items and *less* for abstractions.

He would do very well if he had fewer cakes and sweetmeats sent him from home.
I wanted to tease you a little to make you less sad.

—Charlotte Bronte, *Jane Eyre*

In comparisons using *more . . . fewer* and *more . . . less*, *more* and *less* can act as either adverbs or adjectives, and *the* can act as an adverb.

We searched (the) more thoroughly. We found (the) fewer treasures.
I offered (the) more love. He showed (the) less enthusiasm.

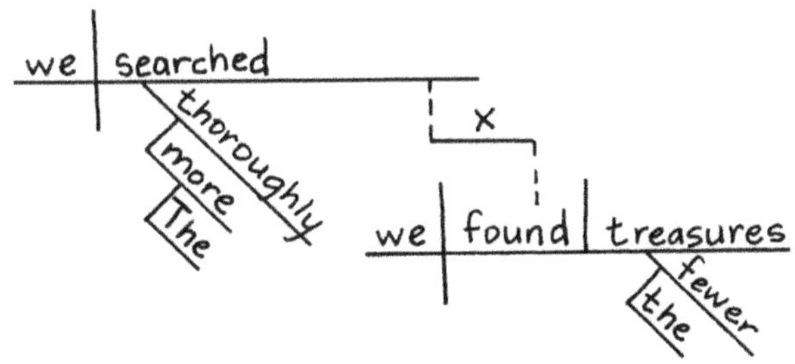

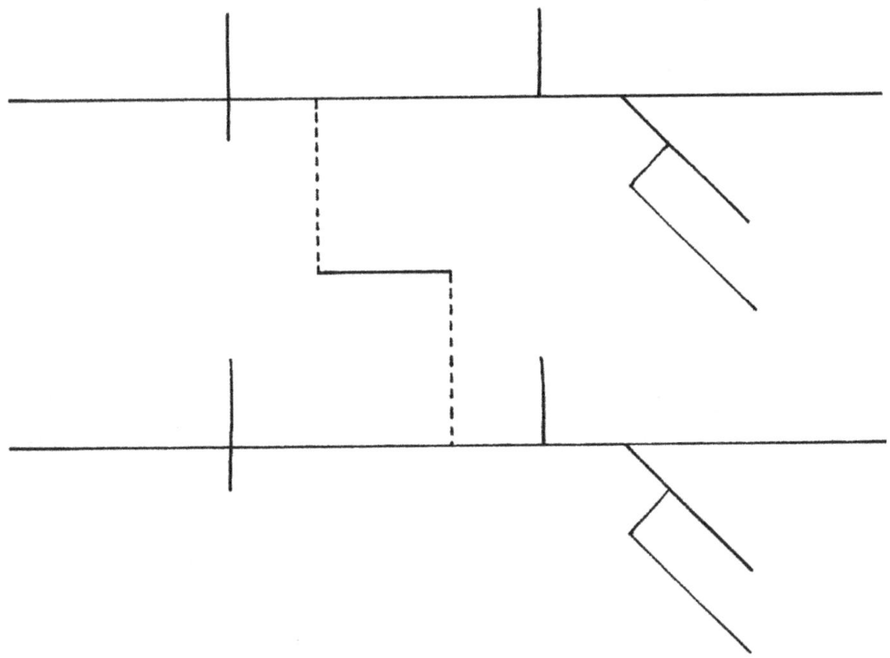

The more the building shook, the less he wanted to be there.

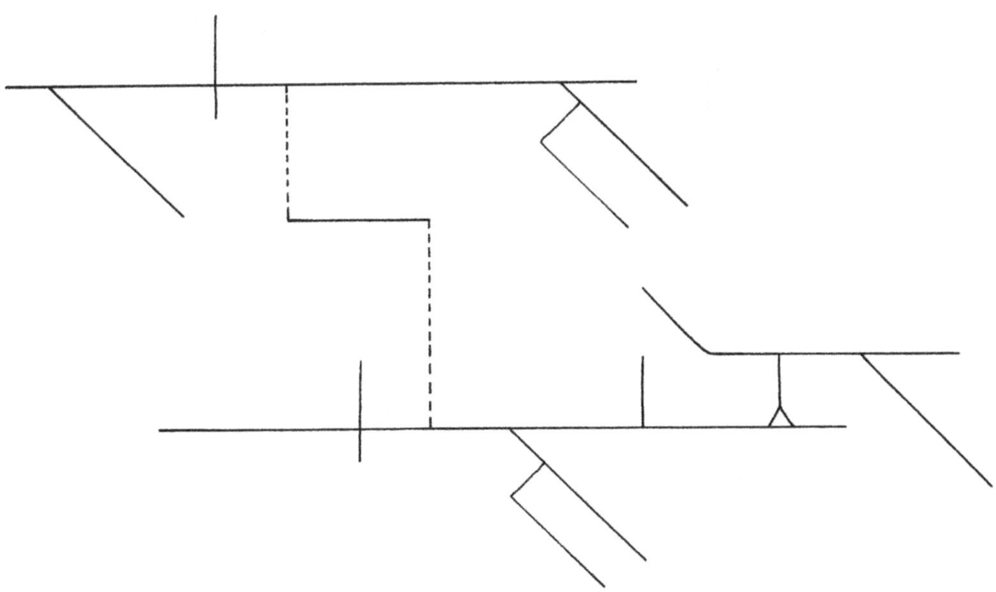

The more the building shook, the more we held on.

The less we saw, the less we knew.

The more the wave rose, the faster we ran.
The less we worried, the better we felt.
The happier we were, the more we rejoiced.
The louder the wind, the fewer words we were able to exchange.

The better we felt, the longer we stayed.
The longer the tail grew, the better the horse could swat flies.

The better we felt, the longer we stayed.

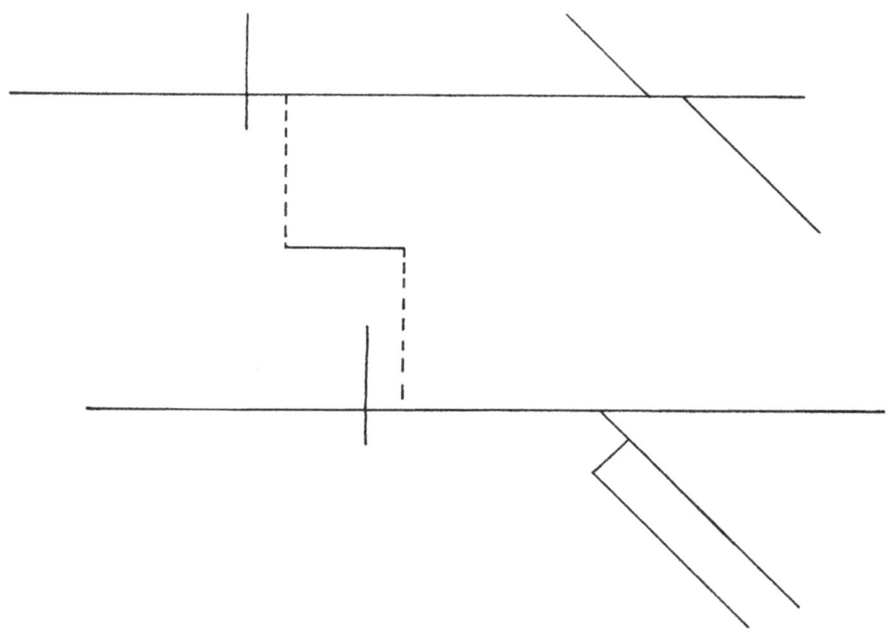

The longer the tail grew, the better the horse could swat flies.

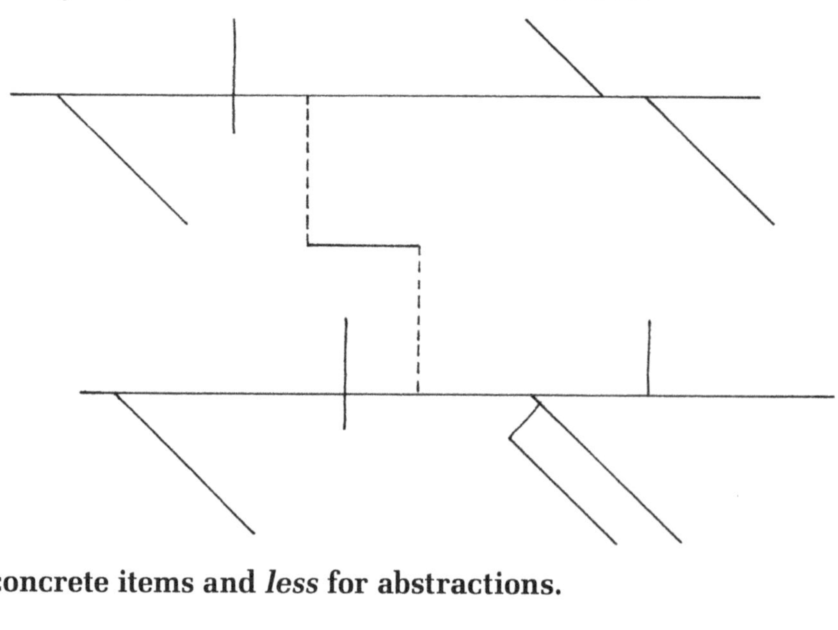

Use *fewer* for concrete items and *less* for abstractions.

Comparisons can be formed using a combination of *more* and *fewer* or *less*; a combination of *more* and *more* or *fewer/less* and *fewer/less*; a combination of *more* or *fewer/less* with a comparative form; or simply two comparative forms.

In comparisons using *more*, *fewer*, and *less*, *more* and *less* can act as either adverbs or adjectives, and *the* can act as an adverb.

In comparisons using two comparative forms, the forms may act as either adverbs or adjectives, and *the* can act as an adverb.

Exercise 104A: Positive, Comparative, and Superlative Adjectives

Using the following chart to review spelling rules for forming degrees of adjectives. Fill in the missing forms. Then, fill in the blank in each sentence with each adjective indicated in brackets (properly spelled!).

These sentences are all drawn from Emily Bronte's classic novel *Wuthering Heights.*

Spelling Rules

If the adjective ends in *-e* already, add only *–r* or *–st.*

noble	nobler	noblest
pure	purer	purest
cute	________	________

If the adjective ends in a short vowel sound and a consonant, double the consonant and add *–er* or *–est.*

red	redder	reddest
thin	thinner	thinnest
flat	________	________

If the adjective ends in *–y*, change the *y* to *i* and add *–er* or *–est.*

hazy	hazier	haziest
muddy	________	________

A wild, wicked slip she was—but she had the ____________________ eye, the ____________________ smile, and the ____________________ foot in the parish. [in order, the superlatives of *bonny*, *sweet*, and *light*]

Our young lady returned to us ____________________ and ____________________, and ____________________ than ever. [in order, the comparatives of *saucy, passionate,* and *haughty*]

"It is not so buried in trees," I replied, "and it is not quite so large, but you can see the country beautifully all round; and the air is ____________________ for you— ____________________ and ____________________." [in order, the comparatives of *healthy, fresh,* and *dry*]

Catherine, his ____________________ days were over when your days began. [superlative of *happy*]

"But you have been ____________________," persisted his cousin; "____________________ than when I saw you last; you are ____________________." [in order, the comparatives of *bad, bad* again, and *thin*]

I went, at the ____________________ opportunity, and besought him to depart. [superlative of *early*]

He had grown ____________________, and lost his colour. [comparative of *spare*]

Many a time I've cried to myself to watch them growing ____________________ daily. [comparative of *reckless*]

I discerned a soft-featured face, exceedingly resembling the young lady at the Heights, but ____________________ and ____________________ in expression. [in order, the comparative of *pensive* and the positive of *amiable*]

Your presence is a moral poison that would contaminate the ____________________: for that cause, and to prevent ____________________ consequences, I shall deny you hereafter admission into this house. [in order, the superlative of *virtuous* and the comparative of *bad*]

That is the ______________________ deed that ever you did. [superlative of *diabolical*]

Linton was very reluctant to be roused from his bed at five o'clock, and astonished to be informed that he must prepare for ______________________ travelling [comparative of *far*]

Let them say the ______________________ word to her, and she'll curl back without respect of any one. [superlative of *less*]

Exercise 104B: Forming Comparisons

Rewrite each set of independent clauses so that they form a comparative sentence making use of *more*, *less*, *fewer*, and/or comparative forms of the adjectives indicated. The first is done for you.

When you are finished, ask your instructor to show you the original sentences, which are taken from Charlotte Bronte's novels *Villete* and *Shirley*.

The humor is inflexibly stubborn.
The tone is sadder and softer.

The more inflexibly stubborn the humor, the sadder, the softer the tone.

My mien was impassible and prosaic.
She laughed more merrily.

I did more.
I worked harder.
He seemed less content.

They say.
They have more to say.

I look further into this matter.
I see plainly.

We live longer.
Our experience widens.
We are less prone to judge our neighbour's conduct.

____

____

Exercise 104C: Using *Fewer* and *Less*

Complete the sentences by filling in each blank with either *fewer* or *less*.

The original sentences are taken from Charlotte Bronte's novels *Villete* and *Shirley*.

Her attainments were ________ than were usually possessed by girls of her age and station.

With little ceremony, and ________ courtesy, he pointed out what he termed her errors.

I am cheated in ________ things than you imagine.

Once or twice she addressed him with suddenness and sharpness, saying that he hurt her, and must contrive to give her ________ pain.

Such men may have ________ originality, ________ force of character than you, but they are better friends to mankind.

Exercise 104D: Diagramming

On your own paper, diagram every word of the following sentences from *Wuthering Heights.*

The more the worms writhe, the more I yearn to crush out their entrails!
The nearer I got to the house the more agitated I grew; and on catching sight of it I trembled in every limb.
By his knack of sermonizing and pious discoursing, he contrived to make a great impression on Mr. Earnshaw; and the more feeble the master became, the more influence he gained.

WEEK 27

Double Identities

—LESSON 105—

Clauses with Understood Elements

Than as Conjunction, Preposition, and Adverb

Quasi-Coordinators

I like chocolate better than vanilla.
Other than pistachio, I'll eat any flavor of ice cream.
I am more than satisfied with chocolate, but less than happy with pistachio.
I will starve rather than eat pistachio.

A coordinating conjunction joins equal words or groups of words together.
A subordinating conjunction joins unequal words or groups of words together.

He worked more efficiently than his brother.
He worked more efficiently than his brother [worked].

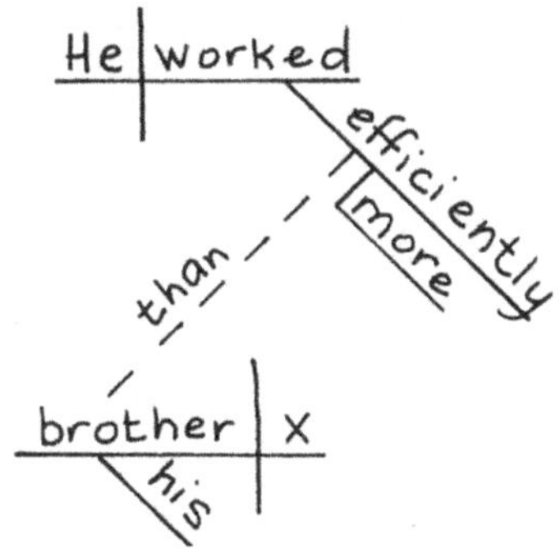

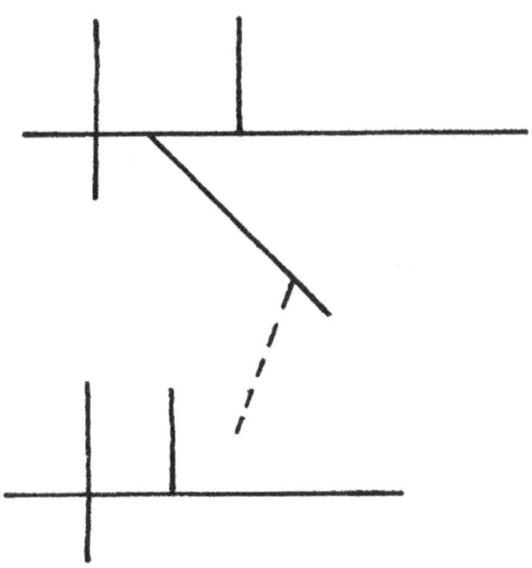

Tomorrow should be sunnier than today.
A new broom sweeps better than an old one.
The cook added more salt than he should have.

I love him more than you.

He is stronger than I.

INCORRECT: He is stronger than me.

He is stronger than I am.

not He is stronger than me.

When *than* is used in a comparison and introduces a clause with understood elements, it is acting as a subordinating conjunction.

Other than pistachio, I'll eat any flavor of ice cream.

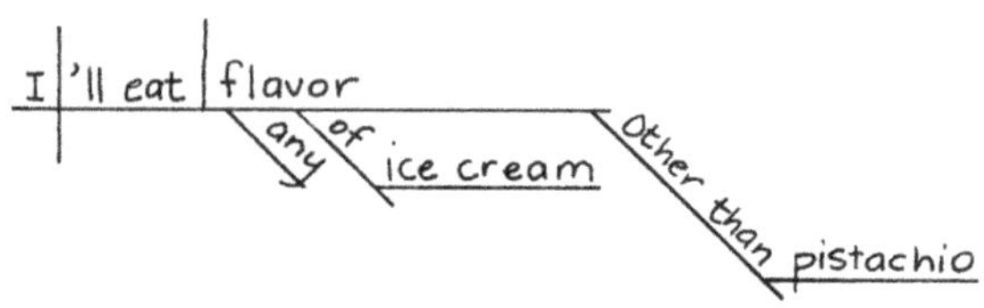

***Other than* is a compound preposition that means "besides" or "except."**

I am more than satisfied with chocolate, but less than happy with pistachio.

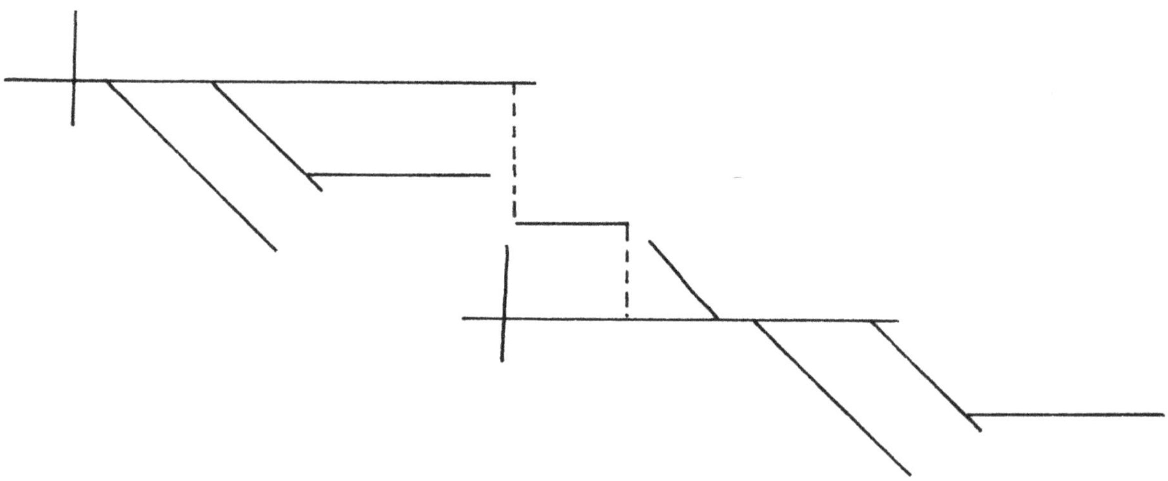

***More than* and *less than* are compound modifiers.**

I will starve rather than eat pistachio.

I will starve *and* eat pistachio.

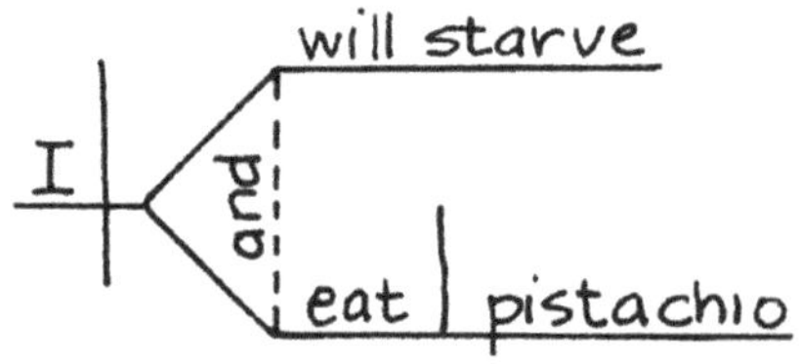

Quasi-coordinators link compound parts of a sentence that are unequal. Quasi-coordinators include *rather than*, *sooner than*, *let alone*, and *not to mention*.

I will starve rather than eat pistachio.

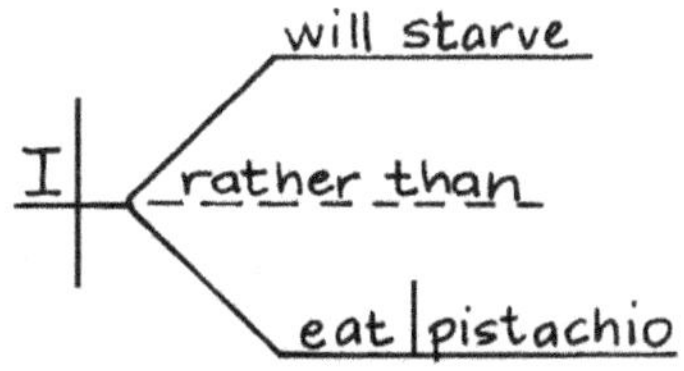

Rather than going home, she drove back up to the lake.

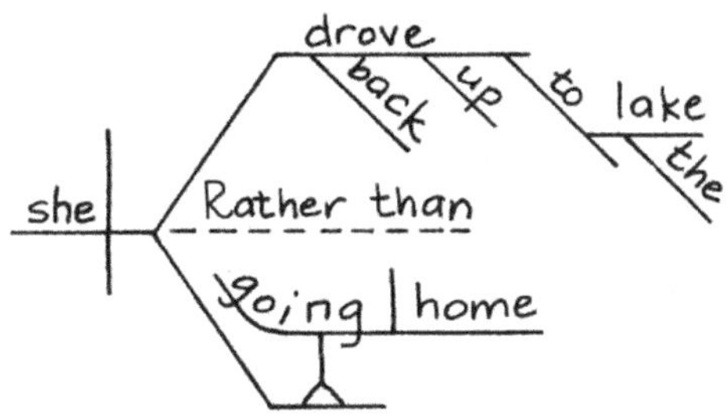

He could not keep up with Patel, let alone Krishna.

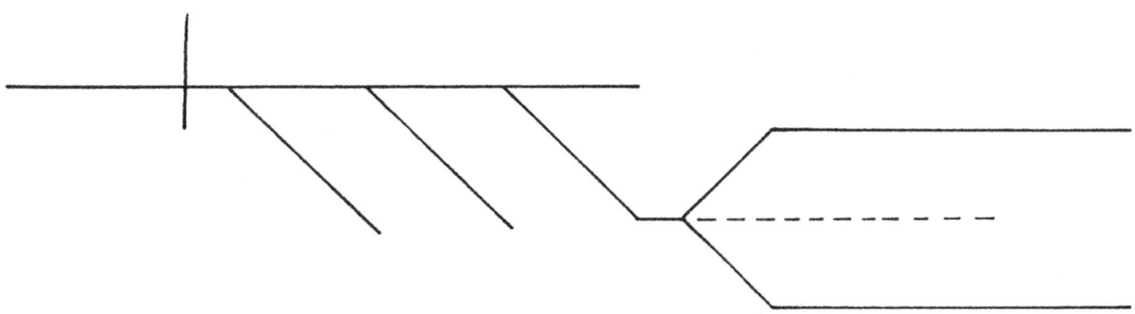

The expense, not to mention the risk, was simply too great.

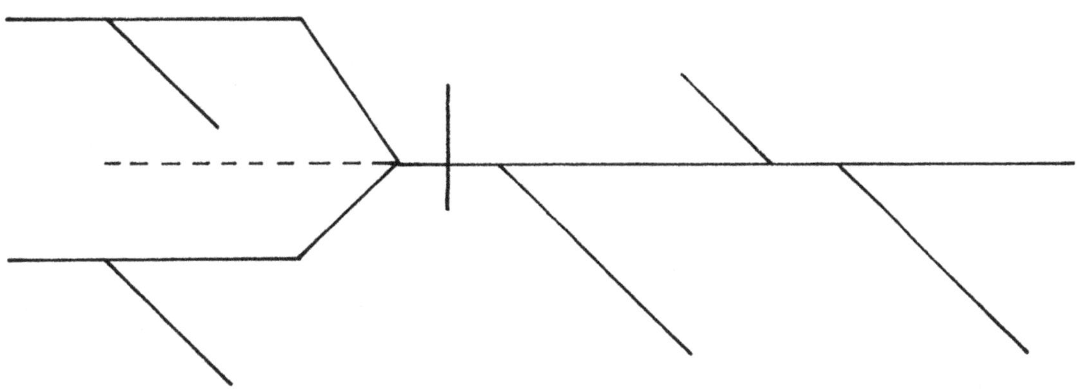

He would walk in a hailstorm sooner than pay ten dollars for a cab.

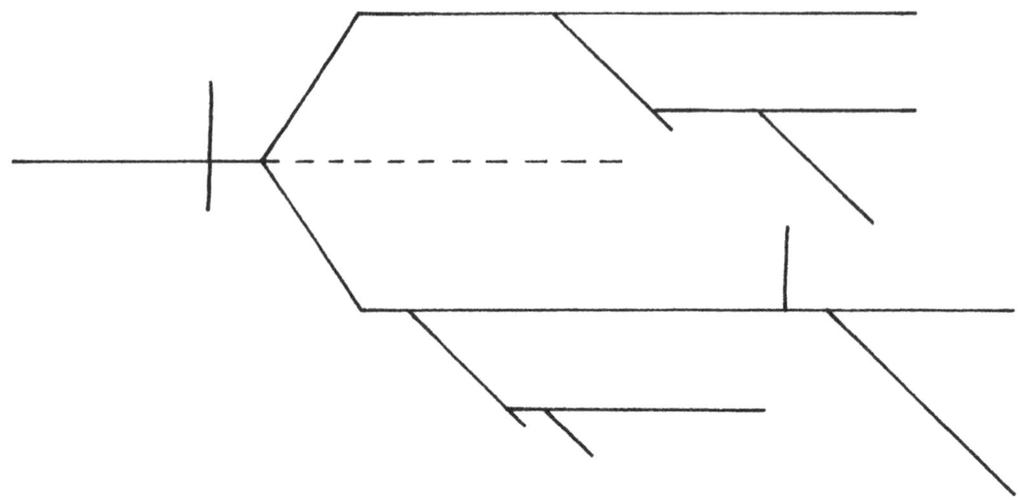

When *than* is used in a comparison and introduces a clause with understood elements, it is acting as a subordinating conjunction.
Other than* is a compound preposition that means *besides* or *except.
***More than* and *less than* are compound modifiers.**

Quasi-coordinators link compound parts of a sentence that are unequal. Quasi-coordinators include *rather than, sooner than, let alone,* and *not to mention.*

Exercise 105A: Comparisons Using *Than*

Each of the following sentences, taken from Charles Darwin's account of his travels in *The Voyage of the Beagle,* contains a comparison clause introduced by *than* and missing some of its words. Using carets, do your best to insert the missing words.

Considering that there is no natural boundary between the two places, and that the character of the country is nearly similar, the difference was much greater than I should have expected.

At Bahia Blanca, a recent establishment in Northern Patagonia, I was surprised to find how little the deer cared for the noise of a gun; one day I fired ten times from within eighty yards at one animal; and it was much more startled at the ball cutting up the ground than at the report of the rifle.

I allude only to the butterflies; for the moths, contrary to what might have been expected from the rankness of the vegetation, certainly appeared in much fewer numbers than in our own temperate regions.

Nothing can be more striking than the effect of these huge rounded masses of naked rock rising out of the most luxuriant vegetation.

It is as flat and elastic as an ivory paper-cutter, and the lower mandible, differing from every other bird, is an inch and a half longer than the upper.

Exercise 105B: Identifying Parts of the Sentence

In the following sentences, drawn from *The Life and Letters of Charles Darwin*, Vol. I, identify each bolded word or phrase as *SC* for subordinating conjunction, *QC* for quasi-coordinator, *PREP* for preposition, or *ADV* for adverb.

In the old days the practice of bleeding largely was universal, but my father maintained that far more evil was thus caused **than** good done; and he advised me if ever I were myself ill not to allow any doctor to take **more than** an extremely small quantity of blood.

He gave one the idea that he had been active **rather than** strong; his shoulders were not broad for his height, though certainly not narrow.

I think I shall go for a few days to town to hear an opera and see Mr. Hope, **not to mention** my brother also, whom I should have no objection to see.

I am nothing **more than** a lions' provider: I do not feel at all sure that they will not growl and finally destroy me.

The author begins by stating that varieties differ from each other less **than** species.

The origin of a new species by **other than** ordinary agencies would be a vastly greater "catastrophe" than any of those which Lyell successfully eliminated from sober geological speculation.

We felt that we saw more of him in a week's holiday **than** in a month at home.

He had more dread **than** have most people of repeating his stories, and continually said, "You must have heard me tell," or "I dare say I've told you."

Your engraving is exactly true, but underrates **rather than** exaggerates the luxuriance.

How much **more than** delightful to go to some good concert or fine opera.

Exercise 105C: Diagramming

On your own paper, diagram every word of the following sentences, slightly condensed from *The Voyage of the Beagle.*

In five little packets which I sent him, he has ascertained no less than sixty-seven different organic forms!

One is a small kingfisher (*Ceryle Americana*); it has a longer tail than the European species, and hence does not sit in so stiff and upright a position.

Much of the snow at these great heights is evaporated rather than thawed.

If Vesuvius, Etna, and Hecla in Iceland (all three relatively nearer than the corresponding points in South America), suddenly burst forth in eruption on the same night, the coincidence would be remarkable.

—LESSON 106—

The Word *As*

Quasi-Coordinators

Middle English *alswa* "similarly" *as*

> The twenty-fourth object would be as big as a sugar cube, the twenty-seventh would be about the size of a large mammal, the fifty-fourth would be the size of the planet Jupiter and the fifty-seventh would be about as big as the Sun, where even atoms are destroyed by gravity, leaving a mixture of nuclei and free electrons called a plasma.
>
> —John R. Gribbin, *The Scientists: A History of Science Told Through the Lives of Its Greatest Inventors*

is big
The twenty-fourth object would be as big as a sugar cube ^.

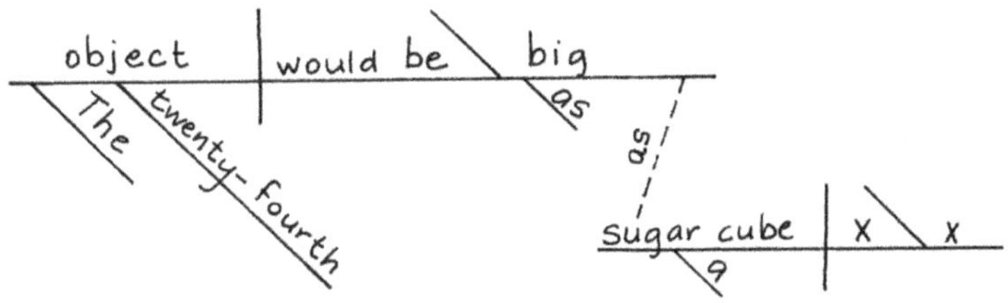

(The following sentences are all from Gribbin's *The Scientists* as well.)

An equally important factor, as many people have argued, was the depopulation of Europe by the Black Death.

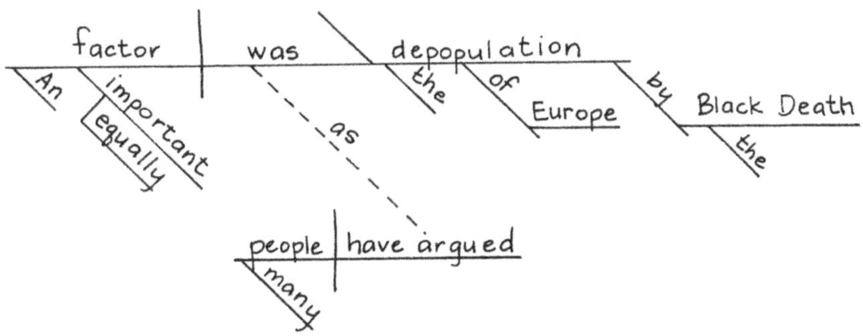

As long as Frederick remained on the throne, Tycho was able to enjoy an unprecedented amount of freedom to run his observatory just as he liked.

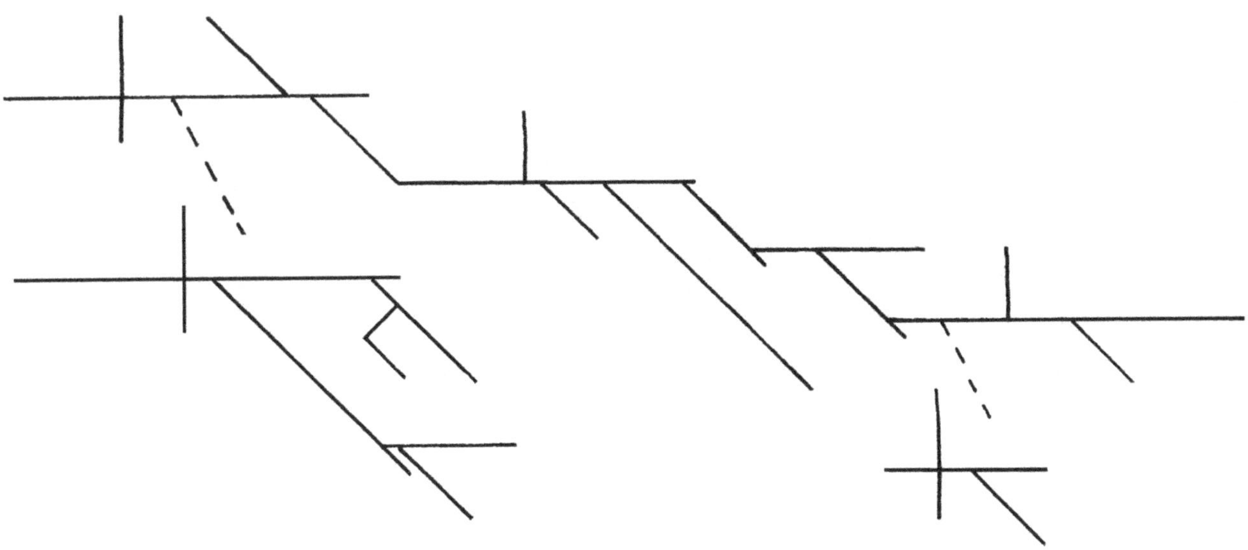

There were many translations and new editions of the book, which laid the foundations for chemistry as a genuinely scientific discipline.

Lavoisier . . . played a full part in the activities of the Academy, and during his time as a member worked on very many reports covering topics as diverse as . . . meteorites, cultivation of cabbages, the mineralogy of the Pyrenees and the nature of the gas arising from cesspools.

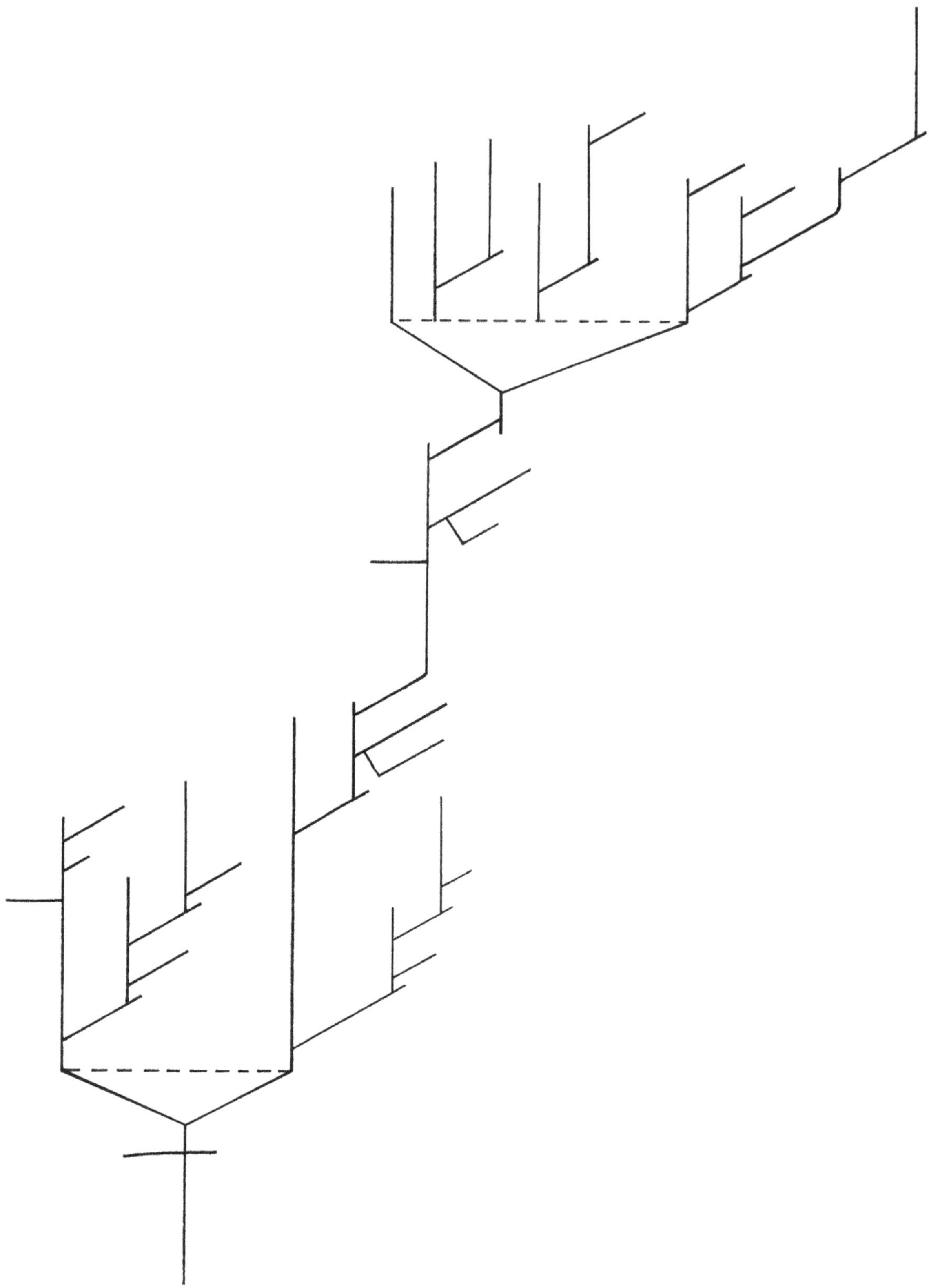

At the time of his marriage, as well as considerable property, Charles Cavendish had a disposable annual income of at least £2000, which grew as time passed.

Quasi-coordinators link compound parts of a sentence that are unequal. Quasi-coordinators include *rather than*, *sooner than*, *let alone*, *as well as*, and *not to mention*.

As well as his fame as a geologist, Darwin also received acclaim as a writer, in the mould of Lyell.

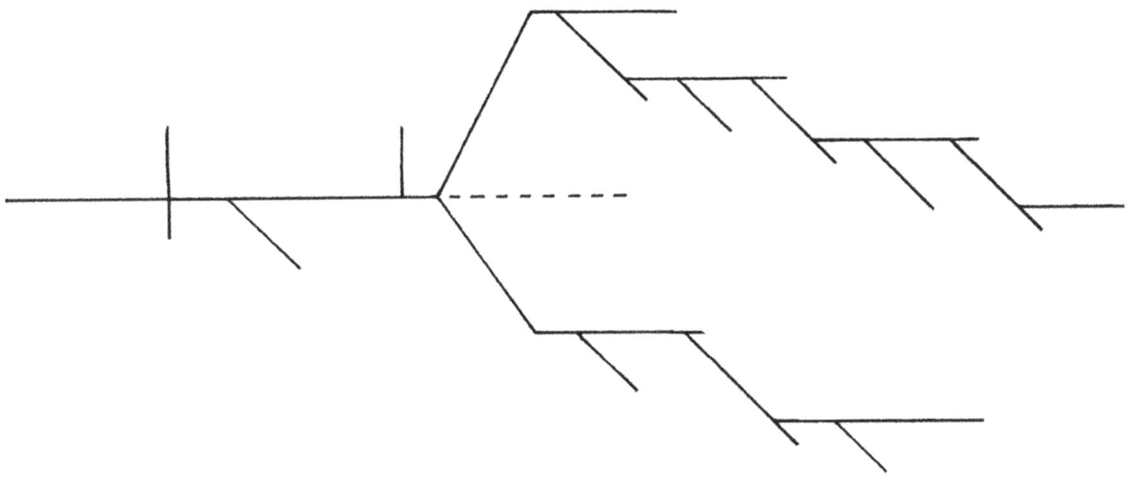

Exercise 106A: Identifying Parts of the Sentence

In the following sentences, find and underline every adverb, preposition, conjunction, and quasi-coordinator. Then label each as *ADV* for adverb, *PREP* for preposition, *CC* for coordinating conjunction, *SC* for subordinating conjunction, and *QC* for quasi-coordinator. Remember that a quasi-coordinator can be a short phrase as well as a single word.

These sentences are adapted from Oliver Goldsmith's 1816 scientific study, *A History of the Earth and Animated Nature.*

Pectoral fins serve the same purpose to fish as wings do to birds.

Fishes are as deaf as they are mute.

The frogs began to be agitated, more than before.

The tail of the whale serves as a great oar to push its mass along.

The sword-fish is as active as the whale is strong.

He describes his countrymen as living for part of the year upon salted gulls.

Sharks, as well as rays, bring forth their young alive.

The animal, in less than two days, grows a hard skin over its body.

The land tortoise is much more nimble upon land than the sea turtle.

The Pike-headed Whale and the Round-lipped Whale differ from each other, as their names obviously imply.

Larger fish will swallow a living small fish upon a hook, sooner than any bait that can be put on it.

The fish seems as well furnished with the means of happiness as quadrupeds or birds.

Those tiny bones are dangerous as well as troublesome to be eaten.

Exercise 106B: Diagramming

On your own paper, diagram every word of the following sentences, slightly adapted from Oliver Goldsmith's 1816 scientific study, *A History of the Earth and Animated Nature.*

These are difficult! Do your best to think through the sentences, but ask for help if you need it.

A roach appears more bony than a carp, because it is leaner and smaller; and it is actually more bony than an eel, because it has a greater number of fins.

In a single season, a cod can produce as many potential offspring as there are people in England; the cod spawns in one season more than ten million eggs.

The scorpion's head seems, as it were, joined to the breast, in the middle of which are seen two eyes.

It is a good thing that scorpions are so destructive to each other, or they would multiply so greatly as to make some countries uninhabitable.

—LESSON 107—

Words That Can Be Multiple Parts of Speech

(The sentences from this lesson have been slightly adapted and condensed from *Bleak House*, by Charles Dickens.)

But ______________________ ______________________

I had an illness, but it was not a long one.

He has never hurt anybody but himself.

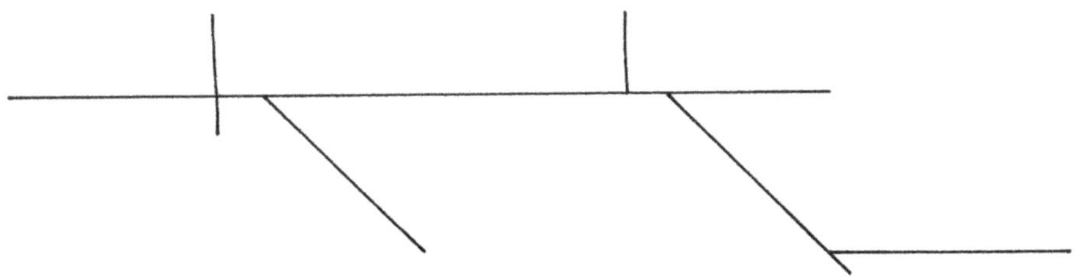

For ______________________ ______________________

I can answer for him as little as for you.

I should have been ashamed to come here to-day, for I know what a figure I must seem to you two.

About ______________________ ______________________

You could hear the horses being rubbed down outside the stable and being told to "Hold up!" and "Get over," as they slipped about very much on the uneven stones.

What with making notes on a slate about jams, and pickles, and preserves, and bottles, and glass, and china, and a great many other things; and what with being generally a methodical, old-maidish sort of foolish little person, I was so busy that I could not believe it was breakfast-time when I heard the bell ring.

Yet ______________________ ______________________

Is he here yet?
At this time, Jo has not yet died.
It is good, yet it could be improved.

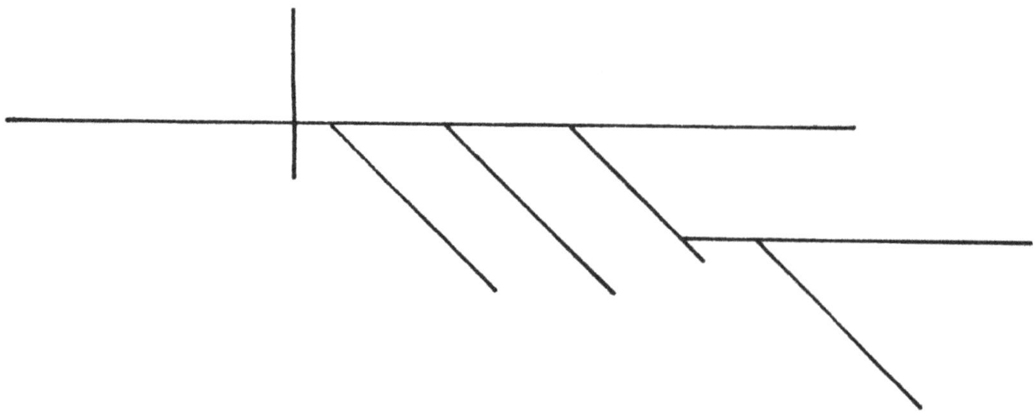

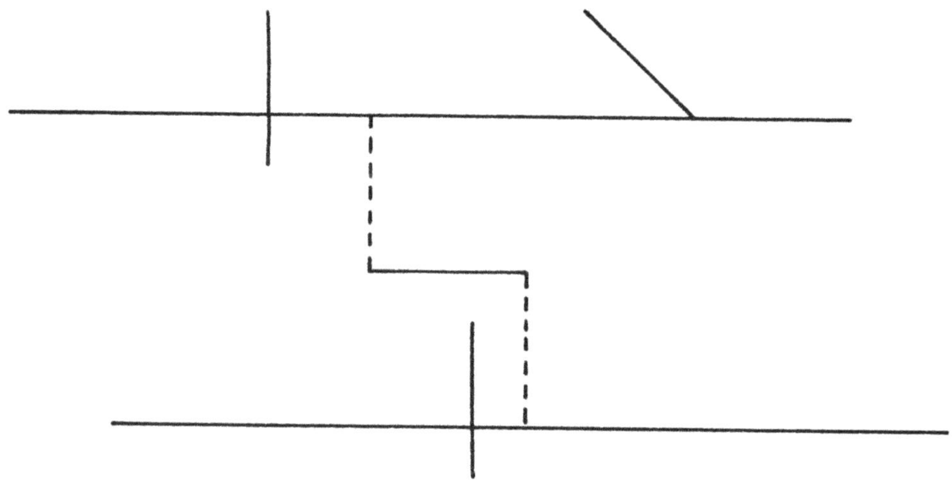

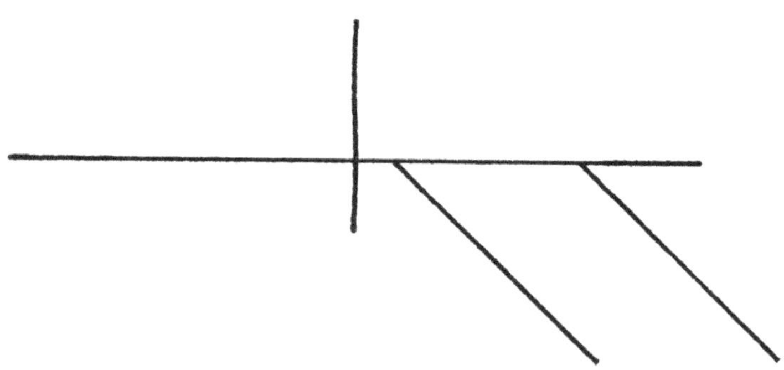

Any pronoun adjective adverb

I could not reproach myself any less.

It would be an insult to the discernment of any man with half an eye to tell him so.

I wonder whether any of the gentlemen remembered him.

I then asked Richard whether he had thought of any more congenial pursuit.

I thought it was impossible that you could have loved me any better.

Before ______________ ______________ ______________

Weariness of soul lies before her, as it lies behind.

It was past twelve before he took his candle and his radiant face out of the room.

He seemed to have been completely exhausted long before.

Above preposition ______________ ______________

The flame of gas was burning so sullenly above the iron gate.

His eyes were fixed high above.

But it is all blank, blank as the darkness above.

After preposition adverb ______________

In half an hour after our arrival, Mrs. Jellyby appeared.

I once more saw him looking at me after he had passed the door.

He presented himself soon after.

Otherwise ______________ ______________ ______________

We are not so prejudiced as to suppose that in private life you are otherwise than a very estimable man.

How could you do otherwise?

Love her and all will go well; otherwise, all will go ill.

Still

It is quite still and silent. ______________

She remained perfectly still until the carriage turned into the drive. ______________

The cause was hopeless; still, they fought. ______________

Still yourself, my dear, and wait in patience. ______________

In the still, the woods seemed massively hushed in sleep. ______________

Exercise 107A: Identifying Parts of Speech

Identify the part of speech of each underlined word (adapted from *Bleak House*, by Charles Dickens) by writing the correct abbreviation above it: *N* (noun), *PRO* (pronoun), *V* (verb), *ADJ* (adjective), *ADV* (adverb), *PREP* (preposition), *CC* (coordinating conjunction), or *SC* (subordinating conjunction).

I came off laughing, and red, and anything but tidy.

After we got home, he haunted a post opposite our house.

We stood aside, watching for any countenance we knew.

They meet again at dinner—again, next day—again, for many days in succession.

Mr. Snagsby is doubtful of his being awake and out—doubtful of the reality of the streets through which he goes—doubtful of the reality of the moon that shines above.

We were charmed by his fine hilarious manner and his engaging candour and his genial way of lightly tossing his own weaknesses about.

Business has prevented me from mixing much with general society in any but a professional character.

As the bell was yet ringing and the great people were not yet come, I had leisure to glance over the church, which smelt as earthy as a grave.

Her fingers were white and wrinkled with washing, and the soap-suds were yet smoking which she wiped off her arms.

Well, my dear, it's a pretty anecdote, nothing more; still I think it charming.

I said I would be ready at half-past six, and after she was gone, stood looking at the basket, quite lost in the magnitude of my trust.

I cannot describe the tenderness with which he spoke to her, half playfully yet all the more compassionately and mournfully.

I don't think there's any harm in that.

The men's consent I bought, but her help was freely given.

In no way wearied by his sallies on the road, he was in the drawing-room before any of us; and I heard him at the piano while I was yet looking after my housekeeping.

The sky had partly cleared, but was very gloomy—even above us, where a few stars were shining.

And have the children looked after themselves at all, sir?

I have no purpose but to die.

On this blooming summer morning, they sat beneath the cloudless sky above.

It appeared to be something droll, for occasionally there was a laugh and a cry of "Silence!"

Keep the whole thing quiet ever after.

Don't you worry any more.

He will get into some trouble or difficulty otherwise.

"I hear a voice," says Chadband; "Is it a still small voice, my friends?"

It was so delicious to see the clouds about his bright face clearing, and to see him so heartily pleased.

Exercise 107B: Diagramming

On your own paper, diagram every word of the following sentences from *Bleak House.*

Weariness of soul lies before her, as it lies behind.

Everything the dear child wore was either too large for him or too small.

They straggle about in wrong places, look at the wrong things, don't care for the right things, gape when more rooms are opened, and exhibit profound depression of spirits.

The next two sentences are **CHALLENGE EXERCISES**—ask for help when necessary!

She should be an upper servant by her attire, yet in her air and step, though both are hurried and assumed—as far as she can assume in the muddy streets, which she treads with an unaccustomed foot—she is a lady.

Beyond it was a burial ground—a dreadful spot in which the night was very slowly stirring, where I could dimly see heaps of dishonored graves and stones, hemmed in by filthy houses with a few dull lights in their windows, on whose walls a thick humidity broke out like a disease.

—LESSON 108—

Nouns Acting as Other Parts of Speech
Adverbial Noun Phrases

Exercise 108A: Nouns

The next five sentences are taken from the classic reader *Animal and Nature Stories,* edited by William Patten. Identify the part of the sentence that each underlined noun plays by labeling it as *S* for subject, *DO* for direct object, or *OP* for object of the preposition.

The afternoon wore on, and the sun got low.
—Anna Sewell, *Black Beauty*

Afterward, he made the round of the camps.
—Rush Hawkins, "Jeff the Inquisitive"

The well, when we reached it, was dried up, and few of the pilgrims survived.
—Lillian Gask, "Ships of the Desert"

She staked her all on the answers to those eager questions.
—John Brown, "Rab and His Friends"

After a while, they carried them all away.
—John Lubbock, "The Intelligence of Ants"

Exercise 108B: Nouns as Other Parts of Speech

Each of the following sets of sentences is missing one of the nouns from the exercise above. Your task: figure out which of those nouns can fill every blank in one set of sentences, according to the parts of speech given in parentheses. Each set must use the *same* noun in each blank!

These sentences are slightly adapted from *Animal and Nature Stories*, edited by William Patten.

The good Doctor did nothing to stop the ______________ of gayeties. (noun)
—Harriet Beecher Stowe, "The Katy-Did's Party"

The wind shook the boughs and scattered the fruit ______________ far and wide. (adv)
—Carl Ewald, "The Beech and the Oak"

The anemones burst into flower and bashfully bowed their ______________ heads to the earth. (adj)
—Carl Ewald, "The Anemones"

He helped ______________ up the cows, casting furtive glances ahead. (verb)
—M. Cornell, "Anna and the Rattler"

I found, in that ______________ walk, some curiously shaped splinters of jasper. (adj)
—Charles C. Abbott, "How the Stone-Age Children Played"

They went one ______________ to drink tea with Lady Margaret. (noun)
—Octave Thanet, "Marcus Aurelius"

I'll take good care of you ______________ you are mine. (subordinating conjunction)
—Octave Thanet, "Marcus Aurelius"

I will ______________ away the time by geologizing. (verb)
—Charles C. Abbott, "How the Stone-Age Children Played"

All the ______________, he continued to be an incorrigible rogue and thief. (noun)
—W. H. G. Kingston, "Some True Stories of Tigers, Wolves, Foxes and Bears"

______________ camels are by nature patient, and strong to endure. (adj)
—Lillian Gask, "Ships of the Desert"

The papa fox took a survey ______________ round. (adv)
—W. H. G. Kingston, "Some True Stories of Tigers, Wolves, Foxes and Bears"

______________ of these arrow-points are very neatly made. (pronoun)
—David Starr Jordan, "The Story of a Stone"

He seemed so glad to give his ______________ that I was ashamed of myself. (noun)
—Louisa May Alcott, *Little Women*

The frosts came early, but we are all ______________. (adj)
—Lillian Gask, "Two Enemies of the Beavers"

We know very ______________ that if we once catch a bad cold we are done for. (adv)
—Carl Ewald, "The Anemones"

______________, you must wait until Father Beaver comes home. (int)
—Lillian Gask, "At Home with the Beavers"

They drank from the ______________ at Blackfriars Wynd. (noun)
—John Brown, "Rab and His Friends"

Tears ______________ in her eyes as she reads the letter. (verb)
—Octave Thanet, "Marcus Aurelius"

Mary and her lamb went into the school.

Mary and her lamb went home.

He followed her to school on Monday.

He followed her to school one day.

An adverbial noun tells the time or place of an action, or explains how long, how far, how deep, how thick, or how much. It can modify a verb, adjective, or adverb. An adverbial noun plus its modifiers is an adverbial noun phrase.

Before the lamb had travelled a mile, Mary turned around.

The road to school was two miles long.

The mud puddle in the road was three inches deep.

The lamb splashed in the puddle until he was covered with inch-thick mud.

The lamb splashed in the puddle until he was covered with mud an inch thick.

The storm continued all night.

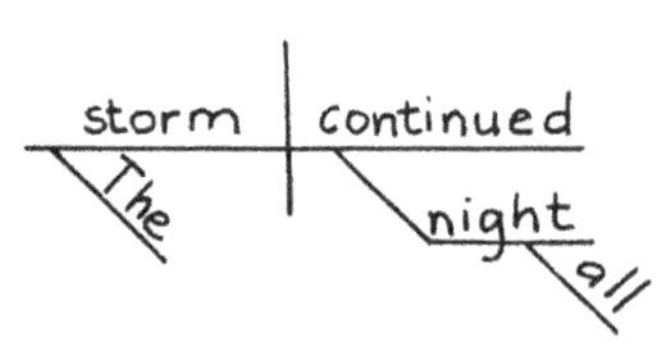

The earth's mantle is roughly 1,800 miles thick.

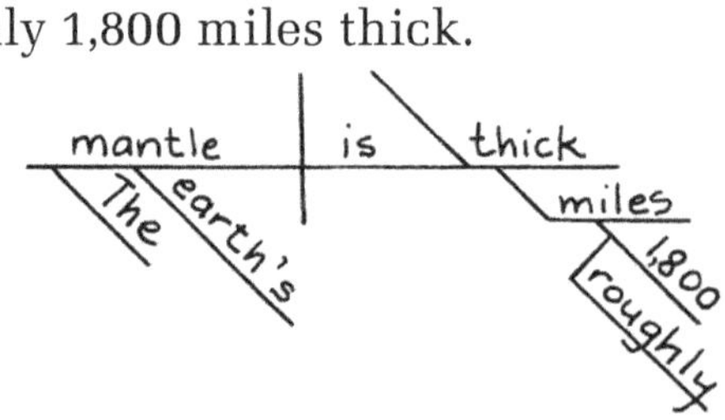

He slept eight hours and then woke up early the next morning.

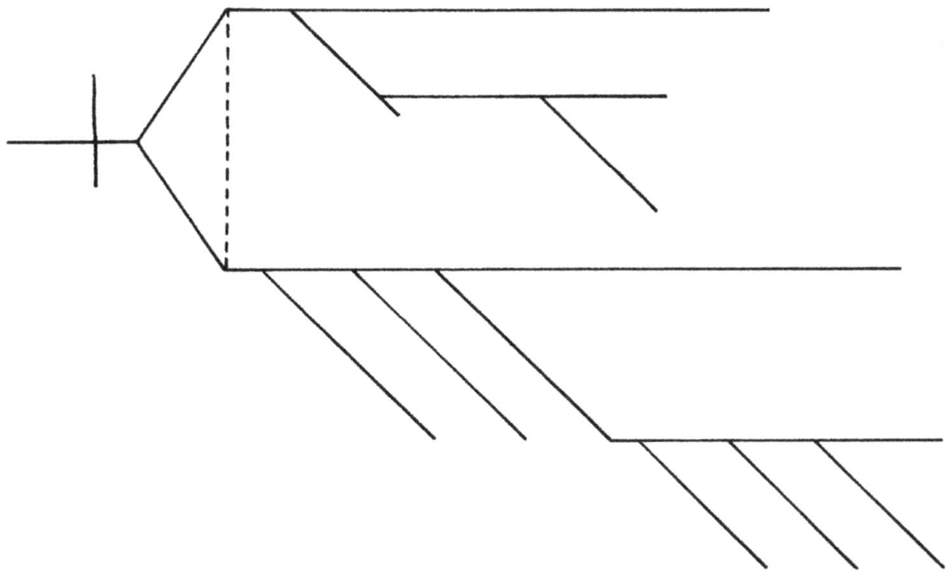

After our delicious picnic lunch, we walked the two miles to the battlefield.

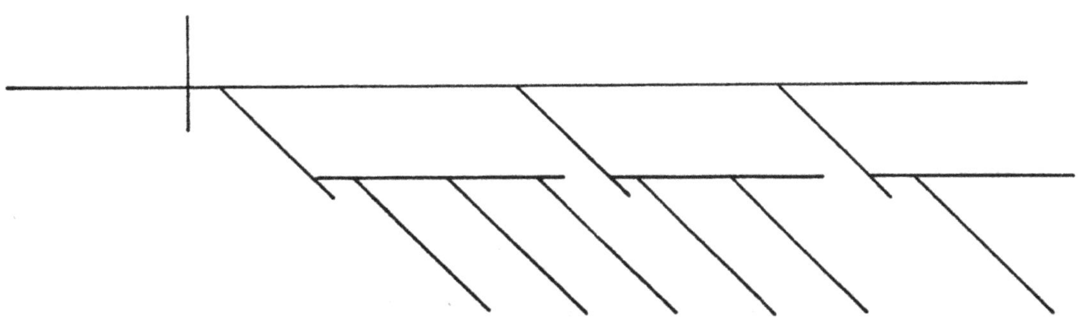

Exercise 108C: Identifying Parts of Speech

Identify the part of speech of each underlined word by writing the correct abbreviation above it: N (noun), ADV-N (adverbial noun), PRO (pronoun), V (verb), ADJ (adjective), ADV (adverb), PREP (preposition), CC (coordinating conjunction), SC (subordinating conjunction), or QC (quasi-coordinator).

These sentences are taken from *Great Astronomers*, by Robert S. Ball.

The effect of this instrument is to show an object at a distance of fifty miles as if it were but five miles.

Kepler had himself assigned no reason why the orbit of a planet should be an ellipse rather than any other of the infinite number of closed curves which might be traced around the sun.

It was, no doubt, not so large as Saturn, it was certainly very much less than Jupiter; on the other hand, the new body was very much larger than Mercury, than Venus, or than Mars, and the earth itself seemed quite an insignificant object in comparison with this newly added member of the Solar System.

There was no argument in favour of this notion, other than the merely imaginary reflection that circular movement, and circular movement alone, was "perfect," whatever "perfect" may have meant.

No doubt others, before Copernicus, had from time to time in some vague fashion surmised, with more or less plausibility, that the sun, and not the earth, was the centre about which the system really revolved.

Tycho, however, speedily made it plain to his teachers that though he was an ardent student, yet the things which interested him were the movements of the heavenly bodies and not the subtleties of metaphysics.

This new Pope, while a cardinal, had been an intimate friend of Galileo's, and had indeed written Latin verses in praise of the great astronomer and his discoveries.

It must be remembered that it was the almost universal belief in those days, that all the celestial spheres revolved in some mysterious fashion around the earth, which appeared by far the most important body in the universe.

The absurdity of this doctrine is obvious enough, especially when we observe that, as it is now well known, there are two large planets, and a host of small planets, over and above the magical number of the regular solids.

Kepler rightly judged that the number of days which a planet required to perform its voyage round the sun must be connected in some manner with the distance from the planet to the sun; that is to say, with the radius of the planet's orbit, inasmuch as we may for our present object regard the planet's orbit as circular.

It would have been almost impossible to refuse to draw the inference that the stars thus brought into view were still more remote objects which the telescope was able to reveal, just in the same way as it showed certain ships to the astonished Venetians, when at the time these ships were beyond the reach of unaided vision.

Exercise 108D: Adverbial Noun Phrases

Circle each adverbial noun or noun phrase, and draw an arrow from the circle to the word modified.

These sentences are taken from *Great Astronomers*, by Robert S. Ball.

It was not unusual for him to work twelve hours at a stretch.

On the 11th of November in that year, he was returning home to supper after a day's work in his laboratory, when he happened to lift his face to the sky, and there he beheld a brilliant new star.

Rouge was then introduced as the polishing powder, and the operation was continued nine hours, by which time the great mirror had acquired the appearance of highly polished silver.

After an uneventful voyage lasting three months, the astronomer landed on St. Helena with a telescope 24 feet long, and forthwith plunged with ardor into his investigation of the southern skies.

The King took so great a fancy to the astronomer that he first, as I have already mentioned, duly pardoned his desertion from the army, some twenty-five years previously.

It appears that sitting one day in the Cathedral of Pisa, Galileo's attention became concentrated on the swinging of a chandelier which hung from the ceiling.

So long as a bird was perched on a tree, he might very well be carried onward by the moving earth, but the moment he took wing, the ground would slip from under him at a frightful pace, so that when he dropped down again he would find himself at a distance perhaps ten times as great as that which a carrier-pigeon or a swallow could have traversed in the same time.

Exercise 108E: Diagramming

On your own paper, diagram every word of the following sentences from *Great Astronomers,* by Robert S. Ball.

In those days the doctrines of Aristotle were regarded as the embodiment of all human wisdom in natural science, as well as everything else.

Brinkley was eighteen years waiting for his telescope, and he had eighteen years more in which he could use it.

On the other hand, constellations new to the inhabitants of northern climes were seen to rise above the southern horizon.

By this reasoning he arrives at the fundamental conclusion that the earth is a globular body freely lying in space, and surrounded above, below, and on all sides by the glittering stars of heaven.

As the earth turns round, the stars over your head will change, and unless it should happen that you have taken up your position at either of the poles, new stars will pass into your view, and others will disappear, for at no time can you have more than half of the whole sphere visible.

WEEK 28

— REVIEW 9 —

Weeks 25-27

Topics

Progressive Perfect Indicative Tenses
Progressive Present and Progressive Perfect Present Modal Verbs
Conditional Sentences
Adjectives in the Appositive Position
Correct Comma Usage
Limiting Adjectives
Misplaced, Squinting, and Dangling Modifier Comparisons
Using *More*, *Fewer*, and *Less* Quasi-Coordinators
Words That Can Be Multiple Parts of Speech
Nouns Acting as Other Parts of Speech
Adverbial Nouns

Review 9A: Definition Fill-in-the-Blank

In the last three weeks, you learned (and reviewed) even *more* definitions than in Weeks 22, 23, and 24! Fill in the blanks in the definitions below with one of the terms from the list. Many of the terms will be used more than once.

abstract noun
adjectives
adverbs
attributive
comma
compound modifiers
dangling modifier
descriptive adjective
future
indefinite pronouns
interrogative pronouns
modal
passive
perfect
plural
predicative
progressive perfect
second conditional
singular
subjunctive
third conditional

active
adverb
apostrophe
cardinal numbers
commas
compound preposition
demonstrative adjectives
fewer
imperative
indicative
less
noun
past
perfect past
positive
present
progressive present
simple
squinting modifier
subordinating conjunction

adjective
adverbial noun
appositive
clause
comparative
coordinating conjunction
demonstrative pronouns
first conditional
indefinite adjectives
interrogative adjectives
misplaced modifier
ordinal numbers
past participle
perfect present
possessive adjective
progressive
quasi-coordinators
simple present
state-of-being
superlative

__________________ verbs express real actions.

__________________ verbs express situations that are unreal, wished for, or uncertain.

__________________ verbs express intended actions.

__________________ verbs express possible actions and situations that have not actually happened.

In a sentence with an __________________ verb, the subject performs the action.

In a sentence with a __________________ verb, the subject receives the action.

A __________________ verb simply tells whether an action takes place in the past, present, or future.

A __________________ verb describes an ongoing or continuous action.

A __________________ verb describes an action which has been completed before another action takes place.

A ________________________________ verb describes an ongoing or continuous action that has a definite end.

The present passive imperative is formed by adding the helping verb *be* to the

___________________________ of the verb.

The present passive subjunctive is formed by pairing *be* with the __________________ of a verb.

Use the simple past subjunctive __________________ verb, plus an infinitive, to express a future unreal action.

__________________ sentences express circumstances that might actually happen. The

predicate of the condition clause is in a __________________ tense. The predicate of the consequence clause is an ____________________ or is in a ____________________ or ____________________ tense.

____________________ sentences express circumstances that are contrary to reality. The predicate of the condition clause is in a ____________________ tense. The predicate of the consequence clause is in the ____________________ or ____________________ modal tense.

____________________ sentences express past circumstances that never happened. The predicate of the condition clause is in the ____________________ tense. The predicate of the consequence clause is in the ____________________ modal or ____________________ modal tense.

A ______________________________ tells what kind.

A __________________________ becomes an ____________________ when you add *-ness* to it.

A ________________________________ tells whose.

A ____________________ becomes an ____________________ when it is made possessive.

Form the possessive of a ____________________ noun by adding an ____________________ and the letter *s*.

Form the possessive of a ____________________ noun ending in *-s* by adding an ____________________ only.

Form the possessive of a ____________________ noun that does not end in *-s* as if it were a ____________________ noun.

An ____________________ that comes right before the noun it modifies is in the

______________________________ position.

An ____________________ that follows the noun it modifies is in the ____________________ position.

____________________ adjectives directly follow the word they modify.

When three or more nouns, adjectives, verbs, or adverbs appear in a series, they should be

separated by ____________________.

When three or more items are in a list, a ____________________________ before the last term is usual but not necessary.

When three or more items are in a list and a ______________________________ is used, a

____________________ should still follow the next to last item in the list.

When two or more adjectives are in the ____________________ position, they are only

separated by ____________________ if they are equally important in meaning.

______________________________ demonstrate or point out something. They take the place of a single word or a group of words.

______________________________ modify nouns and answer the question *which one.*

____________________________________ are pronouns without antecedents.

____________________________________ modify nouns and answer the questions *which one* and *how many.*

______________________________ take the place of nouns in questions.

______________________________ modify nouns.

____________________ represent quantities (one, two, three, four . . .).

____________________ represent order (first, second, third, fourth . . .).

A ____________________ is an adjective, adjective phrase, adverb, or adverb phrase in the wrong place.

A ____________________ can belong either to the sentence element preceding or the element following.

A ____________________ has no noun or verb to modify.

The ________________ degree of an adjective describes only one thing.

The ________________ degree of an adjective compares two things.

The ________________ degree of an adjective compares three or more things.

Most regular adjectives form the ________________ by adding *-r* or *-er.*

Most regular adjectives form the ________________ by adding *-st* or *-est.*

Many adjectives form their ________________ and ________________ forms by adding the word *more* or *most* before the adjective instead of using *-er* or *-est.*

In ________________ and ________________ adjective forms, the words *more* and *most* are used as ________________.

Use ________________ for concrete items and ________________ for abstractions.

In comparisons using *more . . . fewer* and *more . . . less, more* and *less* can act as either ________________ or ________________ and *the* can act as an ________________.

In comparisons using two comparative forms, the forms may act as either

_________________ or _________________, and *the* can act as an __________.

A _________________________ joins equal words or groups of words together.

A _________________________ joins unequal words or groups of words together.

When *than* is used in a comparison and introduces a _________________ with

understood elements, it is acting as a _________________________.

Other than is a _________________________ that means "besides" or "except."

More than and *less than* are _________________________.

_________________________ link compound parts of a sentence that are unequal.

_________________________ include *rather than, sooner than, let alone, as well as,* and *not to mention.*

An _________________________ tells the time or place of an action, or explains

how long, how far, how deep, how thick, or how much. It can modify a verb,

_________________ or _________________.

An _____________________ plus its modifiers is an __________________ phrase.

Review 9B: Parsing

Above each underlined verb, write the complete tense, the voice or the label *state-of-being,* and the mood. The first sentence is done for you.

These sentences are from *Otto of the Silver Hand,* by Howard Pyle.

progressive past, active, indicative — progressive past, active, indicative

I was walking there, and my wits were running around in the grass like a mouse.

A moment more, and he might have promised what she besought; a moment more, and he might have been saved all the bitter trouble that was to follow.

A stranger was in the refectory, standing beside the good old Abbot, while food and wine were being brought and set upon the table for his refreshment; a great, tall, broad-shouldered man, beside whom the Abbot looked thinner and slighter than ever.

A few inches more and he would have been discovered;—what would have happened then would have been no hard matter to foretell.

First, it shone white and thin like the moon in the daylight; but it grew brighter and brighter, until it hurt one's eyes to look at it, as though it had been the blessed sun itself.

And then, in her own fashion she related to him the story of how his father had set forth upon that expedition in spite of all that Otto's mother had said, beseeching him to abide at home; how he had been foully wounded, and how the poor lady had died from her fright and grief.

If you be slain, what then would become of me?

One by one those barons who had been carrying on their private wars, or had been despoiling the burgher folk in their traffic from town to town, and against whom complaint had been lodged, were summoned to the Imperial Court, where they were compelled to promise peace and to swear allegiance to the new order of things.

Otto lay watching the rope as it crawled up to the window and out into the night like a great snake, while one-eyed Hans held the other end lest it should be drawn too far.

There was no room now to swing the long blade, but holding the hilt in both hands, Baron Conrad thrust with it as though it were a lance, stabbing at horse or man, it mattered not.

Many folk said that the one-eyed Hans had drunk beer with the Hill-man, who had given him the strength of ten, for he could bend an iron spit like a hazel twig, and could lift a barrel of wine from the from the floor to his head as easily as though it were a basket of eggs.

I wish that I were back in the monastery again; I am afraid out here in the great wide world; perhaps somebody may kill me, for I am only a weak little boy and could not save my own life if they chose to take it from me.

So at last they reached the chasm that yawned beneath the roadway, and there they stopped, for they had reached the spot toward which they had been journeying.

Night will be upon you before you can reach home again, and the forests are beset with wolves.

Review 9C: Provide the Verb

Complete each song lyric by providing an appropriate verb in the tense indicated. You may want to use the chart in Lesson 99 for reference. In some cases, the missing verb is also part of the title of the song!

If there are two blanks for a single verb, the helping verb is divided from the main verb by another part of the sentence.

If you can't think of a verb, ask your instructor for help.

When you are finished, compare your answers to the original lyrics.

progressive perfect present, active, modal

And I'll finally show you how I ______________________________ with you every day.
—"Train," Lincoln Avenue

progressive future, active, indicative

So if you've a date in Constantinople/ She ______________________________ in Istanbul.
—"Istanbul," They Might Be Giants (lyrics by Jimmy Kennedy)

simple present, active, modal

I ______________________________ that I'll always be here for you.
—"I ________________," Lily Allen

progressive perfect present, active, indicative

Time . . . I ______________________________ time watching trains go by.
—"It Might Be You," Steven Bishop

progressive present, active, modal

We ______________________________ now,/ We're wide awake, but we're dead on our feet.
—"We ______________________________," Eddie Money

simple future, active, indicative / *progressive future, active, indicative*

I ______________________________ you free, and then just like me you ______________________________ /
In love with me.
—"My Best Friend," Jefferson Airplane

perfect future, active, indicative

Oh, if only love comes 'round again,/ It ______________________________ worth the ride.
—"It's Only Love," Sheryl Crow

progressive perfect past, active, indicative

You were the answer that I ______________________________ for.
—"The Best I Had," Taken

perfect present, passive, indicative

They may be false; they may be true, but nothing ______________________________.
—"Nothing ______________________________," Dusty Springfield

***both** perfect present, active, indicative*

Since I ______________________________ you, my life ______________________________ just
______________________________.
—"Love, Thy Will Be Done," Martika

progressive present, active, modal

______________________________ I ______________________________ home, with the waves rolling back?
—"______________________________," Sylvan Esso

simple present, active, modal / *simple present, active, indicative*

I ______________________________ this place before they ______________________________ my heart.
—"Shall I Tell You What I Think of You?" Oscar Hammerstein, from *The King and I*

Review 9D: Identifying Adjectives and Punctuating Items in a Series

In the following stanzas (from the poem "Hakon's Lay," by the American poet James Russell Lowell), carry out the following three steps:

a) Underline once and label all adjectives (except for articles), using the following abbreviations:

Descriptive Adjectives		Limiting Adjectives	
Regular	*DA-R*	Possessives	*LA-P*
Present participles	*DA-PresP*	~~Articles~~	~~*LA-A*~~
Past participles	*DA-PastP*	Demonstratives	*LA-D*
Infinitives	*DA-Inf*	Indefinites	*LA-IND*
		Interrogatives	*LA-INT*
		Numbers	*LA-N*

b) Circle all adjectives that are in the predicate or in the predicative position, and draw an arrow from each back to the noun it modifies.

c) The passage contains one indefinite pronoun, two demonstrative pronouns, and two interrogative pronouns. Find each, underline them twice, and identify them as part of the sentence (*SUBJ* for subject, *DO* for direct object, *IO* for indirect object, *OP* for object of the preposition).

Then the old man arose; white-haired he stood,

White-bearded with eyes that looked afar

From their still region of perpetual snow,

Over the little smokes and stirs of men:

His head was bowed with gathered flakes of years,

As winter bends the sea-foreboding pine,

But something triumphed in his brow and eye,

Which whoso saw it, could not see and crouch:

Loud rang the emptied beakers as he mused,

Brooding his eyried thoughts; then, as an eagle

Circles smooth-winged above the wind-vexed woods,

So wheeled his soul into the air of song

High o'er the stormy hall; and thus he sang:

"The fletcher for his arrow-shaft picks out
Wood closest-grained, long-seasoned, straight as light;
And, from a quiver full of such as these,
The wary bow-man, matched against his peers,
Long doubting, singles yet once more the best.
Who is it that can make these shafts as Fate?
What archer of his arrows is so choice,
Or hits the white so surely? They are men,
The chosen of her quiver; nor for her
Will weakened reed suffice, or cross-grained stick
At random from life's vulgar stick-heap plucked:
Such answer household ends; but she will have
Souls straight and clear, of toughest fibre, sound
Down to the heart of heart; from these she strips
All needless stuff, all sapwood; hardens them;
From circumstance untoward feathers plucks
Crumpled and cheap; and barbs with iron will:
The hour that passes is her quiver-boy;
When she draws bow, 'tis not across the wind,
Nor 'gainst the sun, her haste-snatched arrow sings,
For sun and wind have plighted faith to her
Ere men have heard the sinew twang, behold,
In target's heart her trembling messenger!"

Review 9E: Correcting Modifiers

The following sentences all have modifier problems! Correct each sentence, using proofreader's marks, and be ready to explain the problems to your instructor. The first is done for you.

As I was w
^Wandering through the zoo, my attention was caught by the new baby panda.

Explanation: The adjectival participle phrase at the beginning is a misplaced modifier—my attention was not wandering through the zoo, I was!

The goal of this book is the development of correcter grammar.

The patient was whisked to the hospital before more symptoms were suffered by the first responders.

Ghost stories are more scary when it is completely dark.

Once finished with college, my favorite professor was able to find me a great internship.

The dog under the table that tried to snatch food off my plate is badly trained.

While eating the steak, Dr. Mulrooney's pager went off and called him to surgery.

The marathoner ran the most fast of all the competitors.

Realizing that she was two hours late, it seemed simplest for the party guest to give up and go back home.

Rabbits kept in a hutch require fewer food than rabbits that run around outside.

Her favorite sweater was the one she bought at the little thrift store with the asymmetrical hem.

She married a man with a vast country estate in a small church in the Cotswolds.

To do well in school, work must be handed in on time.

January is usually more cold than March.

The young woman in the very high heels I introduced myself to turned out to be my cousin.

After winning the competition, a first-class flight took the singer to Disneyland.

Katsuji gave away his books to his brother that he was finished with.

Nothing is beautifuller than a flower meadow filled with colorful butterflies in the country.

Review 9F: Identifying Adverbs

In the following sentences, taken from J. M. Barrie's novel *Peter Pan,* carry out the following steps:

a) Underline each word, phrase, or clause that is acting as an adverb.
b) Draw a line from the word/phrase/clause to the verb, adjective, or adverb modified.
c) Above the word or phrase, note whether it is a regular adverb (*ADV*), an adverbial noun (*AN*), a prepositional phrase (*PrepP*), an infinitive phrase (*INF*), a present participle phrase (*PresP*), a past participle phrase (*PastP*), or an adverbial clause (*C*).

Remember: within a phrase or clause acting as an adverb, there might also be an adverb modifying an adjective or verb form within the phrase or clause. Underline these adverbs a second time.

"How clever I am!" he crowed rapturously, "oh, the cleverness of me!"

"You see, children know such a lot now, they soon don't believe in fairies, and every time a child says 'I don't believe in fairies,' there is a fairy somewhere that falls down dead."

When at last the heavens were steady again, John and Michael found themselves alone in the darkness.

It was the tail of a kite, which Michael had made some days before.

While that smile was on his face no one dared address him; all they could do was to stand ready to obey.

All night they sat above, keeping watch over the home under the ground and awaiting the big attack by the pirates which obviously could not be much longer delayed.

No watch was kept on the ship, it being Hook's boast that the wind of his name guarded the ship for a mile around.

Left so fearfully alone, any other man would have lain with his eyes shut where he fell: but the gigantic brain of Hook was still working, and under its guidance he crawled on his knees along the deck as far from the sound as he could go.

None too soon, Peter, every inch of him on tiptoe, vanished into the cabin; for more than one pirate was screwing up his courage to look round.

When Wendy returned diffidently she found Peter sitting on the bed-post crowing gloriously, while Jane in her nighty was flying round the room in solemn ecstasy.

Review 9G: Comma Use

The following sentences have lost all of their commas. Insert commas directly into the text (no need to use proofreader's marks) wherever needed.

The first four sentences are from *The Structure of Atoms*, by Suzanne Slade.

Atoms make up every animal plant and rock.

Matter is any solid liquid or gas that takes up space.

Matter that is made of only one kind of atom is called an element.

This book the peanut-butter sandwich you ate for lunch and the helium gas inside a balloon are all matter made from atoms.

(The following sentences are from *Discovering Atoms*, by Margaret Christine Campbell and Natalie Goldstein.)

Rather Empedocles believed that water air fire and earth were the four fundamental "elements" or building blocks of matter.

In medieval Europe alchemists began to gain a bad reputation often being viewed as counterfeiters thieves and cheats.

In 1803 Dalton came up with his own law the law of multiple proportions which stated that the same elements can combine in different ways to form different compounds.

He thought of atoms as solid indestructible spheres that had no internal structure.

Thomson had discovered a particle that was smaller than the atom which was supposedly the smallest indivisible particle that existed.

Rutherford called these rays "beta rays" and they had properties remarkably like electrons which is what they were.

Bohr had created a model of the Rutherford atom that was stable.

Radium emits alpha particles that pierce a sheet of gold foil.

(The following sentences are from *A Tale of Seven Elements*, by Eric Scerri.)

Mendeleev had sketched out a periodic table which included sixty-three known elements.

Mendeleev wrongly placed mercury with copper and silver misplaced lead with calcium strontium and barium and also misplaced thallium along the alkali metals.

Another discovery by Rutherford consisted of the nuclear model of the atom a concept that is taken more or less for granted these days.

In 1913 it was known that there were three main radioactive decay series that began with radium thorium and actinium.

Another unusual aspect of the element argon was its complete chemical inertness which meant that its compounds could not be studied because none existed.

In the minerals which contain these elements a certain amount of weak acid forms.

The next column contains the elements magnesium calcium iron strontium uranium and barium.

Seaborg succeeded in synthesizing and identifying the two new elements which were subsequently named americium and curium.

Review 9H: Conjunctions

In the following sentences from Rudyard Kipling's *The Jungle Book*, find and circle every conjunction. Label each as coordinating (*C*), subordinating (*SUB*), coordinating correlative (*CC*), subordinating correlative (*SC*), or quasi-coordinator (*QC*).

The monkeys never fight unless they are a hundred to one, and few in the jungle care for those odds.

Mowgli had never seen an Indian city before, and although this was almost a heap of ruins, still it seemed very wonderful and splendid.

And yet they never knew what the buildings were made for nor how to use them.

Shere Khan heard the thunder of their hoofs, picked himself up, and lumbered down the ravine, looking from side to side for some way of escape, but the walls of the ravine were straight, and he had to keep on, heavy with his dinner and his drink, willing to do anything rather than fight.

Both beasts dropped down with a snort of disgust, for neither horse nor mule can bear to listen to an elephant's voice.

The boy could climb almost as well as he could swim, and swim almost as well as he could run; so Baloo, the Teacher of the Law, taught him the Wood and Water laws: how to tell a rotten branch from a sound one; how to speak politely to the wild bees when he came upon a hive of them fifty feet aboveground; what to say to Mang, the Bat, when he disturbed him in the branches at midday; and how to warn the water-snakes in the pools before he splashed down among them.

Review 9I: Identifying Independent Elements

The following sentences, taken from J. M. Barrie's novel *Peter Pan*, all contain independent elements: absolutes (*ABS*), parenthetical expressions (*PE*), interjections (*INT*), nouns of direct address (*NDA*), appositives (*APP*), and noun clauses in apposition (*NCA*). Locate, underline, and label each one.

Some elements may legitimately be labeled in more than one way. The difference between an absolute and a parenthetical expression is particularly tricky; generally, a parenthetical element can be removed without changing the meaning of the sentence, while an absolute construction cannot. Be ready to explain your answers.

For reply Peter rose and kicked John out of bed, blankets and all; one kick.

That, Peter had told Wendy, was the way to the Neverland; but even birds, carrying maps and consulting them at windy corners, could not have sighted it with these instructions.

Indeed, sometimes when he returned he did not remember them, at least not well.

One green light squinting over Kidd's Creek, which is near the mouth of the pirate river, marked where the brig, the *Jolly Roger*, lay, low in the water; a rakish-looking craft foul to the hull, every beam in her detestable, like ground strewn with mangled feathers.

Strange to say, they all recognized it at once, and until fear fell upon them they hailed it, not as something long dreamt of and seen at last, but as a familiar friend to whom they were returning home for the holidays.

Poor kind Tootles, there is danger in the air for you to-night.

With the exception of Nibs, who has darted away to reconnoiter, they are already in their home under the ground, a very delightful residence of which we shall see a good deal presently.

They had indeed discovered the chimney of the home under the ground.

He knocked politely, and now the wood was as still as the children, not a sound to be heard, except from Tinkerbell, who was watching from a branch and openly sneering.

Hurrah, I am in a story, Nibs.

Adventures, of course, as we shall see, were of daily occurrence; but about this time Peter invented, with Wendy's help, a new game that fascinated him enormously, until he suddenly had no more interest in it, which, as you have been told, was what always happened with his games.

No watch was kept on the ship, it being Hook's boast that the wind of his name guarded the ship for a mile around.

And then at last they all got into bed for Wendy's story, the story they loved best, the story Peter hated.

Review 9J: Words with Multiple Identities

In the following sentences, taken from *The History of Korea* (2nd ed.) by Djun Kil Kim, identify each underlined word as an adverb (*ADV*), adjective (*ADJ*), pronoun (*PRO*), preposition (*PREP*), subordinating conjunction (*SC*), coordinating conjunction (*CC*), or quasi-coordinator (*QC*).

The nascent Tang dynasty was not yet prepared to make any conquering moves of expansion.

During his reign (391-413), King Gwanggaeto's conquered territory was the largest yet in northeast Asian history.

Yet many Americans know very little about the histories of nations with which the United States relates.

Korea, smaller than China, was a perfect size to become thoroughly orthodox and thoroughly committed to Confucian ideals.

Given the two different ways of life that divided Korea for more than six decades, some language difference, vocabulary in particular, as well as some unique regional dialects have been found between the north and south.

True Bone status consisted of the Kim clan whose maternal lines were other than Bak.

Finally, Yeongjo saw no other alternative but to eliminate his son.

Silla, though grievously insulted, complied, for it was waiting for the right opportunity to circumvent the Tang's imperial ambition for rule of the peninsula.

On April 19, about 20,000 students, mostly from universities and high schools, took to the street in Seoul, shouting, "Down with dictatorship!"

Both the "explode" and "implode" predictions of North Korean scenarios remain possible to bring about the regime change.

In any of the three scenarios, North Korea would change toward the democratic, market-oriented South Korea.

Tang China was distracted by the emerging Tibetan power in the west and therefore could not devote any more resources to Silla.

The sons of Yeon Gaesomun, unable to resolve their bickering, fell easily before the enemy.

After these unexpected victories, Japan strengthened its diplomacy with the United States and Britain before it started peace negotiations with Russia.

Among the high-tech goods mentioned above, the mobile phone and semiconductor productions rank top in the world.

In 589, the Sui dynasty finally unified the Chinese continent after more than three and a half centuries of disunity.

The daughters' descendants were usually not recorded at all, but an exception was made if one of their sons achieved a prominent position in the government; otherwise, the daughters' line ended.

South Korea is globally acknowledged as an advanced country, although some Koreans believe otherwise.

Others were recruited as part of the police or constabulary, and still others became members of political youth groups like the Korean Democratic and Patriotic Youth Union.

The kingdom of Goryeo, however, was still plagued by Chinese rebels from the north and Japanese marauders from the south.

Review 9K: Verb Forms Functioning in Other Ways

The following excerpt, from *Disasters and Accidents in Manned Spaceflight*, by David Shayler, describes the explosion of the space shuttle *Challenger* on January 28, 1986.

In the following sentences, present participles, past participles, and infinitives are used as nouns and modifiers. Circle each of these verb forms and label each one as noun (*N*), adjective (*ADJ*), or adverb (*ADV*).

For adjectives and adverbs, draw a line back to the word modified. For nouns, add a label describing the part of the sentence it fulfills: subject (*S*), direct object (*DO*), indirect object (*IO*), predicate nominative (*PN*), or object of the preposition (*OP*).

By now a rapid sequence of events that had begun the moment that Challenger lifted off the ground was unfolding, unseen by the crew and most of the onlookers on the ground.

Long Range Camera 207—one of several located around the launch complex—recorded a bright glow on the right-hand side of the external tank, which increased in size and brightness until the whole cloud engulfed *Challenger* and her crew.

Unlike earlier programs such as Mercury and Apollo—which employed escape towers to pull the crew module clear of an exploding launch vehicle—the shuttle did not have such an escape system.

What had started as relaxed expectations for the 25th mission, carrying the first schoolteacher into space, ended with the American space program in disarray and its most appalling disaster played out in full view of the world's media.

TV monitors recorded debris splashing into the sea, preventing search aircraft from entering the area for more than an hour, despite being airborne two minutes after the accident.

The plan was to recover all surface debris before starting the much more difficult underwater search.

Whilst the ocean search was running above and below the surface, the investigation panel set up by the President continued to piece together the events leading up to the tragic accident, as well as putting forward recommendations to begin the long road back to space.

Review 9L: Diagramming

On your own paper, diagram every word of the following sentences.

NOTE: The next two sentences contain understood elements that have been left out. If you cannot locate them, ask your instructor for help.

Had it been so with Peter at that moment I would admit it.

A few moments afterwards the other boys saw Hook in the water striking wildly for the ship; no elation on the pestilent face now, only white fear, for the crocodile was in dogged pursuit of him.

—From *Peter Pan*, by J. M. Barrie

NOTE: The next two sentences contain multiple compound elements.

Painters began to create native pastoral scenes in Korea rather than the commonly copied landscapes of south China, which they had never seen.

As tax payments, the government now collected rice, bolts of cloth, or currency, and no longer demanded necessary goods—weapons, paper, nails, ceramics, silks, brassware, and coins.

—From *The History of Korea*, 2nd ed., by Djun Kil Kim

NOTE: The next two sentences both have complicated elements that follow the verbs.

Actinium was the least understood of the recently discovered radioelements, with a still unknown atomic weight.

Lavoisier then rediscovered oxygen but went much further than his contemporaries in making this element the centerpiece for a new theory of combustion that overthrew the notion that burning resulted in the evolution of a substance called phlogiston.

—From *A Tale of Seven Elements*, by Eric Scerri

NOTE: The next three sentences all have at least one part of speech that you may have trouble identifying.

We told your friend here that there was nothing to be afraid of, but he knew so much that he thought otherwise.

This time, if I have any eye-sight, they have pecked down trouble for themselves, for Baloo is no fledgling and Bagheera can, as I know, kill more than goats.

—From *The Jungle Book*, by Rudyard Kipling

Partly as a result of the *Challenger* accident, many astronauts decided to leave the agency to pursue new careers.

NOTE: You can figure this last sentence out without a hint!

Some were critical of the agency and the accident, but many just recognised that the agency and the program they had joined would never be the same again.

—From *Disasters and Accidents in Manned Spaceflight*, by David Shayler

WEEK 29

Still More Verbs

—LESSON 109—

Hortative Verbs

Subjunctive Verbs

A hortative verb encourages or recommends an action.

Latin *hortari*: to encourage or urge

English derivatives:
to exhort (verb): to urge, or to give urgent recommendations
I exhorted him to keep running despite his weariness.
hortative (adjective): encouraging or urging on
Patience, Charity, and Praise-God are all hortative names.

Let's be more careful next time.

Let's run faster.

Let's be finished now.

In first-person plural hortative verbs, the helping verb *let* is used.
The state-of-being verb takes the form *be*.
The active verb is the same form as the present active indicative.
The passive verb combines *be* with the past participle.

May you be happy.

May you walk in joy.

May you be saved from your own foolishness.

In second-person hortative verbs, the helping verb *may* is used.
The state-of-being verb takes the form *be*.
The active verb is the same form as the present active indicative.
The passive verb combines *be* with the past participle.

Let the trumpets be sounded.

May no creature on earth be silent.

Let the Lord of the Black Lands come forth.

Third-person hortative verbs use the helping verbs *let* or *may*.
The state-of-being verb takes the form *be*.
The active verb is the same form as the present active subjunctive.
The passive verb combines *be* with the past participle.

Active indicative, first-person	We **sing** with happiness.
second-person	You **sing** with happiness.
Active hortative, first-person	Let us **sing** with happiness.
second-person	May you **sing** with happiness.
Active indicative, third-person	He **sings** with happiness.
Active subjunctive, third-person	Should he **sing**, he will be happy.
Active hortative, third-person	Let him **sing** with happiness.

May you travel safely.
Let us travel safely.

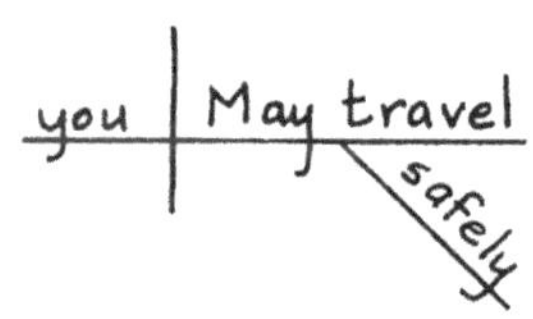

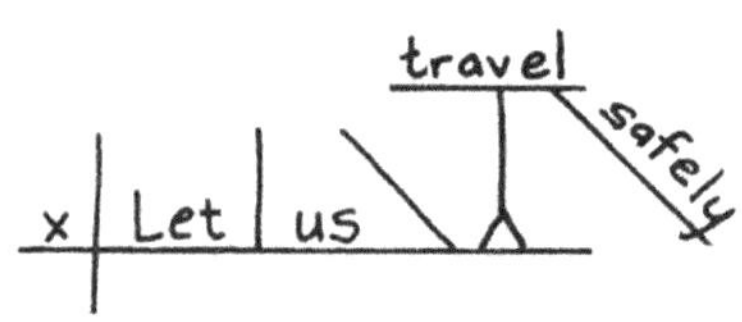

An object complement follows the direct object and renames or describes it.

DO OC
We elected Marissa leader.

May the evildoers come forth.
Let the Lord of the Black Lands come forth.

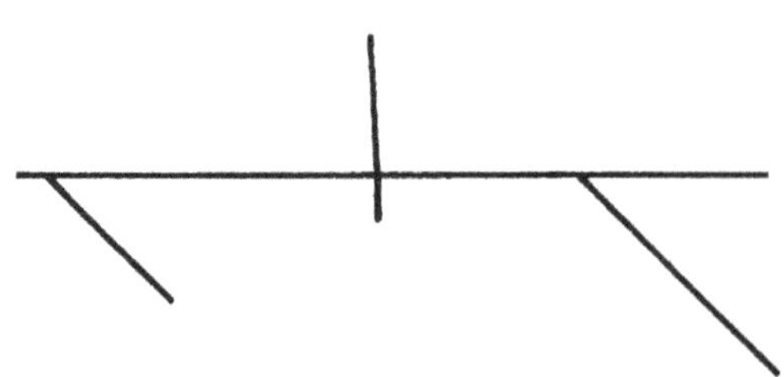

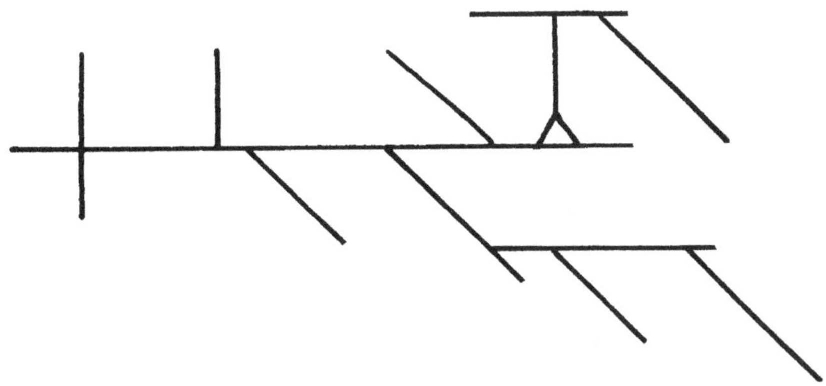

Exercise 109A: Identifying Hortative Verbs

Sacred and religious texts are often exhorting their readers—so they tend to use many hortative verbs! In the following sentences, underline twice every element of each hortative verb (*let* or *may*, any other helping verbs, and the main verb). Above the verb, identify it as state-of-being, active, or passive. If the person or thing being exhorted is present in the sentence, circle the noun or pronoun that identifies him/her/it, and identify it as *S* for subject or *O* for object.

The first is done for you.

state-of-being
O
Let my servants be few and secret: they shall rule the many and the known.
—*The Book of the Law*

May it be thy will, O Lord my God and God of my fathers, to suffer me to lie down in peace and to let me rise up again in peace. Let not my thoughts trouble me.
—*The Authorized Daily Prayer Book*

Let us fill ourselves with costly wine and ointments: and let no flower of the spring pass by us.
—*Wisdom*, Chapter 2 (The Apocrypha)

Let us live happily then, not hating those who hate us! Among men who hate us let us dwell free from hatred!
—The *Dhammapada*

If a man find no prudent companion who walks with him, is wise, and lives soberly, let him walk alone, like a king who has left his conquered country behind.
—The *Dhammapada*

May the radiance of the three wisdoms increase.
—*Aspirations for Mahamudra*

May ignorance and confusion be completely resolved.
—*Aspirations for Mahamudra*

So may this his pyramid endure, and this his temple, likewise, for ever and ever.
—The Pyramid Texts

Without going out of doors one may know the whole world; without looking out of the window, one may see the Way of Heaven.
—The Sayings of Lao-Tzu

O cobbler! mend me this shoe, that I may walk.
—*Liber*

And God said: "Let there be a firmament in the midst of the waters, and let it divide the waters from the waters."
—Genesis 1 (The Bible, King James Version)

So let it come to pass, that the damsel to whom I shall say: Let down thy pitcher, I pray thee, that I may drink; and she shall say: Drink, and I will give thy camels drink also; let the same be she that Thou hast appointed for Thy servant, even for Isaac; and thereby shall I know that Thou hast shown kindness unto my master.
—Genesis 24 (The Bible, King James Version)

And afterward Moses and Aaron went in, and told Pharaoh, Thus saith the Lord God of Israel, Let my people go, that they may hold a feast unto me in the wilderness.
—Exodus 5 (The Bible, King James Version)

Let us therefore, with all haste, put an end to this; and let us fall down before the Lord, and beseech Him with tears, that He would mercifully be reconciled to us, and restore us to our former seemly and holy practice of brotherly love.
—Clement of Rome

In hunger I have come to thee; let me not go unfed. I have come in poverty to the Rich, in misery to the Compassionate; let me not return empty and despised.
—St. Anselm

It casts aside cares, and excludes all thoughts save that of God, that it may seek Him.
—St. Anselm

Exercise 109B: Rewriting Indicative Verbs as Hortative Verbs

Hortative verbs are also common in speeches. In the excerpts from famous speeches below, the statements and commands in bold type originally contained hortative verbs. On your own paper, rewrite each bolded clause so that the main verbs are hortative. Then, compare your answers with the original.

If you need help, ask your instructor.

The enterprise itself, then, the opportunity, your property, your dangers, and the glorious spoils of war should animate you far more than my words.
—Catiline, "To the Conspirators" (c. 70 BC)

Would we be free? If we no longer desire it, **we should perish,** for we have all sworn it. If we wish it, **we will all march to defend our independence.**
—Georges Jacques Danton, "Let France be Free" (1793)

Be generous toward the good, compassionate with the unfortunate, inexorable with the evil, just toward every one.
—Robespierre, "The Festival of the Supreme Being" (1794)

We will perish before we break a pledge which has saved the country and the life of her children.
—Simon Bolivar, "Address at Angostura" (1819)

No matter what happens in the coming days, the French are going to suffer. **They will be worthy of the past of their nation. They will become brothers.**
—Paul Reynaud, "France Will Live Again" (June 13, 1940)

Exercise 109C: Diagramming

On your own paper, diagram every word of each sentence.

These, my friends, are some of the evils visited upon us by a hateful and contentious spirit, from which may the good Lord deliver us.
—Oliver Wendell Holmes

So let us begin anew—remembering on both sides that civility is not a sign of weakness, and sincerity is always subject to proof. Let us never negotiate out of fear, but let us never fear to negotiate.
—John F. Kennedy, Inaugural Address

—LESSON 110—

Transitive Verbs
Intransitive Verbs
Sit/Set, Lie/Lay, Rise/Raise
Ambitransitive Verbs

The reindeer broke the first house apart.

The ice between the two floes broke apart.

Transitive verbs express action that is received by some person or thing.
Intransitive verbs express action that is not received by any person or thing.

ambi- from the Latin: prefix meaning "both"

ambidextrous ______________________________

ambiguous ______________________________

ambitransitive both transitive and intransitive

When I hear my voice on a record I absolutely loathe my voice. I cannot stand my voice.
—Roger Daltrey

Music in the soul can be heard by the universe.
—Laozi

Transitive verbs can be active or passive.
Intransitive verbs can only be active.

I hate thunderstorms.
The goat bleated.

***Sit*, *lie*, and *rise* are intransitive.**
***Set*, *lay*, and *raise* are transitive.**

(simple present) Strong women ______________ above adverse circumstances.

(simple present) The waiter ______________ the coffee carefully on the table.

(progressive past) The hen ______________ four or five eggs every week.

(simple present) She ______________ primly on the elaborate throne.

(simple past) The farmer ______________ corn, wheat, and rye.

(progressive present) The horse ______________ peacefully on its side in the pasture.

The cook tied on his apron and set to work.
The travelers set off first thing in the morning.
As we reached the ocean, the sun was setting.

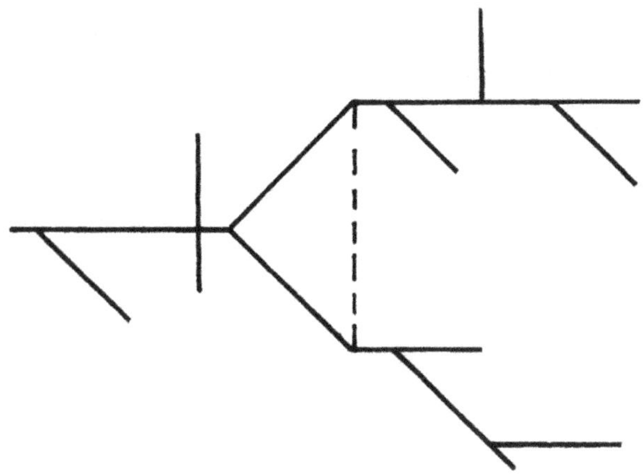

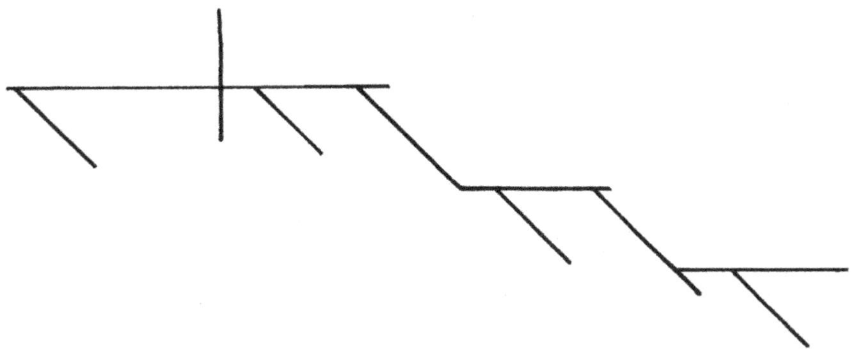

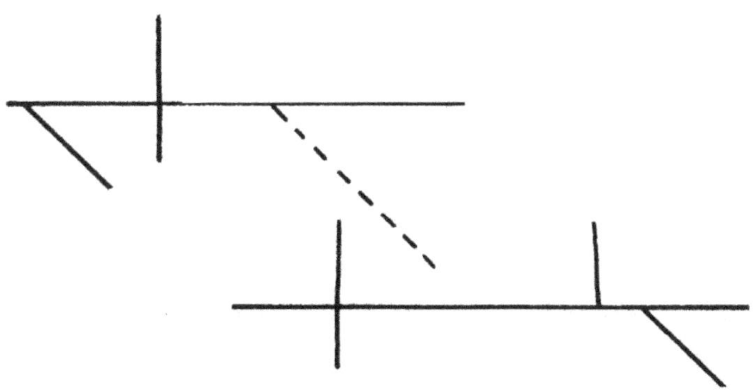

Transitive verbs can be active or passive.
Intransitive verbs can only be active.
Ambitransitive verbs can be either transitive or intransitive.
Transitive verbs express action that is received by some person or thing.
Intransitive verbs express action that is not received by any person or thing.

Exercise 110A: Ambitransitive Verbs

Each one of the sentences below (adapted from traditional Eskimo folk tales) contains at least one ambitransitive verb. For each sentence, carry out the following steps:

a) Underline the verbs that are acting as predicates, and label each one as *TR* for transitive or *INTR* for intransitive.
b) Label each transitive verb as *A* for active or *P* for passive.
c) Label the direct object of each active transitive verb as *DO* (*TR*) and the subject of each passive transitive verb as *S* (*TR*).
d) Choose two sentences with active transitive verbs. On your own paper, rewrite them so that the verb becomes passive.

A lamp burned at one end of the house.

The man burned the tops of the grass blades down.

The grass plant changed itself quickly into a small tuber plant.

The mouse was changed at once into a beautiful white owl.

The white owl changed immediately into a fine young man.

In those days people grew very fast, so that the earth would be peopled.

The new earth grew grass thickly across her surface.

I will not eat the meat of a whale!

You must eat, or you will die.

And then the man was eaten by the young thunderbirds.

I will cook you a very good supper.

The grandmother cooked for the guests.

The bear entered, and frightened her very much.

I will enter the house; do not shoot me!

We have followed him a long way.

Run quickly, and I will follow.

Exercise 110B: The Prefix *Ambi-*

Using a dictionary or thesaurus, find two more words using the prefix *ambi* where the prefix carries the meaning of *both*. On your own paper, write the words and their definitions, and then use each correctly in a sentence. If the word is too technical for you to write an original sentence, you may locate a sentence using an Internet search and write it down.

Exercise 110C: Diagramming

On your own paper, diagram every word of the following quotations.

When you are finished, label each action verb occupying a predicate space with *T* for transitive or *INT* for intransitive.

Progress is impossible without change, and those who cannot change their minds cannot change anything.
—George Bernard Shaw

Just when I think I have learned the way to live, life changes.
—Hugh Prather

Space can bend and twist and stretch, and probably the best way to think about space is to imagine a big piece of rubber that you can twist.
—Alan Guth

If a man can't manage his own life, he can't manage a business.
— S. Truett Cathy

When evil acts in the world it always manages to find instruments who believe that what they do is not evil but honorable.
—Max Lerner

— LESSON 111 —

Ambitransitive Verbs
Gerunds and Infinitives
Infinitive Phrases as Direct Objects
Infinitive Phrases with Understood *To*

I may not succeed, but I will try.

Try the chocolate cake.

The concert-goers tried arriving early.

Every night, he tries to go to bed by ten.

A gerund is a present participle acting as a noun.
An infinitive is formed by combining *to* and the first-person singular present form of a verb.

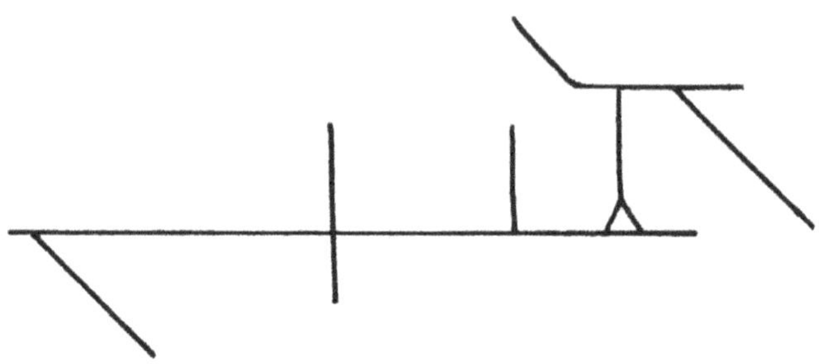

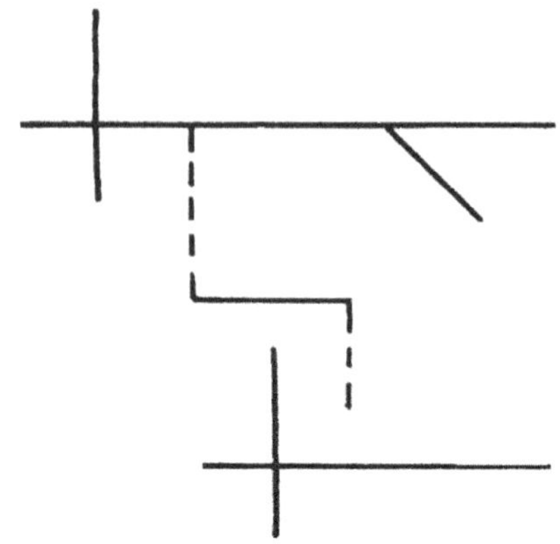

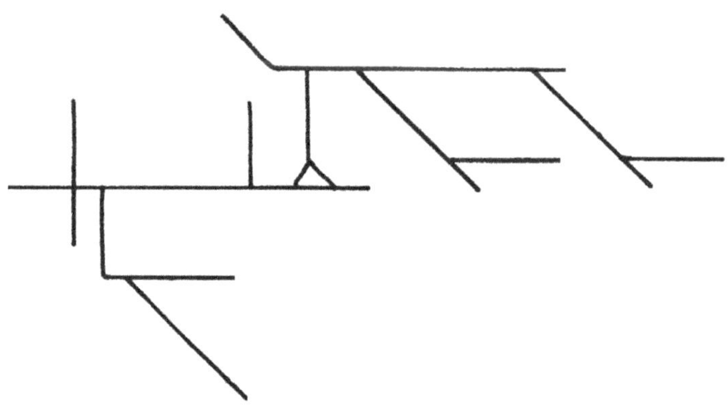

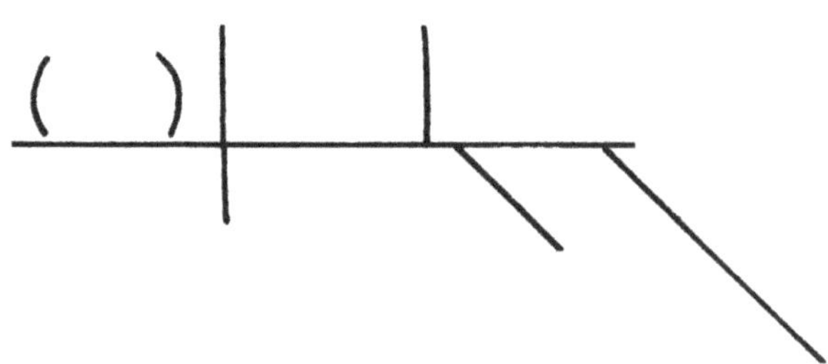

Mother told me to clean my room.

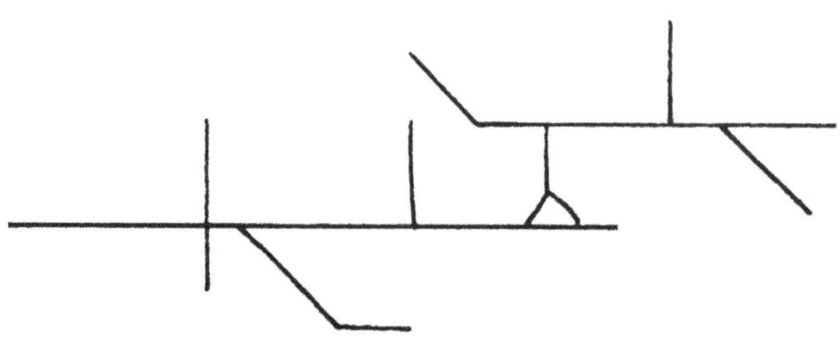

The duchess ordered the maid to arrange the flowers.

His mistake made me lose money.

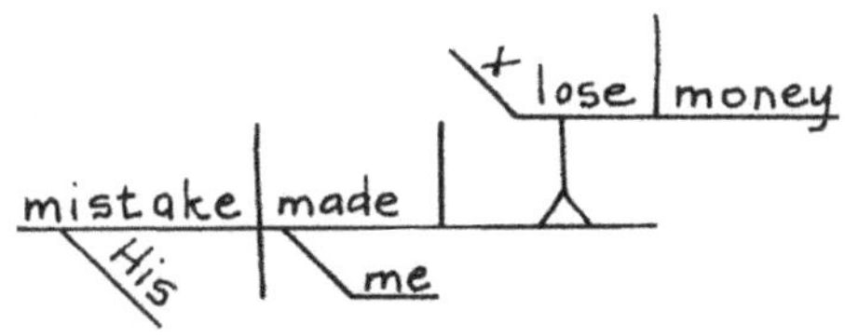

You must come and make Lizzy marry Mr. Collins, for she vows she will not have him.
—*Pride and Prejudice*

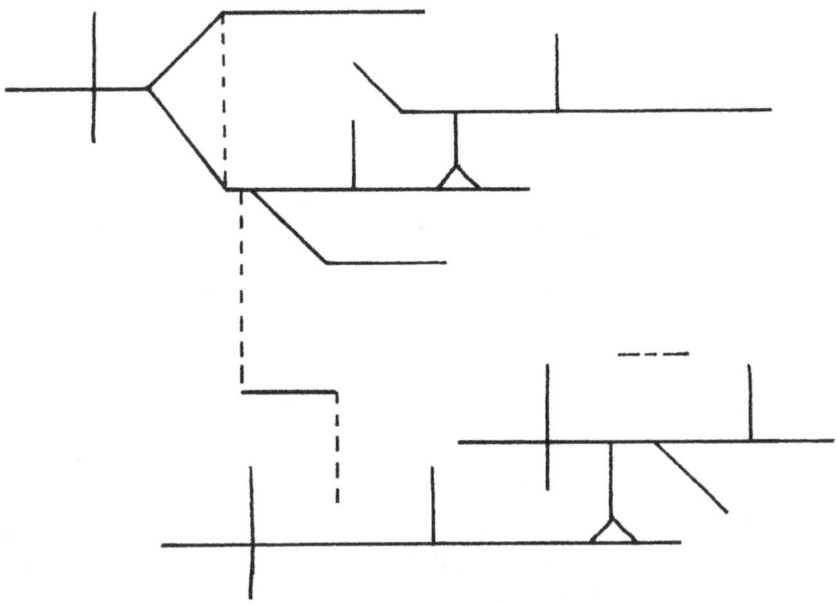

I was made to love you.

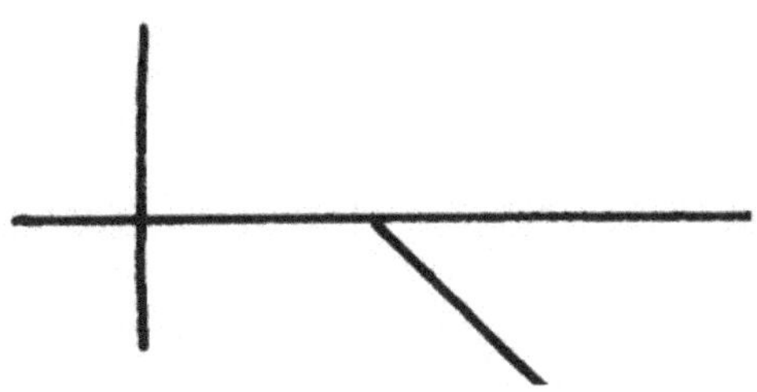

He was good enough to sing.

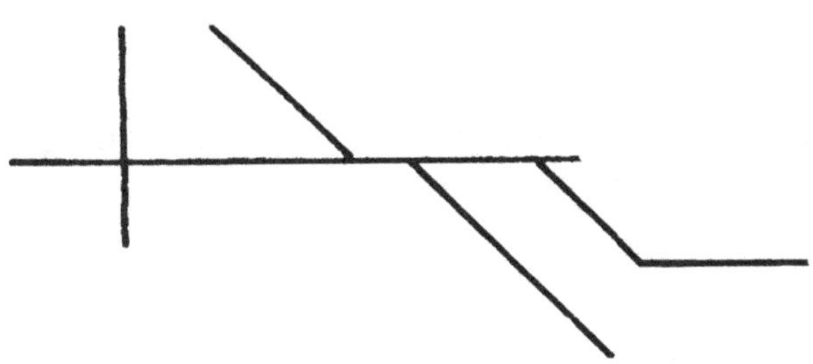

You ought to go home.

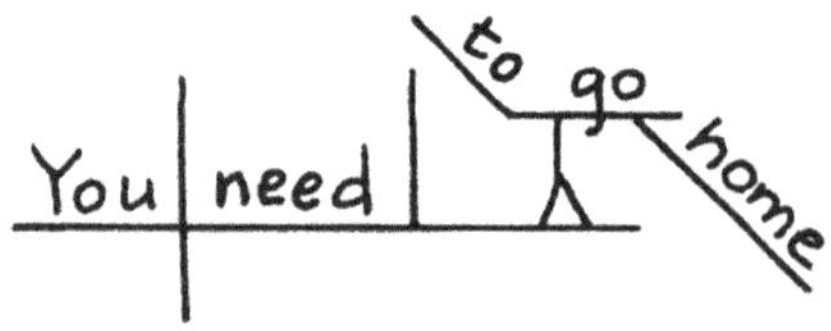

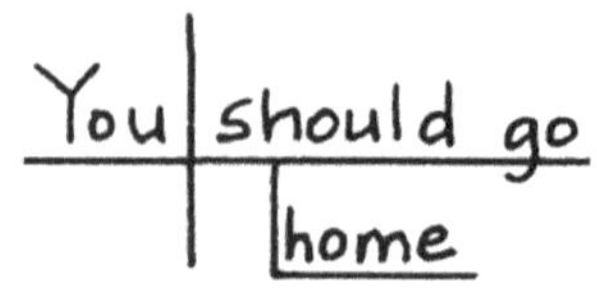

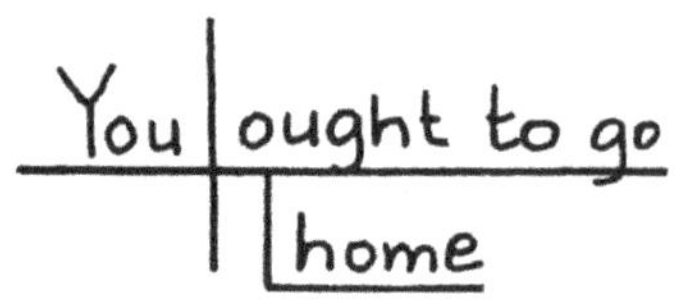

The politician ought to have been thrown in jail.

The politician should have been thrown in jail.

Exercise 111A: Infinitives and Other Uses of *To*

In the following sentences from Howard Pyle's classic novel *The Merry Adventures of Robin Hood*, underline every phrase that incorporates the word *to*. For infinitives, underline just the infinitive itself; for prepositional phrases, underline just the preposition and its object (and any words that come between); for verb phrases, underline the entire verb.

- Label each phrase as *INF* for infinitive, *PREP* for prepositional, or *V* for verb.
- For infinitives, further identify the phrase as *S* for subject, *DO* for direct object, *PA* for predicate adjective, *PN* for predicate nominative, *ADJ* for adjective, or *ADV* for adverb.
- For prepositional phrases, label the object of the preposition as *OP*.
- For verb phrases, parse the verb, giving tense, voice, and mood.
- For infinitive adjective and adverb phrases, draw an arrow back to the word modified.

  The first is done for you.

When Robin was a youth of eighteen, stout of sinew and bold of heart, the Sheriff of Nottingham proclaimed a shooting match and offered a prize of a butt of ale to whosoever (PREP: to; OP: whosoever) should shoot the best shaft in Nottinghamshire.

But his heart was bitterly angry, for his blood was hot and youthful and prone to boil.

And so he came to dwell in the greenwood that was to be his home for many a year to come, never again to see the happy days with the lads and lasses of sweet Locksley Town; for he was outlawed, not only because he had killed a man, but also because he had poached upon the King's deer, and two hundred pounds were set upon his head, as a reward for whoever would bring him to the court of the King.

Besides this, they swore never to harm a child nor to wrong a woman, be she maid, wife, or widow; so that, after a while, when the people began to find that no harm was meant to them, but that money or food came in time of want to many a poor family, they came to praise Robin and his merry men, and to tell many tales of him and of his doings in Sherwood Forest.

Then when the feast was ready they all sat down, but Robin placed Little John at his right hand, for he was henceforth to be the second in the band.

And now I will tell how the Sheriff of Nottingham three times sought to take Robin Hood, and how he failed each time.

Then he told how none could be found in all Nottingham Town to serve this warrant, for fear of cracked pates and broken bones, and how that he, the messenger, was now upon his way to Lincoln Town to find of what mettle the Lincoln men might be.

As the Sheriff looked around ere he ordered his men to string the three youths up to the oak tree, his eyes fell upon this strange old man.

Then of a sudden it came to him like a flash that were he to proclaim a great shooting match and offer some grand prize, Robin Hood might be over-persuaded by his spirit to come to the butts; and it was this thought which caused him to cry "Aha!" and smite his palm upon his thigh.

"I take thy meaning, Robin Hood," said the Queen, "and that thou dost convey reproach to me, as well thou mayst, for I know that I have not done by thee as I ought to have done."

Exercise 111B: Diagramming

On your own paper, diagram every word of the following sentences from *The Merry Adventures of Robin Hood.*

Truly, no one likes to go on this service, for fear of cracked crowns and broken bones.

So saying, he went within and whispered to the host to add a measure of Flemish strong waters to the good English ale, which the latter did and brought it to them.

Then he bade all his servants and retainers to make ready to go to London Town, to see and speak with the King.

At last Robin gave the stranger a blow upon the ribs that made his jacket smoke like a damp straw thatch in the sun.

Then, of a sudden, with a twist and a wrench, the stranger loosed himself, and he of the scar found himself locked in a pair of arms that fairly made his ribs crack.

— LESSON 112 —

Principal Parts

Yet More Troublesome Verbs

Exercise 112A: Verb Definitions

Match the terms on the left with the definitions on the right by drawing lines between them.

hortative	formed by combining *to* and the first-person singular present form of a verb
first principal part	expresses possible actions
transitive verb	describes an ongoing or continuous action
indicative	present participle acting as a noun
gerund	describes an action which has been completed before another action takes place
infinitive	expresses action that is received by some person or thing
present participle	the simple present (first–person singular)
ambitransitive verb	the perfect past verb form, minus helping verbs
simple verb	the same as the simple past verb form
modal	encourages or recommends an action
perfect verb	expresses situations that are unreal, wished for, or uncertain
second principal part	simply tells whether an action takes place in the past, present, or future
progressive verb	can be either transitive or intransitive
intransitive verb	expresses intended actions
subjunctive	affirms or declares what actually is
imperative	expresses action that is not received by any person or thing
third principal part	a verb form ending in *-ing*

English verbs have three principal parts.

First principal part: The Simple Present (Present)

(I) pontificate	(I) sing	(I) cut	(I) become

Second principal part: The Simple Past (Past)

(I) pontificated	(I) sang	(I) cut	(I) became

Third principal part: The Perfect Past, Minus Helping Verbs (Past Participle)

(I have) pontificated	(I have) sung	(I have) cut	(I have) become

pontificate, pontificated, pontificated
sing, sang, sung
cut, cut, cut
become, became, become

***Sit*, *lie*, and *rise* are intransitive.**
***Set*, *lay*, and *raise* are transitive.**

lie **Simple Past**		**lay** **Simple Present**		**lay** **Simple Past**	
I lay	we lay	I lay	we lay	I laid	we laid
you lay	you lay	you lay	you lay	you laid	you laid
he, she, it lay	they lay	he, she, it lays	they lay	he, she, it laid	they laid

(simple past) The child ____________ out her clothes for the birthday party the night before.

(simple past) She got sunburned because she ______________ out in the sun too long.

(simple present) ______________ down and go to sleep now.

(simple present) ______________ your head down and close your eyes.

	First Principal Part **Present**	**Second Principal Part** **Past**	**Third Principal Part** **Past Participle**
I	lie	lay	lain
	lay	laid	laid
	sit	sat	sat
	set	set	set
	rise	rose	risen
	raise	raised	raised

Exercise 112B: Using Troublesome Verbs Correctly

In the following sentences from Indian myths, fill in the blanks.

The first blank (above the sentence) should be filled in with the first principal part of the correct verb: *lie* or *lay* in the first set of sentences, *sit* or *set* in the second set, and *rise* or *raise* in the third set of sentences.

You will be able to tell from the context of the sentence whether you should use the transitive verbs *lay, set,* and *raise* (if the verb is passive, or has a direct object), or the intransitive verbs *lie, sit,* and *rise* (if the action of the verb is not passed on to any other word in the sentence).

The second blank (in the sentence itself) should be filled in with the correct form of that verb.

The first sentence in each section is done for you.

The first eight sentences are from *Hindu Tales from the Sanskrit,* by N. D'Anvers and Siddha Mohana Mitra.

simple past active indicative of lie

Then, thinking she had been dreaming, Patala lay down again.

perfect past active indicative of ______

The princess too was tired, because she ____________ awake so many nights.

simple past active indicative of ______

Buddhi-Mati led her husband to the garden where she had found the beetle and ______ it tenderly on the ground.

simple present active indicative of ______

"Whoever wins the fight will get them all. There they ________ on the ground."

infinitive of ______

If he wishes my death, I am ready ______ down my life.

simple past passive indicative of ______

Very happily Buddhi-Mati obeyed, and soon the cotton thread and twine __________ aside.

The piles of seed were gone, and flocks of birds were gathering in the hope of securing

simple past active indicative of ______

some of the seed as it ________ in the furrows.

infinitive of ______

The lizard loved ________ and bask in the sunshine, catching the flies on which he lived,

gerund of ______

________ so still that they did not notice him.

The following sentences are from Volume 1 of *The Mahabharata of Krishna-Dwaipayana Vyasa*, trans. by Kisari Mohan Ganguli.

simple past active indicative of ___rise___

And saying this, she quickly ___rose___, with tearful eyes, to go to her father.

perfect present active indicative of ______

The low ____________, and the high have fallen.

simple future active indicative of ______

And the lowest orders of men ______________ to the position of the intermediate ones.

simple past active indicative of ______

He ______________ a great quantity of dust that overspread the firmament.

simple present active indicative of ______

And this will slake their thirst after they ______ refreshed from sleep.

simple past active indicative of ______

That wicked youth who had nectar in his tongue and a razor in his heart, ______ at length, and in a friendly way.

simple past passive indicative of ______

His tail, covered with long hair and a little bent at the end, ____________ like a banner.

perfect past passive indicative of ______

In that lake, a pillar ______________.

gerund of ______

Both Arjuna and Vasudeva, hastily ______________ from their seats, stood waiting.

gerund of ______

And the monarch, promptly ________________ her from the pit, sweetly and courteously returned to his capital.

perfect past active indicative of ______

Kunti, frightened by a tiger, ________________ up suddenly, unconscious of the child that lay asleep on her lap.

simple past active indicative of ___sit___

What also did all the kings who ___sat___ in that assembly say?

perfect past active indicative of ______

And when all ______________ down, Salya spoke.

simple present active modal of _______

After carefully deliberating on all things, a person ______________ before the king those topics that are both profitable and pleasant.

Those princes, the sons of Draupadi, rivalling their fathers in valour, strength, grace, and

simple past active indicative of _______

prowess, ______ upon excellent seats inlaid with gold. And when those mighty heroes

perfect past active indicative of _______

wearing shining ornaments and robes ________________ themselves down, that gorgeous assembly of kings looked beautiful, like the firmament spangled with resplendent stars.

simple past passive indicative of _______

Upon that chariot ________________ a tall standard bearing a lion of golden maces.

simple past active indicative of _______

None of his friends or kinsmen could venture to look at or speak to Arjuna, as he ______ there exceedingly afflicted with grief on account of his son, and with face bathed in tears.

progressive present active indicative of _______

Let these rulers of earth that ________________ here say what the answer should be!

simple present active modal of _______ simple present active modal of _______

A learned man _______________either on the king's right or the left; he ________ not ______

infinitive of _______

behind him for that is the place appointed for armed guards, and _____ before him is always forbidden.

	First Principal Part Present	Second Principal Part Past	Third Principal Part Past Participle
I	give	gave	given
	come	came	come
	write	wrote	written
	go	went	gone
	eat	ate	eaten

She had gave her outgrown shoes to her sister.

Has she came home from the movies yet?

The policeman had wrote her a speeding ticket.

When Mom got home, I had already went to bed.

He has ate his dinner too fast.

Exercise 112C: More Irregular Principal Parts

Fill in the chart below with the missing principal parts of each verb. (You may use a dictionary if necessary.) Then, in the sentences below (from *Watership Down*, by Richard Adams), fill in the blanks with the correct verb, in the tense, mood, and voice indicated in brackets at the end of each sentence. Each verb is used one time.

	First Principal Part **Present**	Second Principal Part **Past**	Third Principal Part **Past Participle**
I	fight		
	shake		
	weave		
	split		
	fly		
	draw		
	show		
	freeze		
	tear		

Then the Black Rabbit told such a tale of fear and darkness as ____________________ the hearts of Rabscuttle and El-Ahrairah where they crouched on the rock, for they knew that every word was true. [simple past, active, indicative]

Dandelion took up his cue with the same plucky readiness that he ____________________ in the wood. [perfect past, active, indicative]

They noticed for the first time that the grass in front of it ____________________ and scored with lines. [simple past, passive, indicative]

The does, disturbed from their thoughts, looked at him resentfully and ______________ back. [simple past, active, indicative]

More than once he ______________ alone and imposed his will on crowds of other rabbits. [perfect past, active, indicative]

Fiver looked as though he were about to speak, but then ______________ his ears and turned to nibbling at a dandelion. [simple past, active, indicative]

But down in the grass itself, between the bushes, in that thick forest trodden by the beetle, the spider, and the hunting shrew, the moving light was like a wind that danced among them to set them scurrying and ______________ . [gerund (present participle)]

The bird ______________ the stick three ways in as many seconds and snapped up the few insects inside. [simple past, active, indicative]

"What does that prove?" said Blackberry, his teeth chattering. "He ______________ off the surface or put his great webbed feet down. It's not he that's soaked through and shivering and twice as heavy with wet fur." [perfect present, active, modal]

WEEK 30

Still More About Clauses

—LESSON 113—

Clauses and Phrases

The sentences in this lesson are taken from *Redwall,* by Brian Jacques.

> All eyes were on the Father Abbot. He took a dainty fork loaded precariously with steaming fish. Carefully he transferred it from plate to mouth. Chewing delicately, he turned his eyes upwards then closed them, whiskers atwitch, jaws working steadily, munching away, his tail curled up holding a napkin which neatly wiped his mouth.
>
> —Brian Jacques, *Redwall*

A clause is a group of words that contains a subject and a predicate.

An independent clause can stand by itself as a sentence.

A sentence is a group of words that usually contains a subject and a predicate. A sentence begins with a capital letter and ends with a punctuation mark. A sentence contains a complete thought.

A phrase is a group of words serving a single grammatical function.

A dependent clause is a fragment that cannot stand by itself as a sentence.

Dependent clauses can act as adjective clauses, adverb clauses, or noun clauses.

An adjective clause is a dependent clause that acts as an adjective in a sentence, modifying a noun or pronoun in the independent clause.

Relative pronouns (*who, whom, whose, which, that*) introduce adjective clauses and refer back to an antecedent in the independent clause.

Relative adverbs (*where, when, why*) introduce adjective clauses when they refer back to a place, time, or reason in the independent clause.

Matthias started to slide down the rope on the Mossflower side of the wall, where the woods came close up to the Abbey.

The Father Abbot halted in front of the wall on which hung a long tapestry.

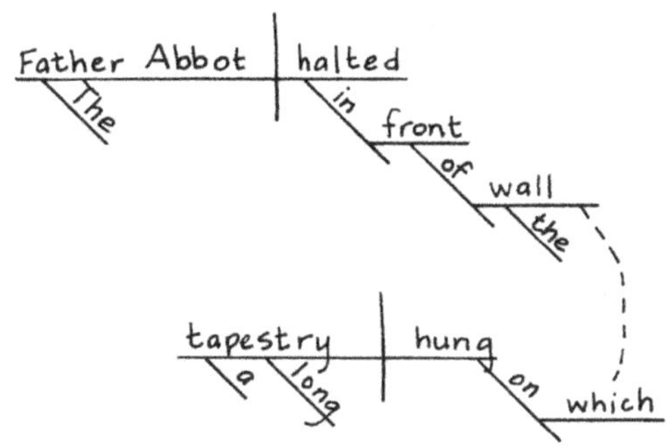

He arrived here in the deep winter when the Founders were under attack from many foxes, vermin, and a great wildcat.

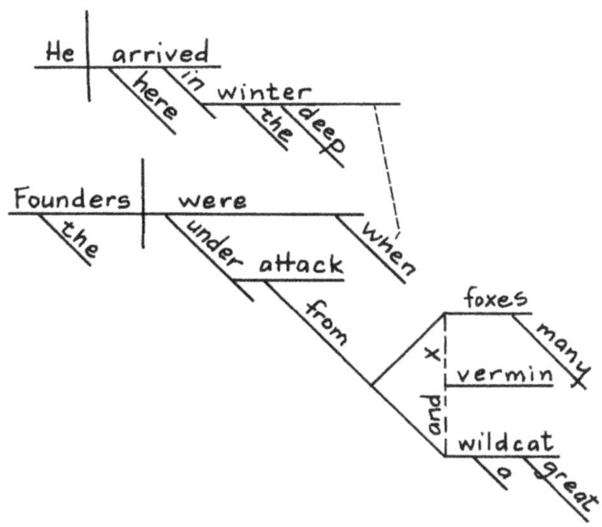

Adverb clauses can be introduced by adverbs.

Common adverbs that introduce adverbial clauses are as follows:

as and its compounds (as if, as soon as, as though)
how and its compound (however)
when and its compound (whenever)
whence
where and its compounds (whereat, whereby, wherein, wherefore, whereon)
while
whither

Her blunt claws churned the roadside soil as she propelled the cart through a gap in the hawthorn hedge, down to the slope of the ditch where she dug her paws in, holding the cart still and secure while John Churchmouse and Cornflower's father jumped out and wedged the wheels firmly with stones.

A subordinating conjunction joins unequal words or groups of words together.

Subordinating conjunctions and subordinating correlative conjunctions often join an adverb clause to an independent clause.

Common subordinating conjunctions are:

after
although
as (as soon as)
because
before
if
in order that
lest
since
though
till
unless
until
although/though . . . yet/still
if . . . then

All the mice took a solemn vow never to harm another living creature, unless it was an enemy that sought to harm our Order by violence.

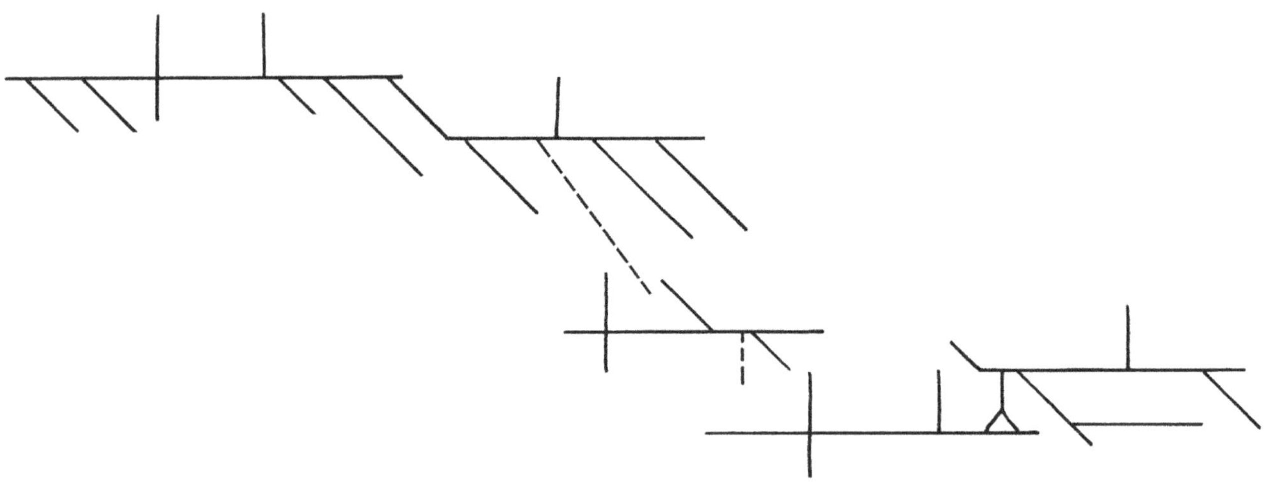

A noun clause takes the place of a noun. Noun clauses can be introduced by relative pronouns, relative adverbs, or subordinating conjunctions.

Somewhere there had to be a clue, a single lead that might tell him where the resting place of Martin the Warrior could be found, or where he could regain possession of the ancient sword for his Abbey.

The defenders stood and cheered in the depression above what had once been Killconey's tunnel.

It is because you are kind and good.

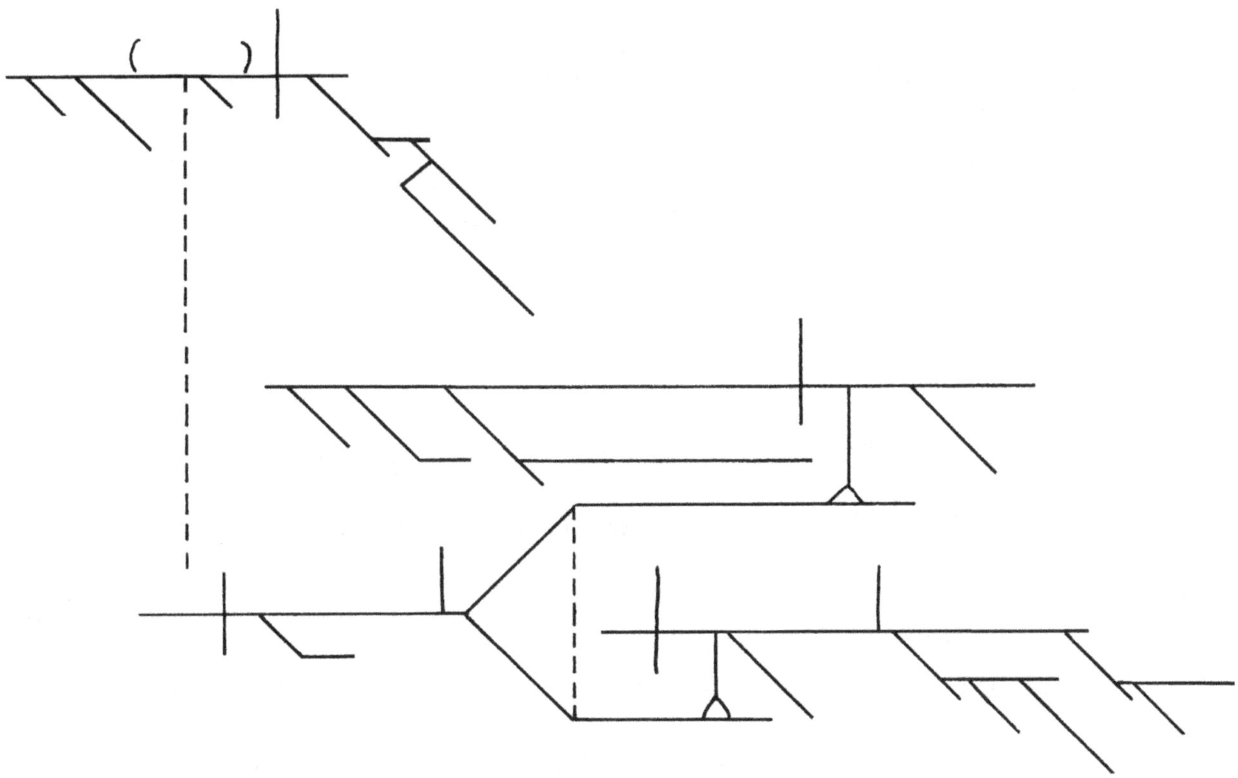

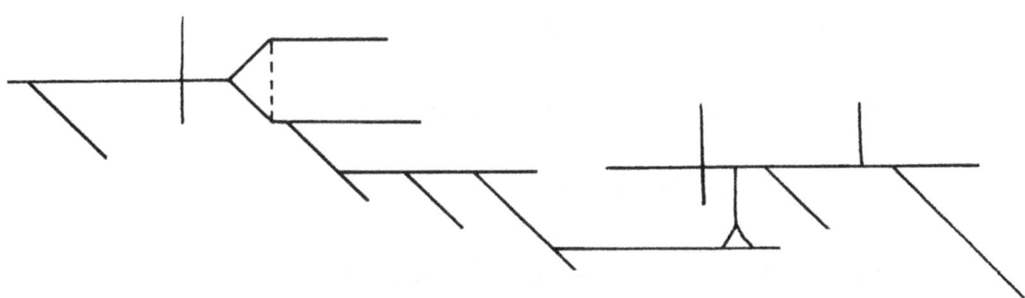

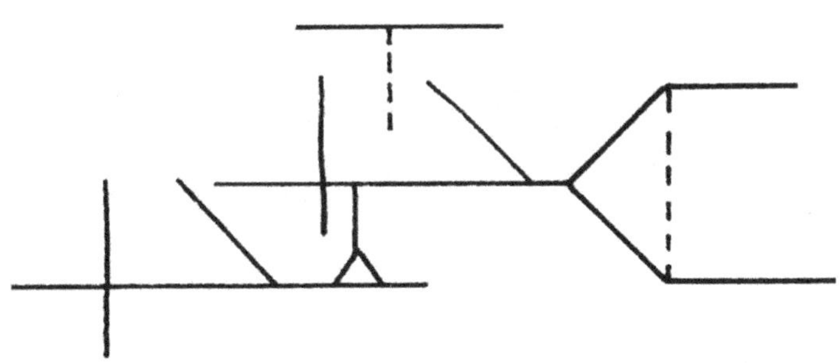

Exercise 113A: Phrases and Clauses

Identify each bolded set of words as *PH* for phrase or *CL* for clause.

Then, identify the part of the sentence (*S, DO, IO, OP, PN, PA, ADV, ADJ*) that each set of words functions as.

- For adjective and adverb phrases and clauses, draw an arrow to the word modified.
- For phrases, further identify the phrase as *PREP, INF* (infinitive), *GER* (gerund), or *PP* (past participle).
- For clauses, underline the subject of the clause once and the predicate twice.

The first is done for you. All of these sentences are taken from *Martin the Warrior*, by Brian Jacques.

PH ADV PREP

The mole gazed at it **for a while** before giving his verdict.

Their foraging had proved extremely fruitful: apples, early wild plums and some green acorns, parsley, dandelion, wild oats and a piece of honeycomb, **which Pallum had found floating in a small rivulet of ice-cold mountain water.**

Rising above the mists into the summer day, it towered in solitary splendor, the lower slopes clad **in verdant pine**, rising to shrub and wild lupin, **which gave way to naked dun-hued rock all the way to its majestic peak**.

Brome sighed and voiced aloud the thought that tormented him constantly, **whenever he looked out over the deep waters of the main**.

A small cloud **of dust** arose **where the otter toiled away**, digging the sandy clayish ground **with both paws**.

She had been following his paw tracks **since early noon**; they stood out clearly in the smooth wet sand, marked with a straight furrow **where the sword point trailed at Martin's side.**

She had thought **of giving her eagle call**, but if Martin or Dinjer were in the nest they would be crushed under the gannet, **which would naturally sit on its nest to defend the chicks against anything.**

The lizards stood motionless, tongues in, eyes filmed over **as if completely cowed** by the mad intensity **of the heron's stare.**

The marks **of the deep scratches on his cheeks** were still there, and his face was thinner though the resolute jaw was firm and the eyes **that stared back at him** shone with the light of determination.

There was a considerable interval **when nobeast was on the walltop**, and she took advantage of this **to sneak up to the fortress.**

You were coming this way **because a band of ruffians were chasing you.**

Unable to see **because of the bright light burning in their eyes**, the walltop troops were hit hard.

While the wounded were treated by Rose and Brome, food was divided up among the groups of creatures **seated around the low hillock.**

They continued **to play the game**, this time **with Clogg's paw straying close to his cutlass**, while Badrang toyed with the bone handle of a long skinning dagger.

Exercise 113B: Diagramming

On your own paper, diagram every word of the following sentences, taken from *Rakkety Tam*, by Brian Jacques.

The volethief munched on his rations whilst he analyzed what he had just witnessed.

Snow, that silent invader, fell deep and soft upon Redwall Abbey in Mossflower Country.

Turning his attention to the trembling king, Tam tried to make sense of all that was going on.

It was some twelve seasons since they had arrived and had enforced their authority over the tree groves.

Those two beasts were the only creatures who moved through this territory since the rats have been here.

It had been a long time since the traveller's last visit, and the Abbey creatures were anxious to hear the news from places beyond Redwall.

Where the sun falls from the sky, and dances at a pebble's drop, where little leaves slay big leaves, where wood meets earth I stop.

—LESSON 114—

Restrictive and Non-Restrictive Modifying Clauses

Punctuating Modifying Clauses

Which and *That*

Why does the mechanism of the p-value, which seems so reasonable, work so very badly in this setting?

If the first throw is tails and the second is heads, an event which happens 1/4 of the time, Paul gets two ducats.

—From *How Not to Be Wrong: The Power of Mathematical Thinking*, by Jordan Ellenberg

A non-restrictive modifying clause describes the word that it modifies. Removing the clause doesn't change the essential meaning of the sentence. Only non-restrictive clauses should be set off by commas.

A restrictive modifying clause defines the word that it modifies. Removing the clause changes the essential meaning of the sentence.

I especially like the "Methods" section, which starts "One mature Atlantic Salmon (*Salmo salar*) participated in the fMRI study."

I especially like the "Methods" section which starts "One mature Atlantic Salmon (*Salmo salar*) participated in the fMRI study."

A noun clause takes the place of a noun. Noun clauses can be introduced by relative pronouns, relative adverbs, or subordinating conjunctions.

In principle, if you carry out a powerful enough study, you can find out, which it is.

The reason the 0.999 . . . problem is difficult is, that it brings our intuitions into conflict.

An appositive is a noun, noun phrase, or noun clause that usually follows another noun and renames or explains it. Appositives are set off by commas.

The Goldbach conjecture, that every even number greater than 2 is the sum of two primes, is another one that would have to be true if primes behaved like random numbers.

The chocolate brownies that
The chocolate brownies which

The chocolate brownies that were on the counter are gone now.

The chocolate brownies, which were made with olive oil instead of butter, have been sitting on the counter since lunch time.

When the relative pronoun introducing a modifying clause refers to a thing rather than a person, *which* introduces non-restrictive clauses and *that* introduces restrictive clauses.

"These are but shadows of the things that have been," said the Ghost.

It was shrouded in a deep black garment, which concealed its head, its face, its form, and left nothing of it visible save one outstretched hand.

He lived in chambers which had once belonged to his deceased partner.

At last she said, and in a steady, cheerful voice, that only faltered once, "I have known him walk with—I have known him walk with Tiny Tim upon his shoulder, very fast indeed."

—From *A Christmas Carol*, by Charles Dickens

That's certainly an impressive figure, but one which clearly indicates that the percentage doesn't mean quite what you're used to it meaning.

—From *How Not to Be Wrong*, by Jordan Ellenberg

He lived in chambers that had once belonged to his deceased partner.
At last she said, and in a steady, cheerful voice, which only faltered once, "I have known him walk with—I have known him walk with Tiny Tim upon his shoulder, very fast indeed."
That's certainly an impressive figure, but one that clearly indicates that the percentage doesn't mean quite what you're used to it meaning.

Exercise 114A: Restrictive and Non-Restrictive Adjective Clauses

Find every adjective clause in the following sentences, taken from *A History of Mathematics*, by Florian Cajori, and then follow these steps:

a) Underline each adjective clause.
b) Circle the relative pronoun that introduces each clause.
c) Draw an arrow from the pronoun back to the word modified.
d) Label each clause as *R* for restrictive or *NR* for non-restrictive.
e) Draw an asterisk or star next to each sentence that does *not* follow the *which/that* rule.

In it are also found the theorems that the sum of the three sides of a spherical triangle is less than a great circle, and that the sum of the three angles exceeds two right angles.

The principal defect of Egyptian arithmetic was the lack of a simple, comprehensive symbolism—a defect which not even the Greeks were able to remove.

During middle life he engaged in commercial pursuits, which took him to Egypt.

Later another regular solid was discovered, namely the dodecahedron, which, in absence of a fifth element, was made to represent the universe itself.

The fact that trigonometry was cultivated not for its own sake, but to aid astronomical inquiry, explains the rather startling fact that spherical trigonometry came to exist in a developed state earlier than plane trigonometry.

The geometry of the circle, which had been entirely neglected by the Pythagoreans, was taken up by the Sophists.

The equations which constitute the foundation of the theory of fluid motion were fully laid down at the time of Lagrange.

It contains the proposition that the number of primes is greater than any given number.

Two questions which have occupied geometers of all periods may be regarded as having originated with them.

Poisson drew from Fresnel's formulæ the seemingly paradoxical deduction that a small circular disc, illuminated by a luminous point, must cast a shadow with a bright spot in the centre.

Exercise 114B: Dependent Clauses Within Dependent Clauses

The following sentences all contain dependent clauses that have other dependent clauses within them.

Underline the entire dependent clause, including additional dependent clauses that act as nouns or modifiers within it. Draw a box around the subject of the main dependent clause, and underline its predicate twice. In the right-hand margin, write the abbreviation for the part of the sentence that the main dependent clause is fulfilling: *N-SUB* for a noun clause acting as subject, subject, *N-PN* for predicate nominative, *N-DO* for direct object, *N-OP* for object of the preposition, and then *ADJ* for adjective and *ADV* for adverb.

Then, circle any additional clauses that fall within the main dependent clause. Label each clause, above the circle, in the same way: *N-SUB* for a noun clause acting as subject, *N-PN* for predicate nominative, *N-DO* for direct object, *N-OP* for object of the preposition, and then *ADJ* for adjective and *ADV* for adverb. For adjective and adverb clauses, draw a line from the circle back to the word in the main dependent clause modified.

The first sentence is done for you.

The following sentences are from *Philosophy & Fun of Algebra*, by Mary Everest Boole.

It often happens that two or three problems are so entangled up together that it seems impossible to solve any one of them until the others have been solved. ADV

ADV ADV

That is what will happen to you (if you learn your algebra properly) when you are no longer tied down to a, b, c, and √–1, as the values of x.

The next sentences are from *Zero: The Biography of a Dangerous Idea*, by Charles Seife.

Hippasus had revealed a secret that threatened to undermine the entire philosophy that the brotherhood had struggled to build.

The bad news was that the river destroyed many of the boundary markers, erasing all of the landmarks that told farmers which land was theirs to cultivate.

The only real difference was that instead of basing their numbers on 60 as the Babylonians did, the Mayans had a vigesimal, base-20 system that had the remnants of an earlier base-10 system in it.

Pythagoras noticed that plucking the string segments creates two notes that form a perfect fifth, which is said to be the most powerful and evocative musical relationship.

The following sentences are from *Things to Make and Do in the Fourth Dimension: A Mathematician's Journey Through Narcissistic Numbers, Optimal Dating Algorithms, at Least Two Kinds of Infinity, and More*, by Matt Parker.

To do that, we'll prove that no sum of consecutive numbers can give a total which is a power of two.

> **NOTE:** Be careful—the next sentence has a missing word, *and* a clause within a clause within a clause! Ask your instructor if you need help.

You'll notice we're not using the original number as one of its own factors, which means we're adding the so-called "proper factors", i.e., all the factors including 1 but excluding the number itself.

> **NOTE:** Don't relax yet—the next sentence has even more clauses within clauses, plus unusual word order. Ask your instructor if you need help.

The factors of 220 are 1, 2, 4, 5, 10, 11, 20, 22, 44, 55, and 110, which may not seem very special—until you realize that, if you add them all together, the total is 284.

NOTE: See if you can figure out what makes this last sentence difficult! You've already met these complications in your other sentences—just not in this particular combination.

Mills' constant is a great reminder that, if we want a number with a certain property, we can simply construct it ourselves—which is not to say it isn't a real number.

Exercise 114C: Diagramming

On your own paper, diagram every word of the following sentences. If you need help, ask your instructor.

In fact, this idea underlies what in mathematics we call the law of the excluded middle—which says that there is no middle ground between true and not true.

—From Amir D. Aczel, *Finding Zero: A Mathematician's Odyssey to Uncover the Origins of Numbers*

But nowadays everybody knows that zero can't really sit anywhere on the number line, because it has a definite numerical value of its own.

This violates a basic principle of numbers called the axiom of Archimedes, which says that if you add something to itself enough times, it will exceed any other number in magnitude.

—From Charles Seife, *Zero: The Biography of a Dangerous Idea*

We've already used whole numbers as well as fractions, which are what I call the "well-behaved" numbers.

If you list all the factors of any composite number, they form pairs which multiply to give you back the original number, but square numbers have an extra lonely factor which has to pair with itself.

—From Matt Parker, *Things to Make and Do in the Fourth Dimension: A Mathematician's Journey Through Narcissistic Numbers, Optimal Dating Algorithms, at Least Two Kinds of Infinity, and More*

—LESSON 115—

Conditional Sentences
Conditional Sentences as Dependent Clauses
Conditional Sentences with Missing Words
Formal *If* Clauses

The sentences in this lesson are from *Pride and Prejudice and Zombies*, by Jane Austen and Seth Grahame-Smith.

I have nothing to say against him; he has felled many a zombie; and if he had [simple past, active, subjunctive] the fortune he ought to have, I should think [simple present, active, modal,] you could not do better. SECOND

Active verbs are active or passive in voice.
State-of-being verbs do not have voice.
Subjunctive verbs express situations that are unreal, wished for, or uncertain.

If my children are silly, I must hope to be always sensible of it. ______________

If I had known as much this morning I certainly would not have called him. ___________

If I were not afraid of judging harshly, I should be almost tempted to demand satisfaction.

____

First conditional sentences express circumstances that might actually happen.
The predicate of the condition clause is in a present tense.
The predicate of the consequence clause is an imperative or is in a present or future tense.

Second conditional sentences express circumstances that are contrary to reality.
The predicate of the condition clause is in a past tense.
The predicate of the consequence clause is in the simple or progressive present modal tense.

Third conditional sentences express past circumstances that never happened.
The predicate of the condition clause is in the perfect past tense.
The predicate of the consequence clause is in any modal tense.

In her postscript it was added that if Mr. Bingley and his sister pressed them to stay longer, she could spare them.

However, I recollected afterwards that if he had been prevented going, the wedding need not be put off.

If he fears me, why come hither?

If he no longer cares for me, why silent?

Should you wish to, meet me in the drawing room.

Formal conditional sentences drop *if* from the condition clause and reverse the order of the subject and helping verb.

Were you not otherwise agreeable, I should be forced to remove your tongue with my saber.

If he fears me, why come hither?

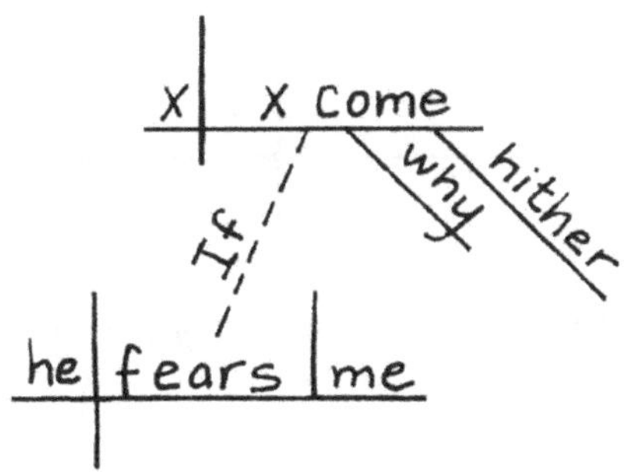

If he no longer cares for me, why silent?

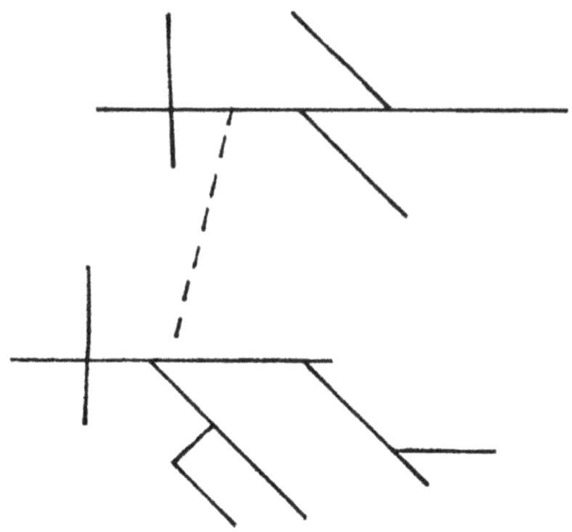

Should you wish, meet me in the drawing room.

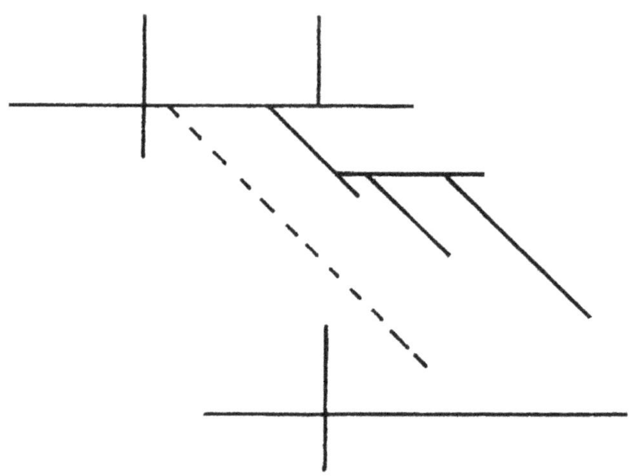

Were you not otherwise agreeable, I should be forced to remove your tongue with my saber.

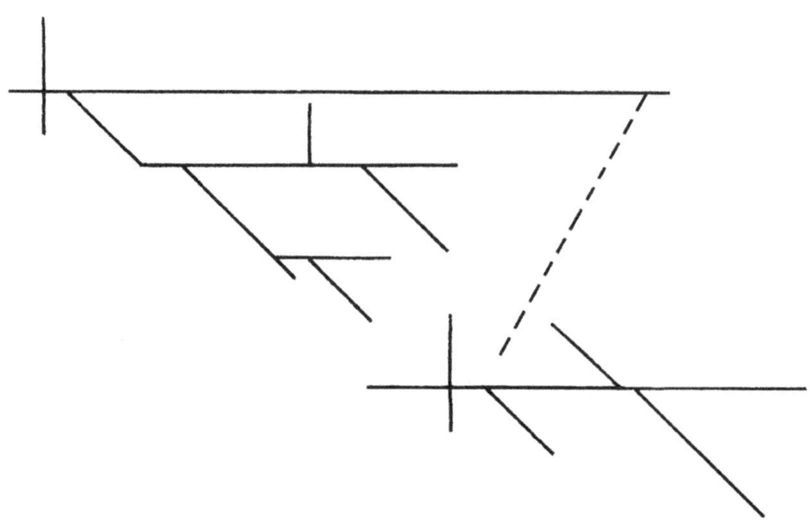

Exercise 115A: Conditional Clauses

In the following sentences from *Pride and Prejudice and Zombies*, by Jane Austen and Seth Grahame-Smith, circle every conditional sentence. This may mean circling the entire sentence, or circling simply the part of it that makes up the conditional-consequence clause set, or circling the conditional and consequence clauses separately if they are divided by other words.

After you have circled the conditional sentences, underline twice and then parse the predicate in each conditional and consequence clause.

Finally, write a *1, 2,* or *3* in the blank to indicate *first, second, or third* conditional. The first is done for you.

simple future, state-of-being, indicative — simple present, active, subjunctive

Will you be very angry with me, my dear Lizzy, if I take this opportunity of saying how much I like him? 1

All Elizabeth's anger against him had been long done away, but had she still felt any, it could hardly have stood its ground against the unaffected cordiality with which he expressed himself on seeing her again. ______

If this be the case, he deserves you. ______

I now give it to you, if you are resolved on having him. ______

Had she her dagger, Elizabeth would have dropped to her knees and administered the seven cuts of dishonor without a moment's hesitation. ______

"If he does not come to me, then," said she, "I shall give him up for ever, and shall never again divert my eyes from the end of my blade." ______

And, if I may mention so delicate a subject, endeavour to check Miss Bennet's unladylike affinity for guns, and swords, and exercise, and all those silly things best left to men or ladies of low breeding. ______

Elizabeth highly approved his forbearance, which was greater than her own, for she confessed that a duel would have almost certainly ensued, had she been in his place. ______

Prattle on if you must, but leave me to the defense of my estate! ______

But if I go on, I shall displease you by saying what I think of persons you esteem. ______

If Mr. Darcy is neither by honour nor inclination confined to his cousin, why is not he to make another choice? ______

I should prefer you have speed at your disposal; besides, if it rains, you must stay all night. ______

If they believed him attached to me, they would not try to part us; if he were so, they would not succeed. ______

He really believed, that were it not for the inferiority of her connections, he should be in some danger of falling in love, and were it not for his considerable skill in the deadly arts, that he should be in danger of being bested by hers—for never had he seen a lady more gifted in the ways of vanquishing the undead. ______

Had he done his duty in that respect, Lydia need not have been indebted to her uncle for whatever of honour or credit could now be purchased for her. ______

Exercise 115B: Diagramming

On your own paper, diagram every word of the following two sentences from Exercise 115A.

All Elizabeth's anger against him had been long done away, but had she still felt any, it could hardly have stood its ground against the unaffected cordiality with which he expressed himself on seeing her again.

> **NOTE:** This is a hard one! Use scratch paper, and ask for help if you need it.

He really believed, that were it not for the inferiority of her connections, he should be in some danger of falling in love, and were it not for his considerable skill in the deadly arts, that he should be in danger of being bested by hers—for never had he seen a lady more gifted in the ways of vanquishing the undead.

—LESSON 116—

Words That Can Be Multiple Parts of Speech
Interrogatives
Demonstratives
Relative Adverbs and Subordinating Conjunctions

Exercise 116A: Words Acting as Multiple Parts of Speech

Use these sentences, taken from Zane Grey's classic western novel *Riders of the Purple Sage* (some very slightly adapted), to identify the parts of speech that the bolded words can serve as. The first blank is filled in for you. Fill in the blanks with the correct labels from the following list:

coordinating conjunction	subordinating conjunction	interjection
preposition	adverb	adjective
noun	verb	

But coordinating conjunction ____________________ ____________________

The rider did not bridle him, but walked beside him, leading him by touch of hand, and together they passed slowly into the shade of the cottonwoods.

There never was any one but her in my life till now.

I never had but one idea. I never rested.

For ____________________ ____________________

A thousand excuses he invented for himself, yet not one made any difference in his act or his self-reproach.

But death, while it hovered over him, did not descend, for the rider waited for the twitching fingers, the downward flash of hand that did not come.

Yet ____________________ ____________________ ____________________

"The world seems very far away," he muttered, "but it's there—and I'm not yet done with it."

He smiled a flinty smile that was more than inhuman, yet seemed to give out of its dark aloofness a gleam of righteousness.

But that's a good many miles yet.

Before ____________________ ____________________ ____________________

Her clear sight intensified the purple sage-slope as it rolled before her.

Once, long before, on the night Venters had carried Bess through the canyon and up into Surprise Valley, he had experienced the strangeness of faculties singularly, tinglingly acute.

I lost all before I knew it.

Out ____________________ ____________________ ____________________

A sharp clip-crop of iron-shod hoofs deadened and died away, and clouds of yellow dust drifted from under the cottonwoods out over the sage.

I reckon, Jane, that marriage between us is out of all human reason.

Out! Out! Leave Utah and leave me in peace!

Around ____________________ ____________________ ____________________

But I feel something dark and terrible closing in around me.

When the two men entered the immense barnyard, from all around the din increased.

I've seen them drunk with joy and dance and fling themselves around.

Below ____________ ____________ ____________ ____________

Venters had a moment's notice of the rock, which was of the same smoothness and hardness as the slope below, before his gaze went irresistibly upward to the precipitous walls of this wide ladder of granite.

Next on the slope, just below the third and largest lake, were corrals and a wide stone barn and open sheds and coops and pens.

He knew that behind the corner of stone would be a cave or a crack which could never be suspected from below.

The dog growled below and rushed into the forest.

Except ____________________ ____________________

I've no more to lose—except my life.

Swiftly, resolutely he put out of mind all of her life except what had been spent with him.

Up ____________ ____________ ____________ ____________

On the morrow he was up bright and early, glad that he had a surprise for Bess.

Once again he upped his bet.

Low swells of prairie-like ground sloped up to the west.

A group of riders cantered up the lane, dismounted, and threw their bridles.

Since ____________________ ____________________ ____________________

It was he of whom Judkins had long since spoken.

Bess, I haven't seen that since last summer.

How many years had passed since the cliff-dwellers gazed out across the beautiful valley as he was gazing now?

---

who, whom, whose, what, which

Interrogative pronouns take the place of nouns in questions.
Interrogative adjectives modify nouns.

Interrogative Pronouns	**Interrogative Adjectives**
Who was Dragging Canoe?	Whose side was Dragging Canoe on?
With whom did Dragging Canoe fight?	What war did he fight?
What did Dragging Canoe do?	Which tribe did Dragging Canoe belong to?
Which of his countrymen followed him?	

In the American Revolution, Dragging Canoe fought against the colonists who were rebelling against the British.

Dragging Canoe and his brother chiefs, whom he had known for many years, joined together and allied with the British.

Dragging Canoe told his tribesmen to consider the case of the Delaware, whose land had been swallowed by the American colonies.

At first, the American colonists did not know what Dragging Canoe was planning.

Dragging Canoe led attacks on the settlements which were in southeast North America.

The interrogative words *who*, *whom*, *whose*, *what*, and *which* can also serve as relative pronouns in adjective clauses or introductory words in noun clauses.

What was the name of Dragging Canoe's father? ____________________

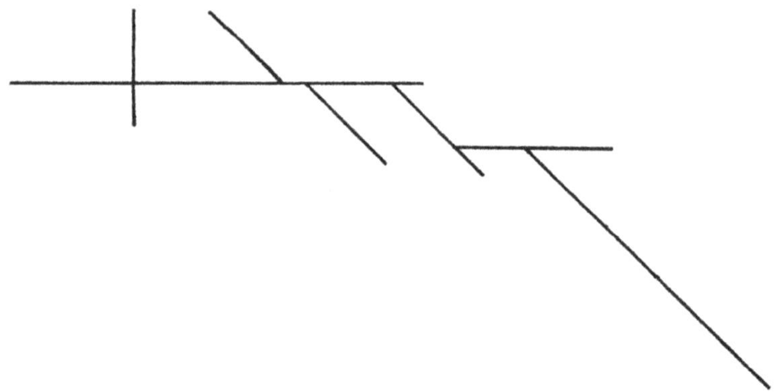

What five towns did Dragging Canoe build? ____________________

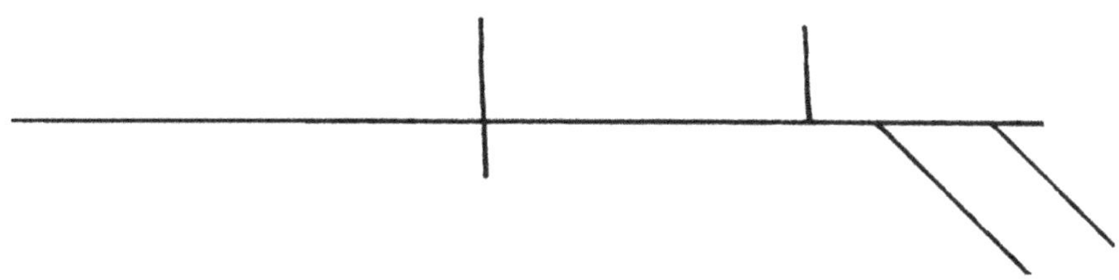

Dragging Canoe did not believe what the governor of North Carolina told him. ____________________

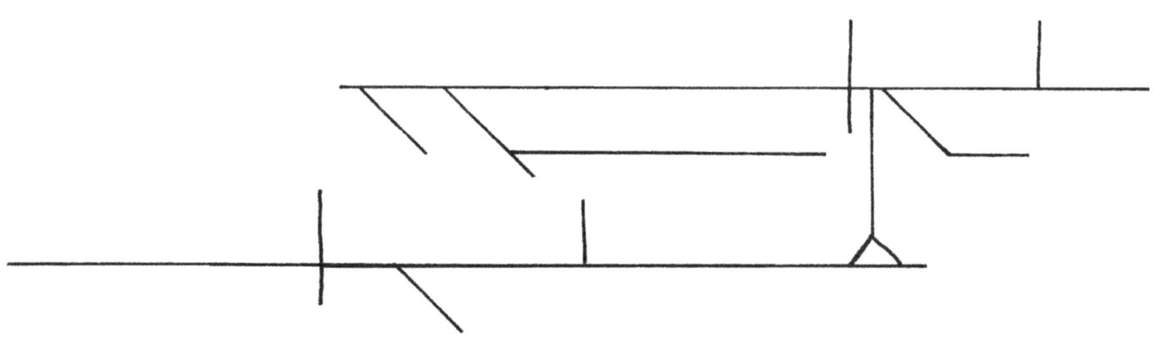

Dragging Canoe led the Cherokees who refused to stay neutral.

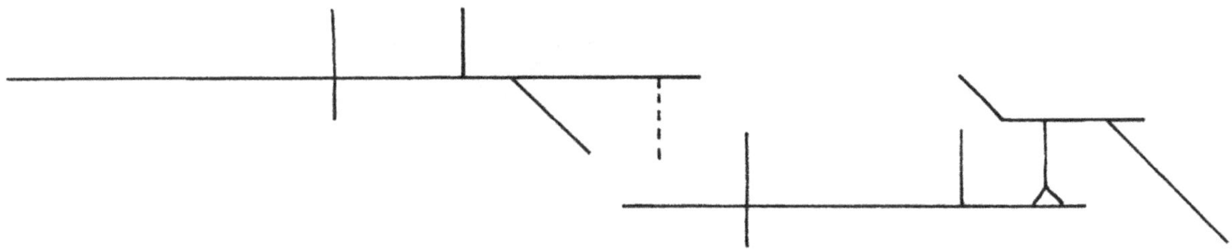

this, that, these, those

Demonstrative pronouns demonstrate or point out something. They take the place of a single word or a group of words.

Demonstrative adjectives modify nouns and answer the question *which one*.

Those were the first Spanish ships to touch American shores.

While a young boy, this future chief wanted to accompany his father, Attakullakulla, and a Cherokee war party going to battle the Shawnee.

During one of these council sessions, a young chief named Dragging Canoe exploded into prominence.

Now that hope is gone.

This was the first invasion of the Middle Towns by an enemy force on record.
—From Pat Alderman, *Nancy Ward: Cherokee Chieftainess, Dragging Canoe: Cherokee-Chickamauga War Chief*

He had come to the council because of his admiration for that great chief.

They set off at a rapid pace, little guessing that a silent scout followed them.

That would be a catastrophe for the Cherokee and their allies.

An adverb describes a verb, an adjective, or another adverb.
Adverbs tell how, when, where, how often, and to what extent.

Relative adverbs introduce adjective clauses and refer back to a place, time, or reason in the independent clause.

where, when, why

(The remaining sentences in the lesson are slightly adapted from *Trail of Tears: The Rise and Fall of the Cherokee Nation*, by John Ehle.)

It was the orderly village to which he was heir, and where his mother was the pivot of the world.

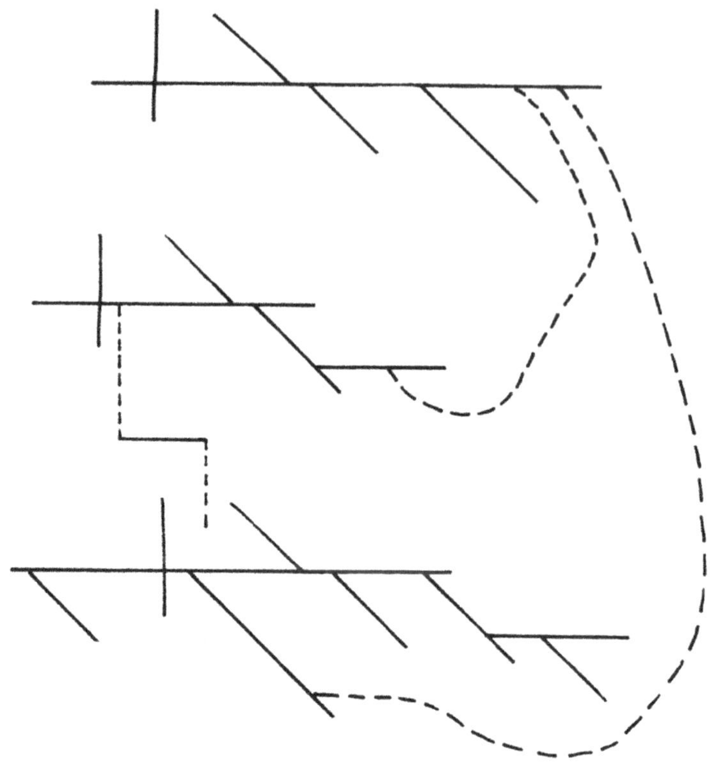

My heart rejoices when I look upon you.

Adverbs can act as subordinating conjunctions when they connect adverb clauses to a verb, adjective, or adverb in the main clause.

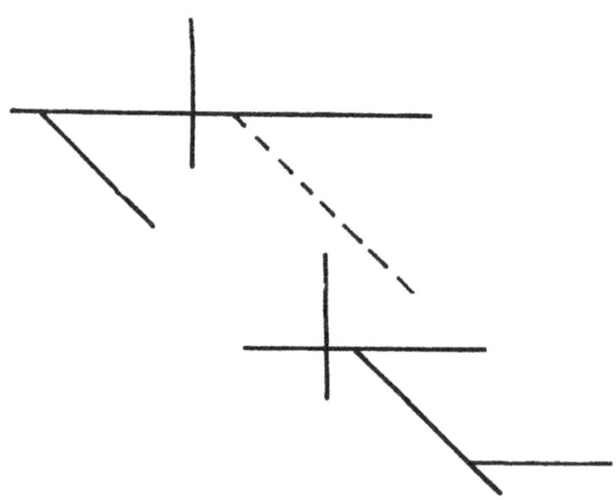

Their land was taken away because they fought for the British.

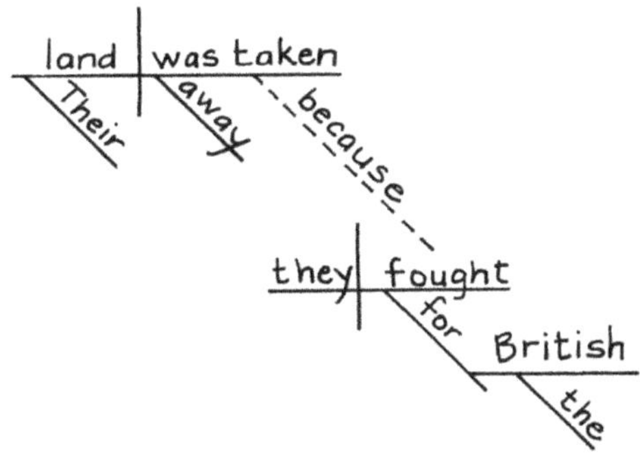

Exercise 116B: Words Introducing Clauses

In the following sentences, taken from Zane Grey's classic Western novel *The Lone Star Ranger* (some slightly condensed), underline every subordinate clause. Then, carry out the following steps:

a) Circle the introductory word of the clause.
(**NOTE**: When the introductory word is the object of a preposition, circle the word itself, not the preposition that precedes it. See the sample sentence.)
b) Label the clause as *N* (for noun), *ADJ* (for adjective), or *ADV* (for adverb).
c) For noun clauses, further identify them as *S* (for subject) or *OBJ* (for object).
d) For adjective or adverb clauses, draw an arrow back to the word modified.
e) Finally, label the introductory word as one of the following: *RP* for relative pronoun, *RAdj* for relative adjective (a relative pronoun functioning as an adjective and introducing an adjective clause), *RAdv* for relative adverb, *SC* for subordinating conjunction, or *A-SC* for adverb functioning as a subordinating conjunction.

And these images naturally are of the men with whom I have dealt.

When he had looked after the needs of his horse he returned to the group before the inn.

These riders, whoever they were, had approached too closely.

The reward was offered by the woman's husband, whose name appeared at the bottom of the placard.

Without the horse he made better time and climbed through deep clefts, wide canyons, over ridges, up shelving slopes, along precipices—a long, hard climb—till he reached a divide.

Who heads the gang, anyway?

About three in the afternoon he came to a little river which marked the boundary line of his hunting territory.

The bottom-lands through which the river wound to the southwest were more inviting.

He looked among his effects for a hobble, and, finding that his uncle had failed to put one in, he suddenly remembered that he seldom used a hobble, and never on this horse.

He's the only person in this awful place who's been good to me.

Hardly once since Jennie had entered into his thought had those ghosts returned to torment him.

There were four other men whom Duane knew by sight, several whose faces were familiar, and half a dozen strangers, all dusty horsemen.

Darkness had about set in when he reached his destination.

Those who were his real friends on the border would have been the last to make inquiries.

There were more coming round the cut where the road curved.

He had gathered from the words of one of his pursuers that the brake was a kind of trap.

The way out of it was along the bank where he had entered, and where obviously all night long his pursuers had kept fires burning.

After supper the guests assembled in a big sitting-room where an open fire place with blazing mesquite sticks gave out warmth and cheery glow.

He followed it until a late hour, when he picketed his horse and lay down to rest.

It can't be done unless you want to sacrifice everything.

Wellston was a small town, but important in that unsettled part of the great state because it was the trading-center of several hundred miles of territory.

Exercise 116C: Diagramming

(You didn't think you'd escape diagramming, did you?)

On your own paper, diagram every word of the following sentences from Zane Grey's classic Western novel *The Rainbow Trail.*

If you need help, ask your instructor.

By and by they had a little girl whom they named Jane.

We raised corn and fruit, and stored what we didn't use.

When he assured her he was unhurt she said he had agreed to go where she went.

In the gray of dawn, when the hush of the desert night still lay deep over the land, the Navajo stirred in his blanket and began to chant to the morning light.

He had not often walked with her beyond the dark shade of the pinyons round the cottage, but this night, when he knew he must tell her, he led her away down the path, through the cedar grove to the west end of the valley where it was wild and lonely and sad and silent.

WEEK 31

Filling Up the Corners

After the feast (more or less) came the Speech. Most of the company were, however, now in a tolerant mood, at that delightful stage which they called "filling up the corners." They were sipping their favourite drinks, and nibbling at their favourite dainties, and their fears were forgotten. They were prepared to listen to anything, and to cheer at every full stop.

—J. R. R. Tolkien, *The Fellowship of the Ring*

—LESSON 117—

Interrogative Adverbs
Noun Clauses
Forming Questions
Affirmations and Negations
Double Negatives

An adverb describes a verb, an adjective, or another adverb.
Adverbs tell how, when, where, how often, and to what extent.

Relative adverbs introduce adjective clauses and refer back to a place, time, or reason in the independent clause.

where, when, why

I found a shop where I could buy cheese and chocolate.

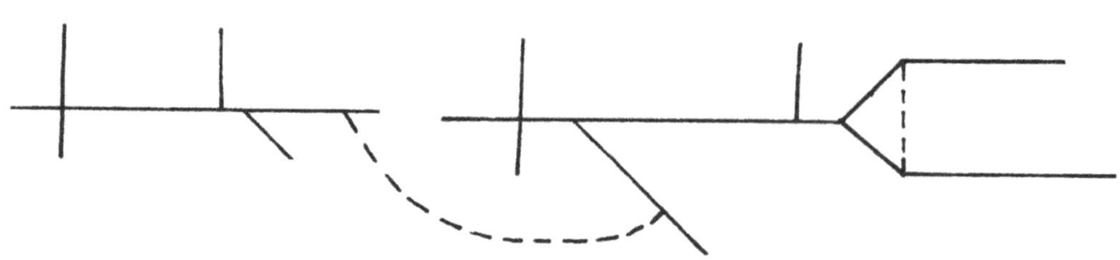

Where did you get the cheese and chocolate?

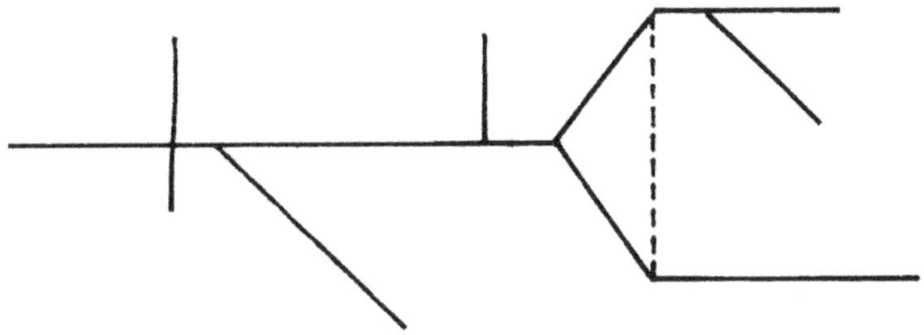

He asked me where I got the cheese and chocolate.

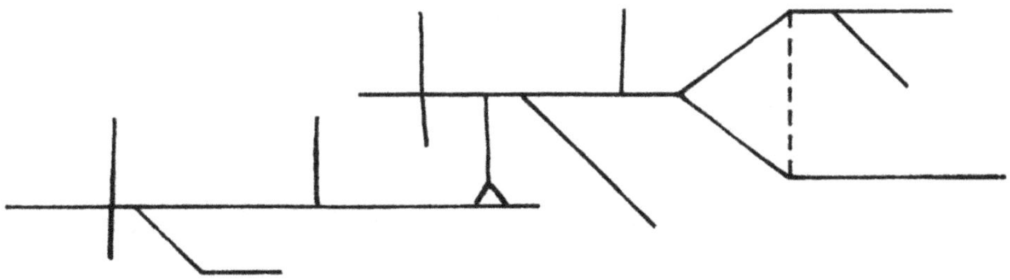

An interrogative adverb asks a question.

where, when, why, how

The interrogative adverbs can also introduce noun clauses.

I desired to know how this thing came to Gollum, and how long he had possessed it.

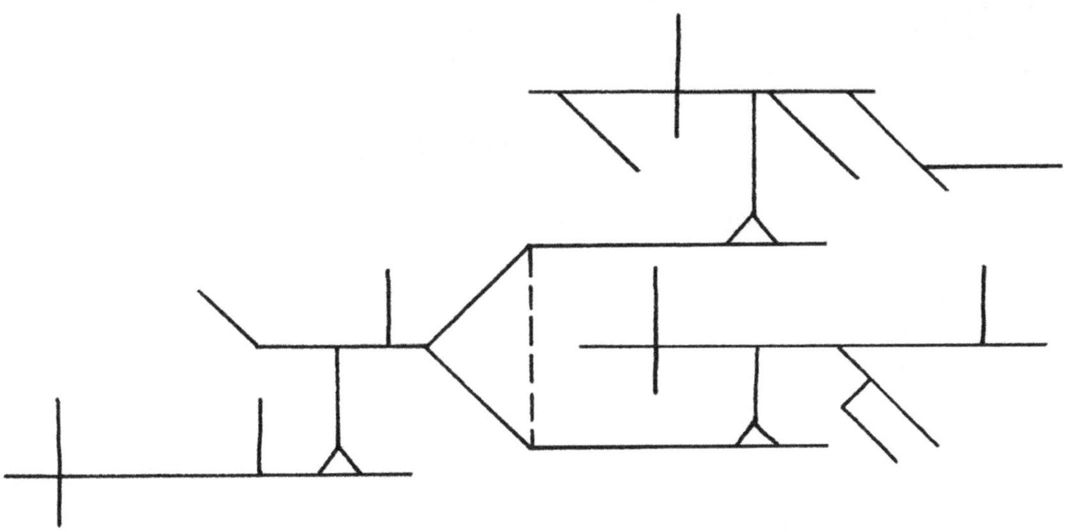

How do the Wise know that this ring is his?

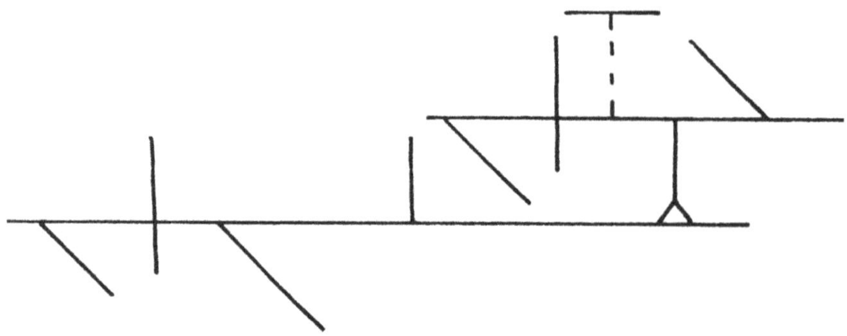

You are hungry.
Are you hungry?

You would like a big bowl of pozole.
Would you like a big bowl of pozole?

Use the helping verbs *do, does,* and *did* to form negatives, ask questions, and provide emphasis.

He fixed green pozole with sliced avocados.
Did he fix green pozole with sliced avocados?

Simple Present		**Simple Past**	
I do	we do	I did	we did
you do	you do	you did	you did
he, she it, does	they do	he, she it did	they did

They love to nibble on chalupas.
Do they love to nibble on chalupas?

Who is bringing the bread pudding with flaming brandy?

What kind of frosting are you using for the cake?

When will the mangos be ripe enough to make mango cake?

Which limes did you use in the lime pudding?

Whom have you invited to the party?

How many loaves of challah did you bake?

Whose presents are those?

An affirmation states what is true or what exists.
A negation states what is not true or does not exist.

Adverbs of affirmation
yes, surely, definitely, certainly, absolutely, very

Did he invite her in?
And he invited her in; yes, he did.

Were they merry?
Surely they were very merry.

Was the roast chicken ready?
The roast chicken was definitely ready to eat.

Were the mushrooms good?
The mushrooms were absolutely delicious.

Adverbs of negation	**Adjective of negation**
no, not, never	no

Did anyone go hungry?
No man, woman, or child went hungry.

When did they stop feasting?
They did not stop feasting until well after sundown.

How much merriment was there?
Never was there so much merriment.

There is not no doubt.

I haven't heard no good of such folk.

I don't know nothing about jewels.

Do not use two adverbs or adjectives of negation together.

Exercise 117A: Identifying Adverbs, Interrogative and Demonstrative Pronouns and Adjectives, and Relatives

In the following sentences from *Charlie and the Chocolate Factory*, by Roald Dahl, follow these steps:

a) Label each bolded word as one of the following:

ADV for adverb

Draw an arrow from the adverb to the word modified.

If the adverb also introduces a clause, underline the clause.

PRO for pronoun

If the pronoun has an antecedent, label the antecedent as *ANT*.

If the pronoun introduces a clause, underline the clause.

Label each pronoun as *S* for subject, *PN* for predicate nominative, *DO* for direct object, *IO* for indirect object, *OP* for object of the preposition, or *ADJ* (see below).

ADJ for adjective

Draw an arrow from the adjective to the word modified. If the adjective introduces a clause, underline the clause.

SC for subordinating conjunction

Underline the dependent clause introduced by the conjunction.

b) Label each underlined clause as *ADV-C* for adverb clause, *ADJ-C* for adjective clause, or *N-C* for noun clause.

c) Draw an arrow from each *ADV-C* and *ADJ-C* clause back to the word modified. Label each *N-C* noun clause as *S* for subject, *DO* for direct object, *IO* for indirect object, or *OP* for object of the preposition.

The first is done for you. Notice that *whose* has two labels because it is both an adjective and a relative pronoun.

ANT ADJ/PRO ADJ-C

Mr. and Mrs. Bucket have a small boy **whose** name is Charlie Bucket.

I shall now tell you **how this** amazing television set of mine works.

And oh, **how** he wished he could go inside the factory and see **what** it was like!

They suck up the chocolate and carry it away to all the other rooms in the factory **where** it is needed!

Why do we have to go rushing on past all **these** lovely rooms?

The wallpaper has pictures of all **these** fruits printed on it, and **when** you lick the picture of a banana, it tastes of banana.

So **who** is going to run the factory **when** I get too old to do it myself?

If **these** people can break up a photograph into millions of pieces and send the pieces whizzing through the air and **then** put them together again at the other end, **why** can't I do the same thing with a bar of chocolate?

But **there** was one other thing **that** the grownups also knew, and it was **this: however** small the chance might be of striking lucky, the chance was **there**.

What sort of nonsense is **this**?

He worked in a toothpaste factory, **where** he sat all day long at a bench and screwed the little caps onto the tops of the tubes of toothpaste **after** the tubes had been filled.

Exercise 117B: Forming Questions

On your own paper, rewrite the following statements as questions.

Use each of the three methods for forming questions (adding an interrogative pronoun, reversing the subject and helping verb, or adding the helping verb *do, does*, or *did* in front of the subject and adjusting the tense of the main verb) at least once. You may change tenses, add or subtract words, or alter the statements in any other necessary ways, as long as the meaning remains the same.

These statements are all adapted from famous questions in books and movies. When you have transformed your statements into questions, compare them with the originals.

The rum is gone.

I feel lucky.

The air speed velocity of an unladen swallow is unknown.

You're a little short for a storm trooper.

We shall play a game.

Mirror, mirror on the wall, the fairest one of all is unknown.

You are Sarah Connor.

It always has to be snakes.

It has something in its pocketses.

A white dove must sail many seas before she sleeps in the sand.

While you're at it, give me a nice paper cut and pour lemon juice on it.

Exercise 117C: Affirmations and Negations

On your own paper, rewrite each of the following affirmative statements as a negation, using one adverb or adjective of negation. You may add or subtract words or change tenses as necessary.

- Rewrite each negative statement as an affirmative, using at least one adverb of affirmation.
- Rewrite each double negation as an affirmative, also using at least one adverb of affirmation.

When you are finished, compare your answers with the original sentences, slightly adapted from Lamar Underwood's *1001 Fishing Tips: The Ultimate Guide to Finding and Catching More and Bigger Fish.*

Fishing in the big wind is not tough.

The mealworm isn't a deadly bait.

The fish sucked the worm into its mouth.

The film *Bigmouth 35* will not help you catch more bass.

You can't count on the seven lures featured here.

Chum salmon get respect.

A hair-trigger reaction to a strike is the way to go.

People who tell you that bass don't school don't know nothing about what they're talking about.

Worm fishing doesn't make anglers yawn.

—LESSON 118—

Diagramming Affirmations and Negations
Yet More Words That Can Be Multiple Parts of Speech

Comparisons Using *Than*
Comparisons Using *As*

Are you ready for your lesson?
   Absolutely.
Do you remember the definition of a noun?
   Definitely.
How sure are you?
   Very.
Have you forgotten it?
   No.
Will you ever forget it?
   Never.

Affirmative and negative adverbs can also act as interjections.

Never
Absolutely

I can be **very** deaf when I need.

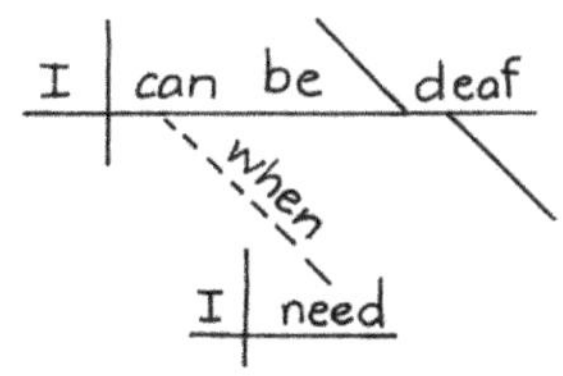

Yes, I will paint you, Juanico.

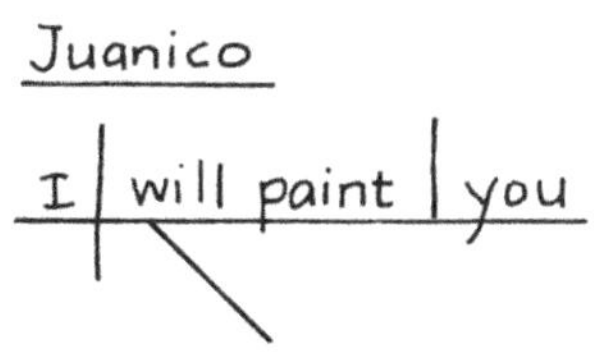

You will **never** be beaten again.

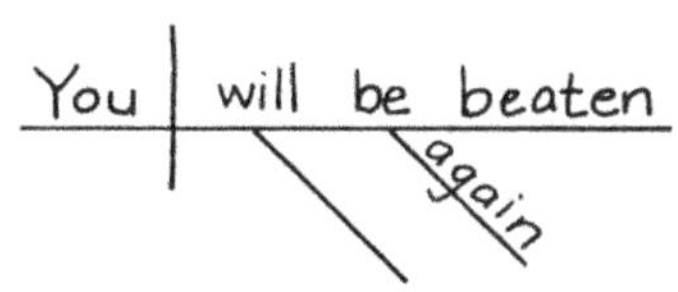

I am **no** longer a slave.

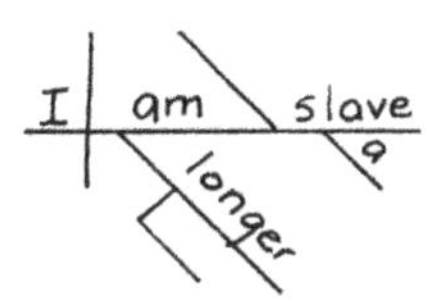

(From *I, Juan de Pareja*, by Elizabeth Borton de Treviño.)

Yes, I said.

He's unbeatable and drops the dehuller with a fat Yes.

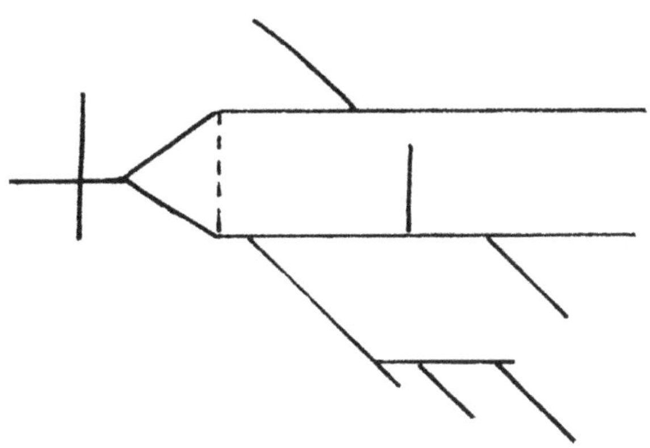

(From *Drown*, by Junot Diaz)

Father might say no.

It has no shoestrings.

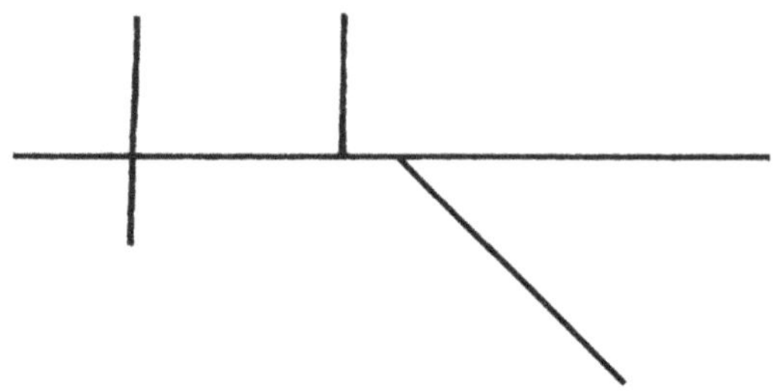

(From *The Dreamer*, by Pam Muñoz Ryan.)

QC: quasi-coordinator *PREP*: preposition *ADV*: adverb *SC*: subordinating conjunction

The stone was black and shiny, so you could see your reflection as well as the blooming trees and the clouds in the sky.
—From *Return to Sender*, by Julia Alvarez

Mamadre nodded and smiled as she left the room.

As my partner, how do you think we should proceed?
—From *The Dreamer*, by Pam Muñoz Ryan

When we arrived, nothing was as promised.
—From *Esperanza Rising*, by Pam Muñoz Ryan

His affections became poems, as warm and supple as the wool of a well-loved sheep.
—From *The Dreamer*, by Pam Muñoz Ryan

When *than* is used in a comparison and introduces a clause with understood elements, it is acting as a subordinating conjunction.

That wool is warmer than my wool.

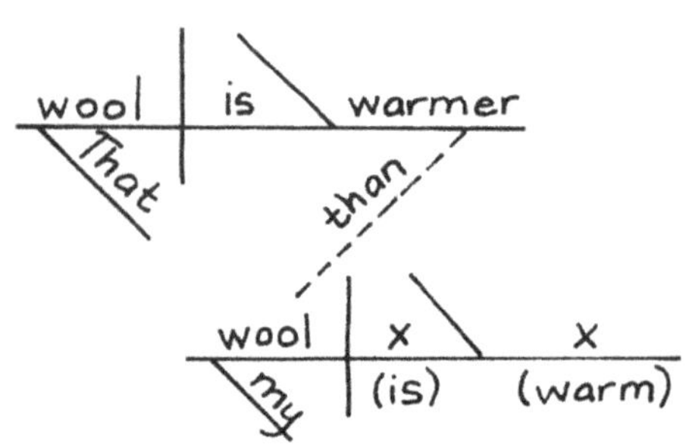

His affections became poems, as warm and supple as the wool of a well-loved sheep.
—From *The Dreamer,* by Pam Muñoz Ryan

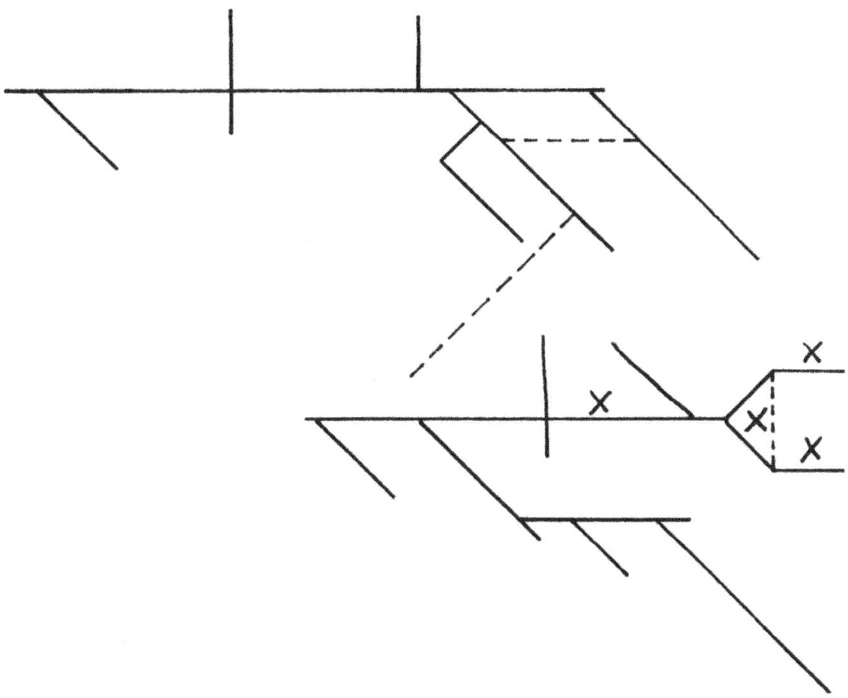

I did as he asked.

He had the same concerns as you have had.

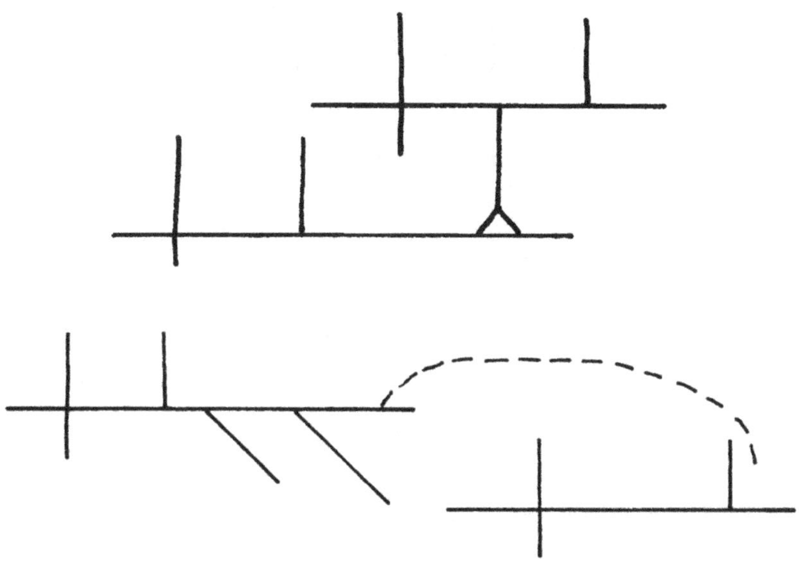

The farmer struggled with the same difficulties as you.

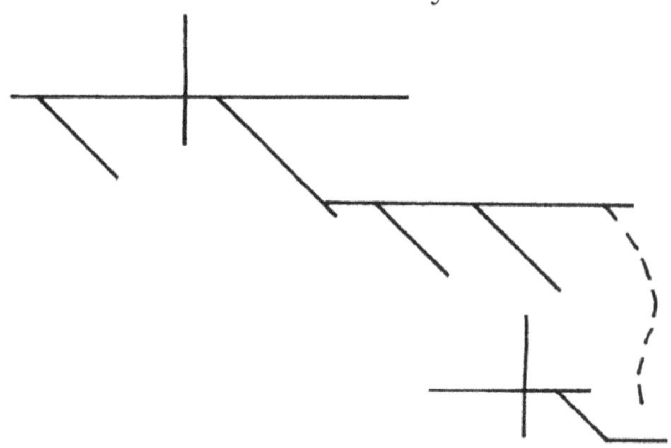

Exercise 118A: Identifying Parts of Speech

Label each of the bolded words in these sentences (from Roald Dahl's novel *The BFG*, about a big friendly giant) with one of the following abbreviations: *ADV* for adverb, *ADV-N* for adverb of negation, *ADV-A* for adverb of affirmation, *ADV-R* for relative adverb, *SC* for subordinating conjunction, *PREP* for preposition, *RP* for relative pronoun, or *N* for noun.

Where a subordinating conjunction introduces a comparison clause with missing words, draw a caret and insert the missing words.

It was **as** clear **as** crystal.

Yes, **now that** you come to mention it, I did.

They had never seen the likes of it **before.**

The Giant reached **out** and rolled the stone to one side **as easily as** if it had been a football, and **now, where** the stone had been, **there** appeared a vast black hole.

Suddenly, **there** was a crunch **as** the Bloodbottler bit a huge hunk **off** the end.

By now Sophie was beginning to feel **not** only **extremely** hungry, but **very** thirsty **as well**.

The wind rushing **against** Sophie's face became **so** strong **that** she had to duck **down** **again into** the blanket to prevent her head **from** being blown **away**.

It was **as** big **as** a house.

The ninth, **who** happened to be the Fleshlumpeater, was causing trouble for the soldiers **because** he was lying with his right arm tucked **underneath** his enormous body.

Fleshlumpeater says he is **never** eating a queen and he thinks **perhaps** she has an **especially** scrumdiddlyumptious flavour.

It is the same with trees **as** it is with flowers.

No noise came **out**, but it was obvious to Sophie **that whatever** had been in the jar had **now** been blown through the trumpet into the Goochey children's bedroom.

Exercise 118B: Diagramming

On your own paper, diagram every word of the following sentences. Ask your instructor for help if you need it.

Do you know what they are really thinking?

His memories of the understory of the great forest burst into lyrical phrases, as resinous as the sap of a pinecone, as crisp as the shell of a beetle.

—From *The Dreamer*, by Pam Muñoz Ryan

Yes, really and truly, I want you to keep it.

Well, Diary, I was about to say, No!

After that call, we were all very nervous as we always are when we hear news of someone being nabbed by *la migra*.

We have missed you terribly the eight months and a day (yes, Mama, I am keeping count!) that you have been gone.

Papa kept reassuring us that the journey home was no problem, as you would be entering your birth land on an airplane, not on foot through a desert.

—From *Return to Sender*, by Julia Alvarez

—LESSON 119—

Idioms

I'm confused because I don't know what you are **driving at**.

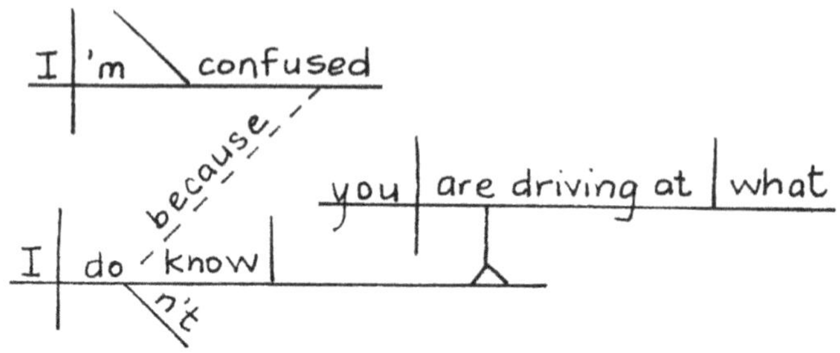

We did our best, but we failed, and now it is **back to the drawing board**.

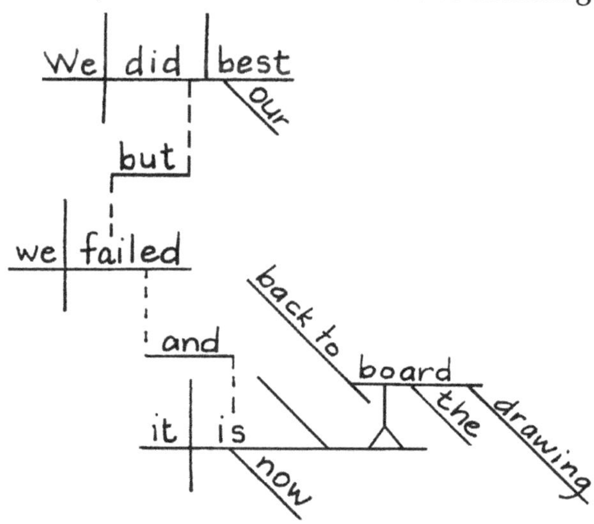

One day it's sunny and warm and the next it's raining cats and dogs.

—From *Final Flight: The Mystery of a WWII Plane Crash and the Frozen Airmen in the High Sierra*, by Peter Stekel

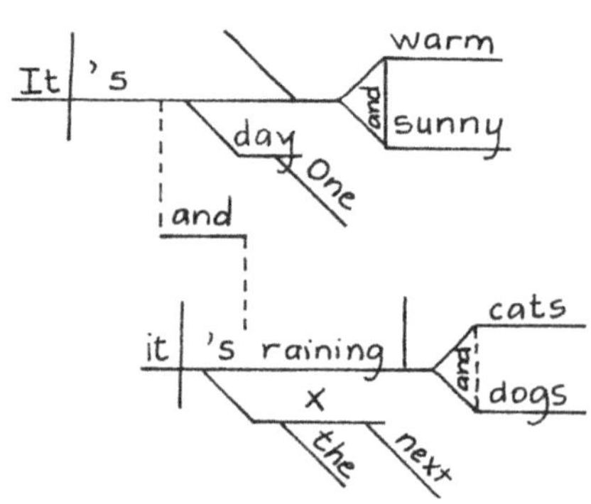

The king rained gifts and favors upon the lucky knight.

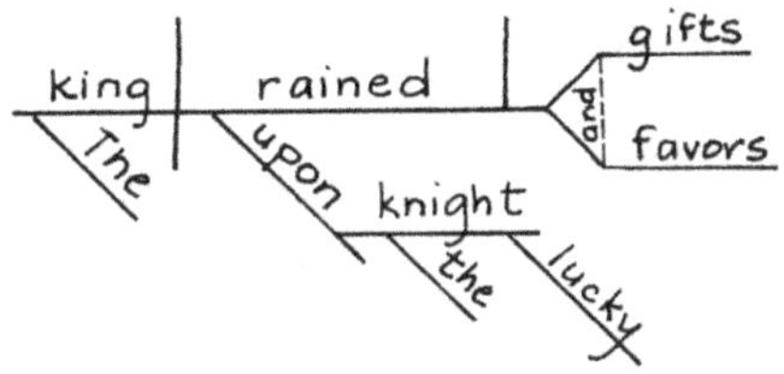

The pilot was getting into the groove of the airplane, was flying it every day.
—slightly adapted from *Final Flight: The Mystery of a WWII Plane Crash and the Frozen Airmen in the High Sierra,* by Peter Stekel

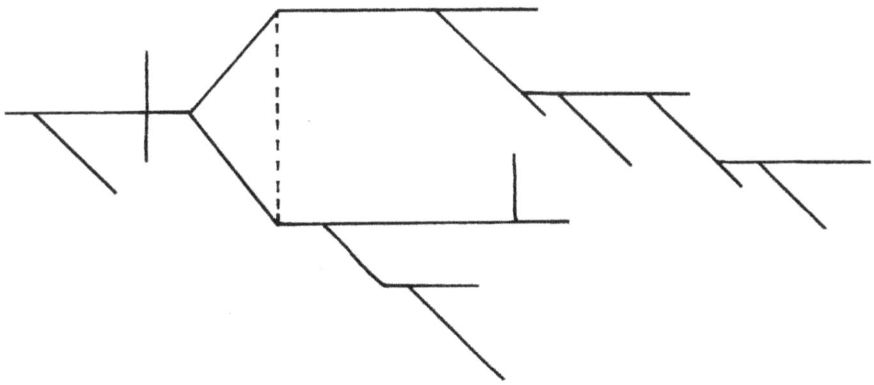

No doubt the gypsy had stolen my earring as I lay unconscious.
—From *I, Juan de Pareja,* by Elizabeth Borton de Treviño

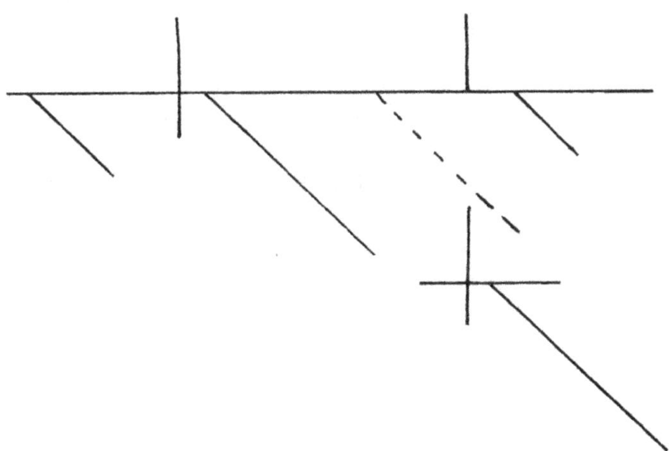

When my arms began to ache, she would wash the butter with ice water in order to separate the curd from the whey.

—From *Where the Flame Trees Bloom,* by Alma Flor Ada

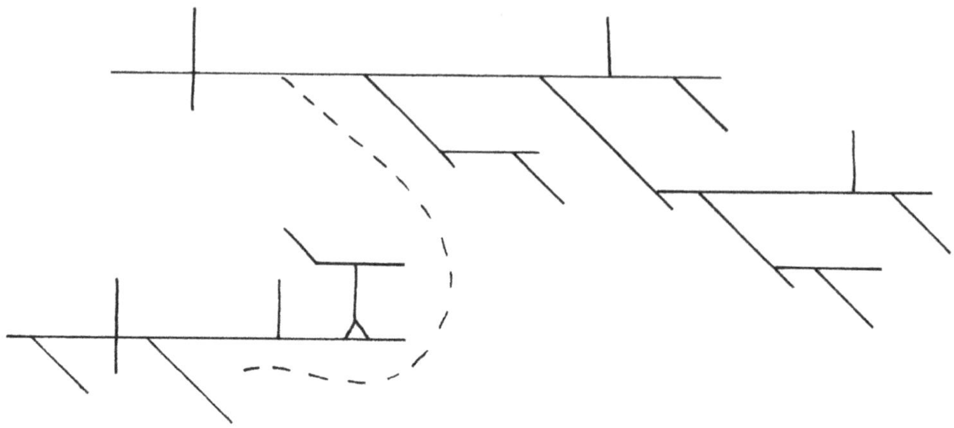

As for the ghosts, we ourselves had never seen nor heard them.

—From *Where the Flame Trees Bloom,* by Alma Flor Ada

An absolute construction has a strong semantic relationship but no grammatical connection to the rest of the sentence.

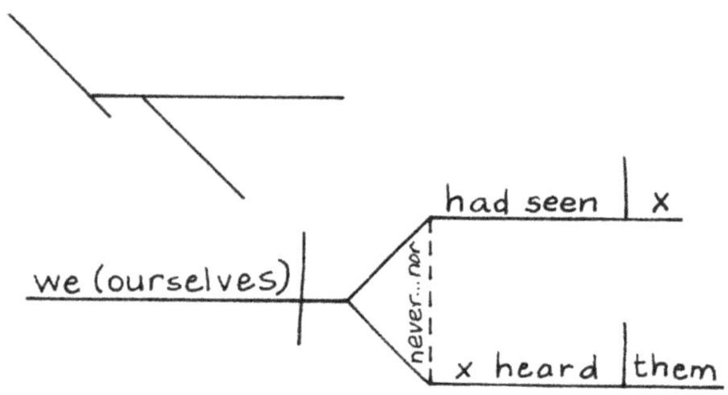

Well, Thomas Keller and Jean-Georges wouldn't be caught dead using the same salt in their kitchens as you use in yours, so they had to up the ante, turning to such exotics as African clay salt and black lava salt from Hawaii.

It felt kind of weird.

—From *52 Loaves: A Half-baked Adventure,* by William Alexander

And he could use a job after school, no?

—From *The Dreamer,* by Pam Muñoz Ryan

Exercise 119A: Identifying Idioms

In the following sentences, circle each complete idiom. Write its meaning above it in your own words. (You can use more than one word!)

The first is done for you.

somewhat like, similar to

The tea was beautiful, served in a tall glass filled with mint leaves, kind of like the mojito I'd have greatly preferred, but without ice.

If I were baking a different kind of bread each week, no one would blink an eyelash, but somehow this pursuit of trying to do one thing very well made me eccentric.

I took a step back so as to not destroy an entire production cycle with my clumsiness.

A third row of tables, reserved for guests, ran plumb down the center, just so everyone could keep an eye on us.

This was apparently her cue to invite a most unwelcome eight-hundred-pound gorilla into the garden.

Chlorine, it turned out, wasn't even the half of it.

—From *52 Loaves: A Half-Baked Adventure*, by William Alexander

You'd think he'd come off his high horse after the fool he made of himself at the mine, but he's worse than ever.

She rather expected that Mrs. Mablett would cut her dead, but she had reckoned without that lady's firm grasp on mine politics.

You'll be right out on your ear in nothing flat.

—From *Foxfire*, by Anya Seton

Because nothing in the world is so disheartening as being in dire straits after once enjoying prosperity, the formerly rich man suffered terribly from the plight he found himself in.

Persuading her husband that it was a good idea for him to visit some of his estates, because she had heard that things were going to rack and ruin there, she got him out of the house for an indeterminate number of days.

Many ignorant people, when lauded to their face by flatterers, tend to take them at their word, but this king, who was truly meritorious, wanted people to think the opposite.

The seventh and last unit was led by the emperor himself, with four thousand Germans, all tried and true, who looked as if they had been born in armor.

—From *Medieval Tales and Stories*, ed. Stanley Appelbaum

Exercise 119B: Diagramming

On your own paper, diagram every word of the following sentences.

After all, he had often used this excuse in order to avoid going back to school on Monday.

He pushed an old ice-cream cart throughout the city, visiting a new neighborhood each day, as if to give everyone a chance to taste the delicious flavors of his ice cream: pineapple, coconut, cherimoya, and more.

Ever since their mother had died when my father was fifteen and my uncle only ten, my father had taken care of Mario.

—From *Where the Flame Trees Bloom*, by Alma Flor Ada

I was fighting tooth and nail with them and wanted you to help me.

Katerina Ivanovna had just begun, as she always did at every free moment, walking to and fro in her little room from window to stove and back again, with her arms folded across her chest, talking to herself and coughing.

—LESSON 120—

Troublesome Sentences

Grammar is the art of speaking or writing a language correctly.

—William Greatheed Lewis, *A Grammar of the English Language* (1821)

Perfect grammar—persistent, continuous, sustained—is the fourth dimension, so to speak: many have sought it, but none has found it.

—Mark Twain, *Autobiography* (posthumous edition, 1925)

Grammar is to literary composition what a linch-pin is to a waggon. It is a poor pitiful thing in itself; it bears no part of the weight; communicates nothing to the force; adds not in the least to the celerity; but, still the waggon cannot very well and safely go on without it; she is constantly liable to reel and be compelled to stop, which, at the least, exposes the driver to be laughed at, and that, too, by those who are wholly unable to drive themselves.

—William Cobbett, *Grammar of the English Language* (1818)

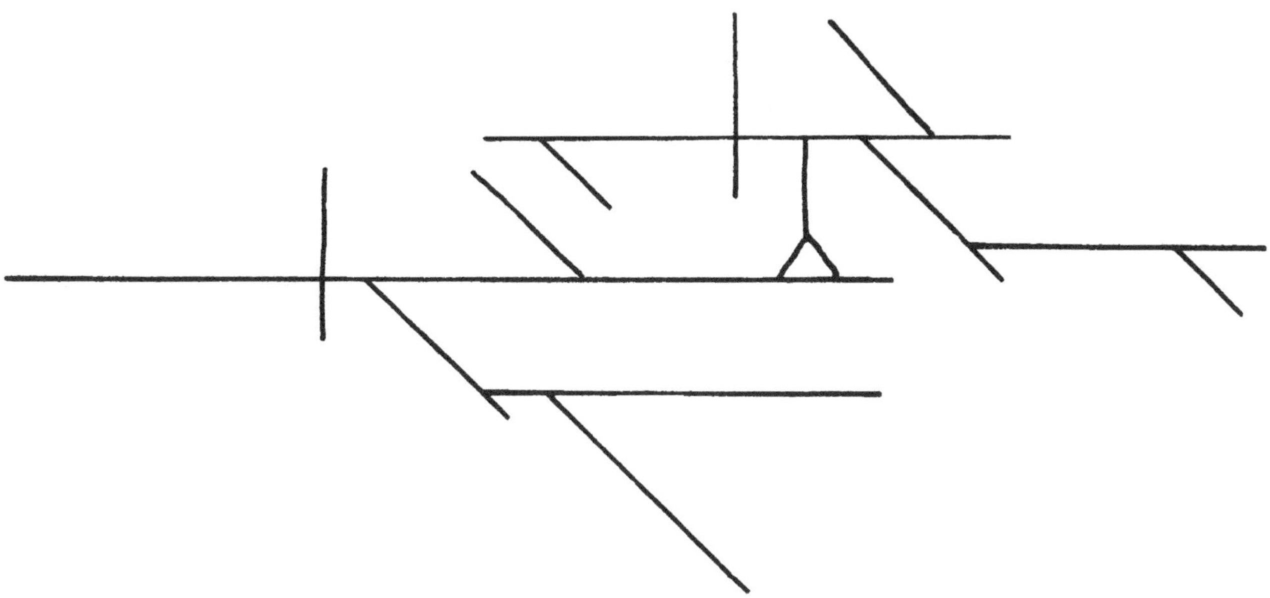

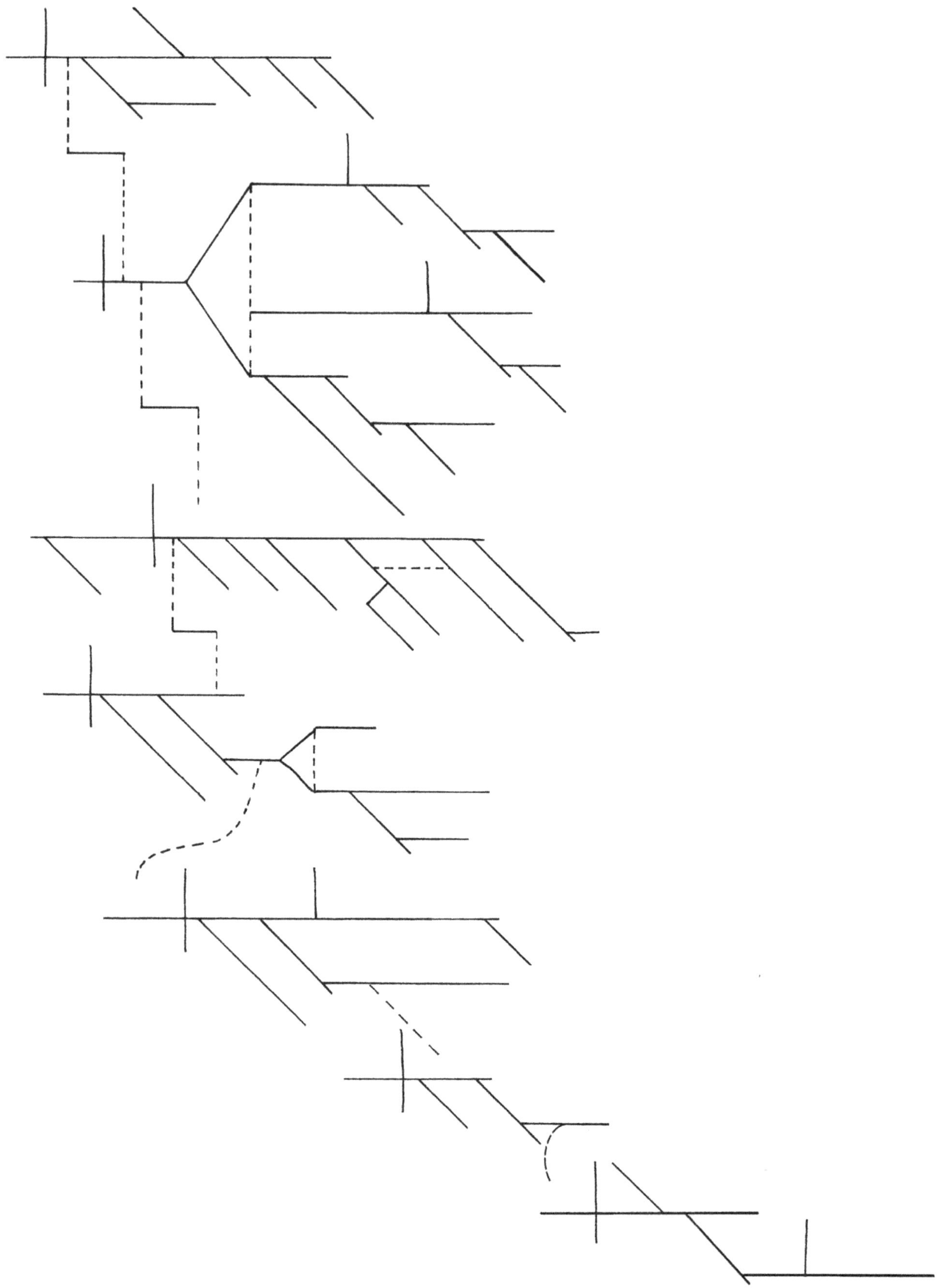

Exercise 120A: A Selection of Oddly Constructed Sentences

After your instructor discusses each sentence with you, diagram it on your own paper.

No, do not hand it to me, fan me with it!

Now I had never been called Señor Pareja in my life.

—From *I, Juan de Pareja*, by Elizabeth Borton de Treviño

Neftali felt the river breathing beneath him, as if keeping time to the slow and sorrowful tune.

He felt as if a piece of himself had been left behind, too.

—From *The Dreamer*, by Pam Muñoz Ryan

And if at that moment he had been capable of seeing and reasoning more correctly, if he had been able to realize all the difficulties of his position, the hopelessness, the hideousness and the absurdity of it, if he could have understood how many obstacles and, perhaps, crimes he had still to overcome or to commit, to get out of that place and to make his way home, it is very possible that he would have flung up everything, and would have gone to give himself up, and not from fear, but from simple horror and loathing of what he had done.

—From *Crime and Punishment*, by Fyodor Dostoyevsky, trans. Constance Garnett

WEEK 32

—REVIEW 10—

Weeks 29-31

Topics
Hortative Verbs
Ambitransitive Verbs
Infinitive Phrases as Objects
Infinitive Phrases with Understood *To*
Principal Parts of Irregular Verbs
Noun Clauses as Appositives
Which/That in Restrictive and Non-Restrictive Clauses
Formal Conditionals
Words Acting as Multiple Parts of Speech
Affirmations and Negations
Idioms

All of the sentences in this review are taken from (or slightly adapted from) the 19th-century magazine called *Prairie Farmer: A Weekly Journal for the Farm, Orchard and Fireside*. It first appeared in 1841 and continued to be published from the city of Chicago for the next half-century.

Review 10A: The Missing Words Game

Fill in each blank below with the exact *form* described—but choose your own words!

Show your answers to your instructor, who will insert them into the matching blanks in the short essay in the *Answer Key*.

Your instructor will then show you the original essay—and your version.

regular adverb	______________________
past participle acting as adjective	______________________
adjective	______________________
active infinitive of transitive verb	______________________
plural concrete noun	______________________
adverb of affirmation	______________________
adjective	______________________

adjective ____________________

adjective ____________________

coordinating conjunction ____________________

plural noun ____________________

interrogative adverb ____________________

regular adverb ____________________

simple present modal passive verb, third-person plural ____________________

abstract singular noun ____________________

present participle of transitive verb ____________________

adverb of affirmation ____________________

singular noun ____________________

plural concrete compound noun ____________________

plural concrete compound noun ____________________

plural concrete noun ____________________

adjective ____________________

regular adverb ____________________

adjective ____________________

adjective ____________________

passive infinitive ____________________

plural noun ____________________

plural demonstrative pronoun ____________________

adverb ____________________

adjective ____________________

simple present modal passive verb, third-person plural ____________________

compound adjective ____________________

present active imperative, singular, of transitive verb ____________________

perfect present active indicative transitive verb, first person-singular ____________________

adverb of affirmation ____________________

present participle of transitive verb ______________________

singular concrete noun ______________________

adjective ______________________

present participle of transitive verb ______________________

present participle of transitive verb ______________________

subordinating conjunction introducing an adverb clause ______________________

adverb of negation ______________________

adjective ______________________

present active imperative, singular, of transitive verb ______________________

active infinitive of transitive verb ______________________

present active imperative, singular, of transitive verb ______________________

indefinite pronoun that can be either singular or plural ______________________

plural concrete noun ______________________

singular concrete noun ______________________

plural object pronoun ______________________

singular concrete noun ______________________

present participle of transitive verb ______________________

subordinating conjunction ______________________

adverb of negation ______________________

singular demonstrative pronoun ______________________

regular adverb ______________________

plural concrete noun ______________________

simple future active indicative verb, first-person plural ______________________

adjective ______________________

singular concrete noun ______________________

simple future active indicative of transitive verb, third-person singular ______________________

adverb of affirmation ______________________

regular adverb ______________________

Review 10B: Identifying Infinitive Phrases, Noun Clauses, and Modifying Clauses

In the following essay, follow these four steps:

a) Identify every set of underlined words as *INF* for infinitive phrase, *PREP* for prepositional phrase, or *CL* for clause.
b) Label each phrase or clause as *ADV* for adverb, *ADJ* for adjective, or *N* for noun.
c) For adjective and adverb phrases and clauses, draw an arrow from the label to the word modified.
d) For noun phrases and clauses, add the appropriate part of the sentence label: *S* for subject, *DO* for direct object, *IO* for indirect object, *PN* for predicate nominative, *OP* for object of the preposition, *APP* for appositive.

The first is done for you.

RAISING ONIONS

CL ADJ

There are two causes of failure that make this crop uncertain. One is because the soil is not kept clear of weeds, and the other is that it is not properly enriched.

To raise a good crop of onions requires a light, loamy soil, worked to as fine a condition as possible, to render cultivation easy. The greater part of the preparation should be done in the fall, especially the application of the manure. Well-rotted manure is the best, and that which is free from grass, oats, or weed seeds should always be selected. Of course, if the manure is properly rotted the vitality of the larger portion of the seed in it will be killed, but unless this is done it will render the cultivation much more difficult. Stiff, clayey, or hard, poor land can be made a great deal better for the onion crop by a heavy application of ashes. I prefer to apply ashes to the soil as a top dressing in the spring, working it in the surface, as I find by experience that they are not only valuable as a fertilizer, but are also of great benefit in keeping down the weeds.

A plot of ground that is seeded with crab-grass should not be selected, as the pulling up of the grass injures the growth of the onions. Of course it is too late now to talk about fall preparation. If we want a crop of onions from seed this spring, whatever preparation there is must be done between now and seeding.

Another important point in raising a good crop of onions is to have good seed and sow it early. The first favorable time in the spring must be taken advantage of, if you would have the best success with your crop. I always take advantage of the first chance in March to sow my onion seed. We usually have a few warm days sometime about the middle of the month when this work can be done. Of course I do not say that this is the case every year. That the first favorable opportunity should be taken advantage of is what I want to impress upon those who expect to make a crop; let this time come when it will, any time early in the spring.

If you have well-rotted poultry manure, now is the best time to apply it. This strategy, that you begin your spring cultivation by working fertilizer into the top of the soil with a rake, will guarantee a healthy sprouting of the seeds.

As soon as the shoots make their appearance above the ground a good raking with a fine steel rake can be given. This will give them a good start and destroy the young weeds that will make their appearance at the same time. After the onions start growing, cultivation is the making of the crop.

Review 10C: Parsing

Parse every bolded verb in the following essay.

Provide the following information:

Person: First, second, or third
Number: Sing. or pl.
Tense: Simple past, present, or future; perfect past, present, or future; progressive past, present, or future; or progressive perfect present
Voice: Active, passive, or state-of-being
Mood: Indicative, subjunctive, imperative, hortatory, or modal
If the verb is also emphatic, add this label to the mood.

The first bolded verb is done for you.

CHICKEN CHAT

3rd sing., simple present, active, indicative

One of my correspondents **writes**: "My hens don't eat well—they just **pick** over the food as if it **were** not good enough for them—and they don't lay well; in fact they don't do much of anything except to mope about—not as if sick, but as if lazy."

Probably you **have fed** the same thing every day for the last six months, and the hens **are getting** tired of it. Hens **are** like other people—they like a change of provender once in a while, especially when confined indoors. Sometimes over-feeding **will cause** indigestion, and then the biddies will exhibit the symptoms you describe. In either case, **let** the fowls **fast** for a whole day, and then for a few days **feed** lightly with food that is different from what they **have been living** on.

Another correspondent wants to know why I always advise giving cooked food to fowls and chicks when uncooked food **is** the natural diet. I advise cooked food because experience **has taught** me that it is much better for poultry than the raw articles would be. Because raw bugs and worms constitute the "natural diet" of fowls in their wild state, it

does not **follow** that raw meal and potatoes **would be** the best and most economical food for our domestic fowls. Other things being equal, chicks that **are fed** on cooked food grow fatter, are less liable to disease, and thrive better generally than those who worry along on uncooked rations.

If you are short of sitting hens and don't own an incubator, **make** the hens do double duty. Set two or more at the same time, and when the chicks come out, give two families to one hen, and set the other over again. To do this successfully, the chicks **must be taken** from the nest as soon as dry and given to the hen that is to raise them; for if a hen once leaves the nest with her chicks, no amount of moral persuasion **will induce** her to go back. Before giving the hen fresh eggs, the nest **should be renovated** and the hen dusted with sulphur or something to prevent lice.

Review 10D: *Which* and *That* Clauses

In the following sentences, underline each clause introduced by *which or that.* If *that* is understood, use a caret to insert it. If a *which* or *that* clause falls within another clause, underline the entire larger clause once, and the clause-within-a-clause a second time.

- Label each clause as *ADJ* for adjective, *ADV* for adverb, or *N* for noun.
- For adjective and adverb clauses, draw an arrow back to the word modified.
- For noun clauses, label the part of the sentence that the clause fulfills (*S, PN, DO, IO, APP*).
- Finally, label each adjective clause as *R* for restrictive or *NON-R* for non-restrictive.

The first sentence is done for you.

ADJ R

We have been looking for a grass that would supply good grazing to our cattle and sheep after the native grasses have become dry and tasteless.

Two twisted No. 11 wires were used for this fence, and the posts are the best that could be procured.

I came away satisfied that it was reliable; it ought to be in the home of every farmer in this great country of ours, so that their children can learn and know what a grand heritage they have got.

The weather was so nice the first part of this month that the farmers did a large amount of plowing.

Those who planted seed of their own raising and got a stand have fair corn, while much of that which was raised from Kansas and Nebraska seed was caught by the frost.

For some reason a barrel that has once held beef will never do for a pork barrel.

The potato which has sold for the highest price in Boston all season is the Early Rose; this has been one of the most remarkable potatoes known.

I remarked that this was pretty rough farming.

The red ears of maize have a constancy of color which is truly remarkable.

Every Northern farmer knows the common coarse grass called door-yard grass, which has long, broad leaves, a tough, bunchy root, and a three-fingered spreading head, which contains large, round seeds.

Great numbers of these caterpillars were killed by a contagious disease, which swept them off just as they were ready to transform to the chrysalis.

We often see in the papers the amount, in dollars and cents, that strong drink costs the people of this country.

That year he grew about 1,000 bushels of oats, some 250 bushels of wheat, and raised 100 hogs.

We must have a grass that the hogs will relish, and on which they will both grow and fatten.

In three or four days after the cheeses are placed in the drying-room they become speckled; in another week they are covered with a thick crop of white mold, which by degrees deepens to a dark yellow, the outside of the cheese becoming less and less sticky.

In about two hours, when it is dark, go out again with a lantern and a pail containing salt and water, and pick up each piece on which the slugs are found feeding, and throw slugs and bran into the brine, where they instantly die.

He thought that Iowa was one of the best places in the world in which to raise sheep.

Review 10E: Words Acting as Multiple Parts of Speech

In each set of sentences below, underline the repeated word. Label each occurrence as *N* for noun, *V* for verb, *PRO* for pronoun, *ADV* for adverb, *ADJ* for adjective, *PREP* for preposition, *CC* for coordinating conjunction, or *SC* for subordinating conjunction.

At day-break we rode home.

For a hardy, early, red raspberry that is sweet and delicious for home use, plant the Turner.

The new home will be established on the fertile prairie next summer.

Shaffer's Colossal raspberry is excellent for canning, or for table use, if you like a fruit full of raspberry flavor though a little tart.

The honest breeder, though a man of ideas, acknowledges he does not know all.

Though blue grass is the best for pasture, timothy is the best for hay.

Our race horses of to-day would make a sorry comparison to those in the days of the pony express.

There are some people in every business who, in the race for success, far outrun their competitors.

Huge cakes of ice of every shape and size race past us.

Prudent farmers spare neither time nor expense in providing themselves with a full set of improved furnishings for their dairies, all the way down to good, substantial three-legged milking stools.

It set him to thinking, and before next morning he was of the same opinion.

A set smile was fixed upon his round face.

Should the ground prove weedy, cut the weeds down with the mowing machine in June, and leave them upon the surface.

It is quite appalling how much the average lawyer in Congress expects, in money down, in the way of a retainer.

A large cake of ice had come floating down the river.

She sells duck eggs, breeding ducks, and feathers and down at the local market.

Mr. I. L. Ellwood was experimenting to accomplish a like result with a thin band of metal, the barbs cut and curved outward from the strip.

The blueberry, like the cranberry, appears to be a potash plant.

Some members did not like to have hogs running in their orchards.

Musty stained drawers, dusty baskets, old barrels, and the like do not help to sell fruit.

Does the basket willow have to be cultivated like a field crop?

I have found the very opposite to be true, and I believe I have carefully and faithfully tested the matter.

Mr. Glidden had had in his mind the idea of a barb of wire twisted about the main wire of the fence, leaving two projecting points on opposite sides.

The statue stands opposite the far corner, next to the path.

Review 10F: Idioms

Circle each idiom in the following sentences. Above each one, write its meaning within the sentence. The first is done for you.

suitable for, will do well in

Strawberries are (at home) in a young orchard.

To begin the work, I have set my own house in order.

I think the Kieffer pear is better than the Bartlett, but I have no axe on the grindstone in this matter.

I must brush up my memory by asking you a question or two.

I have always tried to keep a lock on the stable door before the horse is stolen.

Who can be indifferent in the face of our great perils?

If you think best, you can blow the candle out and allow the wick to cool.

I used to think a great deal of Mrs. Goode, who was always so kind to me.

An orchard owner who could import European pear varieties that will fill the bill required by the necessities of our soil and climate would have a fortune at his command.

Review 10G: Ambitransitive Verbs

Underline each predicate in the following sentences. Mark each verb as *T* for transitive or *IT* for intransitive. For transitive verbs, circle the word that receives the action of the verb. The first is done for you.

This mill will stand a heavier wind, run steadier, and last longer than any other mill.

Two men run the old-fashioned cross-cut saw, which makes two backs sore every day that they use it.

The trees should then be set against the sloping side of the trench.

The cells of the frosted corn ruptured when hard weather set in.

She set several hens and the incubator at the same time.

The corn-plant louse, an early and destructive enemy of the crop, throttled the young shoots before they had broken ground.

The lark broke into song.

The snow will melt away when warm air rises from the unfrozen earth.

The engineers melted copper for the strong but thin wire.

Young horses frighten easily at every fresh or strange object that they see.

The raging torrent frightened him.

He strung two wires between two trees and twisted them together with a stick.

The vines will twist around the arbor if you tie them up with twine.

Gates open from each field into a private central road belonging to the farm.

Linnæus opened the way in botany, and the world profited by his blunders.

Review 10H: Hunt and Find

In the following essay, find, underline, and label each of the following:

- Infinitive phrase acting as a noun
- Infinitive phrase acting as an adjective
- Infinitive phrase acting as an adverb
- *To* as a preposition
- Hortative verb
- *That* acting as a demonstrative pronoun
- Restrictive clause introduced by *which*
- Non-restrictive clause introduced by *which*
- Noun clause in apposition
- Indirect object
- Clause with an understood *that*
- Comparison
- Participle phrase acting as a noun
- Compound subordinating conjunction
- Adverbial noun

THE HORSE AND HIS TREATMENT

The horse is naturally a wild animal and therefore, though domesticated, he demands such food as nature would provide for him. But man forgets this. Nature's food would be largely grass. It is true that when domesticated and put to hard work he needs some food of a more concentrated and highly nutritious nature than grass; but while labor may necessitate grain, the health of his system yet demands a liberal allowance of grass.

I have found that when the horses were allowed the range of a blue grass pasture at night, they endured work the best because they digested their grain and hay better, and good digestion made good appetites. In fact, I consider pasture the best food and the best medicine a horse can be given. If his coat is rough, if he is stiff and lifeless, if he is losing flesh and strength, turn him on pasture and he will soon grow better.

For winter, hay is provided. I am convinced that the great majority of farmers do not feed their horses enough forage. I know of farmers who do not feed hay at all when their horses are at work, which is more than half the year. Grain is fed exclusively. Yet they wonder why their horses lose flesh and have rough coats. Feeding a horse all grain is like feeding a man all meat. The food is so oily and difficult of digestion that it soon deranges the digestive organs. The horse should have all the hay he wishes, at all seasons of the year.

The horse should have at least ninety minutes for each meal. A large number of farmers do not give him this much time. Their reason for neglecting to do so, that it would be a loss of time, is untrue. Time is gained. The horse has the opportunity to eat slowly, can eat all he wishes, and can rest after eating, giving the organs of digestion a chance to work. Let him have an hour and a half to eat his noon-day meal, at least, and at the end of the season you will find that you have gained time. He may not have walked before the plow and harrow so many hours, but he has stepped faster and pulled more energetically.

Another error is the feeding of too much grain. Some farmers have grain in the feeding troughs all the time during the spring and summer. This may do for a hog, whose only business is to lie around, grunt, and put on fat; but for a horse it will not do.

One more error which I notice is the giving of too much dry food. The horse does best upon moist food, or that which has a large percentage of water in its composition. Carrots, turnips, beets, pumpkins, etc., may be given in small quantities with decided advantage, especially in the winter. In summer the hay should be sprinkled with water, and the oats soaked. This will make the food more palatable and easily digested.

One of the other evils of stable management often allowed is the accumulation of manure. The accumulation of the manure in the stable hurts the horse. Its fermentation gives off obnoxious gases which pollute and poison the air the horse is compelled to breathe.

The manure should be cleaned out morning, noon, and again at night. Use sawdust or straw liberally for bedding. It will absorb the urine, and as soon as foul, should be removed to the compost heap with the dung, where it will soon be converted into fine, excellent manure.

Review 10I: Conditionals and Formal Conditionals

In each of the following conditional sentences, parse the underlined verbs, giving tense, voice (*active, passive*, or *state-of-being*), and mood. Then, classify the sentences as first, second, or third conditional by placing a *1, 2,* or *3* in the blank at the end.

If the sentence is a formal conditional, write *FC* next to the blank.

The first is done for you.

simple future, active, indicative — simple present, passive, indicative

Oak planks will last many years if they are turned over occasionally. 1

If pork is to be kept all summer, twice boiling the brine may be necessary. ______

Much loss from frost would have been avoided had the seed been carefully selected from the best corn grown in the immediate neighborhood. ______

If arbors or rests are needed, let them be placed at the points where they are obviously required, and be made of graceful patterns. ______

The coat is rough and staring if the horse is in lean condition. ______

Were they successful, it would be a sad commentary upon our system of government. ______

She labored early and late to make both ends meet, something she would not have been able to accomplish had she not possessed skill as a dressmaker. ______

If every scientist had attempted to master the majority of scientific truths before concentrating his time on some special branch of science, science would have progressed little or none at all. ______

Were I the owner of a whole herd of Jerseys, I should endeavor to engage this genius to write them up for me. ______

If you want a crop of onions from seed this spring, whatever preparation there is must be done between now and seeding. ______

If farmers expect a good crop of corn they should not get seed from a southern latitude. ______

Review 10J: Affirmations and Negations

The following sentences all contain adverbs of affirmation and negation. Circle each one, and label them as *AFF* or *NEG*.

Then, choose three sentences and rewrite them on your own paper, turning affirmatives into negatives and vice versa. Show your sentences to your instructor.

The first is done for you.

NEG
There is (no) new thing under the sun.

There is certainly a new thing under the sun.

Never since I was a boy can I remember experiencing so perfect a repose.

Indeed, the whole tribe of willows love cool, moist situations.

If at the end of forty-eight hours the water turns milky, there can be no doubt of its impurity.

No crop is free from immaturity or imperfection.

The eucalyptus proved to be no more hardy than the orange.

I have never seen a large variety of corn that suited me so well.

The cattle there were certainly fine animals.

Surely every farmer can afford to build a wind break, at least a pile of brush and old hay, around the stock yards.

This is indeed a fearful showing.

In fields of maize, the cornroot worm was again very destructive.

It surely will not be lasting.

Review 10K: Diagramming

On your own paper, diagram every word of the following sentences.

The railway folks feared it would injure stock, the damages for which they would be forced to pay.

Now why could we not make some use of this grass, and of others, such as quack-grass, which defy so persistently all our efforts to destroy them?

With the first of June the field was green indeed, and from then until frost we pastured sixty large hogs, which, with one ear of corn for each, morning and evening, became thoroughly fat.

A good farmer must be quick in his judgment of what should be done at the present time, and he should have a good perception to show him the best thing to do for the future.

With a liberal supply of corn fodder for winter feeding and a good pasture, with hay and corn during the coldest weather, this branch of farming is not only easy, but certain and profitable.

Review 10L: Explaining Sentences

Tell your instructor every possible piece of grammatical information about the following sentences. Follow these steps:

a) Underline each clause. Describe the identity and function of each clause and give any other useful information (introductory word, relationship to the rest of the sentence, etc.)
b) Circle each phrase. Describe the identity and function of each phrase and give any other useful information.
c) Parse all verbs acting as predicates.
d) Describe the identity and function of each individual remaining word.

If you need help, ask your instructor.

Have you no butter, eggs, fowls, honey, or bees-wax to sell from this good farm?

How has science advanced—is it not by the invaluable aid of men who have given their whole lives to the solution of some special problem?

This is a mistaken idea that many possess who think there is no brain work needed on a farm.

WEEK 33

Mechanics

—LESSON 121—

Capitalization Review
Additional Capitalization Rules
Formal and Informal Letter Format
Ending Punctuation

what an amazing place london was to me when i saw it in the distance and how i believed all the adventures of all my favourite heroes to be constantly enacting and re-enacting there and how i vaguely made it out in my own mind to be fuller of wonders and wickedness than all the cities of the earth i need not stop here to relate

What an amazing place London was to me when I saw it in the distance, and how I believed all the adventures of all my favourite heroes to be constantly enacting and re-enacting there, and how I vaguely made it out in my own mind to be fuller of wonders and wickedness than all the cities of the earth, I need not stop here to relate.

—Charles Dickens, *David Copperfield*

A proper noun is the special, particular name for a person, place, thing, or idea. Proper nouns always begin with capital letters.

1. Capitalize the proper names of persons, places, things, and animals.

boy	manuel
store	macy's
car	ford
horse	secretariat

2. Capitalize the names of holidays.

lent

ramadan

new year's day

3. Capitalize the names of deities.

zeus

buddha

holy spirit

god

4. Capitalize the days of the week and the months of the year, but not the seasons.

wednesday	february	spring
thursday	april	fall
saturday	september	winter

5. Capitalize the first, last, and other important words in titles of books, magazines, newspapers, stories, poems, and songs.

book	*green eggs and ham*
magazine	*the new yorker*
newspaper	*the philadelphia inquirer*
movie	*the hunger games: catching fire*
television show	*agents of s.h.i.e.l.d.*
story	"the lottery"
poem	"stopping by woods on a snowy evening"
song	"happy birthday to you"
chapter in a book	"an unexpected party"

6. Capitalize and italicize the names of ships, trains, and planes.

ship	*santa maria*
train	*hogwarts express*
plane	*air force one*

The titles *mister*, *madame*, and *miss* are capitalized and abbreviated *Mr.*, *Mrs.*, and *Miss* when placed in front of a proper name.

Miss Snevellicci made a graceful obeisance, and hoped Mrs. Curdle was well, as also Mr. Curdle, who at the same time appeared.
—Charles Dickens, *The Life and Adventures of Nicholas Nickleby*

A proper adjective is formed from a proper name. Proper adjectives are capitalized. Words that are not usually capitalized remain lowercase even when they are attached to a proper adjective.

	Proper Noun	**Proper Adjective**
Person	shakespeare	the shakespearean play
	kafka	a kafkaesque dilemma
Place	italy	an italian city
	korea	a non-korean tradition
Holiday	labor day	the labor day picnic
	christmas	an anti-christmas sentiment
Month	september	september storms
	december	the post-december blues

Capitalize the personal pronoun *I*.

Interjections express sudden feeling or emotion. They are set off with commas or stand alone with a closing punctuation mark.

I have prayed over them, oh, I have prayed so much.
Ahem! That is my name.
Ha, ha! The liars that these traders are!
—Charles Dickens, *David Copperfield*

Capitalize the interjection *O*. It is usually preceded by, but not followed by, a comma.

For a few weeks it was all well enough, but afterwards, O the weary length of the nights!

But, O dear, O dear, this is a hard world!
—Kenneth Grahame, *The Wind in the Willows*

After an interjection followed by an exclamation point, the next word may be lowercase.

Oh! let me see it once again before I die!
Alas! how often and how long may those patient angels hover above us!
—Charles Dickens, *The Life and Adventures of Nicholas Nickleby*

Capitalize the address, date, greeting, closing, and signature of a letter.

Your Street Address
Your City, State, and ZIP Code

June 14, 2018

Well-Trained Mind Press
18021 The Glebe Lane
Charles City, Virginia 23030

Dear Editors:

Thank you for *Grammar for the Well-Trained Mind.* It is the most exciting grammar book I have ever read. I only wish I could spend more time doing grammar.

Please publish more grammar books immediately.

Sincerely,

SIGNATURE

Your Greatest Fan

Your Street Address
Your City, State, and ZIP Code

June 14, 2018

Well-Trained Mind Press
18021 The Glebe Lane
Charles City, Virginia 23030

Dear Editors:

Thank you for *Grammar for the Well-Trained Mind.* It is the most exciting grammar book I have ever read. I only wish I could spend more time doing grammar.

Please publish more grammar books immediately.

Sincerely,

SIGNATURE

Your Greatest Fan

Abbreviations are typically capitalized when each letter stands for something.

The WHO has expressed concern about the Zika virus and its rapid spread.
Why did NASA cancel the lunar exploration program?
OPEC was founded in 1960 in Baghdad.

Capitalize the first word in every line of traditional poetry.

"The Elephant"
by Hilaire Belloc

When people call this beast to mind,
They marvel more and more
At such a little tail behind,
So large a trunk before.

A sentence is a group of words that contains a subject and a predicate. A sentence begins with a capital letter and ends with a punctuation mark.

A statement gives information. A statement always ends with a period.
An exclamation shows sudden or strong feeling. An exclamation always ends with an exclamation point.
A command gives an order or makes a request. A command ends with either a period or an exclamation point.
A question asks something. A question always ends with a question mark.

Look ahead, Rat

Hooray, this is splendid

I wonder which of us had better pack the luncheon-basket

Presently they all sat down to luncheon together

Exercise 121A: Proofreading

Use proofreader's marks to insert the missing capital letters and punctuation marks into the following sentences.

capitalize letter: ≡	make letter lowercase: /
insert period: ⊙	insert exclamation point: ↑
insert comma: ^,	insert question mark: ^?

If a word or phrase should be italicized, indicate this by underlining.

oh dear the subject is difficult

i was a moviegoer, a magazine-reader, a cnn-watcher

and so, after my sophomore year, i had moved out of the dorms with friends and into an apartment on 112th street between broadway and amsterdam, and i had escaped whenever possible into the city—to carnegie hall or folk clubs in the village or to the movie revival houses on the upper west side

in 1897, the distinguished architectural firm of mcKim, mead & white had given the campus an integral design, but i had never encountered anyone who was passionate about the neo-renaissance, red-brick buildings with limestone trim and pale green copper roofs that surrounded the large open space between low library to the north and the blockish, herbert hooverish butler library to the south

i now understood better than ever that my dismay when odysseus kills the suitors at the end of the *odyssey* was an emotion homer couldn't possibly have intended his listeners to feel

—david denby, *great books: my adventures with homer, rousseau, woolf, and other indestructible writers of the western world*

oh i am a smart toad, and no mistake

for a few weeks it was all well enough, but afterwards o the weary length of the nights

alas what am I saying

well well we won't linger over that now

but the mole was bent on enjoying everything, and although just when he had got the basket packed and strapped up tightly he saw a plate staring up at him from the grass, and when the job had been done again the rat pointed out a fork which anybody ought to have seen, and last of all, behold the mustard pot, which he had been sitting on without knowing it—still, somehow, the thing got finished at last, without much loss of temper

—kenneth grahame, *the wind in the willows*

nicholas was standing with his back to the curtain, now contemplating the first scene, which was a gothic archway, about two feet shorter than mr crummles, through which that gentleman was to make his first entrance mr crummles lived in thomas's street, at the house of one bulph, a pilot, who sported a boat-green door, with window-frames of the same colour, and had the little finger of a drowned man on his parlour mantelshelf, with other maritime and natural curiosities

smike, the boys, and the phenomenon went home by a shorter cut, and mrs grudden remained behind to take some cold irish stew and a pint of porter in the box-office

at mr wackford squeers's academy, dotheboys hall, at the delightful village of dotheboys, near greta bridge in yorkshire, youth are boarded, clothed, booked, furnished with pocket-money, provided with all necessaries, instructed in all languages living and dead, mathematics, orthography, geometry, astronomy, trigonometry, the use of the globes, algebra, single stick (if required), writing, arithmetic, fortification, and every other branch of classical literature. terms, twenty guineas per annum. no extras, no vacations, and diet unparalleled. mr squeers is in town, and attends daily, from one till four, at the saracen's head, snow hill.

—charles dickens, *the life and adventures of nicholas nickleby*

Exercise 121B: Correct Letter Mechanics

The following text is the actual rejection letter written to Edgar Rice Burroughs, the author of *Tarzan of the Apes*, when he sent his story to the Chicago publisher Rand McNally & Company in 1913.

On your own paper (or with your own word processing program), rewrite or retype the text so that it is properly formatted, punctuated, and capitalized. You may choose either letter format from this lesson.

Notice that there are no ZIP codes, because ZIP codes were only created by the U.S. Post Office in 1963.

Each sentence in the letter is a separate paragraph. The last sentence/paragraph ends with the comma after *we are*, and the closing is *Yours very truly*. This is an old-fashioned but correct way to end a letter.

When you are finished, compare your letter with the two versions in the *Answer Key*.

rand mcNally & company 168 adams street chicago illinois august 20, 1913 mr edgar rice burroughs 2008 park avenue chicago illinois dear sir we are returning under separate cover *the all-story* magazine (oct. 1912) containing your story, "tarzan of the apes." we have given the work careful consideration and, while interesting, we find it does not fit in with our plans for the present year. thanking you for submitting the story to us, we are, yours very truly, rand mcNally & company

—LESSON 122—

Commas
Semicolons
Additional Semicolon Rules
Colons
Additional Colon Rules

1. A comma and coordinating conjunction join compound sentences.
2. Commas separate three or more items in a series.
3. Commas separate two or more adjectives that come before a noun (as long as the adjectives can exchange position).
4. A comma follows the second -to-last item in a series of three or more (the "Oxford comma").
5. Commas set off terms of direct address.
6. Commas set off non-restrictive adjective clauses.
7. Commas set off parenthetical expressions that are closely related to the sentence.
8. Commas set off most appositives (unless the appositive is only one word and very closely related to the word it renames).
9. Commas may surround or follow interjections.
10. Commas may surround or follow introductory adverbs of affirmation and negation.
11. Commas may set off introductory adverb and adjective phrases.
12. In dates, commas separate the day of the week from the day of the month and the day of the month from the year.
13. In addresses, commas separate the city from the state.
14. Commas follow the greeting and closing of a friendly letter, and the closing of a formal letter.
15. Commas divide large numbers into sets of thousands.
16. A comma follows a dialogue tag or attribution tag that precedes a speech or quote.
17. A comma comes after a speech or quote if a dialogue tag or attribution tag follows.
18. A comma may divide a partial sentence from the block quote it introduces.
19. Commas may be used at any time to prevent misunderstanding and simplify reading.

Exercise 122A: Comma Use

In the blank at the end of each sentence, write the number from the list above that describes the comma use. If more than one number seems to fit equally well, write all suitable numbers.

These sentences are taken from *Fifty Famous People*, by James Baldwin.

This happened six hundred years ago, in the city of Florence in Italy. ________

And you, grandfather, were as bad as the rest. ________

There was one such king who had four sons, Ethelbald, Ethelbert, Ethelred, and Alfred. ________

"Shoe him quickly, for the king wishes to ride him to battle," said the groom who had brought him. ________

Two children, brother and sister, were on their way to school. ________

Daniel, you must be up early in the morning. ________

King Solomon lived 3,000 years ago. ________

His grandfather, whose name was Astyages, was king of Media, and very rich and powerful. ________

The caliph, Al Mansur, lived nearly twelve hundred years ago. ________

He looked at the bright, yellow pieces and said, "What shall I do with these coppers, mother?" ________

He saw that Cyrus had a will of his own, and this pleased him very much. ________

He was always reading, learning, inquiring. ________

He sang of war, and of bold rough deeds, and of love and sorrow. ________

They looked, or so they thought, in every place where the lambs might have taken shelter. ________

He shouted, "A horse! A horse! My kingdom for a horse." ________

Oh, yes, I know she is anxious, and I will go. ________

"Let us call the neighbors together and have a grand wolf hunt tomorrow," said Putnam. ________

No, no, I am going to be a sailor; I am going to see the world. ________

The independent clauses of a compound sentence must be joined by a comma and a coordinating conjunction, a semicolon, or a semicolon and a coordinating conjunction. They cannot be joined by a comma alone.

> He knew—as the Athenians and Persians did not—exactly when the flooding of the Nile was about to occur, and he managed to hold the combined invasion force off until the waters began to rise rapidly around him.
>
> Thousands of years ago, groups of hunters and gatherers roamed across Asia and Europe, following mammoth herds that fed on the wild grasses. Slowly the ice began to retreat; the patterns of the grass growth changed; the herds wandered north and diminished.
>
> They eat and drink, and thank him for his generosity; but Atrahasis himself, knowing that the feast is a death meal, paces back and forth, ill with grief and guilt.
>
> —Susan Wise Bauer, *The History of the Ancient World*

Block quotes should be introduced by a colon (if preceded by a complete sentence) or a comma (if preceded by a partial sentence).

> Piankhe did not try to wipe out his enemies. Instead, he chose to see Egypt as a set of kingdoms, with himself as High King over them:
>
> > Amun of Napata has appointed me governor of this land,
>
> he wrote in another inscription,
>
> > as I might say to someone: "Be king," and he is it, or: "You will not be king," and he is not.
>
> —Susan Wise Bauer, *The History of the Ancient World*

Use a colon after the salutation of a business letter.

The White House
1600 Pennsylvania Ave NW
Washington, DC 20500

Dear Mr. President

Use a colon to separate the hour from minutes in a time.

I went to bed at 11 59 on December 31.

Use a colon to separate the chapter from verse in a Biblical reference.

According to Ecclesiastes 12 12, "much study wearies the body."

If items in a series contain commas within the items, semicolons may separate two or more items in a series.

If semicolons separate items in a series, a colon may set off the series.

> Around the tomb complex, buildings recreated in stone the materials of traditional Egyptian houses: walls of stone, carved to look like reed matting; stone columns shaped into bundles of reeds; even a wooden fence with a partly open gate, chiseled from stone.
>
> Like the Great Pyramid, the Sphinx has attracted its share of nutty theories: it dates from 10,000 B.C. and was built by a disappeared advanced civilization; it was built by Atlanteans (or aliens); it represents a zodiacal sign, or a center of global energy.
>
> Between 4000 and 3000 B.C. is known as the Naqada Period, and was once divided into three phases: the Amratian, which runs from 4000 to 3500 B.C.; the Gerzean, from 3500 to 3200 B.C.; and the Final Predynastic, from 3200 to 3000 B.C.
>
> —Susan Wise Bauer, *The History of the Ancient World*

A colon may introduce a list.

> Stripped of personality, prehistoric peoples too often appear as blocks of shifting color on a map: moving north, moving west, generating a field of cultivated grain, or corralling a herd of newly domesticated animals.
>
> Many thousands of years ago, the Sumerian king Alulim ruled over Eridu: a walled city, a safe space carved out of the unpredictable and harsh river valley that the Romans would later name Mesopotamia.
>
> Plague, drought, and war: these were enough to upset the balance of a civilization that had been built in rocky dry places, close to the edge of survival.
>
> —Susan Wise Bauer, *The History of the Ancient World*

For emphasis, a colon may introduce an item that follows a complete sentence, when that item is closely related to the sentence.

But the historian's task is different: to look for particular human lives that give flesh and spirit to abstract assertions about human behavior.

But the historian's task, to look for particular human lives that give flesh and spirit to abstract assertions about human behavior, is different.

Exercise 122B: Commas, Capitals, Closing Punctuation, Colons, and Semicolons

Insert all missing punctuation and correct all capitalization in the text that follows. Use these proofreader's marks:

capitalize letter: ≡	make letter lowercase: /
insert period: ⊙	insert exclamation point: ^!
insert comma: ^,	insert question mark: ^?
insert colon: ^:	insert semicolon: ^;

122B.1: Sentences

we have divided time into segments of every conceivable size nanoseconds milliseconds seconds minutes hours days weeks months years decades centuries millennia eons eras and on and on.

the watches on our wrists today are the culmination of a long slow arduous process of invention and discovery which ultimately began about four millennia ago when someone stuck a stick in the ground and watched its shadow change throughout the day.

our Ancestors of course had no idea of any of the things discussed in the previous chapter

Early efforts at time-counting still did not quite deal with the whole day/night unit instead they usually tallied repetitions of an easily recognized event within the unit namely sunrise or sunset

in addition to the flat dial with which we are most familiar sundials were also invented in the form of sunken hemispheres and cones cubes columns open rings and opened tablets to name only a few

—Jo ellen Barnett, *Time's Pendulum: From sundials To Atomic Clocks, the Fascinating History of timekeeping and How Our Discoveries Changed the world*

Jewelers also regulated maintained and repaired timepieces

the Jewelers who crowded beneath the chicago clock when it debuted might have recalled the years when they belonged to the ranks of time specialists those artisans, tinkerers, and scientists who reckoned the time and made clocks for its conveyance

the clock itself was an elaborate period piece illuminated with electric lights decorated in the oriental motifs favored in twenties' design and topped with a figure of father time holding a scythe and an hourglass

the parameters within which the earliest clocks functioned were broad a hand moved either direction (rather than only "clockwise") and dials indicated three four sixteen or twenty-four hours in addition to the now conventional twelve hours

they decorated their homes with clocks included clocks and watches in their poetry Sermons stories and songs and enlivened their visual culture with representations of Timekeepers

and even on land calculating longitude was no small feat just an estimation of it required a well-regulated clock astronomical instruments and observatory charts

steam engines gas-light telegraphs telephones electricity phonography photography combustion engines and wireless communications fundamentally changed our experiences of time and space

—Alexis McCrossen, *marking modern times: A History of Clocks, Watches, and Other Timekeepers in American life*

122B.2: Letter Format

The following letters are adapted from the book *Mark Twain's Letters*, Vol. 1 (1917).

september 28 1860

Orion Clemens

keokuk Iowa

dear brother

yesterday I spent ten dollars on dinner at a french restaurant, where we ate sheep-head fish with mushrooms shrimps and oysters birds and coffee with brandy burnt in it.

Please find $20 enclosed

in haste

Sam

---

january 27 1868
american publishing company
hartford connecticut

dear sir

i agree to your propositions and will furnish you with manuscript sufficient for a volume of 500 to 600 pages for a book to be sold by the American Publishing Company by subscription.

For this manuscript, the apc will pay me a copyright of 5 percent upon the subscription price of the book for all copies sold.

very truly yours,
samuel l. Clemens

122B.3: Quotes

In his book *About Time,* bruce koscielniak writes "the greeks used three ten-day weeks per month" He adds "The romans used an eight-day week with the eighth day reserved for market festivities.

We think of time as something natural normal and inevitable. But in *About Time,* bruce koscielniak points out that our ideas of time are invented

> Time is what is measured by a regular or standard interval—a second, a minute, an hour, for example—that is chimed ticked beeped or in some way displayed by a time-measuring device called a clock.

—LESSON 123—

Colons
Dashes
Hyphens
Parentheses
Brackets

> But the historian's task is different: to look for particular human lives that give flesh and spirit to abstract assertions about human behavior.

> But the historian's task is different—to look for particular human lives that give flesh and spirit to abstract assertions about human behavior.
> —Susan Wise Bauer, *The History of the Ancient World*

A colon may introduce an item that follows a complete sentence, when that item is closely related to the sentence.

Dashes — — can enclose words that are not essential to the sentence.
Dashes can also be used singly to separate parts of a sentence.

> A dash is twice as long as a hyphen.
> When you write a dash, make it a little longer than a hyphen.
> When you type a dash, use two hyphens for each dash.

> well-educated (hyphen)
> Well—that was a mistake. (dash)

Hyphens connect some compound nouns.

self-confidence
wallpaper
air conditioning

Hyphens connect compound adjectives in the attributive position.

self-confident woman
the woman was self confident

Hyphens connect spelled-out numbers between twenty-one and ninety-nine.

seventy-one balloons
he turned seventy-one on Friday

Hyphens divide words between syllables at the end of lines in justified text.

. . . worth inhabiting by reason of its barrenness; and indeed, both for-
saking it because of prodigious number of tigers, lions, leopards,
and others of the furious creatures which harbour there; so that the . . .

. . . worth inhabiting by reason of its barrenness; and indeed, both
forsaking it because of prodigious number of tigers, lions, leo-
pards, and others of the furious creatures which harbour there;
so that the . . .

Parentheses ( ) can enclose words that are not essential to the sentence.
Parenthetical expressions often interrupt or are irrelevant to the rest of the sentence.
Punctuation goes inside the parentheses if it applies to the parenthetical material; all other punctuation goes outside the parentheses.
Parenthetical material only begins with a capital letter if it is a complete sentence with ending punctuation.

I had no sooner said so, but I perceived the creature (whatever it was) within two oars' length.

Commas make a parenthetical element a part of the sentence.
Dashes emphasize a parenthetical element.
Parentheses minimize a parenthetical element.

"Particularly," said I, aloud (though to myself), "what should I have done without a gun, without ammunition, without any tools to make anything, or to work with, without clothes, bedding, a tent, or any manner of covering?"

Accordingly, having spent three days in this journey, I came home (so I must now call my tent and my cave); but before I got thither the grapes were spoiled; the richness of the fruit and the weight of the juice having broken them and bruised them, they were good for little or nothing; as to the limes, they were good, but I could bring but a few.

Well, to take away this discouragement, I resolved to dig into the surface of the earth, and so make a declivity; this I began, and it cost me a prodigious deal of pains (but who grudge pains who have their deliverance in view?); but when this was worked through, and this difficulty managed, it was still much the same, for I could no more stir the canoe than I could the other boat.

> I first laid all the planks or boards upon it that I could get, and having considered well what I most wanted, I got three of the seamen's chests, which I had broken open, and emptied, and lowered them down upon my raft; the first of these I filled with provisions—bread, rice, three Dutch cheeses, five pieces of dried goat's flesh (which we lived much upon), and a little remainder of European corn, which had been laid by for some fowls which we brought to sea with us, but the fowls were killed.
> —Daniel Defoe, *Robinson Crusoe*

Exercise 123A: Hyphens

Some (but not all) of the following sentences (from *Around the World in Eighty Days*, by Jules Verne) contain words that should be hyphenated. Insert a hyphen into each word that needs one.

Phileas Fogg passed ten hours out of the twenty four in Saville Row.

He was never seen in the counting rooms of the City.

He was served by the gravest waiters, in dress coats, and shoes with swan skin soles.

The club decanters contained his sherry, his port, and his cinnamon spiced claret.

I've been an itinerant singer and a circus rider.

From this moment, twenty nine minutes after eleven, you are in my service.

Seen in the various phases of his daily life, he gave the idea of being perfectly well balanced.

He appeared to be about forty years of age, with handsome features, and a well shaped figure.

A moderate sized safe stood in his bedroom.

A package of banknotes, to the value of fifty five thousand pounds, had been taken.

On the day of the robbery, a well dressed gentleman of polished manners, and with a well to do air, had been observed going to and fro in the paying room where the crime was committed.

The other was a small, slight built personage, with a nervous, intelligent face.

According to habit, he scrutinized the passers by with a keen, rapid glance.

This is a family watch, monsieur, which has come down from my great grandfather!

Three quarters of an hour afterwards we were off.

The celebrated East India Company was all powerful from 1756.

He lost no time in knocking down two of his long gowned adversaries with his fists.

In the semi obscurity they saw the victim, quite senseless.

The whole multitude prostrated themselves, terror stricken, on the ground.

Exercise 123B: Parenthetical Elements

The following sentences are all from *Robinson Crusoe*, by Daniel Defoe. Defoe liked to write very long sentences filled with parenthetical elements! Set off each bolded set of words with commas, dashes, or parentheses. Choose the punctuation marks that seem to fit best. Then, compare your answers with the original punctuation in the *Answer Key*.

NOTE: Depending on what punctuation marks you choose, you may have to add an additional comma or semicolon following some the parenthetical elements. Be sure to look at the entire sentence to decide whether additional punctuation should be added. Keep in mind that, in contemporary English punctuation, a parenthesis can be followed by another punctuation mark, but a dash almost never is.

Nature **as if I had been fatigued and exhausted with the very thoughts of it** threw me into a sound sleep.

About a year and a half after I entertained these notions **and by long musing had, as it were, resolved them all into nothing, for want of an occasion to put them into execution** I was surprised one morning by seeing no less than five canoes all on shore together on my side of the island, and the people who belonged to them all landed and out of my sight.

I loaded all my cannon, as I called them **that is to say, my muskets, which were mounted upon my new fortification** and all my pistols, and resolved to defend myself to the last gasp **not forgetting seriously to commend myself to the Divine protection, and earnestly to pray to God to deliver me out of the hands of the barbarians**.

So **after some days** I took Friday to work again by way of discourse, and told him I would give him a boat to go back to his own nation; and, **accordingly** I carried him to my frigate **which lay on the other side of the island** and having cleared it of water **for I always kept it sunk in water** I brought it out, showed it him, and we both went into it.

While this was doing, I sent Friday with the captain's mate to the boat with orders to secure her, and bring away the oars and sails **which they did** and by-and-by three straggling men, that were **happily for them** parted from the rest, came back upon hearing the guns fired; and seeing the captain **who was before their prisoner** now their conqueror, they submitted to be bound also; and so our victory was complete.

Accordingly we went on board, took the arms which were left on board out of her, and whatever else we found there—which was a bottle of brandy, and another of rum, a few biscuit-cakes, a horn of powder, and a great lump of sugar in a piece of canvas **the sugar was five or six pounds** all which was very welcome to me, especially the brandy and sugar **of which I had had none left for many years**.

As the bear is a heavy, clumsy creature, and does not gallop as the wolf does **who is swift and light** so he has two particular qualities, which generally are the rule of his actions; first, as to men, who are not his proper prey **he does not usually attempt them, except they first attack him, unless he be excessively hungry, which it is probable might now be the case, the ground being covered with snow** if you do not meddle with him, he will not meddle with you; but then you must take care to be very civil to him, and give him the road, for he is a very nice gentleman; he will not go a step out of his way for a prince; nay **if you are really afraid** your best way is to look another way and keep going on; for sometimes if you stop, and stand still, and look steadfastly at him, he takes it for an affront; but if you throw or toss anything at him **though it were but a bit of stick as big as your finger** he thinks himself abused, and sets all other business aside to pursue his revenge, and will have satisfaction in point of honour **that is his first quality** the next is, if he be once affronted, he will never leave you **night or day** till he has his revenge, but follows at a good round rate till he overtakes you.

—LESSON 124—

Italics

Quotation Marks

Ellipses

Single Quotation Marks

Apostrophes

In *Around the World in Eighty Days*, Jules Verne describes the arrival of the steamer *Mongolia* at the port of Suez.

Capitalize and italicize the names of ships, trains, and planes.

Italicize the titles of lengthy or major works such as books, newspapers, magazines, major works of art, and long musical compositions.

Use quotation marks for minor or brief works of art and writing or portions of longer works such as short stories, newspaper articles, songs, chapters, and poems.

Watership Down	"The Chief Rabbit"
The Hobbit	"An Unexpected Party"
The New York Times	"In Julia Child's Provençal Kitchen"
National Geographic	
The *Mona Lisa* of Da Vinci	"Saint Jerome in Penitence," by Dürer
The *David* of Michelangelo	
1812 Overture, by Tchaikovsky	
The opera *Carmen*, by Bizet	"Toreador Song"
	"Scarborough Fair"
	"The Lottery"
The *Odyssey*	"Stopping by Woods on a Snowy Evening"
	"The Raven"

Italicize letters, numbers, and words if they are the subject of discussion. In plural versions, do not italicize the *s*.

The letter *A* begins the alphabet, and a *Z* concludes it.

Most Americans hate the word *moist.*

*A*s and *F*s are hard to write in calligraphy.

Italicize foreign words not adopted into English.

What we call "rapid-eye-movement sleep" the French call *sommeil paradoxal* (paradoxical sleep) because the body is still but the mind is extremely active.

—Pamela Druckerman, *Bringing Up Bébé*

Mark Twain was the nom de plume of Samuel Langhorne Clemens.

English doesn't borrow from other languages. English follows other languages down dark alleys, knocks them over and goes through their pockets for loose grammar.
—Sir Terry Pratchett

Use quotation marks for minor or brief works of art and writing or portions of longer works such as short stories, newspaper articles, songs, chapters, and poems.

Then there crawled from the bushes a dozen more great purple spiders, which saluted the first one and said, "The web is finished, O King, and the strangers are our prisoners."

Dorothy did not like the looks of these spiders at all. They had big heads, sharp claws, small eyes and fuzzy hair all over their purple bodies.
—L. Frank Baum, *Glinda of Oz*

Direct quotations are set off by quotation marks.

Fear of spiders might come in part from children's stories, which often portray spiders as hostile predators. In *Glinda of Oz,* L. Frank Baum writes about a Spider King and his army of "great purple spiders, which . . . said, 'The web is finished, O King, and the strangers are our prisoners.'"

A quote within a quote is surrounded by single quotation marks.

An apostrophe is a punctuation mark that shows possession. It turns a noun into an adjective that tells whose.

Form the possessive of a singular noun by adding an apostrophe and the letter *s*.

spider	wand
web	sorceress

Form the possessive of a plural noun ending in *-s* by adding an apostrophe only.

spiders	troubles
fields	lakes

Form the possessive of a plural noun that does not end in *-s* as if it were a singular noun.

sheep	hangmen
geese	teeth

A contraction is a combination of two words with some of the letters dropped out. An apostrophe shows where the letters have been omitted.

they are ____________________

was not ____________________

were not ____________________

I am ____________________

Exercise 124A: Proofreading Practice

The sentences below have lost most punctuation and capitalization. Insert all missing punctuation marks, and correct all capitalization errors. When you are finished, compare your sentences with the originals.

Use these proofreader's marks:

capitalize letter: ≡	make letter lowercase: /
insert period: ⊙	insert exclamation point: ^!
insert comma: ^,	insert question mark: ^?
insert colon: ^:	insert semicolon: ^;
insert dash: (—)	insert quotation marks: ∨"
insert hyphen: ^-	

all of the sentences in this exercise are from g*linda of oz* by l. frank baum this book has twenty four chapters, including the magic stairway the enchanted fishes and glinda's triumph

when evening came they saw the diamond swan still keeping to the opposite shore of the lake walk out of the water to the sands shake her diamond sprinkled feathers and then disappear among the bushes to seek a resting place for the night

the fairy ruler of oz only needed her silver wand tipped at one end with a great sparkling emerald to provide through its magic all that they might need

she placed her two hands before her mouth forming a hollow with them and uttered a clear thrilling bird like cry

ive lost all the poison i had to kill the fishes with and i can't make any more because only my wife knew the secret of it and she is now a foolish pig and has forgotten all her magic

a different sort of person was jack pumpkinhead one of ozmas oldest friends and her companion on many adventures

the one who had been a goldfish had beautiful golden hair and blue eyes and was exceedingly fair of skin the one who had been a bronzefish had dark brown hair and clear gray eyes and her complexion matched these lovely features

the others too seemed to think the wizards plan the best and glinda herself commended it so on they marched toward the line of palm trees that hid the skeezers lake from view by this time ozma had made up her mind as to the character of this haughty and disdainful creature whose self pride evidently led her to believe herself superior to all others

at ordinary times ozma was just like any little girl one might chance to meet simple, merry, lovable as could be yet with a certain reserve that lent her dignity in her most joyous moods.

there is more magic in my fairyland than i dreamed of remarked the beautiful ozma with a sigh of regret

that is all that makes life worth our while to do good deeds and to help those less fortunate than ourselves

Exercise 124B: Foreign Phrases That Are Now English Words

The following phrases and words are now part of English and are usually not italicized. Using a dictionary, look up each one. In the blank, write the original language that the word belongs to, the meaning in English, and the meaning in the original language. The first is done for you.

cul-de-sac	French, a dead-end street, "bottom of the sack"
status quo	______________________
résumé	______________________
doppelganger	______________________
en masse	______________________
vice versa	______________________
non sequitur	______________________
addendum	______________________
hors d'oeuvre	______________________
per diem (noun)	______________________

WEEK 34

Advanced Quotations & Dialogue

—LESSON 125—

Dialogue

Additional Rules for Writing Dialogue

Direct Quotations

Additional Rules for Using Direct Quotations

Use dialogue in fiction and to bring other voices into memoir, profiles, and reporting.

> A man was thought to be the painter of "Portrait of an Unknown Lady" when it went on sale in 2014 at an auction in the southern English city of Salisbury. It was bought by Bendor Grosvenor, an art dealer and historian who recognized the work as Carlile's.
>
> In an interview with *The Telegraph*, Mr. Grosvenor said that the artist's style "is quite recognizable if you know what it looks like."
>
> —Roslyn Sulcas, "A 17th-Century Portrait Will Be the Earliest Painting by a Woman at the Tate," *The New York Times,* Sept. 21, 2016

A dialogue tag identifies the person making the speech.

When a dialogue tag comes after a speech, place a comma, exclamation point, or question mark inside the closing quotation marks before the tag.

When a dialogue tag comes before a speech, place a comma after the tag. Put the dialogue's final punctuation mark inside the closing quotation marks.

> "There goes Tommaso the painter," the people would say, watching the big awkward figure passing through the streets on his way to work.

> Diamante said to Filippo, "You have learned well, and it is time now to turn your work to some account."

Speeches do not need to be attached to a dialogue tag as long as the text clearly indicates the speaker.

> The father gave a hopeless sigh and turned away. "So, you will be a painter."

Usually, a new paragraph begins with each new speaker.

> Michelangelo said nothing, but he mounted the scaffolding and pretended to chip away at the nose with his chisel. Meanwhile he let drop some marble chips and dust upon the head of the critic beneath. Then he came down.
>
> "Is that better?" he asked gravely.
>
> "Admirable!" answered the artist. "You have given it life."

> "I am growing too old to help you," Leonardo said, but Raphael shook his head.
>
> "I will go with you to the ends of the earth," he said.

When a dialogue tag comes in the middle of a speech, follow it with a comma if the following dialogue is an incomplete sentence. Follow it with a period if the following dialogue is a complete sentence.

> "The boy!" said one brother, nudging the other, "has found his brains at last."

> The painter's quick eyes examined the work with deep interest. "Send him to me at once," he said. "This is indeed marvellous talent."
>
> —Amy Steedman, *Knights of Art: Stories of the Italian Painters*

RULES FOR USING DIRECT QUOTATIONS

Direct quotations are set off by quotation marks.

Every direct quote must have an attribution tag.

When an attribution tag comes after a direct quote, place a comma, exclamation point, or question mark inside the closing quotation marks.

> "Frederick, is God dead?" asked Sojourner Truth.

When an attribution tag comes before a direct quote, place a comma after the tag. Put the quote's final punctuation mark inside the closing quotation marks.

> The orator paused impressively, and then thundered in a voice that thrilled his audience with prophetic intimations, "No, God is not dead; and therefore it is that slavery must end in blood!"

When an attribution tag comes in the middle of a direct quotation, follow it with a comma if the remaining quote is an incomplete sentence. Follow it with a period if the remaining quote is a complete sentence.

> "A new world had opened up to me," Douglass wrote. "I lived more in one day than in a year of my slave life."

> "It was my good fortune," he writes, "to get out of slavery at the right time, to be speedily brought in contact with that circle of highly cultivated men and women, banded together for the overthrow of slavery, of which William Lloyd Garrison was the acknowledged leader."

Direct quotes can be words, phrases, clauses, or sentences, as long as they are set off by quotation marks and form part of a grammatically correct original sentence.

> In his autobiography Douglass commends Mr. Johnson for his "noble-hearted hospitality and manly character."

Ellipses show where something has been cut out of a sentence.

If a direct quotation is longer than three lines, indent the entire quote one inch from the margin in a separate block of text and omit quotation marks.

> In a footnote to the *Life and Times of Garrison* it is stated:
>
> > This enterprise was not regarded with favor by the leading abolitionists, who knew only too well the precarious support which a fifth anti-slavery paper . . . must have . . . As anticipated, it nearly proved the ruin of its projector; but by extraordinary exertions it was kept alive.

If you change or make additions to a direct quotation, use brackets.

> Parker Pillsbury reported that "though it was late in the evening when the young man closed his remarks, none seemed to know or care for the hour. . . . The crowded congregation had been wrought up almost to enchantment during the whole long evening, particularly by some of the utterances of the last speaker [Douglass], as he turned over the terrible apocalypse of his experience in slavery."

A quote within a quote is surrounded by single quotation marks.

ADDITIONAL RULES FOR DIRECT QUOTATIONS

Use direct quotations to provide examples, cite authorities, and emphasize your own points.

An attribution tag may be indirect.

> In the wild songs of the slaves he read, beneath their senseless jargon or their fulsome praise of "old master," the often unconscious note of grief and despair.

A colon may introduce a direct quote.

> Douglass spent a year under Covey's ministrations, and his life there may be summed up in his own words: "The overwork and the brutal chastisements of which I was the victim, combined with that ever-gnawing and soul-destroying thought, 'I am a slave—a slave for life,' rendered me a living embodiment of mental and physical wretchedness."
>
> —Charles W. Chesnutt, *Frederick Douglass*

To quote three or fewer lines of poetry, indicate line breaks by using a slanted line and retain all original punctuation and capitalization.

> Likewise, Paul Laurence Dunbar's 1895 poem "We Wear the Mask" anticipates the "two-ness" of African-American existence expressed most poignantly and poetically by Du Bois nearly a decade later. Dunbar most famously writes: "We wear the mask that grins and lies,/It hides our cheeks and shades our eyes,—/This debt we pay to human guile".
>
> —Rebecka Rutledge Fisher, *Habitations of the Veil*

Four or more lines of poetry should be treated as a block quote.

> In his poem, "We Wear the Mask," Dunbar speaks of a double-consciousness that had been forced on African-Americans:
>
> > We wear the mask that grins and lies,
> > It hides our cheeks and shades our eyes,—
> > This debt we pay to human guile;
> > With torn and bleeding hearts we smile,
> > And mouth with myriad subtleties.
>
> Dunbar's biographer, Benjamin Brawley, wrote that Dunbar's poetry "soared above race and touched the heart universal."
>
> —Joseph Nazel, *Langston Hughes*

Any poetic citation longer than one line may be treated as a block quote.

Direct quotes should be properly documented.

—LESSON 126—

(Optional)
Documentation

> In *101 Gourmet Cookies for Everyone*, author Wendy Paul claims that her Chocolate Chip Pudding Cookies are "by far the softest chocolate chip cookies" that can be found.[1]
>
> [1] Wendy Paul, *101 Gourmet Cookies for Everyone* (Bonneville Books, 2010), p. 18.

A sentence containing a direct quote should be followed by a citation.

A superscript number may lead to a citation at the bottom of the page (a footnote) or the end of the paper (an endnote).

1. Footnotes and endnotes should follow this format:

   Author name, *Title of Book* (Publisher, year of publication), p. #.

   If there are two authors, list them like this:

   Author name and author name, *Title of Book* (Publisher, year of publication), p. #.

   If your quote comes from more than one page of the book you're quoting, use *pp.* to mean "pages" and put a hyphen between the page numbers.

   Author name, *Title of Book* (Publisher, year of publication), pp. #-#.

   If a book is a second (or third, or fourth, etc.) edition, put that information right after the title.

   Author name, *Title of Book*, 2nd ed. (Publisher, year of publication), p. #.

If no author is listed, simply use the title of the book.

Title of Book (Publisher, year of publication), p. #.

All of this information can be found on the copyright page of the book.

2. Footnotes should be placed beneath a dividing line at the bottom of the page. If you are using a word processing program, the font size of the footnotes should be about 2 points smaller than the font size of the main text.

3. Endnotes should be placed at the end of the paper, under a centered heading, like this:

ENDNOTES

[1] Wendy Paul, *101 Gourmet Cookies for Everyone* (Bonneville Books, 2010), p. 18.

[2] Author, *Title of Book* (Publisher, year of publication), p. #.

For a short paper (three pages or less), the endnotes can be placed on the last page of the paper itself. A paper that is four or more pages in length should have an entirely separate page for endnotes.

4. The second time you cite a book, your footnote or endnote only needs to contain the following information:

[2] Author last name, p. #.

5. If a paragraph contains several quotes from the same source, a single citation at the end of the entire paragraph can cover all quotations.

Every work mentioned in a footnote or endnote must also appear on a final Works Cited page.

WORKS CITED

Paul, Wendy. *101 Gourmet Cookies for Everyone.* Springville, UT: Bonneville Books, 2010.

1. List sources alphabetically by the author's last name.
2. The format should be as follows: Last name of author, first name. *Title of Book.* City of publication: Publisher, year of publication.
3. If the work has no author, list it by the first word of the title (but ignore the articles *a*, *an*, and *the*).
4. If the city of publication is not a major city (New York, Los Angeles, London, Beijing, New Delhi, Tokyo), include the state (for a U.S. publisher) or country (for an international publisher).
5. For a short paper (three pages or less), the Works Cited section may be at the bottom of the last page. For a paper of four or more pages, attach a separate Works Cited page.

Additional Rules for Citing Sources (Turabian)

1. Magazine articles

   In a footnote or endnote, use the following style:

   [1] Author name, "Name of article." *Name of Magazine*, Date of publication, page number.

   [2] Jacqueline Harp, "A Breed for Every Yard: Black Welsh Mountain Sheep Break New Ground." *Sheep!*, September/October 2013, p. 27.

   In Works Cited, use the following style:

   Author last name, first name. "Name of article." *Name of Magazine* volume number: issue number (Date of publication), total range of pages article takes up in magazine.

   Harp, Jacqueline. "A Breed for Every Yard: Black Welsh Mountain Sheep Break New Ground." *Sheep!* 34:5 (September/October 2013), pp. 26–28.

2. Websites

   In a footnote or endnote, use the following style:

   [3] Author/editor/sponsoring organization of website, "Name of article," URL (date accessed).

   [4] Mallory Daughtery, "Baa Baa Black and White Sheep Treats," http://www.southernliving.com/home-garden/holidays-occasions/spring-table-settings-centerpieces-00400000041389/page8.html (accessed Sept. 12, 2013).

   In Works Cited, use the following style:

   Author/editor/sponsoring organization of website. "Name of article." URL (date accessed).

   Daughtery, Mallory. "Baa Baa Black and White Sheep Treats." http://www.southernliving.com/home-garden/holidays-occasions/spring-table-settings-centerpieces-00400000041389/page8.html (accessed Sept. 12, 2013).

3. Ebooks with flowing text (no traditional page numbers)

   In a footnote or endnote, use the following style:

   [5] Author name, *Name of book* (Publisher, date), Name of ebook format: Chapter number, any other information given by ebook platform.

   [6] Paul de Kruif, *Microbe Hunters* (Harvest, 1996), Kindle: Ch. 7, Loc. 2134.

   In Works Cited, use the following style:

   Author last name, author first name. *Title of book.* City of publication: Publisher, date. Name of ebook format.

   de Kruif, Paul. *Microbe Hunters.* Fort Washington, PA: Harvest, 1996. Kindle.

In-text citations may be used in scientific or technical writing.

The chemical reactions that take place within Chocolate Chip Pudding Cookies make them "by far the softest chocolate chip cookies" (Paul 2010, 18) that can be found.

About Turabian

The style described in this lesson is the most common one for student papers. It is known as "Turabian," after Kate Turabian, the head secretary for the graduate department at the University of Chicago from 1930 until 1958.

Kate Turabian had to approve the format of every doctoral dissertation and master's thesis submitted to the University of Chicago. These papers were supposed to follow the format of the *University of Chicago Manual of Style*, but the *Manual of Style* is huge and complicated and many students couldn't figure out exactly how to use it. So Kate Turabian wrote a simplified version of the *Manual of Style*, intended just for the use of students writing papers. It was called *A Manual for Writers of Research Papers, Theses, and Dissertations*, and her book has sold over eight million copies.

Alternative Styles for Citation

A. **Turabian** (most common for students)

FOOTNOTE/ENDNOTE

[1] Susan Cooper, *Silver on the Tree* (Atheneum, 1977), p. 52.

IN-TEXT CITATION

(Cooper 1977, 52)

WORKS CITED

Cooper, Susan. *Silver on the Tree.* New York: Atheneum, 1977.

B. **Chicago Manual of Style**

FOOTNOTE/ENDNOTE

[1] Susan Cooper, *Silver on the Tree* (New York: Atheneum 1977), 52.

IN-TEXT CITATION

(Cooper 1977, 52)

WORKS CITED

Cooper, Susan. 1977. *Silver on the Tree.* New York: Atheneum, 1977.

C. **APA** (American Psychological Association, the standard for science writing)

FOOTNOTE/ENDNOTE

APA does not recommend the use of footnotes or endnotes.

IN-TEXT CITATION

(Cooper, 1977, p. 52)

WORKS CITED

Cooper, S. (1977). *Silver on the tree.* Atheneum.

D. **MLA** (Modern Language Association, more often used in the arts and humanities)

FOOTNOTE/ENDNOTE

MLA does not recommend the use of footnotes or endnotes for citations. They should only be used to direct the reader to additional books or resources that should be consulted.

IN-TEXT CITATION

(Cooper 52)

WORKS CITED

Cooper, Susan. *Silver on the Tree*. New York, NY, United States: Atheneum, 1977. Print.

—LESSON 127—

Practicing Direct Quotations and Correct Documentation

Your assignment: Write a short essay called "Four Famous Pirates." It should be at least 250 words, although it will probably need to be longer.

You must quote directly from all four of the sources listed below, footnote each direct quote, and put all four on your Works Cited page.

Your essay must include the following:

a) A brief quote that comes before its attribution tag.
b) A brief quote that comes after its attribution tag.
c) A brief quote divided by its attribution tag.
d) A block quote.
e) A quote that is incorporated into a complete sentence and serves a grammatical function within that sentence.
f) A quote that has been altered with either brackets or ellipses.
g) A second quote from the same source.

One quote can fulfill more than one of these requirements.

If you need help, ask your instructor.

Author: Daniel Defoe
Title of Book: *A General History of the Pyrates, From Their First Rise and Settlement in the Island of Providence, to the Present Time*
City of Publication: London
Publisher: T. Warner
Date: 1724

Page 44
In the Times of Marius and Sylla, Rome was in her greatest Strength, yet she was so torn in Pieces by the Factions of those two great Men, that every Thing which concerned the

publick Good was altogether neglected, when certain Pyrates broke out from Cicilia, a Country of Asia Minor, situated on the Coast of the Mediterranean, betwixt Syria on the East, from whence it is divided by Mount Tauris, and Armenia Minor on the West. This Beginning was mean and inconsiderable, having but two or three Ships, and a few Men, with which they cruised about the Greek Islands, taking such Ships as were very ill arm'd or weakly defended; however, by the taking of many Prizes, they soon increased in Wealth and Power: The first Action of theirs which made a Noise, was the taking of Julius Cæsar, who was as yet a Youth, and who being obliged to fly from the Cruelties of Sylla, who sought his Life, went into Bithinia, and sojourned a while with

Page 45
Nicomedes, King of that Country; in his Return back by Sea, he was met with, and taken, by some of these Pyrates, near the Island of Pharmacusa: These Pyrates had a barbarous Custom of tying their Prisoners Back to Back and throwing them into the Sea; but, supposing Cæsar to be some Person of a high Rank, because of his purple Robes, and the Number of his Attendants, they thought it would be more for their Profit to preserve him, in hopes of receiving a great Sum for his Ransom; therefore they told him he should have his Liberty, provided he would pay them twenty Talents, which they judg'd to be a very high Demand, in our Money, about three thousand six hundred Pounds Sterling; he smiled, and of his own Accord promised them fifty Talents; they were both pleased, and surpriz'd at his Answer, and consented that several of his Attendants should go by his Direction and raise the Money; and he was left among these Ruffians with no more than three

Page 46
Attendants. He pass'd eight and thirty Days, and seemed so little concerned or afraid, that often when he went to sleep, he used to charge them not to make a Noise, threatening, if they disturbed him, to hang them all; he also play'd at Dice with them, and sometimes wrote Verses and Dialogues, which he used to repeat, and also cause them to repeat, and if they did not praise and admire them, he would call them Beasts and Barbarians, telling them he would crucify them. They took all these as the Sallies of a juvenile Humour, and were rather diverted, than displeased at them.

At length his Attendants return'd with his Ransom, which he paid, and was discharged; he sail'd for the Port of Miletum, where, as soon as he was arriv'd, he used all his Art and Industry in fitting out a Squadron of Ships, which he equipp'd and arm'd at his own Charges; and sailing in Quest of the Pyrates, he surpriz'd them as they lay at Anchor

Page 47
among the Islands, and took those who had taken him before, with some others; the Money he found upon them he made Prize of, to reimburse his Charges, and he carry'd the Men to Pergamus or Troy, and there secured them in Prison: In the mean Time, he apply'd himself to Junius, then Governor of Asia, to whom it belonged to judge and determine of the Punishment of these Men; but Junius finding there was no Money to be had, answered Cæsar, that he would think at his Leisure, what was to be done with those Prisoners; Cæsar took his Leave of him, returned back to Pergamus, and commanded that the Prisoners should be brought out and executed, according to Law in that Case provided; which is taken Notice of, in a Chapter at the End of this Book, concerning the

Laws in Cases of Pyracy: And thus he gave them that Punishment in Earnest, which he had often threatened them with in Jest.

Author/Editor/Sponsoring Organization: *Time* Magazine
Name of Web Article: "Peril on the High Seas: Francis Drake Raids Cadiz: 1584"
URL: http://content.time.com/time/specials/packages/article/0,28804,1860715_1860714_1860707,00.html
Date of access: Use the date on which you are writing your essay

The Englishman may be remembered for circumnavigating the world, but Sir Francis Drake also happened to be Queen Elizabeth I's favorite pirate. Indeed, part of his globetrotting mission was to take treasure from the Spaniards, which he brought back to his appreciative monarch (who got a half-share of the loot). The pirate-patriot's greatest act was also a blow against the King of Spain: a raid on the Spanish port of Cadiz that destroyed several ships being assembled for the great Armada that was to be launched against England.

Author: Ta Chen
Title of Book: *Chinese Migrations, With Special Reference to Labor Conditions*
City of Publication: Washington, DC
Publisher: Government Printing Office
Date: 1923

Page 41

EXPLOITS OF KOXINGA

At this time the Ming dynasty was declining and the Chinese coast fell into the hands of Cheng Ch'in-kung (Koxinga), a pirate patriot, who checked the invading Manchus. Koxinga's father, Tse-lung, was a tailor of Chuanchow, who, because of his defeat of the pirate Liu Hiang-lao in 1639, was promoted to a high rank by the court of Ming. In 1644, Brigadier General Ching Hung-tah proclaimed himself Emperor of Fukien and made Tse-lung a prince, and Ch'in-kung, his son, a marquis. When Tse-lung was executed in Nanking, Ch'm-kung (Koxinga) succeeded him in control of the coast of Fukien and Formosa. Using the Kulan Islands off Fukien as the base for food supplies, Koxinga made raids upon the coast villages of the Province. Ho Bien, who was known to the Dutch as Pinqua, had been with the Japanese pirates, but was dismissed by them because of crimes he had committed. He was now in the employ of the Dutch in Formosa as a treasurer and was heavily in debt. In order to meet his own debts, as well as for the political and commercial advantages to Koxinga, he persuaded Koxinga to invade Taiwan.

With about 25,000 men, in 400 junks, Koxinga attacked Fort Provintia, which was surrendered May 4, 1661. Castle Zeelandia fell soon after. A treaty of peace was signed by Koxinga and the Dutch on February 1, 1662, by which the fort was evacuated by the Dutch.

KOXINGA'S SUCCESSORS

Koxinga's advisor, Chen Yung-hua'tiien persuaded him to promulgate just laws, open lands for cultivation, appoint civil officers, make adequate military preparations, establish schools, and treat emigrants of the old Ming dynasty with magnanimity. He founded the prefecture of Chen Tien on the site of the old Tayouan, and also put two districts under its jurisdiction: Tien Shun and Wan Nien.

When Yin, his son, came to succeed him from Amoy, the Manchus persuaded him to submit himself to the Emperor, but his conditions of surrender were refused, and frequent fighting ensued.

Name of Article: "Morgan the Buccaneer"
Author: None listed
Magazine: *Harper's New Monthly* Magazine
Date: June 1859
Volume and issue number: Volume 11, No. 6
Page range of article: 20-37

Page 20
About the year 1666 there was an old pirate at Jamaica named Mansvelt. At the same time an adventurer by the name of Morgan, a Welsh man by birth, and the commander of a good vessel, had acquired the reputation of being a bold and successful cruiser. Mansvelt having resolved to make a descent on Costa Rica, fitted out an expedition consisting of fifteen vessels, manned with 900 men. Making Morgan his vice-admiral, he set sail for St. Catherine's Isle, near Costa Rica. The Spaniards in possession of it were unprepared for such a force, and after a mere

Page 21
show of resistance surrendered. Demolishing all the forts but one, Mansvelt laid a bridge over the channel to an adjacent isle, and soon became master of that also. Leaving a hundred men here he re-embarked, intending to plunder the coast of Costa Rica as far north as Nata. But finding that the Governor of Panama had been informed of his approach, he turned back with his fleet to St. Catherine's. The Sieur Simon, whom he had left as Governor, having during his absence put the main island in a good state of defense, and begun to cover the smaller one with fertile plantations, Mansvelt determined to keep possession of it. To carry out this plan he went to Jamaica with proposals to the Governor for its retention. Being met with a refusal, and knowing he could not hold it against the Spanish force in those seas, he retired to Tortuga, where he suddenly died.

Morgan succeeded to the command, and hoped, like his predecessor, to retain St. Catherine's; but the Spaniards, during his absence, made a sudden descent upon it and took it. He then resolved to collect a large force in some of the ports of Cuba; and in two months' time he succeeded in assembling twelve vessels and 700 men. It was first proposed to plunder Havana, but fearing that his force was insufficient, he resolved to attack Puerto del Principe.

Having arrived abreast of the place in the night, he waited for daylight to land and surprise it. But a Spanish prisoner aboard one of the vessels contrived to escape unobserved, and swimming ashore alarmed the town. The news spread consternation through the place; and the inhabitants, aroused from their slumbers by the cry, "The pirates have come!" swarmed through the trees in affright, bearing bags of gold and other valuables and fled—men and women and children—into the surrounding forest. Soon every house was empty; and nothing was heard save the steady tramp of 800 soldiers as they defiled through the streets toward the port, which lay some distance off. Halting where the road was narrow, they cut down trees and made barricades, behind which they were stationed by the Governor, and awaited the approach of the pirates. Morgan, finding the high-road to the town thus defended, landed his men some distance off, and taking a circuitous march through the woods, at length emerged on the open plain in front of the place. As the troops defiled from the forest and formed into line, they saw the Governor with a large body of horse drawn up in order of battle. Morgan had scarcely time to throw his men into the form of a half moon when the Spanish bugles sounded the charge, and the horse came gallantly on. The pirates, reserving their fire till the enemy were within close range, took deadly aim, and emptied nearly a hundred saddles at the first discharge. The Spaniards wheeled and charged again and again, but were unable to break the firm formation, while the deadly volleys mowed them down by scores. At length the few survivors turned and fled.

Morgan then marched on the town, but was met at the entrance by the foot-soldiers, who defended it for a long time with determined bravery. The pirates, made desperate by this protracted resistance, dashed with a loud yell so fiercely on the gate-way that they bore back all opposition, and poured through the street. The Spaniards then retired to their houses, from whence they continued to fire on their assailants until the latter threatened to fire the town, when they surrendered. After the surrender some were locked up in the houses and burned to death; others underwent the most dreadful tortures to make them confess where they had hidden away their riches; their cries and groans mingling in with the shouts and laughter of those who, in the meantime, grew merry over the deep potations of liquor which the inhabitants had left behind.

Having tried every other means in vain, Morgan told them if they did not pay a handsome ransom he would take them all to Jamaica and sell them as slaves. The Spaniards then deputized four of their number to get the required contribution. These brought back word that they could not find any of their own party, but that they would raise the money in fifteen days. This was granted, and the pirates gave themselves over to reveling and pleasure.

In a few days, however, a servant was caught with letters on his person from the Governor of Santiago to the chief officers of the town urging them to detain the pirates as long as they could, for he would soon be there with a large force to their assistance. Morgan immediately ordered all the booty he had collected to be sent aboard his vessel, and demanded that the ransom should be paid next day. This being declared impossible, he directed them to send him immediately five hundred sides of beef, with salt enough to cure them. This being done, he liberated the prisoners and set sail for an uninhabited island to divide the plunder.

WEEK 35

Introduction to Sentence Style

The definitions in this lesson use the categories laid out by Thomas Kane in the *New Oxford Guide to Writing.*

—LESSON 128—

Sentence Style: Equal and Subordinating
Sentences with Equal Elements: Segregating, Freight-Train, and Balanced

But, in a larger sense, we cannot dedicate—we cannot consecrate—we cannot hallow this ground.
—Abraham Lincoln, "The Gettysburg Address"

We shall defend our island, whatever the cost may be; we shall fight on the beaches, we shall fight on the landing grounds, we shall fight in the fields and in the streets, we shall fight in the hills; we shall never surrender.
—Winston Churchill, "We Shall Fight on the Beaches"

An equal sentence is made up of a series of independent grammatical elements.

Years and years ago, when I was a boy, when there were wolves in Wales, and birds the color of red-flannel petticoats whisked past the harp-shaped hills, when we sang and wallowed all night and day in caves that smelt like Sunday afternoons in damp front farmhouse parlors, and we chased, with the jawbones of deacons, the English and the bears, before the motor car, before the wheel, before the duchess-faced horse, when we rode the daft and happy hills bareback, it snowed and it snowed.
— Dylan Thomas, *A Child's Christmas in Wales*

Even when pressed by the demands of inner truth, men do not easily assume the task of opposing their government's policy, especially in time of war.
—Martin Luther King, "Beyond Vietnam—A Time to Break Silence"

A subordinating sentence is made up of both independent and dependent elements.

Equal sentences can be segregating, freight-train, or balanced.

Segregating sentences express a single idea each, and occur in a series.

The barn was still dark. The sheep lay motionless. Even the goose was quiet.
—E. B. White, *Charlotte's Web*

He hadn't found any doweling that day. He hadn't checked the generator. He hadn't cleaned up the pieces of mirror. He hadn't eaten supper; he'd lost his appetite. That wasn't hard. He lost it most of the time.
—Richard Matheson, *I Am Legend*

They disappear among the poplars. The meadow is empty. The river, the meadow, the cliff and cloud. The princess calls, but there is no one, now, to hear her.
—John Fowles, *The Ebony Tower*

Freight-train sentences link independent clauses together to express a combined idea.

He was energetic and devout; he was polite and handsome; his fame grew in the diocese.
—Lytton Strachey, *Eminent Victorians*

There was much game hanging outside the shops, and the snow powdered in the fur of the foxes and the wind blew their tails.
—Ernest Hemingway, "In Another Country"

I'm very young, I have no real friend here in the barn, it's going to rain all morning and all afternoon, and Fern won't come in such bad weather.
—E. B. White, *Charlotte's Web*

Balanced sentences are made up of two equal parts, separated by a pause.

Darkness is cheap, and Scrooge liked it.
—Charles Dickens, *A Christmas Carol*

It is a far, far better thing that I do, than I have ever done; it is a far, far better rest that I go to than I have ever known.
—Charles Dickens, *A Tale of Two Cities*

But there is something that I must say to my people, who stand on the warm threshold which leads into the palace of justice: In the process of gaining our rightful place, we must not be guilty of wrongful deeds.
—Martin Luther King, "I Have a Dream"

Exercise 128A: Identifying Sentence Types

In the blank that follows each sentence, write *S* for segregating, *FT* for freight-train, or *B* for balanced.

Her good will could not be denied, and her capacity could not be disregarded.
—Lytton Strachey, *Eminent Victorians* ______

I make them. But they are not mine. The artillery is not mine. I must put in for it.
—Ernest Hemingway, *For Whom the Bell Tolls* ______

The rain is beating on the windows. It was not midnight. It was not raining.
—Samuel Beckett, *Molloy* (translated by Patrick Bowles) ______

It had rained in the night, and the lane was awash with thin red mud, and puddles stood in the ruts and potholes.
—Berton Roueché, *What's Left* ______

The nurse sat down again. The nurse's shoes were white. Pelletier's and Espinoza's shoes were black. Morini's shoes were brown.
—Roberto Bolaño, *2666: A Novel* ______

Then God said, "Let there be lights in the firmament of the heavens to divide the day from the night; and let them be for signs and seasons, and for days and years; and let them be for lights in the firmament of the heavens to give light on the earth"; and it was so.
—Genesis 1:14-15 ______

We are such stuff as dreams are made on, and our little life is rounded with a sleep.
—William Shakespeare, *The Tempest* ______

The shadows are lengthening for me. The twilight is here. My days of old have vanished, tone and tint.
—Douglas MacArthur, "Duty, Honor, Country" ______

What the white whale was to Ahab, has been hinted; what, at times, he was to me, as yet remains unsaid.
—Herman Melville, *Moby-Dick* ______

Let freedom ring from the mighty mountains of New York. Let freedom ring from the heightening Alleghenies of Pennsylvania. Let freedom ring from the snow-capped Rockies of Colorado. Let freedom ring from the curvaceous slopes of California.
—Martin Luther King, "I Have a Dream" ______

Cowards die many times before their deaths; the valiant never taste of death but once.
—William Shakespeare, *Julius Caesar* ______

The grass was wet and the earth smelled of springtime.
—E. B. White, *Charlotte's Web* ______

They are waiting on the street in the late afternoon. The air is thin as paper. The day is raw.
—James Salter, *A Sport and a Pastime* ______

Mrs. Cratchit made the gravy (ready beforehand in a little saucepan) hissing hot; Master Peter mashed the potatoes with incredible vigour; Miss Belinda sweetened up the apple-sauce; Martha dusted the hot plates; Bob took Tiny Tim beside him in a tiny corner at the table; the two young Cratchits set chairs for everybody, not forgetting themselves, and mounting guard upon their posts, crammed spoons into their mouths, lest they should shriek for goose before their turn came to be helped.
—Charles Dickens, *A Christmas Carol* ______

—LESSON 129—

Subordinating Sentences: Loose, Periodic, Cumulative, Convoluted, and Centered

In a loose sentence, subordinate constructions follow the main clause.

People always think that happiness is a far away thing, something complicated and hard to get.
—Betty Smith, *A Tree Grows in Brooklyn*

He was pacing the room swiftly, eagerly, with his head sunk upon his chest and his hands clasped behind him.
—Arthur Conan Doyle, "A Scandal in Bohemia"

The spotlight has often been focused on me because I was a late bloomer who turned out to be a prodigy, and perhaps, more than that, because I am a black woman excelling in a white world.
—Misty Copeland, *Life in Motion: An Unlikely Ballerina*

In a periodic sentence, subordinate constructions precede the main clause.

To be, or not to be: that is the question.
—William Shakespeare, *Hamlet*

When Galileo and Newton looked at nature, they saw simplicity.
—Edward Dolnick, *The Clockwork Universe: Isaac Newton, the Royal Society, and the Birth of the Modern World*

Some years ago—never mind how long precisely—having little or no money in my purse, and nothing particular to interest me on shore, I thought I would sail about a little and see the watery part of the world.
—Herman Melville, *Moby-Dick*

A cumulative sentence puts multiple subordinate constructions before or after the main clause.

Beyond the obvious facts that he has at some time done manual labour, that he takes snuff, that he is a Freemason, that he has been in China, and that he has done a considerable amount of writing lately, I can deduce nothing else.
—Arthur Conan Doyle, "The Red-Headed League"

Lastly, she pictured to herself how this same little sister of hers would, in the after-time, be herself a grown woman; and how she would keep, through all her riper years, the simple and loving heart of her childhood; and how she would gather about her other little children, and make their eyes bright and eager with many a strange tale, perhaps even with the dream of Wonderland of long ago; and how she would feel with all their simple sorrows, and find a pleasure in all their simple joys, remembering her own child-life, and the happy summer days.

—Lewis Carroll, *Alice's Adventures in Wonderland*

In a convoluted sentence, subordinate constructions divide the main clause.

The dorm, with two narrow beds to a room, didn't just house dancers studying with ABT.

—Misty Copeland, *Life in Motion: An Unlikely Ballerina*

We, the people of the United States, in order to form a more perfect union, establish justice, insure domestic tranquility, provide for the common defense, promote the general welfare, and secure the blessings of liberty to ourselves and our posterity, do ordain and establish this Constitution for the United States of America.

—The Constitution of the United States

They knew, without my needing to spell it out, every setback or curve in the road: that I had fought for ten years to be recognized, to show that I had the talent and ability to dance in classical ballets.

—Misty Copeland, *Life in Motion: An Unlikely Ballerina*

In a centered sentence, subordinate constructions come on both sides of the main clause.

With an apology for my intrusion, I was about to withdraw when Holmes pulled me abruptly into the room and closed the door behind me.

—Arthur Conan Doyle, "The Red-Headed League"

And having got rid of this young man who did not know how to behave, she resumed her duties as hostess and continued to listen and watch, ready to help at any point where the conversation might happen to flag.

—Leo Tolstoy, *War and Peace*

Exercise 129A: Identifying Subordinating Sentences

In each sentence, underline the subject(s) of the main clause once and the predicate twice. Label each sentence in the blank that follows it as *L* for loose, *P* for periodic, *CUMUL* for cumulative, *CONV* for convoluted, or *CENT* for centered.

For the purpose of this exercise, any sentence with four or more phrases and dependent clauses before or after the main clause should be considered cumulative. If three or fewer phrases or dependent clauses come before or after the main clause, the sentence should be classified as loose or periodic.

If phrases or clauses come before *and* after the main clause, the sentence is centered, no matter how many phrases or clauses there are.

If any phrases or clauses come between the subject, predicate, and any essential parts of the main clause (objects, predicate nominatives or predicate adjectives), the sentence is convoluted.

A phrase serving as an object or predicate nominative should be considered a single part of speech, not a subordinate phrase.

All emotions, and that one particularly, were abhorrent to his cold, precise but admirably balanced mind.
—Arthur Conan Doyle, "A Scandal in Bohemia" ______

She had heard Papa sing so many songs about the heart; the heart that was breaking—was aching—was dancing—was heavy laden—that leaped for joy—that was heavy in sorrow—that turned over—that stood still.
—Betty Smith, *A Tree Grows in Brooklyn* ______

I am a convicted prisoner serving five years for leaving the country without a permit and for inciting people to go on strike at the end of May 1961.
—Nelson Mandela, "I Am Prepared to Die" ______

The answer, Galileo came to see, was that four objects were in orbit around Jupiter.
—Edward Dolnick, *The Clockwork Universe: Isaac Newton, the Royal Society, and the Birth of the Modern World* ______

As she read, at peace with the world and happy as only a little girl could be with a fine book and a little bowl of candy, and all alone in the house, the leaf shadows shifted and the afternoon passed.
—Betty Smith, *A Tree Grows in Brooklyn* ______

Shall we acquire the means of effectual resistance, by lying supinely on our backs, and hugging the delusive phantom of hope, until our enemies shall have bound us hand and foot?
—Patrick Henry, "Liberty or Death" ______

Seeing the self-confident and refined expression on the faces of those present he was always expecting to hear something very profound.
—Leo Tolstoy, *War and Peace* ______

The other students—most of them white, some of them Asian, and from Russia, Japan, and Spain, as well as from cities and small towns throughout the States—had been dancing their entire lives.
—Misty Copeland, *Life in Motion: An Unlikely Ballerina* ______

In this land, he may be what he will, if he has the good heart and the way of working honestly at the right things.
—Betty Smith, *A Tree Grows in Brooklyn* ______

For my part, whatever anguish of spirit it may cost, I am willing to know the whole truth—to know the worst and to provide for it.
—Patrick Henry, "Liberty or Death" ______

And when he speaks of Irene Adler, or when he refers to her photograph, it is always under the honourable title of "the woman."
—Arthur Conan Doyle, "A Scandal in Bohemia" ______

The San Bernardino Valley lies only an hour east of Los Angeles by the San Bernardino Freeway but is in certain ways an alien place: not the coastal California of the subtropical twilights and the soft westerlies off the Pacific but a harsher California, haunted by the Mojave just beyond the mountains, devastated by the hot dry Santa Ana wind that comes down through the passes at 100 miles an hour and whines through the eucalyptus windbreaks and works on the nerves.
—Joan Didion, "Some Dreamers of the Golden Dream" ______

While the spread of the plague could be charted from the Bills, its origins were uncertain.
—Stephen Porter, *The Great Plague* ______

It is a big, airy room, the whole floor nearly, with windows that look all ways, and air and sunshine galore.
—Charlotte Perkins Gilman, *The Yellow Wallpaper* ______

But you must believe me when I tell you that I have found it impossible to carry the heavy burden of responsibility and to discharge my duties as King as I would wish to do without the help and support of the woman I love.
—Edward VIII, Abdication Speech ______

Often, after shows, the dancers would do outreach, speaking to young people who'd been in the audience.
—Misty Copeland, *Life in Motion: An Unlikely Ballerina* ______

The last of the great naked-eye astronomers, Tycho was a meticulous observer with an unsurpassed knowledge of the sky.
—Edward Dolnick, *The Clockwork Universe: Isaac Newton, the Royal Society, and the Birth of the Modern World* ______

No thinker of that age, no matter how brilliant, could imagine an alternative.
—Edward Dolnick, *The Clockwork Universe: Isaac Newton, the Royal Society, and the Birth of the Modern World* ______

If his father was a carpenter, he may be a carpenter.
—Betty Smith, *A Tree Grows in Brooklyn* ______

She had so much of tenderness in her, so much of wanting to give of herself to whoever needed what she had, whether it was her money, her time, the clothes off her back, her pity, her understanding, her friendship or her companionship and love.
—Betty Smith, *A Tree Grows in Brooklyn* ______

Tonight, I will become the first black woman to star in Igor Stravinsky's iconic role for American Ballet Theatre, one of the most prestigious dance companies in the world.
—Misty Copeland, *Life in Motion: An Unlikely Ballerina* ______

With the exception of the aunt, beside whom sat only one elderly lady, who with her thin careworn face was rather out of place in this brilliant society, the whole company had settled down.
—Leo Tolstoy, *War and Peace* ______

In the loveliest town of all, where the houses were white and high and the elm trees were green and higher than the houses, where the front yards were wide and pleasant and the back yards were bushy and worth finding out about, where the streets sloped down to the stream and the stream flowed quietly under the bridge, where the lawns ended in orchards and the orchards ended in fields and the fields ended in pastures and the pastures climbed the hill and disappeared over the top toward the wonderful wide sky, in this loveliest of all towns Stuart stopped to get a drink of sarsaparilla.
—E. B. White, *Stuart Little* ______

When he smiled, his grave, even rather gloomy, look was instantaneously replaced by another—a childlike, kindly, even rather silly look, which seemed to ask forgiveness.
—Leo Tolstoy, *War and Peace* ______

If a physician of high standing, and one's own husband, assures friends and relatives that there is really nothing the matter with one but temporary nervous depression—a slight hysterical tendency—what is one to do?
—Charlotte Perkins Gilman, *The Yellow Wallpaper* ______

If you had somehow happened to guess the Pythagorean theorem, how would you prove it?
—Edward Dolnick, *The Clockwork Universe: Isaac Newton, the Royal Society, and the Birth of the Modern World* ______

These mothers, instead of being able to work for their honest livelihood, are forced to employ all their time in strolling to beg sustenance for their helpless infants.
—Jonathan Swift, *A Modest Proposal* ______

Wrapped in their torn blankets, they would sit or lie on the ground, staring vacantly into space, unaware of who or where they were, strangers to their surroundings.
—Elie Wiesel, "The Perils of Indifference" ______

If they but knew it, almost all men in their degree, some time or other, cherish very nearly the same feelings towards the ocean with me.
—Herman Melville, *Moby-Dick* ______

The stout gentleman half rose from his chair and gave a bob of greeting, with a quick little questioning glance from his small fat-encircled eyes.
—Arthur Conan Doyle, "The Red-Headed League" ______

—LESSON 130—

Practicing Sentence Style

Choose one of the following assignments:

Exercise 130A: Rewriting

The following list of events, from the Brothers Grimm tale "The Mouse, the Bird, and the Sausage," needs to be rewritten as a story.

This story must have at least one of each of the following types of sentences:

Segregating (at least three sentences in a row)
Freight-Train
Balanced
Loose
Periodic
Cumulative (with four or more subordinate phrases/clauses; main clause can come either first or last)
Convoluted
Centered

You may add, change, and subtract, as long as the finished story is at least 400 words long and makes good sense.

mouse, bird, sausage lived together
it went well
they were comfortable
they were prosperous
they all had different duties
the bird fetched wood for the fire
the mouse fetched water
the sausage cooked
the sausage jumped in the broth
the sausage rolled in the vegetables
this seasoned them
the bird met another bird
he told the other bird about the duties
the other bird called him a simpleton
the other bird said that the bird did too much hard work
the other bird said the mouse could spend all day in her room
the other bird said the sausage did nothing until dinner
the first bird went home
the next morning he refused to fetch wood for the fire
the mouse and sausage begged
he refused to go

the sausage went for wood
the bird made the fire
the mouse got ready to cook
the sausage never came back
the bird flew out to find him
a dog had eaten him
the bird went home and told the mouse
they were unhappy
the bird set the table
the mouse got ready to cook
she jumped into the broth
she got cooked
the bird could not find the mouse
the bird hunted for the mouse
no one watched the fire
a coal fell out of the fire
the kitchen began to burn
the bird went to the well for water
he fell in the well and drowned

Exercise 130B: Original Composition

Write an original composition of at least 400 words, with at least one of each of the following types of sentences:

Segregating (at least three sentences in a row)
Freight-Train
Balanced
Loose
Periodic
Cumulative (with four or more subordinate phrases/clauses; main clause can come either first or last)
Convoluted
Centered

This composition may be one of the following:

a) A plot summary of one of your favorite books or movies,
b) A narrative of some event, happening, trip, or great memory from your past,
c) A scene from a story that you create yourself, or
d) Any other topic you choose.

WEEK 36

—REVIEW 11—

Final Review

Review 11A: Explaining Sentences

Tell your instructor every possible piece of grammatical information about the following sentences. Follow these steps (notice that these are slightly different than the instructions in your previous "explaining" exercise):

1) Identify the sentence type and write it in the left-hand margin.
2) Underline each subordinate clause. Describe the identity and function of each clause and give any other useful information (introductory word, relationship to the rest of the sentence, etc.)
3) Label each preposition as *P* and each object of the preposition as *OP*. Describe the identity and function of each prepositional phrase.
4) Parse, out loud, all verbs acting as predicates.
5) Describe the identity and function of each individual remaining word. Don't worry about the articles, though.
6) Provide any other useful information that you might be able to think of.

The Sound in front of me was like a sheet of blue silk, with just the distant murmur of moving water as a reminder that there were tides here.

—Hans Kruuk, *Wild Otters: Predation and Populations*

I had come to cooking late in life, and knew from firsthand experience how frustrating it could be to try to learn from badly written recipes.

Along the quay, dozens of wooden fishing boats were parked, stern in, and wizened old men and enormous fishwives sold the day's catch from little stalls or sometimes right from the back of their boats.

—Julia Child, *My Life in France*

The wind was blowing a gale now, and there was little danger of oars being heard.

Frankly, had I been the King, the further they had gone the better should I have been pleased.

—Anthony Hope, *The Prisoner of Zenda*

But whatever the incarnation of the "small difference," whether it be a missing horse shoe nail, a butterfly, a sea gull, or most recently, a mosquito "squished" by Homer Simpson, the idea that small differences can have huge effects is not new.

—Leonard Smith, *Chaos: A Very Short Introduction*

Review 11B: Correcting Errors

Rewrite the following sets of sentences on your own paper (or with a word processing program), inserting all necessary punctuation and capitalization.

Include the citations in your corrections!

one night it was on the twentieth of march 1888 i was returning from a journey to a patient for i had now returned to civil practice when my way led me through baker street

let me see said holmes hum born in new jersey in the year 1858 contralto hum la scala hum prima donna imperial opera of warsaw yes retired from operatic stage ha living in london quite so your majesty as i understand became entangled with this young person wrote her some compromising letters and is now desirous of getting those letters back

—arthur conan doyle, a scandal in bohemia

i have always understood that the word mob was derived from the latin expression mobile vulgus, which is i believe in virgil

in some of the most beautiful pictures of the virgin and child of raphael and other old masters the right foot of jesus is placed upon the right foot of the virgin what is the symbolism of this position

the letter is fully quoted by mr tytler in his book england under edward vi and mary

—notes and queries: a medium of inter-communication for literary men artists antiquaries genealogists etc. Number 243, june 24 1854

this lady was the countess amelia, whose picture my sister in law wished to remove from the drawing room in park lane and her husband was james fifth earl of burlesdon and twenty second baron rassendyll a knight of the garter

i could see only three yards ahead i had then good hopes of not being seen as i crept along close under the damp moss grown masonry

they came one by one and kissed my hand de gautet a tall lean fellow with hair standing straight up and waxed moustache bersonin the belgian a portly man of middle height with a bald head though he was not far past thirty and last the englishman detchard a narrow faced fellow with close cut fair hair and a bronzed complexion

—anthony hope, the prisoner of zenda

Review 11C: Fill-in-the-Blank

Each of the following sentences is missing one of the elements listed. Provide the correct required form of a word that seems appropriate to you. When you are finished, compare your sentences with the originals.

On all __________ (plural noun), except the wash by __________ (relative pronoun) we __________ (simple past active indicative verb) the river, the place appeared __________ (passive infinitive) in by towering mountains whose bare sides __________ (simple past passive indicative verb) into __________ (adjective) and __________ (adjective) forms.

From a dark, __________ (adjective), __________ (present participle) mass, the river __________ (simple past passive indicative verb) into a __________ (present participle), __________ (present participle) stream which seemed __________ (infinitive) its gratitude at __________ (present participle) from the gloom of the great canyon.

—Josiah F. Gibbs, *Kawich's Gold Mine: An Historical Narrative of Mining in the Grand Canyon of the Colorado*

In a posthumous vindication of Charles's belief in the Divine Right of Kings, __________ (indefinite pronoun) rushed forward __________ (active infinitive) their handkerchiefs in the royal blood, __________ (present active participle) it to have sacred properties.

—Charles Spencer, *Killers of the King*

I felt we __________ (present active modal indicative verb) to show our readers __________ (subordinating adverb) to make everything top notch, and explain, if possible, __________ (subordinating adverb) things work one way __________ (coordinating conjunction) not another.

The little restaurant __________ (present active modal indicative verb) only __________ about twenty patrons, but it __________ (perfect past active indicative verb), quite nicely, largely on the strength of its *beurre blanc*—a thick, creamy sauce __________ (relative pronoun) is really nothing but warm butter __________ (past participle acting as adjective) in suspension by an acidic flavor base of shallots, wine, vinegar, salt, and pepper.

—Julia Child, *My Life in France*

This book __________ probably never _______________ if it had _____________ been for
perfect present passive modal verb adverb of negation
____________ first few years in the ______________ study area in Shetland, at Lunna, and
possessive pronoun adjective
I ______________ some of its details ______________ a background for ________________ of
simple future active indicative verb infinitive indefinite pronoun
the results ________________ here.
past participle acting as adjective

__________________________, we ________________ or lie in full view of the animals, ____
idiom introducing an alternative point of view simple present active modal verb adverb
long ________ we ______________ absolutely still, ______________ rather dark clothing
subordinating conjunction simple past active indicative verb present participle
and ________________ against a bank or a rock or ___________.
present participle indefinite pronoun

—Hans Kruuk, *Wild Otters: Predation and Populations*

But whatever solution we choose (and most modern speculation ________ not ________
progressive perfect present
very ________), an even bigger puzzle is ___________ fact ___________ one of the
active indicative verb demonstrative pronoun subordinating conjunction
founding twins really was ______________— since Remus ______________ by Romulus, or
adjective simple past passive indicative verb
in other versions by, one of his henchmen, on the very first day of the city.

—Mary Beard, *SPQR: A History of Ancient Rome*

If the blob ________ far out in space, ______________ as an unresolved point of light in the
present state-of-being subjunctive present participle
sky, ________ five senses would offer us ________ insight to its distance, velocity through
possessive pronoun adjective of negation
space, or ________ rate of rotation.
possessive pronoun

—Neil DeGrasse Tyson, *Death by Black Hole and Other Cosmic Quandaries*

Review 11D: Diagramming

On your own paper, diagram every word of the following sentences.

To ignore the Romans is not just to turn a blind eye to the distant past.

Romulus and the new citizens of his tiny community were fighting their neighbours, a people known as the Sabines, on the site that later became the Forum, the political centre of Cicero's Rome.

—Mary Beard, *SPQR: A History of Ancient Rome*

Either there's a missing part of Einstein's gravity that enables it to acept the tenets of quantum mechanics, or there's a missing part of quantum mechanics that enables it to accept Einstein's gravity.

—Neil DeGrasse Tyson, *Death by Black Hole and Other Cosmic Quandaries*

Yet, at about the same time that I was sitting there along the Yell Sound, the last otter disappeared from Holland, the land where I grew up with its sea, lakes, dykes, and rivers, a paradise for otters if ever there was one.

—Hans Kruuk, *Wild Otters: Predation and Populations*

A tiny brook moved through the meadow, then noisily tumbled over the sharp descent toward the river, ten miles distant by the winding trail.

On the southeast side of the river the walls rose terrace above terrace, like giant stairs, composed of granite, marble, lime and sandstone, and each so variegated with sculptured forms and tints as to baffle the most skillful artist.

—Josiah F. Gibbs, *Kawich's Gold Mine: An Historical Narrative of Mining in the Grand Canyon of the Colorado*

Charles was determined to talk of his innocence, particularly on the greater charges against him; he insisted with disdain that he had not begun the war with Parliament, pointing instead to how his opponents had taken his militia from him; that had been, he said, the first act of the hostilities.

—Charles Spencer, *Killers of the King*

An intellect which at a certain moment would know all forces that set nature in motion, and all positions of all items of which nature is composed — if this intellect were also vast enough to submit these data to analysis, it would embrace in a single formula the movements of the greatest bodies of the universe and those of the tiniest atom; for such an intellect nothing would be uncertain and the future, just like the past, would be present before its eyes.

—Pierre Laplace, quoted in Leonard Smith, *Chaos: A Very Short Introduction*

NOTES